Forgotten Laughs

An Episode Guide to 150 TV Sitcoms You Probably Never Saw

by

Richard Irvin

BearManor Media

Albany, Georgia

Forgotten Laughs: An Episode Guide to 150 TV Sitcoms You Probably Never Saw
© 2012 Richard Irvin. All rights reserved.

All photographs are from the author's personal collection.

No part of this book may be reproduced in any form or by any means, electronic, mechanical, digital, photocopying or recording, except for the inclusion in a review, without permission in writing from the publisher.

Published in the USA by:
BearManor Media
PO Box 1129
Duncan, OK 73534-1129
www.BearManorMedia.com

ISBN: 1-59393-225-1

Printed in the United States of America

Table of Contents

Acknowledgments ix

Introduction xi

Chapter 1: Growing Up Is Hard to Do 1
Better Days; Brutally Normal; Go Fish; M.Y.O.B.; Molloy; Someone Like Me

Chapter 2: Lusting, Loving, and Making a Living 25
As If; Black Tie Affair; Co-Ed Fever; Coupling; Dreams; Emily's Reasons Why Not; Grapevine; Happy Hour; Life on a Stick; My Guide to Becoming a Rock Star; Party Girl; The Random Years; Romantically Challenged; The Singles Table; Welcome to the Captain; Wild Oats; A Year at the Top

Chapter 3: Finding True Romance 111
Common Law; Herbie, The Love Bug; If Not for You; It Had to be You; Love & Money; You're the One

Chapter 4: Male Bonding 139
The Boys; Flatbush; Local Heroes; Misery Loves Company; The Trouble with Normal

Chapter 5: Raising Kids and Making Ends Meet 163
Another Day; Arresting Behavior; Baby Makes Five; Bringing Up Jack; Fathers and Sons; Free Country; Love and Marriage; The O'Keefes; Raising Caines; 704 Hauser; Tall Hopes; You Take the Kids

Chapter 6: Single Parenting   **209**

Daddy's Girls; Danny; Dudley; In the Motherhood; My Guys; Regular Joe

Chapter 7: Rooming Together   **235**

Lush Life; Princesses; The Return of Jezebel James; Semi-Tough; Some of My Best Friends; Trial and Error; Twenty Good Years

Chapter 8: Welcome to My World – Male Version   **263**

Bob Patterson; Come to Papa; Doc Corkle; First Impressions; Imagine That; Life . . .and Stuff; Lost at Home; Luis; The Martin Short Show; The Paul Reiser Show

Chapter 9: Welcome to My World – Female Version   **303**

Frannie's Turn; Julie; Laurie Hill; My Wildest Dreams; Roxie; Talk to Me; The Tammy Grimes Show

Chapter 10: Starting a Brand New Job   **331**

Charlie Lawrence; Checking In; Dorothy; The Jake Effect; Katie Joplin; Mister Dugan /Hanging In; The Sanford Arms; Secret Service Guy; Teech; Waverly Wonders; Wednesday 9:30 (8:30 Central)

Chapter 11: Mostly Mismatched Workmates   **377**

Ace Crawford, Private Eye; Buddies; Clerks; Cutters; Harry; In the Beginning; Nick & Hillary; Rewind; Singer & Sons; Work with Me; Working Stiffs; Zorro and Son

Chapter 12: Working as a Team   **423**

A.E.S. Hudson Street; Ball Four; Battery Park; Do Not Disturb; A League of Their Own; No Soap, Radio; The Nutt House;

The Office; On the Air; On the Spot; Park Place; Public Morals; The Rollergirls; Shaping Up; The Six O'Clock Follies

Chapter 13: Returning Home — 475

The Building; Built to Last; Costello; Crumbs

Chapter 14: Failing at Marriage — 495

It's Not Easy; Snip; The Stones

Chapter 15: Starting Over — 511

Ask Harriet; The Brian Benben Show; The Dictator; Hank; Kitchen Confidential; Take Five

Chapter 16: Surprising Arrivals and Unexpected Inheritances — 539

Beware of Dog; Bram & Alice; God, the Devil and Bob; Highcliffe Manor; Misconceptions; Over the Top; Pauly; Scorch; Struck by Lightning; That's Life; The Trouble with Larry

Chapter 17: Not Exactly the Family Next Door — 587

Apple Pie; Everything's Relative; The Grubbs; Ivan the Terrible; The Kallikaks; Mr. T and Tina; Nearly Departed; The Ortegas; The People Next Door; The Pitts; The Secret Diary of Desmond Pfeiffer

Appendix — 633

Endnotes — 641

Index — 653

Acknowledgments

I wish to thank the following writers, producers, and directors for their various contributions to this work: Al Aidekman, Lee Aronshon, David Baldy, Richard L. Bare, Stephen Black, Peter Bonerz, Stan Cutler, Robert Dames, Matthew Diamond, Richard Dresser, Michael Elias, Ken Estin, David Frankel, Tracy Gamble, Rob Gilmer, Rowby Goren, Howard M. Gould, Elizabeth Forsthye Hailey, Charlie Hauck, Bruce Kalish, Allan Katz, Dave Ketchum, Alicia Kirk, Marvin Kupfer, Dee LaDuke, Harvey Laidman, Sheldon Larry, David Latt, Norman Lear and his assistant Jean Anderson, Rob LaZebnik, Robert Leighton, Richard Christian Matheson, Lisa Medway, Frank Mula, Stephen Neigher, Andrew Nicholls, Bob Nickman, Jerry Perzigian, Lynn Phillips, Nate Reger, Eugenie Ross-Leming, Donald Reiker, Don Roos, Mike Schiff, Mindy Schneider, Brian Scully, Bob Shayne, Michael Short, Dan Staley, Joshua Sternin, Bill Taub, Richard Vaczy, Russ Woody, and George Yanok.

I would also like to thank the staffs at the following libraries and facilities for access to video and script collections relating to little-known sitcoms: Brooklyn College Library (for access to the Devery Freeman Script Collection); the Motion Picture Reading Room of the Library of Congress (and, in particular, Josie Walters-

Johnson, Rosemary Hanes, Zoran Sinobad, and Dorinda Hartmann); the New York Public Library for the Performing Arts, Dorothy and Lewis B. Cullman Center, Billy Rose Theatre Division (for access to the Peter Stone Papers); The Paley Center (especially, Richard Holbrook); The Writers Guild Foundation Library; UCLA TV script collection; the University of North Carolina (for access to the Frank Shaw Collection), and the University of Wyoming (for access to the William Dozier papers).

In addition, a big thanks to Rachel Rosenfeld for her work in researching various scripts in the UCLA TV script collection for several of the comedies profiled in this book, as well as to my good friend Garry Settimi for his assistance with different aspects of this work.

Introduction

Brad Pitt had a small part in an episode of one, while George Clooney played a former boyfriend on one. Jennifer Aniston and Michelle Williams each portrayed teenagers on different ones. Oscar winners Julie Andrews and Faye Dunaway were stars of their own. Some aired only once and were never seen again. A handful produced several episodes that never aired at all.

Forgotten Laughs: An Episode Guide to 150 TV Sitcoms You Probably Never Saw profiles little-known, short-lived situation comedies that aired less than six episodes when originally broadcast. As many as thirteen episodes were produced for some of these comedies, but they were canceled before all of them could air. Others made only a limited number of episodes as try-out series that were never renewed. *Forgotten Laughs* also describes certain sitcoms that were canceled before any episodes were televised, including several series (e.g., *Rewind*, *Secret Service Guy*, *The Grubbs*, *The Ortegas*) that the Fox network ordered but never broadcast.

In addition to airing less than six episodes, the other requirement for a comedy to be featured in *Forgotten Laughs* is that it had to have more than one episode produced; thus, pilots that never resulted in a series are excluded. This also means that a comedy like *Kid Mayor* is not included. *Kid Mayor* was a sitcom about a nineteen-year-old guy who became the mayor of a small town. The show had an order from the WB network for six episodes, but the series was canceled in the middle of taping its first episode. The head of the WB was present at the taping, hated the episode, and canceled the sitcom on the spot.[1]

For each of the comedies in *Forgotten Laughs*, a brief description is provided of the series concept and its main characters along with background information about the show and an episode guide for both aired and unaired episodes. Episode descriptions in this guide were obtained from the following sources:

1. If videos of the sitcom were available, descriptions were based on viewing the episodes. Over 700 episodes were viewed, primarily at the Library of Congress and The Paley Center.

2. If videos were not available, episode descriptions were obtained from reviewing scripts written for the series or requesting summaries of episodes from writers and producers. Descriptions based on a script or contributed by a writer or a producer are so noted in the guide.

3. As a last resort, episode descriptions were extracted from print or electronic media such as reviews of the sitcom and TV logs printed in newspapers or found online.

Most of the episode descriptions contained in *Forgotten Laughs* are being published for the first time.

While attempts were made to keep all of the episode descriptions for a particular series more or less equal in detail, this was not always possible. Videos may exist for some episodes of a comedy but not all. The same can be said for scripts. Even summaries provided by writers or producers can vary in length with some recalling very little about their series. As one writer told the author about his inability to remember the storyline of an episode he scripted, maybe it's psychological protection—in response to working on that series.

Despite multiple attempts to obtain episode descriptions for particular comedies, in some cases, little information could be found. A situation comedy is excluded if descriptions could not be procured for the majority of its episodes. At least four comedies fall into this category: the unaired *The Men's Room* and *Thick and Thin* ordered by NBC, the unaired HBO series *12 Miles of Bad Road*, and the twice-aired *The Mike O'Malley Show*. Since information could be found for only a few episodes of each of these series, they are not profiled in this book.

Also, any comedy that aired less than six episodes on a broadcast network but was later resurrected with new episodes on a cable network is not included. The animated sitcom *Home Movies*, which was broadcast briefly on UPN and then was brought back by the Cartoon Network, falls into this category.

Even for situation comedies described in the book, details about the number of episodes produced, what they were about, and who wrote and directed them were not always easy to obtain. If the information could not be found for a particular comedy, its profile simply indicates that a writer, director, or storyline of an episode is "unknown."

In *Forgotten Laughs*, sitcoms are organized around their main theme related to different stages in life, from "growing up" to "raising kids," from "starting a new job" to "starting over." Within each thematic category, the comedies are listed in alphabetical order. These categories are not mutually exclusive, and one could argue that some sitcoms could be placed in more than one category. The comedies covered in the book range from 1952's *Doc Corkle* to 2011's *The Paul Reiser Show*. An appendix is included listing each series in chronological order by the TV season in which it premiered.

As noted in the Acknowledgments, over fifty writers, directors, and producers provided information about the various short-lived sitcoms on which they worked. They not only helped with descriptions of episodes, but several also provided insights into the development of their comedy and behind-the-scenes anecdotes. For example, one writer related the story of the son of the star of the sitcom being such a poor actor that he was directed to read his one line with his head in a waste paper basket (see *Harry*, Chapter 8). Another writer indicated that the producer of a comedy hid the tapes so the network could not air the series (see *Mister Dugan*, Chapter 10). Such anecdotes are included in the series' profiles.

When contacted by the author about the short-lived comedy *Life... and Stuff* (Chapter 8) which he co-created, Lee Aronsohn, who also helped to create the hit comedy *Two and a Half Men* with Chuck Lorre, said that, "I've been involved with quite a few 'little-known TV comedies' (aka abysmal flops) during my career."[2] While not all of the sitcoms described in *Forgotten Laughs* may be characterized as utter failures, they certainly cannot be said to have been successes.

The reason a series expired after only a few episodes is generally because of its Nielsen ratings as evaluated by various network executives who saw little potential for the ratings of the sitcom to improve. Generally, the lower the rating, the more likely a series is to be canceled quickly or not be renewed after a few episodes. However, low ratings in and of themselves do not explain the abrupt demise of all of the comedies profiled. Some shows are canceled, or not renewed, even when they get respectable ratings but lose a large share of the audience from the series that preceded it. This phenomenon, known as the "falloff factor," is viewed by network executives in the same way a real estate developer does not like to see an ugly property being built in a fancy neighborhood – the overall value of the area is decreased.[3]

A series being canceled before it airs any of its episodes is almost always due to a change in top executives at a network with the new management thinking it is in a no-win situation. If the comedy developed under the preceding regime is aired and becomes a hit, then no doubt the previous management will get the credit. However, if the sitcom bombs, then the new management will most likely receive the blame. The exception to this is when the producer of a series decides not to let the comedy air, as was the case with two Norman Lear sitcoms – the first version of *A Year at the Top* (Chapter 2) and *Mister Dugan* (Chapter 10).

Finally, while all of the comedies in *Forgotten Laughs* aired less than six episodes when originally televised, in some cases, all the episodes of the series were subsequently broadcast on cable channels such as the Cartoon Network, Universal HD, or the now-defunct Trio channel. Also, in a few instances, DVDs or videotapes of these little-known series have been released. This often happens when the star of the sitcom becomes more popular. For example, in 2005 Buena Vista Home Entertainment released ten of twelve episodes of Dave Chappelle's short-lived comedy *Buddies* (Chapter 11) on DVD and billed it as "the show Dave Chappelle doesn't want you to see." These cases are noted in the profile for the applicable series. However, unlike the DVD for *Buddies*, this book contains comprehensive descriptions of all the episodes for this series as it does for most of the other sitcoms profiled.

Raphael Sbarge and Dick O'Neill in *Better Days*

Chapter 1
Growing Up Is Hard to Do

From *Leave It to Beaver* to *Malcolm in the Middle*, many situation comedies have focused on the trials and tribulations of tweens and teens living at home, going to school, making friends, and dating. Often times, the writers of long-running comedies dealing with kids have had to contend with the child actor maturing, losing his or her cuteness, and perhaps also losing their natural acting ability. The writers of the sitcoms profiled in this chapter had no such problems.

Better Days

Premiered Wednesday, October 1, 1986, at 8:30 PM on CBS

Better Days was kind of a fish-out-of-water comedy involving teenager Brian McGuire (Raphael Sbarge) moving from his parents' home in Beverly Hills to his grandfather Harry Clooney's (Dick O'Neill) place in Brooklyn. Brian's parents broke up when his dad found he was in financial trouble and left the family. His mother sent him to live with her father. Brian joined his new high school's basketball team, and his street-smart teammates, Luther (Chip McAllister) and Anthony "Snake" (Guy Killum), helped him adjust to life in Brooklyn. Brian's other classmates included Terence Dean (Randall Batinkoff) and Beat-Box (Richard McGregor). His grandfather ran a deli-candy store, and Harriet Winners (Randee Heller), nicknamed "Dirty Harriet" because she was in the police reserves and carried a gun, was Brian's homeroom teacher.

Background

The sitcom, originally called *Squad 'R'*, was created by Jeff Frelich, Arthur Silver, and Stuart Sheslow who indicated that *Better Days* would deal with issues like drugs, the generation gap, homelessness, and nuclear war, and not dwell on the "culture shock" premise of a kid from Beverly Hills adapting to Brooklyn. Magnum/Thunder Road Productions in association with Lorimar-Telepictures produced the comedy. The series theme song was "These Are My Better Days."

Episode Guide: 4 aired; 7 unaired

Episode 1: October 1, 1986   "Squad 'R'"

Director: Joel Zwick   Story: Jeff Frelich, Arthur Silver, and Stuart Sheslow
Teleplay: Arthur Silver

Brian finds it difficult getting accepted by the other students at Broxton High School. He tries to help Luther, who is afraid of public speaking, by telling their substitute teacher, Harriet Winners, that Luther is an African-exchange student who doesn't speak English. Ms. Winners asks Brian to interpret Luther's speech for the class, which he does. She then asks Brian to be the interpreter when she speaks to Luther's parents at Parent-Teacher Night. While Brian, Luther, and Snake try to prevent Ms. Winners from talking to Luther's parents, Harry informs Brian and his friends that the teacher knows that the story of Luther being unable to speak English is not true. Brian tells everyone at Parent-Teacher Night that he and Luther pretended Luther was an exchange student to gauge everyone's reactions to a newcomer at the school. Luther loses his fear of public speaking, and Ms. Winners announces that she will be their permanent homeroom teacher.

Raphael Sbarge was named after the painter Raphael and began his acting career at age four and a half on *Sesame Street*.

Episode 2: October 8, 1986   "Cheaters Never Win"

Director: Bill Bixby   Writer: Rob Edwards

Faced with the prospect of failing English and having to attend summer school, Brian thinks about cheating on an exam. Terence has set up an elaborate scheme to cheat on the test by having another student who is good in English listen to the questions the teacher poses and project the answers on a wall outside the classroom windows. In the end, Brian refuses to participate, and Ms. Winners uncovers the scheme. Brian gets a C on the test.

While directing many TV series episodes, Bill Bixby was probably better known for his acting in series like *My Favorite Martian* and *The Incredible Hulk*.

Episode 3: October 15, 1986   "Wendell and the Three Sure Things"

Director: Howard Storm   Writer: David Nichols

Snake's promise to take his little brother, Wendell, to Coney Island goes unmet when the guys get three hot dates. Wendell sneaks out while Snake, Luther, and Brian are dancing with their dates in the living room. When they find Wendell missing, the three go looking for him. They think he broke into Harry's deli but discover that a real thief broke into the store. Finally, Wendell appears, and Snake apologizes and says he will take him to Coney Island as promised.

Episode 4: October 22, 1986   "Double-D"

Director: Stan Lathan   Writer: Ralph Farquhar

A pro-basketball star, nicknamed "Double-D," returns to his alma mater to award a scholarship in his name. He invites Luther, who idolizes him, to hang out. Brian sees Double-D doing cocaine and tells Snake. The two of them confront Luther about the drug use. Double-D reveals to Luther that he is not as good as Luther thinks he is. Later Luther finds Double-D dead from a drug overdose and vows never to get involved with drugs.

Episode 5: Unaired   "Never Blow Up the World" (summary based on final draft script)

Director: Bill Bixby   Writer: Ronald Rubin

The students have to come up with an idea for a "Peace Week" project. Brian suggests they have a summit meeting by dividing the class between the NATO countries and the Eastern Bloc countries. Luther will be President Reagan, and Snake will be Gorbachev, the head of the Soviet Union. Meanwhile, a new student, Odessa Williams, enrolls in school, and both Snake and Luther are attracted to her. Although Luther and Snake agree not to let a girl ruin their friendship, Odessa ends up dating both guys. Brian moderates the summit meeting between Luther and Snake, but the two guys proceed to argue over Odessa. For the meeting, Brian hooked up a world globe that glows when either Luther or Snake push buttons on their podiums indicating a nuclear strike. As Luther and Snake argue, both press their buttons at the same time. The globe explodes and causes the lighting fixtures in the classroom to burst and the sprinklers to spray water. When their teacher asks them what they learned, they say they learned never to blow up the world.

Episode 6: Unaired   "A Car is Not a Home" (summary based on final revised script)

Director: Mel Ferber   Writer: Jeff Frelich

Brian, Snake, and Luther discover a man named Fred (Bill Macy) living in his car. The guys have to do a report for school about their "Man of the Year," and initially they want to do the report about an exterminator. But when they find other classmates are doing their reports on judges and surgeons, the guys decide to have Fred come to their class and do their report about him. Their teacher scolds them for embarrassing Fred in front of the class, and the boys apologize to him. Brian decides to take Fred home for a meal and a good night's sleep. He also works to get Fred's car started. Brian is distracted by some girls when he gets the car running, and someone steals the vehicle. After informing Fred that his car was stolen, the guys try to get him back with his family. However, the people whom they think are

Fred's family simply share the same last name with him. Fred thanks the guys for caring and says he wants to start over. In the end, the guys do get Fred's car back from the guy who stole it.

Episode 7: Unaired   "Ground Rules" (summary based on final draft script)

Director: Bill Bixby   Writers: Jeanne Baruch and Jeanne Romano

Brian promises his granddad that he will be at the deli to accept a delivery of soda so Harry can go bowling with his friends. However, Brian wants to get free tickets to a Rolling Stones concert and forgets his promise. Harry misses his bowling match and grounds Brian for two weeks which means he can't attend the concert. Brian decides to let fate decide if he can go to the concert or not. He plans to walk by the deli in full view. If his grandfather sees him, he will not go to the concert, but if he doesn't see him, he will go. Brian ends up going to the concert and, on the way home with Snake and Luther, his foot gets stuck in a hole in the street that has been dug up for repairs near the deli. Harry discovers him and, realizing he sneaked out to the concert, begins yelling at him. But by the end, Harry says he really loves Brian, and they hug.

Episode 8: Unaired   "West Coast Girl" (summary based on final draft script)

Director: Howard Storm   Writer: Marty Nadler

Tracy, Brian's girlfriend from L.A., is spending a few days in New York before flying to Europe with a friend. When she arrives, Brian and Harry have dinner with her, and Harry makes Brian sleep in the living room while Tracy sleeps in Brian's bedroom. At a dance the school is having, Brian meets Tracy's male friend Leslie. Leslie, Tracy, and Brian wind up back at Harry's place where Tracy kisses Leslie good night, and both Leslie and Brian sleep in the living room. The next day, when Tracy and Leslie come to the school to talk with Brian, Leslie and Brian fight. Later, Brian tells Tracy he is sorry, and they kiss several times before she leaves for the airport.

Episode 9: Unaired "Wooly Bully" (summary based on final draft script)

Director: Stan Lathan   Writers: Eric Blakeney and Gene Miller

Snake accidentally knocks the lunch tray out of the hands of a new student named Curtis who just got out of reform school. Curtis says that he won't kill Snake but that he needs to disappear anytime Curtis is around. Snake tries to avoid Curtis at school; however, when Curtis comes to Harry's deli and tells Snake to leave, Snake stands his ground. After Harry asks Curtis to leave, Curtis demands that Snake meet him in the alley later after school. Ms. Winners informs Curtis that, since he is on probation, he can stay in school only if he doesn't get in trouble. Brian and Luther try to talk Curtis out of fighting Snake but are unsuccessful. When Snake shows up for the fight, Curtis attempts to get him to hit first so Curtis can claim self-defense. Curtis lets Snake know that if Snake doesn't hit him first, he goes back to reform school, but Snake won't hit him.

Episode 10: Unaired "29 Minutes" (summary based on final draft script)

Director: Stan Lathan   Writers: Phil Kellard and Tom Moore

The vice principal informs Ms. Winners that she needs to stick to the curriculum and not try to be experimental in class. He also wants her to drop the show she has on the school's public access television channel and gives her an ultimatum—either stay at Broxton and do things his way or leave. Ms. Winners decides to leave the school, and the vice principal hires a former wrestler to take over her class who doesn't challenge students to learn anything. The guys get the vice principal and Ms. Winners together in the school's TV studio so they can broadcast the real reasons she left the school. When he discovers he is on a live broadcast, the vice principal asks Ms. Winners to return to Broxton High.

Episode 11: Unaired "All Rapped Up" (summary based on final draft script)

Director: Stan Lathan   Writer: Ralph Farquhar

A TV music channel is holding a contest to win a free concert by Run-D.M.C. at the winner's high school. Each school is to submit an original rap song, and Run-D.M.C. will pick the winning entry. Snake wants to compose the song for

Broxton High but has writer's block. Brian and Terence also try to write a rap song just in case Snake doesn't come up with one. Finally, Snake completes his rap, and Broxton High wins the contest. However, the vice principal forbids Run-D.M.C. from appearing because he has heard that rap concerts start riots. Brian reads the lyrics to a Run-D.M.C. rap for the principal who likes them and lets the group give their concert.

Good-bye *Days*

Better Days was originally on Wednesdays at 8:30 PM for a few weeks before it moved to the 8:00 PM time slot. The comedy faced tough competition from *Highway to Heaven* on NBC and the sitcoms *Perfect Strangers* and *Head of the Class* on ABC. *Better Days* lasted for four episodes before it was canceled because of low ratings. Its third episode ranked forty-seventh out of sixty-four programs. It was one of the first casualties of the 1986-87 TV season.

Brutally Normal

Premiered Monday, January 24, 2000, at 9:00 PM on the WB

Brutally Normal focused on the lives of four best friends attending Wicker M. Normal High School: Robert "Pooh" Cutler (Mike Damus), who was well meaning but slightly neurotic; Russell Wise (Eddie Kaye Thomas from the *American Pie* films), a handsome but insecure teen; Anna Pricova (Lea Moreno), a precocious girl whose family had emigrated from Russia, and Dru Pape (Tangie Ambrose), the bright, cynical member of the group. Joanna Pacula played Anna's mother, Gogi. The comedy was sometimes punctuated with fantasy sequences that brought the characters' imaginations to life.

Background

Michael Goldberg and Tommy Swerdlow created *Brutally Normal* and originally tried to sell it to ABC. However, ABC wanted the series to be an hour-long teen drama instead of a half-hour comedy, and so the creators took the show to the WB as a half-hour comedy. The one-hour pilot for the series was filmed in July 1999, but never aired.[4] Supposedly, the character of Russell was based on Swerdlow's own experiences in school, and the character of Anna was based on Swerdlow's wife.[5] The pilot dealt with AIDS awareness week at the school Pooh, Russell, and Anna attended. Pooh was studying for his PSAT's, but, after viewing a website about HIV, he became convinced that he had the virus. Anna was wondering about her sexual identity after defending a fellow student who might have been a lesbian. She was also concerned about her mother's dating habits and urged her to take an AIDS test. Anna propositioned Russell to have sex with her. But, when he went to her place at night for the encounter, she changed her mind, and he left. In the end, Anna confessed that she wanted Russell to make love to her to see if she could become physically aroused by a man; Russell admitted that he was still a virgin; Pooh walked out of his PSAT's still worried that he had HIV, and Anna's mother took the test for AIDS. *Brutally Normal* was produced by The Shephard/Robin Company and Touchstone Television.

Episode Guide: 5 aired; 2 unaired

Episode 1: January 24, 2000   "You Get What You Get"

Director: Marc Buckland   Writer: Stephen Chbosky

Russell receives a kiss from an older woman at an art gallery only to find out later that she is his new substitute teacher. No one believes Russell when he says he kissed the teacher. His friends want to see photographic evidence. Russell has Pooh hide in a tree with a camera, while he goes to the teacher's classroom to position her in such a way that it will appear through the window that he is kissing her. When Anna finds out about the photo, she tells Russell that it will ruin the teacher's career if they put the photo on a website. Anna dates the yearbook editor to not only retrieve the photo of the teacher that Russell gave him but also to get back a bad candid photo of herself that is to appear in the yearbook. At the end, the three friends find that the photo Pooh took of the teacher didn't come out.

Episode 2: January 24, 2000   "Barricade"

Director: Marc Buckland   Writers: Tommy Swerdlow and Michael Goldberg

Russell's civics teacher encourages his students to express themselves which Russell does by mooning the class. When the vice principal sees this, Russell has to go to the principal's office. While the principal is not in his office, Russell, trying to access his file on the principal's computer, accidently crashes the PC. In a panic, he locks himself in the principal's office, and, unwittingly, becomes the leader of a protest movement against the possible termination of the popular civics teacher. Thomas Jefferson appears to him, and they discuss what being a revolutionary really means. Anna and Russell speak with the principal who assures them that he will not terminate the civics teacher, but he does give Russell a two-day suspension.

Ken Jenkins, better known as Dr. Bob Kelso on *Scrubs*, played the civics teacher and Thomas Jefferson on this episode.

Episode 3: January 31, 2000   "Mouth Full of Warm Roses"

Director: Marc Buckland   Writers: Will McRobb and Chris Viscardi

Russell asks Pooh to deliver a love letter to the most popular senior girl in school whose boyfriend is the school bully. When confronted by the girl's boyfriend who casts aspersions on his manhood, Pooh pretends the letter is from him. Pooh and Russell argue over who should fight the bully since the fight offers Russell the chance to win the girl's affection and Pooh a way to prove his manhood. The bully declines to fight either Pooh or Russell, and they end up fighting each other. Meanwhile, Anna has a secret admirer who turns out to be the school nerd, but he is too shy to say anything to her in person.

Episode 4: February 7, 2000   "Stretching Ethics"

Director: Lev L. Spiro Writer: Stephen Chbosky

Anna and her family are about to be deported back to Russia because the Immigration Service claims their visas were obtained illegally. Anna's mother wants to get another set of fake visas, which cost about $20,000. She has $15,000 but needs the rest. Russell and Pooh scheme to cheat at poker to win the $5000. However, the game they enter is raided by the police. The police don't press charges against Pooh or Russell because of their age, and Russell's mother finds that Anna's family papers are really legal.

Episode 5: February 14, 2000   "Well Solved Sherlock"

Director: Michael M. Robin   Writers: Tommy Swerdlow and Michael Goldberg

While preparing for the science fair, Pooh thinks his dad is having an affair with Anna's mother, and so he asks Russell to spy on his dad during a late-night business meeting. After the science fair, Pooh and Anna go to Gogi's salon where they find that Pooh's dad was being secretive about meeting with Anna's mother because he was arranging a second mortgage on the building that houses her salon.

Episode 6: Unaired   "Damaged Goods"

Director: Randall Zisk   Writers: Tommy Swerdlow and Michael Goldberg

When a guidance counselor questions Anna's social skills and says she is closed to new experiences, Anna agrees to show Ashley, a new student, around school. Anna invites Ashley to dinner with her and her mother. Both Russell and Pooh find Ashley charming, and she confides to Pooh that Anna says he is neurotic and to Russell that Anna thinks he has a big ego. Anna confesses that Ashley is creeping her out and asks Pooh and Russell to determine what she is up to. Ashley admits that she was so taken with Anna's life that she wanted to be just like Anna, but she has to leave school because her dad is moving to a new town.

Episode 7: Unaired   "Road Trip"

Director: Randall Zisk   Story: Tommy Swerdlow and Michael Goldberg
Teleplay: Tommy Swerdlow

Russell invites Pooh and Anna to go to a nightclub where his father is floor manager, but Pooh's dad won't let him go. Russell and Anna convince Pooh to steal his dad's car and take them to the club. When they arrive, Russell discovers that his father forgot to put their names on the list so they can get in. He climbs through a window to enter the club, and Anna and Pooh follow him. Russell tries to find his dad, while Anna and Pooh attempt to have fun. Having discovered the car missing, Pooh's father turns up at the club and confronts Russell's dad. Eventually, the two fathers find their kids, and Pooh, Russell, and Anna leave with Pooh's dad. Russell's father gives him a prepaid phone card so he can call him, but Russell throws the card away telling Pooh and Anna that the phone cards his dad gives him have always had all of their minutes already used.

Brutally Bombed

This teen comedy was on Mondays up against the CBS powerhouse *Everybody Loves Raymond*, and bombed in the ratings. It scored the lowest rating ever for a WB non-rerun on Mondays at 9:00 PM losing about 70 percent of the audience from its lead-in, *7th Heaven*.

Go Fish

Premiered Tuesday, June 19, 2001, at 8:00 PM on NBC

Go Fish was like a combination of *The Wonder Years* and *Malcolm in the Middle*. "Fish" was the nickname of Andy Troutner (Kieran Culkin, Macauley Culkin's brother), a high school freshman who had a plan to become the most popular kid at Westlake High and win the heart of the cheerleader of his dreams, sophomore Jess Riley (Katherine Ellis). Given that this was a comedy, his plan, of course, resulted in many embarrassing situations. Fish's friends at school were Henry "Krak" Krakowski (Kyle Sabihy) and Hazard (Taylor Handley). Fish's plan was complicated by the fact that his older brother, Pete (Will Friedle, *Boy Meets World*, *The Random Years*), taught at the school. Pete was attracted to English teacher Laura Eastwood (Kristin Lehman). Andy Dick from *Newsradio* was also featured on the series as Ernie Hopkins, an over-the-top drama teacher. Andy's mom and dad were played by Molly Cheek and Joe Flaherty.

Background

Go Fish was originally scheduled to premiere at midseason on NBC but was delayed until summer 2001. Adam Herz, who had written *American Pie*, created the series, which was developed by Pam Brady, a writer for the animated series *South Park*.

Touchstone Television produced *Go Fish*.

Episode Guide: 4 aired; 1 unaired

Episode 1: June 19, 2001   "Go Four-Point Plan"

Director: John Fortenberry   Writers: Adam Herz and Pam Brady

On the first day of his freshman year in high school, Fish tells Krak and Hazard that they should maintain a low profile, but things go awry. Fish puts on some cologne his dad gave him, but, when his brother Pete tells him it smells terrible, he goes to the restroom, takes off his shirt, and tries to wash off the cologne. In the meantime, Hazard spills a spicy substance on his pants, goes to the restroom, and takes off his pants to clean himself. Krak is outside the bathroom door, but other students, wanting to use the facility, push him through the door. He falls on Hazard and Fish, and they all end up in embarrassing positions on the bathroom floor in front of their fellow classmates who think they are a gay threesome. Later, Fish is in drama class where the teacher wants someone to perform in front of the class. Because Jess doesn't want to be the one chosen, Fish volunteers, tries to sing "The Wedding Bell Blues," and passes out from not eating anything. When other students go through his pants to find out who he is, they discover a card from his mom saying he is eligible for "three free hugs in mommy land." When Jess sees Fish in the nurse's room, she thanks him for saving her in drama class. Meanwhile, Fish's brother Pete starts his teaching job at the school. In his first class, he tells the students to call him Pete and that he won't give them any tests. After the principal talks to Pete about this, in later classes, Pete advises his students that he is "Mr. Troutner" and that there will be tests.

Episode 2: June 19, 2001   "Go PDA"

Director: Alan Arkush   Writer: Jeff Lowell

When Fish goes out with a girl named Amanda to make Jess jealous, he discovers that Amanda is dating him to make the boy who is dating Jess envious. Fish begins to develop feelings for Amanda. But she stages a public breakup with him, and Jess begins noticing Fish more. Meanwhile, drama teacher Hopkins holds a seminar for teachers to identify students who may be abusing drugs. He instructs the teachers to befriend suspected drug abusers. Pete mistakenly thinks that Hazard is on drugs. Pete tries to be a role model and makes friends with him, but his actions cause Hazard to think that Pete is gay. When Hazard tells Pete that he is straight, Pete thinks that he is saying he is no longer on drugs.

Episode 3: June 26, 2001   "Go Student Council"

Director: Arlene Sanford   Writer: Jeff Lowell

Fish decides that if he runs for student council, girls will notice him. Fish, Krak, and a girl named Lisa get on council because they are the only volunteers for the three open spots. Power-hungry Lisa questions Hopkins, who is student council adviser, when a council member proposes more funds for the drama class. Fish is made student council treasurer, but his plans to lead student council get out to all the members. Hopkins calls an emergency meeting where Fish has to defend himself. He confesses that he is only guilty of being ambitious, which isn't a violation of the school constitution. Later Lisa finds a $49 discrepancy in the council's books maintained by Fish. Fish remembers Hopkins billing the council for $49 for curtains for his office which leads Hopkins to oust Lisa from the council and keep Fish. Meanwhile, Pete would like to date Ms. Eastwood but sees her with Hopkins. Hopkins says that he and Ms. Eastwood have a relationship, but she later says they are only friends.

Episode 4: July 3, 2001   "Go Wrestling"

Director: Arlene Sanford   Writers: Christopher Miller and Phil Lord

Seeing that a letterman jacket impresses the girls, Fish tries out for the wrestling team coached by his brother. There is only one other guy in Fish's weight class whom he figures he can beat. However, when the guy turns out to be tougher than Fish thought, his next plan is to fatten the guy up so that Fish will be the only one in the weight class. While Fish succeeds at this, Pete matches him up against a member of the school's feminist club. Fish doesn't want to wrestle the girl but, to save face, finally does. He wins the match, but no one cheers. However, Jess thinks that wrestling the girl shows that Fish believes in women's equality.

Episode 5: Unaired   "Go Rebel"

Director: Peter Lauer   Writer: Michael A. Kaplan

Fish tries to act like a bad boy to win Jess over, but Pete restrains Fish's rebel yelling in front of half the school. Meanwhile, Fish's dad finds a new way to stay in tune with his wife after signing up for Mr. Hopkins' singing class.

Go Fish Gone

Go Fish premiered with a special double episode on Tuesdays at 8:00 PM. The two episodes ranked seventieth and seventy-second in the Nielsen ratings. The comedy aired two more episodes at 8:30 PM on subsequent Tuesdays, and then it was gone.

M.Y.O.B.

Premiered Tuesday, June 6, 2000, at 9:30 PM on NBC

M.Y.O.B. meant "mind your own business," which was the exact opposite of what the leading character, Riley Veatch (Katherine Towne), a sixteen-year-old girl raised in foster care, did. Riley left her foster home in Ohio and traveled to Northern California in search of her birth mother. In California, she found her Aunt Opal (Lauren Graham), a teacher at Gossett High School where Riley enrolled. Opal was infatuated with the handsome assistant principal at the school, Mitch Levitt (Paul Fitzgerald) with whom she had been friends in college and had a brief affair. Lisa Overbeck (Amanda Detmer) was a sexy teacher whom Mitch had hired. Each episode of this sitcom was narrated by Riley, who looked similar to Paris Hilton and liked to smoke a lot.

Background

Don Roos, writer and director of the 1998 movie *The Opposite of Sex*, created *M.Y.O.B.*, which was a variation of the film. In *The Opposite of Sex*, a teen girl moves in with her gay half-brother who was a school teacher and seduces his boyfriend. In *M.Y.O.B.*, Roos created a character similar to the young girl in the film. He described the teenager as "... basically Eve Arden, after midnight, when she's sour and mean."[6] Nicki Aycox and Elizabeth Perkins were originally cast as Riley and her aunt, but apparently they were not right for the roles and the series' leads were recast. Intended to be a midseason replacement, NBC finally premiered the comedy during the summer. Charade Productions and NBC Studios produced *M.Y.O.B.*

Episode Guide: 4 aired; 3 unaired

Episode 1: June 6, 2000   "The Bad Seed"

Director: Bryan Gordon   Writer: Don Roos

Arriving in California, Riley takes a taxi from the airport with an older man, and they go to his hotel room for lunch. When he makes a pass at her, Riley sticks him in the groin with a toothpick and gets away. She finds Opal Brown and says she is her niece. Opal emails her sister Pearl in Finland to see if Riley's claim is true. Although Pearl responds by stating she was never pregnant, Opal doubts her sister and lets Riley stay with her. Opal happens to be the assistant principal at the school Riley will attend. When the principal of the school dies of a sudden heart attack, Opal is next in line for the position. However, the superintendent gives the position to Opal's ex-boyfriend Mitch. When Riley sees on TV that the superintendent is the man who picked her up at the airport, she calls him, and Riley's aunt is suddenly given the principal's position.

Katherine Towne (Riley) is the granddaughter of 1940s movie stars John Payne and Anne Shirley.

Episode 2: June 13, 2000   "Boys in the Band"

Director: Bryan Gordon   Writer: Ann Donahue

Riley discovers that teacher Mary Beth Farber, Opal's best friend, is in love with Richard, an eighteen-year-old student although they have yet to have sex. Opal wants to terminate Mary Beth, but Riley is suspicious that Richard and the teacher have never consummated their relationship. She breaks into Richard's locker and finds a picture of a semi-naked man. Later, Riley discovers Richard in a compromising position in the back of a van with another male student and forces him to come out to Mary Beth, thereby avoiding Opal from having to fire her.

Ann Donahue, who scripted this episode, became a writer and producer for *CSI* and its spin-offs.

Episode 3: June 20, 2000   "French Connection"

Director: Victoria Hochberg   Writers: Jim Keily and Jimmy Aleck

Riley finds what she thinks is her mother's diary in Opal's attic. She hopes it will reveal some details about her parents, but, since it is in French, she tricks her French teacher into translating it for her by telling him the dairy is about two women kissing. From the diary, she thinks that her real father's name is Phil. Riley finds Phil, but he says he is not her father and that her mother just wanted money from him for an abortion.

Episode 4: June 27, 2000   "Basic Instinct"

Director: Stephen Crago   Writer: Marc Dube

Riley gets romantic with fellow student, Evan, while Opal finds out that Mitch has never signed his divorce papers and so was still married when they had their affair. When Opal discusses this with Mitch, they begin kissing passionately, but she turns down his further propositions. Riley discovers that Evan is still involved with his girlfriend from last year, and when he comes by her house, she doesn't invite him in. By the end, Riley sees that she has something in common with Opal.

Paul Fitzgerald (Mitch) is the grandson of 1964 Vice Presidential candidate William Miller who was on the Republican ticket with Barry Goldwater.

Episode 5: Unaired   "Paper Chase"

Director: Unknown   Writers: Jeanette Collins and Mimi Friedman

After Opal receives flack from the faculty that Riley is uncontrollable, she asks Mitch to help her. He suggests that Riley enroll in work study. Riley thinks Opal is trying to get rid of her and uses Mitch to get a job as Opal's office assistant.

Episode 6: Unaired   "Coming to America"

Director: Unknown   Writers: Amy Engelberg and Wendy Engelberg

Opal sponsors a needy foreign exchange student whom Riley discovers is a con artist who is pregnant. The student wants her child to be born in the U.S. Riley has to choose between protecting Opal and informing on the foreign exchange student.

It appears that this episode, which was originally scheduled to air on July 11, 2000, might also be known as "Out of Africa." When contacted by the author, Don Roos, the creator of *M.Y.O.B.*, apologized for not recalling what "Out of Africa" and the following episode "Arms Akimbo" were about due to the length of time that has passed since *M.Y.O.B.* had been produced.[7]

Episode 7: Unaired   "Arms Akimbo"

Director: Unknown   Writer: Unknown

Storyline unknown

No One Wanted to Watch

At the end of the first episode, Riley, speaking to the camera, said, "So you don't wanna watch? Hey, that's okay. *Law & Order* is bound to be on somewhere." Apparently the viewing audience took her advice; *M.Y.O.B.* lasted only four episodes. Lauren Graham, who played Aunt Opal, subsequently starred on the long-running series *Gilmore Girls* and the TV series remake of Ron Howard's *Parenthood*.

Molloy

Premiered Wednesday, July 25, 1990, at 9:00 PM on Fox

Molloy, if remembered at all, is probably best known as Jennifer Aniston's sitcom debut. However, she did not play the lead role of thirteen-year-old Molloy Martin. Mayim Bialik was Molloy, a teenager who, after the death of her divorced mother in New York, moved in with her father, Paul (Kevin Scannell), her stepmom, Lynn (Pamela Brull), who ran an interior design business, and Lynn's two kids – teenage Courtney (Jennifer Aniston) and young son Jason (Luke Edwards) in Beverly Hills. While Molloy got along with her stepmother and stepbrother, she could not tolerate spoiled, status-conscious sixteen-year-old Courtney. In addition to being committed to social and environmental causes, Molloy was part of the cast of a local children's TV show called *Wonderland* at KQET—the TV station where her father was the program director. Her co-stars on *Wonderland* included veteran performer Simon (I.M. Hobson) who appeared dressed as a squirrel, ditsy teen Sara (Ashley Maw), and hip Louis (Bumper Robinson).

Background

After her performance in the movie *Beaches*, Mayim Bialik was sought for a TV series. She committed to two pilots – *Molloy* for Fox and *Blossom* for NBC. *Molloy* was the first to go into production, and after, the episodes for *Molloy* were produced, Bialik shot the pilot for *Blossom*.

George Beckerman wrote the original pilot of *Molloy*. Stu Kreisman, along with Chris Cluess, recreated the series after Beckerman was let go. *Molloy* was originally about a young girl, Maude Molloy, moving from Brooklyn to Beverly Hills to live with her single, divorced dad after her social activist mother had died. She attended a private school where her father – Malcolm (Robert Desiderio), was the science teacher. He was dating Ms. Deluca (Cindy Morgan), the dean of the school. Actors Donnie Jeffcoat, Ashley Maw, Matt Norero, Bumper Robinson, and twins Aditra and Danielle Kohl played her classmates. None of the students had a social conscience like Molloy. In the pilot, Molloy didn't want to dissect frogs in her science class. The frogs mysteriously disappeared and everyone thought that Molloy had freed them. However, a boy with a crush on Molloy actually let the frogs go, but she still took the blame for the incident. In the end, her dad and Ms. Deluca discovered who really freed the frogs.

Kreisman and Cluess revamped the concept letting all the actors go except for Bialik, Maw, and Robinson. Molloy got a stepmother and two step-siblings, and the role of the father was changed from a teacher to a TV station program director. Kreisman and Cluess also added the idea of Molloy working on a kids' TV show which was supposed to be a parody of *Sesame Street*. Lee Rich Productions in association with Warner Bros. produced *Molloy*. The series had been in the can for about a year before it was aired. *Molloy's* theme song was "Accentuate the Positive."

Episode Guide: 4 aired, 2 unaired

Episode 1: July 25, 1990   "Surprise! We Forgot"

Director: Andrew D. Weyman   Writers: Stu Kreisman and Chris Cluess

Dad promises Molloy a surprise later in the day, which she thinks will be for her thirteenth birthday. When Molloy goes home, she finds that her dad's surprise is a new Mercedes for the family. The next day, Paul wonders why Molloy is in a bad mood. After Courtney discovers a birthday card for Molloy, her dad realizes that yesterday was Molloy's birthday. The family plans a party for Molloy, but all the guests have left by the time Molloy comes home. Mom and dad apologize to her but are upset that she is late.

Episode 2: August 1, 1990   "Blame It on Mio"

Director: Jack Shea   Writer: Dottie Archibald

Everyone is scheduled to go on a weekend ski trip except Molloy and her dad, and she is looking forward to time alone with her father. However, since Courtney is misbehaving as usual, her mother threatens to forbid her from going skiing. Molloy covers for Courtney when she loses one of her mother's earrings so she doesn't get grounded. Courtney takes advantage of the situation by causing trouble on purpose. Finally, Molloy tells her dad that she has been covering for Courtney's bad behavior. Paul informs Lynn, and Courtney confesses what she has been doing. In the end, mom and her two kids go on the ski trip, while Molloy and her dad stay home together.

Episode 3: August 8, 1990   "Hell No, We Won't Mop 'N Glo"

Director: Andrew D. Weyman   Writers: Carrie Honigblum and Renee Phillips

Thanks to Molloy, the Martin house becomes strike headquarters for housekeepers seeking better working conditions.

Episode 4: August 15, 1990   "The Object of Her Obsession"

Director: Andrew D. Weyman   Writer: Dottie Archibald

Molloy experiences puppy love for Courtney's potential boyfriend. She is so impressed with his style that she overlooks his lack of substance.

Episode 5: Unaired   "Business as Usual"

Director: Jack Shea   Writer: Lee Maddux

The storyline of this episode is not known.

Episode 6: Unaired   "The Day the Squirrel Cried"

Director: Jack Shea   Writers: Renee Phillips & Carrie Honigblum

Presumably, this episode was about Simon who dressed in a squirrel costume for the TV show on which Molloy appeared.

Fox's First Victim

Molloy lasted for four episodes. Being a relatively new network, most of Fox's shows ranked near the bottom of the Nielsen ratings. *Molloy*'s premiere ranked eighty-ninth out of ninety shows. The series was the first quick cancelation of a sitcom by the Fox network. The cancelation of *Molloy* allowed NBC the chance to put Mayim Bialik's other series, *Blossom*, into production.

Someone Like Me

Premiered Monday, March 14, 1994 at 8:30 PM on NBC

Attempting to take a realistic look at the world from the viewpoint of a preteen, this comedy, set in St. Louis, was about an opinionated eleven-year-old girl, Gaby Stepjak (Gaby Hoffman). Her stepdad was Steven (Anthony Tyler Quinn), an optician at a local mall; her mom was Jean (Patricia Heaton) who liked natural foods, kept an ultra-clean house, and was a travel agent at Four Corners Travel. Gaby had two siblings – her older teenage sister, Samantha (Nikki Cox) and a four-year-old half brother, Evan (Joseph Tello). Her best friend, Jane Schmidt (Reagan Kotz), had a mother, Dorie (Jane Morris), who would let Jane do almost anything. Gaby attended Walter Mondale Middle School and hung out at the Park Recreation Center where she was a member of the swim team.

Background

Bruce Helford, a former producer of *Roseanne* and *The Drew Carey Show*, created *Someone Like Me*, which was originally titled *Gaby*. He always wanted to do a series about kids. Helford went to a school in St. Louis to do research for the series. "I'd ask questions of the kids . . . like, 'Do you guys date?' . . . No adults have any real idea what life is like because we're used to basically looking at faces that look very young and expecting a certain thing."[8] NBC felt the comedy would be a good companion to its lead-in, *Blossom*. *Someone Like Me* was produced by Mohawk Productions and Sandollar Productions in association with Touchstone Television.

Episode Guide: 5 aired; 1 unaired

Episode 1: March 14, 1994   "The Lying Game"

Director: John Whitesell   Writers: Robert Cohen and Drew Carey

Sam wants Gaby to cover for her so she can go to a skating rink although she has been forbidden by her mother to go there. Gaby tells her stepdad, Steven, that her sister is taking her to the movies. Gaby and her friends really go to the mall, while Sam is at the rink. Sam forgets to pick Gaby up at the mall, and, when Gaby finally gets home, she says that she ditched Sam and went to another movie with her friend Jane whom her mother forbade her to see. Steven has always let Jean punish her daughters when they disobey, but this time he punishes Gaby by taking away her phone privileges.

Drew Carey, who co-wrote this episode, is better known as the star of his self-titled TV sitcom as well as the host of *The Price Is Right*.

Episode 2: March 28, 1994   "When Moms Collide"

Director: John Whitesell   Writer: Lona Williams

Jane is turning twelve but doesn't want to have a birthday party at her home because it is so messy. Gaby says that they can have the party at her place although she has to convince her mom of this. Jean agrees to have the party, but then Jane's mother Dorie shows up bringing a bottle of wine and a slasher movie. Jean doesn't want the kids to have a taste of alcohol or view the movie. The two moms argue, and Gaby blurts out that they are having the party at her house because Jane's house was too dirty. Dorie leaves, but the two mothers continue arguing at Gaby and Jane's swim meet. Eventually, Jean decides to try to make peace with Dorie. She goes to Dorie's house under the guise that Dorie, who sells cosmetics door-to-door, gave her a coupon for a free makeover. Dorie informs Jean that she has gotten over their argument but then gives Jean a hideous makeover.

Episode 3: April 4, 1994   "The Guy"

Director: John Whitesell   Writer: Ruth Bennett

At her first dance, Gaby is infatuated with a handsome boy named Shawn. Inspired by an experience that Steven had when he was in school, Gaby decides to record a love song to Shawn and gives him the tape at the rec center. She later finds out that he already has a girlfriend. Steven and Gaby go to the rec center to retrieve the tape which Shawn has given to the manager of the center snack bar to play. However, they are able to get the tape back and destroy it before it is played.

Episode 4: April 18, 1994   "El Presidente"

Directors: Zane Buzby and John Whitesell   Writers: Holly Hester and Mark Driscoll

Jean encourages Gaby to run for class president against classmate Doug Harper. Harper's campaign manager stops by Gaby's house when she isn't there and pretends he wants to interview Jean about Gaby for the school paper. While Jean is on the phone, he takes an embarrassing baby picture of Gaby out of the photo album and makes posters showing the picture with the slogan, "Gaby's Barely Qualified." To get even, Jane steals Doug's baby blanket from his bedroom. But Gaby's mom doesn't want her daughter to engage in dirty tricks like her opponent's campaign is doing. Gaby learns that Doug has dropped out of the race after finding his blanket was stolen. Gaby gives it back to him without anyone knowing. Doug re-enters the race, but Gaby wins anyway.

Episode 5: April 25, 1994   "What I Did for Art"

Director: Rob Schiller   Writers: Eve Ahlert and Dennis Drake

Gaby's piece of "performance art" thoroughly confuses her tradition-minded coach (Leslie Nielsen) who is also the art teacher. The teacher gives her an "F" for a recitation she does on the teacher's desk while painting herself in different colors. Jean decides to meet with the teacher to get him to reconsider. He agrees to give Gaby a second chance. Gaby shows him a sculpture she did of herself which everyone, including the teacher, says looks like ET. The teacher likes the sculpture, but Gaby tells him that she wants to stick with her original performance art. The teacher decides to raise her grade to a "B" because of her integrity.

Episode 6: Unaired   "Sympathy for the Devil"

Director: John Whitesell   Writer: Bruce Helford

Gaby doesn't want her parents to find out that Jane smokes. However, when Jane's discarded cigarette starts a fire in front of Gaby's home, Steven finds the cigarette, and Jean forbids Gaby from seeing her again. Gaby gives her mother the silent treatment, but Steven advises her to make up with her mom. Gaby talks with her mother and asks to see Jane at least on the weekends.

This episode was the pilot for the series. In it, Gaby's mom Jean was a buyer for a department store and not a travel agent.

Blossom Did Better

Originally scheduled for six weeks, *Someone Like Me* left the air after five episodes. The series ranked in the middle of the Nielsen ratings. However, it did not perform as well in its timeslot as the previous occupant of that spot had done – *Blossom*.

Patricia Heaton (Jean) later starred on *Everybody Loves Raymond* and *The Middle*, while Anthony Tyler Quinn (Steven) went on to another short-lived comedy, *Ask Harriet*.

Chapter 2
Lusting, Loving, and Making a Living

David Keith in *Co-Ed Fever*

John Stamos, Jamie Gertz, and Cain Devore in *Dreams*

The years after high school and before getting married, having kids, and buying a house, called the "random years" by one sitcom creator, is a theme explored by many TV comedies, particularly after the success of *Friends*. Most of the sitcoms in this chapter could be called *Friends* "clones" since they premiered on or after September 1994, and deal mainly with unmarried twentysomethings having sex, wanting relationships, and getting jobs. *Black Tie Affair* is somewhat unique from the other comedies in the chapter. It premiered more than a year before *Friends* and deals with a private detective in his late twenties lusting after an older client during the course of a murder investigation. The client and her husband are not in their twenties but act like twentysomethings when it comes to sex. The other comedies in this chapter that premiered before *Friends* can be traced to cultural phenomena from the seventies and early eighties. *Co-Ed Fever*, somewhat incorrectly, is lumped with other sitcoms that premiered in the late seventies in response to the success of the film *Animal House*; *Dreams* is said to have been inspired by the original music video format of MTV, and *A Year at the Top* was the result of a collaboration between Norman Lear, the iconic producer of *All in the Family*, and seventies music impresario Don Kirshner.

As If

Premiered Tuesday, March 5, 2002, at 9:00 PM on UPN

Based on a British show of the same name, *As If* was shot in the *cinema vérité* style with scenes lasting only a few seconds. The six young, almost twentysomething adults on the series (three women and three men) were: Nicki (Adrienne Wilkinson), sexy and materialistic; Sooz (Emily Corrie, who had played the same role on the British version), cynical and outspoken; career-oriented Sasha (Tracie Thoms); intelligent and gay Alex (Robin Dunne); honest Jamie (Derek Hughes), and hunky Rob (Chris Engen). Each episode was shown from the viewpoint of one of the six young adults picturing his or her relationships with others.

LUSTING, LOVING, AND MAKING A LIVING

Background

The creator of the British series, Amanda Coe, also developed the American version and used the scripts from the British version, which took place in London, for the episodes shown on UPN. The show featured a lot of close-ups of the actors, loud music, and the character who was the focus of the episode spoke directly to the camera in several scenes. *As If* was produced by Carnival Films Production and Columbia Tristar.

Episode Guide: 2 aired; 5 unaired

Episode 1: March 5, 2002   "One"

Director: Brian Grant   Writers: Amanda Coe and Jonathan Collier

This episode is from the point of view of Jamie who has a crush on Nicki. When Jamie goes to a party with Nicki, he doesn't realize, until Sooz tells him, that Nicki is using him to get to someone else. Nicki leaves Jamie holding her hand bag while she goes off with another young man to have sex. She ends up regretting this and apologizing to Jamie. Meanwhile, Rob, who is living with Sasha, misses her award function to go to the party. He goes home with Jamie because Sasha throws him out of their apartment.

Episode 2: March 12, 2002   "Two"

Director: Brian Grant   Writers: Amanda Coe and Jonathan Collier

This episode was from Sooz's perspective. Sooz has a crush on Rob who works at a coffee bar and had been living with Sasha. For an art project, she is taking pictures of guys with tattoos. Jamie tells Sooz that Rob has broken up with Sasha and also that he has a tattoo on his back. Rob, seeing that Sasha is going out with another guy, agrees to pose for Sooz at her place. Sooz takes pictures of the tattoo and ends up doing body painting on Rob's back. However, when she does not reveal how she really feels about him, Rob shakes her hand and leaves.

Emily Corrie who portrayed Sooz gave up acting and joined the British Navy.

Episode 3: Unaired   "Three"

Director: Brian Grant   Writers: Jonathan Collier and Patrick Wilde

This episode is from the point of view of Alex. Alex is attracted to an older man named Dan, a motorcycle cop. Alex says he is twenty and a computer systems analyst. Dan is thirty-years old. Meanwhile, Sasha breaks up with her new boyfriend Chris who wanted her only for sex.

Episode 4: Unaired   "Four" (summary based on final revised script)

Director: Brian Grant   Story: Julian Jones   Teleplay: Jonathan Collier

From Jamie's perspective, he gets a date with Gabi, a thirty-two-year-old woman with whom he has been chatting over the internet. He is apprehensive about the date because he lied to the woman saying he is twenty-five-years old and a pilot. When he finally meets her, he takes her to a nice restaurant, and they go dancing. She reveals she has a sixteen-year-old son. Gabi and Jamie make love in the park, and he reveals he is really eighteen. Although they have a good time together, Gabi breaks off the relationship because she feels Jamie needs to be with women his own age. Meanwhile, Sasha tries to reconcile with Rob.

Episode 5: Unaired   "Five" (summary based on final revised script)

Director: Brian Grant   Story: Tom Higgins   Teleplay: Jonathan Collier

This episode is from Nicki's point of view. Alex wants Nicki to accompany him to his grandmother's birthday celebration so she can see him with a girl before she dies, but Nicki has other plans. She is tired of dating boys and wants to date an older man. She hooks up with an older guy named Sebastian who takes her to an expensive hotel for dinner. Nicki tells Jamie to call her every half hour so that Sebastian will think she is a very in-demand model. Sasha goes with Alex to his grandmother's birthday party since Nicki didn't make herself available. After dinner, Nicki spends the night with Sebastian in his room. When she wakes up the next morning, she finds that Sebastian stole her money and credit cards and has disappeared. She panics and calls Alex for help since his boyfriend Dan is a cop. Nicki is mortified when questioned by the hotel manager and Dan because she doesn't really know anything about Sebastian, and she had tried to leave the hotel by the fire escape to avoid paying the tab Sebastian had run up. Nicki admits she is eighteen. Since the hotel had served her champagne and since the hotel manager knows that act can get him in trouble, he doesn't press charges.

Episode 6: Unaired   "Six" (summary based on final revised script)

Director: Brian Grant   Story: Julian Jones   Teleplay: Cynthia Greenburg

From Sasha's perspective, Sasha asks Rob to dinner at her place. She goes shopping with Nicki for a dress for the date with Rob. Meanwhile, Rob got Sooz, Jamie, and Alex jobs as waiters at a garden party. However, Rob and Sooz are dismissed by the maitre d' because they are not patient with a demanding guest. After they leave, Rob and Sooz kiss in a secluded spot in the park. Rob shows up at Sasha's a little late and threatens to leave after they argue over Chris, Sasha's former boyfriend. However, Rob stays for dinner, they have sex, and he tells Sasha he loves her. Rob later mentions to Jamie that he is moving back in with Sasha, and Sooz breaks down when she finds this out.

Tracie Thoms (Sasha) later became a regular on the detective series *Cold Case*.

Episode 7: Unaired   "Seven" (summary based on final revised script)

Director: Brian Grant   Story: Amanda Coe   Teleplay: Greg Fiering

Sooz says she is over Rob, but she really isn't. She hooks up with a guy named Josh. When Nicki flirts with Josh in a club, Sooz gets mad at Nicki but eventually leaves the club with her. Later, Josh sees Sooz at a café, and they go to bed together back at her apartment. But Sooz, thinking of Rob while she is with Josh, doesn't want to have sex with him. Josh leaves, but then Rob shows up and kisses Sooz. Meanwhile, Alex goes to Dan's house to wish him happy birthday. Dan informs Alex that he knows Alex is not a systems analyst and is not twenty-years old, and wonders if Alex realizes how much trouble Dan could be in because Alex lied about his age. Dan is not sure what kind of relationship they can have.

At the Bottom

As If lasted only two weeks. It ranked at the bottom of the Nielsen's in its two outings – 123rd and 134th respectively.

Black Tie Affair (aka Smoldering Lust)

Premiered Saturday, May 29, 1993, at 10:00 PM on NBC

On *Black Tie Affair*, Bradley Whitford played Dave Brodsky, a dealer of rare records and a private detective in his late twenties. He had a van advertising "Ed's House of Hammers" on the side which he used for surveillance. The comedy-drama followed the case of wealthy entrepreneur Christopher Cody (John Calvin) who, with his wife, had founded Cody Canyon, a mail order house for wilderness gear and clothing. Cody's wife, Margo (Kate Capshaw) had hired Brodsky to find out if her spouse was cheating on her with one of the clothing-catalog models, Eve Saskatchewan (Alison Elliott). Other characters on the series included Cookie (Maggie Han), Brodsky's assistant; Margo's business manager, Philip (Patrick Bristow), apparently a closeted homosexual who planted the idea in Margo's head that her husband was having an affair and who turned out to be Eve's long-lost brother, and Hal Kempner (Bruce McGill), the inventor of an special athletic shoe called the "Toad" that he wanted Cody Canyon to market. Brodsky, sometimes speaking directly to the camera, narrated each episode.

Background

The idea for the series started with Brandon Tartikoff (the late NBC entertainment chief) who mentioned to Jay Tarses that he would like a show about a stylish, urban couple where the husband and wife were each having affairs and titled, *Black Tie Affair*.[9] Tarses, under contract with NBC to create a series, developed the idea into *Smoldering Lust*, a show about characters doing things they really shouldn't be doing, basically attempting to have affairs but never really consummating them. Episodes involved liaisons between almost all of the major characters – Chris and Margo, Margo and Brodsky, Chris and Eve, Chris and Cookie, etc. Two weeks

LUSTING, LOVING, AND MAKING A LIVING

before the series premiere, NBC changed the name back to the *Black Tie Affair*, thinking audiences would be confused by the title *Smoldering Lust*. The series was produced by Brillstein/Grey Entertainment and Columbia Pictures Television.

Episode Guide: 5 aired; 8 unaired

Episode 1: May 29, 1993 "One"

Director/Writer: Jay Tarses

In the opener, Brodsky is hired by Margo Cody to find out if her husband is having an affair and with whom. The Cody's are attending a testimonial dinner for Chris at a San Francisco hotel, the Fleetwood. Brodsky, disguised as a hotel bellboy to keep an eye on Chris, sees him slip out of the dinner for a rendezvous with Eve. Chris thinks the rendezvous is in Room 1216 but mistakenly knocks on the door to Room 1218 where he meets a black guy named Felton (John Cothran, Jr.) who lives in the hotel and is a fan of Cody Canyon. Chris then enters Room 1216 where he thinks he is supposed to meet Eve and discovers the body of a dead woman. Meanwhile, Margo finds Brodsky in a secluded hotel hallway, and they passionately kiss as witnessed by Hal Kempner whom they don't see. Chris Cody hurries back to the dinner but loses his eyeglass case near the scene of the crime when he smashes into a bellboy carrying a tray of food. Brodsky goes to Room 1216 and finds the body. While Chris is giving his speech at the dinner with food smeared all over his clothes, he eyes Eve in the doorway and passes out.

Kate Capshaw (Margo Cody) is the wife of director Steven Spielberg.

Episode 2: May 29, 1993 "Two"

Director/ Writer: Jay Tarses

Brodsky, still dressed as a bellboy, sees Eve calling for a ride and offers to take her home, but she refuses. He calls the police about the murder. However, when they arrive, they find the hotel room empty and clean. After Margo informs Chris that she saw Eve at the hotel, Chris tells Margo that he and Eve did nothing. Margo doesn't believe him, and they end up sleeping in separate rooms. Chris realizes that he left his eyeglass case in the hotel. He also learns that Eve was in Room 2161 –

not 1216. After Chris informs Eve of the dead body in 1216, she recommends that he go to the police.

Before John Calvin was chosen for the role of Chris Cody, Michael Ontkean, John Shea, Victor Garber, and Ryan O'Neal were under consideration for this role.

Episode 3: June 5, 1993   "Three"

Director: Jay Tarses   Writer: Richard Dresser

Brodsky considers giving up the case since he doesn't get involved in murder investigations. He confesses to Margo that he has no pictures of Eve and Chris together and wants to refer Margo to another private investigator. Meanwhile, Chris goes back to the hotel to try to find his glass case and runs into Felton again who tells him to see the maid about his lost item. In the end, Brodsky reconsiders dropping the case. He breaks into the Cody's bedroom, makes sure that both of them are aware that each knows about the murder, but thinks that Chris is innocent.

Jay Tarses is the father of Matt Tarses (producer of *Worst Week*) and Jamie Tarses (producer of *Happy Endings*) and created series like *The Days and Nights of Molly Dodd*, *Buffalo Bob*, and the very short-lived *Public Morals*.

Episode 4: June 12, 1993   "Four"

Director: Lesli Linka Glatter   Writer: Russ Woody

Chris Cody takes the hotel maid out to lunch to see if she knows about the murder and his eyeglass case. Margo visits Brodsky in his surveillance van where, after talking with Cookie about the case, he tells Margo that he now thinks her husband murdered the woman in the hotel room. Margo warns Eve to be careful, and Margo and Chris have sex in their bedroom while under surveillance by Brodsky who fantasizes about making love to Margo.

Episode 5: June 19, 1993   "Five" (summary based on final draft script)

Director: Lesli Linka Glatter   Writer: Russ Woody

LUSTING, LOVING, AND MAKING A LIVING

Margo goes to Brodsky's office to fire him, but he tells her that he is not dropping the case of the dead woman. She kisses him passionately and then leaves. That afternoon, Brodsky has Cody under surveillance at a seedy motel where Cody meets Eve. Cody is nervous about having sex with Eve and says that having an affair is probably not the best way to salvage his marriage. Eve replies that she understands and departs. Brodsky goes to the motel room where Cody is alone and confronts him about the murder. Cody tells Brodsky he could never kill anyone. Brodsky believes him, and they end up becoming friends. Now Brodsky has no primary murder suspect and wonders if the murderer could really have been Felton, Eve, the room service guy, Kempner, Margo, or someone else.

Episode 6: Unaired   "Six" (summary based on final draft script)

Director: Unknown Writer: Richard Dresser

Teddy Gilooly (Christopher Barnes) comes to Brodsky's office with a missing person's case. His girlfriend, Susan Wells, who looks very much like the woman murdered at the Fleetwood, has disappeared, and he wants Brodsky to find her. Brodsky goes to see Margo. They kiss and want to make love, but Brodsky has guilt feelings about betraying his new friend Chris Cody, and so he leaves Margo. Cody goes to Eve's apartment which she shares with twenty-seven-year-old Billy (David Packer) who is very wealthy and likes to watch a lot of TV. Eve moved into the apartment after Billy's former roommate died. Cody apologizes to Eve for letting her walk out of the motel room. He now wants to have sex with her, but she wants him to go and speak to Margo about how much he appreciates his wife. That night, Cody does tell Margo how grateful he is for her, and Brodsky goes back to the Fleetwood to talk with Felton who is apparently not in his hotel room.

Episode 7: Unaired   "Seven" (summary based on final draft script)

Director: Jay Tarses   Writer: Russ Woody

Cody Canyon Catalog is sponsoring a political fund-raiser at the Fleetwood for U.S. Senate candidate, Peter "Dutch" Van der Klugle, and the Cody's, Eve, Philip, Kempner, and Felton and his date are all in attendance. Brodsky is undercover disguised as a waiter, but everyone recognizes him anyway. Lust continues to smolder between Margo and Brodsky and between Cody and Eve. When Van der Klugle chokes on a tamale husk, Brodsky saves his life. While everyone is looking at the incident, Felton holds up an eyeglass case for Cody to see. Felton tells Cody to stop Brodsky's investigation into the murder and that he will hold the eyeglass case as his insurance policy. After the fund-raiser, Brodsky walks Eve home to her apartment where she kisses him. Now he is fantasizing about both Margo and Eve. Late that night, Felton is sobbing in his hotel room when the room service guy, Chandler Bacon (Jake Crawford), comes by unannounced but then departs. He waits outside the door and hears Felton begin sobbing again.

Episode 8: Unaired   "Eight" (summary based on first draft script)

Director: Peter Baldwin   Writer: Richard Dresser

Felton is moving out of the Fleetwood, and, late at night, a masked man breaks into Margo's office and spray paints a toad on her wall. The next day, Margo is aghast when she sees the vandalism. Felton and the room service guy from the Fleetwood come to see Cody in his office. Felton gives Cody back his eyeglass case. After Felton leaves, the room service guy meets with Cody to ask if he can be a model for his catalog. Hal Kempner comes to see Margo to continue to insist that his toad shoes appear in the Cody Canyon catalog. He pulls a can out of his jacket and sprays the painting on Margo's office wall which starts to disappear. Later Felton goes to see Brodsky. He says he is looking for a particular record album but relates the story of a state politician who had an affair with a woman, wanted to break it off but she wouldn't let him, and apparently murders her. Still later, Cody, Margo, Philip, and Brodsky are to have dinner at a restaurant. Brodsky brings Eve with him and informs Cody that he has nothing to worry about. Margo suggests keeping Brodsky on retainer to investigate Kempner.

Episode 9: Unaired   "Nine" (summary based on final draft script)

Director: Peter Baldwin   Writer: Richard Dresser

Margo advises her husband that they both need more "space." While Cody makes it clear to Margo that he never had sex with Eve, Margo confesses to him that she has lusted for Brodsky. Also, Cody tells Margo that Dutch Van der Klugle is the one

LUSTING, LOVING, AND MAKING A LIVING

who murdered the girl at the Fleetwood Hotel. The next day, Margo announces to Philip that she and Chris are separating, and, when she meets with Brodsky about what his duties will be at Cody Canyon, Margo advises him of the separation as well. At his health club, Chris talks with Van der Klugle about the murder. Dutch says that the girl was already dead when he got to her hotel room. That night, Brodsky is entertaining Eve at his office/record store and mentions to Eve that the Cody's are separating.

Episode 10: Unaired "Ten" (summary based on final draft script)

Director: Unknown   Writer: Russ Woody

Cody and Margo have separated in order to strengthen their marriage. Cody is going to live in a cabin he owns in the woods. Meanwhile, after Billy and Eve argue about his continuing addiction to TV watching, she leaves their apartment. Margo goes to Brodsky's office because Kempner has sent her a death threat. The police won't do anything because the message from Kempner says he will "thrill" Margo – instead of "kill" her, and the police don't believe it is a typo. Later that afternoon, Cookie informs Teddy Gilooly that Susan Wells is dead and that Van der Klugle murdered her. Cody then stops by Brodsky's office to talk with him about his separation, but Brodsky isn't there. He meets Cookie for the first time. Late that afternoon, Margo finds Kempner on the terrace of the Cody house where he threatens her with the picture of a gun and makes her sit through a presentation about his toad shoes. She finally agrees to put the shoes in the company's catalog. Brodsky is outside the Cody house but can't get his surveillance equipment to work when Cody finds him and asks him to spend time at the cabin. Eve comes by the Cody house to ask Margo if she can stay there for awhile, and Margo reluctantly agrees.

Episode 11: Unaired "Eleven" (summary based on final draft script)

Director: Unknown   Writers: Lee Blessing and Jeanne Blake

Cody and Brodsky are driving to Cody's cabin in Brodsky's van which breaks down. While waiting for road service, Cody says that he asked Van der Klugle if he murdered the girl in room 1216, and the candidate said he got to the room after the girl was already dead. Brodsky starts to worry about Margo's safety since the murder really hasn't been solved. He heads back to his office leaving Cody alone at the cabin. Kempner comes to Brodsky's office to tell him that his services are not needed anymore since he is no longer a threat to Margo given that she agreed to include his shoes in Cody Canyon's next catalog. Later Cookie mentions to Brodsky that she thinks Margo murdered the girl in the hotel. Brodsky goes to see Margo at the company's photo studio and informs her of what Kempner said. She points out to Brodsky that he is still working for her and also that she would do anything to save her marriage. Brodsky is beginning to believe that Cookie might be right about Margo, but he still lusts for her.

Episode 12: Unaired "Twelve" (summary based on final draft script)

Director: Unknown   Writer: Cindy Lou Johnson

Margo comes home from a bad day at the office. Eve tries to comfort her when she says that she thinks Philip is getting too much power at the company and is keeping the company's financial statements from her. The next day, Felton informs Brodsky that he thinks he saw Margo in the hallway outside the room of the woman murdered in 1216. While Brodsky and Felton are talking, Susan Wells shows up. She says that Teddy Gilooly is not her boyfriend; he is just someone she once dated. Chris Cody is making dinner for himself at the cabin and reminisces about the time Margo suggested they start a catalog company together. Later, after receiving an anonymous note from someone who has something to tell him, Brodsky is at an abandoned merry-go-round to meet the note sender. Cookie shows up, and the two of them talk about the possibility that Margo is the murderer. Cookie confesses that she lusts for Chris Cody.

Maggie Han (Cookie) previously starred on the short-lived comedy *Teech*.

Episode 13: Unaired "Thirteen" (summary based on final draft script)

Director: Unknown   Writer: Richard Dresser

Brodsky is getting ready for a date with Margo whom he still thinks might be the murderer. Meanwhile, Philip is upset that Margo doesn't pay more attention to his efforts at the company and doesn't really know him. Eve stops by Philip's office as he is shredding possibly incriminating financial documents concerning the company. As they talk, Eve discovers that Philip may be her long-lost brother. Later that afternoon, Brodsky meets Margo in the Cody Canyon photo studio where they begin kissing. Margo confides that she really doesn't love him but just lusts for him. Eve sees Margo crawl on top of Brodsky and advises Philip she is going to the cabin to inform Cody. At the cabin, Cookie stops by to tell Cody that she knows that Margo murdered the girl at the Fleetwood. She bases this on her gut feeling and also mentions to Cody that Brodsky is with Margo. Eventually, Cookie and Cody are together in front of the fireplace and begin to kiss as Eve stares at them through the cabin window. The episode ends with Brodsky, speaking directly to the camera, saying that solving a murder is easy but figuring out why people lust for one another, that's the real mystery.

Even after thirteen episodes, the writers never did divulge who murdered the girl in room 1216.

The End of the *Affair*

NBC delayed the premiere of the series for several months, finally deciding to debut it on the Saturday of Memorial Day weekend at 10:00 PM with back-to-back episodes. The show's premiere ranked fifty-ninth out of eighty-four shows. Only five episodes of the series aired before the network removed it from the schedule.

Co-Ed Fever

Previewed Sunday, February 4, 1979, at 10:30 PM on CBS

The setting for *Co-Ed Fever* was an off-campus co-ed house at fictional Baxter College, formerly all-girls', which had just allowed male students to enroll. The main characters on the series were:

- ■ Tuck Davis (David Keith) – a regular college student whose dad didn't really want him to attend a formerly all-girls school;

- ■ Doug (Christopher S. Nelson) – a wealthy, sophisticated student;

- Gobo (Michael Pasternak)— a wacky, unconventional student;

- Sandi (Heather Thomas)— the most popular co-ed on campus;

- Hope (Tracey Phillips) – an independent feminist;

- Maria " Mousie" (Alexia Kenin) – a compulsive overeater;

- Elizabeth (Cathryn O'Neil) – a smart, wholesome co-ed;

- Mrs. Selby (Jane Rose)—the housemother and cook.

Background

In 1978, the movie *Animal House* was a big hit at the box office, and each major TV network developed comedies focused on kids in college. ABC actually had the rights to *Animal House* and turned it into a series called *Delta House*, which debuted on January 18, 1979, and lasted until the spring. NBC put on a series titled *Brothers and Sisters*, another midseason replacement which began on January 21, 1979, and lasted until April of that year.

The producer of *Co-Ed Fever*, Martin Ransohoff, said he got the premise for the series from his own son enrolling in Vassar in 1976 that had gone co-ed in the early 1970s. He, along with Frank Shaw and Michael Elias, developed his idea into a series.

The original concept of *Co-Ed Fever* was very different from the show that finally aired. In a 1976 version of the script, the school's name was Finley College – not Baxter College, and the main characters were Tuck Davis; Doug Compton; Charles Bernstein; Mousie, a plump brunette; Hope, an attractive blonde junior; Elizabeth, a new student; Sandi, who dressed like a model, and Mrs. Selby, the housemother. The action took place on the first day of enrollment at Finley College that had just become co-ed. Tuck met the residents of Brewster House with Doug suggesting to Tuck that they smoke some weed, steal a car, and go to Boston to visit a house of prostitution. Tuck got acquainted with Elizabeth whom he thought was his new roommate, but she ended up rooming with Mousie. There was a scene where Tuck and Bernstein went to a class taught by Professor Burroughs. Tuck later met the professor's wife whom he mistook for a co-ed at the school. Tuck also became friendly with a girl named Judy who wanted to spend the night with him in his room. However, Tuck's real roommate turned out to be Billie Ray Bonzone who arrived with his poodle and two motorcyclists from Greenwich Village who helped him move in. Billie was gay, and, when Judy came by with her overnight case, Billie told her he got there first.

By the time the first pilot was filmed in spring, 1978, the whole concept of a gay roommate for Tuck was dropped, there were no references to smoking pot or going to a house of prostitution, and the college name was changed from "Finley" to "Brewster." In the first pilot, directed by Alan Myerson, Hope was played by Laurie Chock, Bernstein by Michael Corbett, and the rest of the characters were played by the actors mentioned above except for Gobo who wasn't in the initial pilot. In the pilot, Tuck was working at Peabody's Sporting Goods store when Mousie came in to purchase a ski jacket and jumped to the conclusion that Tuck was in love with her. Another co-ed named Melba came in after Mousie. Tuck was really attracted to her and eventually invited her back to his room. However, word was relayed to Mousie that Tuck wanted to date her. She made him a homemade pizza and delivered it to his room only to find Melba there.

CBS's Program Practices department did object to several items in the script for this pilot. For instance, when Mousie came to the store to buy a ski jacket, CBS said that the action must avoid taking on "graphic sexual overtones" when Tuck "zips it up slowly." They cautioned that Tuck not delay the zipping in the vicinity of Mousie's breasts. Also, there was a scene in the pilot script showing both males and females using the same bathroom. The network objected to the unisex bathroom and to any impression of nudity.

When CBS tested the completed pilot, it tested below average with a number of adults complaining that the openness of sex in the show was not appropriate, and, even worse, CBS found that the test audience felt the show was basically dull and humorless. Viewers of the pilot thought that the idea of a group of college students running around a dormitory (even a co-ed dorm) wasn't that interesting.

Martin Ransohoff blamed CBS for not permitting him to deal with real college issues on the series since the show was intended for early Monday evenings at 8:30

PM. The producers wanted to have more sex on the series if it had been scheduled for a 9:30 PM time slot.

Apparently, CBS had misgivings about the series almost from the start of production. The network received the pilot before the popularity of the movie *Animal House* and sat on it until that film became a success. Another pilot was filmed in December 1978, based on a revised script, and it is described in the episode guide below as the special preview episode broadcast on February 4, 1979.

Episode Guide: 1 aired; 5 unaired

Episode 1: February 4, 1979   "Pepperoni Passion" (summary based on final revised script)

Director: Marc Daniels   Writers: Michael Elias and Frank Shaw

In this revised pilot, the character of Bernstein was dropped in favor of the more goofy character of Gobo, and Tracey Phillips replaced Laurie Chock as Hope. Like in the first pilot, Tuck is working at Peabody's Sporting Goods Store where Mousie thinks that Tuck is attracted to her and mentions this to Sandi. Tuck's next customer is Melba whom Tuck finds attractive. The following day, Tuck tells Sandi about a guy and a girl meeting in a store who both like each other and seeks her advice on how to ask the girl out. Elizabeth informs Mousie of what Tuck said to Sandi, and the girls think that Tuck wants to date Mousie. However, Tuck asks Melba for a date and orders a pepperoni pizza to share with her when she comes to his room. Mousie overhears the order, cancels it, and decides to make her own pizza for what she thinks is a date with Tuck. Mousie enters Tuck's room with a pizza and discovers Tuck with Melba. When Melba talks to Tuck most of the night about spiritual love, he is so tired that he asks her to leave. The next morning, Tuck and Mousie discuss their relationship and declare their friendship for each other.

Alexia Kenin, who played Mousie, died in September 1985, at the age of twenty-three.

LUSTING, LOVING, AND MAKING A LIVING

Episode 2: Unaired   "Disco Tuck" (summary based on final draft script)

Director: Jim Drake   Writer: Jack Handey

Sandi asks Tuck to dance with her at a party, but he says he is too tired. However, the real reason he won't dance is because he doesn't know how to. Hope volunteers to take Tuck to her next dance class. When Tuck's beer accidentally spills on Sandi, she and Tuck go upstairs so she can change. It is intimated that Sandi and Tuck try to have sex, but he is too anxious to perform. Meanwhile, Gobo has lost his pet boa constrictor, Billy, which ends up eating Elizabeth's hamster. Gobo eventually finds his pet snake on a table next to Mrs. Selby. Later at another dance, Tuck asks Sandi to dance mentioning to her about the dance lessons he took with Hope. Gobo accidentally spills Tuck's beer again on Sandi, and Tuck goes with her to "help her change."

Heather Thomas (Sandi) later starred with Lee Majors on *The Fall Guy*.

Episode 3: Unaired   "Double Exposure" (summary based on first draft script)

Director: Unknown   Writer: Marc Sheffler

Tuck receives a letter from his dad saying that if he wants to continue at Baxter, he'll have to pay his own way. Tuck wants to find another part-time job to finance his education but decides he can't handle two part-time jobs and go to school at the same time. Doug has a deal with the Dean at Baxter to handle the merchandising of school paraphernalia and wants Tuck to invest in his scheme to make money. Doug takes pictures of Sandi in her night gown through a hole in the ceiling without her knowledge and has Gobo develop the photos in the attic. While developing the pictures, Gobo thinks he was bitten by a bat and is turning into a vampire. Sandi finds out that the pictures of her were published in an underground school newspaper, and Gobo confesses that he developed the photos at Doug's direction. Doug tries to apologize to Sandi. However, to get back at him, Tuck photographs Doug taking a shower. To scare Doug, Sandi tells him that she sent the photo to the underground paper. Tuck's dad calls to say that Tuck's mom convinced him to continue to pay for Tuck's education, and, when he doesn't melt in the daylight, Gobo realizes he is not really a vampire.

Episode 4: Unaired   "Mid-Term Panic" (summary based on first draft script)

Director: Unknown Writers: Ian Praiser and Howard Gewirtz

While most of the students at Brewster House are preparing for mid-terms, Mousie brings home a black poodle with a sprained paw and decides to keep it until she can find the owner. Gobo is installing a "Mr. Radio Kit" antenna so he can do his own campus broadcasts. As he is signing on to air his first broadcast, he gets sick to his stomach. He thinks eating so many pork chops at the school's cafeteria caused the upset. Hope broadcasts to the entire campus that anyone who ate pork chops may have trichinosis and should go to the health center. It turns out that Gobo really got sick from eating too much candy. Meanwhile, the poodle Mousie found disrupts the house with its barking until it eats Doug's "Mauie-Wowie" which calms it down. Mousie eventually finds the dog's owner.

The actor who portrayed Doug, Christopher S. Nelson, is the son of actor Ed Nelson who starred on the TV series *Peyton Place*.

Episode 5: Unaired   "Mousie's Turn" (summary based on first draft script)

Director: Unknown   Writer: Iris Rainer

A friend of Doug's – Dave Ellis, visits the house to borrow a book since he is writing Doug's theme paper about Shakespeare for him. All the girls think Dave is really cute. When everyone is out of the house except Mousie, Dave visits to return Doug's book. Dave likes Malomars as much as Mousie does, and she offers him some. Mousie ends up spending the night at Dave's place. Everyone in the house thinks that Mousie is depressed when she hasn't heard from Dave after their night together, but it is really Dave who is depressed because Mousie rejected him. Dave had invited Mousie over to his place for popcorn and all-night movies and, unlike other girls, that is all Mousie had wanted from him. Mousie thinks Dave is a great guy – just not for her.

Iris Rainer, who wrote this episode, later authored the novel *Beaches* on which the movie starring Bette Milder was based.

LUSTING, LOVING, AND MAKING A LIVING

Episode 6: Unaired   "Good-bye, Mrs. Selby" (summary based on revised draft script)

Director: Unknown   Writer: Iris Rainer

Gobo is bringing several girls up to his room at Baxter House – like six in three days. He comes down the steps with a beautiful coed whom he thanks for being so good. Girls keep going in and out of Gobo's room as witnessed by Mrs. Selby and the other housemates. The gang then discovers that Mrs. Selby has left—presumably out of disgust over Gobo's behavior. Tuck talks with Gobo about all the women he has been bringing to his room. Gobo explains that he is not making love to them but instead is doing research for a term paper by psychoanalyzing the girls. In the meantime, Mrs. Selby has returned to the house to get her fuzzy slippers, and Tuck asks her to go upstairs to speak with Gobo. They talk and she decides to stay at the house.

Jane Rose (Mrs. Selby) died of cancer four months after *Co-Ed Fever* was canceled.

Episode Never Produced

At least one script titled "Battle of the Sexes," written for *Co-Ed Fever* by Dave Ketchum and Tony DeMarco, was never filmed. In the script, Sandi finds out that she is not eligible to run for Homecoming Queen since her grade point average is a tenth of a point below the minimum needed to qualify. Gobo decides to run since the rules don't specify that candidates for Homecoming Queen have to be female–the rules not being changed since Baxter College went co-ed. Gobo wins Homecoming Queen, and, at the end, he gets to meet the Princeton Homecoming King who turns out to be a girl.

Fever Not Contagious

Previewing to mostly negative reviews, the special Sunday night airing of *Co-Ed Fever* did fairly well in the ratings – ranking nineteenth, but it did lose a lot of the audience from the movie *Rocky* which ranked number one for the week. In any event, after airing the first episode, CBS pulled the show from its intended February 19, 1979 regular start date because of "production problems." The comedy never returned. *Co-Ed Fever* has the dubious distinction of being the first sitcom canceled after only one episode.

Coupling

Premiered Thursday, September 23, 2003, at 9:30 PM on NBC

With great fanfare, NBC announced that an American adaptation of the British hit sitcom *Coupling* would be on its 2003–04 season schedule. Since the comedy *Friends* was in its final season, *Coupling* was seen as the next incarnation of *Friends*.

Like *Friends*, *Coupling* centered on six young singles—three men and three women—who frequented a bar in Chicago, not a coffee shop in New York as in *Friends*. Following were the characters on the show:

- Susan Freeman (Rena Sofer), who was dating Steve Taylor (Jay Harrington), a music critic;

- Jane Honda (Lindsay Price), a traffic reporter who was Steve's former threesome-loving, bisexual girlfriend and would not let go of the relationship;

- Patrick Maitland (Colin Ferguson), Susan's sex-driven former boyfriend who hung out with the group and was an investment adviser;

- Sally Harper (Sonya Walger), Susan's neurotic best friend who owned a beauty salon, and

- Jeff Clancy (Christopher Moynihan), who happened to be Susan's coworker at an advertising agency and was Steve's best friend.

Background

Coupling was supposed to be racier than *Friends* in dealing with sexual matters such as genital size, threesomes, performance issues, and such. Two church-owned NBC affiliates—one in Indiana owned by the University of Notre Dame and one in Utah owned by the Mormon Church—refused to carry the series because of its purported sexual content.[10]

The comedy was adapted for American TV by its British creator, Steve Moffat, who later wrote episodes of the sci-fi classic *Doctor Who* and the mystery series *Sherlock*. The original pilot for the U.S. version starred Melissa George as Susan, Breckin Meyer as Jeff, and Emily Rutherford as Sally in addition to Colin Ferguson, Jay Harrington, and Lindsay Price. It was titled "Flushed." The storyline was basically the same as described below for the first episode with Steve trying to end his relationship with Jane. Jeff called Jane "unflushable," meaning that she was the type of woman a person couldn't break up with. The initial script also had such "witty" dialogue as Susan telling Sally, "one swallow does not a summer make," and Steve confessing to Jeff that "one swallow doesn't make her (i.e. Jane) my girlfriend."

The scripts for several of the episodes described below such as "Size Matters," "Sex, Death, and Nudity," and "A Foreign Affair" were taken directly from the British version which lasted four seasons in England. The U.S. series was produced by Universal Television.

Episode Guide: 4 aired; 6 unaired

Episode 1: September 25, 2003   "The Right One"

Director: Andrew D. Weyman   Writer: Steven Moffat

Steve tries to end his relationship with Jane, but she keeps tempting him with sex. Patrick thinks he is in a relationship with Susan, but she isn't so sure. Steve asks Susan out while still trying to break up with Jane. When Susan comes to a restaurant to see Steve, Jane introduces herself as Steve's girlfriend and then dumps him. Jeff, Susan's co-worker, also shows up at the restaurant as does Patrick with Susan's friend Sally. All six meet each other and have dinner together.

Episode 2: October 2, 2003   "Size Matters"

Director: Andrew D. Weyman   Writer: Steven Moffat

Susan tells Sally and Steve that Patrick is very well endowed. Sally asks Jeff to check out Patrick in the men's room to see if Susan is telling the truth. Also, Susan invites Steve for dinner at her place, and after their dinner, they have sex. Meanwhile, Jane is dating a gay man which to her is logical since she is bisexual.

Jay Harrington (Steve) later starred on the sitcom *Better Off Ted*.

Episode 3: October 9, 2003   "Sex, Death & Nudity"

Director: Andrew D. Weyman   Writer: Steven Moffat

Up for a promotion, Jeff is apprehensive about the giggle loop – laughing at an inappropriate time after trying to stifle it. Jane's aunt has died, and she asks Steve to attend the funeral with her since she hasn't told her family that they are no longer dating. Susan says Steven can go if she can attend since she doesn't want Steve passing himself off as Jane's boyfriend. Susan asks Patrick to go as her "date;" he, in turn, asks Sally to go. Jeff attends as well since he knew the aunt. At the funeral, the guys succeed at stifling their laughter during a moment of silence.

Episode 4: October 23, 2002   "Check/Mate"

Director: Andrew D. Weyman   Writer: Danny Zuker

Since Steve and Susan feel that it is too early in their relationship to be brutally honest with each other, they lie about their preferences in music, sports, dancing, and movies. Susan picks up the check for dinner one evening, and then she and Steve have remarkable sex. The next time, Steve picks up the check, and Susan is very creative sexually, leading their friends to say that they are paying each other for sex. Susan asks Steve's friends for advice about what Steve really likes in bed, and they say he prefers earthy sex. Steve asks Susan's friends the same question, and they tell him to be romantic. When they each follow their friends' advice, Susan and Steve realize they should be more honest with each other. Meanwhile, Jane has a stalker that she feels is not paying enough attention to her, and Patrick keeps looking for a new car that will reflect his manhood.

LUSTING, LOVING, AND MAKING A LIVING

Episode 5: Unaired "Present Tense"

Director: Andrew D. Weyman   Writers: Paul Corrigan and Brad Walsh

Susan is celebrating Yom Kippur which Steve knows nothing about. His friends convince him it is Moses' birthday. Jeff is celebrating his birthday for which he doesn't want anything special, but Sally overhears the guys' conversation and thinks that it is really Steve who is having a birthday. Susan buys Steve a watch for what she believes is his birthday. He thinks the gift is for Yom Kippur and so rushes out to purchase a Yom Kippur gift for Susan. Steve and Susan again find that their friends gave them wrong advice. Meanwhile, Jane takes up charity work to prove she is not self-centered and ends up rearranging a blind man's furniture to improve the décor in his apartment.

Episode 6: Unaired "A Foreign Affair"

Director: Andrew D. Weyman   Story: Steven Moffat   Teleplay: Steven Moffat and Phoef Sutton

Jeff is attracted to a new girl at the bar who, it turns out, doesn't speak English, which is just as well since Jeff babbles to her about collecting women's ears. The girl is from Israel and only speaks Hebrew. The next night Jeff flirts with the girl again, and she believes he is interested in her less attractive translator. Jeff also thinks he knows the girl's name but what he believes is her name is actually the Hebrew word for "breast." Meanwhile, Jane has a picture of Sally at a club showing her with her hands on the zipper of a guy's pants. The man turns out to be Patrick although Jane and Susan can't see the man in the photo. They question Sally about the photo, but she says it was a private matter. Apparently, Patrick had gotten his penis caught in his zipper, and Sally was trying to get it uncaught.

Episode 7: Unaired "Nipple Effect"

Director: Andrew D. Weyman   Writer: J.J. Philbin

Patrick is dating a woman who likes his nipples. Sally is dating an environmental lawyer who doesn't like women to wear make-up. She discovers that he is a serial de-glamourizer – after six weeks, his girlfriends look worse than they did when he met them since he tells them he likes the natural look. However, when Sally makes over one of his former girlfriends, he dumps Sally for his ex. Meanwhile, Susan and Steve are into role playing as strangers trying to pick up each other. But, when another guy at the bar thinks Steve is coming on too strong with Susan, he punches him. Jane wants to hook up with the male news anchor at her station but then switches her attention to the weather girl.

J.J. Philbin, who wrote this episode, was the story editor for *Coupling* and is also the daughter of Regis Philbin

Episode 8: Unaired   "Dressed"

Director: Andrew D. Weyman   Story: Steven Moffat   Teleplay: Steven Moffat and Phoef Sutton

Jeff and Susan are working on a presentation in his apartment and end up getting hooked on playing video games. Jane goes to the apartment of a man she met at the bar wearing nothing but an overcoat and finds that instead of the two being alone, he is having a party. She locks herself in his bathroom to find something to wear and makes contact through the bathroom window with the little girl in the adjacent apartment. She trades her overcoat for what the girl tells her is a little black dress that turns out to be a doll's dress. Meanwhile, one of Patrick's clients bets him that he can pick up a woman in the bar quicker than Patrick. The client tries to pick up Sally who demands Patrick pay her $400 to rebuff the client.

Episode 9: Unaired   "Object Lessons"

Director: Andrew D. Weyman   Writer: Liz Astrof

When Susan finds that Steve hasn't given all of Jane's belongings back to her since they broke up, she has Steve return Jane's stuff. Steve also has things at Jane's apartment that he needs to retrieve. Jane gets upset about the exchange and wants to have break-up sex with Steve. He reacts by leaving in a hurry and doesn't get his stuff but pretends to Susan that he did. Steve is also concerned that Susan never leaves anything of hers in his apartment. When Jane comes to Steve's apartment to pick up the rest of her stuff, Susan gets upset that Steve hasn't been honest with her. Susan tells Steve she is not afraid of commitment – just afraid of getting hurt, which is why she doesn't leave things at his apartment. In the meantime, Jeff can't get the attention of any women at the bar because a group of firemen are hanging out there and all the women are attracted to them. However, he finally gets some attention from a burly female firefighter.

Episode 10: Unaired   "Holiday" (aka "Thanksgiving")

Director: Andrew D. Weyman Writers: Paul Corrigan and Brad Walsh

On Christmas Eve, Jane has to track Santa's sleigh for the station where she works. Sally is dating a new guy and is having dinner with his parents. Susan is spending Christmas Eve with Steve who says his parents are on an Alaskan cruise. However, she hears a message on Steve's answering machine from his parents wondering why he and his girlfriend don't visit them. Susan thinks Steve is ashamed of her, but he says he really is ashamed of his parents for fighting all the time and that is why he didn't want to visit them. Jeff is spending Christmas Eve at the bar where he hooks up with Molly, the bartender, who has an evil side that includes spitting in drinks before they are served. Patrick is spending Christmas Eve alone in his apartment when Jane arrives to keep him company. Sally leaves her date's family to go to Patrick's place because she thinks he is lonely. She sees Jane trying to sneak out of Patrick's apartment, and, when another girl shows up, all three women leave.

Episode Never Produced

"The Man with Two Legs" was supposed to be the eleventh episode of the series but was never filmed. In the script for the episode, Jeff meets the woman of his dreams on the train but doesn't see her face. One morning she sits beside him, and they talk but then he says something he cannot take back – that he has only one leg.

Coupling Uncoupled

Coupling lasted only four episodes. The series scored lower ratings and lost more viewers from its lead-in, *Will & Grace*, than did the series (*Good Morning, Miami*) that it replaced in the 9:30 PM time slot.

Dreams

Premiered Wednesday, October 3, 1984, at 8:30 PM on CBS

The popularity of rock music videos and the movie *Flashdance* in the 1980s inspired *Dreams*, a sitcom about a struggling Philadelphia rock group. Music videos were part of each episode. Dreams was the name of the rock band made up of Gino Minnelli (John Stamos), the lead singer and a welder at a truck plant during the day; Phil Taylor (Cain Devore), Gino's coworker who wrote the songs and was the lead guitarist; Morris Weiner (Albert Macklin), the keyboard player who held various temporary jobs during the day; Martha "Marty" Spino (Jami Gertz), a back-up singer, bass player, shoe store clerk, and secretly in love with Gino, and Lisa Copley (Valerie Stevenson), also a singer and the daughter of a wealthy U.S. Senator, who became a member of the band when they needed money from her. In addition, the band had a male drummer, Angie, who never had any speaking lines.

While waiting for their big break, the Dreams performed at a small neighborhood club, Club Frank, owned by Gino's uncle and former cop Frank Franconi (Ron Karabatsos) who was married to Louise (Sandy Freeman).

Background

The sitcom's executive producers were Peter Guber and Jon Peters, who had produced *Flashdance*. Andy Borowitz, who later developed more successful comedies like *The Fresh Prince of Bel-Air* with his wife, Susan, created *Dreams*. The series was produced by Guber-Peters Entertainment Company.

Episode Guide: 5 aired; 8 unaired

Episode 1: October 3, 1984 "What Dreams Are Made Of"

Director: Bill Bixby Writer: Andy Borowitz

After the group's amplifying system is stolen, the band attempts to borrow $1000 from Frank to buy a new system, but he won't lend them the money. Gino then tries to sell his record collection to raise money. In the record store, he sees Lisa, the girl of his dreams, who is the daughter of a rich, U.S. Senator. Phil wants Gino to ask Lisa for the money they need. When he does, Lisa says that she will lend Gino the $1000 on the condition that she becomes part of the band. The other members balk at the idea, and Lisa asks Gino to at least allow her to audition. She nails the audition at Frank's club, and Frank offers the band a loan to buy new amplifiers.

Episode 2: October 10, 1984   "Friends"

Director: Tom Trbovich   Writers: Janis Hirsch

To Gino's dismay, Phil is quoted out of context in a magazine article which makes him sound like he is the main force behind Dreams. Meanwhile, Weiner unwittingly becomes the missing link in a councilman's kickback scheme.

Episode 3: October 17, 1984   "Boys Are the Best"

Director: Bill Bixby   Writers: Neil Thompson and Nancy Steen

When Martha loses the apartment she is subletting, Lisa invites her to move in with her. Martha reluctantly accepts the invitation, but tension between the two women escalates as Martha is jealous of Lisa's wealth and the attention Gino gives her. Lisa wants Martha to leave, but the guys come by and tell them they will all work things out. The women order the guys to go. Lisa then apologizes to Martha and says that she is envious of some of Martha's traits such as her looks and the fact that she is a survivor. They both agree to try to get along, and they perform "Boys Are the Best."

Episode 4: October 24, 1984 "Suspicion"

Director: Bill Bixby   Writers: Neil Thompson and Nancy Steen

Martha begins receiving fan letters from an anonymous person and thinks she may have a stalker. Weiner moves in to protect her, and she decides not to perform with the band. After Phil goes to her apartment to try to convince her to rejoin the band, she shows up at Frank's to perform and discovers that the person who wrote the letters is a newspaper columnist who had written about the band. Gino tells the guy to get lost. Meanwhile, Phil and Gino's jobs are in jeopardy because a truck whose disc assembly they had worked on was in an accident. However, they later find out that they are off the hook.

Episode 5: October 31, 1984 "Fortune and Fame"

Director: Tom Trbovich Writer: Andy Borowitz

Frank is having an agent attend a talent night at his club. Phil is trying to come up with a new song to perform at the talent show but is having writer's block. When he sees that an old classmate of his, who went on to higher education, is applying for a high-paying managerial position at the place he works, Phil wants to give up music and go to computer school. Phil decides to leave the band because the first class at computer school is on the same night as the talent show. However, when he goes to the school, he freaks out about spending the rest of his life working on computers. Phil is inspired to write a new song, and the band still has time to perform it at Frank's place on talent night even though the agent had to leave.

Episode 6: Unaired "Working Life"

Director: Bill Bixby Writers: Barbara Hall

Gino and Phil report their plant supervisor for extorting money from co-workers, and then find themselves working the night shift which obviously interferes with their nighttime performances.

Barbara Hall, who wrote this episode, subsequently created the drama *Joan of Arcadia*.

Episode 7: Unaired "Head Over Heels"

Director: Tom Trbovich Writers: Neil Thompson and Nancy Steen

Phil is in love with a girl named Kim whom Gino had dated. Even though Gino advises Phil not to get involved with her, Phil still dates her. Kim says that Gino just wanted her for his trophy case. The two guys argue when Phil mentions that he is going away with Kim for the weekend. Gino lets Phil know that he also was in love with Kim once but she stood him up when he planned for the two of them to go on a ski weekend. Phil goes to the hotel anyway to meet Kim who, of course, doesn't show up. Gino comes to the hotel room to console his friend telling him that Kim is a game player – that once she hooks a guy, she is no longer interested in him.

Episode 8: Unaired "Alone"

Director: Tom Trbovich   Writers: David Chambers

Gino's Uncle Frank and his wife Louise are celebrating twenty-five years of marriage when they get into an argument over Frank's opinion about wives needing to obey their husbands. Louise decides to spend a few days apart from Frank to see who is more dependent on whom. Frank then goes to Phil and Gino's place to spend the night. Louise comes back and admits that she missed Frank, but Frank still won't acknowledge that he needs Louise. When Louise leaves Frank again, Gino and Phil tell him that he has to be honest with Louise. Frank goes back to the bar, sees Louise, and finally admits that he needs her. Meanwhile, Gino cannot understand why Lisa is not susceptible to his charms. He confesses that he cares about Lisa, and she says she appreciates his honesty. At Frank and Louise's twenty-fifth anniversary party, the band sings "Alone" which Phil composed based on a poem Frank had written about being away from Louise.

Episode 9: Unaired "Rusted Dreams"

Director: Will MacKenzie   Writers: Chris Lucky

Gino and Phil try to persuade a loading dock worker who used to be a rock star to perform at a benefit.

Episode 10: Unaired "Stuttering"

Director: Bill Bixby   Writers: David Chambers

Weiner gets the band a chance to perform in New York City. However, after they arrive at the place, they find it is near the airport, and they have to wait tables before they perform. When Dreams finally starts its first number, most of the audience gets up to catch their flight. The band goes back to Philadelphia where Frank reluctantly agrees to give them a raise so they continue to play at his club.

Episode 11: Unaired "Tears in the Night" (formerly "Second Chance")

Director: Tom Trbovich   Writers: Susan Borowitz and Richard Raskind

When Martha's brother, Danny, a successful investment counselor visits, she feels ignored as everyone lavishes attention on him. Martha suggests that her brother and her double date. She wants to date Gino with whom she is in love despite Gino lusting after Lisa. Danny ends up with Lisa and Martha with Gino who is jealous of Danny for dating Lisa. After dinner, Danny and Lisa go for a stroll in the park leaving Gino and Martha alone in Danny's car. Gino leaves Martha to find Danny and Lisa and accuses Danny of stealing his girl. After stating that she and Gino are just friends, Lisa walks away from both the guys. Martha finds Danny and tells him that she is crazy for Gino and thought that, since Gino liked Danny, he would fall for her as well.

Episode 12: Unaired "Kiss Me Red"

Director: Bill Bixby Writer: Andy Borowitz

The band has an audition for a TV show called "Single Platinum." Meanwhile, Billy, a former classmate of Lisa's shows up at Frank's club. Billy was a geek in school but now is a handsome stockbroker who likes to work out. When he hits on Lisa, Gino becomes jealous, and Billy challenges him to a weight-lifting competition. In preparation for the contest, Gino starts working out with weights and injures his back making it difficult for him to perform at the audition. After the audition, Frank is able to get Gino's back in shape for the weight-lifting competition which Billy ends up winning anyway. However, Lisa decides to spend time with Gino after the contest instead of going out with Billy. Frank informs the band that they won the audition for the TV show where they perform "Kiss Me Red."

Episode 13: Unaired "The Birthday Party"

Director: Will MacKenzie   Writer: Andy Borowitz

Lisa is turning twenty-one, and her parents want to give her a party at their country club. However, the band is having a celebration at Frank's place. The parents agree to go to Frank's club for Lisa's birthday. The band dresses up for the party, and Phil and Gino finally meet Lisa's parents. Gino talks to Lisa's mother about what he has in mind for a future with Lisa, but mom is not impressed. When the band performs with Lisa as the lead singer, her parents enjoy the entertainment.

***Dreams* Dashed**

Dreams was part of CBS's Wednesday lineup debuting right after another new sitcom, *Charles in Charge*. Both shows ranked in the top thirty, but ratings went down from there. *Dreams* aired just five episodes up against the second half of *Highway to Heaven* on NBC and *The Fall Guy* on ABC. While low ratings killed *Dreams*, the series did result in the actors recording an album of music performed on the show. The album included songs, most of which were episode titles, like "Kiss Me Red" performed by Valerie Stevenson, "Tears in the Night" sung by Jami Gertz, and "Stuttering" done by Cain and Albert. The series also resulted in a paperback book titled *Dreams* written by Barbara Hall. The novel was based on two episodes of *Dreams* – the first one where the band's amplifiers are stolen and Lisa joins the band, and the episode called "Boys Are the Best" where Martha needs a place to stay and moves in with Lisa.

Emily's Reasons Why Not

Premiered Monday, January 9, 2006, at 9:00 PM on ABC

Emily's Reasons Why Not appeared to be ABC's answer to the successful HBO series *Sex and the City*. The show revolved around a female editor of self-help books who was unsuccessful at finding true romance. Emily Sanders (Heather Graham) had a rule that if she could list five reasons to break up with a guy, she would. In addition to Heather Graham, the series co-starred Nadia Dajani as Reilly, Emily's best friend since childhood; Khary Payton as Josh, her gay friend; Smith Cho as Glitter Cho, Emily's rival at Paperoom Publishing who had once been her assistant but then stole one of Emily's ideas to get ahead, and James Patrick Stuart as Midas, a consultant at the publishing company. Each episode of the series was narrated by Heather Graham. During an episode, the five reasons a relationship was not working would display on the TV screen.

Background

Emily's Reasons Why Not was based on the novel of the same name by Carrie Gerlach and adapted for television by Emily Kapnek. Gerlach published her book in 2004 about the problems Emily Sanders had getting past the ninety-day trial period with a guy. In the novel, Emily goes to a psychologist to discuss her problems with developing a lasting relationship with a member of the opposite sex, and he advises her to write down ten reasons why she should not be with a new man in her life before she becomes serious with him. Given it was a thirty-minute show, the series changed the ten reasons to five. Emily had two best friends in the book – Reilly, an Asian-American who was adopted and Grace. In the series, Reilly was not Asian-American, but Emily's rival at the publishing company was. Also there was no mention of Grace in the sitcom. However, both the novel and series mentioned Josh, Emily's gay best friend who in the book was initially Emily's co-worker in public relations. In the series, Josh was supposed to be a "makeup technician" who worked at the Chanel counter in a department store. But his occupation was changed to a waiter at Chi for Two Tea House and Emporium. Also, Josh had a permanent relationship with a yoga instructor.

Each chapter in the book dealt with Emily's description to her psychologist of a different man with whom she had had a relationship and the ten reasons why the relationship did not work. Emily's dates included the CEO of her company; Craig, a man whom she met on vacation whose fiancé had just walked out of their marriage ceremony because he was too controlling; Reese Callahan, a pro-baseball player with the San Diego Padres; Stan, a guy with intimacy issues who might be gay; Lance, a young surfer, and Charlie, an older guy. Gerlach had intended to write a sequel to *Emily's Reasons Why Not*, but the quick cancelation of the TV series put an end to those plans.

The comedy, produced by Sony Pictures Television and Pariah Productions, was filmed with a single camera and no laugh track. In the few episodes that were made, the series did try to go beyond storylines involving Emily's particular man of the week to explore Emily's relationships in general and why they didn't always work out. Still the sitcom was limited by its premise of always coming up with five reasons a relationship could not continue.

LUSTING, LOVING, AND MAKING A LIVING

Episode Guide: 1 Aired; 5 Unaired

Episode 1: January 9, 2006   "Pilot"

Director: Michael Patrick Jann   Writer: Emily Kapnek

In the first act, Emily breaks up with her boyfriend Reese Callahan (Mark Valley), who, unlike the character in the novel, is the author of a book about manipulating women called *Hook, Lie and Sinker: The Lies Men Tell Women, The Lies Women Tell Themselves*. However, like the Reese character in the novel, Emily found that he had two different cell phones – one used to call Emily; the other used to contact other women.

Emily begins dating Stan (Victor Webster), a new guy from the firm's marketing division who doesn't seem to want to get physical with her.

Reasons Why Not to Date Stan: 1) He means he wants to **sleep** with you when he says he wants to sleep with you; 2) He wears make up (bronzer); 3) He has a subscription to *Martha Stewart Living* magazine; 4) He is into Brazilian ju-jitsu which, because of its ground fighting and submission holds, Emily thinks is the gayest sport there is; 5) Josh, Emily's gay friend, thinks Stan is gay.

Emily leaves a message on Stan's office voice mail saying: ". . . I'm going to open the closet door and just come right out and say it. Stan, you're gay. Now I'm not sure if you have fully embraced your gayness yet, but as the woman in your life, I can tell you that I most certainly have." Glitter informs Emily that she learned from Stan's sisters that he is a Mormon who has been saving his virginity for marriage. Emily attempts to erase the voice message that she left Stan, but it is too late—he already played the message when his co-workers were in his office.

Emily Kapnek, who wrote several episodes of *Emily's Reasons*, later created the comedy *Suburgatory*.

Episode 2: Unaired   "Why Not to Date a Twin"

Director: Michael Patrick Jann   Writer: Emily Kapnek

Emily's friend Josh introduces her to Vincent (Matthew Marsden), a British architect, who invites her to his house.

Reasons Why Not to Date a Twin: 1) Emily finds two toothbrushes in Vincent's bathroom and thinks he has a girlfriend. However, it turns out that Vincent has a twin sister, Vinessa (Fay Masterson), who is staying with him while her floors are being done; 2) The twins start playing a game together which requires only two players leaving Emily out; 3) After Emily prepares dinner for Vincent with all his favorite foods that Vinessa told Emily he liked, Vincent gives all the credit to his twin.

For their next date, Vinessa decides to let Vincent and Emily alone in his house for the night. However, the next morning, Vinessa enters Vincent's bedroom and begins to play with his feet, while Emily is naked in his bed. Emily gets upset, but her friends tell her that she has "same-sex" naked issues. When the twins subsequently come to Emily's apartment as she is just getting out of the shower, she answers the door naked to prove she does not have "same-sex" naked issues.

Other Reasons Why Not: 4) Emily in the buff finds not only Vincent and Vinessa at the door but also some Girl Scouts selling cookies, and 5) Vincent hurts himself at yoga class and chooses his sister and not Emily to accompany him to the hospital.

Episode 3: Unaired   "Why Not to Date Your Gynecologist"

Director: Craig Zisk   Writer: Cynthia Greenburg

Emily tries to prove to everyone that she does date mature men and not just boys. She begins dating Dr. Dan (Jay Harrington), her gynecologist, but finds that at dinner he just talks about his medical experiences in France and says he cannot spend the night with her because he has a fibroid procedure in the morning.

Reasons Why Not to Date Your Gynecologist: 1) Emily's date is cut short because of the fibroid procedure; 2) On their second date, Dr. Dan plays backgammon with Emily; 3) The doctor repeats the same stories about his medical experiences at Emily's workplace that he originally told her; 4) Dan discusses ovarian cysts with

Emily's friends at a nightclub, and 5) Dr. Dan tells her how many cells she will shed after they make love.

Episode 4: Unaired "Why Not to Invite Your Vacation Date Home"

Director: Daisy von Scherler Mayer   Writer: Tom Caltabiano

Emily went to Martinique on a book assignment and had a fling with Alain (Ehjan Alexander), a "fun facilitator" at her hotel, whom she invites to visit her in the U.S. He comes to this country and keeps her busy with his lovemaking which causes her not to have time to review an urgent manuscript.

Reasons Why Not to Invite Your Vacation Date Home: 1) Emily gives Alain the keys to her apartment, and Glitter tells her he will rent a truck and steal everything; 2) Alain does body painting on Emily, and she doesn't realize that he painted her back until she takes off her coat at work in front of her coworkers; 3) Emily thinks Alain's body pumping dance looks stupid; 4) Alain pours sand all over her carpet to bring the beach to her, and 5) At a restaurant, Alain hears a cell phone with an island ring tone and begins to dance.

In the end, Alain goes back to Martinique.

The director of this episode, Daisy von Scherler Mayer, co-wrote the screenplay for the film *Party Girl* and helped develop the TV series version of that movie.

Episode 5: Unaired   "Why Not to Cheat on Your Best Friend"

Director: Julie Anne Robinson Writer: Emily Kapnek

Emily begins to discover that she does not have a lot in common with Reilly even though they have been friends since childhood. She decides to contract with a "Girl Dating" service to find a new best friend—someone with whom she has more in common. Through the service, she meets Bethany Marsh (Kristin Bauer) who looks and dresses like her and also works for a publisher. Emily and Bethany go to a book event together and the next day, they go for a walk.

Reasons Why Not to Cheat on Your Best Friend: 1) Reilly calls Emily, and Bethany answers the phone; 2) Emily finds that Bethany is really obsessed with her own career and will do anything to get ahead; 3) Bethany makes appointments for both of them to have their teeth whitened; 4) Reilly becomes friends with Glitter, and 5) Emily throws a shoe at Bethany upon seeing her walking with a new friend and after learning that Bethany signed Emily's former boyfriend to a book deal and had sex with him.

Episode 6: Unaired   "Why Not to Hire a Cute Male Assistant"

Director: Michael Patrick Jann   Writer: Emily Kapnek

When Midas wants Emily to hire an assistant to help her out, she hires Milo (Nick Cornish), a cute guy who turns out to be very efficient and loyal to her. He likes taking care of her, and they begin to act more like boyfriend and girlfriend. They do everything together except have sex.

Reasons Why Not to Hire a Cute Male Assistant: 1) Emily's text to Milo, asking him to read her a bedtime story, is mistakenly sent to the entire division at her firm; 2) Milo gives Emily a small gift for their two-week anniversary; 3) Emily is introduced to Milo's girlfriend and spills water on herself; 4) Emily would like to fire Milo for having a girlfriend, and 5) Emily argues with Milo over the fact that he never told her he had a girlfriend.

Emily asks Milo to quit, but then they kiss. Glitter sees the kiss, and, in the end, Milo is transferred to another floor.

Episode Never Produced

At least one script titled "Why Not to Look at Bridal Magazines" was written but never produced. According to Alicia Kirk, who authored this script, the gist of this potential episode was Emily getting caught up in wedding fever when a friend wants to suddenly get married.[11]

Reasons Canceled

After a big promotional campaign by ABC, *Emily's Reasons Why Not* premiered to poor reviews and low ratings. The comedy did not perform well opposite CBS's *Two and a Half Men*. The first episode came in fourth in its timeslot. Six episodes of *Emily's Reasons Why Not* were produced, but ABC canceled the series after airing a single episode, stating that the show "was not going to get better, and we needed to make a quick change."[12] There was an online petition to save the series, but it garnered only seven signatures. Even though only one episode was broadcast in the U.S., the entire series did air in other countries such as Finland.

Grapevine

Premiered Monday, February 28, 2000, at 9:30 PM on CBS

Grapevine centered around the relationships of four friends in Miami's South Beach: Susan Crawford (Kristy Swanson, Buffy in the movie *Buffy the Vampire Slayer*), a marketing director for a cruise line; David Klein (Steven Eckholdt), a former lawyer turned South Beach restaurateur and Susan's best friend who was secretly in love with her; David's brother, Thumper Klein (George Eads), a bachelor and local sportscaster, and Thumper's friend, Matt Brewer (David Sutcliffe), a newly-divorced manager of a South Beach hotel. Each week's episode involved the characters' sexual and romantic escapades with the characters often speaking directly to the camera explaining what was going through their heads during a previous scene.

Background

When remakes are done, they are usually of a successful TV series. For example, the hit 1960s detective drama *Hawaii 5-0* was remade in 2010 for CBS. *Grapevine* was unusual in that it was a remake of an unsuccessful six-episode series of the same name originally broadcast in 1992. Apparently, CBS brought it back in 2000 because the setting for the series, Miami's South Beach, had become very popular by then. Each episode of the original 1992 series recounted a different male-female relationship story through the words of assorted characters talking directly to the camera. David Frankel, who created the original series, kept lobbying CBS to bring *Grapevine* back, and the network eventually did. *Grapevine* was produced by Paramount Television.

Episode Guide: 5 aired; 1 unaired

Episode 1: February 28, 2000   "Pilot"

Writer/Director: David Frankel

The characters and their relationships are introduced. Susan realizes that she is in love with David who, in turn, loves her but has never admitted his feelings to Susan.

Episode 2: March 6, 2000   "Thumper"

Writer/Director: David Frankel

Thumper falls in love with his friend Matt's former wife Yancy. He bears his heart to Yancy, but she is not as interested in him as he is in her. Susan tells Matt to give his relationship with Yancy another try but not before she fixes him up with Gina, who had a bad experience with Thumper. Meanwhile, Susan and David realize that it might make sense for them to move in together since they constantly commute between each other's apartments.

George Eads, who played Thumper, became Nick Stokes on the hit drama *CSI*. The character of Thumper was supposedly based on David Frankel's real-life brother Jon.

Episode 3: March 13, 2000   "David"

Writer/Director: David Frankel

David purchases an engagement ring for Susan but can't work up the courage to actually propose. However, Matt tells Susan that David plans to propose to her making her wonder why it is taking him so long. A decision about David and Susan's relationship must be made when he receives an offer to manage a restaurant in Los Angeles.

Steven Eckholdt, who played David, portrayed Thumper on the first *Grapevine*.

Episode 4: March 20, 2000   "Jamie"

Writer/Director: David Frankel

Thumper and Jamie have been friends for a long time, but now Jamie wants to change the relationship from friends to lovers since she has fallen in love with Thumper, much to Thumper's horror. Meanwhile, Matt reluctantly gives his blessing to his sister Heather's marriage to Rick who dumped her at the altar three years earlier.

Lynn Clark, who played Susan in the prior version of *Grapevine*, guest starred as Matt's sister in this episode.

Episode 5: March 27, 2000   "Jack"

Writer/Director: David Frankel

Thumper's high school sweetheart asks him to be her final fling before she gets married. David returns to Miami to help Matt manage his new restaurant. Susan is dating Jack (Michael Weatherly), a former co-worker who is now a magician; while David sees a former girlfriend for whom he still has feelings.

Episode 6: Unaired   "Matt" (summary provided by David Frankel)

Writer/Director: David Frankel

Matt meets Paulina (Amanda Pays) at a casual party and falls in love with her very quickly, not realizing that she is wealthy and married. Paulina briefly considers leaving her husband for Matt before recognizing that they're wrong for each other and dumping him unceremoniously.

This episode was essentially a remake of an episode from the 1992 version of *Grapevine* titled "Fran and Joey."

The Second Time: Not the Charm

The comedy aired on Mondays—first at 9:30 PM and then at 8:30 PM. Scheduled for six episodes like the original, it was canceled after five shows – one less than the 1992 version. The premiere episode following the CBS hit *Everybody Loves Raymond* ranked fortieth out of ninety-three series, losing many of the viewers from its lead-in, and the ratings for subsequent episodes in the 8:30 timeslot kept declining.

Happy Hour

Premiered Thursday, September 7, 2006, 8:30 PM on Fox

"*Friends* with alcohol instead of coffee" is how some characterized this series. *Happy Hour* was about a young man, Henry Beckman (John Sloan), losing not only his girlfriend Heather (Brooke D'Orsay), a former Miss Missouri who wanted to be single again, but also his job with her uncle and his apartment and moving in with a neighbor, Larry Cone (Lex Medlin), who needed a roommate. The title of the series came from one of Larry's rules that every day at 4:00 PM was happy hour when he played Dean Martin songs and drank martinis.

Of course, the roommates on *Happy Hour* had opposite personalities—Henry was the sensitive romantic, and Larry the insensitive womanizer. The concept was that both roommates had their personalities shaped by their previous relationships with women – Henry was blinded by love, while Larry had been damaged by love.

Happy Hour focused not only on the love lives of the twentysomething roommates, but also on their friends: Brad Cooper (Nat Faxon), Larry's former roommate who worked in a pharmacy; Brad's controlling fiancée, Tina DiFabio (Jamie Denbo); and Larry's friend and Henry's new boss, Amanda Pennington (Beth Lacke). The friends often hung out at Teddy's bar.

Background

The husband and wife team of Jeff and Jackie Filgo created *Happy Hour* as an edgier *Friends*. The series was produced by Double Double Bonus Entertainment and Werner Gold Miller in association with Warner Bros. Television.

Episode Guide: 4 aired; 9 unaired

Episode 1: September 7, 2006   "Pilot"

Director: Andy Ackerman   Writers: Jeff and Jackie Filgo

After moving from Missouri to Chicago to be near his girlfriend, Henry Beckman is dumped by her because she needs to "blossom." He loses his job and his apartment and is forced to move into an apartment with Larry Cone who has a T-shirt business. Larry lost his former roommate Brad when he fell in love with Tina. Larry helps Henry get a job at the Second Community Bank where Larry's friend Amanda is Henry's boss. When Larry throws a party for Henry, Henry ends up in bed with Amanda. Henry's ex-girlfriend, Heather, comes by Larry's apartment the next morning to see if Henry has been able to move on after their breakup and sees Amanda and Henry together.

Episode 2: September 14, 2006   "The Mix CD"

Director: Mark Cendrowski   Writer: Rob Des Hotel

Henry is frustrated that Larry has yet to make any room in the apartment for his stuff, and so, he cleans out the closet in his room and finds a mix CD of love songs. Henry asks Amanda, Brad, and Tina the significance of the CD. He receives details from them about Molly for whom Larry violated his own rule about not dating anyone longer than six weeks. It turns out that, when Larry gave Molly the mix CD and told her he loved her, she didn't feel the same about him and broke off the relationship. Meanwhile, Amanda is concerned when a new doctor in her gynecologist's office cancels their date. She thinks it has to do with her pubic area but finds out that the doctor was told he couldn't date patients.

Episode 3: September 21, 2006   "Larry's Birthday"

Director: Andy Ackerman   Writers: Jeff and Jackie Filgo

Everyone forgets Larry's birthday except for Henry who gives him an evening of camping as a present. Heather stops by the apartment to deliver Henry's tent and is introduced to Larry's friends. Henry and Larry go camping on the roof of their apartment building where Henry sings and plays his guitar. Needless to say, this is not Larry's idea of a fun evening, and so he orders steaks and some girls to come up to the roof for a party. Amanda tells Henry that Larry never really had birthday celebrations when he was a kid and that is why he makes such a big deal out of them now. Amanda gives Larry her toy elephant that shoots cigarettes out its butt as her perfect gift for him. When Heather ends up at the party on the roof, Henry invites her to stay.

Episode 4: November 2, 2006   "The Ring and I"

Director: Mark Cendrowski   Writers: Casey Johnson and David Windsor

Henry still has the engagement ring that he planned to give Heather. Larry tries to get Henry to sell the ring on eBay so they can buy a wine refrigerator. Amanda borrows the ring to show a former date that she is now married. Meanwhile, Tina is jealous that she is engaged to Brad but has no ring. She questions Brad if he really wants to marry her and then kicks him out of their apartment. Amanda gives the ring to Brad who goes back to Tina to formally propose and present her with the ring. Heather talks to Henry and says she misses him and wants to get back together. However, after witnessing Brad's proposal to Tina, Henry realizes that he and Heather are just friends and asks Brad for the ring back.

Nat Faxon (Brad) won an Oscar in 2012 for co-adapting the screenplay for the film *The Descendants*.

Episode 5: Unaired   "Crazy Girls"

Director: Shelley Jensen   Writer: Jim Reynolds

Larry warns Henry about dating a girl named Shauna, who works in the local coffee shop. Larry had dated her but had to lie about his sexuality in order to break off the relationship. Despite Larry's warnings, Henry takes her out and later finds she hacks into his emails and stalks him. Henry asks Larry to get him out of the relationship, but eventually Henry has to get Tina to tell Shauna that her relationship with him is over. Meanwhile, Amanda meets Lucy, an old college friend, who gives her a gift certificate for an online dating service. Offended by the suggestion, Amanda wants to show she can get a man on her own. Amanda starves herself to look good for an upcoming benefit her old friend will be attending.

Episode 6: Unaired   "Boo! This Party Sucks"

Director: Mark Cendrowski   Writer: Sally Bradford

Larry and Tina host separate Halloween parties. Brad begs everyone to attend Tina's party, but Amanda, Henry, and Heather first go to Larry's party and then plan to attend Tina's. Heather and Amanda both dress as Catwoman; Larry and Henry are Big Elvis and Little Elvis respectively. When Heather, Amanda, and Henry finally go to Tina's party, they discover they are her only guests which complicate their plans to leave quietly. Brad suggests to Tina that they all attend Larry's party, but they don't want to make Tina unhappy. Finally, Larry and Tina work out an arrangement where, in the future, he will host Halloween parties and she will be in charge of Thanksgiving.

Episode 7: Unaired   "Thanksgiving"

Director: Asaad Kelada   Writers: Jackie & Jeff Filgo

For Thanksgiving, Tina's mother, Nanette (Jessica Walter), and sister, Alicia (Laura Bell Bundy) are planning to visit. Brad invites Larry, Henry, and Amanda to join them. Brad cannot seem to make a good impression on Tina's mother. However, Henry apparently makes a very good impression on Nanette since she puts the moves on him.

Episode 8: Unaired "The Election"

Director: Asaad Kelada   Writer: Shawn Simmons

Larry gets a satellite dish that Tina, as President of the tenant's association, wants to have him take down. Henry advises Larry to campaign against Tina in the upcoming tenant's association election with Henry as his running mate. Don, an older resident in the building, decides to run as well. Since Tina and Larry don't want to split the "youth" vote, they decide to run together with her as president and Larry keeping his satellite dish. However, Don wins anyway. Meanwhile, Amanda likes how Tina controls Brad; so she gets herself Chucky, a man she can control.

Episode 9: Unaired "The Family Affair"

Director: Shelley Jensen   Writers: Jeff and Jackie Filgo

Henry's parents, Boots and Tucker, are coming to visit, and he is afraid they will be disappointed in him when they find that he broke up with Heather and moved in with Larry. Larry and Amanda like Henry's parents because they cook and clean for them. Boots and Tucker want to tell Henry that they have separated but are afraid to. They want Larry to reveal their secret, which he eventually does. Meanwhile, Heather and Amanda get jobs as tequila girls at Teddy's bar.

Episode 10: Unaired "A Dead Man's Ham" (aka "Xmas")

Director: Gail Mancuso   Writer: Rob Des Hotel

Larry's friends leave to be with their parents for Christmas but, when all the flights are canceled because of a snowstorm, they come back to spend the holiday with him at the apartment. However, the only food available is a mail-order ham that came for Mr. Pickwick, a neighbor who died suddenly. They take the ham but then can't bring themselves to eat it.

Episode 11: Unaired "New Year's Eve"

Director: Shelley Jensen   Writer: Sally Bradford

When Larry meets Amanda's new boyfriend Ross, he has bad "vibes" about him. Amanda asks Larry to be honest with her about why he doesn't like Ross. He says that she should not date someone just because the guy is into her. This upsets Amanda, and she leaves. On New Year's Eve, Larry and Henry see Ross kissing another woman. When Larry informs Amanda of what he saw, she says she already knows, and Larry says he is sorry. Also, Tina and Brad dress in formal attire for their New Year's Eve midnight kiss picture.

Episode 12: Unaired "11:30 Snuggles"

Director: Shelley Jensen   Writers: Casey Johnson and David Windsor

Heather offers to throw a bridal shower for Tina, while Brad suggests a 'guys' night' out to Larry and Henry. Tina says he can go with Larry and Henry provided he is back for 11:30 snuggles with her. At the club, Brad takes on his alter ego of a police officer to impress women. However, another guy interferes when he zeroes in on a particular woman, and Henry, Larry, and Brad almost get into a fight with three other guys. Henry calls the cops, and he, Larry, and Brad are arrested. Meanwhile, at Tina's bridal shower, Amanda meets a friend of Tina's who is an assistant district attorney, and Amanda discovers she is gay. After Larry calls Amanda to bail him and the other guys out of jail because Brad is concerned he won't make 11:30 snuggles, Amanda asks the lesbian she met to get the guys released.

Episode 13: Unaired "The T-Shirt"

Director: Gail Mancuso   Writer: Shawn Simmons

Larry's T-shirt business takes off after George Clooney is seen wearing one on a magazine cover, but the reverse happens when Kevin Federline is seen in a magazine in one. The slogan on the T-shirt is "I'm not that into Me." Heather helps Larry's business by changing the slogan to "I'm not that into Men" and sells them at a Melissa Etheridge concert. Meanwhile, after Brad has forgotten certain wedding preparations, he gives Tina an experimental pill for her migraine that makes her very mellow and compliant. Also, Amanda complains to her boss about his sexual comments, but, when he hits on other women, she gets jealous.

Not So Happy Ending

The sitcom followed another new comedy on Fox – *'Til Death* and was on opposite *Ugly Betty* on ABC, *Survivor* on CBS, and *The Office* on NBC. It ran for three episodes with each episode receiving lower ratings than the one before it. The last episode in September ranked fourth in its timeslot. *Happy Hour* was pulled from the schedule, and then brought back for one more episode in November, after which it was finally canceled due to low ratings. However, all thirteen episodes of the series were subsequently broadcast in other countries such as Australia, Poland, and New Zealand.

Life on a Stick

Premiered Thursday, March 24, 2005, at 9:30 PM on Fox

Life on a Stick centered on recent Seattle high school graduate Laz Lackerman (Zachary Knighton); his best friend, Fred (Charlie Finn), and his girlfriend, Lily (Rachelle Lefevre). All of them worked in the mall at Yippee Hot Dogs which was managed by Mr. Hut (Maz Jobrani). The hot dog stand served corn dogs on a stick, hence the title of the series.

Laz had an arrangement with his dad, Rick (Matt Glave), and his stepmother, Michelle (Amy Yasbeck), that if he looked out for his sixteen-year-old stepsister Molly (Saige Thompson), he could continue to live at home rent free. The parents ran a mail-order beauty products internet business from home. Also on the series was Laz's nine-year-old half brother, Gus (Frankie Ryan Manriquez) on whom the parents lavished most of their affection, and Molly's study partner, Jasper (Ryan Belleville) on whom she had a crush.

Background

Created by Victor Fresco, *Life on a Stick* was initially titled *Related by Family*. In speaking about the comedy, Fresco, who has created such sitcoms as *Andy Richter Controls the Universe* and *Better Off Ted*, said: "…my experience in life and with kids that I've known is they don't know what they want to do when they get out of high school. That's what these guys are. And I don't know why it's taken so long to set up a show in a food court; but it's about time."[13]

Life on a Stick was supposed to premiere in January but was delayed until the spring. Garfield Grove in association with Paramount produced the series.

Episode Guide: 5 aired; 8 unaired

Episode 1: March 24, 2005   "Pilot"

Director: Andy Ackerman   Writer: Victor Fresco

Instead of going to college after graduating from high school, Laz and his friend Fred start working at Yippee Hot Dogs. There Laz develops a crush on co-worker Lilly and doesn't like it when the boss, Mr. Hut, yells at her. Laz is fired after talking back to Mr. Hut and is afraid that he will have to move out of his parents' house. They tell him that he doesn't have to move as long as he spends time with Molly who only seems to speak to Laz. Laz and Fred go back to Yippee Hot Dogs to collect wages due them, but Mr. Hut won't pay them. Laz, Fred, and Lilly decide to deep fry everything on Mr. Hut's desk. Lilly tells Hut it was her idea, but then, like in the movie *Spartacus*, everyone else also claims responsibility.

Episode 2: March 30, 2005   "Liking Things the Way They Aren't"

Director: Andrew D. Weyman   Writer: Michael A. Ross

Fred and Laz have to work for free at Yippee Hot Dogs until they pay for the damages to Mr. Hut's office. Lilly doesn't want a relationship with Laz; she just wants to fool around since she has so many other commitments such as helping her disabled brother and unemployed father. The guys start bartering corn dogs for other services at the mall like free manicures and tanning. Laz gets Lilly and Fred new jobs working at the Pretzel Hut, but they find the working conditions worse than at the hot dog stand. All three eventually quit the pretzel stand and go back to Yippee Hot Dogs. Meanwhile, Molly goes on a 'date' with Jasper only to find that it is a group date that includes his girlfriend Susan.

Michael A. Ross, who wrote this episode, is married to Markie Post, one of the stars of *Night Court*.

Episode 3: April 6, 2005   "Fish Song"

Director: Andrew D. Weyman   Writer: Miriam Trogdon

The staff from the mall's fast food fish place begins singing about their food, and the Yippee staff doesn't like it. However, Mr. Hut wants his staff to sing as well with hopes of increasing business. Laz, Fred, and Lilly plot to stop the competing fast food staff from singing and try to get other food court workers to join them. But Fred goes over to the 'enemy' because he feels excluded by Laz who is devoting all his attention to Lilly. Laz and Lilly decide to eat the shrimp at the fish place and pretend they get food poisoning, but, before Lilly begins throwing up from some medicine she took, she gets Fred and Laz to reconcile.

Episode 4: April 20, 2005   "The Defiant Ones"

Director: Andrew D. Weyman   Writer: Adam Chase

Molly is taking a German class to be with Jasper. The teacher thinks that she is a troublemaker like her stepbrother was when he was in class. She questions the teacher's arbitrary rules and is assigned the 'wobbly' desk at the front of the class. Molly becomes very popular with the class when she puts a Hitler-like moustache on the teacher. After Rick and Michelle give Laz a motor scooter as a reward for helping Molly, Laz doesn't want them to know about Molly's trouble in class. He goes to see the teacher and ends up breaking the 'wobbly' desk. Meanwhile, Mr. Hut has been kicked out of his house by his wife for not shaving his body and has Fred, Lilly, and Laz keep him company at the mall after it closes. Laz and Fred finally get Mr. Hut to go back to his wife.

Amy Yasbeck, who played Michelle, is the widow of John Ritter.

Episode 5: April 27, 2005   "Gangs of the Mall"

Director: Andrew D. Weyman   Writer: Maggie Bandur

The Sports City guys at the mall intimidate the food court workers so they don't date the girls from the store, Rendezvous. Fred longs for Allison from Rendezvous, but Evan, the biggest Sports City guy, who dated Allison in the past, wants to fight Fred over her. Although Fred doesn't want to fight, Allison tells him that someone needs to teach Evan a lesson. Fred changes his mind about fighting, but, before he and Evan go to it, Fred puts on glasses since he knows no one can hit a man with glasses. Evan also puts on thick glasses, and the two can't see each other to fight.

Episode 6: Unaired   "We'll Always Have Bowling"

Director: Andy Ackerman   Writer: Mike Teverbaugh

Molly gets her younger brother to take the blame for her spilling soda on the family's PC by bribing him with iced cappuccinos, and he becomes hooked on caffeine. Fred has an affair with one of Michelle's friends, and Laz takes Lilly bowling but then decides to date an older woman when Lilly won't commit to their relationship. However, Laz doesn't want to have sex with the older woman because he is still in love with Lilly.

Episode 7: Unaired   "Breaking Away"

Director: Andrew D. Weyman   Writers: Kat Likkel and John Hoberg

Mr. Hut hires Nancy, a student intern, whom Laz dates since he says his relationship with Lilly is over. Lilly retaliates by dating Brad, the hot dog bun delivery guy. Laz doesn't really like Nancy because of her hatred of old people, and Lilly doesn't like Brad singing all the time. When Lilly admits to Laz that she is not over him, he confesses the same to her. Meanwhile, Molly sees her parents trying to destroy her childhood teddy bear that they said was lost several years ago but was actually hidden in their garage. Her parents feel so bad about lying about the bear that they will do anything for her. She asks for a pony but really wants cable TV in her bedroom. The parents figure that Molly knew all along that her teddy bear was hidden in the garage, and so, when they decide to get her a real small-size pony, she says that she knew about the teddy bear.

Episode 8: Unaired "Things People Stand For"

Director: Andrew D. Weyman   Writer: Jeff Westbrook

Lilly, Fred, and Laz enter a contest to win a car by being the last ones to remove their hands from the vehicle. Fred drops out right away, but Laz thinks Fred should still get a share of the car if they win. He and Lilly fight, and they move away from each other around the car. Later, they both make up, and Laz kisses her while she is sleeping by the car. She is startled, and they both take their hands off the automobile. Meanwhile, her parents want to throw a surprise party for Molly's sixteenth birthday although she doesn't want them to. She throws a surprise party for her parents to embarrass them and then believes that her parents called off her surprise party. Molly thanks them by saying how lame her friends are only to discover that her friends hear her comments while hiding in a closet for the surprise party.

Episode 9: Unaired   "The Things We Do For Love"

Director: Sheldon Epps   Writer: Michael A. Ross

When Laz is teaching Molly how to drive, she ends up hitting him with the car which causes him to pee his pants. Everyone at Yippee Hot Dogs learns of the incident. Molly tries to do something nice for Laz to make up for the accident, while Lilly pities him. Laz feels he has to prove his manhood and decides to sit in a crab tank in the mall's Oriental restaurant. After he breaks a record by spending three hours in the tank, Lilly says she really cares about him.

Episode 10: Unaired   "Some Drinkin' and Some Foolin' Around"

Director: Lee Shallat Chemel   Writer: Mike Teverbaugh

After Laz and Lilly make love in the Nature Store at the mall, Lilly now wants to be in a committed relationship with him. Laz claims that he "won" by getting Lilly to commit to their relationship which makes her mad, and she leaves. Laz, thinking the relationship is over, takes a former female classmate to the movies where Lilly finds him, and they reconcile. Meanwhile, Rick and Michelle want to teach Molly about the effects of alcohol, and so they have wine with dinner. Molly begins to bond with Rick when he tells her he used to be a nudist. Much to her dismay, Molly then sees him in the nude in the kitchen.

Episode 11: Unaired   "Soupless in Seattle"

Director: Lee Shallat Chemel   Writer: Miriam Trogdon

When Lilly makes a lot of soup for Laz since he has been sick, he doesn't want to tell her she is going overboard. After Molly mentions to Lilly that Laz thinks she is getting too intense with him with all the soup, Lilly gets miffed at Laz for not being honest with her. In the meantime, Michelle and Rick want to renew their wedding vows on their tenth anniversary, and Rick wants a new wedding photo because he thinks he looked too feminine in the original photo. As part of the preparations for the renewal of vows, Lilly puts on a wedding dress to make Laz think she wants to marry him. When Fred tells Laz that Lilly has been messing with him for not being honest about the soup, Laz, to get back at her, proposes. She says "yes" and has a marriage license ready. They have the parents' minister begin the marriage ceremony, but Molly speaks up and says they need to be honest with each other. Molly also informs Jasper, who recently broke up with his girlfriend and is there for the renewal of the parents' vows, that she is crazy about him, and he says he likes her.

Episode 12: Unaired   "Wouldn't It Be Nice"

Director: Lee Shallat Chemel   Writer: Maggie Bandur

Lilly and Laz have a friend allow them to spend nights at a furniture store in the mall in order to be together more. They find that they each have habits that irritate one another. Laz likes to listen to jazz at night, and Lilly prefers to have a fan blowing. They don't agree on anything especially when Lilly wishes to have a party in the furniture store, while Laz wants to be alone with her. Fred, who has also been sleeping on the various kids' beds in the store at night, convinces the two to make up. Meanwhile, Molly goes to meet Jasper's parents and grandmother. Since they are out and only Jasper is at home, Molly decides to play a trick on him by hiding in the closet with a water pistol. The parents and grandmother come home early, and, when grandma opens the closet, Molly literally scares her to death. Although Molly tries to apologize to Jasper's parents, they want her to go away. Only when Jasper insists that he likes Molly, do the parents say he can still date her.

Episode 13: Unaired "The Gods of TV"

Director: Andy Ackerman   Writer: Adam Chase

Molly and Lilly are taking a self-defense class. Laz and Jasper are invited to a self-defense demonstration at the same time as a Beastie Boy's concert for which Fred has tickets. Laz says that if they go to the concert and make up an excuse as to why they couldn't attend the demo, they will be punished for it like husbands are when they lie to their wives on TV sitcoms. Fred decides to burn the tickets on the way to the self-defense demo. However, the guys pick up the Beastie Boy's stage manager whose motorcycle crashed after Fred threw the flaming tickets out of the car window and take him to the concert where he gives them great seats. After the concert, Laz tells the girls they didn't make it to their demonstration because they had a flat tire and hit a deer. The guys end up taking baseball bats to the front of Laz's vehicle to try to show that they hit a deer.

Life Interrupted

When it finally debuted in the spring, Fox scheduled the first episode on Thursdays after the hit *American Idol*, where it lost half of the viewers from its lead-in. Fox moved the show to Wednesday nights at 9:30 PM and then 8:30 PM, where relatively low ratings led to its cancelation after five episodes. The entire series subsequently aired on the cable channel Universal HD.

Zachary Knighton (Laz) later starred on *Flash Forward* and *Happy Endings*, and Rachelle Lefevre (Lilly) subsequently became a regular on *Off the Map* and *A Gifted Man*.

My Guide to Becoming a Rock Star

Premiered Thursday, March 14, 2002, at 8:00 PM on the WB

The son of Goldie Hawn and the brother of Kate Hudson, Oliver Hudson starred on this series as Jason "Jace" Darnell, the lead singer of a struggling rock band called SlipDog out of Becker, Washington – a suburb of Seattle. Jace narrated each episode illustrating the steps a rock group takes to become a success. Other members of the group included a spaced-out guitarist, "Doc" Pike (Kevin Rankin), and a punky female bassist, Joe Delamo (Lauren Hodges). In the debut episode, Jace, who had been unemployed for about eighteen months, offered the young woman from the unemployment office, Sarah Nelson (Emmanuelle Vaugier), a job with the band as a DJ and keyboard player. Ex-rocker Michael Des Barres played Jace's dad Eric who was a former rock star and now ran an amplifier and guitar repair store; Shannon Tweed (wife of KISS's Gene Simmons) was Jace's mother Gina. Originally, John Lydon played Jace's dad, but the pilot was reshoot with Des Barres in that role.

Background

Based on a British comedy, *The Young Person's Guide to Becoming a Rock Star*, the sitcom was adapted for American television by its British creator, Bryan Eisley, and by John Riggi. Thirteen episodes of the comedy were produced, and originally the WB planned to air *My Guide* in Fall 2001. However, the network pushed the series to the spring and promoted it as the first ever "Super Series". The situation comedy was produced by Tiny Hut in association with Warner Bros..

The British series on which *My Guide* was based, broadcast in 1998, had only six episodes which followed essentially the same overall storyline. However, in the British version, the band, from Glasgow, was called "Jocks-Wa-Hey" and the lead singer was Jeremy "Jez" MacAllister (Ciaran McMenamin). The other members of the band were: bass player "Psycho" MacPhail (Duncan Marwick), the equivalent of Doc in the American series; drummer Wullie MacBoyne (Stephen McCole); lead guitarist Joe Nardone (Nicola Stapleton), and welfare office worker Fiona Johnstone (Simone Lahbib) who was recruited by Jez to play the keyboard. Unlike the American version, in the final episode of *The Young Person's Guide to Becoming a Rock Star*, the band, having recorded an over-budget album and going on a promotional tour, ended up with a top ten single and a massive 3 million pound debt. Also, in the British version of the show, Gerard Butler had a role early in his career as Marty Claymore, an over-the-top rock star.

Episode Guide: 5 aired; 8 unaired

Episode 1: March 14, 2002   "Pilot"

Director: Rodman Flender   Writers: John Riggi and Bryan Eisley

Jace makes a deal with Doyle Greyson (Rick Overton), owner of a salvage and reconditioning center, to manage the band because he is unable to pay what he owes Doyle for rehearsal space and other services. When Jace meets Sarah, his employment counselor who is interested in his music, he wants her to join the band. SlipDog's drummer is Danny Whitaker (James DeBello), a not-so-bright jock.

Episode 2: March 14, 2002   "The New Drummer"

Director: Rodman Flender Writer: John Riggi

Jace attempts to convince Sarah to contribute her DJ skills to the band, and she reluctantly agrees to a six-month time frame. However, Joe is upset about having another female band member and wants Sarah to try out for the group. Sarah will audition only if Joe plays as well. Meanwhile, Danny, the band's drummer, drowns in a mud puddle while playing football when he ends up at the bottom of the heap during practice. Sarah is able to provide a new drummer Lucas Zank (Kris Lemche), a gay friend of hers.

Episode 3: March 15, 2002   "Fame"

Director: Michael Engler   Writers: Alec Holland and Melissa Samuels

After the band plays a concert at a local middle school, three young girls become obsessed with Jace. They follow him everywhere, come to rehearsals, and show up at a performance where they jump on stage and ruin the show. Jace tells the girls to "get a life." Later he feels guilty and tries to apologize, but they have already chosen someone else to idolize – the band's bassist, Joe.

Episode 4: March 21, 2002   "The Road Gig"

Director: Michael Engler Writer: Steve Rudnick

The band goes on a road trip for a performance in Idaho. When they arrive at their destination, they find the club that booked them is closed because of a fire. The band looks for another place to perform and ends up at a Potato Festival. Jace gets the band booked at the festival, but the audience, attuned to country and western music, doesn't like them.

Episode 5: March 21, 2002   "Pay to Play"

Director: Michael Engler   Writer: Vince Calandra

SlipDog gets a job at a club where the band has to pay the owner unless at least one-hundred patrons show up for their performance. The band members blanket the town with posters advertising their gig. Meanwhile, Sarah has a growing distaste for her job at the unemployment office and quits to devote full time to SlipDog.

Episode 6: Unaired   "Inspiration"

Director: Michael Engler   Writer: J. Elvis Weinstein

The band needs more songs to perform, but Jace and Doc are unable to come up with any. When Jace hears one of his father's unfinished compositions on an old tape, he is finally inspired to complete it. Meanwhile, Jace's dad is trying to fight growing older and is depressed at having to get eyeglasses. At a performance attended by Jace's mother and father, Jace invites his dad on stage to perform the song, "Your Love Rocks Me," with the band, and his dad feels young again.

J. Elvis Weinstein, who wrote this episode, was the original voice of robot Tom Servo on the cult classic *Mystery Science Theater 3000*.

Episode 7: Unaired   "The Yoko Factor"

Director: Craig Zisk   Writer: Leonard Dick

Doc dates an Indian performance artist named Siobahn (Christine Zimmer) who clashes with the other members of the band. He tries to add a sitar to the band's sound and allow Siobahn to sing. Lucas becomes so frustrated with Siobahn's critique of the band and the ensuing arguments that he quits, leaving the band without a drummer.

Episode 8: Unaired   "The Session"

Director: John Payson   Writer: J. Elvis Weinstein

The band gets set to record their first song, "Shining Star," at a cheap recording studio at night when the rates for renting the studio are cheaper. Owen (Brian Dietzen), the inexperienced engineer at the studio, is also a drummer, and so he joins the band for the recording session. Siobahn is still dating Doc and continues to criticize the band, finally causing Doc to end their relationship.

Episode 9: Unaired   "The Competition"

Director: Craig Zisk   Story: Peg Healey   Teleplay: Melissa Samuels and Alec Holland

SlipDog enters a "battle of the bands" competition, and the members of the group meet a former member of SlipDog, Dominic, who left when Jace would not get rid of Joe. Even though Dominic was dating Joe, he felt she was not a good musician but didn't tell her that. When Joe and Dominic begin dating again, she reveals the song SlipDog will perform in the contest. Dominic's band performs that song meaning that Jace's group has to play something different at the last minute. SlipDog ends up winning the competition anyway.

Episode 10: Unaired   "The Wedding Singers"

Director: Lev Spiro Writer: Vince Calandra

As a favor for Sarah, the band performs at a wedding. They are so good that they get other bookings for weddings and other parties which they find very profitable. Despite Doc's objections that they are selling out, the other members of the band decide to use an alternative name for the group when they perform at such functions. They use the alias "Happily Ever After" and wear blue tuxedos and gowns (everyone except Doc). But when the band forgets to play at one of their regular gigs and

LUSTING, LOVING, AND MAKING A LIVING

performs at a wedding instead, they realize that Doc is correct. The members end up burning their tuxedos and gowns.

Episode 11: Unaired   "One Night Only"

Director: Peter Lauer   Writer: Peg Healey

The band gets its first concert as an opening act for the boy band, Boulevard Boys. They are impressed by the professionalism of Boulevard Boys' manager compared to their own manager, Doyle. Jace fires Doyle; then the Boulevard Boys' manager fires SlipDog out of concern that they are better than his boy band and will upstage them. After Jace informs Doyle they were fired, Doyle strong arms Boulevard Boys' manager into giving SlipDog the job back. Doyle then resumes his position as manager of SlipDog.

Episode 12: Unaired   "The Betrayal"

Director: John Riggi   Writers: Leonard Dick and Steven Rudnick

After their performance at the Boulevard Boys concert, Jace only wants the band to play big venues which frustrates the other members. They decide to take a two-week break from rehearsals and performing. But when Jace visits a club and finds that the other members of the band have formed a jazz ensemble and are performing jazz songs, he feels betrayed. At SlipDog's next regular performance, Jace announces to the audience that this will be his last show and that he is leaving the band. However, after the show, Jace meets a representative from a major record label, and he reconsiders his decision to leave SlipDog.

Episode 13: Unaired   "The Deal"

Director: Rodman Flender   Writer: John Riggi

In the final episode, the band goes to Seattle to meet the staff of a record company. They find that Doc's former girlfriend, Siobahn, now works at the record label, and she advises Doc that the company only wants to sign Jace to a contract and not the other band members. Jace is told the same thing by the record label representative. Although the other members of SlipDog are disappointed, they tell Jace to accept the deal. The record company asks the band to give a rooftop performance to celebrate Jace's signing. After the performance, Jace refuses to sign on his own and abandon the other members.

Fallen *Star*

The WB said the series would run for six weeks with back-to-back episodes, but only five episodes were broadcast—two back-to-back on Thursdays at 8:00 PM for two weeks and one episode on Friday following the first Thursday broadcast. *My Guide to Becoming a Rock Star* averaged only about 2 million viewers. The series ranked 167th out of 170 shows.

Oliver Hudson (Jace) later starred on the comedy *Rules of Engagement*. Kevin Rankin (Doc) subsequently became a regular on the crime series *Unforgettable*.

Party Girl

Premiered Monday, September 9, 1996, at 9:00 PM on Fox

In *Party Girl*, Christine Taylor (Marcia in *The Brady Bunch Movie*) played Mary, a single young woman whose mother had recently died. She got a job working with her godmother, Judy Burkhart (Swoosie Kurtz), as a clerk in the New York City Public Library. Wanda (Merrin Dungey), Mary's co-worker at the library, was always pointing out to Judy, Mary's shortcomings as a library clerk. At night, Mary liked to party with her friends, including Derrick (John Cameron Mitchell), a gay fashion designer who sometimes tried to flirt with Mary's dates. Oneal (Matt Borlenghi) was the handsome but dense bartender at the bar where Mary and Derrick liked to hang out.

Background

Party Girl was based on a 1995 independent film of the same name directed by Daisy von Scherler Mayer and written by Harry Brickmayer. They both created the *Party Girl* series. The movie *Party Girl* starred Parker Posey as Mary who earned money from parties she held in her loft. After she was arrested for selling liquor without a license, for unauthorized showing of videos, etc., Mary asked her godmother Judy, a librarian, for a loan. Judy hired Mary as a library clerk, and eventually Mary wanted to major in library science so she could become a full-fledged librarian.

The TV series was developed by Efrem Seeger and produced by Warner Bros.. There were several changes in the supporting cast from the sitcom's initial inception. Originally the part of Mary's godmother was played by Sasha von Scherler – the mother of series co-creator Daisy von Scherler Mayer, and Mary had a DJ friend named Leo (Alexis Cruz). Alexis Cruz was dropped from the pilot, and Bumper Robinson (*Molloy*) took over the role before the character was eliminated altogether. The character of Oneal, the bartender was then added to the show. Also, Swoosie Kurtz took over the role of Judy – Mary's godmother.

Episode Guide: 4 aired; 2 unaired

Episode 1: September 9, 1996 "Pilot"

Director: Michael Lembeck
Writers: Daisy von Scherler Mayer, Harry Brickmayer, and Efrem Seeger

After being arrested for running a nightclub in her apartment, Mary gets a job as a library clerk working in the Seward Park Branch for her responsible godmother, Judy. Among other duties, Judy has a class for adults to learn conversational English, but she is not successful at getting anyone to speak in the class. During her first day of work, Mary hides the books she is supposed to shelve, and Judy fires her. But because Mary likes working in the library, she breaks into the place at night with help from Derrick and Oneal to learn the Dewey Decimal System. She returns to the library the next day to get her job back and impresses Judy with her knowledge of the system. She also sits with the conversational English class and gets them to talk, and so Judy rehires her.

The pilot episode was a mini-remake of the movie. Son of actor Harvey Lembeck (*The Phil Silvers Show*) and former actor, Michael Lembeck has directed many sitcom episodes including *Friends*.

Episode 2: September 16, 1996   "Virgin Mary"

Director: Steve Zuckerman   Writer: Beth Fieger Falkenstein

After Judy loses her bid to display a collection of priceless medieval artifacts at her branch, Mary sets up a meeting with the head of the Winslow Foundation which owns the artifacts. She pretends she is the head librarian at the Park Avenue Library which is getting the collection to display and that she is very clumsy. The Foundation head decides to move the collection to Judy's branch which makes Judy very happy. However, once the collection is at the library, Mary tries on a chastity belt from the collection and can't get it off. She decides to model the belt, and her friends model other parts of the exhibit which goes over well with the guests invited to the opening.

Episode 3: September 23, 1996   "Just Say No"

Director: Steve Zuckerman   Writer: Eric Weinberg

After Mary forgets to take Judy to the dentist, Judy tells her that she is spreading herself too thin and is not dependable. Derrick advises Mary that she needs to learn to say "no" and gives her a date book to keep track of everything. Derrick is having a "Fountain of Youth" party on the same night that Judy needs Mary to take her back to the dentist. Also, a teenage boy who stole and then returned some library books on sex asks Mary to go to a dance with him on that same night. Mary decides that she can do all three events sequentially. However, Judy takes too many pain pills after the dental appointment and can't be left alone, and so Mary takes her to the teen dance. When Mary wants to leave the dance early to go to Derrick's party, all the teens want to go with her. Everyone ends up at Derrick's party which impresses Derrick's client since the theme is the "Fountain of Youth."

Christine Taylor (Mary) is married to Ben Stiller and, after *Party Girl*, she was a regular on the unaired comedy *Rewind*.

Episode 4: September 30, 1996   "A Charming Tale"

Director: Shelley Jensen   Writer: Susan Seeger

LUSTING, LOVING, AND MAKING A LIVING

Lillian Todd, Judy's favorite author, and her son Jason are in New York for a book party. Mary, through her contacts, gets Judy an invitation. She wants to go with Judy to the party, but Judy asks Mary to work at the library and takes Wanda instead. Mary decides to crash the party anyway with Derrick who gives her a dress to wear that he needs back by midnight to ship to a client on the West Coast. She meets Lillian's handsome son Jason at the party. They kiss, but it is near 12:00 AM and so she has to leave. The next day, Jason goes to the library to find Mary and asks her to go to England with him. However, she says she wants her freedom and doesn't go. Derrick, seeing a possible opening for himself with Jason, pursues him.

John Cameron Mitchell who played Derrick in the series later wrote, directed, and appeared in the films *Hedwig and the Angry Inch* and *Shortbus*.

Episode 5: Unaired   "Art History" (summary based on final draft script)

Director: Ted Wass   Writer: Beth Fieger Falkenstein

Mary is forced to clean out her storage unit in the basement that is full of her mother's things. Instead of going through it all and dealing with unresolved emotions about her mother's death, she decides to sell everything at a garage sale. A lot of people come to purchase the stuff including Judy and Wanda. A nun buys a painting of Mary's mother, Annie. The next day at work Mary sees Judy wearing her mom's old clothes and gets very emotional. She decides to reclaim all the items she sold. When she goes to get the painting the nun purchased, the nun says it was sold to the Met for $600,000 after an appraiser said it was actually a Picasso. Upset, Mary schemes to steal the painting by dressing as a nun and going to the Met. However, before she takes the painting, she hears a tour guide describe her mother's painting as a masterpiece that might be the next Mona Lisa. Mary feels bad and talks to the painting telling her mother that she misses her but that her spirit will always be alive within her. Mary leaves the museum without the painting but feeling very happy.

Best known as Nick Russo, the dad on *Blossom*, Ted Wass is now a full-time director.

Episode 6: Unaired "The Falafel Guy" (summary based on final draft script)

Director: Shelley Jensen   Writer: Lisa Rosenthal

Mary is awakened by a man selling falafels outside her apartment. She goes downstairs to yell at him, but when they talk, she finds she likes the guy and can't stop thinking about him. The falafel guy, Rashid, finds Mary at the library, and she asks him out. On their first date, they have dinner, while he attends to his falafel cart. On their next date, Rashid is late from having to work, and Mary begs him to quit his job so they can spend more time together. That night Mary has a dream that Rashid becomes a couch potato in her apartment and ends up chaining her to the couch so she will never leave his side. When she wakes up, Mary realizes that she only likes Rashid because he wasn't chasing her. She tells him that she wants to break off the relationship. Meanwhile, Judy bleaches her hair and gets a fake tan to date her old boyfriend from college, who turns out now to be blind.

Party Over

Fox paired *Party Girl* with *Lush Life* (see Chapter 7) on Mondays beginning at 9:00 PM. The third episode of *Party Girl* rated ninety-fifth out of 107 shows. It did a little better in the ratings than did *Lush Life*, which is probably why Fox announced that *Party Girl* was going on hiatus after four episodes and would return later in the season. However, that never happened.

The Random Years

Premiered Tuesday, March 5, 2002 at 9:30 PM on UPN

The relationship among three twentysomething guys and a girl living in New York City was the premise of *The Random Years*. Alex Barnes (Will Friedle, *Boy Meets World, Go Fish*), who worked as a magazine researcher but really wanted to be a music critic; Todd Mitchell (Sean Murray), unemployed and not very motivated to find work, and Wiseman (Joshua Ackerman), a wacky dental hygienist, were three lifelong friends sharing a loft. Living across the hall from them was Casey Parker (Natalia Cigliuti), whom Alex had originally hired to work on his Internet music website. Steve (Winston J. Rochas) was the building's maintenance man. Most of the episodes related to the guys' dating problems, with all of them wanting to date Casey.

Background

Originally titled *Life as We Know It*, *The Random Years* was created by Mike Lisbe and Nate Reger, who were writers for the series *Spin City*. Big Phone Productions in association with Paramount produced the comedy. Will Friedle, who played Alex on the series, was scheduled to co-star on the WB comedy *Off Centre* when UPN gave the go ahead to *The Random Years*. Eddie Kaye Thomas (*Brutally Normal*) took over his role on *Off Centre*, which lasted one and a half seasons on the WB.

Episode Guide: 4 aired, 3 unaired

Episode 1: March 5, 2002 "Pilot"

Director: Lee Shallat Chemel   Writers: Mike Lisbe and Nate Reger

Alex hires college student Casey Parker as a temp to work on his music website and arranges a meeting with Megan, an old girlfriend. Wiseman uses sexy sheets to attract a woman at the laundromat. Both Alex and Wiseman take their dates to the same restaurant where Alex finds that Megan lies about her achievements and Wiseman discovers that the woman he met at the laundromat has a bad temper. Because both want to escape from their dates, Alex feigns an allergic reaction to the food and leaves with Wiseman. Meanwhile at the loft, Todd finds that he and Casey both like *Antiques Roadshow*, and they play their version of strip poker by betting on the appraisers' verdicts on items presented during the show. Todd loses.

Episode 2: March 12, 2002 "Don't Make Me Have Sex in the Hamptons"

Director: Matthew Diamond   Writers: Mike Lisbe and Nate Reger

Alex is now an assistant to a rock critic for *Music Scene* magazine – his music website having crashed. He is dating Melissa who is very clinging. When he tries to break up with her, she doesn't get the message. Meanwhile, Casey is looking for a new apartment, and Wiseman suggests that Melissa, who is a real estate agent, find her one. To accomplish this, Alex has to go for a weekend in the Hamptons with Melissa. Because Casey feels awful about putting Alex in this position, she informs Melissa that Alex really wants to end their relationship. Wiseman and Todd tell Melissa the same thing. Casey ends up getting an apartment across the hall from the guys. The apartment was used as a storage unit by Steve, the building's super, who stored merchandise his brother got from working at the docks.

Joshua Ackerman (Wiseman) had been a regular on *The All New Mickey Mouse Club*.

Episode 3: March 19, 2002   "Men Behaving Sadly"

Director: Matthew Diamond   Writers: Judd Pilot and John Peaslee

Casey's boyfriend is coming to visit her for the weekend, but then has to cancel when he finds he has to work. The guys tell Casey to call her boyfriend to discuss their relationship. When she does, he breaks up with her. The guys all try to win Casey's affections, but her boyfriend eventually makes up with her. Meanwhile, Wiseman discovers that a frequent patient at his dental office is interested in more than good dental hygiene. She keeps coming to have her teeth cleaned because she likes to be naked in the dental chair, but Wiseman is too dim-witted to realize she wants to have sex with him.

Episode 4: March 19, 2002   "Dangerous Liaisons"

Director: Matthew Diamond   Writer: Maisha Closson

Alex dates Sydney, one of Todd's ex-girlfriends who's into magic. Things get awkward when Alex brings Sydney to the loft. After Todd and Sydney argue about who broke off their relationship first, they end up apologizing to each other at the coffee shop. Subsequently, Sydney confesses to Alex that she still has feelings for Todd and wants to wait a few days to figure things out. However, both Todd and Alex declare that neither wants to have a relationship with her. Meanwhile, Wiseman wants to date Tanya, the new barista at the coffee shop. He gets Casey to play his girlfriend, pretends to breakup with her, and then asks Tanya out. Tanya tells Wiseman that she wants to go out with both Casey and him leading Wiseman to think she wants a three-way. Wiseman and Tanya go to Casey's apartment where Tanya explains that she wanted to hang out with both of them – not have a threesome.

Episode 5: Unaired   "Inherit the Windbreaker"

Director: Matthew Diamond   Writer: Jonathan M. Goldstein

The three guys, envious of the parties thrown by an upstairs neighbor, decide to throw one of their own. However, a dispute with their landlord gets them locked out of their apartment on party day. Meanwhile, Wiseman is pressured into taking his aunt to see a play.

Episode 6: Unaired   "Losin' It"

Director: Matthew Diamond   Writer: Mike Lisbe and Nate Reger

The guys' cable, which they obtained illegally through Steve, is out interfering with their desire to watch the big boxing match. Meanwhile, Wiseman, who always thought he was the first of the three to lose his virginity, finds out that Alex and Todd ditched him on junior prom night so they could become "men." Learning this causes Wiseman to lose his confidence with women. He subsequently leaves his date at the movie theatre and talks with Steve who suggests that he should take revenge on Todd and Alex. Wiseman gets a guy from the cable company to visit the loft and warn Todd and Alex about the unauthorized use of the cable system. Later, Alex confesses to Wiseman that he really didn't have sex on junior prom night, and Todd says the same thing. Wiseman's confidence is restored, and he goes back to the theatre to be with his date.

Sean Murray (Todd) became a regular on the hit series *NCIS*.

Episode 7: Unaired   "Boy Meets World" (aka "Corrupting Jacob") (summary provided by Nate Reger)

Director: Matthew Diamond   Writer: Jonathan M. Goldstein

Alex's sister drops off his nephew for the guys to babysit.

Random Cancelation

The Random Years followed *As If* on UPN and lasted three weeks when the network broadcast back-to-back episodes of the series during the third week. Like *As If*, *The Random Years* ranked at the bottom of the Nielsen ratings.

Romantically Challenged

Premiered Monday, April 19, 2010 at 9:30 PM on ABC

Romantically Challenged was another *Friends*-like sitcom focusing on the love lives of recently-divorced Rebecca Thomas (Alyssa Milano, *Who's the Boss?*, *Charmed*), her younger sister Lisa (Kelly Stables), her best friend Perry Gill (Kyle Bornheimer), and his roommate Shawn Goldwater (Josh Lawson). The setting for the series was Pittsburgh, PA. Rebecca was a lawyer with a fifteen-year-old son, Justin (Israel Broussard); her sister was a kindergarten teacher. Perry, who had known Rebecca since childhood, was a financial planner and, for six years, had shared an apartment with Shawn, a struggling writer.

Background

Ricky Blitt created the comedy, which was produced by Warner Bros., Bonanza Productions, and Candy Bar Productions. Blitt grew up in Montreal, but was always a big fan of the Pittsburgh Penguins hockey team, which is why Pittsburgh was the setting for *Romantically Challenged*.

Originally, the sitcom was to center on the Shawn character with Eric Christian Olsen (*NCIS: Los Angeles*) cast in the role. The comedy, then called *Threesome*, was about a single man in his early thirties, Shawn Gordon, an aspiring novelist who worked as a telemarketer, caught between his best friend roommate, Perry Martin, and his girlfriend, Rebecca Ulrich, a lawyer and single mother of two – fourteen year-old Justin and twelve year-old Scout. Shawn had met Rebecca at a global warming event and told her he was in marketing (leaving her under the impression he was wealthy). In turn, Rebecca did not mention to Shawn that she had two children. Eventually they both disclosed the truth to each other, and Shawn met Rebecca's children. Rebecca's sister Lisa was the receptionist at her law office.

The title of the sitcom was changed from *Threesome* to *Single with Baggage* and then to *Romantically Challenged*. Also, the concept was changed to make the series more an ensemble comedy instead of focusing on the Shawn character, and the role of Shawn was recast. Initially ABC ordered thirteen episodes of *Romantically Challenged*, but the order was reduced to seven episodes.

Episode Guide: 4 aired; 3 unaired

Episode 1: April 19, 2010 "Don't Be Yourself"

Director: James Burrows   Writer: Ricky Blitt

Rebecca's ex is getting married four months after their divorce, and she feels she needs to start dating. She meets a man at a restaurant who asks her out, while her best friend Perry meets a girl at cooking class that he wants to date. Rebecca's sister and friends advise her not to tell her date the age of her son, and, when he says he has a seven-year old, she says that she has a child the same age. She also states that the picture of the teenage boy in her wallet is that of her ex-husband. Meanwhile, Perry's date wants to be spanked and called dirty names which he can't do. Rebecca finally confides to her date that she is a lawyer, and then her teenage son, calling her "mom," walks into the restaurant. Her date ends the relationship as does Perry's date when he can't give her what she wants.

Episode 2: April 26, 2010 "The Charade"

Director: James Burrows   Writer: Ricky Blitt

Perry is having his wisdom teeth pulled and asks Shawn to pick him up at the dentist's. Shawn is distracted by a cute girl he meets outside the apartment and forgets about Perry. When Perry finally gets home, he tells Shawn that he doesn't care about anyone but himself and kicks him out of their apartment. Shawn moves into Rebecca's place temporarily, but he eventually apologizes to Perry. Meanwhile, Rebecca believes that her sister always dates creeps and not nice guys. Rebecca wants Lisa to date Neil, the nice-guy waiter at their restaurant, but, after the first date, Lisa is no longer interested in him. When Lisa suggests that Rebecca go out with him, Rebecca finds how overly-solicitous Neil can be, and she apologizes to Lisa for hooking her up with him.

James Burrows, who directed all the episodes of *Romantically Challenged*, has won ten Emmys for directing such comedy series as *Taxi*, *Cheers*, *Frasier*, and *Will & Grace*.

Episode 3: May 3, 2010   "Perry and Rebecca's High School Reunion"

Director: James Burrows   Writer: Ricky Blitt

Perry reveals to Shawn that Rebecca's prom date from high school—Jessie—stood her up as a prank and that Perry was in on it. At their high school reunion, Jessie apologizes to Rebecca for the incident and asks her to dinner, but Perry doesn't want her to go for fear that Jessie will confess that Perry knew about the prank. When Perry tells Jessie that he is in love with Rebecca, Jessie doesn't take her to dinner. Jessie mentions to Rebecca what Perry told him, and Shawn reveals to Rebecca that Perry knew that Jessie was going to stand her up at the prom. To make Perry feel guilty, Rebecca says that she loves him and comes on to him. She eventually asks Perry to be honest with her in the future. Meanwhile, Shawn is upset because his cable company took away the hockey channel. He hooks up with one of Lisa's friends who coincidentally has the hockey channel. Shawn duplicates her key so he can watch hockey even when she is away. Lisa's friend orders him out of her apartment when she finds him there after visiting her mother.

Episode 4: May 11, 2010   "Rebecca's One Night Stand"

Director: James Burrows   Writers: Ted Cohen and Andrew Reich

Rebecca has her first one-night stand with Leo, an attractive but boring guy who likes to talk about mushrooms. Ignoring Lisa's advice, Rebecca calls him after the one-night stand to thank him, and he asks her out again. She tries to ignore him, but that just makes him want her more. Lisa tells Rebecca to really get in tune with him to frighten him off. However, when she does, they start talking about other things, and she becomes genuinely interested in him. Meanwhile, Perry is staying home for awhile after completing a big project at work. He gets on Shawn's nerves so much that Shawn starts looking for a regular job. He finally lands one as a delivery person for a Chinese restaurant but quits when Perry submits one of Shawn's stories that is accepted for publication.

Episode 5: Unaired   "Perry Dates His Assistant"

Director: James Burrows   Writers: Ted Cohen and Andrew Reich

Rebecca wants to take her relationship to the next level with a guy until she discovers a giant tattoo of a scantily-clad girl on his chest. Perry tries to fire his enthusiastic but lousy assistant Erin (Anna Camp), who incorrectly anticipates his every need, but ends up in a relationship with her. Shawn is hesitant to watch Lisa's coworker's cute dog until he realizes what a great chick magnet a dog is.

Episode 6: Unaired   "Hey-Now, Hey-Now, Perry's Girlfriend's Back"

Director: James Burrows   Writer: Ricky Blitt

Storyline unknown

Episode 7: Unaired/Unproduced   "Rebecca's Spunky Little Sister"

Director: Unknown   Writer: Unknown

Based on available information, it is not known if this episode was ever produced or what is was about. While other episodes of *Romantically Challenged* are recorded in the files of the Writer's Guild of America, this title is not.

Ratings *Challenged*

The comedy premiered after *Dancing with the Stars* and lost about half of the audience from its lead in; it also did not do well with advertiser-coveted viewers eighteen to forty-nine years of age, ranking fifty-ninth with this group. The sitcom was gone after four episodes.

The Singles Table

Supposed to debut midseason 2006-07 on NBC

At the wedding reception of Doug (Jordan Belfi) and Martina (Sheetel Sheth), five young adults were assigned to the "singles table." While they were all strangers to begin with, over the course of the reception, they became friends. Georgia Setliff (Alicia Silverstone), a doctor in residency; Stephanie Vogler (Rhea Seehorn), a dolls clothes designer; Ivan Throckmorton (John Cho), a freelance tech products creator; Eli Braxton (Conor Dubin), owner of a coffee distribution company, and Adam Leventhal (Jarrad Paul), a rabbi, comprised the guests at the singles table.

Background

Bill Martin and Mike Schiff created and produced the series, which initially received an order for thirteen episodes, but NBC later reduced the order to six episodes. The pilot for the series had Pascale Hutton in the role of Georgia. The part was then recast with Alicia Silverstone in the role, and the scenes with Hutton were reshot with Silverstone and edited into the pilot described below. Mike & Bill Productions and Twentieth Century-Fox were the production companies.

Episode Guide: 6 unaired episodes

Episode 1: "Pilot"

Director: Adam Bernstein   Writers: Bill Martin and Mike Schiff

The five twentysomethings at the singles table for Doug and Martina's wedding reception are all kind of bitter. Ivan is really bitter because his ex-wife Lexi is there as a bridesmaid and with a date. Georgia, who is working all the time and lacks social skills, realizes that she doesn't want to be that way anymore. Adam is there as Doug's rabbi, and Eli is at the reception because he is Doug's boss. Stephanie is attending with her parents. An inebriated Ivan makes a toast to the bridal couple mentioning Doug's former girlfriend and commenting on his ex-wife Lexi. Ivan had introduced Doug and Martina to each other. However, after his divorce, Lexi became Martina's bridesmaid, and Ivan was relegated to the singles table. Eli and

LUSTING, LOVING, AND MAKING A LIVING

Adam have to hold Ivan back from getting into a fight. All of the singles decide to hang out together in the future. When Stephanie drives Ivan back to his place, they hook up for the night.

Episode 2: "The Work Dinner" (summary based on shooting script)

Director: Gail Mancuso   Writer: Christine Zander

While Ivan is working on the servers and operating system at Eli's business, Eli invites his staff to a Saturday night dinner at a restaurant. Since Doug, who works for Eli, will be at the dinner, his wife Martina asks Stephanie to a girls' night out with her and some of her friends. Stephanie then invites Georgia, but Georgia wants to go out with Eli on Saturday not knowing he has already scheduled a dinner with his employees. When Georgia calls Eli saying she is free on Saturday, he reluctantly asks her to the work dinner. Ivan would also like to attend, but Eli says he is not a regular employee, and so Ivan ends up at a coffee shop with his laptop. Adam is having dinner with a couple from his synagogue who have a gorgeous, single daughter. After Eli announces to his staff that attendance at his work dinner is not mandatory, only Doug and one other employee show up along with Eli and Georgia, and Doug leaves the dinner early. Without Eli knowing, Georgia, trying to save the evening for Eli, calls Stephanie to ask her to come to the restaurant where the dinner is being held, and Stephanie phones Ivan to invite him. Georgia also calls to ask Adam to the restaurant, and he is relieved to have an excuse to leave his dinner after the daughter confesses that she is in love with a married Catholic man and the parents want Adam's advice on how to deal with the situation.

Episode 3: "The Brawl"

Director: Adam Arkin   Writer: Chris Kelly

The guys try to play squash at Ivan's club, but another party won't give up the court. Ivan interrupts the other party's game and gets into a fight with one of the players. He has a hearing before the head of the club and is placed on probation. Meanwhile, Stephanie, who still lives with her parents, is having a birthday and is concerned that nothing she thought as a child that she would accomplish has happened yet.

To cheer her up, Georgia puts on a surprise party for her that features line dancing at a country and western bar.

Robert Pine (*CHIPs*) was featured as Stephanie's dad on this episode.

Episode 4: "The Housewarming Party"

Director: Roger Nyard   Writers: Bill Martin and Mike Schiff

The group is invited to Doug and Martina's housewarming party. All five show up at the party separately. Doug and Martina are surprised at Ivan's presence since he got drunk at their reception. His ex-wife, Lexi, is at the party with her boyfriend, and Ivan asks Stephanie to tell Lexi that they had sex so his ex doesn't feel sorry for him. Stephanie eventually gives Ivan a passionate kiss in front of Lexi. Meanwhile, Eli, who has been trying to ask Georgia out but she never returned his calls because of her busy schedule, arrives at the party with a date—much to Georgia's disappointment. Eli tells Georgia that he never really had a chance to talk with her because of her work. She apologizes to him. At the end, the singles all decide to go to a bar.

John Cho (Ivan) is better known for his role as Harold in the *Harold and Kumar* films.

Episode 5: "The Emergency"

Director: Don Scardino   Writer: Mary Fitzgerald

Since Ivan seems to be jealous of Eli's success, Adam suggests that Eli allow Ivan to win at squash to make him feel less envious. But Eli gets mad at Ivan's insults, and then Ivan injures his head during the squash game and has to go to the emergency room. Adam and Eli leave Ivan at the hospital, while they go to the movies. Meanwhile, Georgia has invited Stephanie to a gynecological symposium, but Stephanie convinces Georgia to ditch the symposium and go shopping with her. The two end up at a bar where Georgia gets drunk. In need of an emergency contact that can stay with him in case he has a concussion, Ivan calls Stephanie at the bar and asks her to come to the hospital. Both Stephanie and an inebriated Georgia show up at the hospital as do Eli and Adam who decided they should be with Ivan instead of seeing a film.

LUSTING, LOVING, AND MAKING A LIVING

Episode 6: "Georgia's Big Move"

Director: John Blanchard   Writer: Abraham Higginbotham

After receiving a job offer in New York City, Georgia decides to move from Connecticut. Eli is concerned about the move since he feels she is moving because of him. Stephanie suggests that both Georgia and she find an apartment together. Georgia gets the guys to help her move, but, by the time they reach her new apartment, the manager won't let them unload the truck since the service elevator is not available. Georgia wants to sleep in the truck with all of her belongings so they are not stolen. No one wants to stay with her until Eli grudgingly volunteers. When Georgia tells him that she is not moving to New York because of him, he feels slighted because he was not a factor at all in her decision. Eli finally admits to Georgia that he likes her.

Tabled

Although *The Singles Table* was the first sitcom NBC picked up for the 2006-07 season, the network decided to schedule *30 Rock* and *Twenty Good Years* for the fall and pushed back *The Singles Table* to midseason. However, when it came time to announce their midseason shows, NBC chose the Andy Richter comedy *Andy Barker, P.I.*, which was produced by their own NBC Universal Studios, and Conan O'Brien over *The Singles Table*, which was produced by Twentieth Century-Fox. After that, Kevin Reilly as President of NBC Entertainment was replaced by Ben Silverman. Because Silverman saw no upside in ever airing his predecessor's projects, *The Singles Table* was never scheduled by the network.

Welcome to the Captain

Premiered Monday, February 4, 2008, at 8:30 PM on CBS

Twentysomething Josh Flug (Fran Kranz) was a young filmmaker in Hollywood who had won an Oscar five years earlier for a film short but hadn't done much recently. Josh was thinking of moving back to New York when his friend and accountant Marty Tanner (Chris Klein) persuaded him to stay in L.A. and move into the apartment building, El Captain, where he was staying. While moving in, Josh met Uncle Saul (Jeffrey Tambor, *Arrested Development, Everything's Relative, Twenty Good Years*), a former writer for the sitcom *Three's Company*, Jesus (Al Madrigal, *The Ortegas*), the desk attendant who preferred the English pronunciation of his name, Astrid (Valerie Azlynn), a wannabe actress, and Charlene Van Ark (Raquel Welch), a former soap opera star. Josh also encountered the girl of his dreams – Hope (Joanna Garcia), an acupuncturist who was staying in her brother's apartment, a movie special effects guy, while he was on location.

Background

Originally titled *The Captain*, the comedy was created by John Hamburg, who wrote the *Meet the Parents* films. There were some differences between the pilot episode that premiered in 2008 and an early script for the pilot written in 2006. In the script, the Marty Tanner character was married to Claire – his live-in girlfriend in the pilot episode. Also, Marty and Claire had a three-month old baby named Eunice, and the Raquel Welch character was Charlene Van Ness, instead of Charlene Van Ark. CBS Paramount and Bernard Gayle Productions produced *Welcome to the Captain*.

Episode Guide: 5 aired episodes

Episode 1: February 4, 2008   "Pilot"

Writer and Director: John Hamburg

Josh, who hasn't been able to complete his screenplay and has just broken up with his girlfriend, moves into the El Captain apartment building at the urging of his friend Marty. Marty, who has an apartment in the building, moves in with Josh when his live-in girlfriend Claire finds he is having an affair with another woman. Josh becomes infatuated with acupuncturist Hope and asks her to treat his sciatica. When she mentions that she will be moving back to New York after passing her certification exam, he says he will be moving to New York as well. That evening Josh is seduced by Charlene, and the next day Hope informs him that she won't be going to New York because she failed her exam. She also lets him know she has a boyfriend in New York.

Episode 2: February 11, 2008   "Weekend at Saul's"

Director: Mark Mylod   Writers: Andrew Reich and Ted Cohen

Hope's brother Brad returns from his film shoot for the weekend, and, since he plans to propose to his girlfriend, Hope has to find a place to stay. Josh invites her to stay with him, but after she treats Josh as just a friend, he decides to make her jealous by going to Uncle Saul's weekend place. Saul's weekend getaway turns out to be another apartment on the eighth floor of the building. When Josh looks out the window of Saul's place and sees Hope have a car accident in the parking lot, he races to her side. After he confesses that he was with Saul on the eighth floor, Hope thinks it was sweet for him to leave her alone for the weekend to study.

Episode 3: February 18, 2008   "The Letter"

Writer and Director: John Hamburg

Josh invites Hope to his place for dinner. Saul and Jesus take it upon themselves to go through Hope's garbage to find what foods she likes. Based on what she threw away, they think she is a vegan. They also find part of a letter Hope was writing to her boyfriend Lucas that they believe is a break-up note. Since Saul and Jesus have convinced Josh that Hope is a vegetarian, he serves her tofu turkey, which she hates. She explains to Josh that she throws away all the vegan food that her friends give her. When Hope finds part of her letter in Josh's trash, she is irritated and leaves. After Jesus locates the rest of Hope's letter, he and Saul tell Josh that it definitely was a break-up note. Josh takes his garbage to Hope and asks her to go through it. She says that she has decided not to break off her relationship with Lucas and that he will probably be moving to L.A.

Episode 4: February 25, 2008   "The Wrecking Crew"

Director: Beth McCarthy-Miller   Writers: Sherry Bilsing and Ellen Plummer

Since Hope is still treating him like a friend, Josh wants to move on. He goes to a club with Marty, Saul, and Jesus to pick up women. However, Saul doesn't want Josh to give up on Hope, and so, when Josh meets a girl at the club, Saul makes up a story about Josh being a gay ex-con. After the guys leave the club, Saul takes them to the roof of El Captain which he has set up as his own club, TGIS – Thank God It's Saul's. From the roof, Josh sees new tenant Heather through her apartment window, and the guys encourage him to visit Heather. When he goes, he finds Heather watching a video with Hope. In front of Hope, Josh asks Heather out for a drink, and she says "yes."

Writer Ellen Plummer is the daughter of actress Marion Ross from *Happy Days*.

Episode 5: March 3, 2008 "Mr. Big Meeting"

Director: John Hamburg   Writers: Tucker Cawley and Mary Fitzgerald

Marty gets Josh a meeting with Vin Kelso, the head of Paramount, so he can pitch his screenplay. However, Saul insists on helping him with the pitch. Meanwhile, Astrid takes over for Jesus at the front desk while he is busy checking the building's smoke detectors.

Goodbye *Captain*

Welcome to the Captain debuted at thirty-fifth in the ratings, but, by its fifth episode, the sitcom had sunk to fifty-ninth. Fran Kranz signed on for the Josh Whedon series *Dollhouse* on Fox, effectively canceling the series. The comedy later aired on the Universal HD cable channel.

Wild Oats

Premiered Sunday, September 4, 1994, at 9:30 PM on Fox

In September 1994, a sitcom about the lives of twentysomethings in New York City debuted. *Friends* was an immediate hit and lasted for ten seasons. Also in September 1994, a sitcom about the lives of twentysomethings in Chicago premiered on Fox. *Wild Oats* was an immediate failure which lasted for four episodes.

Like *Friends*, *Wild Oats* focused on the lives of young adults after they graduated from college but before they married and had a family. The series centered on

LUSTING, LOVING, AND MAKING A LIVING

two male roommates—Jack Slayton (Tim Conlon), a shallow, womanizing photographer, and his best friend, Brian Grant (Paul Rudd), a sensitive social worker who, not being able to get a job in his field, worked as a temp. Jack's idea of a good date was "anonymous sex with some cheap girl who doesn't eat too much." Others on the series included two female roommates – Shelly Thomas (Paula Marshall), a schoolteacher and one of Jack's former girlfriends, and Liz Bradford (Jana Marie Hupp), a hair stylist who could not maintain a romantic relationship, and Gordon Walker (Timothy Fall), a geeky guy who worked at the McCormick Convention Center and liked Liz. Most of the episodes of *Wild Oats* took place in the twentysomethings' apartment and, instead of a coffee shop like on *Friends*, at the neighborhood singles club called The Hanger.

Background

Wild Oats was created by Lon Diamond who had previously created the Fox comedy, *Parker Lewis Can't Lose*. K-Rule Productions in association with Twentieth Century-Fox produced the sitcom.

Episode Guide: 4 aired; 2 unaired

Episode 1: September 4, 1994 "Pilot"

Director: James Widdoes   Writer: Lon Diamond

Shelly and Liz run into Jack and his roommate Brian at a bar who are there on a double date with two Russian models. Shelly hits it off with Brian, but it is obvious she still has feelings for Jack – her ex-boyfriend. The next day, when Brian asks Jack for Shelly's phone number, Jack secretly listens in on their phone conversation. Jack visits Shelly at the school where she teaches and tells her that she has his permission to date Brian, which antagonizes Shelly. Shelly and Brian go on a date, but Jack spies on them when they come home and start kissing. Jack cannot stand Brian making out with Shelly. He bursts in on them, and Shelly asks to speak with him in another room. They end up kissing, but stop and say that was a bad idea. Shelly leaves flustered. When Brian asks what happened, Jack lies and says Shelly told him to back off.

James Widdoes, who directed the pilot, played fraternity President Robert Hoover in the film *Animal House*.

Episode 2: September 11, 1994 "Dream Date"

Director: Stan Lathan   Writer: Tom Straw

Shelly and Brian are celebrating their two-week anniversary together, but Shelly is disappointed that Brian hasn't committed to her yet. When she meets Adam, a guy who wanted to take her out when she was dating Jack, she wonders if she should date him. She and Brian argue about their relationship, and he tells her that she needs to make up her own mind about the relationship. She decides to go on a date with Adam, while Jack encourages Brian to go out with someone else also. After Adam says he didn't really have fun on their date, Shelly gets back together with Brian.

Episode 3: September 18, 1994 "Tickets"

Director: Stan Lathan   Writers: Barbara Wallace and Thomas R. Wolfe

Brian is trying to get football tickets to a Bears–Packers game, and the dad of a girl Jack dated offers him four tickets to the game if he stays away from his daughter. Jack promises to treat his friends to the sold-out game, but his plans get sidelined when he meets a beautiful woman named Ingrid who also wants to go to the game. Jack seeks an extra ticket and trades his four tickets at the fifty-yard line to a scalper for five tickets in a different part of the stadium – so different that that part of the stadium doesn't exist. After Jack confesses to Brian, Liz, and Shelly that he now only has counterfeit tickets, he approaches Gordon Walker who has four valid tickets for the game. The gang tries to get on Gordon's good side so he will ask them to the game. They do such a good job that Gordon decides to get an extra ticket for Ingrid, and ends up trading his tickets for counterfeit ones like Jack had done.

Episode 4: September 25, 1994 "Slice o' Life"

Director: Stan Lathan   Writer: Mark Nutter

A local TV show called *Slice o'Life* wants to film the friends. Jack is really the only one of the four who wishes to appear on TV. Shelly wants to make sure that no one talks about her previous relationship with him. However, when the producer of the reality show decides that the gang is boring and wants to stop filming them, Jack reveals his prior relationship with Shelly. Jack divulges that he and Shelly had sex after they broke up which upsets Brian who announces that Jack cheated on Shelly. After the camera crew leaves, Jack and Brian argue about Shelly. Jack apologizes to Shelly for not being able to commit, and he also apologizes to Brian. When Shelly views the TV show and sees Brian saying that he wishes he could tell her all the things he is too shy to say, she runs to the bar where Jack and Brian are and makes up with Brian.

Episode 5: Unaired   "Renaissance Woman" (summary based on final draft script)

Director: Stan Lathan   Writers: Lon Diamond and Tom Straw

Brian and Shelly go on a double date with Jack and his new girlfriend Jolie (Emily Proctor). Unlike most girls Jack has dated, Jolie is very smart and chic which causes Shelly to become jealous. Jolie gets a job offer to teach at Oxford and asks Jack to go with her. At their going-away party, Shelly invites all of Jack's crazy ex-girlfriends to scare Jolie. Jack calls out Shelly on trying to sabotage his new relationship. Jolie takes Jack aside and says she doesn't want to be with him anymore since it is obvious he still has feelings for Shelly. Brian breaks up with Shelly after the party because he also sees that Jack and Shelly have feelings for each other. Shelly comes over the next day to Jack's place, confesses her feelings for Jack, and they end up sleeping together.

Episode 6: Unaired   "Move-In" (summary based on final draft script)

Director: Stan Lathan   Writer: Mark Nutter

Shelly and Jack move in together, while Brian and Liz have found their own places to live. Shelly and Jack have planned a romantic night when their friend Kirby mentions to Jack about a "party of the year." After their romantic dinner, Jack tries to convince Shelly to go to the party with him. They fight, and Jack goes alone. He stays only for a little while since he feels guilty leaving Shelly. However, when he gets home, Shelly is not there. She returns home late and a little drunk having gone with friends to the same party that Jack had attended. They fight a bit more and talk about what a big step it is for them to live together, and then they make up.

Not So Wild about *Oats*

Wild Oats followed the hit comedy *Married with Children* on Sundays but did not retain the audience *Married with Children* enjoyed. Its premiere episode ranked sixty-eighth out of eighty-five programs.

Paul Rudd (Brian) later, coincidentally, guest-starred on several episodes of *Friends* and then starred in films like *I Love You, Man* and *Our Idiot Brother*. Paula Marshall (Shelly) became a regular on several short-lived series like *Snoops*, *Cupid*, and *Out of Practice* and more recently co-starred on *Gary Unmarried*, while Jana Marie Hupp (Liz) became a regular on the little-known comedy, *Public Morals*.

A Year at the Top

Supposed to premiere January 19, 1977, on CBS

Partnering with Don Kirshner, who had been the music supervisor for *The Monkees* and *The Archies*, Norman Lear attempted to develop a fantasy, rock music situation comedy. *A Year at the Top* was based on the Faust legend in which ambitious people make a deal with the devil in order to achieve a year of success in the music business.

Background

A Year at the Top went through several conceptual and cast changes. It began as an unsold pilot for NBC called *Hereafter*, written by Woody Kling, which was broadcast on Thanksgiving Day in 1976. In this pilot, three old vaudevillians: Joe (John J. Fox), Frank (Robert Donley), and Lou (Phil Leeds) sold their soul to the devil's youngest son, Nathan, played by Josh Mostel, for a chance to be rock stars. Paul Shaffer, Greg Evigan, and Don Scardino were Lionel, Cliff, and Rick—members of the rock band called "Hereafter," and Vivian Blaine played Lillian, their agent.

After NBC rejected the series, Lear took the concept to CBS, which gave him the go-ahead to produce several episodes. Originally, *A Year at the Top* was to debut on January 19, 1977. This version starred Vivian Blaine, Robert Alda (father of Alan Alda), Phil Leeds, and Mickey Rooney as Lillian, Cliff, Studly, and Mickey—an over-the-hill lounge act, "The Four Tunes," which never made it big. The devil's daughter (Kelly Bishop) offered the lounge act a deal to which they all agreed except for Mickey. They would become younger and form a rock group called "Top." Playing the younger versions of Blaine, Alda, and Leeds were Judith Cohen as Young Lillian, Greg Evigan as Young Cliff, and Paul Shaffer as Young Studly. This version of the series had two sets of casts—an older one and a younger one, and four episodes were produced.[14] Each episode was to feature the older characters, the younger ones, and a concert segment, with little time left for the storyline. T.A.T. Communications and Don Kirshner Productions produced the comedy.

Version 1 Episode Guide: 4 episodes unaired

Episode 1: "The Contract" (summary based on third draft script)

Directors: Jim Drake and Alan Myerson   Writer: Gy Waldron

Cliff, Lillian, Studly, and Mickey are trying out for a bug spray commercial which they do not get. They all complain about their age and not making it in the music world when a young woman named DeeDee (Devil's Daughter) offers them a deal. In return for their souls, the group will have one year at the top after they have a gold record, and they will all be thirty years younger. To prove that she can do this, she makes Cliff, Studly, and Lillian young for a few minutes. All three are younger, but thin Lillian gains 100 pounds in the process. Mickey, who is against the idea, makes DeeDee zap them back to being old. While they are considering the offer, Cliff suffers a heart attack, so Cliff, Lillian, and Studly all decide to become young to prevent Cliff from dying. Once they are young, DeeDee says that she has booked them a show at a packed arena. However, Mickey pleads with the group to think about what is important in their lives right now. They decide not to make the contract with the devil right away. DeeDee allows them to perform as a young group anyway so they can get a taste for performing in front of an enthusiastic audience. She is correct; the band wants to stay young. In the last scene, Mickey, who is still old, vows to find a loophole in the contract to get them back.

Writer Gy Waldron subsequently created the CBS action-adventure series *The Dukes of Hazard*.

Episode 2: "The Visits" (summary based on final draft script)

Director: Jim Drake   Writers: Gerald Gardner and Dee Caruso

Now that the band has chosen to have their year at the top in return for their souls, Mickey thinks that if they all go to say good-bye to their families, it will make Lillian, Cliff, and Studly choose to stay old. DeeDee grants them one hour to turn themselves old again and say farewell. Studly visits his ex-wife with whom he has a love-hate relationship. She yells at him for the whole hour, not giving him anytime to say good-bye. When Cliff tries to visit his estranged brother, the doorman keeps him waiting almost the entire hour with only enough time for the brothers to recognize each other before Cliff turns young again. Lillian visits her mother who is so busy talking the whole time that she doesn't really get to say farewell either. Mickey is disappointed when the rest of the group ends up a little more depressed and wanting to stay young.

Gerald Gardner and Dee Caruso previously wrote several episodes of *The Monkees*.

Episode 3: "Grey is Beautiful" (summary based on final draft script)

Director: Hal Cooper   Writer: Rowby Goren

DeeDee is throwing a party with young Lillian, Cliff, Studly and other young people in order to entice Mickey to sign the contract. She thinks that if Mickey is the only old person at the party, he will feel out of place and want to become young like the others. When Mickey is not too successful at striking up a conversation with the young party guests, he leaves early. DeeDee encourages him to sign the contract to be young again, but he refuses. Young Studly, Cliff and Lillian become concerned when they don't see Mickey for three days after the party. They discover that he is appearing at a theatre with three other older people billed as "The Four Tunes." They go to see the act along with DeeDee. When they find that the new act Mickey put together is not working, DeeDee zaps the trio back to their older selves so they can appear as the original Four Tunes. While they are a hit and agree that they all need each other, Mickey still refuses to sign the contract.

Episode 4: "Hit Man" (summary based on final draft script)

Director: Jim Drake   Writer: Warren Murray

Pop sensation Billy Worthy (Ed Begley, Jr.,) who is represented by DeeDee, wants Cliff, Lillian, and Studly to open his arena show. He has the deal with the devil that if he can make the new band famous, he can have one more year at the top before going to hell. The concert is to be recorded for an album which should go gold and start the year at the top for the band. However, Mickey wants them to stay unknowns for as long as possible; it's his loophole. Mickey overhears Billy's bodyguard say the concert will be recorded, but the band doesn't believe him. When DeeDee pushes the band on stage to perform, Mickey gets on stage as their drum player and ruins their set so that it can't be recorded. DeeDee is foiled again and pledges to get Mickey soon.

Another *Year at the Top*

Norman Lear decided that this version of *A Year at the Top* would be too confusing for viewers, and so he pulled the show from the CBS winter schedule. All of the cast were let go except for Greg Evigan, Paul Shaffer, and Mickey Rooney. In the revised *A Year at the Top* that debuted Friday, August 5, 1977 at 8:00 PM, Greg and Paul played two rock musicians who were seeking a promoter to give them a big break. Mickey Rooney starred as Mickey Durbin, their uncle in the first special one-hour episode, and the actor Gabe Dell was brought in to play the son of the devil, Frederick J. Hanover. Nedra Volz was Grandma Belle Durbin; Julie Cobb played Paul's friend Trish; Priscilla Lopez was featured as Greg's girlfriend Linda, and Priscilla Morrill was Miss Worley. The revamped concept had Hanover as the head of Paragon Records whose dad, the devil, was the chairman of the board. Musicians with Paragon Records would receive fame and fortune and then would have to sign a contract selling their souls. If they didn't sign, they would lose everything.

Version 2 Episode Guide: 5 episodes aired

Episode 1: August 5, 1977   "The Big Deal" (summary based on final draft script)

Directors: Alan Rafkin and Marlena Laird   Writer: Sandy Veith

Mickey is trying to pitch to Paragon Records Greg and Paul as composers and Greg's girlfriend Linda as the star of a new musical. Initially they get turned away from Hanover's office, but when the devil tells his son that he needs two more souls, Hanover becomes interested in having Greg and Paul sign their souls away for success in the music world. He books Greg and Paul for a show and says that if they do well, he will have a verbal agreement to sign them, and once they get famous, they will sign a written contract.

In the second half of the one-hour episode, Mickey and Linda decide to produce the new musical themselves, but they need money. Belle, a cleaning lady in Hanover's office, recognizes Mickey and tells Hanover a story about Mickey being infamous for having two wives. Hanover bribes Belle for photographic evidence of the two wives so he can blackmail Mickey. As it turns out, Belle is really Mickey's mother, and the photos she gave Hanover in return for money were of Mickey's sisters. The money she got from Hanover is used to finance the new musical.

Episode 2: August 12, 1977   "The Handshake"

Director: Unknown   Writers: Terry Hart, Sandy Veith, Ann Gibbs, & Joel Kimmel

Greg and Paul have second thoughts about Hanover's ability to handle their careers when they learn that his previous clients were only successful for one year.

Episode 3: August 19, 1977   "Identity Crisis"

Director: Unknown   Writers: Ann Gibbs & Joel Kimmel

Greg and Paul have a falling out which makes Hanover desperate to get their act back together to avoid incurring the devil's wrath over the loss of two souls.

Episode 4: August 28, 1977   "Love Story"

Director: Unknown   Writer: Terry Hart

Greg falls in love with a popular singer at Paragon Records, unaware that she has a binding contract with Hanover.

CBS decided to move the series from Friday nights to Sunday nights at 8:30 PM beginning with this episode.

Episode 5: September 4, 1977   "The Sun Also Rises"

Director: Unknown   Writers: Mary Willard & Steve Bluestein

Much to Hanover's disappointment, Paul decides to give up his musical career and spend time with his newfound love – an attractive girl.

Another *Year* Over

Ratings for *A Year at the Top* were not great, and CBS did not renew the series. However, an album was made from the second version of the series. Titled *A Year at the Top: Greg and Paul*, it included songs like "She's A Rebel," "Give Me More," "Love Just Comes and Goes," and "Like a Rising Star" from the comedy performed by Greg Evigan and Paul Shaffer. According to Paul Shaffer, Don Kirshner thought that "Like a Rising Star," which Paul co-wrote with Don Scardino, would be a bigger hit than "I'm a Believer" was for the Monkees.[15] Of course, that didn't happen. The album was released in 1977.

Megyn Price and Greg Giraldo in *Common Law*

Chapter 3
Finding True Romance

The history of situation comedies has been strewn with little-known series about a male and a female, usually from different backgrounds and usually young, who fall hopelessly in love with each other. Think of the TV version of *Barefoot in the Park*, *Bridget Loves Bernie*, *Joe and Valerie*, *Loves Me, Loves Me Not*, and *Love on a Rooftop*, for example – all of which lasted one season or less. The romantic comedies in this chapter are among the briefest runs in sitcom history.

Common Law

Premiered Saturday, September 28, 1996 at 9:30 PM on ABC

As the title implies, *Common Law* was a comedy about cohabitating attorneys. John Alvarez, played by stand-up comedian Greg Giraldo, was a Harvard-educated Hispanic lawyer hired by a conservative New York City law firm who fell in love with Nancy (Megyn Price), another attorney at the firm. They moved in together but had to keep it a secret because the law firm frowned on interoffice romances. John's father on the series, Luis (Gregory Sierra), was a barber. Other characters at John and Nancy's law firm included insecure Peter Gutenhimmel (Carlos Jacott), the son of one of the partners in the firm; Henry Beckett (David Pasquesi), an ambitious associate, and Maria Marquez (Diana-Maria Riva who later starred on *Luis*), the office manager.

Background

Before the start of the 1996-97 TV season, ABC had been picketed by interest groups reacting to the perceived lack of shows on the network featuring minority characters. Responding to such assertions, the network scheduled *Common Law*. Greg Giraldo, a Harvard-trained lawyer himself, worked with producer and creator Rob LaZebnik to turn his experiences into a comedy series. Witt-Thomas Productions produced *Common Law*.

Episode Guide: 4 aired; 5 unaired

Episode 1: September 28, 1996   "Pilot"

Director: Robby Benson   Writer: Rob LaZebnik

Nancy and John work on a big class action suit against a corrupt developer. The pair has thirty-six hours to get the brief to the judge. However, John's former roommate Francis, a messenger at the law firm, is being sued by Nancy's old boyfriend whom he had punched. John stops work on the brief to bail Francis out of jail and has to go to his dad for the bail money. He works all night to finish the brief. The suit against Francis is dismissed because Nancy's ex- boyfriend provoked the altercation.

Robby Benson, who directed this episode, is also an actor who did the voice of the Beast in the animated feature *Beauty and the Beast*.

Episode 2: October 5, 1996   "In the Matter of: John's Fifteen Minutes"

Director: Will MacKenzie   Writers: Drew Vaupen and Phil Baker

John's court victory over a corporate polluter makes a favorable impression on Nancy's parents as well as on the media, but the elation wears off when, instead of asking John questions about the case, the media is interested only in topics such as what it is like to be a successful Latino lawyer, whether he was ever in a gang, and what winning the case meant for the Latino community.

Before he became a director, Will MacKenzie acted on *The Bob Newhart Show* and several other comedy series.

Episode 3: October 12, 1996   "In the Matter of: Acceptance"

Director: Will MacKenzie   Writer: Rob LaZebnik

Nancy tries to win over John's father by offering to take Rosa, a visiting cousin from Columbia sightseeing. Nancy loses Rosa, who speaks no English except for "I'm from Columbia," in a crowd. When Nancy tells John's dad that Rosa is missing, he bawls her out, but John says that means his dad likes her. Eventually, they find Rosa sitting on a bench at Columbia University.

Episode 4: October 19, 1996   "In the Matter of: Luis in Love"

Director: Will MacKenzie   Writer: Roger Garrett

   Nancy wants to fix Luis up with Ruta Peirce, a co-worker at the law firm. Both John and Nancy encourage Luis to go out with Ruta on a double date with them. At dinner, Luis does most of the talking. Although Ruta explains to Nancy that she doesn't want to date him again, Luis is still interested in her. Nancy tries to get Ruta to change her mind about Luis, but she won't hear of it and pepper sprays Nancy in the parking lot. Meanwhile, John and his dad go to a bar, and John encourages his dad to ask out a woman he meets there.

Episode 5: Unaired   "In the Matter of: Need"

Director: Will MacKenzie   Writer: Regina Stewart

John is chosen for a job in Washington D.C. but hesitates to leave Nancy despite her seeming approval. Nancy's independent pride doesn't allow her to admit that she doesn't want John to leave. Meanwhile, Henry uses every kiss-up technique possible to get the job for himself.

Episode 6: Unaired   "In the Matter of: Attention"

Director: Will MacKenzie   Writer: Regina Stewart

A woman sues Luis for refusing to give her a haircut. When John tells him he doesn't have a case, he hires Nancy.

Episode 7: Unaired   "In the Matter of: John's Hero"

Director: Will MacKenzie   Writer: Peter Murrieta

John invites a sixties activist to stay at the apartment, but the hippie's lifestyle chases Nancy away.

Episode 8: Unaired   "In the Matter of: Thanksgiving"

Director: Will MacKenzie   Writer: Gary Janetti

John and Nancy can't decide to spend Thanksgiving with Luis or with Nancy's parents, and so John hosts Thanksgiving at the apartment.

Episode 9: Unaired   "In the Matter of: John and Nancy's Secret" (summary provided by Rob LaZebnik)

Director: Will MacKenzie   Writer: Rob LaZebnik

When ambitious Henry from the law firm wants an apartment in the same building as John and Nancy's apartment, he learns that they are living together. John decides to tell Maria that he is living with Nancy, and she intentionally gossips the secret to the rest of the firm. To their surprise, when John and Nancy go in to announce their relationship to the firm's partners, many other "secret" couples appear in the conference room, and all is excused. Meanwhile, Maria needs help in the typing pool, and Peter reveals that he was a champion typist in high school. He gladly helps type and finds himself in a pitched battle with another champion typist in the pool.

Episodes Not Produced

When *Common Law* was canceled, it appears that four episodes out of the original order of thirteen were never produced. One of the unproduced episodes was titled "In the Matter of: John's Buddy," but the storyline of this script is not known.

Law Repealed

The debut episode of *Common Law* ranked ninetieth out of 107 series. By the end of the third episode, it ranked ninety-sixth out of 122 shows. After the fourth episode aired, the series was history.

Commenting on the demise of *Common Law*, Greg Giraldo confessed that "My acting was an abomination. I had absolutely no business having a sitcom. I want to go back in time and slap myself."[16] Greg Giraldo resumed his stand-up career after the series. He died in 2010 from an accidental drug overdose. Megyn Price became a regular on several comedies: *Lateline*, *Grounded for Life*, and more recently, *Rules of Engagement*.

Herbie, The Love Bug

Premiered Wednesday, March 17, 1982, at 8:00 PM on CBS

In *Herbie the Love Bug*, a white VW Beetle with human emotions and mental capabilities, paired up with Jim Douglas (Dean Jones) and found him a wife. Douglas, a former race car driver, ran the "Famous Driving School" and supplemented his income teaching driver's education at the local high school. Jim and Herbie stopped a bank robbery and met Susan MacLane (Patricia Harty), a divorced mother of three, who was being held hostage by the robbers. Jim romanced Susan and eventually married her. She had three children: Julie (Claudia Wells), a teenager just beginning to learn how to drive, Matthew (Nicky Katt), the middle child, and her youngest son, Robbie (Douglas Emerson) who really, really loved Herbie. Bo Phillips (Richard Paul) was Jim's rotund assistant at the driving school.

Background

The comedy was based on the *Love Bug* movies made by Walt Disney Productions and was adapted for television by Arthur Alsberg and Don Nelson. In turn, the films were based on the 1961 book by Gordon Buford titled *Car, Boy, Girl*. Dean Jones, who had starred in the *Love Bug* films, reprised his role in this limited-run one-hour sitcom.

Episode Guide: 5 aired episodes

Episode 1: March 17, 1982   "Herbie, the Matchmaker"

Director: Charles S. Dubin   Writers: Arthur Alsberg and Don Nelson

When Herbie's owner Jim Douglas goes to the bank to get a loan for his driving school, he sees the bank being robbed. Herbie helps capture the robbers, and Jim meets Susan, who had been held hostage. Susan asks Jim to help teach her daughter, Julie, to drive. While taking Julie for a driver's lesson, Jim encounters Susan and her boyfriend, Randy Bigelow (Larry Linville). After Herbie pushes Randy's car into some lawn sprinklers, Jim takes Susan out on a date. Randy becomes jealous of Jim and wants to marry Susan as soon as possible. When the couple goes to Santa Barbara for the ceremony, Herbie takes Jim to that city as well to stop the marriage. Herbie drives right into the chapel, and Susan ends up not marrying Randy.

Claudia Wells (Julie) played Marty McFly's girlfriend in the movie *Back to the Future*; Kirk Cameron (*Growing Pains*) had a small role on this episode.

Episode 2: March 24, 1982   "Herbie to the Rescue"

Director: Vincent McEveety   Writers: Don Nelson and Arthur Alsberg

Randy stops by the driving school and offers Jim a loan to save his struggling business. Under the guise of granting the loan, Randy has the DMV inspect the cars owned by Jim's school. When they don't pass inspection, the DMV closes the school. Meanwhile, Jim and Susan argue over whether he wants to make a commitment. Susan's sons think they are coming between their mom and Jim. After the boys don't come home after school, Susan calls the police to report them missing. Jim goes looking for them, and so does Herbie. Herbie finds the boys in an abandoned house and tries to break down the door but becomes stuck. Jim and Bo see Herbie and get the boys out of the house. Jim then asks Susan to marry him, and she accepts. Later the DMV inspector returns to the driving school and re-inspects the cars, which pass his time. Randy gives Jim the loan.

Writer Don Nelson is the brother of the late Ozzie Nelson of *Ozzie and Harriet* fame.

Episode 3: March 31, 1982   "My House Is Your House"

Director: Bill Bixby   Writer: Don Tait

Although Randy is still trying to end Jim and Susan's relationship, he proposes giving Jim a bachelor party. Meanwhile, Jim wants to rent a larger apartment in his building for Susan and the kids once they are married, while Susan wants Jim to move into her place. Randy invites Jim's old girlfriend Diane, a race car driver, to the bachelor party and decides to move the party to Jim's apartment after Susan mentions that she will be looking at the new apartment while Jim is at the celebration. At the party, Randy instructs Jim to take an inebriated Diane to the apartment he wants to rent so she may lie down. Susan discovers Jim and Diane together and thinks they have rekindled their relationship. Susan then decides to go out to dinner with Sergio, an old racing car driver buddy of Jim's. After Herbie takes Jim to where Susan and Sergio are having dinner, Susan and Jim fight, and Jim decides to go back to racing, despite Susan's dislike for that occupation. At the race, Susan and Randy see that Herbie won but that Diane was the driver – not Jim as they thought. Susan learns to trust that Jim really gave up racing, and Jim says that if she marries him, he will move into her house.

Episode 4: April 7, 1982   "Herbie, the Best Man"

Director: Vincent McEveety   Writers: Arthur Alsberg and Don Nelson

Jim and Susan are preparing for their wedding ceremony, while Randy is still trying to sabotage the pending nuptials. He hires a guy to plant a stink bomb in Herbie so that Jim will not make it to the ceremony on time. After several futile attempts to drive Herbie, Randy decides to have the car towed to a junk yard and have another VW fixed to look like Herbie with the bomb inside. He parks the lookalike outside Jim's apartment, but, when Jim finds cigarettes in the ashtray, he knows the car is not Herbie. Jim saves Herbie from the scrap yard but arrives too late at the church. Susan and the kids have left with Randy, but Jim catches up with them and finally gets married.

Episode 5: April 14, 1982 "Calling Dr. Herbie"

Director: Bill Bixby   Writers: Arthur Alsberg and Don Nelson

Susan wants to trade her vehicle for a family station wagon, but Herbie, feeling ignored, doesn't like the idea. Jim and Susan take Herbie to Wally's motors to look for a new car. While on a test drive, Wally tries to move Herbie who drives himself into a fire hydrant. Upset with Herbie, Wally sends the car to the impound lot. Meanwhile, Robbie gets a high fever and is taken to the hospital. Back at the impound lot, Herbie escapes when he hears two teenagers planning to steal him. After learning from Jim that Robbie is in the hospital, Herbie drives himself there, goes up in the elevator, and drives down one of the widest hospital halls ever to see Robbie. The next day Jim finds Herbie in his garage, and goes to the hospital where he finds Robbie no longer has a fever. Apparently, Robbie was sick because his mother was paying more attention to Jim than to him. In the end, Jim pays the impound lot for the cost of the fire hydrant destroyed by Herbie.

The late George Lindsay played the owner of Wally's Motors, reminding the audience that he once worked at Wally's garage on *The Andy Griffith Show*.

Not Quite the End of Herbie

Because of low ratings, CBS did not order additional episodes of *Herbie, the Love Bug*. However, the Disney Channel did later air the comedy. Herbie went into semi-retirement after the series ended but made a comeback on an episode of *The Wonderful World of Disney* in 1997 and again in the 2005 movie *Herbie, Fully Loaded*.

If Not for You

Premiered Monday, September 18, 1995, at 9:30 PM on CBS

Elizabeth McGovern and Hank Azaria starred in this romantic comedy about two people who were instantly attracted to each other while out on dates with the individuals they originally intended to marry. McGovern played Jessie Kent, an anthropologist who narrated her own books on tape and who was engaged to Elliot (Peter Krause), an architect; Azaria portrayed Craig Schaeffer, a record producer who coincidently worked at the same company where Jessie was recording her book and was engaged to Melanie McKee (Jane Sibbett), a social worker. Among others at Gopher Records in Minneapolis were Eileen (Debra Jo Rupp, *The Office*, *That 70's Show*), who did voiceovers, Bobby Beaumont (Reno Wilson, *Mike & Molly*), a composer and singer, and Cal (Jim Turner), a sound engineer.

Background

Larry Levin created *If Not for You*. ABC, CBS, and NBC each waged a bidding war for the pilot script he wrote for what would become *If Not for You* with CBS winning the bidding. They guaranteed him thirteen episodes on Mondays at 9:30 PM, but CBS didn't really like the pilot which was reshot with a different supporting cast. [17] The pilot had the same storyline as the first episode described below, but the supporting cast had different actors for Craig and Jessie's prospective partners. Heidi Swedberg was Melanie McKee, and Zeljko Ivanek was Elliot Gordon.

Apparently between the pilot and the actual series, CBS lost faith in Levin's meandering romantic comedy. The network decided to change the title of the series to *One of Those Things*, but then changed it back to *If Not for You* before its premiere. Rock Island Productions and Touchstone Television produced the series.

Episode Guide: 4 aired; 3 unaired

Episode 1: September 18, 1995   "Detour Ahead"

Directors: Barnet Kellman and Thomas Schlamme   Writer: Larry Levin

Jessie and Craig lock eyes at a Chinese restaurant while dining with their prospective marriage partners. Craig later meets Jessie when she comes to the recording studio where he works to record her book titled *Breeding Strategies* about human mating habits. He invites her to meet him at a restaurant to see if she is having any second thoughts about marrying Elliot as he is about marrying Melanie. However, when she shows up at the restaurant, she bumps into a coworker of Elliot's and can't talk to Craig in public. She meets Craig later in a secluded spot and tells him that, after reflection, she thinks they should keep their commitments to their respective fiancés.

In a prior draft script for this episode, Jessie's book was titled *What's Love Got to Do With It: The De-Evolution of Love* – a scientific look at the myth of romantic love.

Episode 2: September 25, 1995   "Taking a Shower with My Two True Loves"

Director: Robert Berlinger   Writer: Dennis Klein

Craig gives Jessie an expensive gift and then shows up unexpectedly at her engagement party to apologize. Jessie invites him to stay. He meets Elliot, and Jessie attempts to explain to everyone at the party that she is still faithful to Elliot.

Episode 3: October 2, 1995   "The Kiss"

Director: John Rich   Writer: Leslie Caveny

At the recording studio, Craig confesses that he loves Jessie, and they kiss. Elliot invites Craig to lunch causing Craig to think that Elliot knows about his relationship with Jessie. However, what Elliot wants to talk to Craig about is recording an album because Elliot thinks he's a great singer. Jessie phones Craig while he is having dinner with Melanie to tell him that he doesn't need to say anything to Melanie about their relationship. Craig and Elliot both have lunch, but Craig doesn't want to produce his album. Back at the studio, Jessie and Craig kiss again.

Jane Sibbett (Melanie) was later considered for the part of Debra, Ray's wife, on *Everybody Loves Raymond*.

Episode 4: October 9, 1995 "Snap!"

Directors: John Rich and Dennis Erdman   Writer: Leslie Caveny

Craig and Jessie agree to breakup with their respective fiancés. When Jessie informs Elliot that she doesn't want to marry him, he says that he is going to fight to win her back. Melanie returns from a camping trip she was on with juvenile delinquents and has a neck injury after one of the kids pushed her off a cliff. Craig feels sorry for her and doesn't say anything about breaking up. After Melanie stops by the studio, Jessie sees her condition and understands why Craig said nothing to her about ending their relationship.

Episode 5: Unaired "The Day the Halo Came Off"

Director: John Rich   Writer: Larry Levin

During a two-week grace period after Jessie said she was not going to marry him, Elliot tries to win Jessie back. Craig is chomping at the bit to end his relationship with Melanie but can't because she is still wearing a halo neck brace for her neck injury.

Episode 6: Unaired "Who Are You"

Director: John Rich   Writer: Wil Calhoun

His engagement with Melanie has finally ended, and so Jessie and Craig can be together. They go on their first real date.

Episode 7: Unaired "Rise and Shine" (summary provided by David Latt)

Director: John Rich   Writer: Larry Levin

Jessie and Craig try living together, which comes after sleeping together, which doesn't go well.

The Falloff Factor

Viewers never saw Jessie and Craig's romance develop because the comedy was canceled after the fourth episode even though it ranked twenty-fifth overall in the ratings. *If Not for You* was on Mondays after *Murphy Brown* and before *Chicago Hope*, usually a good spot for a new show sandwiched between established hits. However, the series did not maintain the audience from its lead-in; it was another victim of the "falloff factor."

Following the cancelation of the series, Elizabeth McGovern (Jessie) went on to show business projects in England, such as *Downton Abbey*. Hank Azaria (Craig) later starred on two other short-lived sitcoms – *Imagine That* and *Free Agents*.

It Had to Be You

Previewed Sunday, September 19, 1993, at 8:00 PM on CBS before moving to Fridays at 8:00 PM

With lush music and white silk behind the opening titles, *It Had to Be You* was an adult romantic comedy that CBS thought would be a good alternative to the kid-friendly comedies on ABC at the time. In *It Had to Be You*, Faye Dunaway was twice-divorced, book publisher Lauria Scofield who fell in love with a widowed carpenter Mitch Quinn (Robert Urich) who had three boys—oldest son, David (Justin Whalin); middle son, Christopher (Will Estes), and youngest son, Sebastian (Justin Jon Ross). Mitch had been a widower for about four years since his wife Jenny died. Eve Parkin (Robin Bartlett) was Laura's assistant. The setting for the series was Boston.

Background

Originally the title of the sitcom was *For Love or Money*. It had been created by John Steven Owen and a pilot was filmed in 1992 about a widowed plumber who fell in love with an heiress. Twiggy Lawson of *Princesses* and Terence Knox (*St. Elsewhere*) played the leads.[18] When Faye Dunaway became involved with the project, the title was changed and Robert Urich was brought in to play the male lead—a carpenter.

The network thought the star power of Dunaway and Urich would make the series a hit. Highest Common Denominator Productions in association with Warner Bros. Television produced the series. Andrew Nicholls, Darrell Vickers, Brad Buckner, and Eugenie Ross-Leming were all producers and writers for *It Had to Be You*.

Episode Guide: 4 aired; 5 unaired

Episode 1: September 19, 1993 "Pilot"

Director: David Steinberg   Writers: Darrell Vickers and Andrew Nicholls

Wealthy publisher, Laura Scofield phones carpenter, Mitch Quinn, to install a set of book shelves in her office. She gets his address from his tool bag, and calls him at home on a Saturday to fix her credenza. Later, when she goes to his house to thank him, he invites her to stay for dinner. Laura tries to help in the kitchen with disastrous results, and leaves before dinner. Next day, Mitch shows up at Laura's office to invite her to lunch, and they kiss.

Before becoming a director, comedian David Steinberg wrote and performed for *The Smothers Brothers Comedy Hour*.

Episode 2: September 24, 1993   "Long Date's Journey into Night"

Director: David Steinberg   Writer: Jenny Bicks

Laura pries the book shelves in her office lose so she has an excuse to have Mitch fix them again. It has been a week since they first met and kissed. Mitch invites Laura to his house for BBQ, and she accepts. But, before she goes, she finds out that a manuscript she paid $1 million for is a fake. She tells Eve to call Mitch to cancel the dinner date. Sebastian takes the message that Laura will not be coming to dinner, but David mistakenly throws it in the trash. When Laura doesn't arrive, Mitch feels he has been stood up and goes to Laura's apartment. She explains that Eve left him a message that she wouldn't be able to have dinner with him. She wants him to leave so she can be left alone with her problem. After Mitch suggests that she should release her frustrations by hitting him with a pillow, they end up in a pillow fight, which leads to kissing. When her phone rings, Laura lets the answering machine take the message that Immigration caught the fake author trying to cross the border into Canada.

Episode 3: October 1, 1993   "Let's Spend Termite Together"

Director: David Steinberg   Writer: Rick Cunningham

Mitch's house is infested with termites and needs to be fumigated. He cannot find a hotel for him and the boys, and so Laura spontaneously invites everyone to spend the night at her place even though the next day people from an exclusive French magazine are coming to do an article about her. The boys bring their dog with them, and they mess up Laura's very neat apartment. Eve calls and says that the people from the magazine will be at her place earlier than expected. Mitch and the boys try to clean the apartment before the reporter and photographer arrive, but then their dog starts to have puppies. The French magazine staff arrives and takes a picture of all of them and the newborn pups.

Episode 4: October 15, 1993   All About Dave

Director: David Steinberg   Writer: Lindsay Harrison

When Dave gets fired from his job dressed as an "eager beaver" at a car wash, Laura offers him an entry-level job at her office as a gopher so he can earn money to buy a CD player. Because she wants Dave to like her, she gives him a big office and praises his work. However, he becomes increasingly irresponsible. When he mistakenly sends photocopies of his butt instead of contracts to important clients, Laura goes ballistic. Mitch tries to retrieve most of the photocopies from the air express service before they are delivered, and Dave resigns. However, Mitch was unable to get one of the photocopies back – one that is delivered to the Queen of England.

Justin Whalin (Dave) later starred as Jimmy Olsen on *Lois & Clark*.

Episode 5: Unaired   "Truth or Dare" (summary based on first draft script)

Director: David Steinberg   Writers: Brad Buckner and Eugenie Ross-Leming

Mitch's son Christopher telephones Laura and says he is in trouble. When Christopher arrives at her apartment, he is with an off-duty police officer who caught him shoplifting a tie. The officer thinks Laura is his mother and turns Christopher over to her. Christopher explains to Laura that he took the tie because his friends dared him. She says he must tell his dad about the incident. The next day Laura finds out Christopher still hasn't told Mitch about the theft, and, when Mitch visits Laura's office, she sees him wearing the tie which he thinks Christopher bought for his upcoming birthday. Laura tells Mitch the truth, and Mitch informs his son that he must take the tie back to the store and confess to the manager what happened. Christopher talks Laura into going with him, and, when Laura finally has a chance to talk to the manager, she has the tie, but Christopher is nowhere to be seen. Laura is accused of stealing the tie and has to be bailed out of jail.

Will Estes (Christopher) later became a regular on the drama *Blue Bloods*.

Episode 6: Unaired   "London Calling" (summary based on table draft script)

Director: David Steinberg   Writer: Jenny Bicks

Laura is offered a job with a London publishing firm and discusses the pros and cons of leaving with Eve. When she talks with Mitch about the job offer, she suggests that the boys and he go with her. But Mitch says "no". Mitch and Laura discuss her leaving at a party Mitch throws for some friends. Laura feels that Mitch is not communicating his real feelings to her, but Mitch doesn't want to make the decision for her. Laura goes to the airport to fly to London expecting Mitch to come and talk her out of going. However, she boards the plane, and, as it taxies down the runway, Laura has the plane stopped and gets off. Waiting for her when she deplanes is Mitch.

Episode 7: Unaired   "Shrink Resistant" (summary based on table draft script)

Director: David Steinberg   Writer: Art Everett

Mitch gives Laura a key to his house and wonders why Laura does not want to reciprocate. Mitch is working on a project for Steven Singer, who happens to be Laura's psychiatrist whom she calls to ask for advice about giving Mitch a key to her place. Laura decides to surprise Mitch whom she thinks is out playing poker by going to his house in a night gown. She discovers that the poker game was moved to his place and that one of the players is her psychiatrist. Since Mitch doesn't believe in psychotherapy, he has problems when he finds that Laura is seeing Dr. Singer. The next afternoon, Mitch has Steven over to watch football, and he tries, to no avail, to get Steven to discuss what Laura has told the doctor about him. Laura drops by and suggests that she and Mitch have a therapy session while Steven is there. The session doesn't go that well in Laura's eyes. Steven leaves, and Laura confesses to Mitch that she doesn't want to lose him like she has lost everyone else in her life. When Mitch says he is there for her, she gives him the key to her apartment.

Episode 8: Unaired   "Wheel of Laura"

Director: David Steinberg   Writer: Marianne Meyer

Laura goes to Sebastian's little league baseball game with Mitch and Debbie (Shelly Fabares), a neighbor. Debbie seems to be competing against Laura for Mitch. Unlike Laura, Debbie cooks, knows how to play baseball, and has chaired the Carnival Committee for Sebastian's school. In an effort to bond with Sebastian, Laura wants to get more involved in activities that interest him. She visits Mitch while he is hosting a fund-raising meeting for the Carnival Committee and is nominated along with Debbie for chairperson. When voting results in a tie between the two, Mitch has to break the tie. He flips a coin, and Debbie wins the toss. Mitch suggests that the two work together on the committee. Debbie puts Laura in charge of the posters and crepe paper. At the carnival, Laura volunteers for the Super Splash to impress Sebastian, not realizing it is where people throw balls to dunk others in a tub of water. Both Laura and Sebastian get dunked.

Episode 9: Unaired   "Just Hold (aka Please Hold!)" (summary based on table draft script)

Director: David Steinberg   Writer: Bernie Keating

Mitch and Laura are too busy with their respective jobs to spend time with each other. Mitch is building a house, while Laura is endeavoring to get an author to finish the last chapter of his novel. Mitch and Laura finally attempt to have a romantic evening together at her place. However, the guy who is trying to complete his book arrives drunk at Laura's place. While Mitch is miffed that Laura wants to spend time to help the author with his book, he eventually joins Laura in helping to finish the last chapter. They both dictate a chapter about a princess and a serf that sounds like their own romance. Finally, the author leaves promising to have his book done in a few days.

Episodes Never Produced

At least two scripts were written for this series but never filmed:

"Take My Kids….Please!" (summary based on studio draft script) Writer: Brian Scully

Mitch moves some heavy furniture at Laura's place and injures himself requiring hernia surgery. Since Mitch is afraid of doctors and hospitals, the next day he pretends to be okay, but, when Laura makes him bend to pick something up, it is obvious that he needs surgery. At home with his sons, he worries about what will happen if he dies. Mitch makes Laura promise to temporarily take guardianship of his sons if something happens to him. While at the hospital, Laura realizes the implications for Mitch to put her in charge of his kids and feels that she isn't ready for this responsibility. The surgery turns out fine, and, after speaking with Mitch, Laura is more comfortable about taking this step in their relationship.

"Three's a Lounge Act" (summary based on studio draft script)   Writer: Michele Wolff

When Eve asks Mitch to get a date for her with one of his friends, he invites all of his friends over to watch a baseball game so Eve can choose a guy. She picks a fellow named Jeff who seems normal. However, when Eve goes on the date with Jeff, he brings along his ventriloquist dummy. Even though Eve tells Mitch and Laura that the date was terrible, they ask her to give Jeff another chance. They all go on a double date, which goes well until Jeff brings out his dummy again, and it begins insulting Laura and Mitch. Jeff sends them all apology cards and flowers the next day, but, when Eve has him come to the office to apologize in person, he brings along the dummy that continues to insult everyone.

"Dun" Away

It Had to Be You lasted only four episodes. Its special preview on Sunday after *60 Minutes* got respectable ratings, but, when the comedy moved to its regular time on Fridays up against ABC's *Family Matters*, the series was killed in the ratings. The sitcom ranked eighty-seventh out of 101 shows.

Reportedly, Dunaway was dissatisfied with her role on the sitcom, and the viewing audience didn't much care for her character. Dunaway's costumes were changed, her hairstyles varied, and her living room set underwent three complete makeovers. Moreover, the results of CBS testing of the first five episodes showed that her likeability rating was in the minus column.[19] After the series was canceled, there was an attempt to rework the sitcom by deleting Dunaway's character. The idea was to focus just on the Urich character and his three sons and make the series a nineties version of *My Three Sons*.[20] Robert Urich, Robin Bartlett, Will Estes, Justin Whalin, and Justin Jon Ross were brought back to film a pilot called *The Mighty Quinn's*.[21] However, CBS decided not to pick it up as a series.

Love & Money

Premiered Friday, October 8, 1999, at 8:30 PM on CBS

Like other sitcoms where two people from different backgrounds fall in love (e.g., *It Had to Be You*), *Love & Money* involved a relationship between the daughter of a billionaire living in a fancy Manhattan high-rise and the building's young, hunky maintenance man. Allison Conklin (Paget Brewster) was about to marry a stuffy socialite when she locked herself in the bathroom to avoid the marriage. The new building superintendent, Eamon McBride (Brian Van Holt), was called to unlock the bathroom door. It so happened that Allison and Eamon were former childhood sweethearts. Much to the dismay of Allison's father, Nicholas (David Ogden Stiers), who wanted her to marry into money, the wedding was canceled. While Nicholas tried to discourage the romance between his daughter and Eamon, Allison's mother, Effie (Swoosie Kurtz), looked for ways to help the couple. Other characters on the sitcom included Puff Conklin (Judy Greer), Allison's horny sister; Nicky Conklin

(John Livingston), her young brother who didn't have a job but would go out every night for unexplained reasons, and Finn McBride (Brian Doyle-Murray), Eamon's father—the doorman for the apartment building.

Background

This rich versus poor culture clash sitcom was created by Dan Staley and Rob Long, who had previously developed the Bob Newhart/Judd Hirsch comedy *George & Leo*. *Love & Money* was originally called *The Super*. Staley and Long Productions in association with CBS Productions and Paramount TV produced the series.

Episode Guide: 5 aired; 8 unaired

Episode 1: October 8, 1999   "Pilot"

Director: Pamela Fryman   Writers: Dan Staley and Rob Long

On her wedding day, Allison Conklin locks herself in the bathroom, and the building superintendent, a former pro-hockey player who had to quit the sport because of an injury, is called to open the door. When he goes through the bathroom window to get to the door, he discovers that Allison is the girl he had an affair with several years earlier. Eamon had broken off the affair at the time because he didn't want to become the spouse of a rich girl, but now he has changed his mind. Allison and Eamon have sex in the shower. He tells Allison's mother that he loves her daughter; Allison's father offers him a blank check to leave his daughter alone. Of course, Eamon doesn't accept the check, and Allison calls off her wedding.

Episode 2: October 15, 1999   "When WASP's Collide"

Director: Michael Lessac   Writer: Daphne Pollon

Two weeks after the wedding was canceled, Eamon and Allison are still together. After he spends the night in Allison's bedroom, the next morning the parents give him the silent treatment at the breakfast table. Eamon then invites Allison to spend the night in his apartment where he lives with his dad. The dad doesn't like the fact that the two will be sleeping together, but he relents after an argument with his son. Allison finds that Eamon and his dad really communicate with one another unlike her family. Allison and her family try to be more honest with one another but find that the "truth hurts."

Episode 3: October 22, 1999   "The Music Box"

Director: Michael Lessac   Writer: Howard Margulies

Since Allison's parents want to get to know Eamon's father, they invite him for cocktails. However, the parents find they have nothing to talk about, but Finn still invites them to his apartment in the basement. When they go, Nicholas Conklin finds his old music box there and accuses Finn of stealing it. After they leave, Effie confesses that she threw the music box away because it reminded her of Nicholas' former girlfriend who gave the box to him. Nicholas apologizes to Finn who says he found the music box in the trash.

Episode 4: July 11, 2000   "Howard's End" (aka "Babe in the City")

Director: Michael Lessac Writer: Cindy Collins

Allison gives Eamon's dad a large-screen TV for his birthday. Eamon thinks the gift extravagant, tells Allison she is a spoiled rich girl, and sends the gift back. Allison's father is happy the two are fighting and tries to get Allison back with Howard whom she dumped at the wedding. Eamon comes to apologize to Allison, but she is not available. Although Nicholas says he will give Allison the message that Eamon was there, of course, he doesn't. When Effie visits Eamon and learns that he tried to apologize, she demands that Nicholas correct the situation. Nicholas invites Allison and Eamon together for dinner and says that he forgot to give Allison the message. At the end of the episode, Finn gets his new TV back.

Brian Doyle-Murray (Finn) is the brother of actor Bill Murray.

Episode 5: July 18, 2000   "A Night at the Opera"

Director: Michael Lessac   Writer: Ross Abrash

Effie takes Eamon's father to the opera with her since Nicholas hates the opera and Effie's "walker" says he has a headache. Finn pretends to be a South American general to Effie's friends and to a gossip columnist at the opera. The next day, the *New York Post* reports that Effie and her husband are breaking up which Nicholas finds humorous. Effie tries to make her husband envious by going out for pizza with Finn. When Nicholas finds out from Finn that Effie is trying to make him jealous, he flatters Effie by forbidding her to see the "general" again.

Episode 6: Unaired   "Five Week Itch"

Director: Michael Lessac   Writers: Dan Cohen and F.J. Pratt

Eamon and Allison have a bad date when Allison takes him to a Thai puppet theater in which he has no interest. Later, Allison gets dressed up for a romantic evening with Eamon, but he is too tired to go out. Allison is upset and wants to know where the romance in their relationship has gone. Her mother advises her to stop expecting so much from Eamon, while at the same time, Eamon's dad tells him to be more romantic. Eamon then goes to the school where Allison is a kindergarten teacher and invites her out for a romantic night, but she suggests they simply take a walk which turns out to be romantic.

Episode 7: Unaired   "Make Room for Daddy"

Director: Michael Lessac   Writers: Phil Baker and Drew Vaupen

Nicholas goes to the hospital after passing out and is found to be suffering from stress. He has to wear a meter to determine the cause of the stress. Most of his stress is coming from his slacker son and from Allison and Eamon. Since Nicholas believes that trying to get to know Eamon better by spending time with him might reduce his stress, both of them go to a hockey game, which Nicholas doesn't really like. With regard to Nicky, Jr., Nicholas meets with him to find out what his goals in life are. When the meeting doesn't go well, the son says he is moving out but ends up going to Eamon's apartment where Nicholas finds him and says he loves him. After Effie tells Nicholas that he is too controlling, he tries to be less controlling to reduce his stress.

Episode 8: Unaired   "The Stepmummy"

Director: Michael Lessac   Writer: Howard Margulies

Effie's stepmother, Beverly, is coming to lunch, and Effie thinks the stepmom will leave her a vacation home that her late father built. At lunch with Effie, Allison, Eamon and Puff, Beverly (Cloris Leachman) says she is leaving the vacation home to her cats at which point Effie orders her to leave. Beverly tells the doorman, Finn, that she has lost all of her money and is living in a flop house in the Bowery. When Effie learns of this, she and Eamon go to the flop house to see Beverly, and Effie gives her some money. Beverly informs Effie that she was just testing her to see if she really cared for her. Beverly is not penniless and decides to leave the vacation home to Effie.

Previously, Swoosie Kurtz (Effie) had starred on the short-lived *Party Girl* and more recently became a regular on *Mike & Molly*.

Episode 9: Unaired   "Career Daze"

Director: Michael Lessac   Writers: Phil Baker and Drew Vaupen

Career Day at the school where Allison teaches has Finn, Eamon, and Nicholas describing what they do. In front of the kids, Eamon confesses that he never completed high school. He went right into pro-hockey. Eamon then decides to study for his GED. Nicholas re-evaluates his career as head of Conklin & Associates – a real estate management firm he inherited from his dad, after the kids ask why he does what he does. He decides to spend more time with his family. However, his late father appears to him in a dream and says that he was more successful than Nicholas. The dream makes Nicholas want to go back to work to be more successful than his late father.

This episode involved a mini-*M*A*S*H* reunion with the late Harry Morgan playing the ghost of David Ogden Stiers' father.

Episode 10: Unaired   "Puff the Magic Sister"

Director: Michael Lessac   Writer: Bob Sand

Apartments in the building where the Conklin's live are being burglarized, and the tenants think that Nicky, Jr. is the culprit. Effie and Nicholas confront Nicky with the allegation. However, another young man in the building is arrested for the thefts when the police find the stolen items in his apartment. It turns out that Nicky framed the guy for the burglaries by planting the items in his apartment. Nicky felt that the guy was psychotic and needed counseling and figured the best way to have him see a psychiatrist was to have him arrested and have the court order counseling. Meanwhile, although Eamon doesn't think that Allison would have fun with his friends, she goes with Puff to a bar where he and his friends are hanging out. Puff seems to fit right in with Eamon's friends, while Allison is more reserved. Eamon's friends wonder why he hasn't introduced Allison to them before and eventually she begins to fit in with the group.

John Livingston (Nicky, Jr.) is the younger brother of actor Ron Livingston.

Episode 11: Unaired   "Diagnosis: Effie"

Director: Michael Lessac   Writer: Daphne Pollon

Effie invites the new tenants, Hugh and Emma Lanston (David Warner and Judy Geeson), who are British, to dinner with the family, and the couple begins arguing with each other. Later, Effie goes to their apartment where she hears the couple having a violent argument again. When she keeps trying to see Emma, Hugh keeps her away leading Effie to conclude that Hugh murdered Emma. However, Emma subsequently appears at Eamon's apartment with a large trunk and asks to borrow a saw, and so now Effie thinks that Emma killed Hugh. When Effie accuses her, Emma simply says that her husband left her and she is moving back to England. New tenants move in to Hugh and Emma's apartment and find Hugh's head in the freezer.

Episode 12: Unaired   "Guess Who's Paying for Dinner"

Director: Michael Lessac   Writer: F.J. Pratt and Dan Cohen

Allison tells Eamon that the reason her father doesn't like him is because her father is the "alpha dog" and Eamon is the new dog invading the "alpha dog's" space.

Eamon decides to take the Conklin family out to dinner to get Nicholas on his turf. Also, Eamon's dad is now dating Gloria, a nurse with a nervous laugh. Eamon and the Conklin's have to take the subway to the Chinese restaurant Eamon chose for dinner. When they arrive, the owner of the restaurant turns out to be one of Nicholas' tenants on whom he just raised the rent. During dinner, Effie's face begins to swell from an allergic reaction to the food, Nicholas asks for squab but is served some type of mystery meat, and Eamon's father turns up with his new girlfriend. Soon it appears that Eamon is judging his father's girlfriend like Nicholas judges him. Eamon apologizes for his remarks to his dad's girlfriend, and Nicholas apologizes to Eamon.

Episode 13: Unaired   "Everybody Doesn't Love Eamon" (aka "Slapshot")

Director: Michael Lessac   Writers: Michael Fitzpatrick and Rob Fox

At Molly's, the bar where Eamon and his friends hang out, Eamon sees Stupak, a man who heckled him when he was a hockey player. Allison tries to counsel Stupak about his heckling, and he tricks Allison into mentioning April 17 to Eamon – a day Eamon lost a playoff game and made a fool of himself trying to go after Stupak. Eamon keeps imagining the face of Stupak and decides to beat him up. When Eamon goes to Stupak's place of work, he finds him working in a fast food restaurant with a high-school kid as his abusive young boss. Eamon thinks he is pathetic and leaves him alone. Meanwhile, an article in *Business Week* magazine profiles Nicholas but barely mentions Effie. Effie decides to go back to college to prove her worth. She enrolls in a feminist theory class, but, when during a study session at her apartment her fellow students tell her to get rid of her jewelry, she revolts.

The End of *Love & Money*

For some strange reason, CBS scheduled *Love & Money* on Fridays after the child-oriented *Kids Say the Darndest Things*. *Love & Money* was up against *Boy Meets World* on ABC and the second half of NBC's drama *Providence*. The series ranked fifty-fifth for its premiere episode. The next week it rated sixty-fifth, and for its third episode – eighty-first. *Love & Money* was put on hiatus with CBS promising it would return in January. It didn't. CBS attempted to burn off the remaining episodes in July 2000, with only two episodes broadcast before the series was taken off the air for good.

Paget Brewster (Allison) later starred on *The Trouble with Normal* and *Criminal Minds*. After *Love & Money*, Brian Van Holt appeared on the sitcom *Cougar Town*.

You're the One

Premiered Sunday, April 19, 1998, at 9:30 PM on the WB

Promotional ads for *You're the One* read, "Love makes you do crazy things. Like get married." Another sitcom about a newly married couple from totally different backgrounds, the series starred Cynthia Geary (*Northern Exposure*) as Lindsay Metcalf, a descendent of a Civil War general (on the losing side) and a landscape architect who worked at a plant wholesaler, and Elon Gold as Mark Weitz, her husband, a descendent of Romanian horse traders, who ran a successful fantasy baseball team business on the Internet – www.checkthescore.com. Their respective parents were stereotypical opposites as well—Southern WASP versus Jewish New Yorkers. Lindsay's father, Bo Metcalf (Leo Burmester), a "lovable bigot," ended up buying Mark's company. Kip (Jayce Bartok) was Lindsay's sensitive brother; Mark's mom Lenore (Dori Brenner) and dad Sy (Lenny Wolpe) lived in Florida. Mark also had a sister named Robin (Julie Dretzin) and a business partner, Howie (Troy Winbush).

Background

According to Cynthia Geary, *You're the One* was based on the experiences of its creator and executive producer, Julia Newton.[22] Initially titled *Them!*, the pilot's opening showed film clips from 1950's horror movies to emphasize the interfering relatives. But, the title and opening sequence were changed before its premiere. Love That Mike Productions and Castle Rock Entertainment produced *You're the One*.

Each episode of the sitcom dealt with a single subject that affected the newlyweds—romance, fights, turf, secrets, friendships, and money. However, the series never got beyond "romance," the second episode.

Episode Guide: 2 aired; 5 unaired

Episode 1: April 19, 1998   "Pilot"

Director: Will MacKenzie   Writer: Julia Newton

Mark proposes to Lindsay, and they each advise their parents they will soon marry. Mark's relatives and Lindsay's mother argue over wedding preparations with Lindsay, while her father Bo takes Mark and Kip duck hunting. Because of the arguing, Lindsay wants all of the relatives out of their apartment and changes her mind about marrying Mark. Meanwhile, Mark tells Bo that he is not a hunter, and Kip and he leave the hunting blind. When Lindsay informs Mark she no longer wants to get married, Mark says he stood up to her dad, and they need to set limits on their parents. In the end, Mark and Lindsay marry in Central Park with their parents in attendance.

Episode 2: April 26, 1998   "Romance"

Director: John Rich   Writer: Gail Lerner

It's the first anniversary of the day when Mark and Lindsay consummated their relationship, but Mark doesn't think it is a big deal like Lindsay does. He then has to find a way to get back into Lindsay's good graces. He plans a special romantic evening including a limo and dinner out, but, when leaving, they get stuck in their building's elevator. Meanwhile, Kip, who is now working at Mark's internet business, begins romancing Mark's sister Robin.

Episode 3: Unaired   "Fights"

Director: Max Tash   Writer: John Wierick

A fight over movies – Lindsay likes British art films, Mark likes action movies – has Lindsay concerned that she and Mark are not compatible. Before they go to bed for the night, Lindsay wants to talk about what they said to one another. Mark says that fighting is part of marriage, while Lindsay claims she never saw her parents fight. The next day, Lindsay tells Mark that she will be staying with her parents to do some thinking about their relationship. From her mother, Lindsay learns that her mom sometimes thinks about poisoning Bo after they argue. Lindsay comes to recognize that fighting may indeed be a natural part of marriage, and she apologizes to Mark.

Episode 4: Unaired   "Turf"

Director: James Hampton   Writer: Julia Newton

Lindsay moves her numerous possessions into Mark's apartment. He would like to keep his sofa bed, but Lindsay wants to replace it with her bed. After Lindsay says that she will put all of her stuff in storage, Mark, wanting her to be happy, tells her "no." Later, when Mark comes home, he finds that Lindsay placed both her furnishings as well as his in storage and got her grandmother's giant bed for them. Although Mark doesn't like the bed, he won't admit that to Lindsay and make her unhappy. In the end, however, he does say he dislikes the bed, and Lindsay replies that he needs to be more honest with her.

Episode 5: Unaired   "Secrets"

Director: Max Tash   Writer: Bill Canterbury

Mark's sister Robin plays a game with the family called "Secrets" which leads to her fighting with her husband. Lindsay says that she never wants to keep secrets from Mark. He reveals that when he said he was working late, he was really attending a game with Howie. Lindsay divulges that she was engaged for six months before she met Mark which really upsets him. Later Lindsay learns from Howie's wife that Mark wasn't at the game like he said. She makes up a story for him that she will be having lunch with her ex-fiancé, Reinhold. Mark goes to a health club to meet Reinhold where Lindsay finds him. She tells Mark that she fabricated the story about the lunch date and found that Howie had lied to his wife about not attending the game with Mark.

Episode 6: Unaired   "Friendships"

Director: Max Tash   Writer: Bill Canterbury

Lindsay is excited by a visit from an old friend, Truffy, and her husband Brad. Truffy is very perky, while Brad doesn't say much. Lindsay invites them for a weekend at a beach house in the Hamptons. Mark endures them only to please Lindsay. Truffy announces that she and Brad have decided to move to New York City permanently since her husband received a job offer. She wants Lindsay and Mark to move into a more exclusive neighborhood with her and Brad so they can build a social network together. Lindsay is turned off by the suggestion and tells Truffy that the two of them have grown apart. Truffy and Brad leave the beach house early, and Howie visits for the rest of the weekend. Meanwhile, Bo has had Kip's latest girlfriend deported.

Episode 7: Unaired   "Money"

Director: James Hampton   Writer: John Wierick

Cousin Marvin gives Mark and Lindsay $1000 as a wedding gift. Mark suggests that they open a joint checking account with the money, but Lindsay is concerned about having a joint account given her husband's rather loose financial style which clashes with her obsessive attitude. When their refrigerator needs to be replaced, they use their new joint checking account to pay for another refrigerator, but the store later repossesses the new appliance because their check bounced. Mark confesses that he made an ATM withdrawal that Lindsay didn't know about. After Lindsay gives Mark one last chance to make the joint account work, Mark loses a check. However, Lindsay reveals she used the check Mark thought he had lost, and she didn't enter it in the check book. Meanwhile, Kip moves into Mark's office when Bo evicts him.

Not the One

You're the One was the first WB sitcom to get the axe after two low-rated episodes. It rated no better than the sitcom *Alright Already* that it had replaced.

Chapter 4
Male Bonding

Dennis Boutsikaris, Christopher Meloni, Julius Carry, and Stephen Furst in *Misery Loves Company*

Camaraderie is the theme of the comedies in this chapter. The sitcoms all involve men who are friends – small-town friends, neighborhood friends, high-school friends, friends with relationship problems, and guys who are paranoid.

The Boys

Premiered Friday, August 20, 1993, at 9:00 PM on CBS

In the opening episode of *The Boys*, Doug Kirkfield (Christopher Meloni), a New York novelist who had written *Slopes* about a beast that terrorizes a ski resort, and his girlfriend, Molly Rich (Isabella Hoffman) moved to a small town outside of Seattle, Washington, so he could work on his second novel in peace and quiet. In his new neighborhood, Doug met "the boys," three older men who hung out together. They wanted him to take the place of Ed, the former owner of Doug's home who had passed away. Doug ended up joining them for their weekly get-togethers. Irascible Bert Greenblatt (Ned Beatty), a retired fireman married to Doris (Doris Roberts); closeted Harlan Cooper (John Harkens), an unmarried antique shop owner, and goofy Al Kozarian (Richard Venture), a widower who worked in a tar factory made up the group of older men.

Background

Dan O'Shannon, who had been a writer and producer on *Cheers* and would later script episodes of the Kelsey Grammer sitcoms *Frasier* and *Back to You*, created this comedy. Originally, Anthony Edwards and Jessica Lundy were cast as Doug and Molly but were replaced by Meloni and Hoffman. Hughes-O'Shannon Productions in association with 20th Century-Fox and CBS Entertainment produced *The Boys*.

Episode Guide: 5 aired; 1 unaired

Episode 1: August 20, 1993   "Don't Call Me Ed"

Director: Terry Hughes   Writer: Dan O'Shannon

Doug, a divorced writer, and Molly, his girlfriend, move to a house that belonged to a deceased man named "Ed" who had been friends with three other guys in the neighborhood. Doug is invited to play Monopoly with Bert, Al, and Harlan who treat him as if he were Ed. Doug learns from Doris that the real Ed died five years earlier and that the guy who bought Ed's house was also called Ed by "the boys" in order to keep the memory of the original Ed alive. The "second Ed" passed away six months ago. Doug gains some understanding of the relationship Bert, Al, and Harlan had with Ed.

Before *The Boys*, Christopher Meloni had been on *The Fanelli Boys*, an NBC comedy that lasted one season.

Episode 2: August 27, 1993   "Ladies' Night"

Director: Terry Hughes   Writer: Dan O'Shannon

The boys are having movie night, and Doug asks Doris to visit Molly. Molly mentions to Doris that she will be giving piano lessons to people in the town and that women shouldn't have to give up their careers when they get married like Bert forced Doris to do. Doris tells Bert that he is a selfish ogre and that she is going to apply for her old job as a ticket taker at a movie theatre. However, what she doesn't realize is that the theatre at which she once worked now shows porno films. Bert and the boys go to bring Doris back from the theatre. After Bert says he needs Doris, she decides not to pursue a job.

Doris Roberts eventually became Ray Romano's mother on *Everybody Loves Raymond*.

Episode 3: September 3, 1993   "Strike One, You're Out"

Director: Terry Hughes   Writer: Dan O'Shannon

When Doug joins the boys to do a jigsaw puzzle, he disagrees with Bert on how the puzzle should fit together. They discuss physical fitness, and Bert says he is as strong now as he ever was. While Al and Harlan are out of the room, Bert asks Doug to punch him in the stomach to prove how strong he is. When Doug does, Bert collapses and is rushed to the hospital with appendicitis. Too proud to admit that he isn't what he used to be, Bert tells Doris that Doug punched him because he got mad at him over the puzzle. Harlan and Al kick Doug out of the group. After Doris finds that Bert lied about what happened with Doug, Bert and the others apologize and invite him back.

Episode 4: September 10, 1993   "The Writing Class"

Director: Terry Hughes   Writer: Dan O'Shannon

Doug is giving a class in creative writing in which Al, Bert, and Harlan all enroll. Doug's confidence in his writing ability is shaken when Bert starts writing like Hemingway.

Episode 5: September 17, 1993   "Ninety-Five in the Shade"

Director: Terry Hughes   Writers: Dan O'Shannon and Clay Graham

There is no boys' night out because it is too hot. Everyone is sitting on the front porch at Bert's place on an August evening, and Bert is upset that one of his neighbors, with whom he has had an ongoing feud, still has his Christmas lights up. Bert tries to tear the lights down, but the neighbor's dog (also named Bert) bites him. The neighbor subsequently comes over to Bert's home to try to end their feud. After he says he will take down his lights, Doug comments to the neighbor that he was the last hold out in bowing to Bert's dictates about how the neighborhood should look. The neighbor has second thoughts about his Christmas lights and decides to leave them up.

Episode 6: Unaired   "The Wicker Moosehead" (summary based on first draft script)

Director: Terry Hughes   Writer: Dan Staley

At Doug and Molly's housewarming party, Doris suggests that Molly visit Harlan's antique store, called "Give Antiques," for some items for her home. At the store, Molly points to a lamp she likes, but Harlan thinks she is pointing to a hideous wicker moose head he had made. Not wanting to hurt Harlan's feelings, Molly takes the moose head home with her. Harlan subsequently brings her a second moose head because, when pointing to the lamp in the store, Molly asked if Harlan had two of them. Harlan is so appreciative over that fact that Molly and Doug like his artistic side that he makes moose heads for Bert and Al and decides to invest all his savings in producing them. Molly finally tells Harlan that the moose heads are ugly and explains to him that she really wanted the lamp from his store. While Harlan is depressed because no one likes his moose heads, they do inspire Doug to write a second horror novel about an evil, red-eyed, jagged-toothed wicker moose head which he dedicates to Harlan.

Rating *The Boys*

The Boys was originally on at 9:00 PM Fridays, but CBS then flip-flopped the show with the Bonnie Hunt series *The Building* which had debuted at 9:30 PM to see if it would do any better in the ratings. The first episode of *The Boys* ranked sixty-third in the Nielsen's. The switch didn't improve the ratings, and the series was canceled after five episodes.

Flatbush

Premiered Monday, February 26, 1979, at 8:30 PM on CBS

According to CBS publicity for this series, "The Flatbush Fungos drove girls wild, parents crazy, and neighbors up the wall!" *Flatbush* focused on the adventures of five recent high school graduates, all single, who lived in the Flatbush section of Brooklyn, New York. The five guys, known in the neighborhood as the "Flatbush Fungos," included Presto Prestoppolos (Joseph Cali who had been John Travolta's sidekick in *Saturday Night Fever*), a cabdriver and unofficial leader of the group; Socks Palermo (Adrian Zmed), a clothing store clerk and the group's fashion plate; muscular Turtle Romero (Vincent Bufano), who worked at his family's restaurant; Joey Dee (Randy Stumpf), an apprentice plumber attending law school at night and unofficially engaged to Carma (Donna Ponterotto), a girl in the neighborhood, and Figgy Figueroa (Sandy Helberg), a grocery delivery boy. Also appearing on the sitcom was Anthony Ponzini as Esposito (Espo), the local pool hall owner.

Background

The series started out as a one-hour comedy-drama. According to Harvey Laidman, who directed the never-aired, one-hour pilot, the storyline concerned the guys saving a baseball field from being destroyed.[23] Discos scenes were added while the pilot was being shot, but, overall the show tended toward other family dramas produced by Lorimar at the time such as *Apple's Way* and *The Waltons*. *Flatbush* then evolved into a half-hour adventure comedy. CBS ordered six episodes. As George Yanok, a producer for the series, stated, *Flatbush* "... was an obvious attempt to cash in on *Saturday Night Fever* with the added Bowery Boys element and didn't work."[24] *Flatbush* was originally scheduled for 8:00 PM on Monday nights but then its time slot was changed to 8:30 PM when the network decided not to air *Co-Ed Fever*.

During the production of the series, *Flatbush* ran into some scheduling problems with available sound stages and crew at MGM studios. Lorimar assured the producers that as soon as another show they were doing got canceled, which the company expected would happen quickly, *Flatbush* would get the first choice of stages and crew.[25] The series Lorimar thought would be canceled—*Dallas*.

Episode Guide: 3 aired; 2 unaired

Episode 1: February 26, 1979   "Kar Kannibals" (summary based on second draft script)

Director: Unknown   Writer: Dennis Palumbo

The "Fungomobile," the gang's car, is stolen, and then Esposito's '57 Continental is taken. Joey Dees' little sister walks into the pool hall with the steering wheel for the Fungomobile and claims she took it from a kid who found it down by a warehouse. Presto and Socks go to the warehouse and are caught by the car thieves. When they pretend they want to become part of the car theft ring, one of the thieves tells Presto that he has to steal a certain car within the hour to prove his worth. The thieves keep Socks as collateral, while they give Presto a tow truck to steal the vehicle. After Presto picks up the rest of the gang, they go to find the marked car. Once they start towing the car, a police officer, hiding in the vehicle, gets out and orders them to stop. The police listen to the gang's story and ask Presto to work undercover with them. Presto returns to the warehouse where the thieves permit Socks and him to join their operation. Later, Presto is caught by the thieves when he makes a phone call to Figgy to try to get everyone down to the warehouse. The thieves are finally captured by the gang and the police. Esposito gets his car back, and the gang gets the Fungomobile.

Dennis Palumbo, who wrote this episode, later became a licensed psychotherapist specializing in creative issues.

Episode 2: March 5, 1979 "Moving Out" (summary based on second draft script)

Director: Unknown   Writer: Dennis Palumbo

After the Rent Commission Office has granted a rent increase, Flatbush resident, Mrs. Fortunato (Helen Verbit), can't afford to stay in her apartment and is planning to move. Socks wants the Fungos to come up with a plan to keep her in the neighborhood. They go to the Rent Commission Office to speak with the supervisor who approved the increase. The supervisor declines to change his decision unless he can be shown that the landlord didn't do the promised renovations to the building that justified the rent hike. When the Fungos bring the supervisor to Mrs. Fortunato's apartment building, he leans against a banister which collapses, and he cancels the rent hike.

Episode 3: March 12, 1979 "The Heist"

Director: Unknown   Writer: David Epstein

Socks and Presto are hanging out by Socks' cab in front of Esposito's. When Socks leaves the cab to get some sodas, a tough looking, baldheaded man named Clean Otto gets in the vehicle and has Presto drive to a local bank. While Presto waits outside, the man runs into the bank, returns with a full satchel, and gives Presto $50. Later that day, with the entire gang hanging outside Esposito's, the police come and arrest Presto for taking part in a bank robbery. The gang bails Presto out of jail and attempts to find the real robber. They discover him in a deserted warehouse with the money. Havoc ensues when Presto and Socks sneak in the warehouse to get the satchel which gives rise to a football-like sequence of the satchel being thrown around. Esposito arrives just in time with the police to catch the bag of money.

Adrian Zmed (Socks) subsequently starred on the police drama *T.J. Hooker* with William Shatner.

Episode 4: Unaired   "The Littlest Fungo" (summary based on second draft script)

Director: Tony Mordente   Writer: Mike Weinberger

Espo's sister Annette wants her brother to babysit her nine-month-old son, but, when Espo isn't around, Figgy volunteers to babysit. The other Fungos see Annette with a suitcase leave in a cab. She apparently had a fight with her husband who joined the Merchant Marines. When the Fungos can't find anyone to take care of the baby, they take turns watching him. Figgy puts the baby in a box and mistakenly delivers him thinking he is delivering a box of groceries. Presto and Espo track down Annette and bring her back to Flatbush just as a friend of the Fungos returns the baby.

The actor who portrayed Figgy (Sandy Helberg) is the father of Simon Helberg from *The Big Bang Theory*.

Episode 5: Unaired   "The Wedding" (summary based on second draft script)

Director: Unknown   Writer: Terry Hart

Joey's girlfriend Carma wants to marry him as soon as possible since her younger sister is about to marry. However, Joey would rather hang out with the other Fungos. When he says that he doesn't want to marry right now, Carma breaks off their relationship. To cheer up a depressed Joey, the guys take him out to meet other girls, but, when Joey sees Carma with a new guy at a restaurant, he proposes marriage. Mrs. Palermo and Mrs. Fortunato describe all the pitfalls of marriage to Carma, and, when the other Fungos say that they will all be over to Joey and Carma's apartment a lot, they both agree not to get married right away.

Episode 6: Unaired   "Vooo Dooo" (summary based on revised draft script)

Director: Unknown   Writer: David Epstein

Mr. Scravane, a medium, is romancing Socks' mom, and Mrs. Palermo wants to give him $1000 to help her contact her late aunt. Socks is suspicious of Scravane, but the gentleman tells him to come by with his mother and, if Socks is not convinced that Scravane can contact the dead, he will refund the $1000. At the séance, Socks and his mom hear the ghostly voice of Mrs. Fortunato's former border and are impressed. However, the other Fungos want to prove that Scravane is a fraud. They go to see Madam Kazools, the witch lady of Flatbush, who confirms that Scravane is indeed a fake and that he works with an accomplice who impersonates the voices of the dead. When Scravane holds another séance, the Fungos rush in to reveal the accomplice and break up the séance.

Flattened

Although the premiere episode ranked forty-sixth and the second episode ranked forty-seventh, the ratings for subsequent episodes were lower, leading to the show's cancelation. Apparently the borough president of Brooklyn at the time was so offended by the ethnic Italian stereotypes on the series that he publicly protested to have the series taken off the air.[26] Considering the characters' names and dialogue like, "Which one of yous meatballs parked the car?," his offense was probably understandable. However, the reason CBS canceled the show so quickly was because it faced stiff competition in the ratings from NBC's *Little House on the Prairie*.

Local Heroes

Premiered Sunday, March 17, 1996, at 9:30 PM on Fox

The "local heroes" were four twentysomething guys—friends since high school—who all hung out at Blue Lou's Bar in Pittsburgh, PA. They included:

- Jake Bartholomew (Jay Mohr), a former high school quarterback, who now sold TV sets;

- Eddie Trakacs (Ken Campbell), a factory worker who lived at home with his widowed mother (Rhoda Gemignani) and a rather promiscuous teenage sister, Nikki (Tricia Vessey);

- Stan "Stosh" Stoskolowski (Jason Kristofer, *Teech*), the "intellectual" of the group who drove a cab, and

- Richard "Mert" Mertola (Louis Ferreira aka Justin Louis), who worked with Eddie and was the only member of the group who was engaged to be married. His fiancée was Bonnie Sullivan (Kristin Dattilo-Hayward).

All of the guys except Mert wanted to stay single. Also in the cast was Paula Cale as Gloria Pappas, the barmaid at Blue Lou's.

Background

Local Heroes, created by Frank Mula, was produced by Only Humans Were Harmed Productions and Witt-Thomas Productions in association with Warner Bros. Television. According to Mr. Mula, he had not seen a comedy about real blue-collar guys like those with whom he had grown up. He intended *Local Heroes* to be a cross between *Roseanne* and the movie *Diner*. The studio wanted the series sold to Fox and tried to make it more like *Animal House*. Mula further commented that the executives running Fox at the time understood blue-collar Americans about as much as he understood Martians, and so the sitcom got off to a bad start, and things didn't get any better from there.[27] The Eddie character in *Local Heroes* was loosely based on Mula himself, and the Mrs. Trakacs character was a composite of several of his relatives.

Episode Guide: 5 aired; 2 unaired

Episode 1: March 17, 1996   "Pilot"

Director: Jeff Meiman   Writer: Frank Mula

At a wedding for one of their friends, the guys all wear black armbands mourning the loss of another single guy to marriage. In order to reinvigorate their singlehood, the guys steal the mascot – a goat, from a rival to the high school they attended.

They keep the goat in Eddie's basement but soon discover that they stole the wrong goat. They take the animal back to the country in Stosh's cab and go to another farm to steal the right goat.

Episode 2: March 24, 1996   "Big Bad Stosh"

Director: Ted Wass   Writer: Regina Stewart Larsen

Stosh's dad, a former mailman, breaks out of prison after having been incarcerated for not delivering mail. He wants to stay at Stosh's place but ends up living with Eddie. When Eddie and Stosh find his dad in bed with Eddie's mother, Stosh asks his dad to leave. Meanwhile, Mert thinks that Bonnie prefers Jake to him when she confesses that she previously dated Jake in high school. However, after Jake tells Mert that Bonnie dumped him for Mert, Mert and Bonnie get back together.

Jay Mohr (Jake) subsequently starred on the sitcoms *Action* and *Gary Unmarried*. Stosh's dad was played by Brian Doyle-Murray.

Episode 3: March 31, 1996   "Mertster Meister"

Director: Ted Wass   Writers: Regina Stewart Larsen and David Richardson

The Henkenmeister girl giving out free shots at the bar is attracted to Mert and kisses him. Bonnie is upset with Mert until Gloria explains the situation. Meanwhile, Eddie has paid off his credit card and wants to now use it to purchase a big-screen TV to watch the fights but finds that his mother has used his card to book a cruise. Jake borrows a big-screen TV from work, brings it to Eddie's place, and, on the way back to the shop to return it, the set falls off the back of his convertible.

Louis Ferreria (Mert) went by the stage name Justin Louis in this series as well as two other little-known comedies – *Public Morals* and *Battery Park*, before going back to his birth name.

Episode 4: April 7, 1996   "Not the Booth Who Shot Lincoln"

Director: Ted Wass   Writer: David Richardson III

Eddie wins a Steelers-Browns luxury box in a contest by putting five cats in his pants. Since the luxury box holds twelve people, Eddie advises the guys to bring only one guest. However, Jake brings two dates; Stosh, who thinks he is part native American and wants to open a casino, brings other members of his "tribe;" Bonnie invites her parents so her father will be favorably impressed with Mert; Gloria's entire Greek family shows up, and so do Eddie's sister, her boyfriend, and his mother. The box gets so crowded that the windows steam up, and no one can see the game.

Episode 5: April 14, 1996   "The Unfriendly Skies"

Director: Ted Wass   Writers: Marc Bryan Abrams and Michael P. Benson

Gloria bets the guys that she can go a week without being rude to prove to them that she has the right temperament to become a flight attendant. Meanwhile, Eddie schemes to win the lottery.

Paula Cale (Gloria) later starred on the comedy *Buddies*.

Episode 6: Unaired   "The Birds and the Beers"

Director: Ted Wass   Writer: Brian Scully

The guys challenge each other to dangerous stunts such as bungee jumping. Mrs. Trakacs gets revenge on a neighbor, but Eddie is the one who suffers.

Episode 7: Unaired   "Eddie's Secret"

Director: Ted Wass   Writer: Frank Mula

Eddie gets laid off and takes a job selling women's underwear. Mert tries to resume his career as a pianist.

A Fox executive apparently couldn't understand why a blue-collar guy would be embarrassed selling women's lingerie since, according to the executive, in his house they always had an open copy of *Women's Wear Daily*.[28]

No More *Heroes*

Still trying to find a successful show to follow *Married with Children*, Fox scheduled *Local Heroes* on Sundays at 9:30 PM. It didn't do as well in that timeslot as the series it replaced, *What's So Funny?* The sitcom ranked near the bottom of the Nielsen ratings and was canceled after five episodes.

Misery Loves Company

Premiered Sunday, October 1, 1995, at 9:30 PM on Fox

"Guys with relationship problems" pretty well summed up the premise of this series. *Misery Loves Company* starred Dennis Boutsikaris as Joe DeMarco, a film professor at New York University who had recently divorced his wife Karen after twelve years of marriage and had moved in with his unmarried younger brother Mitch, played by Christopher Meloni. Rounding out the cast were Joe's two best friends, Perry (Julius Carry, *Cutters*), a black guy with a teenage son who had been married and divorced numerous times, and Lewis Fingerhutt (Stephen Furst), a heavy-set dentist who was in counseling trying to save his marriage to Evelyn. The guys often hung out together at Nicky's St. Hubbins bar where they were friends with Nicky Sullivan (Kathe Mazur), the owner.

Background

Misery Loves Company was one of many little-known sitcoms that changed from its original concept. Initially, the series was about three divorced male friends dealing with their relationship problems, worshipping ESPN, and eating a lot of junk food, but executives at Fox rejected that darker version of the show.[29] Bob Young, Michael Jacobs, and David Trainer, the creators of the series, added a fourth friend who had never been married and kept one of the original three men married although in a troubled relationship. Also, in the original pilot, Rick Rossovich played Dennis Boutsikaris' brother Mitch, but the role was recast with Christopher Meloni. This version of *Misery Loves Company* debuted on Sunday nights after *Married with*

Children. Michael Jacobs Productions and Touchstone Television produced the series.

Episode Guide: 4 aired; 4 unaired

Episode 1: October 1, 1995   "Advice & Dissent"

Director: John Tracy   Writers: Rick Singer and Andrew Green

Joe likes to "mother' Mitch even though both are adults. Mitch tells him to stop interfering in his life. While at Nicky's bar, Joe thinks that Sasha, the woman Mitch is hitting on, might really be a man when he sees her urinating in the men's room. However, Perry advises Joe that Mitch will not like it if he mentions what he witnessed. After spending time with Sasha, Mitch says that he will fall in love with whomever he desires. It turns out that Sasha is really a woman, and that Mitch was playing a trick on Joe to make him stop butting into his life. Meanwhile, Perry is upset that his son Connor seems to be bonding with his former wife's boyfriend – Dennis Rodman – instead of with him. Perry challenges Rodman to a game of one-on-one, and Connor, showing that he still likes his father, tells his dad how to score points against Rodman.

Former NBA star Dennis Rodman played himself on this episode. Julius Carry (Perry) passed away in 2008 from pancreatic cancer.

Episode 2: October 8, 1995   "Uneasy Rider"

Director: John Tracy Writer: Harry Dunn

Joe buys a Harley and wants the other guys to join him in riding motorcycles and going to a biker bar. At the bar, Mitch dances with a biker chick; Perry talks with a biker who turns out to be gay, and Lewis helps a biker with a toothache. Meanwhile, Joe is intimidated by other bikers at the bar, one of whom asks him to leave. Joe ends up selling his bike and later finds that the biker who bullied him is really a pharmacist. The guys return to the bar and discover that all the bikers are white-collar professionals. In the end, they all put on cowboy attire and go line dancing at a country and western bar.

MALE BONDING

Episode 3: October 15, 1995   "That Book by Nabokov"

Director: John Tracey   Writers: Linda Mathious and Heather MacGillvray

Kim, a graduate student and former student of Joe's, asks him to watch a film she made which appears to be about Joe and her. Joe's friends encourage him to date Kim. When Joe meets Kim in his office to tell her his thoughts on the film, they end up making love on his desk. However, later, Joe feels that Kim agrees with everything he says and disagrees with nothing. The two break off their relationship. Meanwhile, Lewis decides he needs to get into better shape after a waiter confuses him with the hugest man in the world at Nicky's based on his wife's description to the waiter. Perry takes Lewis to his gym to work out. Lewis doesn't like the experience, but he sticks with it for awhile since he wants his wife to be attracted to him.

In one of her first television appearances, Maria Bello portrayed Kim on this episode.

Episode 4: October 22, 1995   "Pilot"

Director: David Trainer   Story: Michael Jacobs and Bob Young   Teleplay: Michael Jacobs, Bob Young, and David Trainer

The pilot has Joe showing up at his brother's door seeking a place to stay after a brutal meeting about his divorce settlement where he finds that his wife and her attorney were having an affair. Mitch is about ready to have sex with his girlfriend and tries to get rid of Joe. But Perry and Lewis show up, and they all go to Nicky's bar. Mitch's date leaves, but he still doesn't want Joe to stay at his place. After Joe ends up in a cheap motel with Perry and Lewis, they decide to go to a strip club where Mitch finds them. Mitch then invites Joe back to his place.

Christopher Meloni, probably the best known of the actors on the series, went on to star on the long-running *Law & Order: Special Victims Unit*.

Episode 5: Unaired   "The Witches of East 6th"

Director: John Tracy   Writer: Rich Halke

In a Halloween episode, Joe and Mitch accept an invitation to a party from two gorgeous women they meet while out trick or treating with Joe's son. They learn that the women are actually witches who entice them into their hot tub and then handcuff them. Joe and Mitch eventually get away down the fire escape in their swimsuits. Meanwhile, Dr. Fingerhutt is having special office hours on Halloween to take care of all the kids who injure their teeth eating candy, and Perry is depressed on Halloween because he broke up with his first wife around that time.

Episode 6: Unaired   "The Streak"

Director: John Tracy   Writer: Sandy Frank

Mitch is having a "dry" spell in his love life. He has never gone an entire month without having sex. Nicky's advice to all the guys is that they need to be more emotionally honest with women. Perry tries to be open with the woman he is dating even though he has to make up stories about himself based on movies he has seen. Joe is dating a traffic reporter who takes him up in her helicopter. He is nervous and afraid about the flight, and the woman says she likes it when guys express fear and wants to make love to him in the copter. Later, Joe picks up a woman at the bar for Mitch by telling her that Mitch doesn't have long to live. However, Mitch decides to go somewhere to talk with the woman instead of having sex, thus breaking his streak.

Episode 7: Unaired   "Wu's Company"

Director: John Tracy   Writer: Sandy Frank

Mr. Wu, the owner of a local Chinese laundry, counsels Mitch about life, and Mitch introduces him to Joe. Mr. Wu advises Joe that, to be one with the universe, he has to apologize to all the people he ever wronged. Joe asks forgiveness from all the guys for different things, but then he is struck by a car. Wu informs Joe that the universe is trying to tell him something – that he wronged someone when he was sixteen. Joe thinks that when he played high school football with NFL quarterback Jim Kelly, he gave him bad advice. When he meets Kelly in a bar, Kelly says the advice Joe gave him was not bad and didn't lead to his NFL team, the Buffalo Bills, losing Super

MALE BONDING

Bowl games. Wu then advises Joe that he injured himself when he sacrificed fun for work and that he needs balance in his life.

Pat Morita played Mr. Wu in this episode, and Jim Kelly appeared as himself.

Episode 8: Unaired   "Joe DeMarco, Boy Wonder"

Director: John Tracy   Writer: Charlie Kaufman

Joe cannot find a company willing to show his film, *Alone Again*. He decides to change the credit on the film to indicate it was directed by one of his students – Jake Piscotto (David Lipper), in order to trick potential distributors into thinking a "boy wonder" made the movie. The trick works, and a film company offers Jake a two-picture deal. After Joe proves to the company that he actually made the film, the company says they love the movie but, to sell the film, they need a young name associated with it. In other storylines, Mitch gets a date with Anna Nicole Smith, and Lewis goes to a comedy club where Jack Carter is the emcee and Jackie Silver (Phil Leeds) is a comic who insults Lewis. Lewis returns the insults, and Jackie leaves show business. Lewis hires Jackie as his dental assistant, and Jackie begins insulting the patients and then returns to performing. Anna Nicole Smith breaks off her relationship with Mitch when the news media lose interest in covering the affair. She takes up with Jake Piscotto, and after him, she starts a relationship with Jackie Silver.

Charlie Kaufman, who wrote this episode, is better known for his inventive screenplays such as *Being John Malkovich* and *Eternal Sunshine of the Spotless Mind*.

Misery No Longer

Misery Loves Company was not popular with viewers or with critics. The first episode ranked sixty-fourth; the fourth and last episode ranked ninety-second. As one critic wrote – "*Misery Loves Company* doesn't boast an original thought or characterization."[30]

The Trouble with Normal

Premiered Friday, October 6, 2000, at 8:30 PM on ABC

Opening with a graphic of an inkblot, *The Trouble with Normal* focused on four paranoid young men in group therapy: Bob Wexler (David Krumholtz), who thought everyone was spying on him; Bob's friend Max Perch (Brad Raider), who worked at a surveillance equipment store; Zack Mango (Jon Cryer), Bob's neighbor, who along with his friend, Stansfield Schlick (Larry Joe Campbell), were actually spying on Bob. The four men ended up in a neurotics support group led by therapist Claire Garletti (Paget Brewster) and became so dependent on her that they often all hung out at her apartment.

Background

The series, created by Victor Fresco, went through various changes before it aired. The title for the show ranged from *People Who Fear People* to *The Mighty Scared Guys* to *Like* and *You're So Normal* before *The Trouble with Normal* was chosen. In the original script for the pilot, the character who later became Max Perch was called Louis Finch and Bob's last name was Perrin – not Wexler. Also Bob had just adopted a dog which he had not yet named. While Bob's dog appears on the first episode described below, it is not alluded to as much as it was in the initial script where Bob goes through several names before deciding to call the dog "Jackson" after Claire's boyfriend. On the series itself, Bob's dog was named Maggie.

Fresco indicated that he tried to make the characters relatable to the viewing audience, saying that they represent fears we all have, but the characters are not afraid to verbalize them.[31] As one of the characters on the series said, "I have fears that are so old, they grew up and have fears of their own." Garfield Grove in association with Touchstone Television and Paramount produced the comedy.

Episode Guide: 5 aired; 8 unaired

Episode 1: October 6, 2000   "Pilot"

Director: Andy Ackerman Writer: Victor Fresco

MALE BONDING

Bob Wexler thinks that his new neighbor is spying on him. His friend Max brings him a small camera from the surveillance store where he works to see if Bob's suspicions are true, but the neighbor sees the camera under his apartment door and takes it away from Bob and Max. Bob and Max's therapist Claire comes by and goes next door to prove that Bob is just paranoid about the neighbor. But she finds that neighbor Zack Mango and his friend Stansfield are really spying. Bob invites Zack and his friend to join him and Max in his group therapy sessions.

Jon Hamm (*Mad Men*) played Claire's boyfriend in this episode.

Episode 2: October 13, 2000   "Not the Pilot"

Director: Andy Ackerman   Writer: Victor Fresco

Claire persuades the guys to go out to a bar on a group date with her and four girls. Stansfield meets Audry, a wealthy blonde who ends up being a stalker; Zack dates Dora, a girl who works for the FBI, and Max and his date Amanda get married after knowing each other for just a few hours. Bob's date doesn't show up, but he helps Claire impress a female colleague of hers at the bar. In the end, the guys all admit they had fun.

Episode 3: October 20, 2000   "Psychologists without Borders"

Director: Lee Shallat Chemel   Writer: Gail Lerner

The guys quit Claire's therapy group to protest her ban on their late-night visits to her apartment after they try to quiet a noisy neighbor (Sherri Shepherd) that has been keeping Claire up at night. The guys try to form their own therapy group. However, when they find they are not making any progress without Claire, they return to her therapy sessions, and Claire relents somewhat on her ban.

Episode 4: October 27, 2000   "Mail Trouble"

Director: Andy Ackerman   Writer: David Walpert

Stansfield is Claire's postman, but she is concerned about him being too meddlesome in her life so she gets him transferred to another route. On the new route, Stansfield is threatened by a middle-school bully and believes that an "old lady" complained about him to get him transferred. Claire confesses that she had him transferred and asks the post office to give him back his old route.

Episode 5: November 3, 2000 "Owl Show Ya"

Director: Lee Shallat Chemel   Writers: Jim Bernstein and Michael Shipley

Bob is fascinated with owls and finds Kristen (Constance Zimmer), a girl from work, with the same interest. However, when Max gives Bob an owl as a pet, he becomes afraid of it and loses Kristen for the moment. Meanwhile, Claire helps Stansfield find his hidden talent as a ballroom dancer which he keeps as a secret from Zack fearing Zack would be too judgmental of his talent. Since he misses Stansfield, Zack comes to the dance studio, and they end up dancing together.

Episode 6: Unaired "Clairanoia"

Director: Andy Ackerman   Writer: Michael A. Ross

The guys investigate Claire's background and find that she has another therapy group made up of rich people who have low self-esteem. They become jealous of the other group because they think Claire might abandon them. When the four guys go to Claire's other group, Max and Stansfield stall Claire so that Bob and Zack can persuade the other group that they are all cured and no longer need a therapist. In the end, Claire tells the guys she is not going to leave them.

Episode 7: Unaired "Unconventional Behavior"

Director: Andy Ackerman   Writer: Jennifer Celotta

There is a conspiracy convention in town, and Claire advises the guys not to date anyone they meet at the convention because they might be as paranoid as the guys are. After Claire finds that her new boyfriend has a booth at the convention, she dumps him when she sees him performing an alien autopsy. Meanwhile, Bob is the only one who is honest with Max and tells him that his marriage was a mistake which makes him mad at Bob.

Episode 8: Unaired   "Say Cheese"

Director: Lee Shallat Chemel   Writers: Steve Faber and Bob Fisher

A large corporation has bought Bob and Zack's building and installed a surveillance camera in the lobby, which causes the guys to be even more paranoid. Claire offers to call the company, which also owns Claire's building, to complain about the new camera. The guys warn her not to do so because the corporation will come after her. After Claire makes the call, she finds that her apartment is available for rent, that her water and heat are turned off, and that a smoked fish is mailed to her. The guys and Claire all go to the company to see what is going on. They meet the company's CEO in the elevator where he explains that everything that happened to Claire was a mistake.

David Ogden Stiers was the CEO in this episode. He had co-starred with Brewster on the short-lived series *Love & Money*.

Episode 9: Unaired   "Speech! Speech!"

Director: Andy Ackerman   Writer: David Walpert

The guys try to raise Claire's profile through a website, flyers, and press releases in order for her to get a book deal similar to one a former colleague of hers has. They also get her booked at a psychology conference to present one of her papers. However, Claire has a fear of public speaking which she attempts to overcome and eventually does after talking with Bob about fear.

Episode 10: Unaired   "Help Yourself"

Director: Andy Ackerman   Writer: Michael A. Ross

Zack gets a temporary job at Bob's company and finds he can order all sorts of office supplies. He thinks that giving people things makes them like him, and he convinces the other guys to also believe this. Bob starts giving his cubicle neighbor Kristen office supplies as gifts and gets a lunch date with her. Max begins giving office supplies to the elderly woman he visits at an assisted living facility. Claire explains that bribing people with office supplies is not a good thing, but no one listens to her. When the boss at Bob's company finds out what Zack is doing, he fires him along with Bob. But Zack confesses it was his fault and convinces the boss to keep Bob.

Episode 11: Unaired "Spy vs. Guy"

Director: Andy Ackerman   Writers: Steve Faber and Bob Fisher

Bob is dating Kristin from the office again, while Zack's old girlfriend, Dora, the FBI agent, asks him out. After spending the night with Zack, Dora starts questioning him about his likes and dislikes which he feels is intrusive. Claire advises the guys that sharing is important in any relationship. Bob and Kristen share everything until she mentions to him that she plans to take her old boyfriend back. Zack is persuaded that sharing is good and apologizes to Dora, while Stansfield and Max decide to spend time with each other.

Episode 12: Unaired "Chez Schlick"

Director: Jeff McCracken Writer: Jennifer Celotta

When the guys visit Claire's apartment, they find her younger, hipper sister Lindsey there who takes them all to a rave party. They wake up the next morning at Bob's apartment where Bob finds that he had his nipple pierced. He goes to the hospital to have it removed, but, when the nurse says she thinks it is sexy, he changes his mind. At home, after he takes it off, the nurse calls asking him for a date. He ends up in an awkward situation on the date when the nurse wants to see his nipple, and so he makes up an excuse ending the date. Meanwhile, when Claire's sister hits it off with Stansfield, he decides to move out of his mother's home and into his own apartment. The guys visit him at his new place, and Bob gets body lice from an old chair in the apartment. When Bob goes to have it treated, he bumps into the nurse again. In the end, Claire's sister breaks up with Stansfield, and Claire has to give him the bad news.

Episode 13: Unaired "Manhattan Transference"

Director: Andy Ackerman   Writer: Gail Lerner

Since Kristen is back with her old boyfriend, Bob gets the guys to keep the boyfriend busy in order for him to "accidentally" run into Kristin at a restaurant. However, at the restaurant, Bob sees Claire, and they have a "moment" when they gaze into each other's eyes. Torn between Claire and Kristen, Bob decides to get things straightened out with Claire. After conferring with her old college professor on the issue, Claire decides it is best to pretend she has no feelings for Bob.

Trouble Ceases

The Trouble with Normal was on Fridays after *Two Guys and a Girl*. It struggled with low ratings with each episode losing more and more viewers. Its premiere ranked fifty-eighth, and its fifth and final episode ranked eighty-ninth.

Except for Brad Raider, the stars of *The Trouble with Normal* later obtained roles on more successful series: David Krumholtz on *Numb3rs,* Jon Cryer on *Two and a Half Men,* Larry Joe Campbell on *According to Jim,* and Paget Brewster on *Criminal Minds.*

Another Day with Joan Hackett and David Groh

Chapter 5
Raising Kids and Making Ends Meet

From *The Adventures of Ozzie and Harriet* and *Father Knows Best* in the 1950s to *The Middle* and *Modern Family* in the present day, raising children and maintaining a family has been a classic subject of many successful situation comedies. This chapter includes family sitcoms that were less than successful.

Another Day

Premiered Saturday, April 8, 1978, at 9:00 PM on CBS

This family sitcom set in Philadelphia starred David Groh, familiar as Valerie Harper's husband on *Rhoda*, and Joan Hackett as Don and Ginny Gardner, parents raising a twelve-year-old son, Mark (Al Eisenmann) and a sixteen-year-old daughter, Kelly (Lisa Lindgen). Hope Summers, who had played Clara Edwards on *The Andy Griffith Show* for a number of years, was featured as Olive Gardner – Don's widowed mother. Ginny got a job at an insurance company to help with the family finances thinking that Don, an advertising executive, her kids, and her mother-in-law would help out at home. Many episodes of *Another Day* dealt with changing sex roles in the United States during the seventies.

Background

 James Komack, who was responsible for the hits *Chico and the Man* and *Welcome Back, Kotter*, created and produced this series. He originally offered *Another Day* to ABC but took it to CBS when ABC didn't buy the series.[32]   A total of thirteen episodes of *Another Day* were filmed before CBS scheduled it to air. Originally the network thought the sitcom would premiere in November 1977, but then decided to delay the debut. The network told the producers of several concerns it had about the series—that actress Hope Summers looked as if she could not say all of her lines, that the character of the daughter was too bratty (although Komack contended that the character was patterned after his own daughter), and that the opening title sequence did not quickly introduce the stars of the show. CBS thought they would air *Another Day* in January 1978 on Monday nights as a replacement for *The Betty White Show*, but that did not happen. It finally debuted in April 1978 against ABC's hit series, *The Love Boat*.

There were rumors, reported in gossip columns at the time, of trouble on the set between the two stars of *Another Day* – Groh and Hackett. Supposedly, Groh threw a ten-foot table on top of the actress, bruising and frightening her, and Hackett then obtained the services of a bodyguard. Groh commented that this was all gossip, and Hackett had "no comment."[33]

Episode Guide: 4 aired; 9 unaired

Episode 1: April 8, 1978   "Pilot"

Director: Gary Shimokawa   Writer: Carl Kleinschmitt

Ginny comes home late from work and drunk after a baby shower at the office. She finds that no one has fixed dinner, the daughter doesn't have a clean pair of jeans, the son is worried about undressing in gym class because of his lack of body hair,

RAISING KIDS AND MAKING ENDS MEET

and mother Olive wants a new tombstone for Don's father's grave since the current one is not the tallest in the cemetery.

Episode 2: April 15, 1978 "Room for One More"

Director: Hal Cooper
Writer: Stephen Black & Henry Stern (summary provided by Stephen Black)

Olive doesn't like the fact that Ginny has gone back to work and convinces Don that he and Ginny should have another child which would keep Ginny at home. Ginny, however, doesn't want another child. She feels that at this stage in her life she wants to do something outside the home that makes her happy. In the end, Ginny gets her way.

Both David Groh and Joan Hackett died of cancer – she in 1982 and he in 2008.

Episode 3: April 22, 1978 "The Birthday Present" (summary based on final draft script)

Director: Nick Havinga   Writer: Diana and Julie Kirgo

Don comes home and is startled to see Kelly making out with her new boyfriend Peter (Gary Imhoff). Ginny says that it is better that Kelly does this in their home instead of in a parked car. Later, Peter informs Don that he and Kelly have decided to wait to have sex until Kelly's seventeenth birthday which is soon. Don lets Kelly know that she would be cheating herself to have sex now and that she should wait until she is in a committed relationship. Kelly agrees that she isn't ready to stop dating other boys and would prefer a hair dryer for her birthday. Kelly says that her mother gave her the same advice, and, if both of her parents think this, they are probably right.

This episode was almost pulled off the air by CBS because of sponsor complaints about its subject matter, but it did air as scheduled.

Episode 4: April 29, 1978 "The Audition" (summary provided by William Taub)

Director: Nick Havinga   Writer: William Taub

Kelly wants to audition for one of Don's commercials – a hair commercial, which no one thinks is a good idea except her. She insists she wants to be considered only on merit and even changes her last name so nobody would know she is Don's daughter. Even though she thinks the audition went well, she was really awful and an embarrassment. Kelly gets upset when told she didn't win the audition and, disregarding the merit concept, tells her dad she thought she could count on him. Kelly wants the job even if she replaces the more talented girl who won the audition. Ginny and Don think that if they tell Kelly that her dad will pull strings and fire the more talented girl, she will realize that she wasn't good enough for the part. However, Kelly jumps at the chance to be a "star," but in the end comes to her senses when her mom reads her the riot act. The more talented girl who got the part turns out to be the client's girlfriend.

This was one of the first scripts written by William Taub who had left advertising in New York to become a writer in Hollywood.

Episode 5: Unaired "From Here to Eternity" (summary provided by Richard Christian Matheson)

Director: Unknown   Writers: Richard Christian Matheson and Thomas Szollosi

Olive is depressed and begins to talk about joining her late husband because she feels the family doesn't need her. When nothing seems to cheer her up, the family tries a unique approach. They begin planning her funeral allowing her to overhear and witness the planning. The family has a very odd mortician come to the house to describe the type of "affordable" service he could provide – like putting her away "deeper and cheaper." Mark then reads the eulogy he wrote for his grandmother saying that she would never see him grow-up or fall in love or graduate from college. This really gets to her, and Olive finally admits that she really doesn't want to die but just needs to feel more relevant in the lives of the Gardner family.

This was the first script a very young Richard Christian Matheson and his writing partner Thomas Szollosi had authored. Richard Christian Matheson is the son of writer Richard Matheson.

Episode 6: Unaired   "The Short Story" (summary based on final draft script)

Director: Unknown   Writers: William Whitehead and Marcia Rodd

Ginny comes home from the supermarket covered in whipped cream and recounts a story of how a perfect stranger asked if her name was Mrs. Gardner and, when she said "yes', she was sprayed with the cream. Kelly comes home elated and tells the family how everyone at school loved the short story she wrote. While reading her story called "Seduction in Suburbia" starring "Gina Gardner" to the family, a very mad neighbor, Barbara Ellis, comes by and accuses Ginny of cheating with her husband Robert (in the story Gina has an affair with a neighbor named Roger). Apparently, Kelly's story had been copied by other students and passed around town. The next day at both Ginny and Don's work the story is the main topic of gossip. Ginny thinks the story is hilarious, while Don is outraged. When Kelly says she is writing a sequel, her dad forbids it. Ginny gets mad at Don for caring what everyone may think. Don is upset at Ginny for not caring what others think. They eventually make up and tell Kelly she can write the sequel but only if Don is in the story as Don Juan character that sweeps Gina off her feet.

Marcia Rodd, the co-writer of this episode, played the neighbor Barbara Ellis.

Episode 7: Unaired   "Out in the Cold" (summary provided by Lynn Phillips)

Director: Unknown   Writer: Lynn Phillips

Don's advertising company gives him a rare vacation, and he insists that the entire family spend it with him in a secluded cabin in Vermont. While the family is not terribly enthusiastic about the idea, Ginny, who has only been working for six weeks, submits to Don's pressure and asks her boss for a week off. The boss refuses; she ends up calling him a twit, and he fires her. A friend of Ginny's gets her a better job, but it starts on the same day as Don's vacation. She is ready to turn it down, but the family begs her to accept it. They know she needs to work outside the home, and Mark and Kelly don't like going to a cabin in Vermont anyway. Ginny goes back to work, and the family enjoys a "staycation," having redecorated the living room to resemble a snowy New England scene. At the end, Ginny tells her family that the man she is replacing was let go for asking to join his corporate wife on a vacation in Vermont.

Episode 8: Unaired   "The Dangerous Age" (summary based on final draft script)

Director: Unknown   Writer: Sumner Long

Don comes home from work depressed despite the fact he received a raise and a promotion. He feels that he has reached his peak at age thirty-eight and has nowhere else to go. He says he wishes he could do something more creative and travel. Kelly and Mark, who have been reading a health article, think that their dad may have male menopause. Although Ginny tells them to stop the nonsense, she spends the night worrying about her husband. When she wakes up, Don is gone along with the car and his suitcase. Once the kids and Olive figure out the car is missing, they make up a story that Don has left them. Later that day, as they all sit around the kitchen table depressed, Don comes home. He says that he couldn't sleep and so took an early walk in the neighborhood. When he saw some neighbors struggling with suitcases because they were about to leave on a trip, he gave them his new suitcase and took them to the airport. On the way home, he got stuck in traffic and that delayed his return. Ginny warns him never to do that again and that, whatever they do, they need to do it together.

Episode 9: Unaired   "No Smoking" (summary based on final draft script)

Director: Unknown   Writer: Daniel Gregory Browne

Ginny tells the family that she has been kicked out of her carpool because she complained about others smoking and stinking up the car. Just then Don comes home and says he's been given a new account at his ad firm that has lots of perks and travel to Hawaii for the family. When he says the new account is for a cigarette company, Ginny freaks out. She continues to be mad at Don while he smokes in bed and around the house. The next day, Kelly comes home smoking a cigarette after getting in trouble for smoking in school. Don sees how wrong it is and quits the account. Ginny is grateful, the kids are upset, and mother Olive decides to wear her grass skirt to dinner anyway.

Episode 10: Unaired "New Best Friend" (aka "The Office Guru") (summary based on final draft script)

Director: Unknown   Writer: Pamela Chais

Ginny comes home late and is dropped off by her new best friend from work Dorothy Swasey (Charlotte Rae), who compliments everyone saying they have "good vibes" and calling Don "Cary Grant." She stops back later with Mexican food as the family is about to go out to eat. Don doesn't like Mexican food and quickly becomes weary of Dorothy. Later, while Don is taking an important call about work, the operator breaks in with an emergency call from Dorothy. When he informs the operator to tell Dorothy to buzz off, his client overhears and says he doesn't want to work with Don because he is so mean. The next morning, Dorothy wakes up Ginny and Don with breakfast in bed and a list of chores she wants to do for them. She says she has canceled her vacation plans and will spend a week at their house doing cleaning and other such tasks. After the entire house begins arguing about who is going to do what chores, Dorothy realizes that the Gardner's are not the perfect family of which she wanted to be a part. She feels betrayed by her new best friends and leaves—to Don and Ginny's delight.

Episode 11: Unaired   "Mothers-in-Law" (summary based on final draft script)

Director: Unknown   Writers: Elizabeth and Oliver Hailey

Ginny's mother, Edith Spencer (Neva Patterson), arrives at the Gardner home for her first visit since Don's mother Olive came to live with the family. Edith tells everyone that she has sold the house in which Ginny grew up and has moved to a retirement community. Ginny's mother likes being independent and says she would not move in with Ginny and Don like Olive has. Edith tries to convince Olive that she would be happier on her own. Don calls a family meeting and makes it clear to Edith that the family really wants Olive to live with them. Furthermore, he would like Edith to stay with them while she is visiting instead of staying at a hotel. However, Edith is afraid that having mothers-in-law live under one roof with their offspring would damage Ginny and Don's marriage. She thinks that Don and

Ginny will leave her if she stays with them like her husband left her when Ginny got married. Don then asks Edith to move in permanently. Edith says she is grateful for the invitation but wants to be on her own for now.

As Elizabeth Hailey said about this episode which she co-wrote with her late husband, "It allowed us to laugh at our own situation, with a live-in mother-in-law and a more sophisticated, judgmental, visiting mother-in-law . . ."[34] Elizabeth Forsythe Hailey later wrote the acclaimed novel *A Woman of Independent Means* which was inspired by the life of her grandmother.

Episode 12: Unaired   "The Heist" (summary based on final draft script)

Director: Unknown   Writers: William Whitehead and Marcia Rodd

Ginny comes home to find the first floor of the house completely empty of furnishings. Kelly calls the police who inform the family that burglaries happen all the time and that often the burglars might come back and take everything from the upstairs. Ginny puts the entire house on lockdown making sure that someone is always there, installing an alarm system, and teaching everyone emergency drills. Don tries to reason with her and tells her that if she really wants to scare off someone, she should get a gun. He gives her a .44 Magnum. She realizes that she has gone too far and that Don was testing her to show that family is more important than possessions. In the end, the police return and inform the family that they found their stuff in Maryland in a broken down moving van.

Episode 13: Unaired   "The Convention" (summary provided by Stephen Black)

Director: Unknown   Writers: Stephen Black and Henry Stern

Ginny has been selected to represent her company at an out-of-town convention. In the past, when she attended one of Don's conventions, she always felt like a tag along. However, she invites Don to accompany her. At the convention, he is the only husband attending all the functions arranged for wives. He's miserable and allows himself to be tempted by two different women he meets – a strong, aggressive business woman and a meek, married woman. All the while, Ginny is thriving in this new environment.

Another Day Gone

CBS pulled the series from the air after four low-rated episodes. The producers could not get anyone to sample the show. *Another Day* ended up in a three-way tie for 104th out of 110 shows for the 1977-78 TV season.

Arresting Behavior

Premiered Tuesday, August 18, 1992, at 9:30 PM on ABC

Somewhat different from other sitcoms at the time, particularly family comedies, *Arresting Behavior* did not have a laugh track nor was it filmed in front of a live audience. The series, both a family comedy and a spoof of reality shows like the long-running *Cops* on the Fox network, was filmed with handheld cameras. Subtitles were used for different scenes, curse words were bleeped, and the actors had to create believable characters while showing that they were aware of the cameras.

Arresting Behavior focused on two police officers, Bill Ruskin (Leo Burmester) and his younger partner Donny Walsh (Ron Eldred), as cameras followed their family lives as well as their police adventures. Also in the cast were Chris Mulkey as Officer Pete Walsh, Donny's divorced older brother with a quick temper, Lee Garlington as Connie, Bill Ruskin's wife, and Amy Hathaway, Eric Balfour, and Joey Simmrin as the Ruskin's kids – Rhonda, Bill, Jr., and Seth.

Background

Arresting Behavior was created by Larry Levin, who had written episodes of *Seinfeld*. Referring to *Arresting Behavior*, Levin said that he did not set out to parody reality shows. "I was trying to figure out how to do a new family comedy. I just wanted to explore the family. I wanted to create this fictional town and maybe do my own spin on family values."[35] In addition to creating *Bakersfield P.D.* and another short-lived sitcom, *If Not for You*, Larry Levin wrote the screenplays for the Dr. Doolittle movies starring Eddie Murphy and the screenplay for the film *I Love You, Man*. Dakota Productions and HBO produced this comedy.

Episode Guide (4 aired; 1 unaired)

Episode 1: August 18, 1992 "Pilot"

Director: Betty Thomas   Writer: Larry Levin

Bill and Danny chase and lose a burglar, then fail to notice a stolen car that continually crosses their path. Pete traumatizes an infant that Bill and Donny are trying to rescue from inside a locked car. Meanwhile, Bill wonders what to get Connie for her birthday. Donny suggests lingerie.

Director Betty Thomas played Officer Lucille Bates on *Hill Street Blues*.

Episode 2: August 19, 1992 "Homemakers and Hookers"

Director: Betty Thomas   Writer: Larry Levin

Bill is forced to arrest his daughter's boyfriend for auto theft, and a prostitution sting nets a housewife, who just happens to be Bill's neighbor.

Episode 3: August 26, 1992 "Oaxitajaca"

Director: Edward Solomon   Writer: Edward Solomon

Bill is reluctant to follow through on vacation plans with his wife since he does not want to leave his kids home alone. Donny struggles with his sister's homosexuality.

Episode 4: September 2, 1992 "Labor Day" (summary based on table draft script)

Director: Andy Wolk   Writer: Larry Ketron

While Pete is on duty, his ex-wife and kids attend the Ruskin's Labor Day party. Pete makes an unexpected appearance at the party to ask his wife to come back to him, but she wants to be left alone. Donny reunites with his old band mates, and his band Snowpack puts on a performance.

Episode 5: Unaired "Family Values"

Director: Betty Thomas   Story: Ed Solomon   Teleplay: Larry Levin and Dennis Klein

Donny is attracted to Pete's ex-wife, and the Ruskin's try to survive Bill's family night.

The First Mockumentary Sitcom

The series debuted following the hit sitcom *Roseanne* on Tuesday nights where it was the fifth highest-rated show. However, when it moved to Wednesdays the next day following *Home Improvement*, it ranked twenty-second, and the next episode the following week ranked forty-seventh. It was canceled after four episodes. In some respects, *Arresting Behavior* was the precursor to other mockumentary sitcoms like *The Office* and *Modern Family*.

After *Arresting Behavior*, Leo Burmester appeared on another short-lived sitcom, *You're the One* in 1998. He then guest starred on various series before dying of leukemia in 2007. Ron Eldred became a regular on the sitcom *Bukersfield P.D.*

Baby Makes Five

Premiered Friday, April 1, 1983, at 8:00 PM on ABC

After *Bosom Buddies* and before he became a regular on *Newhart*, Peter Scolari starred in the slight family comedy, *Baby Makes Five*, as Eddie Riddle, a young husband, accountant, and father with five small children. Louise Williams was his wife, Jennie, who in the pilot gave birth to twins. The Riddle's other kids were nine-year-old Michael (Andre Gower), eight-year-old Laura (Emily Moultrie), and Annie (Brandy Gold). Eddie's free-spirited mother, Blanche (Janis Paige) and Jennie's more conservative mother, Edna Kearney (Priscilla Morrill) often helped to take care of the children.

Background

Baby Makes Five was produced by Mort Lachman and Associates and Allan Landsburg Productions. Sy Rosen created the series.

Episode Guide: 5 aired episodes

Episode 1: April 1, 1983   "Pilot"

Director: Tom Trbovich   Writer: Sy Rosen

After Eddie doesn't get the raise he thought he would at work, he initially doesn't want to tell his pregnant wife Jennie. When he finally confesses to Jennie about not receiving the pay increase, she goes into labor. Jennie's mother Edna and Eddie's mom Blanche arrive at the hospital to wait for Jennie to give birth. In the delivery room, after Eddie and Jennie find that they are having twins, Eddie has to be given a sedative.

Janis Paige (Blanche) starred in several movie musicals in the 1940s and had her own sitcom, *It's Always Jan*, in the 1950s.

Episode 2: April 8, 1983   "Eddie's Night Out"

Director: Jim Drake   Writer: Harriett Weiss

Eddie goes to a bar to see a fight where a friend persuades him to pick up two girls which turns out to be really bad advice. Meanwhile, at home, Jennie is coping with a prowler.

Episode 3: April 15, 1983   "Jennie Gets a Job" (summary based on revised final draft script)

Director: Jim Drake   Writer: E. Michael Weinstein

Jennie's unmarried older sister Susan (Hillary Bailey) offers Jennie a temporary job at the department store where she works doing a cooking demonstration. Eddie, his mother, and his mother-in-law take care of the kids, while Jennie is at the store preparing rum balls for the store's Caribbean week. Too much rum gets into the mixture, and Jennie, along with the customers, becomes inebriated. She is fired, and Eddie comes to get her when one of the twins gets sick.

Brandy Gold (Annie), sister of Tracey Gold, later became a regular on the short-lived sitcom, *First Impressions*.

Episode 4: April 22, 1983   "The Matchmakers" (summary based on final draft script)

Director: Lila Garrett   Writer: Robert Van Scoyk

Jennie's mother stops by because she is lonely. Eddie says she needs a man, and Jennie suggests her mom could date an older accountant, Chester Clayton (Eugene Roche) who works at Eddie's firm. Blanche comes over to babysit the kids, and, she answers the door when Chester comes by for Edna. Chester thinks that Blanche is his blind date which upsets Edna. However, Blanche gives Edna a mini-makeover which then makes her appealing to Chester.

Priscilla Morrill (Edna) was featured on many little-known comedies profiled in this book – *A Year at the Top*, *In the Beginning*, and *Dorothy*, but is probably best remembered for playing Lou Grant's wife on *The Mary Tyler Moore Show*.

Episode 5: April 29, 1983   "Jennie's Old Flame" (summary based on final draft script)

Director: Russ Petranto   Writers: Phil Doran and Douglas Arango

Mark Dubbins, Jennie's old boyfriend, calls, and she invites him for dinner. Mark is now a lawyer and successful businessman, and Eddie is jealous. When Mark comes over, he wants to sell the Riddles a solar energy home conversion plan for $10,000. Jennie is disappointed that he didn't really want to see her, and he leaves.

Five and No More

Baby Makes Five replaced *Benson* for five weeks as a spring tryout series. Its first episode won its timeslot and ranked twenty-eighth for the week. However, subsequent episodes rated lower, and the comedy was not picked up by ABC for its fall schedule.

Bringing Up Jack

Premiered Saturday, May 27, 1995, at 8:30 PM on ABC

In *Bringing Up Jack*, Jack Gallagher played Jack McMahon, a recently married sports talk show host in Philadelphia. His new wife, Ellen (Harley Jane Kozak), who was pregnant with their first child, had a teenage son, Ryan (Matthew Lawrence), and ten-year old daughter, Molly (Kathryn Zaremba) from a previous marriage. Jeff Garlin was Artie, Jack's best friend and co-host at radio station WST-AM 1040; Ralph Manza was the station engineer, Lou, who was seen but never heard.

Background

Bringing Up Jack was based on comedian Jack Gallagher's one-man show "Letters to Declain" about life with his son and wife. After seeing his one-man show in San Francisco, ABC signed Gallagher to a comedy development deal with a pilot commitment. In real life, Gallagher had become a dad later in life, and he chose producers Nat Bernstein and Mitchel Katlin to develop a comedy series around that theme. Supposedly the initial concept for the sitcom was about a married couple—both professionals—having to take care of the husband's nephew because his brother had some addiction problem. When that premise was rejected, the idea of a radio talk show host who marries a widow with two kids was developed. AKA Productions, a subsidiary of ABC Studios, and Katlin/Bernstein Productions produced the series.

Episode Guide: 5 aired; 1 unaired

Episode 1: May 27, 1995 "Pilot"

Director: Robby Benson   Writers: Michael Katlin and Nate Bernstein

Jack wants to take Ryan to a hockey game, but Ellen, complaining that she is always the "bad guy" in the family, says that he has to do his homework. Jack suggests that Ryan can do his writing assignment at the game. When Jack and Ryan return home after the game, Ryan says he left his paper at the arena. Stepdad and stepson go back to the arena and sort through dumpsters to find the essay. Meanwhile, Ellen has an ultrasound which shows she is having a boy. After Ryan later asks Jack to write him a note to skip class to attend a game at Madison Square Garden with his stepdad, Jack says "no" and so takes on the responsibilities of a dad.

Roscoe Orman appeared as George, the station manager, on this episode but did not appear on subsequent episodes. Jack Gallagher had his hair dyed dark brown for the pilot but let it go gray for other episodes.

Episode 2: June 3, 1995   "Close Personal Friends"

Director: Pamela Fryman
Writers: Michael Katlin, Nate Bernstein, and Jack Gallagher

Ellen and Jack think they have met the nicest couple, Doug and Sue, at a video rental store while trying to make new friends together. Doug and Sue invite Ellen and Jack to their cabin in the Poconos, but before they leave, Jack and Ellen see Doug kissing another woman at a restaurant. They go to the Poconos anyway because Jack wants to find out what Doug's relationship is with the other woman. At the cabin, Sue confesses to Ellen that her marriage is in trouble and reveals that she and Doug are having an affair. The woman that Doug was seen kissing was really his wife. Sue's husband comes to the cabin, thinks Jack is the guy with whom his wife is having an affair, and delivers divorce papers.

Episode 3: June 10, 1995   "Saturday in the Park with Jack"

Director: Pamela Fryman   Writers: Lisa DeBenedictis and Daryl Rowland

Jack is planning a party to watch a game with his friends at the same time the family wants to go camping. Because Jack feels he cannot disappoint his stepson by telling him he can't go camping with the rest of the family, he reluctantly goes on the trip. Early in the morning on the first day of camping, Jack and Ellen make love in the woods. The kids, thinking it is two bears doing it, take a photo. Jack tries various ruses to get the film from the kids before finally telling Ryan the truth. Ryan gives the undeveloped film to Jack, and when Jack gets the film back from the developer, he finds the developer gave him the wrong pictures.

Episode 4: June 17, 1995 "The Beeper"

Director: Pamela Fryman   Writer: David Sacks

When Ellen learns that she may deliver their baby early, Jack gets a beeper but loses it and has to buy another one, which he loses as well. Jack purchases another beeper which is the same model the sales clerk owns since his wife is also pregnant. When Jack's new beeper goes off, he thinks Ellen is in labor. However, it turns out that he picked up the sales clerk's beeper by mistake, and it is the clerk's wife for whom Jack helps to deliver the baby. Meanwhile, Artie is filling in for Jack at the radio station, and, attempting to be a shock jock, he offends guest Bubba Smith on the air.

Episode 5: June 24, 1995 "Gimme a R-Y-A-N"

Director: Pamela Fryman   Writer: Lee Aronsohn

Ryan is dating a cheerleader who is a year older than he and is already driving. Ellen is concerned that the cheerleader is too sophisticated for Ryan, but, when Ryan informs Jack that he wants to break up with the girl since she is older, Jack talks him out of it. He suggests that Ryan invite his girlfriend and her friends to the house, while he takes Ellen out to dinner and Molly is at a sleepover. After they return home, Jack and Ellen find that Ryan took their station wagon and left with the girl. Ryan's girlfriend tells him that they have to break up. Jack and Ellen go looking for Ryan and find him alone in the station wagon. Jack apologizes to Ryan for leaving him under the impression that it was all right to take the car even though he was too young to drive.

Matthew Lawrence (Ryan) is the middle brother of actors Joey and Andrew Lawrence.

Episode 6: Unaired   "The Contest"

Director: Pamela Fryman   Writers: Rob Kurtz and Eric Brand

When Jack is asked to emcee the Ms. Sportbody Contest in Atlantic City, Ellen says the entire family should attend with him. After arriving, Jack finds that Ellen has decided to enter the contest as Ms. Bella Vista and that his daughter will be appearing on stage with him to deliver the cards containing the contestants' introductions. Ellen indicates that she will bow out of the contest only if Jack says it is degrading to women. He finally admits the contest is sexist, but the head of the contest will not let pregnant Ellen drop out. Jack gets into a fight with an audience member who comments on Molly tripping on stage when she is delivering cards to Jack. The fight ends the contest before Ellen can appear.

Last Minute Change

It's not a good sign for a sitcom's longevity when the network, at the last minute, decides against premiering the show. Originally, ABC was to debut *Bringing Up Jack* on Wednesdays at 8:30 PM on March 28, 1995 but decided to shelve the series until that summer.[36] ABC thought that moving the sitcom *Coach* to Wednesdays would deliver a larger audience than *Bringing Up Jack*. However, according to Gallagher, the real reason his comedy was removed from ABC's spring schedule was to embarrass Brandon Stoddard, the head of ABC Studios that produced the series. When the show finally did air, ABC scheduled it on low-viewing Saturday nights; the sitcom's debut ranked seventy-seventh and the third episode sank to ninetieth. The show aired five low-rated episodes.

Jack Gallagher returned to stand-up comedy after his sitcom was canceled. He later developed another one-man show called "Just the Guy" around his experiences with ABC in developing *Bringing Up Jack*. Harley Jane Kozak became an author, having written four novels to date.

Fathers and Sons

Premiered Sunday, April 6, 1986 at 7:30 PM on NBC

This comedy looked at the relationships of a group of young boys among each other and with their parents. The star of *Fathers and Sons*, the late Merlin Olsen, was a former pro-football player known for his roles in the NBC series *Little House on the Prairie* and *Father Murphy*. On *Fathers and Sons*, Olsen played Buddy Landau, a construction worker and ex-athlete, who coached various little league teams and was married to Ellen (Kelly Sanders). Buddy's twelve-year-old son Lanny (Jason Late), slightly overweight, participated on the teams coached by his dad together with his friends Sean Flynn (Andre Gower, *Baby Makes Five*), whose father was divorced; Matt Bolen (Ian Fried), whose busy dad, Dr. Richard Bolen (Nicholas Guest), was not able to spend as much time with him as he would have liked, and Brandon Russo (Hakeem Abdul-Samad), whose father was a cop.

Background

Nick Arnold and Michael Zinberg created *Fathers and Sons*, a single-camera comedy with a laugh track, which was produced by American Flyer Television in association with Twentieth Century-Fox. The pilot aired on NBC in June 1985 and dealt with the Bolen's son, Matt, suspecting his parents were about to divorce. Sean warned Matt not to be alone with his dad because his father would deliver a heart-to-heart talk about separation. All of the boys, along with their fathers except Brandon's dad, who was working, met at the Bolen's beach house to discuss the situation. In the pilot, Sean's dad Michael (Rick Nelson, *Ozzie and Harriet*), a realtor, dropped his son off at the beach house and didn't pick him up until the next day. The kids weren't successful in keeping Dr. Bolen from talking with Matt. He told his son about the separation, but then, after advice from Buddy Landau, the doctor spent the rest of the weekend with Matt.

RAISING KIDS AND MAKING ENDS MEET

Episode Guide: 4 aired episodes

Episode 1: April 6, 1986   "The Ironman"

Director: Michael Zinberg   Writer: Nick Arnold

Evan, a paraplegic student is trying out for the wrestling team along with Sean and Lanny. Sean befriends Evan who gets really upset when the wrestling coach (Bert Rosario) cuts him from the final team because the coach is afraid that Evan will injure himself in a real match. Buddy talks with the coach and gets Evan added to the team, but he refuses to join because he now thinks everyone feels sorry for him. Buddy enlists the aid of pro-wrestler Ironman (Tony Longo) to encourage Evan to become a member of the team.

Episode 2: April 13, 1986   "We'll Always Have the Mall"

Director: Will Mackenzie   Writer: Nick Arnold

Lanny is infatuated with Rebecca (Natalie Gregory), a pretty girl at school, and wants to get to know her better. After a kickball game, Rebecca asks Lanny to take her to the mall on Saturday – the same day that Buddy has tickets for a basketball playoff game. Lanny tells his dad that he would rather go with Rebecca than attend the game. After a nice day at the mall, Rebecca informs Lanny that she and her family are going to move to Texas and then kisses him.

Episode 3: April 27, 1986   "Desperately Seeking Einstein"

Director: Robert L. McCullough   Writers: Randall Zisk and Michael Zinberg

The science club at school is sponsoring a father-son competition in their science fair. Buddy and Lanny are working on a computer program about exercise and weight gain, and each of Lanny's friends has their own project which they are developing with their fathers except for Sean whose dad is skiing in Colorado. Ellen suggests that all the boys work on a team project with Buddy coaching them, but the guys are reluctant to do this at first. Buddy encourages them to help Sean which they eventually do. They enter a project combining aspects of the separate projects they did using a robot, ball, and track that sets off a volcanic eruption.

Episode 4: May 4, 1986 "Which Championship Season?"

Director: Peter Baldwin   Writer: Nick Arnold

Buddy is coaching his son's basketball team. If the team wins one more game, they will be in the championship. Buddy encourages everyone on the team to play, but his friends from high school, who have returned to town for a reunion, disagree with his coaching method. They suggest that Buddy just have the best players in the game. Coach Landau begins training his team harder for the championship and replaces his son and Brandon with better players. Lanny resigns from the team, while the rest of the players have a meeting without Buddy and decide that he needs to change his coaching methods. After he reads Lanny's resignation note, Buddy asks his son to come back and decides to go back to the "buddy system" of allowing everyone to play.

A Quick Disappearance

While the pilot that aired in June 1985 rated fairly well, the subsequent four episodes did not, and NBC did not pick up the series.

Free Country

Premiered Saturday, June 24, 1978, at 8:00 PM on ABC

Rob Reiner starred in this comedy-drama as Joseph Bresner, a Lithuanian immigrant, married to Anna (Judy Kahan) who struggled to adapt to the United States and start a family. Each episode of the series began with Reiner as eighty-nine-year-old Joseph reminiscing about the time he and later his wife came to this country and settled on the Lower East Side of New York City. The series would then flashback to the young Bresner and his wife; their neighbors, Sidney Gewertzman (Fred McCarren) and his wife Ida (Renee Lippin); their friend, Louis Peschi (Joe Pantoliano) who worked in the basement of the Bresner's apartment building alongside Joseph, and Leo Gold (Larry Gelman), a boarder who worked at a newspaper and slept in their dining room.

Background

After leaving *All in the Family*, Rob Reiner signed a contract with ABC to produce series and specials. One result of the contract was *Free Country* created by Reiner and Phil Mishkin. The character of Joseph Bresner was an amalgam of both Reiner and Mishkin's grandfathers. The overall concept of the comedy-drama was to document the history of an immigrant family in America with each season of the series dealing with a decade in the immigrant family's life. Reiner hoped that the series would cover seventy years over seven seasons in the life of the Bresner family.[37] *Free Country* began with the first decade of the twentieth century when Anna arrived in this country and the Bresner's decided to start a family. The Reiner/Mishkin Co. in association with Columbia Pictures produced the series.

Episode Guide: 5 aired episodes

Episode 1: June 24, 1978   "Anna's Arrival"

Director: Hal Cooper   Writers: Rob Reiner and Phil Mishkin

Initially, only Joseph had enough money for passage to America. He saved for two years to bring his wife Anna to the United States. He had paid his cousin Willie to book Anna in second class so she would not have to pass a medical exam upon entry. However, he finds that Anna was booked in steerage and failed to pass the physical because of her poor eyesight. She is placed in holding, and Joseph has to come up with a $25 bond for her to be released. He goes to Willie for the money, but his cousin doesn't have any cash. Joseph takes his clothes and other stuff to pawn to get the needed money.

Episode 2: July 1, 1978   "Anna's Adjustment"

Director: James Burrows   Writer: Earl Pomerantz

Anna keeps talking about the old country which irritates Joseph. She has second thoughts about coming to America and is afraid to leave their apartment by herself. Joseph encourages her to go outside, and she finally does. When Joseph comes home, Anna isn't there, and he becomes upset. She eventually comes back to the apartment and says she is fine and enjoyed being out.

Episode 3: July 8, 1978   "Citizenship"

Director: James Burrows   Writers: Arnold Kane and Sy Rosen

Joseph and Anna are attending a courthouse ceremony for him to become an American citizen. Before the judge, Joseph says that he was part of a revolutionary group in Lithuania, and the judge indicates that an investigation may be needed before Joseph can become a citizen. He is afraid that he may be deported. Later, back before the same judge, Joseph learns that he will not be deported and that he will indeed become a U.S. citizen.

This was one of the first sitcom episodes directed by James Burrows who credits Rob Reiner with helping him become a director. Burrows indicated that *Free Country* was "too smart for the room."[38]

Episode 4: July 15, 1978   "When Already?"

Director: Hal Cooper   Story: Rob Reiner and Phil Mishkin   Teleplay: Earl Pomerantz

Anna is upset that Joseph is a demanding lover, and the couple hasn't had sex for three months. They each seek advice from their friends about lovemaking. Joseph tells Anna that he loves her, they kiss, and three months later Anna finds she is pregnant.

Episode 5: July 22, 1978   "Special Delivery"

Director: James Burrows   Writer: Sy Rosen

Anna is about ready to give birth. She wants Ida, who is a midwife, to deliver the baby, but Joseph wants her to have a doctor. When Anna goes into labor sooner than expected, Joseph has trouble finding Ida and has to deliver the baby himself. The baby is a boy whom they name Arthur.

A Saga that Never Happened

Reiner never got the chance to make *Free Country* a saga about the Bresner family. At the time, he also wanted to work with a publisher to turn *Free Country* into a series of novels each dealing with ten years in the life of the family. Low ratings killed the series.

Love and Marriage

Premiered Saturday, September 28, 1996 at 9:30 PM on Fox

Still attempting to find the right companion for *Married with Children*, Fox scheduled *Love and Marriage* on Saturdays at 9:30 PM when *Married with Children* moved to 9:00 PM on that day. *Love and Marriage* revolved around a waitress and a parking garage manager married to each other for seventeen years with three kids. The wife, April Nardini (Patricia Healy), worked nights, while the husband, Jack (Tony Denison), worked days. The couple still attempted to find time for each other as they struggled to make ends meet. Their children were eleven-year-old Christopher (Adam Zolotin), who liked to act tough and cut his classes, sixteen-year-old Gemmy (Alicia Bergman), who was in to dyed hair and body piercing, and seventeen-year-old Michael (Erik Palladino), who worked five jobs while attending junior college in hopes of earning enough money to move out. In contrast to the Nardini family, their new neighbors were the "perfect" Begg family – Trudy (Megan Fay); her husband, Louis (Michael Mantell), and their eleven-year-old son, Max (Adam Wylie). Trudy was the perfect stay-at-home wife and mother.

Background

Love and Marriage was originally called *Come Fly with Me*, but the estate of Sammy Cahn who wrote the song "Come Fly with Me" wanted too much money for use of the title and song.[39] The theme song was changed to "Love on Pocket Change." Amy Sherman Palladino, who created, wrote, and produced the series, would subsequently create the *Gilmore Girls* and then the unsuccessful sitcom *The*

Return of Jezebel James. Dorothy Parker Drank Here Productions in association with TriStar Television produced *Love and Marriage*.

Episode Guide: 2 Aired; 7 Unaired

Episode 1: September 28, 1996   "Pilot"

Director: Robert Berlinger   Writer: Amy Sherman Palladino

Jack and April try to make time for each other on their wedding anniversary. After discussing the monthly bills and scolding Christopher for skipping classes again, they are invited to dinner at their new neighbors, and, much to April's dismay, Jack accepts. At dinner, while Jack finds he has little in common with Louis, April finds Trudy to be interesting. Trudy volunteers to walk Christopher to school with her son. Jack tells April that she may not be perfect but that she is a great mom.

Episode 2: October 5, 1996   "Look Who's Talking Now"

Director: Max Tash   Writer: Lois Bromfield

When April and Jack see a boy coming out of Gemmy's room, they hope it is not too late for a talk about sex. Jack says he wants to be there for the talk but then chickens out. Gemmy tells her mom that she knows about sex from TV and school. April replies that she is there for Gemmy, and Gemmy says that if there is something happening, she will discuss it with her mother. In the meantime, Jack and April are afraid their power will be turned off because Jack forgot to pay the electric bill.

Episode 3: Unaired   "Ain't No Way to Treat a Lady"

Director: Max Tash   Writer: Mike Martineau

Michael's girlfriend, Kathleen, wants to celebrate their six-month anniversary of dating. She gives him a heart charm that he doesn't particularly care for and says that she is looking forward to their one year anniversary. Michael wants to break up with her because she is too possessive. He doesn't want to marry at an early age like his parents did. Michael finally tells her that he wants to break off their relationship.

She cries and asks for her charm back. Meanwhile, Max and Christopher are playing spy games and think that a man in the neighborhood has murdered his mother.

Episode 4: Unaired   "Up All Night"

Director: Gail Mancuso   Writer: Amy Sherman Palladino

Trudy wants April to babysit Max so she can have a romantic evening with her husband. Jack has had a bad day at work when a customer accused him of taking money from his car's ash tray and complained to Jack's boss after Jack shoved him. When April says Jack needs to better control his temper and Jack asserts that April is babying Chris, they both argue. April won't go to bed until they make up, and so Jack finally apologizes for how he acted at work.

Episode 5: Unaired   "Here's a Case Where Thomas Wolfe Was Wrong"

Director: Gail Mancuso   Writer: Elaine Arata

Michael announces that he is moving into a friend's apartment which surprises his parents. Jack agrees to let him move, but April is none too happy. When April and Jack make an unannounced visit to Michael's new place, he says they need to respect his privacy. Jack and April concur that they can have a whole other life after all their kids move out, but then Michael moves back since the place he was staying turned out to be his friend's mother's apartment.

Erik Palladino (Michael) later starred as Dr. Dave Malucci on *ER*.

Episode 6: Unaired   "Family Business"

Director: Max Tash   Writer: Sue Tenney

The family is going away for the day to help Tony (Joe Santos), Jack's father, with his parking lot. Jack is concerned that his dad is still managing the lot at age sixty-five with no help from Jack's brother Vic. Jack and his father argue about him retiring, and Jack volunteers to take over the lot without first consulting April. April is upset at the news. Jack asks Vic to help run the lot, and his brother reluctantly agrees.

Episode 7: Unaired   "Back to School Fight"

Director: Jody Margolin   Writer: Moe Jelline

Christopher is in trouble at his school again when he beats up Spencer, a kid who bullied Max. Chris is suspended from school but doesn't want Max to say anything about the incident to his parents. At a back-to-school night, April and Jack try to find out what happened. The bully's parents tell April and Jack that Christopher sucker punched their kid from behind. The two couples argue and start to brawl. Max then explains to Chris' parents what happened. Meanwhile, Gemmy and Michael argue over his smoking cigarettes, and Michael tells her he will quit.

Episode 8: Unaired   "Play Kristi for Me"

Director: John Squeglia   Writer: Elaine Arata

April invites Trudy and Louis to play pool with them, while Gemmy babysits Max who becomes infatuated with her. April and Jack don't have much fun with their neighbors until Trudy gets drunk. Also, April finds that Kristi, the waitress at the pool hall, is flirting with Jack in front of her. April leaves Jack at the table to see if the waitress will hit on him. When she does, Jack tells Kristi that he is the wrong guy for her, and April comes and kisses him.

Episode 9: Unaired   "Sick at Home"

Director: Jody Margolin   Writer: Mike Gandolfi

April and Jack are sick in bed and at the mercy of their kids. Jack doesn't like the fact that Gemmy is working nights even though he has no problem with Michael doing the same. While Jack is sick, his brother Vic is helping out at the parking garage and ends up letting a car get stolen. Meanwhile, at the used clothes store where Gemmy is working, when her co-worker's boyfriend (Eric Balfour) tries to hold up the place, his gun accidentally discharges. Gemmy covers for her co-worker with the police but then Gemmy fires her, and the police capture her boyfriend. After that experience, Michael comes by the store at night to accompany his sister home.

Marriage Annulled

The premiere episode of *Love and Marriage* ranked ninety-eighth out of 107 shows, while the second and last episode of the series ranked eighty-first out of 104 series. The series lost 39 percent of adults aged eighteen to forty-nine from its lead-in, *Married with Children*.

The O'Keefes

Premiered Thursday, May 22, 2003, at 8:30 PM on the WB

Home-schooled kids going off to public school and experiencing the outside world was the subject of *The O'Keefes*. Judge Reinhold played Harry O'Keefe, the veterinarian dad who, apparently because he was bullied in school, decided to home-school his kids; Kristin Nelson was the mother, Ellie O'Keefe. The idealistic parents were so worried about the effect of "mindless popular culture" on their three children that they taught them at home and did not let them have much contact with the "real" world, including not being permitted to watch TV. However, the two oldest children, Danny (Joseph Cross) and Lauren (Tania Raymonde), persuaded their father to let them attend public school and work at the local mall, while the youngest sibling Mark (Matt Weinberg) was still home-schooled. The kids were very intelligent, had extensive knowledge of literature, music, art, science and world events, and spoke several languages. But as much knowledge as they had, they still had a lot to learn about the outside world, particularly about interacting with other kids.

Background

Created by Mark O'Keefe, the sitcom was based on his upbringing as a home-schooled kid. Mark had two other brothers – Larry and Daniel. For the series, Larry became the daughter named Lauren, while the two boy characters were named after Mark and his other brother Danny. The series, initially called *Brave New World*, was produced by Turner Television.

Episode Guide: 5 aired; 3 unaired

Episode 1: May 22, 2003   "Pilot"

Director: Andy Ackerman   Writer: Mark O'Keefe

When the O'Keefe family attends a book sale at the public school, Danny and Lauren become curious about interacting with other kids their age. After overhearing their conversation wishing for more social interaction, Ellie tries to convince Harry to let Danny and Lauren attend public school. The kids compose essays about why they think high school would benefit them, but Harry only agrees to let them go to school when Ellie withholds sex from him. In the end, even though Harry has misgivings, he comes to realize that public school makes his kids happier and more socially adjusted.

Episode 2: May 29, 2003   "Election" (summary based on table draft script)

Director: Bryan Gordon   Writers: Jennifer Konner and Alexandria Rushfield

Lauren decides to run for student body president against the incumbent Stephanie because she feels that Stephanie is ignoring issues of concern to many students. Lauren discovers that Stephanie's campaign posters have been defaced. The principal blames Lauren and tells her that she and her brother will be kicked out of school if something like this happens again. Later, Lauren catches Stephanie defacing her own posters, but Lauren covers for her because she doesn't play dirty politics. In the end, since the election is too close to call, the principal names both Lauren and Stephanie as co-presidents.

Episode 3: June 5, 2003   "Substitute Teacher"

Director: Joanna Kearns   Writer: Craig DiGregorio

Harry volunteers to substitute teach biology at Lauren and Danny's school and uses their personal lives in his lesson plans. After the school offers Harry a permanent teaching position, his family tries to convince him to return to his veterinary practice and to home-schooling Matt.

Joanna Kearns, who directed this episode, formerly starred on *Growing Pains*

Episode 4: June 12, 2003   "Football"

Director: Gil Junger   Writer: Craig DiGregorio

Danny joins the football team to seek the attention of a beautiful cheerleader, and Lauren becomes an honorary cheerleader. She persuades the cheerleading squad to pay less attention to football and more attention to school issues, which forces Danny to choose between his status as a jock and his sister's well-being. Meanwhile, the family makes preparations for the O'Keefe Roman Games.

Episode 5: June 12, 2003   "Jobs"

Director: Gerry Cohen   Writer: Paul Ruehl

Lauren and Danny get jobs at the local mall. Lauren's co-worker sets her up as a thief, while Danny's boss takes advantage of Danny's salesmanship. The entire family works together to correct these wrongs.

Episode 6: Unaired   "Festival of Birth"

Director: Gil Junger   Writer: Mark O'Keefe

Instead of celebrating individual birthdays, Henry has created an annual family celebration known as the "Festival of Birth." Lauren and Danny want to have some friends from school attend the celebration. Harry allows them to each invite one friend, but Lauren's friend Nicole brings several kids from school. The kids find aspects of the celebration strange, like singing a song about the different varieties of festive pies and listening to recordings of the births of Danny and Lauren. Danny is embarrassed and tells his dad that he is too weird to have friends and perhaps should go back to being schooled at home. Harry says he should not give up on public school, and Lauren points out that all holidays have strange aspects. In the end, everyone at the party starts dancing together.

Mark O'Keefe's father had invented a private family holiday called "Festivus" which was the basis for the classic *Seinfeld* episode. Mark's brother Danny wrote that *Seinfeld* episode.

Episode 7: Unaired   "Lauren's Date"

Director: Gil Junger   Writers: Tom Saunders and Kell Cahoon

Lauren is asked out on her first date. Her friends come over to the house to help her get ready and to give her advice, which she doesn't accept. Ellie catches Harry trying to spy on Lauren and her date at a pizza parlor. Eventually, however, Harry learns to trust Lauren. Her date likes Lauren because she is different from other girls, and he wants to have their second date at the O'Keefe home.

Kristin Nelson went on to play the police chief on *Psych*.

Episode 8: Unaired   "Party"

Director: Gerry Cohen   Writer: Kevin Murphy

Lauren and Danny go to a party with other teens. Harry will only let them attend if they contact him every hour on an old walkie-talkie. When they arrive at the party, they learn that the adult chaperone drank too much and is unconscious. All of the partygoers get drunk except for Lauren, her new friend, Danny, and a girl he likes. Harry, Ellie, and Matt sneak into the party to check on Danny and Lauren and are proud of their good conduct.

At Last, a Judge Reinhold Sitcom that Aired

Originally scheduled as a midseason replacement, *The O'Keefes* was delayed until the summer, when five episodes were burned off over a four-week period—the last two episodes were aired back-to-back. The premiere episode ranked eighty-fifth, at the bottom of the Nielsen's. However, unlike two other comedies in which Judge Reinhold starred – *Raising Caines* (see below) and *Secret Service Guy* (Chapter 10) which were never broadcast, at least *The O'Keefes* did air for a few weeks.

Many critics liked *The O'Keefes*. The *Pittsburgh Post-Gazette* called it "...an imaginative, funny comedy about pop culture-hating parents who home-schooled their children."[40] However, the Home School Legal Defense Association, apparently not known for its sense of humor, said that "'The O'Keefes' goes out of its way to reinforce almost every negative myth about homeschooling."[41] They did not like the fact that the kids were portrayed as intelligent but socially inept.

Raising Caines

Supposed to premiere midseason 1995-96 on NBC

The pitfalls of raising kids was the premise of this comedy which starred Mel Harris and Judge Reinhold as Julie and Steven Caine, parents of four children ranging in age from six to fifteen, who lived in Cincinnati, Ohio. Steven, a former architect who had lost his business in an economic downturn, was now selling cars. Julie was taking college courses to complete a degree. Supporting characters included Doc (Barry Corbin), the grandfather, and the Caines children, Riley (Christopher Petrosino), Samantha (Katie Volding), Michael (Dan Sarfati), and Trish (Michelle Williams, *Brokeback Mountain, My Week with Marilyn*). The opening and closing of each episode was narrated by one of the regular characters.

Background

Bob Brush, who had produced *The Wonder Years*, created *Raising Caines*, which was originally conceived as a one hour comedy-drama. Harry Morgan of *M*A*S*H* played the grandfather in the one-hour pilot, and James Naughton was the dad. Their roles were recast when the series became a thirty-minute filmed comedy with no laugh track. The pilot had storylines about each of the Caines: fifteen-year-old Trish dated a junior who crashed her dad's new Mustang; Riley's teacher wanted him to be tested to determine what made his thought processes so unique; Michael tried to impress a new girl at school by playing an electric guitar outside her house at night, and dad accidentally killed Samantha's goldfish for which the family held a funeral. NBC ordered six episodes of the series, which was produced by TriStar

Television. As described below, several episodes were based on the storylines in the pilot.

Episode Guide: 6 unaired episodes

Episode 1: "Venus"

Director: Steve Miner   Writer: Bob Brush

Samantha is the planet Venus in a school play about the solar system. Julie is assigned the task of making her costume, while Steven, who discovers he has no film of his youngest daughter, wants to tape her performance. After trying to make the costume, Julie decides to rent one and finds an angel costume for Sam. Steven buys a new VHS camera when he can't fix his old one, but, at the last minute, finds that he forgot to purchase videotape. He commandeers videotape from the closed-circuit cameras at a convenience store and arrives late at the school after the play has begun. Sam, who can't remember her lines, improvises when she sees her dad with the camera.

Episode 2: "Fathers and Daughters"

Director: Thom Eberhardt   Writer: Bob Brush

Trish wants to go on a date with an older boy named Buck she met in a supermarket parking lot. Steven doesn't want her to date Buck but finally relents. However, instead of allowing Buck to use his own four-wheel drive vehicle, Steven gives him the keys to his classic VW convertible. When Buck takes Trish to the party, she sees her regular boyfriend and wants to be taken back home. After Buck wrecks the father's VW, Steven tells him to leave quickly. However, Steven says to Trish that he still loves her.

Episode 3: "The Goldfish"

Director: Steve Miner   Writer: Bob Brush

Sam's pet goldfish Thumper is sick and, in the process of cleaning the fish bowl, Steven drops the goldfish on the kitchen floor where the family dog gulps it down.

Not wanting to tell Sam about the incident, Steven buys another fish, but Sam recognizes it is not Thumper. She discovers Thumper is dead when the dog spits it out. The parents explain what happened, and they conduct a funeral for the dead fish. Meanwhile, Riley is worried that grown-ups are not telling the truth about the hole in the ozone layer. He is afraid that he will be transported to Jupiter through the hole until he is reassured by his dad.

Episode 4: "Tested"

Director: Rodman Flender   Story: Bob Brush   Teleplay: Bob Brush and Robert Rabinowitz

Steven and Julie have to attend a parent-teacher conference about Riley. The teacher says that Riley is a loner and a dreamer. Because he wrote an essay about Peter Rabbit in "rabbit" talk, the teacher would like to have him tested. Steven and Julie debate whether or not to allow this. They go to the library to do research and argue over the issue. Eventually, when Riley writes a letter to his parents that is the story of Peter Rabbit in regular English, Steven and Julie abandon the idea of having him tested.

Episode 5: "Science"

Director: Steve Miner   Writer: Bob Brush

Michael wants dad to help with his science project, which he forgot about until the last minute. Because Steven has to complete an inventory at the car dealership where he works on the same day as the due date for the science project, he initially advises Michael that he can't help him. Michael has to build a machine with at least one moving part. Steven comes up with the plans for the machine, but Michael still needs assistance. Eventually, Steven builds the machine for Michael. The machine uses a golf ball to ring a bell. When the family's dog, Darth, breaks the project right before it is due, Steven and Michael have to repair it with tape. They take it to school only to find that the other students have much more elaborate projects. However, Michael receives an A on his project since the teacher felt he was the only kid whose father didn't help him build it.

Episode 6: "Up All Night"

Director: Steve Miner   Story: Bob Brush   Teleplay: Bob Brush and Robert Rabinowitz

Mom and dad are trying to put all the kids to bed, but various events interfere with this task. Samantha loses a tooth and expects a silver dollar for it. However, Steven can't find a silver dollar, spills a bag of pennies he is trying to put under Sam's pillow, and loses her tooth in the sink. He calls a plumber in the middle of the night to get the tooth out of the sink's drain. Trish is listening to the radio hoping that she will be on the list of the hottest girls in school which some senior boys made up, but, after listening to the radio for hours, she is disappointed when her name is not mentioned. Riley is not sleeping because he watched the movie *Jurassic Park* and thinks raptors are under his bed. Finally, everyone gets to bed around 4:00 AM only to have the dog wake up the kids.

The Caines Mystery

TriStar Television claimed it never knew why NBC failed to air *Raising Caines*. NBC would say only that the series would be evaluated later to determine if and when it would be scheduled, but it never was.[42]

704 Hauser

Premiered Monday, April 11, 1994 *at* 8:30 PM on CBS

704 Hauser centered on Ernie and Rose Cumberbatch, a black couple, their twenty-three-year-old son, Goodie (named after Supreme Court Justice Thurgood Marshall), and the son's white, Jewish girlfriend, Cherlyn Markowitz (Maura Tierney). Ernie (John Amos) was a Vietnam veteran, a master mechanic at an auto repair shop, and a union member; his wife Rose (Lynnie Godfrey) was a churchgoing woman and worked as a caterer, and conservative Goodie (T.E. Russell) lived at home and was the leader of a group of Young Republicans.

Background

704 Hauser was the address for the Archie Bunker residence of *All in the Family* fame. Because the producer of *All in the Family*, Norman Lear, still had the sets from that series, he decided to develop a new sitcom around them. *704 Hauser* was an imitation of *All in the Family* with a twist. It was similar to *All in the Family* in that it emphasized the intergenerational conflict between young and old and the conflict between liberal and conservative. However, the conflict on *704 Hauser* was between a liberal father and a conservative son—not, as on *All in the Family*, between a conservative father and liberal son-in-law, and the cast was black—not white as on *All in the Family*. In the original unaired pilot for *704 Hauser*, Jennifer Lewis was cast as Jenny, a friend of Rose's, who Rose invited, along with her husband, Murray (George Wallace), to see Goodie on *Face the Nation*. Murray, who was caught between Ernie and Goodie in an argument about Supreme Court Justice Clarence Thomas, talked about reconciliation between people with opposing beliefs. When the pilot was re-shot, the characters of Jenny and Murray were eliminated, and the role of the character Joey Stivic was expanded to be the man in the middle between Ernie and Goodie's discussion of Judge Thomas as described below. *704 Hauser* was produced by Act III and Castle Rock.

Episode Guide: 5 aired; 1 unaired

Episode 1: April 11, 1994 "Meet the Cumberbatch's"

Director: Norman Lear   Story: Norman Lear   Teleplay: Norman Lear and Kevin Heelan

The first episode opened much like the premiere episode of *All in the Family* with the parents at church and Goodie and his girlfriend at home alone. She would like to make love with Goodie, but he is sworn to abstinence. (In *All in the Family*, the character of Mike Stivic took no such oath). Goodie is to appear on *Face the Nation*. Joey Stivic makes an appearance as Mike and Gloria's son from *All in the Family* who comes to 704 Hauser to look at the home where he was born. In the meantime, when the parents return from church, Ernie and Goodie begin to argue over their respective political beliefs and in particular the views of Justice Clarence Thomas, with Joey Stivic caught in the middle of the argument. When *Face the Nation* comes on, Goodie says that his parents taught him to be an independent thinker and that he admires his dad but not his dad's politics.

Episode 2: April 18, 1994   "Here's Why Ernie Should Never Be Left Alone"

Director: Jack Shea   Writers: Roger Shulman and John Baskin

Goodie is attending a hockey game with his girlfriend, and while everyone else in the house is out except Ernie, an encyclopedia salesperson comes to the door. Because she is a black conservative like Goodie, Ernie thinks Goodie might be interested in her and drop Cherlyn as his girlfriend. He invites the salesperson to come back later. After an argument with Cherlyn, Goodie comes home and meets the salesperson. However, Cherlyn appears, and the two kiss and make up. Rose and Cherlyn argue with the salesperson about the credibility of Anita Hill's testimony at the Clarence Thomas' hearings, with the salesperson and Ernie thinking Anita Hill was not telling the truth and Rose and Cherlyn believing the opposite.

Episode 3: April 25, 1994   "Ernie Live on Tape"

Director: Jack Shea   Writer: Janet Lynn Jackson

When Rose wants Ernie to get a new suit for church, he and Goodie go to a department store. Ernie comes back from shopping without buying anything because the store's security guard kept following him around which he thinks was an incident of racial harassment. Goodie says that the guard was just doing his job and that his dad is paranoid. Cherlyn, whose parents know the store's owner, gets a copy of the surveillance tape which shows the guard following Ernie while a white woman shoplifts, and also shows Goodie trying to explain his dad's reaction to the guard. Ernie still feels it was a case of racial harassment.

Episode 4: May 2, 1994   "Tristaidekaphobia"

Director: Jack Shea   Writers: Greg Cope and Sean Dwyer

Ernie and Rose are going to Philadelphia for Rose's cousin's wedding on Friday the thirteenth leaving Goodie alone in the house. Cherlyn comes over all dressed up to tempt Goodie into having sex with her, but Goodie is practicing abstinence.

Goodie has invited one of Cherlyn's friends over so the three of them could watch a video. Before the friend arrives, Cherlyn is ready to leave, but then Goodie agrees to have sex with her. Ernie and Rose come back to the house after missing their train to Philadelphia because someone bumped into Ernie's car. When Cherlyn's friend finally comes to the house, she turns out to be the one who ran into Ernie's vehicle. In the end, Cherlyn decides that Goodie is not yet ready to have sex with her.

Maura Tierney went on to *Newsradio, ER,* and *The Whole Truth.*

Episode 5: May 9, 1994   "All That Jasmine"

Director: Jack Shea   Writer: Andrea Allen

Rose's successful, globe-trotting sister, Jasmine, arrives for a surprise visit before Rose's birthday. Ernie had planned to take Rose to Brooklyn where they got married, but Jasmine gives Rose a round trip ticket to Paris for the weekend as a birthday gift. Rose still wants to go with Ernie, but he insists she go to Paris with her sister. When Jasmine's boyfriend calls, Ernie overhears him telling Jasmine that he found another woman and is breaking up with her. Ernie convinces Rose that her sister needs her now and that she should go to Paris because they can always go to Brooklyn some other time.

Episode 6: Unaired   "Revelations"

Director: Jack Shea   Writer: Walter Allen Bennett Jr.

Ernie finds a way to save on his taxes. He becomes Reverend Ernie and turns his garage into a sanctuary.

Another "Falloff" Victim

704 Hauser was on Mondays as a temporary replacement for *Dave's World* and as a lead-in to *Murphy Brown*. Because of the falloff in ratings from its lead-in, *Evening Shade*, and the uptick in ratings from *Murphy Brown* which followed it, *704 Hauser* was canceled after five of six planned episodes had aired. Overall, the sitcom ranked fortieth for the 1993-94 TV season.

Tall Hopes

Premiered Wednesday, August 25, 1993 at 8:30 PM on CBS

Dealing with the theme of getting ahead by athletic ability versus education, *Tall Hopes* was about an African-American family—a dad, mom, two teenage sons, and a six-year-old daughter, living in Philadelphia. The oldest son, Chet "the Jet" Harris (Terence Howard), was a heavily recruited high school basketball player; the younger son, Earnest (Kenn Michael aka Kenny Blank), would rather shoot videos than hoops. Earnest opened each episode speaking directly into the camera about what was to transpire, and, at the end, he summed up what had happened. Their father George (comedian George Wallace), was a transit cop, and their mother Lainie (Anna Maria Horsford), the family disciplinarian and a court stenographer. The young daughter in the family was Deedee (Karla Green). *Tall Hopes* was one of the few sitcoms on CBS in the early 1990s that pictured an intact working-class black family.

Background

The team who had developed the comedy *Head of the Class*, Rich Eustis and Michael Elias, created *Tall Hopes*. According to Michael Elias, they wanted to do a show about what would happen in a family with a "Michael Jordan" character and a "Spike Lee" character as brothers.[43] Eustis/Elias Productions in association with Warner Bros. Television produced the series.

Episode Guide: 3 aired; 3 unaired

Episode 1: August 25, 1993   "Pilot"

Director: Sam Weisman   Writers: Rich Eustis and Michael Elias

Chet talks Earnest into doing his homework for him so that he and his dad can go to a basketball game. Part of dad's bribe for Earnest to do Chet's homework involves a new pair of expensive sneakers. However, Lainie puts an end to the scheme and busts all involved.

Episode 2: September 1, 1993   "Get the Jet" (summary based on revised table draft script)

Director: Linda Day   Story: David Mulligan   Teleplay: Jerry Colker

After Ernest mentions to his parents that he likes a girl from school; his dad says he has to work up the nerve to talk to her. Ernest makes a video confessing his love, but doesn't want anyone to see it. The next day, Ernest asks the girl to come over to his house. When he leaves the room, Chet shows the video to the girl embarrassing Ernest. To get revenge, Ernest writes a letter that looks like it is from the Temple University basketball coach telling Chet that the school is no longer considering him for its team. Chet becomes depressed, and George calls the coach to chew him out. Ernest feels bad for what he did and tells his mom who makes him call the coach and explain what happened. Temple sends a new letter to Chet advising him to ignore the previous one. The next night George informs Ernest that he saw the letter he wrote on his computer and warns him not to do something like that again. He also advises Ernest to keep the lie between them just like his mother told him.

Episode 3: September 8, 1993   "Will Work for Credit" (summary based on revised table draft script)

Director: Robert Berlinger   Writer: Michael Anthony Snowden

George announces that the family's credit card bills have gotten out of hand and that he wants all the cards destroyed. Lainie says that means no anniversary presents which makes George realize that their anniversary is the next day. George gives Chet the one remaining credit card to go to a department store and pick out an inexpensive gift for Lainie. Chet ends up buying a pair of slippers for his mother and a new CD boom box for himself. Chet tells his mom that his dad bought an anniversary present but it is a surprise. When Lainie uses the credit card to buy George a gift, the card is rejected because the purchase would exceed the credit limit. Lainie assumes the gift George has for her must be expensive to max out the card, and so she uses her spare cash to buy him a present. George sees that Lainie must be buying something expensive for him since her spare cash is missing. He asks Ernest to give him the money that Ernest was saving for a film workshop. When George and Lainie exchange gifts, neither of them really likes their presents, and now no one has any money. Lainie makes them return all the gifts. They realize that neither maxed out the credit card, and it was Chet who caused the problem. Since the boom box was on sale, he can't return it and has to get a job at a donut shop to earn funds to cover its cost.

Episode 4: Unaired   "Scalped" (summary based on revised table draft script)

Director: Robert Berlinger   Writer: Laraine Mestman

Chet is playing in an all-star game and has tickets for his parents and Ernest. Ernest tells Chet he may not need the ticket since he will be taking his friend's place in the team's band. However, he wants to keep the ticket just in case. The next day Ernest gives his ticket to a girl he likes who promises to go on a date with him. Later, Lainie asks Ernest for the ticket to give to a co-worker so she can switch to a more interesting trial. George also asks Ernest for the ticket to give to his boss to help him get a promotion. When Ernest refuses to get the ticket back from the girl, his parents end up giving their tickets away but keep this a secret from Chet. The parents show up outside the locker room to make it look like they are attending the game, but then go home and wait for Ernest to tape the game and bring the tape for them to watch. They manage to watch the tape before Chet comes home, but the tape runs out before the end of the game where Chet made a winning shot. The parents try to play along with Chet, not knowing the game's final outcome. Eventually they confess to missing the game because they traded the tickets for favors.

Episode 5: Unaired   "Fantasy Girl" (summary based on final draft script)

Director: Terri McCoy   Writers: Bob Burris and Michael Ware

Chet is dating a girl named Charisse with whom Earnest is infatuated. However, Chet is thinking of dumping her because he is tired of dating the same girl. He avoids her calls, and, when she comes over to the house, he has Earnest tell her he is not home. When Earnest says that there are a lot of guys who would kill to be with her, she gets the hint that Chet is calling off their relationship. After Earnest fantasizes that Charisse is interested in him, Chet has second thoughts about breaking up with her. When Charisse calls the house, she wants to speak with Earnest – not Chet, and thus Chet learns that Earnest may have said too much to Charisse when she visited their home the last time. Chet says to his dad that Earnest stole his girl, but, after Chet settles down, Earnest tells Chet that Charisse is coming over and gives him a video of the movie *Doctor Zhivago*, which is Charisse's favorite, as a way to win her back.

Episode 6: Unaired "Shorts, Laws and Videotape" (summary based on final draft script)

Director: Linda Day   Writer: Gary Hardwick

George brings home a video for Chet to watch showing another high school basketball player describing all the good deeds he does. The player's dad sent the video to every coach and sportswriter who votes for the high school player of the year. Earnest agrees to do a similar video for Chet. However, Chet doesn't want to follow his brother's directions in making the video. George instructs Earnest that his job is to reveal the real Chet. Earnest shows the family a rough cut of the video a few days later where they see Chet stealing his sister's breakfast, sleeping in the classroom, and showing up late for basketball practice. George gets mad at both sons but later apologizes to Earnest. Lainie talks to Chet about his behavior, and Earnest redoes the video with Chet this time following his directions.

Terence Howard, who played Chet, went on to featured roles in major films such as *Hustle and Flow*, *Ray*, and *Iron Man*.

No Slam Dunk

The sitcom debuted at fifty-fifth in the ratings with each subsequent episode getting lower ratings. *Tall Hopes* followed *The Trouble with Larry* on Wednesdays, and like the show that preceded it, the series was canceled after three episodes.

You Take the Kids

Premiered Saturday, December 15, 1990, at 8:00 PM on CBS

To some, *You Take the Kids* seemed like a black version of the hit sitcom *Roseanne*, just not as sarcastic and not as successful.[44] The series, set in Pittsburgh, starred Nell Carter of *Gimme a Break* and Roger E. Mosley of *Magnum, P.I.* Mosley played Michael Kirkland, a school bus driver, married for seventeen years to Nell, a homemaker who taught piano to provide some extra income. They were raising four kids: sixteen-year-old Raymond (Dante Beze aka Dante Terrell, Mos Def, Yasin Bey); fourteen-year-old Lorette (Caryn Ward); twelve-year-old Peter (Marlon Taylor), and ten-year-old Nate (Trent Cameron). Also living with the Kirkland family was Nell's divorced mother Helen (Leila Danette), who, as mothers do, wished that her daughter had married better.

Background

Stephen Nathan and Paul Haggis created the series. Nathan would later write and produce the dramatic series *Joan of Arcadia* and *Bones*. Haggis subsequently won an Oscar for writing and producing the movie *Crash*. Nell Carter sang the series theme, "Nobody's Got It Easy." *You Take the Kids* was produced by CBS Entertainment, Paul Haggis Enterprises, and MTM Productions.

Episode Guide: 5 aired; 1 unaired

Episode 1: December 15, 1990   "Getaway"

Director: Paul Haggis   Writers: Stephen Nathan and Paul Haggis

Nell and Michael want to take their first vacation in seventeen years. However, complications with the kids and Nell's mother ensue. Nate gets a job delivering car stereos for Mr. Stereo to raise money for his parents' trip, but Nell finds he is delivering stolen merchandise. Nell is also dealing with Lorette who thinks she is not developing bosoms as quickly as other girls in her class. Mother Helen gets into an argument with Michael and refuses to babysit the kids until Michael apologizes to her. In the end, Nell and Michael decide to take everyone with them on their weekend vacation.

Episode 2: December 22, 1990   "Merry Christmas to All and a Pointy Hat to You"

Director: Frank Bonner   Writers: Stephen Nathan and Paul Haggis

A needy family, posing as carolers, steals the Kirkland's Christmas tree and gifts. However, the Kirkland's persist in trying to celebrate Christmas. They describe what gifts they bought each other, but when the police find the carolers and return the gifts to the Kirkland's, the family sees that each one of them exaggerated about what they said they got for the others. The police bring the needy family by so the Kirkland's can identify them. When the Kirkland's realize how poor the family is, they say the police made a mistake and invite the family for Christmas dinner.

As an actor, Frank Bonner, who directed this episode, played Herb Tarlick on *WKRP in Cincinnati*.

Episode 3: December 29, 1990   "The Eggs & I"

Director: J.D. LoBue   Writer: Kathy Slevin

The Kirkland's daughter teams with Terry, a cute boy at school, on a parenting project to care for three egg "babies." However, Lorette is more interested in Terry than in taking care of the eggs, and she learns that Terry has no interest in caring for the eggs. When Lorette returns home after finding Terry, they both discover that grandma Helen has cooked the eggs for breakfast.

Episode 4: January 5, 1991   "Sisters are Like Fishes: You Can't Flush Them Without Feeling Guilty"

Director: Peter Baldwin   Writers: Stephen Nathan and Paul Haggis

Lorette is infatuated with Spunk, one of Raymond's friends. She wants to ask Spunk to the dance, but when she sees him, she is tongue-tied. Spunk agrees to go with her to the dance anyway and lets Raymond know that he will humiliate Lorette before the entire school. Meanwhile, Nate brings home a goldfish that Nell thinks will soon die like the other fishes Nate has had. Nate soon tires of taking care of the fish and wants to get rid of it, but Peter tries to prevent the fish's demise. In the end, Raymond tells Spunk that he doesn't want his sister embarrassed even if this means that he and Spunk are no longer friends, and Peter saves Nate's goldfish after his dad accidentally runs over it in the driveway.

Episode 5: January 12, 1991 "Bad Boy"

Director: J.D. LoBue   Writer: Marcia L. Leslie

All the kids receive their report cards but don't want to show them to their parents except for Peter, who got all A's. Peter becomes upset when his parents pay more attention to his siblings' report cards because of their poor grades than to his. He says he is going to do something bad to get his parents' attention. He takes the family car and moves it twenty feet. The family thinks the car has been stolen. When Nell finds Peter in the car, he tells her that he wanted to get as much attention as his brothers and sister, and so she grounds him.

Episode 6: Unaired   "What I Did for Love"

Director: J.D. LoBue   Writer: Bill Levinson

When Peter wants a computer, Nell agrees to purchase one if he earns half the cost. Meanwhile, Raymond is betting on sports games to get money to date an attractive girl at school. When the girl says she wants to go to an M.C. Hammer concert, Raymond borrows more money from the school's loan shark who charges him 40 percent interest for a week. When he doesn't have funds to repay the debt, the loan shark takes the concert tickets he purchased, and Raymond then steals the money that Peter had been saving toward the computer. He uses the money to enter a crap game to win enough to get the tickets back and pay off the loan shark. However, he loses it all. Raymond's date ends up going to the concert with the loan shark, and Nell makes Raymond get a job to earn Peter's half of the cost of the PC.

Take Off

You Take the Kids premiere ranked seventy-third out of eighty-nine shows. The sitcom expired after five episodes. Nell Carter subsequently guest starred on shows like *Touched by Angel* and *Reba* before passing away in 2003 at the age of fifty-four from a heart attack brought on by complications from diabetes.

Daniel Stern: *Danny* and *Regular Joe*

Chapter 6
Single Parenting

A single parent raising kids is really a subset of family comedies described in the previous chapter but deserves separate consideration because of the fascination of TV comedy writers with households headed by only one parent, usually a dad. Beginning with sitcoms like *Bachelor Father* and *My Three Sons*, seeing a male trying to raise children alone is a classic comedy premise. Over time, the reason for the parent being single has evolved from widows and widowers to divorcees or women choosing to be single mothers.

Daddy's Girls

Premiered Wednesday, September 21, 1994, at 8:30 PM on CBS

CBS must have been a big fan of Dudley Moore because, a little more than a year after the sitcom *Dudley* was canceled (see below), Dudley Moore returned to TV, this time as a divorced father of three girls instead of, like on *Dudley*, a divorced father of a son. In *Daddy's Girls*, Dudley Walker's wife had run off with his business partner, leaving him to manage their apparel business and parent their three daughters. The oldest daughter, Amy (Stacy Galina) had just married Lenny (Al Ruck), an optometrist; the middle daughter, Samantha (Meredith Scott Lynn) wanted to be a partner in the family business, and the youngest daughter, Phoebe (Keri Russell), a not-too-bright, uninhibited teenager, was dating a buff, long-haired guy named Scar (Phil Buckman), a work-study student at Dudley's firm. Harvey Fierstein played Dennis Dumont, Dudley's gay fashion designer. In an early draft of the pilot, the Fierstein character was referred to as "festive." Best known for his work on Broadway, Fierstein was the first openly gay actor to be a regular on a prime-time series.

Background

Daddy's Girls, created by David Landsberg and Brenda Hampton, was produced by Witt-Thomas Productions in association with Warner Bros.. In an early script for the pilot, Dudley's oldest daughter was named Susan, not Amy, and the youngest daughter was Natalie instead of Phoebe. Also, the Harvey Fierstein character's last name was Sinclair – not Dumont. The character of Seymour Fields, Dudley's gruff shop foreman, was in both the early scripts as well as the pilot. However, he didn't appear in later episodes.

Episode Guide: 3 aired; 10 unaired

Episode 1: September 21, 1994 "Pilot"

Director: Barnet Kellman   Writers: David Landsberg and Brenda Hampton

Dudley's oldest daughter is getting married, and she has invited Annette, her mother (Dudley's ex) and her mother's husband, Phil (Dudley's ex- business partner) to the wedding. Dudley's youngest daughter is dating a dim-witted guy named Scar, and his middle daughter, Samantha, wants to be his new business partner. Dudley brings a supermodel to the wedding where his ex-partner tries to apologize for running off with Dudley's former wife. Dudley tells his ex-partner that Samantha is his new partner, and then Dudley walks Amy down the aisle.

SINGLE PARENTING

Episode 2: September 28, 1994   "An American in Paris…Cool"

Director: Greg Antonacci   Writers: Jack Amiel and Michael Begler

When a French importer offers Phoebe a job in Paris after she fills in for a model, Dudley has difficulty telling her she can't go. Initially he says that her mother won't let her go, but Phoebe replies that she spoke with her mother who thinks it is a great idea. Dudley finally puts his foot down and tells her "no" and that she is not ready to be on her own. Phoebe then wants to move in with her mother, but Dudley says "no" to that as well since she is now his responsibility.

Keri Russell (Phoebe) later had her own series, *Felicity* and subsequently starred in films like *The Upside of Anger* and *Waitress* and the sitcom *Running Wilde*.

Episode 3: October 12, 1994   "Keep Your Business out of My Business"

Director: Greg Antonacci   Writer: David Landsberg

Samantha starts dating Eddie, Dudley's biggest client. Amy and Lenny get a large dog that bites Lenny, so they have Dudley take care of the hound. Dudley is concerned that Sam's relationship with Eddie will end badly and cause him to lose a customer. When Sam says she is falling in love with Eddie and would relocate to New York for him, Eddie cancels their next date and informs Sam that he is engaged. Dudley decides Eddie isn't worth having as a customer and kicks him out of the office. Meanwhile, Lenny and Amy eventually decide to take their dog back from Dudley.

As an actor, director Greg Antonacci has played Johnny Torio on *Boardwalk Empire* and Butch DeConcini on *The Sopranos*.

Episode 4: Unaired   "Hit and Run"

Director: Greg Antonacci   Writer: Brenda Hampton

Dudley comes home from a business trip and finds that Samantha let Scar stay overnight in his house with Phoebe even though they slept in separate beds. He gets mad at Sam, forbids Scar from seeing Phoebe anymore, and then fires Scar.

Furthermore, Dudley accidentally runs over Amy's husband in the driveway breaking his legs. To try to make amends, Dudley allows Lenny to recuperate in his house, gives Scar his old job back and lets Phoebe resume dating him, apologizes to Samantha, and fills in for Lenny dressed as Abraham Lincoln at a presentation for kids in juvenile hall.

Brenda Hampton, the co-creator of this series, went on to develop such series as *Fat Actress* for Kirstie Alley, *7th Heaven*, and *The Secret Life of the American Teenager*.

Episode 5: Unaired   "Losin' It"

Director: Greg Antonacci   Writer: Martin Weiss

Dudley is exercising to keep up with Sheila, a young woman he is dating. After injuring himself climbing a mountain with her, he comes home to watch boxing with Scar, Dennis, and Lenny. However, Sheila calls and asks Dudley to go horseback riding during which he is thrown off the horse and lands on a cactus. He admits to Sheila that he has been acting like a fool for his age. When Sheila stops by his office, Dudley confesses that he is not the young, outdoors type. She responds that she finds his maturity and sense of humor charming.

Episode 6: Unaired   "A Month of Sundays"

Director: Greg Antonacci   Writer: Brenda Hampton

Dudley attempts to resume a family tradition of Sunday dinner. On the first Sunday, Amy and Lenny announce that they are going to conceive a baby; Scar and Phoebe break up, and Samantha says she is dating a comedian. For dinner the following Sunday, Amy brings her home pregnancy test so everyone can see the results which turn out to be negative; Scar wants to get back with Phoebe, but Dudley tells him that she is dating someone else – a security guard from Dudley's building whom Dudley quickly gets rid of. On the third Sunday, Amy and Samantha have PMS, and Amy says she doesn't want to try to get pregnant anymore. Dudley tells her to allow more time to conceive a baby, and he gets Scar and Phoebe back together. However, everyone leaves before dinner. Dudley stops the tradition, but, on the next Sunday, everyone drops by Dudley's house anyway for bagels.

Episode 7: Unaired   "Triple Double"

Director: Greg Antonacci   Writer: Howard M. Gould

When Dudley's daughters want him to find the right woman, they decide to each choose a date for him. Phoebe sets him up with her home economics teacher who starts giving tips to clean up the house. Amy chooses her travel agent as a date for her dad, but the agent has braces and lisps a lot. Finally, Samantha has her ex-therapist date Dudley. The therapist keeps asking Dudley what he thinks about various subjects he brings up in conversation and then proceeds to come on to him. Dudley says that he is the only person who knows what he needs, and he phones his ex-wife Annette.

Episode 8: Unaired   "Thank God It's Thursday"

Director/Writer: Greg Antonacci

Phoebe wants her mom at Thanksgiving dinner. Dudley reluctantly agrees, and his ex-wife Annette brings her husband and Dudley's former business partner Phil with her. The girls make it clear to Phil that he has to be nice to Dudley at dinner. However, after Phil keeps interrupting Dudley's conversation at the table, Dudley goes outside where Phoebe joins him, and they bond.

Episode 9: Unaired   "Three Play"

Director: David Landsberg Writers: Jack Amiel and Michael Begler

Three concurrent stories occur in this episode. Sam is going on a date with someone she met online; Scar is training Dudley on how to use a computer, and Phoebe is rehearsing for the lead in a production of *Grease*. Sam's date's name is Chad (Curtis Armstrong) who isn't as handsome as she had imagined. Sam tells Chad that he is not the man of her dreams, but he says that she is the woman of his dreams, and they kiss. Scar teaching Dudley PC skills does not go well, but he encourages Dudley to persist in learning the computer. Scar divulges that his nickname is short for "Oscar" and that his brother's name is Felix. Phoebe reveals to Dennis, who is helping her learn lines, that the rest of the actors in the play do not want her and she threatens to quit, but Dennis encourages her to stick with the play.

Phil Buckman (Scar) later became a regular on the short-lived Jason Alexander comedy, *Bob Patterson*.

Episode 10: Unaired "Hard Sell"

Director: Greg Antonacci   Writer: Martin Weiss

Amy has become a real estate agent and suggests that Dudley sell his house and purchase another one. In thinking about putting his house on the market, Dudley flashes back to bad memories of when his wife left him and decides Amy is right. When Amy holds an open house, no one shows up, but she does finally sell the place. However, Dudley can't find a new house that suits him, and Sam doesn't like the fact that her childhood home has been sold. This makes Dudley flashback to when his daughters were young, and he decides not to go through with the sale. Meanwhile, a female friend of Dennis' from high school, who doesn't know he is gay, moves to L.A. Dennis eventually tells her that he will not change, and she leaves.

Episode 11: Unaired "The Honeymoon's Over"

Director: Greg Antonacci   Writers: Colleen Taber and Ellen Saco

Amy leaves Lenny and moves back to Dudley's place because she feels she has nothing in common with him. Also, Dennis' boyfriend Robert (Steven Banks) is visiting but can't stay long because he performs in dinner theatres and is always on the road. Dennis leaves Robert over his traveling and comes to stay at Dudley's. Initially Dudley wants Amy and Lenny to work things out themselves, but relents and gets Lenny and Amy to talk to each other. Amy says that Lenny betrayed her by wanting to go to his own dentist and not hers. Lenny says Amy is too controlling. Dudley advises Amy that she needs to give her marriage with Lenny another try, and he tells Lenny to change dentists. Meanwhile, Robert informs Dennis that he will quit the road and put on a one-man show in New York.

Episode 12: Unaired "Feed a Cold"

Director: Greg Antonacci   Writer: Jon Hayman

Scar has a cold, which he gives to Dudley. Dudley is infatuated with Colleen Weber, the star of a soap opera that his son-in-law Lenny once dated. Sam wants to go on a TV shopping channel to try to sell the warehouse inventory with Colleen as the celebrity host. Lenny gets Colleen to appear on the shopping channel with Dudley who is looped from taking too much cold medication and mistakenly taking someone else's pills. Initially, no one calls in to buy the dresses, but, in the end, they sell out.

Episode 13: Unaired   "All in the Family"

Director: Greg Antonacci   Writers: Colleen Tubero and Ellen Svaco

A lot of changes occur for the Walker family in this final episode of the series. Dudley meets a new tenant in his office building – Maggie Phillips (Belinda Montgomery) who is divorced and has a design firm. After their first date, she invites Dudley to her family reunion, but Dudley is afraid of getting too serious too soon. However, after thinking about it, he tells Maggie he is ready for another relationship, but Maggie has reconsidered and doesn't want to rush things. Meanwhile, Maggie's son Tim asks Samantha out on a date, and they end up getting engaged. Scar is thinking of going on tour with his band, which means dropping out of school and leaving Phoebe. However, when Phoebe says that he shouldn't quit school, he decides against going on tour. Amy announces that she is pregnant, and Dennis tells everyone that he is going to tour with Bette Milder as her costume designer. At the end of the episode, Dudley's former wife, Annette, appears at the door saying she has left Phil and wants to come home.

Never Again

The series lasted for three episodes. Ratings for each episode were worse than the one before with the first episode ranking sixty-second, the second episode ranking seventieth, and the third episode ranking fourth in its time slot after shows on ABC, NBC, and Fox. CBS indicated at the time that the comedy might reappear later in the season, but it never did.

Dudley Moore did little work after this series was canceled: he passed away in March 2002 from pneumonia related to progressive supra-nuclear palsy.

Danny

Premiered Friday, September 28, 2001, at 8:30 PM on CBS

Danny starred Daniel Stern (best known for roles in *Home Alone* and *City Slickers*) as a recently divorced forty-year old and director of the "Wreck Center," a local community center. Living with him were his teenage son, Henry (Jon Foster); daughter, Sally (Julia McIlvaine), and grumpy father, Lenny (Robert Prosky). Danny's ex-wife was Molly (Joely Fisher). Staff at the community center included Chickie (Roz Ryan), Danny's administrative assistant; Vince (Vincent Burns), the twenty-six-year-old handyman, and Rachel (Mia Korf), a ballet teacher who liked Danny.

Background

Daniel Stern created the series, which was variously titled *Community Center* and *American Wreck*. Presumably the latter title was changed to *Danny* to make it less easy for reviewers to use it in their critiques of the show. *Danny* was a single-camera comedy with no laugh track produced by Big Ticket Television, Acme Productions, and Johnny Bongos Productions.

Episode Guide: 2 aired; 7 unaired

Episode 1: September 28, 2001   "Pilot"

Director: Peter Lauer   Writers: Daniel Stern and Howard J. Morris

It's Danny's birthday, and he doesn't handle turning forty very well, since he still considers himself something of a "kid." At the community center, Danny deals with various problems like doing budget projections for the city's budget director, playing basketball with his son's team, and filling in for Rachel at her ballet class. He finally goes home for the birthday dinner Sally prepared which the whole family including his ex-wife attends.

In 2003, Daniel Stern attempted another sitcom, *Regular Joe* (see below), with a similar theme and with results similar to *Danny*.

SINGLE PARENTING

Episode 2: October 5, 2001   "Donuts and Beer" (summary based on final revised script)

Director: Peter Lauer   Writer: Bob Nickman

Danny insists to his kids that he is a "cool" dad; so cool in fact that, when Henry is invited to a beer party, Danny lets him go. He tells Henry not to drink any beer – just walk around with an open can of beer. However, Henry comes home late from the party drunk. Danny admits to his son that he gave him bad advice about going to the party. Meanwhile, when Vince lets Danny know that Rachel likes him, Danny says he is wrong. Danny wants to have a meeting with Rachel about her schedule for classes at the center. She is bringing donuts, and Danny gets dressed up. But he is late for the meeting, and Rachel already worked out her schedule with Vince.

Jon Foster (Henry) continued acting into adulthood appearing in series such as *Accidentally on Purpose* as Zack.

Episode 3: Unaired   "The Dress Mess" (summary based on final revised script)

Director: Lev L. Spiro   Writers: Ari Posner and Eric Preven

The Wreck Center is having a rummage sale, and Danny's kids are collecting things from the house. Meanwhile, Rachel sets Danny up on a date with her friend Brenda, a District Attorney, with whom Danny doesn't have much in common. At the rummage sale, Danny's dad notices many of his things are up for sale including a special red dress that Danny thinks was his mother's. Danny goes looking for the woman who purchased the dress. She happens to be a street walker, and, when Danny offers her money for the dress, he is arrested. Brenda sees him at the police station and says that the police were just messing with him and he can go home.

Episode 4: Unaired   "Forget About Your Boss"

Director: Timothy Busfield   Writers: Ari Posner and Eric Preven

Danny works up the nerve to ask Rachel to the upcoming annual Wrecking Ball, but stops short when she mentions her new motorcycle-riding doctor boyfriend.

Danny pretends that he already has a date for the fund raiser and ends up asking his married cousin to pose as his date.

Timothy Busfield is an actor as well as a director having appeared on several series such as *thirtysomething*, *The West Wing*, and *Without a Trace*.

Episode 5: Unaired   "Danny's Night Out"

Director: Unknown   Writer: Janet Leahy

Motivated by an old high school rivalry, a drunken Danny and his friends vandalize a house with toilet paper and eggs.

Episode 6: Unaired   "Algebra I"

Director: Unknown   Writers: Bob Fisher and Steve Faber

Danny sleeps with his son's math teacher.

Episode 7: Unaired   "Kid Stays in the Picture"

Director: Unknown   Writers: Ari Posner and Eric Preven

Danny's plans a romantic evening with Henry's math teacher. However, the evening is interrupted by one crisis after another beginning with a woman from the center asking Danny to babysit her six-year-old son.

Episode 8: Unaired   "The Trojan Wife"

Director: Unknown   Writers: Ellen Idelson and Rob Lotterstein

When Danny finds condoms in his fourteen-year-old daughter's purse, he fears she is growing up too fast.

Episode 9: Unaired   "Daughters and Pigs"

Director: Unknown   Writer: Bob Nickman

After Danny learns that Sally's date is nicknamed "Tommy the Tongue," he follows the couple to the movies. Also, a friend and his pet pig stay temporarily with Danny's family.

Episodes Not Produced

According to Bob Nickman who helped to write and produce *Danny*, it appears that only eight episodes in addition to the pilot were filmed before the sitcom was canceled.[45] Presumably the following storylines were for episodes of *Danny* that were never produced:

"When It Rains, It Pours"

A flood on Thanksgiving Day brings a larger than expected crowd to the community center's annual turkey dinner. Danny and his ex-wife Molly share a kiss.

"What about Bob?"

Danny is irritated that there is a new man in Molly's life that his kids like. He lets his frustrations out on Sally whom he is coaching on the girls' softball team.

"Who Gives a Truck?"

Henry receives a new truck for his sixteenth birthday from his wealthy maternal grandfather.

Danny Dumped

Danny was the first sitcom of the 2001–02 TV season to be canceled. It lasted for two episodes; the comedy debuted at seventy-sixth place in the ratings and sank to ninety-third in its second airing.

Dudley

Premiered Friday, April 16, 1993, at 8:30 PM on CBS

"He was a swinging bachelor raising Cain, now he's a struggling parent raising a kid. Join Dudley and his son as they discover that 'father knows least'." That was how CBS advertised Dudley Moore's first TV situation comedy where he played Dudley Bristol, a divorced music composer and pianist trying to raise his incorrigible fourteen-year-old son Fred (Harley Cross). Others in the cast were: Joanna Cassidy as Dudley's ex-wife Laraine; Joel Brooks as Harold Krowten, owner of the nightclub "Liaisons" where Dudley performed; Max Wright as Paul, Dudley's manager and best friend, and Lupe Ontiveros as Marta, Dudley's Hispanic housekeeper, who spoke no English but did communicate with Fred who knew Spanish.

Background

CBS had signed Dudley Moore to a development contract after his success in movies like *10* and *Arthur*. Originally, Moore was to play an accountant in a sitcom. A pilot was made called *Modern Times*, but CBS rejected it and brought in Susan Beavers to rework the premise. She came up with the idea of Dudley as a witty cabaret pianist raising a son who had gotten into trouble running with the wrong crowd. Dudley's character on the series attempted to develop a good father-son relationship, even though he didn't have a clue about parenting. Witz End Productions in association with Twentieth Century-Fox and CBS Entertainment produced the sitcom.

Episode Guide: 5 aired; 1 unaired

Episode 1: April 16, 1993   "It Was a Wonderful Life" (Pilot)

Director: Ellen Falcon   Writer: Susan Beavers

Dudley's ex-wife Laraine, who had been raising their son Fred in California, brings him to New York City to live with his father. Laraine tells Dudley that she can't control the boy who was arrested for stealing a car. She thinks Fred needs a strong male in his life and contemplates sending him to boarding school. But Dudley insists that Fred stay with him. While Laraine hopes Dudley will be successful in keeping Fred out of trouble, she does take an apartment near Dudley's.

Episode 2: April 23, 1993   "Call Me Irresponsible"

Director: Ellen Falcon   Writer: Ron Burla

When Fred tells his dad that there is no school all spring due to spring break, Dudley believes him until he is visited by a truant officer. Laraine suggests that Dudley join the PTA to show some interest in Fred's school and to be more responsible. At the PTA meeting, Dudley volunteers to clean up but forgets to unplug the coffee maker when distracted by an attractive female. Two classrooms at the school burn down due to a wiring problem with the appliance. Dudley contributes $30,000 to the school and confesses to the PTA that he didn't unplug the coffee maker.

Episode 3: April 30, 1993   "Off the Record"

Director: Ellen Falcon   Writer: Ron Burla

Marta breaks up with her boyfriend who believes she is now seeing Dudley. Meanwhile, in the course of an interview with a newspaper reporter to promote his new album "Just an Old-Fashioned Guy," Dudley tells the reporter that his son is sensitive and could use some help with girls. When the kids at school read the interview in the paper, Fred gets mad at his father. To get back at him, Fred intercepts a call from a radio station wanting to interview Dudley and says that his dad has hair plugs, is cheap, and is not naturally witty. A TV station later interviews both Fred and Dudley where Dudley says there are no problems between him and his son. However, Marta's ex-boyfriend breaks into the live interview, punches Dudley, and announces that Dudley stole his girlfriend.

Although this was the third episode broadcast, it was the sixth episode produced.

Episode 4: May 7, 1993   "Whose Therapy Is it, Anyway?"

Director: Ellen Falcon   Writers: Ellen Sandler and Cindy Elias

When Fred informs his dad that he wants to take music lessons, Dudley gives him some cash to cover the cost. Laraine subsequently asks Dudley about Fred's music lessons, and Dudley doesn't know anything about them. They find that Fred lent the money Dudley gave him to a friend at 30 percent interest which leads Larraine to suggest that Fred needs therapy. Dudley and Laraine then discover that Fred's friend was actually attending the therapy sessions pretending that he was Fred. Fred tells Dudley that he was loan sharking to get money to go back to California so he could say a proper goodbye to his friends.

Episode 5: May 14, 1993   "Learnin' The Blues"

Director: Ellen Falcon   Writer: Susan Beavers

Fred is sick, and, when his English teacher drops off his homework, she meets Dudley. Fred has a crush on the teacher and offers to walk her home after school, but she turns him down. Later the teacher goes to see Dudley at his rehearsal, and the two go to dinner. When Dudley takes her to his apartment, Fred sees them kiss, and he gets mad at Dudley for dating his teacher. Dudley tells the teacher that he can't date her again because it is not fair to Fred, and he leaves Fred under the impression that she dumped Dudley. Fred thinks that he and his dad share something in common; they were both dumped by the teacher.

In 1995, Susan Beavers created another short-lived comedy starring Valerie Harper called *The Office*.

Episode 6: Unaired   "Round One"

Director: Ellen Falcon   Writer: Susan Beavers

Dudley wants Fred to live by his rules.

Harley Cross (Fred) did some TV and movie work after *Dudley* and co-founded a breath mint company called Hint Mint.

Dudley Unplugged

Dudley was placed against the family comedy *Step by Step* on ABC. Its first episode came in fifty-third ranking second to *Step by Step*, but ratings dropped after that with its fifth episode ranking eighty-third. A little more than a year later, Dudley Moore tried to find success with another sitcom, *Daddy's Girls* (see above), which was canceled after three episodes.

In the Motherhood

Premiered Thursday, March 26, 2009, at 8:30 PM on ABC

The lives of three different mothers raising kids were the focus of this comedy. Rosemary (Megan Mullally), a freewheeling mom with a teenage son, Syd (Ryan Pinkston), was currently single but had been married numerous times. Rosemary's best friend, Jane (Cheryl Hines), a recent divorcée and an architect, was the mother of two girls: a pre-teen named Annie (Charlotte Foley) and Sophie, an eight-month-old, who had a male nanny, Horatio (Horatio Sanz). Jane's younger married sister, Emily (Jessica St. Clair), the perfect stay-at-home mom, had a young son Bill (Sayeed Shahidi), a daughter Esther (Yara Shahidi), and a black husband Jason (RonReaco Lee).

Background

In the Motherhood was based on an internet series developed by David Lang that featured the stories of real mothers; Leah Remini, Jenny McCarthy, and Chelsea Handler played the moms on the web series. Handler was supposed to be the only one of the three to also star on the TV sitcom, but her work on her E! series, *Chelsea Lately*, prevented that from happening.

Alexandra Rushfield and Jennifer Konner created the TV comedy which was produced by Mindshare Entertainment, Pointy Bird Productions, and ABC Studios. Originally, thirteen episodes were ordered, but after the premiere of the comedy, ABC reduced the number of episodes.

Episode Guide: 5 aired, 2 unaired

Episode 1: March 26, 2009   "It Takes a Village Idiot"

Director: Richard Shepard   Writers: Jennifer Konner and Alexandria Rushfield

After Rosemary discovers the advantages of being a pregnant woman, she passes herself off as one by hiding a stuffed toy under her top. When she fights Horatio over a gift in front of other pregnant mothers, the stuffed toy falls out revealing that she is not really expecting. Jane resumes dating again but her date with coworker, Shep (Ken Marino), is interrupted when her boss decides to give a sexual harassment seminar. After the seminar, Jane wants to be ravished by her date, and her boss finds them in a compromising position. Emily, wanting to be an honest parent, tells her kids that Santa Claus and the Tooth Fairy do not exist. Her son informs all the kids at school that there is no Santa Claus or Tooth Fairy, and the kids go crazy.

Episode 2: April 2, 2009   "Vacation"

Director: Beth McCarthy Miller Writers: Paul Corrigan and Brad Walsh

Horatio is going on vacation and so is Jane who has a week off from work to spend time with baby Sophie. Emily and her husband plan a "staycation," but, when the kids don't enjoy staying at home, she decides that they all should go to Hawaii. Rosemary begins organizing the nannies in the neighborhood including Horatio so they can receive better benefits. When Jane accidentally gets locked out of her house with the baby inside and calls Horatio for help during Rosemary's nanny strike demonstration, both Horatio and Rosemary leave the demonstration to help Jane.

Episode 3: April 9, 2009   "Bully"

Director: Gail Mancuso   Writer: Al Higgins

When Jane's daughter is being bullied at school, Horatio tries, with mixed success, to deal with the young bully. Jane then tries to make her boss and co-workers think she is a bully in order to leave work early to spend more time with her kids. After acting like a bully in front of Horatio and her daughter, Jane realizes that she shouldn't behave that way. Meanwhile, Emily asks Rosemary to get her old band, Pony, back together to perform at a preschool fundraiser. However, another mother takes control of the fundraiser away from Emily and says she can get Eva Longoria to appear. When Eva Longoria cancels, Emily asks Pony to perform.

David Anthony Higgins from *Malcolm in the Middle* had a cameo in this episode as one member of Rosemary's band. He is the brother of Al Higgins who wrote the episode.

Episode 4: April 16, 2009   "Practice What You Preach"

Director: Jamie Babbit Writers: Liz Cackowski and Maggie Carey

In order to keep her daughter from quitting karate, Jane rejoins her office's kickball team even though she is not very good at the sport. After Jane finds she is at least able to kick the ball, Annie decides to support her mom at kickball instead of abandoning her to be with a friend. Meanwhile, Emily and her husband are worried about their son's mischievous imaginary friend, Beebop, whom the son blames for everything he does wrong. Rosemary starts giving parenting advice to new mothers, which turns into parenting seminars. Emily takes her son Bill to one of Rosemary's seminars so Rosemary can convince him that Beebop is imaginary. Bill finally admits Beebop is not real and that he was acting out because his mom had him participating in too many extracurricular activities.

The actors who played Emily's two kids – Bill and Esther, are real-life brother and sister.

Episode 5: June 25, 2009   "Shepfather"

Director: Lee Shallat Chemel Writer: Greg DiGregorio

Jane's boyfriend Shep wants to meet her kids and see her house. Jane is hesitant to show him her messy place, but after seeing the home, he doesn't mind the clutter. He starts cooking dinner for the family, mowing the lawn, and cleaning Jane's house to the point where Jane gets upset that Shep is better at taking care of her family and home than she is. Meanwhile, Emily is jealous of her neighbor Gretchen whose family seems more perfect than hers and whose new mini-van means that

Emily is no longer in charge of the neighborhood car pool. Rosemary suggests that Emily take revenge on the neighbor. Emily works up enough courage to place a "Honk if You're Horny" bumper sticker on Gretchen's van. Gretchen confronts Emily about the bumper sticker and divulges that she used to be a sex addict. Rosemary recommends to Emily and Gretchen that they join forces to improve the neighborhood.

Episode 6: Unaired   "Where There's a Will, There's a Wake"

Director: Linda Mendoza   Writer: Annie Mumolo

Emily tries to secretly mold Jane into a perfect parent so that she can name her as legal guardian for her kids. She gives Jane a gift basket containing healthy foods and gift certificates for organic cooking classes and security systems. After Jane and Emily bond during the cooking class, Emily begins having fun with her sister to the point that she lets her kids sleep over at Jane's. However, to make sure that Jane is taking perfect care of her kids, Emily installs a nanny-cam. When she sees Jane allow her kids to watch *America's Funniest Home Videos*, she breaks in, takes her kids away, and confesses to Jane that she wanted her to be their legal guardian in case something happened to her and her husband. Later, when Emily finds that Jane taught her son to tie his own shoes, she apologizes and begs Jane to be the guardian. Meanwhile, after her aunt dies, Rosemary decides to hold a "fake funeral" for herself so she can enjoy it. She invites only her inner circle of friends, which leaves Emily, Jane, and her son out, but finds that no one shows up.

Episode 7: Unaired   "In Sickness and In Health"

Director: Lee Shallat Chemel   Writer: Joel Madison

Rosemary has the flu, and Jane doesn't want to get it since she is working on a big project. Emily's husband also has the flu and is not getting much sympathy from his wife. Jane is under pressure at work to complete her project early, and she is getting flu-like symptoms. She has to leave work when Horatio falls and hurts his back. Jane brings her baby to work and has a series of co-workers look after the child. When her boss finds that Jane is feeling ill and has her baby at work, she threatens to remove her from the project. But Jane insists she can complete it—which she does, and then passes out and ends up in the hospital along with Emily's husband who was admitted for double pneumonia. Meanwhile, Rosemary is jealous that during her bout with the flu, Horatio became friends with another nanny. Rosemary and the other nanny fight over Horatio and ask him to choose which one should be his BFF. He chooses Rosemary.

In Is Out

In the Motherhood debuted opposite a special episode of Fox's *American Idol*. Needless to say, it did not do well in the ratings with each episode after the debut getting worse ratings than the one before and with the final April episode ranking fourth in its timeslot. ABC took the sitcom off the air after four of the planned seven episodes had been broadcast. The network started to burn off the three remaining episodes beginning on June 25, 2009, but because the ratings for the first episode in June were so poor, the network never aired the remaining two.

My Guys

Premiered Wednesday, April 3, 1996, at 8:30 PM on CBS

Ads for *My Guys* proclaimed, "This single father has his hands full. He's busy raising two sons. They're busy raising something else." A recently widowed father trying to raise two boys on Manhattan's Upper West Side was the premise of this comedy. Sonny Demarco (Michael Rispoli) ran a small limousine company. His fifteen-year-old son, Michael (Michael Damus), was attracted to Angela (Marisol Nichols), the older teenage girl next door, and his twelve-year-old, Francis (Francis Capra) seemed to have more common sense than the dad. Harvey (Peter Dobson), a friend of Sonny's, was one of his drivers. Dori (Sherie Scott), a waitress at the local diner, sometimes gave Sonny advice on child-rearing.

Background

Originally the sitcom was to star Lorraine Bracco as a single mother raising two boys, but it evolved into a single father raising two kids.[46] Created by Paul Perlove, the comedy was produced by Cherp Productions and Witt-Thomas Productions.

Episode Guide: 2 aired; 4 unaired

Episode 1: April 3, 1996 "Pilot"

Director: Ted Wass   Writer: Paul Perlove

Sonny's wife has been dead for fourteen months, and Harvey encourages him to date again. When Dori asks him out, Sonny accepts her invitation. Meanwhile, Angela and her mother move into the apartment next to Sonny's, and Michael is attracted to her. Sonny is very nervous on his date with Dori, and, after she says she wants to get involved, Sonny tells her that he isn't ready for a relationship yet. Michael and Angela see each other in the building's laundry room, and he discovers she is in twelfth grade while he is in tenth grade. This ends the idea of him dating her.

Marisol Nichols (Angela) went on to roles in *24, The Gates*, and *G.C.B.*

Episode 2: April 10, 1996 "Tangled Web"

Director: Ted Wass   Writers: Tom Saunders and Kell Cahoon

Sonny gets two tickets to a Knicks game, but Michael explains to Francis that he doesn't want to go since he has a hot date lined up for the same night as the basketball game. He has Francis ask their dad to attend even though Francis doesn't like basketball. Michael says he needs to study for a make-up test. After Francis and his dad go to the game, Michael has the girl from the fifth floor come to the apartment. She likes to smoke and drink, but, when they start to make out, she falls asleep. After Francis gets sick at the game, he and his dad come home early. Sonny finds cigarette butts, an empty beer can, and the girl sleeping in his bedroom. Michael says he is sorry, but Sonny forces him to apologize to the girl's dad. Michael and Sonny go to the fifth floor of their apartment building, but Michael ends up apologizing to the wrong guy.

Mike Damus (Michael) went on to star on the short-lived sitcom *Brutally Normal*.

Episode 3: Unaired "The Sign"

Director: Ted Wass   Writer: Paul Perlove

After Sonny wrecks the limo, he and Harvey have to figure out where to find the money to have it fixed. Meanwhile, Francis thinks he is being watched over by his dead mother.

Michael Rispoli (Sonny) subsequently became a regular on the situation comedy *Bram & Alice.*

Episode 4: Unaired "Like Father, Like Sonny"

Director: Ted Wass   Writers: Jenny Bicks, Tom Saunders, and Kell Cahoon

Sonny dates a new girl named Terri (Liz Larsen).

Episode 5: Unaired "Five Liars and a Funeral" (summary provided by Dee LaDuke)

Director: Ted Wass   Writers: Dee LaDuke and Mark Alton Brown

With Harvey driving, Sonny is trying to get his sons to school on time in one of his limos accompanied by his girlfriend, Terri. He tells Harvey to cut into a funeral procession to avoid traffic, and, while stopped in traffic, a mourner gets into the limo because she is alone and has no ride to the cemetery. The mourner comes to believe that Sonny is the estranged son of the deceased, and Sonny learns that the mourner was the deceased's long-time secretary and mistress. When they all end up at the cemetery, Sonny delivers the eulogy and eventually the mourner learns the truth about him.

The mourner was played by the late Rue McClanahan. According Dee LaDuke, Ms. McClanahan decided to do the guest spot because she fell in love with the script.

Episode 6: Unaired   "Hot and Bothered" (summary provided by Robert Leighton)

Director: Ted Wass   Writer: Robert Leighton

Sonny's kids are lobbying him for a computer. He gets one cheap and presents it to his sons, temporarily becoming a hero. When the kids turn on the computer, they find that it's stolen since it has someone else's information on it. Michael thinks it's cool, but Francis is really upset. Without telling anyone, Francis decides to take the computer back to the original owner, who, rather than being grateful, presses charges against him thinking he is a thief. In the end, Sonny has to come clean at the police precinct and admit that he bought his kids a hot computer to save money.

The actor who portrayed Francis, Francis Capra (no relation to Frank Capra, the director), later became a regular on *Veronica Mars*. Robert Leighton, who scripted this episode, created a puzzle-writing company called "Puzzability." As an actor, Ted Wass appeared on the sitcom *Soap*.

Hardly Given a Chance

My Guys received very poor ratings and was canceled after only two episodes had aired. The premiere episode lost 17 percent of aged eighteen to forty-nine viewers from its lead-in, *Dave's World*. A reviewer summed up the show with the following dialogue between Sonny and Mike from the first episode:

"Funny, huh?"

"Not so far."[47]

Regular Joe

Premiered Friday, March 28, 2003, at 9:30 PM on ABC

Daniel Stern tried again after the failure of *Danny* to achieve sitcom success with *Regular Joe*, a comedy about four generations under one roof. Stern played Joe Binder, a recent widower with a son Grant (John Francis Daley), a high school student; daughter Joanie (Kelly Kabacz), a college freshman, and Joanie's baby Zoey born out of wedlock. Joe's father Baxter (Judd Hirsch) also lived with the family. The Binder family ran a hardware store where Joe and Baxter worked along with Grant and Sitvar (Brian George) who was from India.

Background

David Litt, who, with Michael Weithorn, were responsible for the hit *The King of Queens*, created *Regular Joe*. Originally *Regular Joe* was about a husband and wife whose empty nest years were interrupted when their eighteen-year-old daughter moved back home with a baby. In the original pilot, Lisa Ann Walter played Joe's wife; Estelle Harris (*Seinfeld*) and Bill Macy (*Maude*) were Joe's parents; Eric Christian Olsen had a role as the daughter's boyfriend, and Emiliano Diez was the employee at the hardware store. When the pilot was redone, Joe became a widower, Hirsch took over the role of the grandfather, the grandmother role was dropped along with the daughter's boyfriend, and Brian George replaced Emiliano Diez as the hardware store employee. Touchstone Television produced *Regular Joe*.

Episode Guide: 4 aired; 2 unaired

Episode 1: March 28, 2003   "Puppetry of the Pennies"

Director: Gary Halvorson   Writer: David Litt

Dad gives Grant more responsibility at work by allowing him to operate the paint stirring machine much to the chagrin of Sitvar. Grant wants his dad to give him a raise, and, when Joe offers an additional fifty cents an hour, his son takes this as an insult. At the urging of Sitvar, Grant presses his demand for a raise, and, when his dad refuses, Grant quits and takes a job as a delivery person for a Chinese restaurant. Meanwhile, after Joanie is accepted at Columbia University, Joe informs her that her college fund was used for expenses for the baby, and they don't have the money to send her to the university. Joanie then takes a job as a waitress to earn money for Columbia. After Joe says that she has been working too hard, she quits her job to spend more time with her daughter and to continue going to Queens College instead of entering Columbia. Concerning Grant's request for a raise, Joe finally relents and gives him the pay increase so he can return to work at the hardware.

When Joe finds that Sitvar was egging his son on about the raise, he has Sitvar dress as a hammer to promote the store.

Episode 2: April 4, 2003   "Time and Punishment"

Director: Ted Wass   Writers: Joe Wiseman and Joe Port

When Joe decides to spend some quality time with his family, he declares a "family night." The family doesn't have a good time at first, but then Grant and Joanie decide to surprise Joe with dinner and a little quality time. However, Baxter calls and tells Joe that he has fight tickets for a major boxing match which Joe wants to attend.

John Francis Daly (Grant) later was a regular on the short-lived *Kitchen Confidential*.

Episode 3: April 11, 2003   "Boobysitting"

Director: Rob Schiller   Writers: Joe Wiseman and Joe Port

Joanie hires her friend Nikki instead of Grant to babysit for her. Grant is attracted to Nikki and attempts to teach her how to correctly babysit. Meanwhile, Sitvar tries to sabotage Joe so he can show him how much the hardware store means to Baxter.

Episode 4: April 18, 2003   "The Mourning After"

Director: Ted Wass   Writer: David Litt

His father and kids pressure Joe to go on his first date since the death of his wife, Angela. As Joe tries to teach Grant to drive, take care of the baby, and get ready for the date, Joanie realizes that she might not really be ready for her dad to move on.

This episode, the last to broadcast, was actually the first episode produced after the initial pilot.

Episode 5: Unaired   "Queens Boulevard of Broken Dreams"

Director: Unknown   Writer: Marco Pennette

Storyline unknown

Episode 6: Unaired   "Butt-Out-Ski"

Director: Rob Schiller   Writers: Amy Engelberg and Wendy Engelberg

Storyline unknown

Second Attempts

Regular Joe did not fare well. The comedy came in fourth in its timeslot. *Regular Joe* was opposite *Ed* on NBC and *Hack* on CBS and disappeared after four episodes – lasting two more episodes than Stern's prior comedy—*Danny*.

In 2010, CMT ordered a pilot from David Litt for an updated version of *Regular Joe*. Tom Arnold was cast in the role of Joe whose last name this time was "Herman." Ed Asner got the role of Joe's father. However, CMT did not pick up the pilot for a series.

Trial and Error with Paul Rodriquez and Eddie Velez

Chapter 7
Rooming Together

Whether friends or siblings, two or three people sharing the same house or apartment—often with completely different personalities—is another classic sitcom theme. The initial seasons of *The Lucy Show* with Lucille Ball and Vivian Vance, *Laverne and Shirley*, and *The Odd Couple* are great examples of long-running sitcoms based on this theme. Here are some other "roomies" who didn't stay together very long.

Lush Life

Premiered Monday, September 9, 1996 at 9:30 PM on Fox

Advertised as "Lucy and Ethel of the 90's," this comedy revolved around two female roommates and friends since childhood—Georgette "George" Sanders (Lori Petty) a struggling painter with a platinum blonde buzz cut who worked as a waitress at a restaurant similar to Hooters (with some additional padding under her shirt), and

Margot Hines (Karyn Parsons), a onetime actress who had just left her philandering, airline pilot husband and moved in with George. *Lush Life* focused on the adventures of the two women as one tried to sell her paintings and the other sought to find work and reenter the dating scene. Other characters on the sitcom included Hal Gardener (Sullivan Walker), the owner of the bar where the two women hung out; Nelson "Margarita" Marquez (John Ortiz), the gay Latino bartender; Lance Battista (Kahil Kain), a restaurant manager and neighbor of George's who often showed up in her apartment wearing only a towel, and Hamilton Ford Foster (Fab Filippo), a wannabe punk rocker and another neighbor. Concetta Tomei appeared as Margot's much-married mother – Ann Hines-Davis-Wilson-Jefferson-Ali.

Background

After starring in films like *Tank Girl* and *Free Willy*, Lori Petty decided to try television. Instead of doing a central character sitcom focusing on her, Petty decided to develop a comedy with her and her friend since the 1980s, Karyn Parsons from *The Fresh Prince of Bel-Air*. The actresses collaborated with Yvette Lee Bowser, who had created the Fox comedy *Living Single*, and the three began putting together *Lush Life*. What is fairly bizarre when watching *Lush Life* is Petty's performance. She speaks her lines with a croaking voice as if she is trying to do a bad impression of Cyndi Lauper. Warner Bros. and SisterLee Productions produced *Lush Life*.

Episode Guide: 4 aired; 3 unaired

Episode 1: September 9, 1996   "The Lush Beginning"

Director: Ellen Gittelsohn
Writers: Lori Petty, Karyn Parsons, and Yvette Lee Bowser

The episode begins with George in bed with a basketball player in her funky loft in Venice beach. Margot, George's best friend, arrives saying that her husband Wallace has cheated on her with a flight attendant and that she wants to stay with George. The next day, Margot's husband calls to inform her that he wants a divorce. Margot and George go to Margot's house while her husband is away to get some of her things and end up having to break in. George tries on one of Wallace's suits, and the flight attendant who had the affair with Wallace visits the house and thinks that

Margot and George are a lesbian couple. The flight attendant says that Wallace told her that he left Margot three months ago. In the end, George lets Margot know that she can stay at her loft in Venice for as long as she wants.

Episode 2: September 16, 1996   "The Dead Lush Artist"

Director: Ellen Gittelsohn   Writers: Richard Levine and Lyn Greene

After George's artwork has been rejected by several galleries, Margo says she can get George's paintings displayed. She shows George's work to an art gallery owner who is disinterested until Margot informs him that George is deceased. When the owner agrees to have a showing of the paintings, George has to work furiously to paint more abstracts to fill the gallery. At the exhibit, she shows up in disguise, and, when the owner tries to sell a painting that George didn't do, she reveals herself, and, of course, all the buyers now want their money back.

Episode 3: September 23, 1996   "The First Lush Date"

Director: Ellen Gittelsohn   Writer: Matt Ember

Margot wants to begin dating again after her break up with Wallace. George asks a guy at the bar, who is an amateur botanist, to go out with Margot. Margot double dates with George and her boyfriend. Margot's boyfriend is very boring, while George and her date are hot for each other. Margot accidentally hits her date in the eye with juice from the lobster she ordered, and he says he is going to the restroom but actually leaves the restaurant. Lance, who manages the restaurant, comes by to console her.

Episode 4: September 30, 1996   "The Lush Ex-Posures"

Director: Ellen Gittelsohn   Writer: Eunetta T. Boone

George gets a commission to do a painting for the city of Santa Monica. Margot receives a call from her ex who wants to meet her. George is against the meeting, but Margot, hoping for an apology from Wallace, goes ahead with it. Wallace tells Margot that he has met someone else who is in politics. He wants some naked photos that Margot took of him so that they do not create a controversy when his new girlfriend runs for state Senate. He offers her $1000 for the pictures. Margot is upset at the offer and wants Wallace to leave. However, after talking to George about the encounter, she phones Wallace to set up a meeting at the bar to exchange the photos for money. When Wallace comes to the bar, Margot takes the money, throws the photos at him, and he leaves. In the final scene, George's painting for the city is unveiled, and it turns out to be a naked Wallace.

Phil Morris (Greg Morris' son) appeared as Wallace on this episode.

Episode 5: Unaired "The Lush Waitress" (summary based on second revised script)

Director: Ellen Gittelsohn   Writer: Sally Lapiduss

Margot's divorce has been finalized, and since she received no money from her ex, she has to get a job for the first time in her life. George convinces her to get a job at the Hooters-like restaurant where she works. Margot finds that she is a great waitress and that all the guys like her, resulting in large tips. George becomes envious since she hardly gets any tips with her surly, lazy attitude. George attempts to get Margot to quit and makes a big speech in front of the whole restaurant about how Margot is ruining her life by keeping the job. George throws her false boobs in the kitchen as part of her dramatic speech where they catch on fire. Margot and George make up with Margot now having money for the rent.

Episode 6: Unaired "The Lush Hex" (summary based on second revised script)

Director: Ellen Gittelsohn   Writer: Charles Randolph-Wright

On Halloween, Margot is in a festive mood, while George hates the holiday because it is too commercial. The pair goes to see Hamilton's band perform at Hal's bar, where there is a fortuneteller who puts four curses on George. George doesn't believe in the curses until three of them come true starting with her getting knocked unconscious. While making a potion to undo the curse, a grim reaper knocks on their apartment door and scares everyone. The grim reaper is really the fortuneteller who instructs George to bring the scariness back to the Halloween she once loved. The fortuneteller instructs George to chant: "There's no place like

Halloween." George wakes up back at the bar after having been knocked out, and goes home to put on her scariest costume.

Episode 7: Unaired   "Not So Lush Rock Star"
(summary based on second revised script)

Director: Ellen Gittelsohn   Story: Matt Ember
Teleplay: Lyn Greene and Richard Levine

For her new job as an "artist liaison" at a record company, Margot must keep a struggling rock star, Johnny James (Davy Jones), out of trouble before his comeback. She and George loved Johnny when they were both in junior high. Johnny talks them into hanging out with him all night and then goes back to their apartment where George asks him to do an old stage move for which he was famous. He falls and hurts his back and becomes an annoying bedridden guest that drives the girls crazy. Margot is afraid she will lose her job if she doesn't get Johnny to his sold out concert which she does just in time.

Life's End

Lush Life was canceled after four episodes – one of the first scheduling moves by Fox's then-new president Peter Roth. Its third episode ranked 100th out of 107 shows.

Princesses

Premiered Friday, September 27, 1991, at 8:00 PM on CBS

The "princesses" were three single women living in a Manhattan penthouse who became roommates in an unusual way. They were Tracy Dillon (Julie Hagerty), Georgina De La Rue (Twiggy Lawson), and Melissa Kirshner (Fran Drescher). Tracy was about to get married when she found that her husband-to-be had already been married twice and that one of his ex-wives was his business partner. As a wedding present, her fiancé's friend had given the couple the use of a Manhattan penthouse rent-free for a year. Although Tracy canceled the wedding, she and her best friend Melissa decided to move into the apartment. There they found Georgy, the Princess of Scilly, who had recently been widowed and who had also been promised the apartment by Tracy's fiancé's friend. The three ended up sharing the penthouse.

Tracy was an adult remedial English teacher, and Melissa was a cosmetics counter clerk at a department store. Tracy and Melissa had been friends since they were roommates in college. While her late husband's family was contesting his will, Georgy, a former showgirl, tried to get work singing and dancing.

Background

Barry Kemp, who had created the hit comedies *Newhart* and *Coach*, created *Princesses* along with Mark Ganzel and Robin Schiff. Bungalow 78 Productions and Universal produced the series. "Someday My Prince Will Come" was the theme song for the comedy.

Episode Guide: 5 aired; 3 unaired

Episode 1: September 27, 1991   "Pilot"

Director: Lee Shallat Chemel   Writers: Mark Ganzel and Robin Schiff

The pilot episode opens the day before Tracy is to be married. Her fiancé, Michael (James Read), has a wealthy friend, who has given the couple the use of an East Side Manhattan penthouse rent-free as a wedding gift. Tracy and her current roommate, Melissa, visit the penthouse and find that Michael's friend has also promised the place to Princess Georgina De La Rue. Tracy goes to Michael's office to discuss the situation and finds that the first name of Michael's business partner Andy is really "Andrea" and that Andy and Michael were once married and are now just getting divorced. Tracy decides to call off the marriage, but Michael visits her at the penthouse, says he was afraid to tell her about his prior marriage, and that is real first name is "Moe" – Moe Michael DeCrow. Tracy reconsiders and goes ahead with the marriage ceremony only to find that Michael had another ex-wife before Andrea. There is no wedding, but Georgy asks Melissa and Tracy to stay in the penthouse with her.

In an early draft of the pilot script, the character played by Twiggy was named Georgina Von Pillot, the Princess of Peaslee.

Episode 2: October 4, 1991 "Her Highness for Hire"

Director: Lee Shallat Chemel   Writers: Sally Lapiduss and Pamela Eells

Georgy needs to find a job to make some money. Meanwhile, Melissa is dating an ad agency executive. Since Georgy can sing and dance, she looks for a job in entertainment and auditions for a film titled *Street Tango* where she would play a hooker. When she doesn't get the role, Melissa's date asks Georgy to be the spokesperson for Buckingham Airlines.

Fran Drescher was the breakout star of *Princesses*. She would go on to co-create and star on *The Nanny* for six seasons on CBS and more recently *Happily Divorced*.

Episode 3: October 11, 1991 "Luv Leddahs"

Director: Lee Shallat Chemel   Writer: Marion Grodin

Tracy receives a love letter from a student as part of a writing assignment and thinks that the letter is really for her. Because the student is shy, Georgy suggests that Tracy write him a love letter, and Tracy also invites the student to her place for tutoring. When he arrives, he thanks Tracy for helping him with his writing since it got him back together with his wife. Tracy is glad that she didn't send her love letter to him. However, she finds that Georgy secretly sent the letter. When the student's wife receives the letter, she decides to leave her husband again, and so Tracy has to clear up the misunderstanding.

Writer Marion Grodin is the daughter of actor Charles Grodin.

Episode 4: October 18, 1991 "Someday My Prince Will Gum"

Director: Lee Shallat Chemel   Writer: John Bowman

Melissa's sister gets her two tickets to a Periodontists' Ball (or as the dentists call it – the "Gum Ball") and asks Melissa to take one of her husband's dentist colleagues.

Tracy suggests that Melissa make an appointment with the dentist to see what he is like. Melissa finds that he already has a girlfriend and further that the colleague's dental hygienist is having an affair with her sister's husband. Melissa takes Tracy to the ball, while Georgy is left home cleaning the apartment. At the ball, when Melissa confronts her brother-in-law about the affair with the hygienist, he says it was a minor affair – he just kissed her and gave her a hickey. Melissa's sister and brother-in-law make up, and Georgy, looking like Cinderella, arrives at the ball with the tickets that Tracy and Melissa had forgotten.

Episode 5: October 25, 1991   "Georgy Sings the Blues"

Director: Lee Shallat Chemel   Writers: Mark Ganzel and Robin Schiff

Melissa meets two Frenchmen at the department store where she works and invites them on a date with her and Tracy. Melissa doesn't tell Tracy that her date is much shorter than she is. Meanwhile, Georgy looks for an agent and finds one who is suicidal because he ran his father's business into the ground. Georgy invites him to live at the apartment until he finds her a job. He finally gets her a singing engagement at a blues club. Melissa and Tracy and the two Frenchmen go to the club to see Georgy where she sings the "Widowed Princess Blues."

Episode 6: Unaired   "The Snob Who Came to Dinner"

Director: Lee Shallat Chemel   Writers: Robin Schiff and Mark Ganzel

In order to meet wealthy men, the three roommates plan to throw a party for all single males who live in their building. Among the guests is a columnist and art critic who offends everyone, but Tracy admires him. Since she wants to be a writer, Tracy hopes the guy can help her. When he and Tracy go on a date to the opera, she sees his real character. She tells him that he is overcritical, arrogant, and picky. Contrary to being hurt by her comment, he seems to be reformed.

Episode 7: Unaired   "The Showuhs in Yonkuhs Fall Mainly on the Flowuhs"

Director: Lee Shallat Chemel   Writer: John Bowman

Georgy agrees to teach Melissa how to lose her Queens accent and speak like a lady so she can impress Fisher Hollinger, a wealthy publisher who's attracted to her.

Episode 8: Unaired   "Tall, Dark and Hansom"

Director: Lee Shallat Chemel   Writers: Robin Schiff and Mark Ganzel

Tracy, Melissa, and Georgy all go to a singles bar so Georgy can meet a new man. She meets a guy who is turned off when she tells him about her love for her deceased husband and how she wants a long-term relationship. Georgy then wanders through Central Park where she meets Edward, a British coachman, who reminds her of her late husband, and she wants to believe that their encounter is a sign from her late spouse.

Farewell, *Princesses*

Princesses originally aired at 8:00 PM on Fridays on CBS because the network thought an adult comedy would do well against ABC's *Family Matters* aimed at kids. CBS was wrong. *Princesses* struggled in the ratings. The network changed its time slot to 8:30 PM, but that did not help. It was CBS' lowest-rated series, ranking eighty-fifth for its final episode. Furthermore, Julie Hagerty was apparently unhappy with the direction of her character. According to magazine articles at the time, Hagerty disliked playing straight woman to Fran Drescher and Twiggy.[48] She quit the series and, before the producers could find a replacement for her, CBS canceled *Princesses*.

The Return of Jezebel James

Premiered Friday, March 14, 2008, at 8:00 PM on Fox

Sarah Tompkins (Parker Posey) had everything—a good career as a children's book editor and a boyfriend—everything except a child. When Sarah learned she could not have a baby, she looked to her estranged, uninhibited younger sister Caroline "Coco" (Lauren Ambrose) to have a baby for her. And so, who was Jezebel James? She was Coco's imaginary childhood friend whom Sarah had turned into a series of kids' books. Other characters on this comedy included Marcus Sonti (Scott Cohen), Sarah's co-worker with whom she was having no-strings attached sex, Buddy (Michael Arden), Sarah's assistant at work, and Ronald Tompkins (Ron McLarty), Sarah and Coco's dad.

Background

The Return of Jezebel James was created by Amy Sherman Palladino, who had previously created the short-lived *Love and Marriage* and the successful *Gilmore Girls*. Regency Television and Fox produced the sitcom.

Episode Guide: 3 aired; 4 unaired

Episode 1: March 14, 2008   "Pilot"

Director/Writer: Amy Sherman Palladino

Sarah Tompkins, having broken up eight months earlier with Matt—a man she had lived with for ten years, wants to become a single mom but discovers that she is unable to conceive. She decides to ask her sister Coco to have her baby. Sarah will pay Coco, but her sister must move in with her so she can monitor the pregnancy.

Lauren Ambrose (Coco) previously was a regular on the HBO drama *Six Feet Under*. Parker Posey's career began on the CBS daytime drama *As the World Turns*.

Episode 2: March 14, 2008   "Frankenstein Baby"

Director/Writer: Amy Sherman Palladino

Sarah gives Coco an emergency Hello Kitty cell phone, and then the siblings' parents, Ronald and Talia (Dianne Wiest), arrive for a surprise visit. Sarah tells her parents that Coco has moved in with her and is going to have a baby for her. The mother is upset and calls the baby a "Frankenstein baby." Meanwhile, Sarah continues her sexual affair with Marcus.

Episode 3: March 21, 2008   "Needles & Schlag"

Director: Gail Mancuso Writer: Amy Sherman Palladino

Sarah seeks to help a precocious fifteen-year-old get his book published. She tries to impress him with tickets to a Knicks game, but he prefers going to "Bed, Bath and Beyond" instead. Meanwhile, Sarah goes with Coco to her gynecologist's office where she finds that Coco is afraid of needles. She helps Coco through the experience of having a blood test.

Episode 4: Unaired   "The Return of the Crazy Jackal Shillelagh Lady"

Director: Gail Mancuso   Writer: Daniel Palladino

After the sisters' mother Talia (the crazy jackal shillelagh lady) drops in on Coco unexpectedly one too many times, Coco decides to get a job so she is not always in the apartment. She becomes a dog walker for a tenant in the building. However, Sarah has an argument with the tenant, and Coco loses her job.

Writer Daniel Palladino is the husband of series creator Amy Sherman Palladino.

Episode 5: Unaired   "I'm With Blank"

Director: Michael Zinberg   Writer: Amy Sherman Palladino

Sarah has a party for one of her most successful author's sequel to his popular book. The author reads a draft aloud to a group of kids who discover that the beloved main character dies. Meanwhile, Coco gets a visit from former boyfriend, Dash. They have sex, but then he leaves, making her very unhappy.

Episode 6: Unaired   "Paragraph Two, Section Three"

Director: Michael Zinberg   Writer: Amy B. Harris

Marcus visits Sarah's apartment for the first time and spends the night where he runs into Dash in the kitchen. Coco informs Dash that she will be a surrogate mother, and wants Sarah to tell Marcus. When she does, Marcus is upset over the changes a baby will bring to their relationship. Meanwhile, because Coco wants to begin receiving payments for the surrogacy, she and Sarah go to a lawyer's office where they argue over the terms of the agreement.

Episode 7: Unaired   "Sarah Takes a Bullet"

Director: Jody Margolin   Writer: Daniel Palladino

The two sisters are invited to dinner with their parents. Sarah promises to defend Coco against the parents' inevitable criticism of her. Ronald and Talia treat Coco like she is not part of the family; all of the pictures in their house are of Sarah. Mom and dad are still upset over Sarah's plans to have Coco have her baby. The episode ends with everyone watching videos of Sarah's performances in her high school musicals.

Coco never did actually get pregnant in the episodes produced.

The Demise of *Jezebel James*

Fox initially ordered thirteen episodes of the comedy but reduced that order to seven. The sitcom was to receive a special launch after an episode of *American Idol*, which never happened. Instead, the show debuted on a Friday night with back-to-back episodes. It aired one more episode the following week in its regular time slot – Fridays at 8:30 PM and then disappeared—another victim of very low ratings.

Semi-Tough

Premiered Thursday, May 29, 1980, at 9:30 PM on ABC

Trying to capitalize on the success of *Three's Company*, ABC commissioned a sitcom version of the movie *Semi-Tough*. The series involved the misadventures of two womanizing football players – Billy Clyde Pucket (Bruce McGill) and Shake Tiller (David Hasselhoff), who shared their apartment with a young woman, Barbara Jane Bookman (Markie Post). Unlike the movie, the relationship among all three on the TV series was platonic. Barbara Jane's parents were Big Ed Bookman (Hugh Gillin) and Big Barb (Mary Jo Catlett). Billy Clyde and Shake played for the New York Bulls, owned by Bart Danby (Jim McKrell) and coached by Coach Cooper (Ed Peck).

Background

Broadway impresario David Merrick, who had produced the film version based on the novel by Dan Jenkins, was the executive producer of the series, which was produced by Universal. The initial pilot for *Semi-Tough* titled "Barbara Jane Moves In" starred Mary Louise Weller as Barbara Jane, Doug Barr as Billy Clyde, and Josh Taylor as Shake. Written by Shelley Zellman, Wally Dalton, and Dan Jenkins, it was scheduled to air on ABC in January 1980, but never did. The show was recast, and ABC scheduled four episodes of the comedy after *Barney Miller* on Thursday nights.

Episode Guide: 4 aired episodes

Episode 1: May 29, 1980   "Barbara Jane Moves Out"

Director: Richard Benjamin   Story: Norman Barasch, Wally Dalton, and Shelley Zellman   Teleplay: Wally Dalton, Shelley Zellman, and Reinhold Weege

Barbara Jane moves out of the guys' apartment, and decides to go with a race car driver to Italy. However, Billy Clyde and Shake have second thoughts and want to stop her.

Actor/director Richard Benjamin is married to actress Paula Prentiss and starred with her in the sixties sitcom *He and She*.

Episode 2: June 5, 1980   "One Bad Apple"

Director: John Tracy   Writers: Ian Praiser and Howard Gewirtz

Billy Clyde is jilted by the woman he loves and wants to marry. Barbara Jane and Shake try to cheer him up by arranging a blind date for Billy Clyde with a "hip chick."

Episode 3: June 12, 1980   "That Catch"

Director: Dick Martin   Writer: Rich Reinhart

Shake gets a swelled head after making a game-winning catch to end the team's losing streak. He offends a defensive player from the opposing team and then disappears.

Episode 4: June 19, 1980   "The First Hurrah"

Director: Dick Martin   Writer: Rich Reinhart

Shake and Billy Clyde help with Barbara Jane's first job – campaign manager for a local politician.

Christopher Lloyd (*Taxi, The Dictator*) played the politician on this episode.

Another Movie-Based Sitcom Bites the Dust

With the exception of *M*A*S*H* and *Alice*, situation comedies based on movies do not seem to last very long. *Semi-Tough* was no exception. The ratings for *Semi-Tough* were not as good as those for the series it had replaced – *The Ropers*, and so ABC never ordered additional episodes.

Some of My Best Friends

Premiered Wednesday, February 28, 2001, at 8:00 PM on CBS

Attempting to duplicate the success of NBC's *Will & Grace*, CBS put on its own sitcom dealing with a gay leading character. *Some of My Best Friends* starred Danny Nucci as aspiring actor Frankie Zito, and Jason Bateman as writer Warren Fairbanks. Warren's lover had just moved out of their apartment after a fight, so Warren placed an ad in the newspaper: "GWM seeks roommate." Since Frankie wanted to move out of his parents' house, he responded to the ad thinking that "GWM" meant "guy with money." Only on a TV sitcom could a handsome, wannabe actor like Frankie misinterpret the meaning of "GWM." Nevertheless, Frankie moved in with Warren and then realized that Warren was gay, but, since they were starting to like each other, they decided to give being roommates a try. Meryl Doogan (Jessica Lundy), Warren's twice-divorced sister, managed the apartment building where Warren and

Frankie lived. Warren's best friend was Vern Limoso (Alec Mapa), and Frankie's best friend was Pino Palumbo (Michael DeLuise).

Background

Some of My Best Friends was based on the 1997 independent film *Kiss Me, Guido*, which in turn was based on a German movie called *Maybe, Maybe Not*. Tony Vitale wrote and directed *Kiss Me, Guido*, and he and Marc Cherry developed *Some of My Best Friends*. In *Kiss Me, Guido*, both Warren and Frankie were pursuing acting careers. When Warren injured his ankle, he got Frankie to play his role as a gay character in an avant-garde off-Broadway play being produced by his ex-boyfriend, Dakota. The sitcom was originally to be titled the same as the movie, but CBS decided *Some of My Best Friends* to be a safer title. Axelrod/Widdoes Entertainment and CBS Television Studios produced the comedy.

Episode Guide: 5 aired; 2 unaired

Episode 1: February 28, 2001   "Pilot"

Director: James Widdoes   Writers: Marc Cherry and Tony Vitale

Twenty-four-year-old Frankie Zito moves out of his parent's place in response to an ad for a roommate placed by Warren Fairbanks, whose boyfriend of two years had just left him. Frankie initially thinks Warren is Jewish but subsequently finds out he is gay. He wants to move out, but, when Warren's ex stops by for his raincoat, Vern tells him that Frankie is Warren's new boyfriend. Wanting to be an actor, Frankie decides to play the part. Later, Frankie's parents visit and ask him to move back with them. They think the real reason he moved is because he is gay, but he informs them he moved because he wants to be an actor, and he decides to stay with Warren.

Marc Cherry, who co-wrote this episode, is better known for having created the ABC series *Desperate Housewives*.

Episode 2: March 7, 2001   "Fight Night"

Director: James Widdoes   Writers: John Pardee and Joey Murphy

Frankie is having some of his friends over to watch a fight on TV, and they don't know that he has a gay roommate. Although he wants Warren to leave before his friends arrive, Warren decides not to go out when he finds that his ex-boyfriend will be at the party he planned to attend. While Frankie and Pino try to portray Warren as straight, Vern comes by, and one of Frankie's friends calls Vern 'queer.' When the television goes out, Vern says he can fix it if Frankie's friends apologize. Frankie insists that they do. After they all apologize, Vern leaves since he really doesn't know how to fix the TV set.

Michael DeLuise (Pino) is the middle son of the late comedian Dom DeLuise.

Episode 3: March 12, 2001   "Blah, Blah, Blah"

Director: James Widdoes Writers: Judd Pilot and John Peaslee

Michelle, the girl Frankie is dating, likes to talk about her feelings and likes to shop. Frankie doesn't like doing either, but Warren does. When Warren begins spending time with Michelle, Frankie wonders if Warren is really gay, but then Warren mentions that Michelle wants to have sex with Frankie. He also tells Frankie that together they make the perfect man for a woman. Finally, Warren gets tired of listening to Michelle talk about her feelings and wants to break up with her. He convinces Frankie that Michelle deserves better than both of them.

Before *Some of My Best Friends*, Jason Bateman (Warren) was a regular on six sitcoms: *Silver Spoons*, *It's Your Move*, *Valerie* aka *The Hogan Family*, *Simon*, *Chicago Sons*, and *George & Leo*. After *Some of My Best Friends*, he starred on two more sitcoms (*Arrested Development* and *The Jake Effect*) before becoming a star in movies such as *Juno*, *The Switch*, and *Horrible Bosses*.

Episode 4: March 28, 2001   "A Brief Encounter"

Director: James Widdoes   Writers: John Pardee and Joey Murphy

Vern thinks that Frankie is gay since he is good at picking out clothes and uses the word "fabulous" a lot; Pino thinks that Warren has a crush on Frankie because he is doing Frankie's laundry and cooking for him. When Frankie can't find a pair of red silk underwear he recently purchased, he thinks that Warren took them because of his crush on him. Meanwhile, Vern sees Frankie going through Warren's underwear drawer looking for his silk underpants, and Vern thinks that Frankie wants some of Warren's underwear. After Pino tells Frankie that Warren must be wearing his silk underpants, Frankie goes into Warren's bedroom while he is asleep and finds that Warren is naked. Warren wakes up and says that he didn't take Frankie's underwear, and Frankie responds that he is not gay. Apparently a heavy-set neighbor lady took Frankie's underwear for a souvenir.

Alec Mapa (Vern) later starred on *Ugly Betty*.

Episode 5: April 11, 2001   "Shaggy Dog Story"

Director: James Widdoes   Writers: Judd Pilot and John Peaslee

Frankie and Warren take home a stray dog which they have to take to the vet because it has a cold. They need $380 to cover the vet bill and take $400 that Meryl owes Vern to cover the expense. Seeing Frankie and Warren together with the dog, a new tenant in the building thinks that they make a cute family. When no one immediately claims the dog, Frankie wants to keep it, but Warren isn't as sure. However, after the new tenant tells Frankie that she thought he was gay since she saw him with Warren and the dog, Frankie wants to get rid of the pooch, but Warren now wants to keep it. The dog's owner finally calls to pick up the dog and leaves a check for the vet expenses, which Warren gives to Vern for the money Meryl owed him.

Episode 6: Unaired   "The Marriage Counselor"

Director: James Widdoes Writer: Marc Cherry

Frankie wants to avoid his mother who is coming for a visit, and so Warren and Vern befriend her. She confides to them that her husband may leave her because she is not that good in the bedroom. Warren offers her some sex tips on how to please a man. Frankie's father subsequently tells his son that his mother must be having an affair to learn such new sexual techniques. Warren finally confesses that he is the one who told Mrs. Zito about the new techniques.

Episode 7: Unaired "Scenes from an Italian Party"

Director: James Widdoes   Writers: Terry Maloney Haley and Mindy Morgenstern

Frankie's parents are celebrating their twenty-fifth wedding anniversary, and Warren is planning the party. Frankie invites Warren's sister to the party on behalf of Pino, and she thinks she will be Frankie's date. When Frankie shows up with another girl, she is disappointed and commiserates with Pino. Warren asks the Zito's to make toasts, but Mr. Zito doesn't know what to say and his wife gets mad at him. To make matters worse, after Warren tells Mr. Zito that he is the better person in the relationship, he doesn't apologize to his wife. However, when the parents hear the singer Warren hired, who was the singer on their first date, the Zito's get back together.

No More *Best Friends*

CBS scheduled *Some of My Best Friends* at 8:00 PM Wednesdays, where it replaced Bette Midler's sitcom, which moved to 8:30 PM. Coincidentally, Bette Midler was one of the executive producers of *Some of My Best Friends*. The comedy's premiere ranked seventy-third and the next episode ranked seventy-fourth. However, CBS decided to air one episode after its hit *Everybody Loves Raymond* on March 12; that episode rated twenty-ninth for the week. When the series returned to its regular Wednesday timeslot, the ratings fell again, and *Some of My Best Friends* was canceled after five episodes. The entire sitcom later aired on the Universal HD cable channel.

Trial and Error

Premiered Tuesday, March 15, 1988, at 8:00 PM on CBS

With a title like *Trial and Error*, at least one of the characters had to be a lawyer. This buddy sitcom focused on two Hispanic childhood friends who shared an apartment in Los Angeles and who had made widely different career choices. John Hernandez (Eddie Valez) was a conservative, recent law-school graduate working for a prestigious law firm, Kittle, Barnes, Fletcher, and Gray; his friend and roommate, Tony Rivera (Paul Rodriguez), was a brash T-shirt vendor. Other characters on *Trial and Error* were fellow attorney at the law firm Bob Adams (John de Lancie), John's secretary Rhonda (Debbie Shapiro), and senior partner Edmund Kittle (Stephen Elliott).

Background

Trial and Error evolved from a comedy pilot called *The Family Martinez* created by comedian Tommy Chong of Cheech and Chong in 1986.[49] *The Family Martinez* was about a former Hispanic gang member who became a lawyer and returned to his family home in East L.A. CBS liked the concept but wanted the show changed from a family comedy to a buddy comedy. The pilot was reworked by Donald Seigel and Jerry Perzigian, recast, and was called *Amigos*. The title was then changed to *Trial and Error* because of objections by Paul Rodriguez that *Amigos* was too stereotypical.[50] Tommy Chong remained an executive producer of *Trial and Error*, even though, according to sources connected with the series, he never showed up in either the writing room or on the set. Columbia Pictures Television produced the comedy. Of note, the sitcom was the first English-language TV series to be simulcast in Spanish on Spanish-language radio stations in certain large cities. The comedy's theme was written and performed by the R & B vocal group Sister Sledge.

Episode Guide: 3 aired; 5 unaired

Episode 1: March 15, 1988   "Pilot"

Director: Andrew D. Weyman   Writers: Donald L. Seigel and Jerry Perzigian

John has a tough first day at his new law firm including being mistaken as a typewriter repairman by his boss' secretary and having a large copying machine installed in his office. Tony takes him to lunch at the expensive Foxboro Inn to cheer him up but embarrasses him by, among other things, yelling to a bus boy: "Raul! When did they let you out?" John tells Tony that he is not sure he is going to fit in at the firm, and, when John meets with Mr. Kittle and asks if he was hired because he is Latino, Mr. Kittle replies that John was among the six most qualified applicants for the position but being Latino did make a difference. Tony says John should be proud he was hired, and Tony sends T-shirts to the entire firm with the slogan "Get Off with John" to celebrate John's first day.

Episode 2: March 22, 1988   "Bon Appetit"

Director: Andrew D. Weyman   Writer: Steven Kunes

Tony suggests inviting Mr. Kittle to dinner at their apartment so John can talk with him about getting more responsibility at work. Tony and John order pickled squid, Mr. Kittle's favorite dish, from a restaurant. They do not like the dish and feed most of their portions to a cat a neighbor asked them to watch. During the dinner, when Mr. Kittle receives a phone call from a woman to meet her at a hotel, John thinks that Kittle is using him as an alibi to have an affair. After Mr. Kittle leaves for the hotel, the two buddies find that the cat is dead. Since they think the pickled squid must have killed the cat, they hurry to the hotel to get Mr. Kittle. There they mistake Mr. Kittle's wife for his mistress and rush Kittle to the hospital to have his stomach pumped. In the end, they find that the cat died of old age.

In one of his earliest credited TV appearances, a twenty-four-year-old Brad Pitt played a hotel bellhop on this episode.

Episode 3: March 29, 1988   "Man's Best Friend"

Director: Andrew D. Weyman   Writer: Al Aidekman

When John is having trouble sleeping, Tony suggests they go for a walk. While on the walk, John is bitten by a dog who turns out to be Arnie, the star of several movies. Although the dog's attorney wants to settle with John so he doesn't sue, Tony convinces him to pursue legal action. The dog has bitten other people in the past and could be put to sleep if John identifies the dog has his attacker. The dog's attorney offers Tony a part in the canine's next film, and now Tony doesn't want John to take action. However, John has second thoughts about not identifying the dog that bit him, and Tony begins to have guilt feelings. Tony says they should do what they should have done in the first place. After John finds out about the movie role offered Tony, he advises Tony that he should have been more honest with him.

Episode 4: Unaired   "Deride and Conquer"

Director: Andrew D. Weyman   Writers: Donald Seigel and Jerry Perzigian

When Tony wants to date "Miss Combustoline," he and John meet her at an auto parts store. Tony has a theory about beautiful women that if a man points out their flaws, they will be attracted to him. However, when Tony meets Miss Combustoline, he gets tongue-tied. After she tells Tony he is holding up the line, John rebukes her. She then gives John her phone number which Tony thinks proves his theory. Later, Tony hires an actress to pretend she is attracted to him based on his pointing out her flaws. Tony is to meet the actress at a bar, but, at the bar, Tony goes to the wrong woman, insults her, and her husband punches him. Tony admits that his theory doesn't work.

Episode 5: Unaired "Ring of Truth" (aka "Why Superman Can't Marry" and "The Informant")

Director: Andrew D. Weyman   Writer: Al Aidekman

John is assigned a major class action suit by his law firm. While waiting for John at a bar, Tony meets Diana who goes home with John and him and bakes cookies for them. At their apartment, John mentions that he found a star witness for his case and that he has to go to his office. Diana leaves shortly thereafter. The next day, the star witness fails to show up. Later Tony tells John that Diana came back to their apartment to clean everything including the papers on John's desk. John becomes suspicious that Diana is really an informant for the defense in his class action suit. John plans to prove this by letting her know of some papers relating to the case concerning another star witness. However, Diana doesn't pursue the tip. John finally catches Diana in a lie about never having to have her car fixed when she told Tony at the bar that her car was being repaired. Diana admits that she is working for the defense.

Episode 6: Unaired "Casino Night" (summary provided by Tracy Gamble)

Director: Andrew D. Weyman   Writers: Tracy Gamble and Richard Vaczy

John and Tony hold a casino night to help refurbish their apartment building with the plan being to bilk the managing partner of John's law firm. Instead, a wealthy female relative of the partner attends and cleans everyone out.

Episode 7: Unaired "Strike Three, You're Out" (summary provided by Al Aidekman)

Director: Andrew D. Weyman   Story: Rick Valentine   Teleplay: Doug McIntyre

John and Tony volunteer to coach Little League. John believes in letting everyone play, while Tony is there to win even if it means using some shady tactics like cheating.

Episode 8: Unaired   "Born to Squirm" (summary provided by Jerry Perzigian)

Director: Andrew D. Weyman   Story: Terence McGovern and Kenneth Kimmons   Teleplay: Doug McIntyre

Rock star Billy Squirm wants Tony to design a T-shirt for him.

No Room for *Error*

Although the series received several negative reviews, an article titled "Two Comedy Series Debut with Promise for Long Runs" in the *Chicago Sun-Times* pronounced *Trial and Error* "a funny, fast-paced comedy."[51] The other new sitcom reviewed in the article was *The Wonder Years*, which, unlike *Trial and Error*, lasted for six seasons.

Trial and Error was canceled after only three episodes. The sitcom did not do well against *Who's the Boss?* on ABC and *Matlock* on NBC. The premiere episode ranked seventy-sixth in the ratings out of seventy-six shows.

Twenty Good Years

Premiered Wednesday, October 11, 2006, at 8:30 PM on NBC

Twenty Good Years starred John Lithgow (*3rd Rock from the Sun*) and Jeffrey Tambor (*Arrested Development, Everything's Relative, Welcome to the Captain*) as two old friends——Dr. John Mason (Lithgow), a thrice-divorced, outgoing orthopedic surgeon forced into semi-retirement at age sixty, and Jeffrey Pyne (Tambor), a conservative, retired judge whose wife had died twenty years earlier. John convinced Jeffrey to make the most out of life during the twenty years they figured they had left. Also in the cast were Jake Sandvig as Hugh Pyne, the nineteen-year-old male model son of Judge Pyne and Heather Burns as Stella Mason, Dr. Mason's daughter who got impregnated through a sperm bank.

Background

Michael Leeson and Marsh McCall created the series, which was produced by Werner-Gold-Miller and Marsh McCall Productions in association with Warner Bros. Television. According to McCall, the idea for the sitcom came from Tom Werner, formerly of Carsey-Werner Productions, who had produced John Lithgow's comedy *3rd Rock from the Sun*.[52] Lithgow agreed to do *Twenty Good Years* once Jeffrey Tambor signed on. Michael Leeson wrote the original pilot, but, because of creative differences with Tom Werner, Marsh McCall replaced Leeson. The two leads chose their own first names for their characters. The last name for Lithgow's character came from a friend McCall had in college whose last name was "Mason," and who had some of the same qualities of the Lithgow character on *Twenty Good Years*. Tambor's character's last name came from a screenwriter mentor of McCall's – Danny Pine.[53] McCall based some of the character traits of John and Jeffrey on his own father, a professor at Stanford, and named John's daughter on the series after his own daughter, Stella.[54]

Episode Guide: 4 aired; 9 unaired

Episode 1: October 11, 2006 "Pilot"

Director: Terry Hughes   Story: Michael Leeson and Marsh McCall   Teleplay: Marsh McCall

John is forced by his hospital into semi-retirement on his sixtieth birthday. He shows up late to the birthday party his pregnant daughter is having for him and proclaims that, for the next twenty years he thinks he has left, he wants to live life to the fullest. John's best friend Jeffrey is at the party with Gina (Judith Light), his girlfriend of three years who wants him to propose. But after listening to John about living life on the edge, he breaks up with her. When Stella tells Jeffrey her dad is having financial problems with paying three alimonies, Jeffrey invites John to move in with him. Stella goes into labor and has a baby girl. In the end, John and Jeffrey take a dip in the frigid Atlantic Ocean.

Episode 2: October 18, 2006   "Big Love"

Director: Terry Hughes   Writer: Patricia Breen

John and Jeffrey meet Mary Frances (Jane Leeves), the owner of a rock music club, who invites them to an after party. Mary Frances likes both John and Jeffrey, and John suggests that they both date her. Stella and Hugh don't like the relationship and ask what the sleeping arrangements are—a subject that has yet to come up with Mary Frances. After Stella and Hugh leave Jeffrey's place, Mary Frances suggests they have a threesome, which in the end Jeffrey and John decline.

Episode 3: October 25, 2006   "The Elbow Incident"

Director: Terry Hughes   Writer: Marsh McCall

When Jeffrey hurts his elbow in a basketball game with two younger players, he refuses to let John operate on it because he doesn't like hospitals ever since he had his tonsils out while in college and, without his knowledge, his roommates posed with him in the recovery room with their penises on his forehead. With Jeffrey in a lot of pain, John gives him sleeping pills and then takes him to the OR for surgery. After the surgery, Jeffrey demands an apology from John for duping him. When Jeffrey doesn't receive an apology, he files a complaint against John with the hospital. Jeffrey points out that John felt humiliated when he was forced into semi-retirement and Jeffrey feels the same way when John tricked him into having surgery. After making this statement, Jeffrey withdraws his complaint.

Episode 4: November 1, 2006   "Jeffrey's Choice"

Director: Terry Hughes   Writer: Kirk J. Rudell

When Jeffrey bumps into his ex-girlfriend Gina at a drugstore, she says she is no longer angry with him. They get back together after having sex. John resents the renewed relationship and thinks that Gina is just as controlling as she always was, but Jeffrey disagrees. Jeffrey and Gina go to Vermont on the same weekend that John had planned to bungee jump with him. John drives to Vermont to try to persuade Jeffrey to leave Gina, but he won't leave her. After finding out for himself that Gina has not really changed, Jeffrey finally shows up at the bungee jumping site where John is.

Episode 5: Unaired "Sorry, Wrong Ship"

Director: Terry Hughes   Writer: Mike Teverbaugh

Hugh invites his dad and John to a yacht party with his model friends. However, by mistake, John and Jeffrey board the wrong ship. The vessel they board is populated with mourners on their way to spread their friend's ashes at sea.

Episode 6: Unaired "The Bong Show"

Director: Terry Hughes   Writer: Eric Zicklin

Jeffrey accidently buys a bong thinking it is a vase. John sneaks it into the background of a picture being taken of the judge to be hung in the courthouse in honor of his twenty years of service.

Episode 7: Unaired "Murder He Thought"

Director: Terry Hughes   Writers: Marsh McCall and Mike Teverbaugh

Jeffrey's former girlfriend Gina claims to have gone into therapy and changed her behavior, but John doesn't believe her. Jeffrey invites her on a rock hunting excursion where she falls and breaks her leg.

Episode 8: Unaired "Between Brock and a Hard Place"

Director: Terry Hughes   Writer: Robert Cohen

Jeffrey and John's neighbor, Brock Manley (Ed O'Neill), invites them to apply for membership in an exclusive all-male club – The Magellan Adventure Club, which leads them into an initiation they hadn't bargained for.

Episode 9: Unaired "They Shoot Turkeys, Don't They?"

Director: Terry Hughes   Writer: Hugh Webber

Preparing for Thanksgiving, Jeffrey tries to teach Hugh how to make the perfect pie, while John plans to hunt for his turkey dinner. Meanwhile, John learns about his daughter's relationship with the doctor hired to replace him.

Episode 10: Unaired   "Remember the Alimony"

Director: Terry Hughes   Writer: Sung Suh

John's ex-wife, Kate, announces that she is engaged which makes him happy since he won't have to pay any more alimony. However, Jeffrey suspects that her fiancé is gay after he admits he is "living a lie."

Episode 11: Unaired   "John's Old Lady"

Director: Terry Hughes   Writers: Marsh McCall & Kirk J. Rudell

Jeffrey notices that John's constant arguing with their attractive middle-aged neighbor is just thinly-disguised flirtation. In the meantime, a sexy law student flirts with Jeffrey, but they find that they do not have much in common.

Episode 12: Unaired   "The Crying Game"

Director: Terry Hughes   Writer: Samantha McIntyre

John's date accuses him of being unemotional, and so he pretends to cry. However, she sees through this emotional display. Meanwhile, Jeffrey cooks in a kitchen full of smoke because the building manager has ignored his pleas to fix the broken vent and a stuck window.

Episode 13: Unaired   "Come Fly with Me"

Director: Terry Hughes   Writers: Roy Brown and Blake J. Williger

Jeffrey finds the woman of his dreams that he wants to spend the rest of his life with, but John is not happy about this. Feeling rejected, John flies to Las Vegas and returns with a new wife – a Korean blackjack dealer.

Years End

The series followed another new NBC sitcom, *30 Rock*. Both comedies had low ratings opposite the *Dancing with the Stars* results show on ABC. The second episode of *Twenty Good Years* ranked seventieth in the Nielsen's and was fifth in its timeslot after baseball on Fox and *Americca's Top Model* on the CW. The comedy was canceled after four episodes.

Eddie Mayehoff in *Doc Corkle*

Chapter 8
Welcome to My World— Male Version

Comedies built around a leading male character have been around since the beginnings of television. *The Life of Riley* and *Make Room for Daddy* (aka *The Danny Thomas Show*) are but two examples of such shows from the fifties, while *The Dick Van Dyke Show* and *The Andy Griffith Show* are examples from the sixties. Unlike family comedies that focus on domestic life and workplace sitcoms that deal primarily with working life, central character comedies attempt to portray an entire world of both family and career situations. Such comedies usually have the star's name or his character's name in the title of the show. This chapter profiles male central character comedies that didn't quite make it.

Bob Patterson

Premiered Tuesday, October 2, 2001, at 9:00 PM on ABC

As Bob Patterson, Jason Alexander (George Costanza from *Seinfeld*) played a neurotic motivational speaker with a messy personal life. Patterson had an ex-wife

Janet (Jennifer Aspen, *Come to Papa*); a son, Jeffrey (James Guidice) by his first ex-wife; an assistant, Landau (Robert Klein); a clumsy, wheelchair-bound secretary, Claudia (Chandra Wilson), and an incompetent intern, Vic (Phil Buckman, *Daddy's Girls*).

Background

Alexander created and produced the comedy along with Peter Tilden and Mike Markowitz. He admitted that the Bob Patterson character was created "... out of the ashes of George (Costanza)."[55] ABC agreed to pay a seven-figure penalty if the pilot was not made into a series. After the pilot was shot, two supporting roles were recast – that of Bob's ex-wife and Bob's intern. The character of Bob's business partner Landau was originally envisioned for Martin Landau, but it was later decided they needed a somewhat younger actor. The sitcom was a joint production of Twentieth Century-Fox and Touchstone Television.

Episode Guide: 5 aired; 5 unaired

Episode 1: October 2, 2001 "Pilot"

Director: Barnet Kellman   Story: Jason Alexander, Mike Markowitz, and Peter Tilden

Teleplay: Jason Alexander, Ira Steven Behr, Tim Doyle, Peter Tilden

Bob Patterson, the third-best motivational speaker in the country, is trying to get over his divorce from his second wife, Janet, when she moves back into his house and announces that she is now celibate. Meanwhile, Bob does not like the infomercial he filmed with John Tesh because of the disparity in their height. Bob needs to be alone to prepare for an upcoming seminar but keeps getting interrupted by John Tesh who thinks he could have been better in the infomercial, by Landau who wants Bob to have a gimmick for the seminar, and by his ex-wife. When Janet says she is moving out again, Bob asks her to stay because he discovers she inspires his presentations. Bob ends up presenting his seminar on a bed of nails and then goes to the hospital for treatment of cuts on his back.

Chandra Wilson, who played Bob's secretary, went on to star as Dr. Miranda Bailey on *Grey's Anatomy*.

Episode 2: October 8, 2001   "Honest Bob"

Director: Barnet Kellman   Writers: Ira Steven Behr and Peter Tilden

The results of a focus group viewing the infomercial suggest that women do not like Bob. Bob decides to get rid of John Tesh and do a new infomercial with Bo Derek. Since Tesh signed a contract for the infomercial, Bob and Landau insult him to trick him into breaking the contract. Bo Derek is impressed by Bob who invites her to dinner, and they sign a contract for her work. However, then John Tesh and his wife Connie Sellecca appear. Connie tells Bob and Landau that they duped her husband into quitting. Bo Derek quits, and Bob does the infomercial with Connie Sellecca.

Episode 3: October 16, 2001   "Naked Bob"

Director: Barnet Kellman   Writer: Barbie Feldman Adler

Bob is invited to pose nude for a coffee table book called *Naked Power* being put together by a female French photographer. He is reluctant to do this until Janet tells him that he has naked body issues. Bob gets aroused when any woman speaks French to him. To address this concern, Janet offers Bob some tea that will keep him down for an hour. Although the photographer is attracted to Bob, when she kisses him, nothing happens. She concludes he must be gay. The photo shoot is delayed, and, when it finally takes place, the photographer decides to surround Bob with a bunch of naked men just as the effects of the tea wear off.

Episode 4: October 24, 2001   "Awards Bob"

Director: Barnet Kellman   Writer: Hayes Jackson

Bob is nominated, along with the country's number two motivational speaker, Warren Wellman (William Shatner), for a motivator of the year award. Since Bob has lost the award for the past seven years, Landau suggests he schmooze the judges. Bob and Jeffrey take one of the judges and his son, who is a dwarf, to a baseball game, and, when Bob catches a fly ball, he accidentally knocks the judge's son over the stadium guard rail. When Bob goes to the hospital to see him, he encounters Warren Wellman already there visiting the judge's son. Bob tries to schmooze the other judge – an eighty-seven-year-old woman who wants to have sex with Bob. But after she sees Bob, she says she prefers Landau. At the award ceremony, Wellman wins again, and Bob can't believe it. He wonders why the elderly lady didn't at least vote for him. It turns out that it was the woman's granddaughter who was the real judge.

Episode 5: October 31, 2001   "Bathroom Bob"

Director: Robby Benson   Writer: Brian Scully

Landau keeps using Bob's private bathroom at work, while Bob wants him to use the company's bathroom. They get into a disagreement over the use of the bathroom which evolves into an argument about who made whom successful. Landau quits, but, before he goes, they each have a flashback to when they both first met. In Landau's version, Bob was a hapless TV salesman whom Landau discovered and taught how to become a motivational speaker; in Bob's version, Landau was down-on-his–luck and Bob inspired him to turn his life around. After Landau leaves, Bob tracks him down at a bar where it is revealed that Landau thought Bob was a natural motivational speaker and Bob thought that Landau was good at marketing. Landau decides to return to the firm.

Episode 6: Unaired   "Family Bob"

Director: Barnet Kellman   Writer: Brian Scully

Landau gets E! Entertainment to do a show about Bob's family. Since they are not the perfect family, to prevent the interview from ruining Bob's career, Bob forbids Janet from saying anything about him and has to pay Jeffrey over $6000 for him to be on the show. When the interviewer finds out the truth, Landau has to pay her to keep it quiet.

Episode 7: Unaired   "Paranoid Bob"

Director: Barnet Kellman   Writer: Justin Adler

The actor Gary Oldman seeks Bob's advice on how to get people to stop confusing him with the awful characters he plays. However, when Bob and Landau overhear a phone conversation where Oldman is threatening someone, Bob tries to have him leave his office as quickly as possible by convincing him that he doesn't need Bob's advice. Patterson becomes paranoid that Oldman is stalking him. He receives a call that Oldman has taken Vic to the hospital, and, when Oldman phones, Bob, accompanied by a guard dog, goes to his office to see him. It so happens that a sandwich had made Vic sick and that Oldman had previously dated Bob's latest girlfriend, Melissa, and was trying to warn him that Melissa is smothering. Oldman's threatening phone call that Bob overheard was dialogue for a proposed movie.

Episode 8: Unaired "Clown Bob"

Director: Barnet Kellman   Writer: Barbie Feldman Adler

When Jeffrey's therapist, Dr. Tepnick (Harry Shearer) takes Bob's word over his son's, Jeffrey gets revenge by kidnapping the doctor's valuable, life-sized, talking clown statue, Mr. Jingles, and holding it for ransom. After Bob and Janet stumble across the statue, they think the clown is alive and end up destroying it. Bob, Jeffrey, and Landau then have to get rid of the "body."

Episode 9: Unaired "Matchmaker Bob" (aka "Mentor Bob")

Director: Barnet Kellman   Writer: Justin Adler

An ambitious high school senior, on whom Jeffrey has a crush, sees Bob as her ticket to fame. Bob takes advantage of the situation to be a matchmaker for Jeffrey.

Episode 10: Unaired "Wheelchair Bob" (summary based on table draft script)

Director: Barnet Kellman   Writer: Hayes Jackson

Claudia is collecting money for her charity – "10 Mile Race for Teen Pregnancy." She is to race in her wheelchair but is not sure she will be able to complete the race. Bob buys her a racing wheelchair which he trips over and fractures his ankle. He then falls off his crutches and breaks his other ankle. Having to use a wheelchair, he decides to race with Claudia. Claudia has to tow Bob to the finish line, but they do come in next to last ahead of a blind guy.

Canceled Bob

Up against the hit NBC comedy *Frasier*, *Bob Patterson* premiered to mediocre ratings; it came in third in its timeslot. Moving the show to Wednesdays at 9:30 PM after *The Drew Carey Show* didn't help. *Bob Patterson* lost 31 percent of the viewing audience from its lead-in. The series was canceled after five episodes. Jason Alexander later put together a stage show playing Danny Clay billed as "America's 4th Leading Motivational Speaker," which grew out of his failed sitcom.

Come to Papa

Premiered Thursday, June 3, 2004, at 8:30 PM on NBC

Stand-up comedian Tom Papa starred as himself on this sitcom playing a married newspaper reporter in New Jersey with hopes of becoming a comedy writer. His wife Karen (Jennifer Aspen, *Bob Patterson*) worked at an animal hospital; his pompous boss, Blevin (Steve Carell, *The Office*, *Over the Top*) was the editor of the *New Jersey Daily Times*, and his slacker, horny best friend, Judah (Rob Benedict) lived off a small trust fund. Former NBA star John Salley was a tall, angry black mailman with whom Tom wanted to be friends. Dan Lauria and Mimi Kennedy played Tom's parents.

Background

Papa along with Greg Malins created the series, which was produced by Stan Allen Productions in association with NBC Studios and Warner Bros. Television. Tom Papa had been Jerry Seinfeld's opening act for several years, and apparently NBC thought *Come to Papa* might be another *Seinfeld*.

Episode Guide: 4 aired episodes

(All episodes were directed by Andy Ackerman, a frequent *Seinfeld* director, and written by Greg Malins and Tom Papa)

Episode 1: June 3, 2004 "The Tire Guy"

Tom interviews a local tire retailing legend, Crazy Benny, who seems to have lost his creativity for the commercial spots he was doing, and so Tom volunteers to write his commercials for him. Meanwhile, Judah is determined to nail the one girl he missed in high school science class, and Blevin can't get a mug of black coffee because he offended the new local coffee girl.

Episode 2: June 10, 2004 "The Pep Talk"

Tom attempts to motivate a losing boys' baseball team with a pep talk about Babe Ruth but the talk has mixed results. Meanwhile, Karen tries to get out of going to Tom's parents' party by lying, which puts her in an impossible situation.

Episode 3: June 17, 2004 "The Salad"

Tom interviews Anderson Miller (John O'Hurley), an eccentric millionaire, from whom he seeks a donation to his wife's animal hospital. Later, he saves the millionaire's life and wants to cash in.

Episode 4: June 24, 2004 "The Crush"

Tom's parents create a variety act based on jokes they steal from their son. Tom interferes in the love life of Karen's best friend whose lover is a semi-pro bowler.

Nobody Came

Originally to be a midseason replacement, NBC finally decided to air the series during the summer to bad reviews and mediocre ratings. It was not renewed after the four-episode order had aired.

Doc Corkle

Premiered Sunday, October 5, 1952, at 7:30 PM on NBC

Dr. Ambrose Corkle (Eddie Mayehoff), a dentist in a small town named Musgrove (or, in some scripts, "Mushgap"), was very active in community affairs and always seemed to have money problems. Living with him were Nellie Corkle (Hope Emerson), his sister and assistant; Laurie Corkle (Connie Marshall), his young daughter, and Simon "Pop" Corkle (Chester Conklin), his dad who continually tried without much success to fix things to save money. Doc Corkle's cousin was Melinda Dill (Billie Burke who had played the good witch in *The Wizard of Oz*). Her son Windfield (Windy) Dill (Arnold Stang), a young millionaire, was attracted to Laurie Corkle, but the feeling was not mutual. Because many of Doc Corkle's patients didn't pay their bills, it seemed that he was forever asking Windy for financial help.

Background

Devery Freeman appears to have created the series which was originally titled *Forever Ambrose*. The title was changed to *Doc Corkle* when the author of the novel *Forever Amber* threatened legal action. *Doc Corkle* was produced by Lou Place and directed by him and Richard L. Bare. In addition to Devery Freeman, other writers for this comedy were Alan Lipscott and Bob Fisher. According to Freeman, the scripts were professional but were not decisive about the direction of the series – whether it should be a comedic farce or a family comedy.[56] *Doc Corkle* was produced by Key Productions.

From undated scripts in the Devery Freeman Collection at Brooklyn College, it appears that the original premise of the sitcom had the Eddie Mayehoff character as a captain at Musgrove Academy, a private military school for teenage boys. Captain Ambrose Corkle had two daughters – Laurie, age twenty and sixteen-year-old Patsy. His sister Harriet was also his secretary. Billie Burke played Gertrude Musgrove – the spinster daughter of Colonel Musgrove, the unseen head of the school. The school's handyman was Mr. Cheever. In the script, a wealthy businessman agreed to give the school money for a gymnasium if they enrolled his playboy nephew,

J. Windfield Dill. Corkle had his hands full dealing with young Dill who bribed other cadets and Mr. Cheever into doing favors for him and became infatuated with Corkle's daughter Laurie. In the end, the uncle gave the school the funds for the gym and told Captain Corkle to use an iron hand with his nephew. But Corkle returned the money and informed him that the school just wanted Windy. One can presume that this premise was dropped because it did not offer the comedic possibilities of "dental humor" such as:

Doc: "I've got to work on Henrietta Donegal's teeth."

Nellie: "Henrietta is going to be at the game."

Doc: "Yes, but I can work on her teeth here."

Later, in the 1970s, Devery Freeman wrote a novel, *Father Sky*, about a military school in New Jersey, which was made into the movie *Taps* starring George C. Scott.

Episode Guide: 3 aired; 5 unaired/unproduced

(According to *Variety*, a total of five episodes of *Doc Corkle* were filmed, which would mean that two episodes never aired. However, the Devery Freeman collection contains five scripts in addition to the scripts for the three episodes that aired. Not knowing which of the remaining scripts were filmed and which were not, the storylines of all the scripts are summarized below.)

Episode 1: October 5, 1952 "Laurie's Dress"

Four men from the finance company come to repossess Doc's dentist chair because he owes $50 on it. Pop Corkle suggests that Ambrose borrow the $50 from his cousin's wealthy son Windy. Windy gives Doc the money if he promises to ask Laurie to go to the senior prom with Windy. When Doc returns home with the $50, Nellie informs him that Laurie needs a new dress for the prom which coincidentally costs $50. Unbeknownst to Doc, Windy and his mother stop by the Corkle's to give Laurie a new dress which Nellie puts in the closet. Later, when one of Doc's patients tells him that his sister cuts down her dresses for her daughter, Doc and Pop take Laurie's new dress out of the closet and begin altering it with scissors. Laurie bursts into tears when she sees what they did, and Doc uses the $50 to buy

Laurie a new dress. However, Laurie returns the new dress to get her dad's money back in order to pay for the dental chair. In the end, Doc's patient brings Laurie one of his sister's dresses for the prom.

After *Doc Corkle*, Eddie Mayehoff went on to star in another situation comedy, *That's My Boy* in 1954, which lasted for about half a year. Richard L. Bare directed this episode and the second one and then quit the series, presumably because of Mayehoff's behavior on the set (see below).

Episode 2: October 12, 1952 "Football Game"

Doc is coaching a football team of boys aged eleven to fourteen at the youth center. Because the team is in desperate need of new equipment, Doc invites Windy over to discuss funding the purchase. Windy gives the team new equipment with the proviso that he becomes the team's coach. Doc is demoted to third assistant coach and has to take orders from Windy. When the two argue over which plays are the best for the team to make, Windy fires Doc. Laurie then goes to Windy's home and locks him in the closet before the big game. She calls her father and tells him that he has to coach the team, but by the time he gets to the game, it is over. He discovers that the team won using Windy's play.

Arnold Stang (Windfield Dill) went on to play Milton Berle's sidekick on the *Buick Berle Show* and was also the voice of the title character in the animated series *Top Cat*.

Episode 3: October 19, 1952 "Carnival"

Laurie discovers that her dad failed to mail her application for a college scholarship, and so she will not be able to complete her education. Doc says he will find some way to raise the money for her tuition and that he already has $150 and just needs another $150. Windy suggests that Doc invest the $150 in a business. With the help of Melinda who is into numerology, Doc focuses on an ad in the newspaper asking readers to see a gentleman at the county fair to invest in a "mechanical wonder." Doc invests his $150 with the man at the fair only to find out that the "mechanical wonder" is something Pop Corkle is trying to invent. Doc tries to get his funds back but is unsuccessful and ends up in the chair of a dunking machine at the fair to earn money. As he is repeatedly dunked, Laurie says that she got the college to accept her scholarship application and so will be able to complete her education after all.

Connie Marshall, who had been one of Cary Grant's daughters in the film *Mr. Blandings Builds His Dream House*, retired from show business after the demise of *Doc Corkle*.

Episode 4: Unaired/Unproduced   "The Other Woman" (aka "Glee Club")

Corkle is directing the local glee club which includes his cousin Melinda, the principal of Mushgap Prep, and his wife. They are rehearsing to perform at a church bazaar. Windy gives the club an organ, but they have no one who can play the instrument. Nellie suggests that they add a dancer to their show like the one who performs at the Zanzibar Club. The principal, his wife, and Corkle go to the club to see the dancer, Dawn Devoe, who turns out to be a friend of Doc's from dental school. The principal's wife demands that Doc close the risqué show at the club, but Miss Devoe wants $200 (two weeks salary) from Corkle in order to leave town. After Doc asks Windy for the money, he goes to meet Miss Devoe and Windy at the club. Corkle ends up leaving Windy with the dancer, and Windy gets Miss Devoe to be the organist for Corkle's glee club.

Episode 5: Unaired/Unproduced   "Rival Dentist"

A new, very handsome dentist, Dr. Bradford, locates his office across the street from Doc Corkle, and all of Corkle's female patients start going to him. Since Doc has few patients now, Windy wants to repossess Corkle's dental equipment and informs him that even Nellie is having the new dentist fill a cavity for her. Nellie confesses to Doc that she is in love with Dr. Bradford. The town is having a reception for the new dentist, which Nellie and Doc attend. Corkle cracks a tooth at the reception when he tries to eat a shelled walnut and so leaves the event early. He tries to fix his cracked tooth himself without success. When Nellie comes home, she says that she learned that the new dentist is married. Corkle goes across the street to have it out with Dr. Bradford who hits Doc on the jaw extracting his injured tooth.

Episode 6: Unaired/Unproduced "House Moving"

A wealthy college friend and his mother are coming to visit Laurie, and she's ashamed of the shabby condition of the Corkle house. Nellie wants Ambrose to ask Windy, their landlord, to redecorate the place. Corkle visits Windy and says that for such a valuable piece of real estate, Windy should fix up the house. Windy agrees but wants to move the house to another part of town so he can build a bowling alley on the current lot. Doc and Pop don't want to tell Nellie and Laurie of Windy's plan to move their home. However, when Windy comes by with an architect and a set of blueprints, he informs Doc, Nellie and Laurie that he wants to move their house that afternoon. Doc, his sister, and daughter try to butter up Windy to get him to change his mind, but he won't and Doc finally kicks him out of the house. When Laurie's guests arrive and are having tea, the house starts moving, and the guests promptly leave.

Episode 7: Unaired/Unproduced "Pop's Amour"

Pop has proposed marriage to a woman named Stella that he met at a trailer camp. He has selected Windy instead of his son to be best man since Windy will finance his honeymoon. When Stella comes to the house for the wedding, she reveals she has five sons aged ten to thirty and a big dog that all plan to live with the Corkle's. Knowing this, Pop wants to call off the wedding. Doc tells Stella's oldest son Tyrone that Pop no longer wants to marry his mother, but Tyrone has recorded Pop's marriage proposal and threatens to go to the local newspaper to give them the story. Late at night, Doc enters Stella's trailer to retrieve the recording. Struggling with Tyrone, the record falls into an electric potato peeler that Melinda gave Pop as a wedding gift. Since the record is destroyed, Tyrone ties up Doc to prevent him from calling off the nuptials. On the day of the ceremony, Pop is nowhere to be found. He sends a telegram stating that he has fled to Florida. Stella and her sons leave town to find another potential husband. Pop appears later announcing that he really spent the day at the Roseview ballroom and that he has proposed marriage to another woman named Daisy.

Episode 8: Unaired/Unproduced   "Leaving Mushgap"

At an auction, Doc has purchased a building full of gym equipment for the community. A friend of the Doc's from dental school stops by and says he quit his job as a dentist for an aircraft company in another city and wonders if Corkle would like the position. Subsequently, an attorney for the estate from which Doc purchased the building visits and tells him that the building was sold to him with the provision that he move the building, which will cost $2000. Not having the money, Doc decides to take the job offer in another city for $7000 a year. Upon hearing the news that they will have to leave Mushgap, Nellie and Laurie along with Windy and Melinda come up with a plan to keep Doc from accepting the job. Mr. Sloane, the head of the aircraft company, and his wife are to visit Doc to have him sign a contract for the new position. When they arrive, Nellie and Windy portray Doc as a gambler and kleptomaniac, and Melinda poses as a relative of Doc's who is a stripper. The Sloane's are not amused and cancel the job offer. However, in the end, it is revealed that one of Doc's patients has collected all of Corkle's past due dental bills and has figured out how Doc can borrow the rest of the $2000 he needs.

The First Quick Cancelation

Doc Corkle aired after *The Red Skelton Show* and before *The Colgate Comedy Hour*. Reynolds Metals (now Alcoa, Inc.) was the sponsor of *Doc Corkle*, and in the early days of TV, when shows normally had only one advertiser, sponsors had great power in deciding the fate of a series. Accounts at the time say that Reynolds Metals and NBC were extremely disappointed with the series, which is why it was canceled so quickly. According to preliminary ratings from Los Angeles, the comedy ranked fifteenth during the week of its premiere, doing poorly against a Jack Benny special.

The Chicago Tribune reported that Mayehoff was miscast in the series and had to contend with bad writing.[57] On the other hand, Richard L. Bare, who directed the initial episodes of the sitcom and quit after directing the second episode, says that Mayehoff had a habit of trying to write, direct, and produce, and, when the network learned of this, NBC could see trouble down the road and ended the comedy[58]. The comedy *Mr. Peepers* starring Wally Cox, which had a brief run during the summer of 1952, replaced *Doc Corkle* on the NBC Sunday night schedule.

First Impressions

Premiered Saturday, August 27, 1988, at 8:00 PM on CBS

Before co-starring on the hit comedy *Everybody Loves Raymond*, Brad Garrett played Frank Dutton, a divorced dad raising a nine-year-old daughter, Lindsay (Brandy Gold) and starting a commercial production company, Media of Omaha, with his best friend and partner, Dave Poole (Thom Sharp). Since he was an impressionist, Frank put those talents to work in producing radio commercials. The staff at Media of Omaha included the sound engineer Raymond Voss (James Noble), who had been in Gamblers Anonymous before he joined Alcoholics Anonymous, and Donna Patterson (Sarah Abrell), the company's naïve receptionist whose father was a conservative minister known as Book-Burner Patterson. Clara Madison (Ruth Kobart) was Frank's eccentric next-door neighbor. Frank Dutton had to cope not only with the fact that his wife had moved to Los Angeles to find herself after twelve years of marriage but also with the pressures of starting a new business.

Background

First Impressions, originally called *Just You & Me*, grew out of a pilot titled *Sounds Like* about the life of a widowed commercial special effects man raising a teenage daughter. The pilot was created by voice actors Frank Welker and Gordon Hunt (father of actress Helen Hunt) and producers Bonny Dore and Leslie Greif. The team of Fred Freeman and Lawrence J. Cohen, who had created the sixties sitcom *Occasional Wife*, contributed to the development of *First Impressions*. Greif-Dore Productions and Humble Productions produced the comedy. The series' theme song was written by Joey Carbone, George Doering, Leslie Greif, and Harry Nilsson and sung by Nilsson. An interesting sidelight was that the producers hired tall actors in supporting roles and raised doors and ceilings on the set to make Brad Garrett's height (he is 6'9") less noticeable.

WELCOME TO MY WORLD—MALE VERSION

Episode Guide: 5 aired; 3 unaired

Episode 1: August 27, 1988   "Pilot"

Directors: Terry Hughes and Phil Ramuno   Writers: Fred Freeman and Lawrence J. Cohen

Frank Dutton is frustrated over his wife who has walked out on him to find herself in L.A. Meanwhile, his company is working on an advertising campaign for the owners of Mullins Muffins.

Brandy Gold (Lindsay) is the sister of Tracey Gold from *Growing Pains* and Melissa Gold from *Benson*.

Episode 2: September 3, 1988   "Frank's Date"

Director: Alan Rafkin   Writers: Fred Freeman and Lawrence J. Cohen

After twelve years of marriage, Frank finds the courage to ask Marsha (Paula Matteson), who is also an impressionist, out on a date.

Episode 3: September 10, 1988   "Raymond vs. the Computer"

Director: Howard Storm   Writers: Fred Freeman and Lawrence J. Cohen

Frank's birthday present to Raymond is the latest in high tech sound equipment. However, the new computer seems to confuse Raymond who is worried about his gambling debts.

Episode 4: September 24, 1988   "The Public Trust"

Director: Phil Ramuno   Story: Mark St. Germain & Bernard M. Kahn   Teleplay: Mark St. Germain

Frank's partner Dave decides to run for city council against Sarge Kominsky. Frank finds that his office has been bugged, and he thinks it was Dave's opponent in the race who did the bugging. However, Raymond admits that he bugged the office when he was first hired because he wanted to know what Dave and Frank were saying about him.

Episode 5: October 1, 1988 "On His Own"

Director: Jack Shea   Writers: Dianne Dixon and Susan Strauss

Lindsay visits her mother, and Donna, Frank's receptionist, moves into her own apartment.

Episode 6: Unaired   "Poor Clara"

Director: Unknown   Writer: Howard Ostroff

Everyone is worried about next-door neighbor Clara Madison.

Episode 7: Unaired   "The Selling of Frank"

Director: Unknown   Writer: Richard Marcus

Frank has to go beyond the call of duty to land a new client.

Episode 8: Unaired   "The Audition"

Director: Unknown   Writers: Dennis Danziger and Ellen Sandler

Frank feels as if he is auditioning with all of the voices in his repertoire to get a new client.

No Lasting Impressions

The comedy was to be a midseason replacement during the 1987-88 season, but the writers' strike delayed production. *First Impressions* was then scheduled for an eight-week run beginning in late August, but poor ratings led CBS to pulling the series after five episodes. The last episode broadcast ranked near the bottom of the Nielsen ratings.

Imagine That

Premiered Tuesday, January 8, 2002, at 8:00 PM on NBC

Imagine That, Hank Azaria's second sitcom failure (after *If Not for You*), centered on Josh Miller (Azaria), a comedy writer for a late night sketch show, who was married to a lawyer, Wendy (Jayne Brook). Josh had trouble telling people what he was really thinking, but he had no problem thinking, daydreaming, and fantasizing about things. Josh's thoughts and fantasies about his marriage and life materialized on screen and became the basis for his comedy sketches. Other staff for the sketch show on which Josh worked included his writing partner Kenny (Josh Malina), their assistant Tabitha (Julia Schultz), and Barb Thompson (Katey Sagal), his boss.

Background

Imagine That, originally titled *The Hank Azaria Show* and then *What Are You Thinking?*, was the product of a development deal Azaria had with Columbia Tristar. The sitcom was first pitched to ABC, and when that network showed no interest, it was taken to NBC. Azaria had the idea that it would be fun to play a bunch of characters and be a supporting character on his own sitcom.[59] He liked the idea of playing different characters about which his main character daydreamed. *Imagine That* was co-created by Seth Kurland who quit the series in November 2001 over disagreements with Azaria. NBC originally ordered thirteen episodes, but only five were made. Touchstone Television produced the comedy in association with Columbia Tristar.

Episode Guide: 2 aired; 3 unaired

Episode 1: January 8, 2002   "The Macho Therapist"

Director: Barnet Kellman   Writer: Seth Kurland

Josh's partner Kenny hires Tabitha, a sexy new assistant about whom Josh fantasizes. Josh and his wife, with different opinions about sex, go to a couples' therapist whom Josh imagines as a crude, super-macho, *Sopranos*-like character. He later uses that image as the basis for a comedy sketch – an idea that is stolen by his boss Barb to which Josh does not initially object. The therapist advises Josh and his wife that they need to communicate better. However, when he and Wendy try to have sex, their communication does not go well. In the next therapy session, Wendy complains that Josh does not discuss his work with her. Josh confides to Wendy that he doesn't want to tell her what a doormat he is at work. She says that letting her know that turns her on, and they make love.

Episode 2: January 15, 2002   "The Married Balladeer"

Director: Barnet Kellman   Writer: Tad Quill

Josh and Wendy think it is time to graduate from couple's therapy, but, when Wendy sees John's latest sketch – the "Married Balladeer" which consists of anti-marriage songs, she realizes that things aren't going as smoothly as she thought. After attempting to work through their issues on their own, they go back to therapy. Meanwhile, Kenny is dumped by his latest true love, and the writing staff is forced into a game of Dungeons and Dragons.

Episode 3: Unaired   "The Inner Critic"

Director: Barnet Kellman   Writers: Ed Solomon and Jennifer Glickman

Josh and Kenny write a great alien sketch, but when Kenny is away, Josh has to write the ending himself which no one thinks is funny. Azaria portrays Josh's inner critic – a Gene Shallit-like guy – who taunts, teases, and tells him he had one brilliant idea in his career – partnering with Kenny. Meanwhile, when Josh and Wendy find a house they would like to buy, Josh gets cold feet about the purchase after his inner critic says he has no talent without Kenny. The house is sold to someone else, and Josh apologizes to Wendy that she didn't get her dream house. But at work, he pitches a sketch about an insecure guy with an inner critic who criticizes him all the time which everyone thinks is funny.

Episode 4: Unaired   "The Psychic"

Director: Barnet Kellman   Writer: Laurie Parres

Barb's psychic said she would meet her soul mate and then she meets Carlo whom Josh thinks is gay. Josh fantasizes himself as Ms. Chloe and asks if he should tell Barb that her boyfriend is gay. He decides that he doesn't want to ruin her happiness and so doesn't say anything. The next day, Barb says that her psychic told her that someone will steal her Carlo away, and she thinks it will be Tabitha. When Josh says that Tabitha will not steal Carlo, Barb informs Josh that Carlo is an ex-gay, having gone through "pray the gay out" therapy, and the two of them stay together.

John Michael Higgins (Carlo) later portrayed Fran Drescher's gay ex-husband on *Happily Divorced*.

Episode 5: Unaired "Lucy"

Director: Barnet Kellman   Writer: Steve Lookner

Josh thinks that Wendy's dad, Jack (John Larroquette), a professional golfer, doesn't like him because he isn't included on Jack's wall of photos. So when Josh and Kenny are invited to write some jokes for the President of the United States, Josh sees the perfect photo opportunity to impress his father-in-law. Josh fantasizes that he and Kenny are Lucy and Ethel in the Oval Office with Lucy spilling ink on a treaty with Russia and ruining a portrait of George Washington. When Josh gets the photo of himself with the President, it shows him staring at Kenny's date's boobs. Kenny uses Photoshop to insert a picture of the President in a photo of Josh with Elliott Gould, and Josh gives that photo to his father-in-law.

Imagine *Imagine That* **Canceled**

NBC scheduled the series for five episodes but axed the show after two low-rated episodes. Its premiere ranked fourth in its timeslot. *Imagine That* averaged a 2.7 Nielsen rating/ 5 share among adults aged eighteen to forty-nine – about the same as its timeslot predecessor – the canceled *Emeril*.

Life... and Stuff

Premiered Friday, June 6, 1997, at 8:30 PM on CBS

Middle-aged Rick Boswell had been married for ten years with a wife, Ronnie (Pam Dawber, *Mork & Mindy*, *My Sister Sam*), and two sons—Jerry (Tanner Lee Prairie) and Shawn (Brandon Allen in the pilot and Kevin Keckeisen in the other episodes). Rick had met Ronnie in college, and was now a creative director in an advertising agency. His only pleasures were his large-screen TV and his satellite dish. Rick's friends at the office included Bernie (Fred Applegate) and Jordan (Anita Barone). His unemployed brother Andy (David Bowe) lived in a Winnebago parked in Rick's driveway. Also appearing on the series was Andrea Martin as Christine, a divorced friend of Ronnie's.

Background

Another stand-up comedian, in this case Rick Reynolds, got a chance to create and star on his own situation comedy. Reynolds adapted his autobiographical stage show *Only the Truth Is Funny* as the basis for *Life... and Stuff*. The series often used movie and TV flashbacks to emphasize a point, such as in the first episode, Dawber and Reynolds played June and Ward Cleaver to illustrate what Rick thought married life would be like with Ward arriving home from work and June dressed up and having dinner ready. In the first episode, when Rick came home late from work and bought fast food to eat, Ronnie had already fed the kids SpaghettiO's. Related to the flashback concept, in the opening sequence for the sitcom, Rick Boswell was shown in a sheriff's uniform taking his two sons fishing supposedly as an homage to the opening of *The Andy Griffith Show*.

Initially, the series was to debut on CBS as a midseason replacement but was bumped to the summer. *Life... and Stuff* was produced by Pergood Productions (Somers/Teitelbaum/David) in association with Tristar Television.

Episode Guide: 3 aired; 3 unaired

Episode 1: June 6, 1997   "The First One"

Director: Andy Cadiff   Writers: Lee Aronsohn and Rick Reynolds

Rick complains to everyone that he and his wife have not had sex in weeks. Ronnie feels that they hardly see each other anymore because he works all the time. Reluctantly, Rick attends a preschool fund raiser with Ronnie where they meet a couple, and the wife happens to be majoring in advertising. Ronnie gets mad at Rick because he spends all his time talking about advertising with the wife. Later, Ronnie finds a love letter Rick wrote her before they got married and wonders what happened to their relationship. In the end they kiss and make love.

In many episodes like this one, the character, Rick Boswell, liked to pose the question, "Which would you rather?" and tell the person to whom the question was directed what the consequences would be if they didn't answer. For example, Rick asked Ronnie would she rather have great sex with another woman or have no sex at all for the rest of her life. If she didn't answer, he said her grandmother would die. Ronnie did respond to the question with the "great sex" answer.

Episode 2: June 13, 1997   "Life ... and Fisticuffs"

Director: Andy Cadiff   Writer: Lee Aronsohn

Rather than playing softball, Rick reluctantly goes with the family to one of their son's best friend, Rob's birthday party. Rick doesn't like to mix with the other parents at the party because he hates small talk. However, Rob's dad Chuck (Christopher Rich) asks Rick to play basketball with some other dads. When Chuck keeps fouling Rick, Rick punches him. Ronnie is upset at her husband for punching Rob's dad in front of the kids and asks him to apologize to avoid being branded the "town psycho." Rick agrees to apologize after learning that Chuck's wife canceled the sleepover with her son and Rick's son.

Lee Aronsohn, who created *Life ... and Stuff* with Rick Reynolds, later helped to create a more successful series, *Two and a Half Men*. Aronsohn has also written and produced episodes of *The Big Bang Theory*. He indicated that he left *Life ... and*

Stuff as its executive producer during the production of this episode even though he wrote many of the other episodes.[60]

Episode 3: June 20, 1997 "Life ... and Therapy"

Director: Andy Cadiff Writer: Lee Aronsohn

Rick and Ronnie go to a restaurant and see Christine back together with her ex-husband. Christine says that she and her ex are seeing a couple's therapist to help their relationship, and Ronnie thinks that Rick and she should try couples therapy. Reluctantly Rick and Ronnie go to a therapist (Martin Mull) who advises them that they need to learn how to argue with each other. He tells them to give each other full body massages every night before their next session with him but not to have sex. However, they cannot hold out until the next session and so have great sex. After they confess to the therapist what happened, he informs them that it is what he thought they would do.

Episode 4: Unaired "Life ... and Matchmaking"

Director: Andy Cadiff Writer: David Emery, Matt Selman, & Jon Ross

Ronnie introduces Bernie to Christine when they come to the office to take Rick to lunch. Christine is interested in dating the thrice-divorced Bernie. Rick invites Bernie to a dinner party at his home. When Bernie discovers that the only other guest is Christine, he says he has a stomach ailment and leaves. Bernie tells Rick that he doesn't want to get involved with another woman given his previous divorces. However, later, Bernie phones Christine, apologizes for leaving the party, and asks her out.

Episode 5: Unaired "Life ... and the Way We Were" (summary provided by Mindy Schneider)

Director: Andy Cadiff Writer: Mindy Schneider

To try to recapture days gone by, Rick and Ronnie decide to spend their tenth anniversary in the same hotel suite where they spent their honeymoon. However, the hotel has not fared as well as their marriage, and the only other guests at the hotel are attending an alien abduction convention. Despite outside pressures from work, family, and an intrusive guy in an undershirt on a balcony across the way, they manage to have a good time – and vow to go somewhere else for their twentieth anniversary.

Pam Dawber essentially retired from acting after marrying *NCIS*'s, Mark Harmon.

Episode 6: Unaired   "Life . . . and the Spirit of Sunday"

Director: Andy Cadiff   Writer: Lee Aronsohn

Ronnie and Rick are remembering Sundays before they had kids when they had time together. Rick wants to go to brunch at a hotel, but, after taking care of their children, they arrive too late. Ronnie then suggests they see a movie together, but they have difficulty finding a babysitter. Andy finally agrees to watch the kids so Ronnie and Rick can go to the movies, but at the theatre, they end up being surrounded by other people's children.

Life's End

The comedy came in third in its time slot and then sank to fourth. CBS canceled the sitcom after three episodes. According to one reviewer, "the show is tasteless, vulgar – and not even vaguely funny for the most part."[61] However, *TV Guide* critic, Jeff Jarvis, published a review the same week that *Life . . . and Stuff* was taken off the air stating the series was ". . . actually pretty good."[62]

Lost at Home

Premiered Tuesday, April 1, 2003, at 9:30 PM on ABC

One day, Rachel Davis (Connie Britton) informed her husband Michael (Mitch Rouse), a workaholic, New York City advertising executive, that he loved his work more than his family and that, unless he reconnected with her and their three children, she would leave him. The three kids were Will (Stark Sands), the oldest son and a high school jock; Sara, (Leah Pipes), a shy thirteen-year old, and seven-year-old Joshua (Gavin Fink). Tucker (Aaron Hill) was Sara's stocky and very polite best friend.

Initially, Michael thought if he cooked breakfast for his family that would resolve the problem. To which Michael's much-divorced boss Jordan King (Gregory Hines) responded, "They want to have breakfast with you? Take 'em to Denny's and leave 'em there." However, Jordan did permit Michael some slack at work so he could spend more time at home. Michael was really "lost at home"—bumbling around the kitchen, interfering with his kids' social lives, and generally revealing his ineptitude for domestic life.

Background

Michael Jacobs created *Lost at Home*, initially titled *My Second Chance*, based somewhat on his own family experiences. As a TV producer, Jacobs' work life was insane, and his wife, who was a doctor, also worked long days.[63] He and his spouse had little time to spend with their four kids let alone with each other. Jacobs took time off to work on the script for *Lost at Home* as well as bond with his family. Michael Jacobs Productions, NBC Studios, and Touchstone Television produced the comedy.

Episode Guide: 4 aired; 4 unaired

Episode 1: April 1, 2003   "Pilot"

Director: Andy Cadiff   Writer: Michael Jacobs

Rachel informs Michael that she has spoken to a lawyer about getting a divorce unless he spends more time at home. After Rachel tells him that he doesn't really know his kids anymore, he finds that he is unaware of who his daughter is dating, that his oldest son plans to have sex with a girl the son doesn't really know, and that his youngest son tries to be too perfect to make sure he pleases his dad. When Michael comes home for dinner on time, he finds that he has no place at the table. In the end, he begins to bond with his kids.

Lost at Home was Gregory Hines' last TV series; he died in August 2003 from liver cancer.

Episode 2: April 8, 2003   "One Bracelet Don't Feed the Beast"

Director: Andy Cadiff   Writer: Mark Blutman

Michael tries to help Rachel with the kids leading to an allergic reaction in Joshua and detention for Sara. Among other things, he finds he isn't on the approved list to get Joshua out of school, so he pulls a fire alarm to illegally achieve that goal.

Episode 3: April 15, 2003   "Good Will Hunting"

Director: Andy Cadiff   Writer: David Sacks

Michael thinks that he has lost touch with his son when Will turns to his mom for advice on buying a car. Michael, of course, ends up disliking Will's choice of vehicle.

Episode 4: April 22, 2003   "Our Town"

Director: Mark Cendrowski   Writer: Amy Welsh

Michael gets a lesson on life in small town Katonah when he takes Josh under his wing after Josh fails to sell even one seed packet for a school fundraiser. Rachel tells Michael that he shouldn't be turning Josh into a salesman. He responds by saying that his family has become a bunch of country bumpkins who won't be able to compete with people raised in the city. Michael then meets mysterious neighbor Arthur Forester (William Daniels) who is resistant to Mike's sales pitch. Arthur turns out to be a retired CEO who informs Mike that he was born and raised in Katonah and did all right.

Episode 5: Unaired   "My Skipped Pages"

Director: Brian K. Roberts   Writer: Matthew Nelson

Michael tries to have "family time" with the kids, but they don't connect. He admits he traded seeing his oldest son and daughter growing up for work. Rachel believes she is losing touch with the oldest kids as much as Mike is. Mike thinks that if he doesn't try so hard and just has fun with his children, he will connect with them.

When the entire family plays throwing a football into a laundry basket, they all begin talking to each other about what they did that day.

Episode 6: Unaired   "The Forgiven"

Director: Brian K. Roberts   Writer: Michael Jacobs

When Michael forgets and goes to work on a Saturday, he asks for forgiveness from Rachel. While he is forgiven, Jordan says it was a mistake to accept exoneration because he really didn't do anything wrong. Mike wants Rachel to take back her forgiveness. She says she will if Mike agrees to start all over with her. They bury their wedding rings in the back yard and start dating again. In the end, they re-wed themselves.

Episode 7: Unaired   "The Story of Us"

Director: Ken Wittingham   Writer: Jeff Menell

Michael likes Will's tutor Lisa because she shares the same values as he does. With Will not knowing, he invites Lisa out to dinner with his wife, Jordan and Jordan's friend Joelle (Aisha Tyler), and Will. He is trying to be a matchmaker for Jordan and Joelle as well as for his son and Lisa. However, Lisa makes it clear that she is just Will's tutor – not his girlfriend.

Episode 8: Unaired   "Best Friends"

Director: Dana DeVally Piazza   Writer: Jennifer Fisher

When Michael and Jordan land a new advertising account, they go out to celebrate at their hang-out Ralphie's. Rachel is disappointed that her husband celebrated with Jordan and not with her. She competes with Jordan to see which one really is Michael's best friend. Rachel goes to Ralphie's with Jordan and Michael to scrutinize the place. Jordan explains that a wife is not a husband's best friend like Michael and Rachel believe. Mike tells Rachel that, while Jordan may be his best friend, the only thing that really matters in his life is being with her. Meanwhile, Lisa is still trying to tutor Will in math, but since he can't seem to learn the subject, the two of them start making out.

Lost No More

ABC only scheduled four episodes of this sitcom, and the ratings were not sufficient for the network to air the other four shows that had been produced.

After *Lost at Home*, Mitch Rouse became a semi-regular on *According to Jim*, while Connie Britton played Coach Tyler's wife, Tami, on *Friday Night Lights* and later starred as Vivien Harmon on *American Horror Story*.

Luis

Premiered Friday, September 19, 2003, at 8:30 PM on Fox

Luis, played by Luis Guzman, was the owner of an apartment building in Spanish Harlem that also housed his donut shop, Park Avenue Donuts. He had to deal with the tenants in his building as well as with his ex-wife, Isabella (Diana-Maria Riva), a realtor; his daughter Marly (Jaclyn DeSantis), a bank teller, who lived in the building with her boyfriend Greg (Wes Ramsey), a freeloading artist, and with his not-so-bright donut shop assistant Richie (Charles Day). Also in the cast were Malcolm Barrett as T.K., a black kid from the neighborhood who tried to sell trash from Luis' dumpster; Reggie Lee as Zhing Zhang, the delivery boy from the Chinese restaurant, who claimed he had been a cardiologist in China and who only spoke Chinese, and Masi Oka (*Heroes*) as Deng Wu, a friend of Zhing Zhang's.

Background

The daughter's boyfriend Greg in the original pilot for *Luis* was played by actor Michael McMillian, but the part was recast with 6'2" Wes Ramsey because the producers thought they needed a stronger presence to go against Luis. The interaction between Luis and Greg was compared to that between Archie Bunker and his son-in-law Mike Stivic on *All in the Family*. The comedy was also noted for the fact that it didn't portray Latinos as a single ethnic group. Luis was Puerto Rican, while his ex-wife was Dominican. Will Gluck created *Luis,* which was produced by Olive Bridge Entertainment.

Episode Guide: 5 aired; 5 unaired

Episode 1: September 19, 2003   "Pilot"
(summary based on fourth revised table draft script)

Director: Jeff Melman   Writer: Will Gluck

Greg's fellowship money has run out, and Marly is now paying all the rent with Luis thinking Greg is taking advantage of his daughter. When he confronts Greg, Greg says he will move out. Marly informs Luis that she is also moving out if her boyfriend does. After Isabella tells Luis to apologize to his daughter, he goes to the bank where she works to make the apology. Marly says that he also has to apologize to Greg. Luis talks with Greg and agrees to sell his paintings in the donut shop.

Charlie Day (Richie) later starred on the sitcom *It's Always Sunny in Philadelphia*.

Episode 2: September 26, 2003   "Placeholder"

Director: Jeff Melman   Writer: Will Gluck

Thinking that Isabella still has feelings for him, Luis is reluctant when she sets him up on a date with one of her friends. Meanwhile, Greg attempts to make a romantic dinner for Marly.

Episode 3: October 3, 2003   "E.P.T."

Director: Andrew Tsao   Writer: Matt Goldman

Luis learns that Marly has purchased a home pregnancy test, and he castigates Greg for being irresponsible. However, further news gets Greg off the hook but not with Marly.

Episode 4: October 17, 2003   "Bodega" (summary based on table draft script)

Director: Jeff Melman   Writer: Tom Saunders

Isabella is trying to sell a property across the street from the donut shop which houses the neighborhood bodega. Andolini's Fine Foods, a gourmet grocery chain, would tear down the bodega to make way for their new store. Greg is upset because he thinks that the new store will change the nature of the neighborhood despite the fact that the bodega is cramped and grubby with almost nothing on its shelves. Luis believes not only that there will be a new store in the neighborhood with a better assortment of food but also that he will not have to pay alimony anymore to Isabella given the commission she will get on the sale of the property. However, Isabella discovers that she will not receive a commission; the buyers just used her to get to the zoning board.

Episode 5: October 24, 2003 "Death Day"

Director: Jeff Melman   Writer: Ira Ungerleider

On the anniversary of Luis' great-grandfather's death, Isabella says she has to go to a weekend real estate retreat and won't be able to make it to the memorial activities. After Luis talks with Isabella's boss about forcing her to work on a weekend, she confesses that she is dating her boss and that they want to go away together for the weekend. This irritates Luis even more. He goes to see Isabella to apologize for his behavior, but things don't go well. Luis and his daughter memorialize his great grandfather alone, but eventually, Isabella shows up at the memorial as well.

Episode 6: Unaired "Rat"

Director: Andrew Tsao   Writer: Michael Davidoff

Greg witnesses Luis hit Isabella's car and drive off. When he confronts Luis about the accident, Luis tells him to butt out. After Isabella is cited for not having break lights due to the accident, she asks Luis for an advance on her alimony. When Luis won't give her an advance, Greg says that Luis caused the damage to her car, and everyone calls Greg a rat. Greg then witnesses Isabella taking money out of the donut shop's cash register. She tells him to keep quiet about it, but, after Luis accuses Richie of stealing, Greg informs on Isabella to Luis. Isabella says she only took what he owed her to repair the car.

Episode 7: Unaired   "Friendship"

Director: Andrew Tsao   Writer: Joe Menendez

Luis is jealous because Marly goes to her mother for advice and not him. Isabella advises him to try to be more of a friend with Marly. He asks Marly out for dinner and the theater where they have a good time together. Marly confides to her dad that Greg won't do certain things to her in bed. While Luis is upset over the confession, Isabella tells him to be cool about it. Appearing to work on his car, Luis gets Greg underneath the vehicle and tries to instruct him on how to properly "service" it. Greg mentions to Marly what her dad said which irritates her. She says she will never trust him again. But then Luis tries to just "listen" to Marly, and they make up.

Episode 8: Unaired   "Bavarian Crème"

Director: Wil Shriner   Writer: Ira Ungerleider

Isabella counsels Luis not to get upset like he did two years ago when an inspector is coming to review the donut shop for a liquor license. Marly tells her dad that she broke up with Greg. When Luis celebrates the good news with champagne in the shop, the inspector denies Luis' application for a liquor license. Marly informs Luis that she has met another guy but won't introduce him to Luis because Luis is so critical of her boyfriends. However, Luis drops in any way to meet the new boyfriend while he is having dinner with Marly and Isabella. The boyfriend, Wolfgang Hemlich, says he is a mime. Marly suggests he put on a performance in the donut shop which he does to less than enthusiastic reviews. In the end, Wolfgang reveals that his real name is "Tony" and that he was just pretending to be an Austrian mime to see if Luis would be supportive of Marly.

Director/comedian Wil Shriner is the twin brother of actor Kin Shriner.

Episode 9: Unaired   "Help"

Director: Wil Shriner   Writer: Cristina Kiaz Booth

A city building inspector stops by Luis' building and threatens to shut it down because of low water pressure. Isabella offers Luis money to hire a real plumber to fix the problem, but he says he doesn't need her help. When he goes to the bank where Marly works to get a loan, Luis finds he has poor credit. Luis and Richie try to fix the water lines, but Richie hooks the water to the gas line and fire comes out of the donut shop's sink. Luis finally relents and demands the money from Isabella, but she won't loan him the funds now because of his attitude. He finally confesses to Isabella that he feels he should be helping her – not vice versa, and asks her to please help him out.

Episode 10: Unaired "Promotion"

Director: Wil Shriner   Writer: Tom Saunders

Diane, Marly's boss at the bank, thinks Luis is cute and asks him to a hockey game. However, she subsequently informs him that she couldn't get tickets and takes him to her place. When Luis wants to leave, Diane says that if he does, she will fire Marly. The next day, Marly announces that she just received a promotion from teller to loan officer. Later, Diane asks Luis to dinner at a restaurant with her parents. At dinner, Diane reveals that she is using Luis to get back at her dad and mom. Marly comes to the restaurant and tells off her boss. Unknown to Diane, Isabella has heard her admit that she is forcing Luis to be with her in order for Marly to keep her job. When Isabella threatens to go to the authorities because of Diane's actions, Diane lets Marly keep her promotion.

When It Is Not Good to Be First

Luis was the first casualty of the 2003–04 TV season—canceled after five episodes. The fourth episode ranked 102nd out of 133 series.

The Martin Short Show

Previewed Thursday, September 15, 1994, on NBC before moving to Tuesdays at 8:30 PM

Former co-star of *SCTV*, *The Associates*, and *Saturday Night Live*, Martin Short played himself on this show within a show. Short portrayed the star of his own TV variety show. Also appearing on the series were his wife Meg (Jan Hooks) and old friend Alice Manoogan (Andrea Martin).

Background

Martin Short created the comedy with his brother Michael and with Paul Flaherty. NBC gave Short a thirteen-week commitment without ever seeing a pilot.

The original concept for the series was closer to a conventional situation comedy centering on Short's interaction with his wife (originally played by Catherine Hicks) and his kids and having separate, self-contained comedy sketches such as fake movie promos, take-offs on commercials, and sketches from Short's fictional variety show. In the script for the initial pilot, Short's wife was named Nora, and the couple had three kids: Charlie, age five; Caroline, age ten, and Andrew, age eight. The pilot, titled "Mommie-in-Law Dearest," had Marty's somewhat eccentric mother-in-law visiting the family for a week. Among other things, she got befuddled by all the types of bread they had at the local supermarket. While taping his variety show, Marty had a problem with a sketch about cooking that really wasn't working, and so he decided to impersonate his mother-in-law in the sketch. When he returned home, Marty confessed to Nora that he had mimicked her mother on his show and played a tape of the sketch. Nora asked him to delete the sketch from the final show. However, Marty's mother-in-law saw the taped sketch and thought that he was impersonating the actress Jessica Tandy. Kristen Johnson (*3rd Rock from the Sun, The Ex's*) was Marty's TV producer on the pilot.

Before the series premiered, the concept was changed to more closely integrate the family setting with the comedy sketches. Jan Hooks replaced Catherine Hicks as his wife, now named Meg, and she was also a regular on Marty's variety show. Instead of having three kids, the Shorts had two – Caroline (Noley Thornton) and Charlie (Zack Duhame), and Andrea Martin was brought on board as his old friend and cast member.[64] In the final product, Martin Short played both the star of a comedy variety show and a family man who got into mishaps when he was not creating some wacky character. Dolshor Productions and NBC produced the sitcom.

WELCOME TO MY WORLD—MALE VERSION

Episode Guide: 3 aired; 2 unaired

Episode 1: September 15, 1994   "Who's Afraid of Snowball Fortensky?"

Director: John Whitesell   Writers: Paul Flaherty and Martin Short

When Charlie and Caroline find a white dog, they put a listening device on it. Marty and his wife discover that the dog belongs to Elizabeth Taylor, who at the time was married to Larry Fortensky. Upon returning the dog, they realize that a wireless microphone was left in the dog's collar and so are able to eavesdrop on Elizabeth (played by Martin Short) and her husband. When the Shorts give a party, all the guests want to listen in to Elizabeth and Larry. Eventually, she finds the microphone and threatens the Shorts with legal action causing Marty to visit her and explain what happened. Elizabeth sends them a dog as a gift, and it has a hidden microphone. Sketches on this episode included a spoof of the Sally Jesse Raphael talk show and a promo for *Ed*, a movie in which Ed Grimly takes over for the President of the U.S.

Later in his career, Zack Duhame (Charlie) became a stunt man in films and TV.

Episode 2: September 20, 1994   "The Steve Martin Show"

Director: Eugene Levy   Writer: Dick Blasucci and Martin Short

Steven Martin is the guest on Short's variety show where the main sketch is a take-off on *Jeopardy* called *Half-Wits*, with two teams of contestants played by Short, Andrea Martin, Jan Hooks, and Steve Martin. The contestants have the dumbest answers to the simplest questions. After the show, Marty invites Steve to stay at his place because Steve has a problem with his hotel. Meg tells Marty that she thinks Steve is coming on to her, but Marty says it is only a joke. However, Steve really is flirting with Meg and confesses that he is drawn to things he can't have. Marty kicks him out of the house. Later Steve appears on an infomercial with Jean and Casey Kasem who are selling tapes to help people overcome urges, and Steve flirts with Jean Kasem.

Eugene Levy not only directed this episode but also played the host of *Half-Wits*.

Episode 3: September 27, 1994   "A Hippo Never Forgets"

Director: Eugene Levy   Writers: Howard Bendetson and Cindy Begel

Martin tries to please his son by appearing on *The Lovey Show*, a children's TV show hosted by a pink hippopotamus played by George Wendt from *Cheers*. However, the host doesn't want Marty to be on the show because he believes that his career as a comic was dealt a serious setback when Short gonged him on *The Gong Show*. Meg convinces the kid's show's host to let Marty appear so Charlie won't be disappointed. When on the show, the host gets his revenge on Marty by tarring and feathering him which leads to the cancelation of *The Lovey Show*.

On this episode, Jo Anne Worley and Rip Taylor appeared with Martin Short as the panel on *The Gong Show*, and Fred Willard played Marty's agent.

Episode 4: Unaired   "The Joker is Mine"

Director: Eugene Levy   Writer: Frank Mula

Marty along with Bruno Kirby are playing poker at Hollywood producer, Arthur Spellman's house. Marty loses $12,000 in the game but tells his wife that he only lost $1200. When Marty and Bruno go back to Spellman's house to try to get out of paying the debt, Kirby suggests Marty bet double or nothing on running a foot race with the elderly Spellman. Spellman wins the race. Kirby then suggests another double or nothing bet on who can do the best Katherine Hepburn impersonation. Spellman wins this contest as well. To get out of paying what is now $48,000 to Spellman, Marty has to appear in one of his movies.

Brian Keith played Arthur Spellman. The comedy team of Allen and Rossi had a cameo in this episode in a sketch about singer Jackie Rogers, Jr. played by Short.

Episode 5: Unaired   "Me, the Jury" (summary based on final draft script)

Director: Eugene Levy Writer: Doug Steckler

Marty and his wife are flying first class. Sitting in front of him on the plane is Aileen Parkins (Jan Hooks in a dual role), a former movie star in her fifties. Marty and Aileen get into an altercation when she pushes her seat back and hits him. He then accidentally removes her wig revealing she is bald which is caught on camera. Parkins files a civil suit against Marty for $2 million. When Marty and his attorney and Aileen and her attorney appear in court, they find that they are all on Courtroom TV, which makes Marty's lawyer very nervous, causing him to run out of the courtroom leaving Marty to defend himself. As Marty cross-examines Aileen, he accidentally gets her wig attached to his ring finger pulling it off again. In the end, the civil suit is thrown out as frivolous.

Episodes Never Produced

At least three scripts were written for the series but never taped:

"Back to Nature" (summary based on rough draft script)   Writer: Andy Robin

Marty and Caroline are going camping with other fathers and their kids. Typical sitcom antics ensue with one of the kid's dads insisting that Marty read a script he wrote, and another dad getting stuck in an abandoned Port-A-Potty when the door won't open. Caroline is infatuated with a boy who is on the trip, but the boy is attracted to another girl. In a secondary storyline, Marty and Meg are both reading a book about a sordid affair between Marilyn Monroe and Jerry Lewis, and sketches depict passages from the book.

"Boyfriend'z a Hood" (summary based on final draft script)   Writers: Paul Flaherty, Michael Short, and Martin Short

Meg and Marty are to be interviewed by a Barbara Walters-type newsperson, Paula Davidson. Meg confesses to Alice that she has an embarrassing incident in her past that she is afraid might be brought up in the interview and wants Alice to contact a producer for Paula Davidson that she knows to see if they have found out about it. Later, after Alice hands Meg a photo she got from Davidson's producer, Meg shows Marty the picture of her at seventeen with her boyfriend at the time who was a gangster. Marty goes to Paula's office to talk her out of discussing the photo during the interview. When Paula becomes irritated at Marty for asking about the picture, he says she is a parasite feeding off celebrities. She confides that she could have been a Broadway dancer if she had let producers have their way with her. Marty asks, if he could make her dream come true, would she drop the idea of discussing the photo from the upcoming interview. He gets Paula a spot dancing on his variety show and the interview comes off without any mention of the photo.

According to Michael Short, this script was originally titled "Mother of All Blind Dates."[65] The premise was similar to the one above but, instead of Meg having dated a gangster, she had gone on a blind date with a young Saddam Hussein while she was a graduate student in London. The script included a flashback where Meg and Saddam get into an argument with a drunken Henry Kissinger (Eugene Levy) at a restaurant. NBC thought the story was too controversial, and so the writers redid the script and called it "Boyfrend'z a Hood."

"Movie of the Weak" (summary based on table draft script)   Writer: Laurie Parres

Alice's made-for-TV drama, *Fried Bitter Corn*, is premiering in which she plays a widow trying to keep her family together during the Great Depression. Marty and Meg don't like the movie, but Alice thinks they do. Pat Morita is the guest on Marty's variety show and thinks that Alice's movie was a comedy. The reviews for the film are bad, and Alice wonders if she was that terrible. Meg says that they were just trying to spare her feelings in not revealing the truth about her performance. Marty, Meg, and Alice argue over Marty and Meg not being honest with her. When Pat Morita tells a story of a young martial arts student who sought the nature of truth, Marty thinks the story is boring and pointless. Morita walks off the show. Meg says the moral of the story is that you should always lie through your teeth with which Alice and Marty agree.

According to Laurie Parres, the script for this episode was based on an experience Marty Short had had when a friend acted in a movie that was horrible.[66] Sets for the episode were built, graphics were designed, and the cast had done a table read of the script when NBC announced that the series was canceled.

Short Run

The Martin Short Show was given a special preview on Thursday at 8:30 PM before moving to its regular time period on Tuesdays between *Wings* and *Frasier*. It did not provide a good lead-in to *Frasier* and was taken off the air after three episodes for "retooling." The series did not perform that badly in the ratings; the third episode ranked thirtieth for the week it aired. However, the third episode was lower-rated than the episode of *Wings* that preceded it and the episode of *Frasier* that came after it. *The Martin Short Show* was another victim of the "falloff factor."

Production did resume on a new Martin Short series in Spring 1995. The cast from the original series was let go except for Jan Hooks, and the show-within-a-show concept was abandoned. The new series was a traditional sketch comedy show. NBC aired *The Show Formerly Known as The Martin Short Show* as a one-time special on May 20, 1995 in place of *Saturday Night Live*. One segment of the special was a commercial advertising the sale of a video containing the "lost" episodes of *The Martin Short Show*. The special did not lead to a new series for Short on NBC.

The Paul Reiser Show

Premiered Thursday, April 14, 2011, at 8:30 PM on NBC

Paul Reiser played himself on this comedy that supposedly showed what his life was like after his prior sitcom *Mad About You* left the air. Appearing on the series with him was Amy Landecker who played his spouse Claire, a psychologist and the mother of Paul's two sons. Paul's friends included Brad (Andrew Daly), who came from an old wealthy family; Jonathan (Ben Shenkman), a tightly wound prosecuting attorney; Fernando (Duane Martin), a successful restaurateur, and Habib (Omid Djalii), who ran a business selling slightly-damaged goods. At the start of each episode, Paul addressed the camera directly, talking about life.

Background

Paul Reiser created and developed the comedy along with Jonathan Shapiro. The sitcom was originally titled *Next* as a way of emphasizing that it was about the next part of Reiser's life after *Mad About You*. The show bore similarities to Larry David's *Curb Your Enthusiasm* in that it was a single-camera comedy created by its star who played himself and was purported to be about his everyday life. Bonanza Productions in association with Nuance Productions and Warner Bros. Television produced the series.

Episode Guide: 2 aired; 5 unaired

Episode 1: April 14, 2011   "The Father's Occupation"

Director: Bryan Gordon   Writers: Paul Reiser and Jonathan Shapiro

Paul is stressed about what occupation to put on a form from his son's school. His inconclusive answer motivates him to audition as host for a new game show against Larry David. Meanwhile, Jonathan, Brad, and Fernando get caught up with their kids' school projects about the different states.

Episode 2: April 21, 2011   "The Play Date"

Director: Daniel Stern   Writers: Paul Reiser and Jonathan Shapiro

Paul is left in charge of picking up Jonathan's son for a play date, while Claire is stuck at the dentist's office with one of their kids. In the meantime, when an angry cat keeps Paul and Claire up at night, Habib offers to capture it. Also, Paul is forced to make amends to the father of one of his son's classmates who thinks he won't get a movie role because Paul told the producer he wasn't funny.

Henry Rollins portrayed the intimidating father who was up for the movie role, and Mel Brooks voiced the angry cat in this episode. Daniel Stern, the star of the short-lived *Danny* and *Regular Joe*, directed the episode. Stern had starred in the film *Diner* with Reiser.

Episode 3: Unaired   "The Generator"

Director: Fred Savage   Writers: Paul Reiser and Jonathan Shapiro

After endorsing a tool company, Paul becomes handy around the house with Claire questioning his behavior. Meanwhile, a near-death experience causes Jonathan to begin acting differently, and Habib tries to lose weight by changing his lifestyle.

The star of *The Wonder Years*, Fred Savage, is now both an actor and a director.

Episode 4: Unaired   "The Batting Cage"

Director: Bryan Gordon   Writers: Paul Reiser and Jonathan Shapiro

Paul and his buddies go to the batting cages with their kids where Paul confronts two batting cage bullies who have harassed his son. Paul also weighs options on a possible movie offer.

Episode 5: Unaired   "The Old Guy"

Director: Unknown   Writers: Paul Reiser and Jonathan Shapiro

Paul reevaluates the choice of his sons' legal guardian should something happen to Claire and him. However, he finds that no one else wants to be the guardian for his kids.

Episode 6: Unaired   "The Fedora"

Director: Unknown   Writers: Paul Reiser and Jonathan Shapiro

Storyline unknown

Episode 7: Unaired   "The Shave"

Director: Unknown   Writers: Paul Reiser and Jonathan Shapiro

Storyline unknown

Pale Imitation

The premiere of *The Paul Reiser Show* was NBC's lowest rated sitcom debut ever in the coveted eighteen to forty-nine year-old demographic. Many critics pointed out the similarities between *The Paul Reiser Show* and *Curb Your Enthusiasm*, but not in a good way. *The New York Times* said the show was "…a pale imitation of Larry David's 'Curb Your Enthusiasm'."[67]

Tammy Grimes in *The Tammy Grimes Show*

Chapter 9
Welcome to My World— Female Version

Like male-centered comedies, sitcoms featuring a female central character date back to the 1950's with series like *The Ann Sothern Show* and *Our Miss Brooks*. *Here's Lucy*, *That Girl*, and particularly the *Mary Tyler Moore Show* are great examples of long-running female-centric comedies with the lead character having both a domestic life as well as some type of career. Some not-so-long-running examples are found in this chapter.

Frannie's Turn

Previewed Sunday, September 13, 1992, at 8:00 PM before moving to Saturdays at 8:00 PM on CBS

Frannie Escobar (Miriam Margolyes), a wife, mother, and seamstress, was tired of being taken for granted by her Cuban-American husband, Joseph (Tomas Millian), an exterminator, and by the arrogant fashion designer, Armando (Taylor Negron) for whom she had worked for nine years. She was also concerned that her daughter, Olivia (Phoebe Augustine), was considering an early marriage to her boyfriend, Robert (Anthony Tyler Quinn), a man as chauvinistic as her father—Frannie's husband. The Escobar household included Frannie's mother-in-law Rosa (Alice Drummond) and Frannie's sixteen-year-old son Eddie (Stivi Paskoski). Vivian (LaTanya Richardson) was Frannie's best friend at work.

Background

Frannie's Turn, originally titled simply *Frannie* and then *The Little Woman*, was the first situation comedy created by Chuck Lorre. Produced by the Carsey-Werner Company, *Frannie's Turn* was a rare failure for Chuck Lorre, who would later create several hit comedies including *Grace Under Fire* (1993), *Cybil* (1995), *Dharma & Greg* with Dottie Dartland (1997), *Two and a Half Men* with Lee Aronsohn (2003), and *The Big Bang Theory* with Bill Purdy (2007).

Episode Guide: 5 aired; 1 unaired

Episode 1: September 13, 1992 "Pilot"

Director: Sam Weisman   Writer: Chuck Lorre

Frannie is concerned that her twenty-year-old daughter is thinking of marrying a man much like her dad. Frannie herself got married at age twenty and is tired of being a servant for her husband. She tells her mother-in-law that she has to wait on Joseph hand and foot including always getting his beers to which the mother-in-law replies: "Sometimes it makes you feel better if you spit in the beer." When her boss calls her a "lowly seamstress," she finally stands up to him because she is tired of men taking advantage of her. Frannie informs her husband that she wants to be treated like a person – not a cook and maid.

LaTanya Richardson, who portrayed Frannie's friend Vivian, is married to actor Samuel L. Jackson.

Episode 2: September 19, 1992   "Money Talks, Olivia Walks"

Director: Asaad Kelada   Writers: Tony Blake and Paul Jackson

Frannie and Joseph argue over their finances. When Joseph finds that Frannie has over $2800 that she has been saving for years, she says that she wants money of her own. He then allows her to handle all of the family's money. Frannie discovers that Joseph has been sending $50 to another woman every month. After she confronts him, he responds that he has been contributing to a Cuban liberation group. Meanwhile, Olivia is celebrating her birthday, and her boyfriend Robert continues to act chauvinistic toward her. He invites a friend to go to the movies with them and doesn't tell her in advance; he gets agitated when she changes her hairstyle without asking him first, and, for her birthday, he gives her an electric shaver. In the end, she finally dumps him.

Episode 3: September 26, 1992   "Sex and Saints"

Director: Asaad Kelada   Writers: Susan Sebastian and Diana Ayers

Frannie wants more romance in her love life; while Frannie's mother-in-law claims to have encountered St. Monica, the patron saint of married women. After Frannie's friends say that she should not be afraid of how she looks to Joseph, she plans a romantic evening. However, Joseph wants to turn off the lights before they make love which upsets Frannie who thinks that Joseph can't stand to look at her. After Joseph's mother tells him to make things right with Frannie, he says it is all right to keep the lights on when they make love and that the only reason he liked it in the dark was so he could pretend he was still young.

Episode 4: October 3, 1992   "How Do You Say Death in Spanish?"

Director: Asaad Kelada   Story: Joyce Burditt   Teleplay: Dottie Dartland Zicklin

Rosa wants to pick out a dress for her funeral before her death which upsets Joseph and requires Frannie to drastically alter an existing dress. Joseph is also concerned about Eddie failing Spanish thinking that the family's Cuban pride may die with him. Frannie wants Joseph to help Eddie learn Spanish. Eddie says he is an American – not Cuban, and is not interested in his heritage. However, his sister is interested in her Cuban roots. In the end, Eddie passes his Spanish test with a little help from the classmate in front of him.

This episode revealed that Joseph has a thirty-year-old son named Joe with whom he has been estranged because Joe is gay.

Episode 5: October 10, 1992   "Gentlemen, Wrap Your Guava"

Director: Asaad Kelada   Writer: Larry Spencer

Frannie has Joseph be the housewife, while she makes a wedding dress. When Eddie wants to date a girl from school, Frannie wants his dad to discuss sex with the boy. At the supermarket, Joseph uses a guava and a plastic bag to demonstrate safe sex techniques for Eddie. After Eddie comes home from his date, he reveals that he just danced with the girl; they didn't have sex. Meanwhile, Olivia reveals that her ex-boyfriend Robert is dating someone else.

Episode 6: Unaired   "Frannie and the Kitchen Sink"

Director: Asaad Kelada   Writer: Chuck Lorre

When Frannie tells Joseph that they need a new kitchen sink, he becomes irritated. Rosa advises Frannie that she gives in to Joseph too much, and so Frannie decides to replace the sink herself which further upsets her husband. Despite Joseph telling their priest about Frannie's attitude, she perseveres with installing the sink. In the end, she lets Joseph know that she doesn't need him in her life but she wants him in her life and that he needs to compromise on things.

This episode was the original pilot for the series. Mel Tormé sang the theme song titled "The Little Woman."

Turn Over

When the sitcom moved to its regular spot on Saturdays, the ratings fell by half. Despite weak competition, *Frannie's Turn* did not do well and was removed from the schedule after five episodes. Its last episode ranked eighty-second out of ninety shows.

Julie

Premiered Saturday, May 30, 1992 at 8:30 PM on ABC

Julie was Julie Andrews' debut as a sitcom star. She played Julie Carlyle, the star of her own network variety show, who fell in love and married a veterinarian, Sam McGuire (James Farentino) with a practice in Sioux City, Iowa. Sam was a widower with two children: fourteen-year-old Allie (Hayley Tyrie) and twelve-year-old Adam (Rider Strong). Not wanting to give up his practice, Julie moved herself and her variety show to Sioux City. Her friend and producer, Wooley Woolstein (Eugene Roche), accompanied Julie to Iowa.

Background

Julie Andrews' sitcom started out as *Millie*, an unsold pilot for ABC, produced and directed by her husband Blake Edwards. *Millie* bore many similarities to *Julie* except for the concept of a major television star moving to rural Iowa. In *Millie*, Julie Andrews was Millie Morale, the star of her own variety hour, married to a former pro-football player (James Farentino) with two kids – Evan and Emily – played by the same child actors who were in *Julie*. Also, Eugene Roche played Max, the producer of Millie's variety hour. Millie was trying to balance her TV career with her family responsibilities. The storyline of the pilot focused on twelve-year-old Evan touching a girl's breast at school. When informed of this, Julie dares her son to feel her breast (which he doesn't) and then punishes him by not allowing him to go to the fights with his dad. After Evan informs his dad that, after apologizing to the girl, the girl said she didn't mind, his father advises Evan to invite the girl to Millie's show so she can tell Millie directly. They meet in Millie's dressing room, and it turns out that the girl is a physically mature fifteen-year-old.

Millie was created by Irving and Alice Shatz. When ABC rejected the pilot concept, the writing team of Madeline and Steven Sunshine were brought in to rework the premise, and they came up with the idea of Julie Andrews marrying a widower and moving her show to Iowa.

Episode Guide: 5 aired; 1 unaired

Episode 1: May 30, 1992   "Pilot"

Director: Blake Edwards   Writers: Madeline and Steven Sunshine

After veterinarian Sam McGuire proposes to TV star, Julie Carlyle, she moves to Iowa to get married. The producer of her variety show moves with her, and they plan to broadcast the show from KCOM, the local TV station. On their wedding night, Sam has an emergency veterinary call and has to leave the marital bed.

Rider Strong who played son Adam on this series later played Shawn Hunter on the comedy *Boy Meets World*.

Episode 2: June 6, 1992   "Allie's Talent" (aka "Happy Face")

Director: Blake Edwards   Writers: Joe and Nancy Guppy

Julie encourages Allie's singing and dancing. However, Julie is afraid that Sam may have problems with Allie performing because she hasn't done so since her mom died. Julie and Allie sing "Put on a Happy Face."

Episode 3: June 20, 1992   "The Ugly Bed" (aka "The Bed")

Director: Blake Edwards   Writers: Harry Cauley and Jenna McMahon

Burglars steal all of the McGuire's furniture and belongings except the ugly bed in the master bedroom which Julie despises. When the family leaves the house again, the burglars return everything and take the bed since they learned from TV reports that the bed is an antique.

With her writing partner, Dick Clair, Jenna McMahon wrote and produced the sitcoms *It's a Living*, *The Facts of Life*, and *Mama's Family*.

Episode 4: June 27, 1992   "The Monkey" (aka "Monkey's Business")

Director: Blake Edwards   Writers: Madeline and Steven Sunshine

Delaney, Wooley's pal from vaudeville, has a heart attack, leaving his orangutan partner, Lowell, with no one to take care of him. The McGuire's attempt to care for the simian. When they learn that Delaney wants to see Lowell, they put the orangutan in a dress to sneak him into the hospital. Delaney sings "Feelings" to the ape while cuddling him on his bed. In the closing scene, while Julie sings "New York, New York" on her live variety show, the monkey climbs a picture of the Empire State Building in the background.

Episode 5: July 4, 1992   "Nick Wyler Visits"

Director: Blake Edwards   Writers: Joe and Nancy Guppy

Robert Wagner plays a move star who is a guest on Julie's variety show and whose past relationship with her is a surprise to Sam. Wagner, along with others from the TV station, sing "Everybody Ought to Have a Maid" as Julie, dressed in a French maid's costume, dances.

Episode 6: Unaired   "Put Up Your Dukes"

Director: Blake Edwards   Writers: Harry Cauley and Jenna McMahon

Finding difficulty in getting guest stars to travel to Sioux City for her show, Julie wants to build her own stock company consisting of her producer, the station's children's show host, and a newsman. They do a hillbilly skit satirizing Julie and her husband getting ready to go out for an evening. Offended at his depiction in the skit, Sam argues with Julie. Sam eventually says he is sorry, and the two make up.

Poor *Julie*

The comedy was supposed to be a midseason replacement for the 1991-92 season, but, after seeing the six episodes that were made, ABC decided to air *Julie* during the summer on Saturdays after reruns of *Who's the Boss?*. When *Julie* was finally scheduled by ABC, neither Andrews nor Farentino did any publicity for the show. Each episode of *Julie* got lower and lower ratings; the third episode was the lowest rated program for the week, ranking ninety-third out of ninety-three shows.

As the *Los Angeles Times* put it: "While the idea of Julie Andrews in a TV series directed and produced by husband Blake Edwards sounds like sure-fire fun, the resultant 'Julie'... is so completely perfunctory a sitcom that it's bound to induce major blahs among fans of either spouse."[68]

Laurie Hill

Premiered Wednesday, September 30, 1992, at 9:30 PM on ABC

In this little-known comedy-drama, Dr. Laurie Hill (DeLane Matthews) was a pediatrician as well as mother of five-year-old Leo (Eric Lloyd). Her husband Jeff (Robert Clohessy), a writer, initially worked from home. Dr. Hill practiced medicine at the Wiseman, Kramer, & Hill Family Medical practice. Dr. Walter Wiseman (Joseph Maher), in his sixties; the younger, handsome Dr. Spencer Kramer (Kurt Fuller); the older office manager-receptionist Beverly Fiedler (Doris Belack), and Nurse Nancy MacIntyre (Ellen DeGeneres) made up the other medical staff. The show centered on Dr. Hill's efforts to balance her career and her family life.

Background

Carol Black and Neal Marlens created *Laurie Hill*; they had previously created the hit comedy, *The Wonder Years*. The Black/Marlens Company and Touchstone Television produced the series. ABC originally ordered twelve episodes in addition to the pilot but that order was subsequently reduced to nine episodes.

Episode Guide: 5 aired; 5 unaired

Episode 1: September 30, 1992   "Pilot"

Director: Steve Miner   Writers: Carol Black and Neal Marlens

At home, Laurie tries to discuss with Jeff what they should get Leo for his birthday. Although Leo wants a toy gun, Laurie doesn't want to get him a gift that promotes violence. At work, Dr. Hill treats Justin, a seven-year-old boy who claims he is unable to go to school. She has Nancy do some blood work on the boy, and that evening she is called to the emergency room to look at Justin who has trouble breathing. She is concerned that he may have HIV. The next day, Jeff questions Laurie on whether he should buy Leo a toy gun. He says that getting Leo a toy gun might distract him from missing his mother who works all the time. Laurie receives the results of Justin's blood test and goes to the hospital to tell the boy's parents that she will help him as much as she can. When she returns home that night with a bag full of toy guns, Jeff puts the guns away and consoles Laurie over her bad day at work.

Episode 2: October 7, 1992   "Woman on the Verge"

Director: L.G. Day   Writer: David Rosenthal

The Hill house is having plumbing problems, and the plumber says that all the pipes need to be replaced. Concerned that Jeff might criticize her for allowing the plumber to take advantage of her, Laurie delays the authorization to do any work for one day too long and the pipes burst bringing the household to a standstill. At the office, Laurie treats a man with a sexually-transmitted disease who refuses to provide a list of his sexual partners. When Laurie informs him that she will advise the health department if he doesn't give her the list, he provides a very short list showing that he is not the lothario he claimed he was.

Episode 3: October 14, 1992   "Crush"

Director: Unknown   Writers: Carol Black and Neal Marlens

A young patient develops a crush on Laurie, and she has to make a difficult decision – accepting a Halloween party invitation from the patient or taking her son trick or treating. Laurie is also busy trying to make a Halloween costume for Leo.

Episode 4: October 21, 1992   "Grasshopper" (aka "Sins of the Mother," "School," "Why Leo Can't Read")

Director: Neal Marlens   Story: Hugh O'Neill, Carol Black, and Neal Marlens
Teleplay: Carol Black and Neal Marlens

Laurie and Jeff are told that Leo is having trouble in school – not paying attention in class, not doing his homework, etc. His report card shows need for improvement in a lot of subjects. During the parent-teacher conference, Jeff comes to his son's defense, while Laurie accepts the teacher's comments that Leo may need to be evaluated. Jeff and Laurie later discover that Leo is indeed having trouble in class because he has been made to feel he is not good enough. When a mother brings her infant daughter in for a checkup and is concerned that her daughter is not the height and doesn't crawl enough compared to other babies her age, Laurie realizes that it's good enough to "just be yourself" and forget about how other people's kids are doing.

Episode 5: October 28, 1992   "Sick and Tired"

Director: Unknown   Writer: Stephen Neigher

Laurie, Jeff, and Leo all have the flu, but it turns out that this gives them a much needed break from stress. They realize they should slow down and enjoy life.

Episode 6: Unaired   "The Babysitter"

Director: L.G. Day   Writer: Kim Friese

Laurie stayed home with Leo the first year he was born, and then Jeff stayed home with their son until he started school. Now Jeff has been offered the city editor job at a newspaper, and they have to find a babysitter to take care of Leo after school. The couple hires Lisa, the perfect sitter, but Laurie is jealous because of the time she has to spend away from Leo. Jeff suggests that she do what she wants by working less hours and being at home for Leo after school. At the office, Spencer invests in a new German coffeemaker and gourmet blend which he restricts to the doctors only. The nurses retaliate with a refreshment center of their own.

Episode 7: Unaired   "The Birds and the Elephants"

Director: L.G. Day   Writer: David Rosenthal

Jeff is starting his new job, and Laurie must tell her colleagues that she is cutting back her workload. Walter is not pleased with her decision, which means that

WELCOME TO MY WORLD—FEMALE VERSION

some of Laurie's workload will have to be divided between him and Spencer. The decision comes home to Laurie when she realizes that she can't be there for a couple whose baby she just delivered because her reduced schedule makes it impossible for timely appointments. In spite of the burden on the family finances and the strained relationships at work, special moments at home with Leo make her know that she made the right decision.

Episode 8: Unaired "The Heart Thing"

Director: Neal Marlens   Writer: Carol Black and Neal Marlens

Laurie's mother Mary (Christina Pickles) tells her that she's been experiencing chest pains and that her doctor has prescribed nitroglycerin pills. Laurie offers to set her mother up with a cardiologist, but Mary decides to stick with her original physician. Mary has a heart attack in the middle of the night. At the hospital, the specialist reassures Laurie that an angioplasty will fix everything. However, Mary's internist suggests a bypass, and Laurie's sister Susan recommends a surgeon who did one for a woman she knows. Mary opts for the bypass and just doesn't understand when Laurie confronts the lifelong problem in their relationship that her mother always takes Susan's advice over Laurie's whom Mary believes can't do anything well.

Episode 9: Unaired "Much Ado About Nancy"

Director: Neal Marlens   Writer: David Rosenthal

Laurie sets up a blind date between Nancy and Bruce, one of Jeff's friends. She invites them both to a dinner party she is having along with other staff from the medical practice. For most of the evening, Nancy ignores Bruce. But she eventually talks with him, and they seem to be having a good time. However, Bruce confesses to Jeff that he's just not interested in blondes like Nancy. Upon learning this, Nancy tells Laurie to stop making her into something that she's not – a warm, loving, secure person.

Episode 10: Unaired "Walter and Beverly"

Director: Neal Marlens   Writer: Rita Hsiao

Walter becomes jealous when Beverly starts dating Bill, an accountant whom she met at a bookstore. Walter's attitude results in him firing Beverly when she leaves the office three minutes early. Laurie invites both Walter and Beverly to her house for reconciliation where Walter admits he loves Beverly and she says she loves him as well.

Another Fall-off Factor Victim

Laurie Hill followed *Home Improvement* on Wednesdays. Five episodes aired before the show was canceled. The series performed respectably in the ratings. Each week ratings improved, and by the third week, it ranked twenty-second out of eighty-nine shows.[69] However, the show was not retaining enough of the audience from its lead-in, the top-rated *Home Improvement*, and so it was taken off the air.

My Wildest Dreams

Premiered Sunday, May 28, 1995 at 9:30 PM on Fox

Married for eight years with a husband and two kids and living in suburban New Jersey, Lisa McGinnis (Lisa Ann Walter) had the wild dream of becoming a rock star. Lisa worked at a recording studio – Mound of Sound, while her spouse Jack (John Posey) ran a sporting-goods store. The couple had a son Danny (J. Evan Bonifant), age seven and a four-month-old baby daughter, Delilah. Chandler Trapp (Miquel A. Nunez, Jr.) was the owner/engineer of Mound of Sound. Gloria James (Kelly Bishop), Lisa's mother, and Lisa's sister, Stephanie (Mary Jo Keenen), were other characters on the comedy.

Background

Originally titled *Something's Gotta Give*, *My Wildest Dreams* was created by Shawn Schepps. In the initial pilot written by Schepps, which never aired, Lisa's husband, named Mel, was portrayed by Robert Clohessy, her son Josh was still played by Evan Bonifant, and Laura Innes was featured as her sister Casey. Lisa was a realtor and her spouse a carpenter. As in the first aired episode described below, Lisa and her spouse were trying to celebrate their wedding anniversary. She planned to have her

WELCOME TO MY WORLD—FEMALE VERSION

mother babysit the kids, but mom got into an argument with Lisa's younger sister and left with Lisa and Mel canceling their night out. Columbia Pictures Television produced the series.

Episode Guide: 5 aired episodes

Episode 1: May 28, 1995   "You Don't Know Me"

Director: Jeff Melman   Writers: Linda and Michael Teverbaugh

Lisa and Jack celebrate their anniversary and buy each other gifts. However, as luck would have it, neither is pleased with what they receive.

Episode 2: June 4, 1995   "The Poker Game"

Director: Alan Myerson   Writer: Jordan Moffet

Lisa invites a client to her weekly poker game, but gets upset when the woman makes a pass at Jack.

Episode 3: June 11, 1995   "Sister's Mister"

Director: Alan Myerson   Writer: Micki Raton

Lisa encourages her sister, Stephanie to continue a romance with a guy who arouses the sister's fear of intimacy.

Episode 4: June 18, 1995   "Take This Job and Love It"

Director: Jeff Melman   Writer: Micki Raton

Jack's plan to purchase a new car comes apart when Lisa accepts a low-paying job. Meanwhile, Lisa returns to school and finds that she will have to work harder as a wife and a mother.

Episode 5: June 25, 1995   "Wedding Bell Blues"

Director: John Tracy   Writer: Micki Raton

Lisa and Jack have to contend with his parents when they visit for a wedding. Meanwhile, Stephanie's wedding gift is destined to make the bride blush.

Dreams Over

The premiere of *My Wildest Dreams* retained almost 90 percent of the audience from its lead-in *Married with Children*. However, Fox failed to renew the sitcom after the initial five episodes. *My Wildest Dreams* was Lisa Ann Walter's first lead role on a TV series. After *My Wildest Dreams*, she co-created and starred on *Life's Work* on ABC and later became a regular on the short-lived comedy *Emeril*, starring Chef Emeril Lagasse.

Roxie

Premiered Wednesday, April 1, 1987, at 8:00 PM on CBS

Roxie Brinkerhoff (SCTV alumnus Andrea Martin) was a program director at a small New York City TV station, WNYU, and married to Michael (Mitchell Laurance), a schoolteacher. Her boss, Leon Buchanan (Jack Riley), the station manager, was also the star of the station's children's show called *Larry the Lizard*. Marcie McKinley (Teresa Ganzel), Roxie's friend as well as the office manager, Vito Carteri (Ernie Sabella), and Randy Grant (Jerry Pavlon) comprised the other staff at the station. Roxie was in charge of various shows like an exercise class for the elderly, starring and sponsored by the owners of a pastry shop.

Background

Andrea Martin had played a similar character on two episodes of *Kate & Allie* (a sitcom about two divorced mothers and their kids who pooled resources and lived in the same apartment). In the December 1, 1986 episode of *Kate & Allie*, when Allie (Jane Curtin) wanted more out of life, she became involved with an underfunded cable channel. The episode guest starred Andrea Martin as Eddie Gordon who worked at the TV station. The character of Eddie Gordon returned in the following week's episode of *Kate & Allie* when New York City was paralyzed by a big snow storm, and Allie helped Eddie fill eighteen hours of public TV programming.

"Eddie" became "Roxie" for the spinoff, got a new staff, and a husband. Initially Jerry Stiller *(Seinfeld, King of Queens, Nick & Hillary)* was cast as Roxie's boss, but was replaced by Jack Riley of *The Bob Newhart Show*. Allan Katz developed *Roxie* from the character Bob Randall created on *Kate & Allie*. The sitcom, initially titled *Andrea Spinelli-Brinkerhoff*, was produced by the Reeves Entertainment Group.

Episode Guide: 2 aired; 4 unaired

Episode 1: April 1, 1987   "You're a Big Girl Now"

Director: Sheldon Larry   Writers: Allan Katz and Bob Randall

Roxie wants to impress an old friend from high school that she hasn't seen in fifteen years. When in school, her friend was the attractive prom queen, class president, and valedictorian. However, she is now fat and shows up while Roxie is padded out for a story on discrimination against the overweight. Meanwhile, at the station, a cooking show is canceled because a cat ate the sushi.

After *Roxie*, Andrea Martin became a regular on two other short-lived sitcoms – *The Martin Short Show* and *Life . . . and Stuff*.

Episode 2: April 8, 1987 "Dog Days"

Director: Sheldon Larry   Writer: Allan Katz

Roxie hosts a telethon for a dog rescue and pleads for the return of a lost dog. The pet – as well as nearly every other stray dog in the city – is delivered to Roxie's TV station.

Mitchell Laurance, who played Roxie's husband Michael, has a twin brother Matthew, who is also an actor.

Episode 3: Unaired   "Group Therapy" (summary based on final draft script)

Director: Sheldon Larry   Writer: Bill Richmond

Roxie is interviewing a psychiatrist on her talk show who has written a book on group therapy titled *Talk Your Way to Mental Health*. Since the doctor gives very short answers to Roxie's questions, to fill time, she decides to have the TV staff participate in a live group therapy session. The staff members discuss what annoys them about their co-workers and proceed to get mad at Roxie and their fellow workers over the remarks being made. When viewers call the station to say they liked the show, Roxie decides to have the doctor back the next day to continue the therapy session.

Episode 4: Unaired   "Here's Roxie"

Director: Unknown   Writer: Allan Katz

The pilot for the series introducing Roxie and other cast members.

Allan Katz subsequently produced the short-lived comedy *Scorch*.

Episode 5: Unaired "It's Not Easy Being Green"

Director: Unknown   Writer: Allan Katz

The storyline for this episode is not known. When contacted, Allan Katz indicated that the specifics about this series have pretty much faded from memory. He said that ". . . executive producing, writing and running *Roxie* was for the most part a horrible experience – and thanks to time, I've forgotten much of it."[70]

Episode 6: Unaired   "Professional Courtesy" (summary based on final draft script)

Director: John Bowab   Writer: Doug Steckler

Marcie has developed an outline for a game show called *Antics and Shenanigans* and wants Roxie to critique it. Roxie asks others at the station for comments about the concept, and everyone seems to hate it. However, after Marcie persists in having Roxie present the outline to Leon, Roxie acts out the premise for Leon who wants to put it on the air. Roxie thinks she can improve the concept. But she really can't, and the pilot turns out badly.

Roxie, We Hardly Knew Ya

Roxie was slotted on Wednesdays against NBC's *Highway to Heaven* and ABC's *Perfect Strangers*. Its debut ranked sixty-fifth out of seventy series and was canceled after two episodes.

Talk to Me

Premiered Tuesday, April 11, 2000, at 9:30 PM on ABC

In *Talk to Me*, Kyra Sedgwick starred as Janey Munro, a bubbly radio talk show host. Her cohorts at radio station WSJB in New York City included her co-host Rob (David Newsom), Marshall (Max Baker), the sound effects guy with a British accent, and Cam (Mike Estime), her black producer. Following her radio show was Dr. Debra (Beverly D'Angelo from the Chevy Chase *Vacation* movies), a conservative psychologist, with whose ideas Janey often disagreed. Sandy (Peter Jacobson) was featured as the station's manager, and Kat (Nicole Sullivan) was Janey's sister and best friend. Janey Munro dealt both with stress at work and the anxieties of being single.

Background

Talk to Me, created by Suzanne Martin, who had been a writer and producer for *Frasier*, was similar to the Kelsey Grammer comedy in several respects. The lead, a radio talk show host, was single. The comedy alternated between the station and the lead character's high-rise apartment, and the lead's best friend was her sibling.

In an early script for the pilot, Kat, instead of being Janey's sister, was described as her roommate since college, and the producer of Janey's radio show was a woman named "Sashi" and not Cam. The script also indicated that Janey and her boyfriend Steve had been in a relationship for five years and had been in pre-marital counseling when Steve confessed that he had met an old girlfriend whom he asked to marry him.

Sam Jen Productions and Heritage Productions in association with Touchstone Television produced *Talk to Me*.

Episode Guide: 3 aired; 2 unaired

Episode 1: April 11, 2000   "About Taking It Like a Man"

Director: Michael Lembeck   Writer: Suzanne Martin

Janey just broke up with her boyfriend Steve and feels miserable. While interviewing Gene Simmons of KISS on her radio show, she asks him his secret for surviving break-ups. Rob says to take it like a man and don't let your feelings get in the way with which Simmons agrees. Janey decides to go out on a date with a different guy each night for two weeks. However, she admits to her staff that she still feels miserable. Rob and Max advise that is because she is not having sex with her dates. Janey beds her next date but bursts out crying. She realizes that she just has to let time pass to feel better.

In the original script for this episode, while Janey talks about her break-up on the radio, she doesn't ask Gene Simmons his secret for surviving the end of a relationship. Simmons doesn't appear at all in the early script. Instead, Dr. Debra advises Janey that Steve dumped her because she held back who she really is, and Janey agrees that she tortured herself trying to please Steve.

Episode 2: April 18, 2000   "About Being Gay"

Director: Ted Wass   Writers: Jonathan Stark and Tracy Newman

At a boring advertisers' party, Janey, on a dare from her co-workers, pretends to be a lesbian and flirts with Teresa (Paulina Porizkova), an attractive fashion designer who turns out really to be gay. Janey decides to go on a date with her in order to tell Teresa that she really isn't gay, but, when Teresa invites another couple on their date, Janey doesn't get the opportunity to explain. Janey starts to like the attention and gifts from Teresa. When she finally confesses that she is straight, Teresa says she could tell because Janey kisses like a straight woman.

WELCOME TO MY WORLD—FEMALE VERSION

Episode 3: April 25, 2000   "About Makeovers"

Director: James Widdoes   Writer: Suzanne Martin

Janey's sister is turning twenty-nine, and since her favorite show is E!'s *Fashion Emergency*, Janey makes up a story about her sister to get her on the show for a free makeover. Janey describes Kat as a wheelchair-bound woman who has shed 100 pounds and has a lost love that she hasn't seen in ten years. Needless to say, the host of *Fashion Emergency* finds out the truth when both Rob and Cam show up as Kat's long-lost love.

Writer Suzanne Martin later created the TV Land sitcom *Hot in Cleveland*.

Episode 4: Unaired   "About Shopping"

Director: Ted Wass   Writers: Ellen Bryon and Lissa Kapstrom

Janey attempts to teach Rob and Marsh the tricks of shopping to attract women. On a shopping spree, she runs into her ex-boyfriend's fiancée. She impersonates a sales clerk to outfit the bride-to-be with an ugly wedding gown.

Dr. Joyce Brothers played herself on this episode.

Episode 5: Unaired   "About Religion"

Director: Ted Wass   Writer: John Levenstein

To live her life on a higher plane, Janey attends Dr. Debra's church-study group and ends up dating a minister. Meanwhile, Rob has difficulty breaking up with an annoying girlfriend.

Sandra Bernhard made a cameo appearance on this episode.

Talk to Me No Longer

Talk to Me was placed between the ABC hits *Dharma & Greg* and *NYPD Blue*. Its ratings were not terrible, but like other shows scheduled between established hits, it did not hold the audience from its lead-in. While the premiere of *Talk to Me* won its time period, it lost about 30 percent of the audience from *Dharma & Greg*.

Married to Kevin Bacon, Kyra Sedgwick (Janey) subsequently starred on the drama *The Closer*.

The Tammy Grimes Show

Premiered Thursday, September 8, 1966, 8:30 PM on ABC

Tammy Grimes played Tamantha Ward who worked as a customer relations officer at her Uncle Simon's bank, the Perpetual Savings Bank of New York. Her twin brother, Terence (Dick Sargent), was the eleventh vice president at the bank. As a stipulation in their parents' will, Uncle Simon (Hiram Sherman) controlled their multimillion dollar inheritance until the twins became thirty-years old so that they, particularly spendthrift Tammy, did not end up penniless. Episodes generally involved Tammy trying to get more money from dear old Uncle Simon. The theme of *The Tammy Grimes Show* seemed very similar to that of *The Lucy Show* with Tammy trying to play a Lucy-like character always attempting to obtain funds from a Mr. Mooney-type character, Uncle Simon. Mrs. Ratchett (Maudie Prickett) was Tammy's housekeeper.

Background

Screen Gems thought that Tammy Grimes, a Tony-award winning actress for *The Unsinkable Molly Brown*, would be a good candidate to play a witch on a situation comedy the company was developing. However, Grimes turned the role down, and Elizabeth Montgomery eventually went on to star on the successful sitcom *Bewitched*.

Tammy Grimes was then approached by William Dozier, executive producer of ABC's *Batman*, about doing another series. In the papers Dozier donated to the University of Wyoming, there is an undated memo outlining the original concept of *The Tammy Grimes Show*. The series was to be a half-hour vehicle for Grimes, ". . . high styled, chic, 'in,' hip, very modern in every aspect –'way out', but neither zany

WELCOME TO MY WORLD—FEMALE VERSION

nor incredible." The concept of the character, then known as Tammy Grenoble, was that she was one of a pair of male-female twins born twenty-four years ago. The twin's mother had died giving birth, and the father was a poor school teacher wanting to advance science. The twin's father decided to allow them to become the subjects of a scientific experiment at the Manhattan Foundation to determine the effects of environment and heredity on human behavior. As wards of the foundation, the twins were separated, and Tammy was allowed to "just grow," bumping up against every obstacle and frustration in life with no help from anyone. Her twin brother Tony, on the other hand, was given every available educational and social advantage. At the beginning of their twenty-fifth year, the twins were brought back together and found that they had completely opposite personalities – one uninhibited, the other an over-conformist.

The memo also described whom the producer had in mind for the roles of Tammy's brother and the other characters on the series. For Tony, the producer suggested someone like Peter Fonda, Roddy McDowell, or Noel Harrison (Rex Harrison's son). The part eventually went to Dick Sargent. For the head of the foundation, Paul Lynde, John McGiver, or Jack Albertson were proposed. Also, reference was made to including in the cast a housekeeper answerable to the foundation. The script for the pilot was to be written by George Axelrod, the playwright who had authored *The Seven Year Itch* and *Will Success Spoil Rock Hunter*.

While the memo provided the basic outline of what resulted in *The Tammy Grimes Show*, it is not clear why the concept of the twins having been raised by a foundation was abandoned in favor of one where the twins inherit a fortune that is managed by their uncle through his bank. One can speculate that the foundation idea was too much like something from a George Orwell novel and that the public could more readily identify with a big inheritance and a parsimonious uncle. However, it is difficult to understand how the concept for the series devolved from an attempt at sophisticated, hip comedy to what is described below in the episode guide.

The unaired pilot for *The Tammy Grimes Show*, titled "My Twin Sister," was directed by Don Taylor, and, as mentioned above, written by George Axelrod. In the pilot, both Terence and Uncle Simon were each seeing psychiatrists about Tammy's spendthrift ways. The episode related a revised back story about how Uncle Simon's sister married Terence Ward, Sr. who had borrowed money from the bank where he worked and bet it on the horses to become super rich. When the parents died, the money was left in a trust for Terence and Tammy. Both Uncle Simon and Terence agreed that Tammy needed to see an analyst herself. When Tammy asked Terence for an advance on her allowance, he told her that he would grant such only if she saw a psychiatrist. She resisted taking money with those strings attached, and, in disguise, went to the bank to borrow money. The bank gave her a credit card which she used to purchase a dress, a sports car, and a new hair style. At a disco, Tammy met a baseball player who was on the disabled list because of an arm injury. She used her credit card to buy the player from the team. When she took the player to the disco again, the dancing made his arm better. The team bought back the player, and Tammy made a profit on the deal – at least enough to pay off her credit card bill.

ABC gave the series a seventeen-week commitment. While William Dozier was the executive producer of the sitcom, Alex Gottleib and Richard Whorf produced the series. According to news accounts at the time, Grimes had Whorf taking tranquillizers on the set because she was not the most cooperative of actresses. Reportedly she did things like keeping everyone waiting to shoot a scene while she finished talking on the telephone.[71] Production companies behind the series were Greenway Productions, Tamworth Productions, and Twentieth Century-Fox.

Episode Guide: 4 aired; 6 unaired

Episode 1: September 8, 1966   "Officer's Mess"

Director: Don Taylor   Writer: Ralph Goodman

Tammy's brother is called to active duty in the Naval Reserve. Tammy goes to the ship to see him off, but, when she can't get on board, she sneaks on and the ship sails with her. Tammy ends up dressing as a sailor and saving the ship from crashing into another vessel.

Director Don Taylor was an actor before becoming a director. He married actress Hazel Court whom he met while directing her in an episode of *Alfred Hitchcock Presents*.

WELCOME TO MY WORLD—FEMALE VERSION

Episode 2: September 15, 1966   "How to Steal a Girl Even if It's Only Me"

Director: Don Taylor   Writer: Roland Wolpert

Uncle Simon refuses to give Tammy $50,000 for her favorite charity. She then is kidnapped by a group of amateurs and has the kidnappers demand $50,000 for her return.

Episode 3: September 22, 1966   "Tammy Takes Las Vegas, or Vice Versa"

Director: Don Taylor   Writers: Hannibal Coons and Harry Winkler

Tammy goes to a casino trying to parlay $20 into $50,000 which her housekeeper Mrs. Ratchett needs in order to save her aunt's Brazilian nut plantation.

Episode 4: September 29, 1966   "Positively Made in Paris"

Director: Don Taylor   Writers: Stan Dreben and Howard Merrill

Uncle Simon and Terence send Tammy to Cobbs Corner for the summer. It has a population of twenty seven, and is so rural that it doesn't have a dress shop. Uncle Simon thinks that will put an end to Tammy's clothes buying sprees. However, Tammy changes the name of the town to Paris and goes into the fashion design business.

Episode 5: Unaired   "George Washington Didn't Sleep Here" (summary from revised final draft script)

Director: Don Taylor   Writers: Jack Raymond and Sidney Morse

When Uncle Simon is about to foreclose on Tammy's friend, Andy McAdam's Old Grant Inn, she tries to prevent the action. Tammy finds that the inn really needs to be renovated. In order to create business and thus raise some money, Tammy spreads the rumor to her society friends that the Marchioness of Mull is staying at the inn. When all of her friends show up, Tammy disguises herself as the Marchioness, and, after Uncle Simon arrives, the Marchioness tells him not to be so miserly. He tears up the foreclosure notice and gives Andy a loan to fix up the inn.

Episode 6: Unaired "Send a Rich Girl to Camp This Summer" (summary based on revised final draft script)

Director: Richard Whorf   Writer: Gene Thompson

As only Tammy can, she thinks that rich little girls are spoiled and need to spend time roughing it at summer camp. Since her uncle is chairman of the board of a private school for rich kids, she asks him for money to start a camp. When he finds that his largest depositor thinks this is a good idea, he gives Tammy the funds, and she, along with Mrs. Pritchett, take six girls on a camping adventure. The girls don't like the experience, but when a bear comes to their campsite, and Tammy, thinking it is one of the girls dressed as a bear, scares it away, the girls hug and kiss Tammy for saving their lives.

Episode 7: Unaired "Tammy Plays Cupid" (summary based on revised final draft script)

Director: Don Taylor   Writers: Stan Dreben and Howard Merrill

Tammy, who is dating Justin Tuxedo, a gossip columnist, makes up a story for his column about Uncle Simon becoming engaged to the Countess de la Valle. When Simon reads the column, he is intrigued and wants to meet the Countess. Tammy invites her uncle, her brother, Justin and the Countess to dinner at her place. However, Uncle Simon is late for the dinner, and Terence becomes infatuated with the Countess. They begin dating, but Tammy finds out through Justin that the Countess had four previous husbands who all died under mysterious circumstances. In order to break up the relationship between Terence and the Countess, Tammy dresses as a psychic and holds a séance with everyone where she summons up the deceased husbands who say they were poisoned by the Countess.

Episode 8: Unaired "A Funny Thing Happened to Me on the Way to the Studio" (summary from final draft script)

Director: Richard Whorf   Story: Bob Reitman and Don Garey
Teleplay: Alex Gottlieb

Uncle Simon is negotiating with the head of a movie studio for a ninety-day extension on the studio's loan. Tammy overhears their meeting and wants the studio to release a film she made with her underground film club. She travels to California and through various disguises (as Charlie Chaplin, Greta Garbo, and a bike messenger) finally gets the studio head to watch her movie titled *The Lost Generation Finds Itself on a Bicycle Built for Two*. The studio head thinks the film is hilarious even though Tammy intended it as a serious film.

Episode 9: Unaired   "Tamantha Nightingale Rides Again" (summary based on revised final draft script)

Director: Mel Ferber   Writers: Al Gordon and Hal Goldman

Tammy is taking lessons at a hospital to train as a nurse's aide. The hospital needs money for a library to house the latest books and magazines for its patients. Uncle Simon, who just happens to serve as the hospital's budget officer, won't allow any funds to be spent on such a library. Tammy schemes to have him admitted to the hospital so he will see how boring it is to read old periodicals. When Uncle Simon and Tammy stop by the hospital, he falls on the steps and injures his ankle. Tammy disguises herself as a nurse to make her uncle's stay at the hospital as uncomfortable as possible. When Simon finds he will be quarantined for a week because Tammy placed a patient with "Siamese Fever" in his room, he agrees to budget the money for the library.

In the original outline for this episode, Tammy was trying to get funds to put a TV in every hospital room instead of money for the hospital's library. Also, in the end, Uncle Simon gives the hospital money that a couple of society ladies raised for him when they saw Simon in a crowded hospital room and thought he had lost all his money.

Episode 10: Unaired   "Diamonds are a Bird's Best Friend" (summary based on final draft script)

Director: Norman Foster   Writers: John Barbour and Whitey Mitchell

Tammy's pet parrot Demmy escapes and flies inside Maxime's jewelry store where a young couple, John and Marsha, are looking at diamonds. When the jewels fall off the tray onto the floor, Maxime and the store clerk try to pick them all up and shoo away the bird. Tammy runs into the store and retrieves Demmy. Maxime then discovers that the largest diamond the couple was looking at is missing. Maxime has a police officer find Tammy and Demmy, and everyone from the store ends up at the police station. Before a judge, Tammy's brother brings a fluoroscope to look at the parrot's insides. It shows no large diamond in the bird's stomach. Demmy gets flustered, tries to attack the jewelry store clerk, and ends up pulling the diamond out of the clerk's pants cuffs.

Episodes Never Produced

At least five scripts for the series were written but never filmed. They are as follows:

"Giver Her Back to the Indians" (summary based on final draft script)   Writers: George F. Slavin and Stanley Adams

Tammy gets involved with an Indian tribe that her uncle's bank wants to evict from property the bank claims it owns. She helps the Indians find an old treaty showing they own the land and, in the course of the search for the treaty, the Indians discover oil on the property.

"The Ski's the Limit" (summary based on final draft script)   Writers: Charles Marion and Irving Cummings

Tammy helps the owner of a ski lodge fix up the place and takes on various roles as cook, chambermaid, switch board operator, and bellhop. She ends up selling the lodge to a Frenchman when she finds that the original owner is a con man.

"The Great Charge Account War" (summary based on final draft script)   Writer: Bill O'Hallaren

Tammy takes on Fogarty's Department Store when they change their return policy to allow no exchanges or returns after forty-eight hours.

"How I Saved the Opera or Did I?" (summary based on final draft script) Writers: Harry Winkler and Hannibal Coons

Tammy drums up support for an opera house that Uncle Simon was going to tear down in order to build a new branch bank.

"It's in the Bag, Dad" Writer: Hal Biller

Storyline unknown

Proposed Scripts Never Written

Among the William Dozier papers, there are three treatments for proposed episodes of the series that appear to have never resulted in scripts.

In one outline, Tammy has taken up skydiving and, coincidentally, her uncle's bank is ready to foreclose on the airstrip owned by the pilot who is teaching her. She promises her brother that if the bank gives the pilot an extra month to resolve his delinquent mortgage, she will give up skydiving. When the pilot's experimental aircraft explodes opening up an oil well on the airstrip, Uncle Simon and Terence are distraught thinking the bank could have owned the land if Tammy had not interfered.

In the second treatment, Tammy convinces the bank to hire the son of a notorious gangster. The gangster's son wants to go straight much to the dismay of his father whose gang ends up kidnapping Terence. The son rescues Terence in a hail of machine gun bullets, and his dad turns out to be delighted that the son is really a chip off the old block.

The third treatment has Tammy investigating her brother to see why he is so preoccupied with Miss Thursday Solder at the Playboy Club. Tammy hopes Terence has fallen in love, but it turns out he is merely doing Miss Solder's income taxes.

A Very Quick End

The Tammy Grimes Show was canceled after only four episodes aired. ABC scheduled the show right before *Bewitched* on Thursday nights. Chevrolet, which sponsored

Bewitched, complained to ABC that *The Tammy Grimes Show* was not a good lead-in to its series.[72] That complaint along with early statistical estimates showing the comedy with very low ratings caused its demise. Critical reaction was also negative. As one reviewer said, "The makers of 'The Tammy Grimes Show' had a million-dollar baby, but they put her in a 10-cent script."[73]

After the cancelation of the series, executive producer Bill Dozier said: "It was the wrong idea for the wrong person at the wrong time."[74] Producer and director Richard Whorf was admitted to the hospital for treatment of a bleeding ulcer right after the series was canceled. He died of a heart attack at age sixty in December 1966 – two and a half months after the end of the series. Ironically, even though Tammy Grimes turned down the lead in *Bewitched*, Dick Sargent, who played her twin, went on to play the second Darrin Stephens on that series.

Chapter 10
Starting a Brand New Job

Checking In with Larry Linville and Marla Gibbs

The little-known sitcoms in this chapter all deal with characters taking on a new job or career. Many comedies have started with this premise (e.g. *Mary Tyler Moore Show*) but then evolve as the newness of the job change wears thin. The series in this section never had a chance to evolve.

Charlie Lawrence

Premiered Sunday, June 15, 2003, at 8:30 PM on CBS

Charlie Lawrence starred Broadway veteran Nathan Lane as a freshman congressman. The premise of the series was similar to that of *Mister Dugan* (see below). Charlie Lawrence, a gay former TV star who had moved to Santa Fe after his series ended, ran for a congressional seat from New Mexico when the Democratic incumbent passed away. He got elected and inherited most of the former congressman's staff. Laurie Metcalf from *Roseanne* played Sarah Grimes, his chief of staff, and T.R. Knight, in his first TV series, portrayed Ryan Lemming, a young intern in the congressman's office. Ted McGinley appeared as Republican congressman Graydon Cord, who disagreed with Charlie on most issues. Stephanie Faracy was Suzette Michaels, Charlie's alcoholic office manager who was a huge fan of Charlie's former TV series, *Do Unto Others*, on which he had played an angel named Guppy Sherman. Most of the episodes had Charlie learning the role of a congressman.

Background

Apparently CBS had a development deal with Nathan Lane which meant they signed him to a contract and then came up with an idea for a sitcom starring him. Originally titled *Life of the Party*, seven episodes of the series were made as a potential midseason replacement for CBS. In an interview with *TV Guide*, Lane was optimistic that *Charlie Lawrence* would be well received by the public and get high ratings.[75] His optimism was premature. CBS delayed the series until summer. Jeffrey Richman, a former writer and producer for *Wings* and *Frasier*, created *Charlie Lawrence*. The comedy was produced by Jeffrey Richman Productions and Twentieth Century-Fox Television in association with CBS Productions.

STARTING A BRAND NEW JOB

Episode Guide: 2 aired; 5 unaired

Episode 1: June 15, 2003   "A Vote of No Confidence"

Directors: Jerry Zaks   Writer: Jeffrey Richman

Charlie settles in to his new place in Washington, D.C. and meets his staff. When he is sworn into office, instead of memorizing the speech written by Sarah, Charlie tries to be extemporaneous and ends up making a speech from a movie of the week he had starred in several years before. He argues with Sarah about who should make the decisions relating to voting on legislation. Charlie addresses the House saying that he takes his job seriously and then tells Sarah that he really needs her help.

Episode 2: June 22, 2003   "New Kid in School"

Director: Jay Sandrich   Writer: Jeffrey Richman

Charlie finds that Congress is like high school when he tries to get on the Ways and Means Committee and discovers that he is not "cool" enough to be considered. However, when the committee chairman reconsiders and hints that he may select Charlie if he supports a congressional pay raise, Charlie must decide whether voting against his conscience is worth getting on the committee.

Episode 3: Unaired   "Dinner and a Breakdown"

Director: Gary Halvorson   Writer: John Riggi

Charlie has a dinner party at his house to bond with his staff. He finds that he does not have a lot to talk about with his staff, but then Suzette reveals that Sarah wants to leave Charlie and work for another congressman. He thinks Sarah wants to leave because she doesn't like him. Eventually, Charlie asks Sarah to reconsider, and she says she won't leave because he needs her more than the other representative.

Episode 4: Unaired   "I'll Take the Low Road"

Director: Jay Sandrich   Writer: Jonathan Goldstein

Graydon embarrasses Charlie on *Face the Issues*, a Sunday morning political show, by saying that Charlie was more convincing as an angel on TV than as a congressman. Graydon tells Charlie it was just politics, but Charlie is tempted to do the same thing to him. Sarah, who had a brief affair with Graydon, informs Charlie that Graydon never really graduated from Harvard – that he was a few credits short of a degree. Charlie reveals this to a newspaper reporter. After Graydon apologizes to Charlie for his remarks on the TV show, Charlie tries to stop the paper from publishing the story about Graydon but is too late. Graydon reveals that he made up the story about not graduating because he really didn't have any secrets to tell Sarah at the time they were having an affair. In the end, Charlie and Graydon reconcile.

Episode 5: Unaired   "If It's Not One Thing, It's Your Mother"

Director: Scott Ellis   Writer: Nancy Steen

When Charlie's mother, Pauline (Anne Meara), visits, he invites her to attend a reception at the British embassy for the Queen of England. He had originally asked Sarah to go, but he wants to impress his mother who is always playing up his married brother, Jerry. Ryan, who is moonlighting as a waiter at the reception, tells Charlie that his mother stole a mantel clock from one of the rooms at the embassy as a memento. Charlie finds the clock in his mother's purse and tries to sneak it back into the room, but the ambassador, through closed circuit TV, saw Pauline taking the clock and Charlie putting it back. Charlie has a serious discussion with his mom about how she could have ruined his career and how he is tired of trying to impress her. She confesses that she is proud of him and that she always talks about his brother because he is average while Charlie is exceptional.

Episode 6: Unaired   "Charlie Got Game"

Director: Gary Halvorson   Writers: Kristin Gore and Nicholas Stoller

When Graydon invites Charlie to play basketball with other congressmen, Sarah says that it will be a great opportunity to get face time with members he wouldn't ordinarily see. He gets knocked out during the game, but Sarah persuades him to go to the next game because he needs to "butch it up." Sarah reconsiders what she told Charlie after Suzette thinks that Sarah is a lesbian. Sarah then informs Charlie that he doesn't need to play sports – he should just be himself.

Writer Kristin Gore is the daughter of Al and Tipper Gore.

Episode 7: Unaired   "What's Wrong with This Picture?"

Director: Scott Ellis Writers: Jonathan Goldstein, John Riggi, and Jeffrey Richman

When Charlie wants his office redecorated, he hires Brad (Thomas Gibson), a very handsome, sophisticated interior decorator. Charlie tries to cover up his TV past from Brad, but Suzette keeps bringing it up. In the office, she displays a portrait of Charlie as Guppy, but Charlie takes it down and tries to hide it from Brad at his apartment which hurts Suzette's feelings. Furthermore, when Charlie and Brad go to dinner, Brad criticizes Charlie's former TV career and makes one of Charlie's TV fans feel bad for asking for an autograph. Charlie tells Brad that he is not ashamed of his TV career and that Brad is too pretentious. Charlie also apologizes to Suzette for hurting her feelings about the Guppy portrait.

Sorry *Charlie*

Ratings for *Charlie Lawrence* were so low (the premiere ranked last in its time slot) that the network canceled the sitcom after only two episodes. The series averaged 1.0/3 share with adults aged eighteen to forty-nine. The remaining five episodes never aired.

Checking In

Premiered Thursday, April 9, 1981, at 8:00 PM on CBS

In this spin-off from *The Jeffersons*, Florence Johnston (Marla Gibbs), the Jefferson's maid, became the executive housekeeper at the St. Frederick Hotel in Manhattan. Helping Florence in her new position of managing the maid staff at the hotel was her assistant, Elena Beltran (Liz Torres). Florence reported to hotel manager Lyle Block (Larry Linville), her stuffy boss. Earl Bellamy (Patrick Collins) was the less than competent hotel detective; Hank Sabatino (Robert Costanzo), the hotel's chief engineer, was in charge of heating and plumbing; Betty (Ruth Brown) was one of the floor supervisors, and Dennis (Jordan Gibbs) was the bellboy.

Background

The "pilot" for *Checking In* was a special one-hour episode of season seven of *The Jeffersons*. George Jefferson was trying to land a cleaning contract with the St. Frederick Hotel and invited its owner Mr. Claymore (John Anderson) to his apartment. Claymore took an interest in Florence and offered her the position of executive housekeeper at the hotel. She accepted the job but then had to do two things she really didn't want – fire a maid who was a friend of hers and tell George Jefferson he didn't get the cleaning contract. Although she had second thoughts about taking her new job, she kept the position – at least for the four episodes of *Checking In*. Jay Moriarty and Mike Milligan created the spin-off series which was produced by T.A.T. Communications and Ragamuffin Productions.

Episode Guide: 4 aired episodes

Episode 1: April 9, 1981   "Boo Who?"

Director: Jack Shea   Writers: Bob and Howard Bendetson

Block wants the sixth floor of the hotel readied for a convention, but Florence can't convince her workers to enter any of the rooms because they think they are haunted by the victim of a sixty-year-old murder. Florence decides to spend a night alone in a room to prove it's not haunted even after she learns that three other people died of fright in the room.

Episode 2: April 16, 1981   "Block's Party"

Director: Jack Shea   Writers: Bob Schiller and Bob Weiskopf

Block hints that he would like a birthday party which inspires Florence to turn the party into a "roast" that will give everyone the opportunity to tell Block what they think of him. Block learns of the plan and devises a description of the party that he is sure will turn the roast into a testimonial for him.

Writers Schiller and Weiskopf wrote several episodes of *I Love Lucy* and *The Lucy-Desi Comedy Hour.*

Episode 3: April 23, 1981 "Whose Side Are You On?"

Director: Jack Shea Writer: Michael G. Moye

Florence tries to find a qualified laundry service manager without antagonizing her co-workers who all insist that they have a friend or relative who would be perfect for the job.

Writer Michael G. Moye later co-created the sitcom *Married with Children.*

Episode 4: April 30, 1981 "Florence and the Salesman"

Director: Jack Shea Story: Cindy Begel and Lesa Kite Teleplay: Cindy Begel, Lesa Kite, Bob and Howard Bendetson

Florence misunderstands the intentions of a linen company salesman vying for the hotel's account. She takes his sales pitch as a come on to her.

Checking Out

CBS did not place an order for additional episodes of *Checking In* because of the 1981 writers strike. In a fall 1981 episode of *The Jeffersons,* after George and Louise have hired a new maid, Florence shows up at their apartment with news that the St. Frederick burned down and that she wanted her old job back. According to Marla Gibbs, her contract at the time included a provision for her to return to *The Jefffersons* if *Checking In* was not renewed.[76]

Dorothy

Premiered Wednesday, August 8, 1979, at 8:00 PM on CBS

A red-haired comic actress in a sitcom co-created by Madelyn Davis and Bob Carroll, Jr. – one might think of another Lucille Ball comedy. But in this case, the actress was Broadway veteran Dorothy Loudon as a divorced former showgirl, Dorothy Banks, who got a position teaching music and drama at the Hannah Huntley School for Girls. The four girls – all roommates—that she spent the most time with were Frankie (Linda Manz), a street-wise kid from a tough neighborhood; Meredith (Susan Brecht), a bespectacled scholar; Cissy (Elissa Leeds), an attractive blonde, and Margo (Michele Greene), a brunette. Burton Foley (Russell Nype) was the school's headmaster whose grandmother had founded the private institution. Jack Landis (Kenneth Gilman), the biology teacher, and Lorna Cathcart (Priscilla Morrill), the French teacher, were two of Dorothy's colleagues. On each episode, Dorothy performed at least one musical number.

Background

In addition to Davis and Carroll, Nick Arnold was also credited with creating this summer comedy which ran for four weeks. The Konigsberg Company and Davis, Carroll Productions, Inc. in association with Warner Bros. Television produced *Dorothy*.

Episode Guide: 4 aired episodes

Episode 1: August 8, 1979 "The Bookworm Turns"

Director: John Rich   Writers: Rick Hawkins and Liz Sage

Meredith becomes infatuated with Mr. Landis when he takes an interest in some rocks her archeologist parents sent her. However, when she sees Dorothy and Mr. Landis go to the movies together, she becomes upset. Dorothy tells her that there is nothing between her and Mr. Landis and that she will learn that not all relationships are permanent. Dorothy sings "There Will Be Some Changes Made."

Episode 2: August 15, 1979 "Hard Hearted Hamlet"

Director: John Rich   Writers: Bob Carroll, Jr. and Madelyn Davis

The school is celebrating Founder's Day, and Frankie's financial backer, Horace Kirkland, who will be attending the ceremonies, will want to know how Frankie is doing in school. She is failing drama class, and Foley informs Dorothy that if

Frankie doesn't pass, she will be dismissed and Dorothy will be fired. Frankie ends up explaining the plot of Hamlet in her own way to Foley's mother, and Dorothy passes her. In this episode, Dorothy performs the song "Hard-Hearted Hannah."

Episode 3: August 22, 1979   "Lies and Whispers"

Director: John Rich   Writers: Rick Hawkins and Liz Sage

Foley thinks his mother (Irene Tedrow) wants to fire him. When Dorothy and her colleagues hear this rumor, they all begin to secretly vie for the position. Dorothy sings "Strike Up the Band."

Episode 4: August 29, 1979   "Give My Regrets to Broadway"

Director: John Rich   Writers: Linda Morris and Vic Rauseo

During a school visit to an art museum, Frankie gets bored, goes off on her own, and is arrested for panhandling which puts an end to the school's future field trips. The staff turns against Frankie, and she threatens to run away until Dorothy convinces her otherwise. After being advised that Dorothy prevented Frankie from leaving the school, Foley reinstates future field trips. The song Dorothy performs in this episode is "Keep Your Sunny Side Up."

Back to Broadway

Dorothy Loudon returned to Broadway replacing Angela Lansbury in *Sweeney Todd* when her sitcom was not picked up. She passed away in 2003 at the age of seventy. When asked about *Dorothy* in an interview, Davis and Carroll could not recall why they got involved with the series.[77]

The Jake Effect

Supposed to premiere in midseason 2002-03 on NBC

Jason Bateman starred as Jake Galvin in this comedy about a high-priced attorney who left his Chicago law firm to become a high school history teacher. His best friend, roommate, and former law colleague, Nick Case (Greg Grunberg) narrated each episode. At the school where he taught, Jake had a romantic interest in Liza Wheeler (Nikki Cox), a fellow teacher. He also had run-ins with Vice Principal Curtis (Patricia Belcher) and her secretary Kimmy Ponder (Leslie Grossman). Kyle Gass played fellow teacher Seissner who thought of teaching as a way to perform comedy material.

Background

Jonathan Groff created *The Jake Effect* which was produced by Red Pulley Productions in association with NBC Studios. The series was a single-camera comedy whose original title was *It's Not About Me*.

Episode Guide: 7 unaired episodes

Episode 1: "Pilot"

Director: Marc Buckland   Writer: Jonathan Groff

Jake Glavin wins a big case but can't stand being a lawyer, and so he quits his job and becomes a teacher at Lincoln High. When he finds that the school badly needs new computers, Jake gets some from Norscom, a former corporate client of his. However, Norscom goes bankrupt, and the computers are repossessed. Jake decides to sell his expensive convertible to pay for the computers.

Episode 2: "Only Connect"

Director: Marc Buckland   Writer: Jonathan Groff

Jake tries to inspire average students with untapped potential. He identifies a smart student who is not planning to go to college and tries to persuade him to take the SAT's. Meanwhile, a student from a wealthy family has bought Jake's convertible. The student that Jake encouraged to take the SAT's turns out to be an undercover cop who arrests the owner of Jake's car for possessing and selling drugs. Later, Nick buys Jake's former vehicle at a police auction, but then the car is stolen.

Episode 3: "Fight School"

Director: Marc Buckland   Writer: Chuck Tatham

A former client of Jake's gives him and Nick access to Michael Jordan's mansion while Jordan is away for a few hours. Meanwhile, Jake is trying to prevent a fight between two students – a nerd, Bill Skidelsky and a jock, Steve Skinner. He ends up taking them to Michael Jordan's house to enjoy the swimming pool.

Simon Helberg (*The Big Bang Theory*) played the nerdy student on this episode.

Episode 4: "Parent-Teacher Conference"

Director: Kevin Dowling   Writers: Peter Huyck and Alex Gregory

Jake unwittingly picks up a student's mother at a bar and goes to bed with her. When the student comes back from visiting his father, he finds Jake at his mother's house. Because Jake is concerned about the type of role model he is for students, he feels he has to again date the mother, who is a real estate agent, to show it was not just a one-night stand. When he finds that the woman wants to sell him a house, Jake takes her out to dinner to try to end the relationship. He decides to be honest and says that he is only going out with her to be a better role model for his students. She confesses that she was dating him to sell him a house. They find out that the reason the son was encouraging the relationship was so he could throw parties at home while his mother was out with Jake.

Episode 5: "Don't Mess with Sloppy"

Director: Marc Buckland   Writer: Brian Reich

Jake takes a black student, Cliff Johnson, who is the son of the school's cook, to his former law library to research a paper on the Dred Scott case. The student discovers how difficult it is to be a lawyer which discourages him from becoming one. Cliff's dad gets mad at Jake since his son no longer wants to pursue a law career. Nick then shows the kid all the perks a lawyer can get. The student is subsequently arrested for scalping tickets. After Jake gets the charges dropped, Cliff gets excited about being a lawyer again. Meanwhile, Liza, who was previously married to a medical student when she was nineteen, tries to rekindle the relationship.

Episode 6: "The Jerk Who Came in from the Cold"

Director: Rodman Flender   Writers: Bryan Behar and Steve Baldikoski

Nick and Jake have a competition to celebrate what an idiot Bankhead (Will Schaub) is. Bankhead is a lawyer at the firm where Jake had worked. The competition involves Jake trying to get Bankhead to a party, while Nick attempts to prevent him from attending. Nick steals Bankhead's car battery, but Jake sends a limo to bring him to the party. Nick then tries to get a cop to intercept the limo. Failing this, he picks Bankhead up in a cab and takes him to another party. Liza brings her ex-husband to Jake's party, but later shows up alone to see Jake at the party Nick is having for Bankhead.

Episode 7: "The Intervention"

Director: Marc Buckland   Writers: Nina DeCastro and Matthew Salsberg

When Jake attends a retirement party at his old law firm, some of the partners try to convince him to rejoin the firm. Jake says he is happy as a teacher, but the partners enlist Nick to convince him otherwise. After Jake finds that his first performance evaluation as a teacher rates him as only satisfactory, he reconsiders the offer to go back to law. When one of Jake's students comes to his apartment for advice on college careers while he is out, Nick counsels her and sees how meaningful dealing with young students can be. He tells Jake not to quit teaching and gets an actor to play one of Jake's former teachers to convince him to stay in the teaching profession. Jake knows it is a ruse but decides to remain a teacher anyway.

No *Effect*

According to Jason Bateman, NBC never aired *The Jake Effect* because the network was reluctant to get behind single-camera sitcoms after *Scrubs* didn't get the ratings NBC thought it should have gotten following *Friends*.[78] The cable network Bravo did air six episodes of *The Jake Effect* in 2006.

… STARTING A BRAND NEW JOB … 343

Katie Joplin

Premiered Monday, August 9, 1999, at 9:30 PM on the WB

Katie Joplin starred Park Overall, best known for her role of Nurse LaVerne Todd on *Empty Nest*, as a single mom and outspoken radio talk show host. In pursuit of her husband who deserted her and her teenage son, Gray (Jessie Head), Katie moved from Knoxville, Tennessee to Philadelphia to live with her niece Liz (Ana Reeder), a fashion editor of a hip magazine. Katie got a job at rock radio station WLBP 87.5 FM as a late-night host on a call-in program. The station's manager was Glen Shotz (Jay Thomas) whose wife just had twins and who had an out-of-wedlock sixteen-year-old daughter, Sara (Majandra Delfino) from a fling he had several years earlier. Other characters on the sitcom were Mitchell Tuit (Jim Rash), the station's manager, and Tiger French (Simon Rex), Katie's young, inexperienced producer.

Background

Katie Joplin, whose working title was *You're on with Katie*, was scheduled as a midseason replacement on the WB, but in October 1998, the network stopped production on the series. Neither the network nor the show's producer, Warner Bros. TV were thrilled with the show.

If Katie Joplin echoed some of the characteristics of Murphy Brown, it was because Tom Seeley and Norm Gunzenhauser, who had produced *Murphy Brown*, created this series.

Episode Guide: 5 aired; 2 unaired

Episode 1: August 9, 1999   "I'd Rather Be in Philadelphia"

Director: Steve Zuckerman   Writers: Tom Seeley and Norm Gunzenhauser

Katie has a job working for a car dealership in Philly. While thinking of purchasing a car from her, the manager of local radio station 87.5 FM is so impressed with Katie's honesty and insight (she talks him out of buying a new car) that he hires her to be a late-night radio host offering advice to callers about their personal problems. Because Mitchell, the program director at the rock station, doesn't want a talk show on the air, he pairs Katie with inexperienced producer Tiger. Meanwhile, when Katie attempts to reunite with the father of her teenage son, she learns that he hasn't changed his cheating ways and so tells him that she doesn't want to see him anymore.

Jim Rash (Mitchell) went on to the role of Dean Pelton on the NBC comedy *Community* and also won an Oscar for helping to adapt the screenplay for *The Descendants*.

Episode 2: August 16, 1999   "Charcoaled Gray"

Director: Steve Zuckerman   Writers: Wendy and Amy Engelberg

After Gray gets detention for refusing a burnt grilled cheese sandwich from the school cafeteria, Katie embarrasses him by telling the story on the air, which leads to harassment from two of his classmates. Since Katie decides not to talk about Gray on her radio show anymore, she starts talking about her niece. Also, Katie and Tiger scheme to steal back a comfortable leather chair for her from Mitchell's office.

Episode 3: August 23, 1999   "Promotion Commotion"

Director: Howard Murray   Writer: Michael Bornhorst

Glen decides to do a city-wide promotional campaign for Katie's show. She gets so caught up in the campaign that she doesn't have much time for Gray. Left alone at home, Gray turns to his new friends and gets into trouble breaking windows at an abandoned building. Katie informs Glen that she needs to cut back on her participation in the promotional campaign. Meanwhile, Tiger fends off the advances of Glen's teenage daughter, Sara.

This was actually the fifth episode produced but aired before episode four, which introduced Glen's teenage daughter.

STARTING A BRAND NEW JOB

Episode 4: August 30, 1999   "Parent Trap"

Director: Howard Murray   Writer: Marc Flanagan

Glen's out-of wedlock, sixteen-year-old daughter Sara, whom he has never seen, arrives to visit and decides to stay in Philadelphia and work at the station. Glen buys her gifts to make up for the time that he wasn't around. Katie intervenes when he refuses to discipline his daughter. After Sara proves to be a lazy and incompetent receptionist at the radio station, Glen finally chastises her. Sara decides to live with Glen permanently. Meanwhile, Katie faces financial trouble when her ex-husband goes on a spending spree with their joint credit cards. After her car breaks down, Katie cannot afford to send Gray on a class trip and is harassed by collection agencies.

Episode 5: September 6, 1999   "Kill the Messenger"

Director: James Hampton   Writer: Marc Flanagan

After Katie learns that Sara has been dating Tiger, she advises him that he must inform Glen. Tiger decides to break off the relationship instead of telling Glen. However, since he is not sure Sara realizes that their relationship is over, Katie talks with Sara who confirms she is no longer dating Tiger. Mitchell inadvertently tells Glen about Tiger and Sara, but when Glen confronts her, he learns that she is now dating an intern from the station's mailroom. Meanwhile, Gray turns to Katie's niece for help in preparing for an upscale Bar Mitzvah.

Episode 6: Unaired   "We're Not in Tennessee Anymore, Toto"

Director: Howard Murray   Writer: Michael Bornhorst

Katie wants the afternoon time slot on the station because it would allow her more time with her son. Also, she worries about Gray observing her niece's relationship with a male model, but Gray understands more about sex than Katie thinks. Furthermore, Katie objects to Liz's choice of furniture and misses her own things which are still en route from Tennessee. When Katie disrupts Liz's business meeting, Gray must mediate an argument between his mom and Liz. Meanwhile, Mitchell dreads a visit from his dad, but is happy when he stays just a few minutes and doesn't have a chance to criticize him, that is until Katie forces reconciliation between the two giving his dad a chance to be critical.

This was the third episode produced but was not aired.

Episode 7: Unaired   "Tiger's Choice"

Director: Joe Regalbuto   Writer: Ed Driscoll

Tiger wants more money and respect at work. Meanwhile, Glen and Gray become pals which doesn't entirely please Katie.

Director Joe Regalbuto played Frank Fontana on *Murphy Brown*.

***Katie* Gets the Gate**

When *Katie Joplin* finally did debut in the summer, only five episodes aired. The show scored the smallest audience the WB ever attracted for original programming on Mondays at 9:30 PM.

Mister Dugan and Hanging In

***Mister Dugan* was to premiere Sunday, March 11, 1979 at 8:30 PM on CBS**

According to CBS ads, Mister Dugan has "…a red-headed knockout for an aide. A good ol' southern boy for an advisor. He's one funny, wild and crazy guy. The town can't put him down…and you won't want to either." This comedy starred Cleavon Little as a newly elected black Congressman. Three episodes of the sitcom were produced, but the series never aired. Bill Davenport, Charlie Hauck, Rod Parker, and Arthur Julian created the series which was executive produced by Norman Lear.

Originally, the concept of a person with little experience occupying a political position was to apply to the seventh season of *Maude*. In the last three episodes of the sixth season, Maude was appointed to complete the term of a deceased congresswoman and moved to Washington DC. She was to have a staff consisting of Maggie Gallagher (Barbara Rhoades), her legal assistant; Sam Dickey (Dennis

Burkley); her pragmatic staff assistant, and a new wisecracking housekeeper, Pinky Nolan (Nedra Volz). However, the star of *Maude*, Bea Arthur, decided to end her series after the sixth season.

Norman Lear's T.A.T. Communications liked the interaction among the new supporting players and decided to rework the concept with a black actor playing the role of a new congressman. John Amos (previously on *Good Times*) was hired to play an ex-football player elected to Congress, and the sitcom was titled, *Onward and Upward*. *Onward and Upward* was to be a midseason replacement on CBS. However, after filming the pilot with the same supporting cast as on the last episode of *Maude*, John Amos quit the series due to "creative differences," or, to paraphrase writer Charlie Hauck, Amos thought he was creative but the producers differed. The sitcom's premiere was delayed while the producers searched for a replacement for Amos. Reportedly, Paul Winfield, James Earl Jones, Billy Dee Williams and even Peter Boyle were considered for the role. Finally, Cleavon Little was selected for the lead. An announcement was made in February that the series would premiere on March 11, 1979 after *All in the Family*.[79]

The comedy was then titled *Mr. Dooley*, but, because of legal issues over a newspaper cartoon called "Dooley," the title was again changed to *Mister Dugan*. Little played Matthew K. Dugan, a former football player from Philadelphia who became a congressman. Again the same supporting cast of Rhoades, Burkley, and Volz were in the three episodes filmed for *Mister Dugan*. Cleavon Little was new to working on a three-camera comedy filmed in front of a live audience and found it difficult to memorize lines.[80] At times, there was hesitancy in his performance vis-à-vis the more experienced supporting cast, and, as he searched for his lines, he rolled his eyes and made other expressions reminiscent of exaggerated characterizations of blacks in old movies.

Mister Dugan Episode Guide: 3 Unaired Episodes

Episode 1: "New Man in Town"

Director: Jeff Bleckner   Story: Rod Parker   Teleplay: Charlie Hauck, William Davenport, and Arthur Julian

Matthew Dugan, head of a successful construction company and a college football player who had won the Heisman Trophy, is elected to Congress to complete the term of his late predecessor. Congressman Dugan inherits his predecessor's office staff including Maggie Gallagher, his legislative assistant whose high-pressure style annoys Dugan and gives him doubts about retaining her on his staff; Sam Dickey, the slick-talking, fast-eating chief of staff, and Aretha Balducci (Sarina Grant), his biracial press secretary. Matt comes to Washington with his ideals about the national legislative process intact, but when he is confronted by the practical politics of the system and the self-assured attitude of his staff, he begins to wonder about his future as a congressman.

Episode 2: "Matt and Sam Go Hunting"

Director: Jeff Bleckner   Writer: Arthur Julian

Other than the title itself, no further information about this episode could be found.

Episode 3: Unaired   "Matt's Team Reunion" (summary based on final draft script)

Director: Jeff Bleckner   Writer: William Davenport

The congressman thinks a photo of him in the newspaper with a flight attendant, taken at the attendant's request, makes him look undignified. He wants to make sure he has a suitable date for his football team's reunion. Matt has been ignoring phone calls from Mona Deaton, a former cheerleader for the team, but, when he finds out that she now has a PhD in psychology, he thinks she would be safe for him to date. When he asks Mona to go with him to the reunion, he explains that he has to be careful about with whom he is seen. A news team is covering the congressman's attendance at the reunion. On camera, Mona says she works in the field of male psychology, and, as she pats Matt's hand, she mentions she is a sex therapist. The next day, Matt doesn't want to read the papers or go to his office since he thinks he's a laughing stock with people assuming he is one of Mona's patients. Mona apologizes to Matt and says she was mad at him when he told her he had to be careful about whom he dates. She agrees to make a statement to the press clarifying that Matt was her date – not her patient.

Episode Never Produced

There was also a fourth episode of *Mister Dugan* written but never taped titled "Sam's Girlfriend." When the premise of *Mister Dugan* was reworked again and became *Hanging In* (see below), it appears that "Sam's Girlfriend" was changed to "Old Girlfriend" and became the second episode of *Hanging In* dealing with compulsive overeater Sam who could not stop devouring food when an old girlfriend of his returns.

Controversy Ensued

Before *Mister Dugan* was scheduled to debut in March, T.A.T. Communications screened an episode for about a dozen black friends of the producers and then for the Congressional Black Caucus. The reaction from these previews was very negative, indicating that the lead character was portrayed as silly and stupid and at the mercy of his white staff. Norman Lear pulled the series from its scheduled premiere and apparently actually hid the tapes so CBS could not air the comedy.[81] His company stated that the series did not meet its goal of presenting a positive and accurate role model of a black congressman.

However, the concept was modified again as the story of an ex-football player becoming a university president, and the show was titled *Hanging In*. Four episodes of *Hanging In* were produced, and the sitcom premiered on Wednesday, August 8, 1979 at 8:30 PM. Ironically, Bill Macy, who had played Maude's husband, starred on the revamped series as Lou Harper, an unmarried former pro-football player who became president of Braddock University and got involved in organizational politics. The same staff, which had been part of the previous iterations of this series, was on *Hanging In*. The character of Maggie Gallagher was the idealistic assistant to Lou Harper, and Pinky Nolan was Lou's officious housekeeper. However, Sam Dickey was now the conservative director of admissions, public relations, and scholarships.

Hanging In Episode Guide: 4 aired episodes

Episode 1: August 8, 1979   "New Man on Campus"

Director: Alan Rafkin   Story: Rod Parker   Teleplay: Bill Davenport, Charlie Hauck, and Arthur Julian

Lou Harper inherits his predecessor's office and staff at Braddock University. His new staff and maid all want to give him their opinions on how things should be done, and he receives his first lesson in the art of fundraising.

Episode 2: August 15, 1979   "Old Girlfriend"

Director: Alan Rafkin   Writer: Sy Rosen

Overweight Sam Dickey can't stop eating when his hometown sweetheart pays him a visit. He wants to tell her that he has outgrown her. Sam looks to his co-workers for support, but they are hard pressed to help him.

Episode 3: August 22, 1979   "Lou's Little Problem"

Director: Alan Rafkin   Writer: Bill Davenport

Lou attends a fund-raising dinner and makes some sexist comments that a news crew catches on tape.

Episode 4: August 29, 1979   "Sleep with the Fishes"

Director: Walter C. Miller   Writers: Arthur Julian and Sy Rosen

The staff begins receiving menacing telephone calls when a mob boss' son is denied acceptance to Braddock University.

In Out

Hanging In followed the sitcom *Dorothy* for four weeks. Neither did well enough in the ratings to be picked up by CBS.

The Sanford Arms

Premiered Friday, September 16, 1977, at 8:00 PM on NBC

The premise of *The Sanford Arms* was that Fred and Lamont Sanford of *Sanford and Son* had moved to Arizona and sold their property to Phil Wheeler (Teddy Wilson), a retired army man and widower with two kids. While Wheeler lived in Fred Sanford's old house, he was turning the rooming house next door into a resident hotel. Supporting characters from *Sanford and Son* continued on this series. Grady (Whitman Mayo) and his wife, Dolly (Norma Miller) were tenants although rarely seen. Aunt Esther (LaWanda Page) was in charge of Fred Sanford's business affairs, and Bubba Hoover (Don Bexley) was the hotel's maintenance man and bellhop. However, the episodes focused mainly on Phil Wheeler his two teenagers—Angie (Tina Andrews) and Nat (John Earl); his girlfriend, Jeannie (Bebe Drake), and his work at the Sanford Arms which also included many side businesses such as a dog obedience school and a dancing school. Phil drove a Corvair convertible, and, because the Wheeler family's residence had only two bedrooms, Phil had to share a bedroom with his son.

Background

The Sanford Arms was a spinoff of the popular *Sanford and Son*, which had been adapted from a British series called *Steptoe and Son* by Norman Lear and Bud Yorkin. Lear was a consultant on *The Sanford Arms*, but the major forces behind the show were its executive producers: Bud Yorkin, Bernie Orenstein, and Saul Turteltaub. When Redd Foxx decided to leave *Sanford and Son* after six seasons, the producers planned to continue the series with Demond Wilson, who had played Lamont. However, because of a dispute over his salary for the new series, Wilson chose not to participate.[82] The producers then decided to introduce a new lead character, Phil Wheeler. Tandem Productions produced *The Sanford Arms*.

Episode Guide: 4 aired; 4 unaired

Episode 1: September 16, 1977 "Bye, Fred, Hi, Phil"

Director: Russ Petranto   Writers: Saul Turteltaub and Bernie Orenstein

Phil Wheeler takes over the Sanford Arms. Grady and his new wife Dolly come by to rent the honeymoon suite, and Aunt Esther stops in to collect the monthly mortgage payment. Phil doesn't have the money for the payment and tries to charm Esther, but she still insists on the money. Phil's kids want to give Aunt Esther the insurance money their mother left them for the mortgage payment, but Esther refuses and gives Phil two more weeks to pay. Meanwhile, Phil's daughter, Angie has found a job as a cocktail waitress at the Funky Fox, but Phil doesn't like her working there because she has to wear a skimpy outfit.

Teddy Wilson passed away in 1991 at age forty-seven, reportedly from a stroke.

Episode 2: September 23, 1977 "The Grandparents"

Director: Unknown   Story: Woody Kling
Teleplay: Woody Kling and Robert J. Hilliard

Phil's in-laws, Walt and Sarah, are visiting from San Diego and want to take their grandkids to live with them. Phil's mother-in-law is not only very critical of him but also of the neighborhood in which he is raising the kids. After Nat decides to go back with his grandparents, Phil misses him and drives to his in-laws to bring him back. He finds that the grandparents were preparing to return Nat anyway because they were exhausted trying to raise a teenage boy. Nat confesses to his dad that the only reason he went to San Diego in the first place was to stop the grandmother from constantly bugging Phil about taking the kids.

Episode 3: September 30, 1977 "Phil's Assertion School"

Director: Dick Harwood   Story: Gene Farmer and David Panich
Teleplay: David Panich

Phil's new school for turning mousy men into assertive ones runs into a problem when his most timid student sues him for fraud because the school is not licensed. Since Phil's daughter is dating Travis, a lawyer, Phil asks his daughter's date for advice. However, when he finds out that Travis is gay and his daughter and the lawyer are just friends, Phil doesn't want any help from him. However, he later changes his mind. When Travis points out to the student that Phil's assertion training must have worked since the student is suing Phil, the student drops the suit. Meanwhile, Aunt Esther objects to the hamsters Nat is keeping, but, when Nat says he will have to put them to sleep since no one wants them, she changes her mind.

Episode 4: October 14, 1977   "Phil's Past"

Director: Dick Harwood   Story: Jim Mulligan and Ron Landry
Teleplay: Gene Farmer

Phil's latest idea to make money is to open a cocktail lounge in the Sanford Arms. He applies for a liquor license but is turned down because of a past felony conviction – assault and battery and resisting arrest. He explains to his kids that he spent time in prison for a civil rights protest in 1957 during which he hit a cop who had called him the N-word. When Travis, Phil's daughter's lawyer friend, gets the Liquor Board to re-open the case, the black police officer who hit Phil agrees that he should not have used the N-word.

Episode 5: Unaired   "The T.V. Show" (summary based on final draft script)

Director: Russ Petranto   Writer: Gene Farmer

A Hollywood location scout comes to the Sanford Arms looking for a place to shoot an episode of the TV show *Angels and Hutch*. Phil agrees to let the production company use the place for $750 and a speaking role for his daughter, Angie. Esther feels the TV show has too much sex and violence and gathers her church ladies for a demonstration. Because of this, the TV crew has to stop filming, and Angie may not be able to perform her role. Phil, Nat, and Grady get the producer of the series to tell the church ladies that they can be story consultants and re-write the script. He gives them a trailer to work in, and Grady drives the trailer away while the filming recommences. The ladies don't realize that they were driven away until after the filming is completed, and Angie has done her part.

Episode 6: Unaired   "Young Love" (summary based on final draft script)

Director: Dick Harwood   Writer: Rick Mittleman

Angie tells Phil that a new piano player is needed at the Funky Fox where she works. Phil, always needing extra cash, auditions and gets the part. Apparently, Phil won the audition because Angie is dating the club owner, Bob, who is her dad's age. Phil walks in on his daughter and Bob kissing and makes Angie quit her job. Phil quits also. Bob comes to the Sanford Arms to reason with Phil, pointing out that Phil hit on a waitress at the club who is Angie's age and that he loves Angie and wants to marry her. Phil and Bob resolve their disagreement particularly when Angie says that she knows she is too young to be married now.

Episode 7: Unaired   "The Wedding Reception" (summary based on final draft script)

Director: Doug Rogers   Writer: Heywood Kling

Phil owes Mr. Sanchez, a plumber, $200 for work at the Sanford Arms and makes an arrangement with Sanchez to have his daughter's wedding reception at the Sanford Arms in lieu of a cash payment for the work. Phil gives the Sanchez's the impression that he offers a real banquet service, and they are so impressed that Mr. Sanchez gives Phil some expensive copper pipes. Phil feels guilty, and so, instead of doing a cheap wedding reception, he plans an expensive one costing more than $200. When the bride and groom's families come over to see the place the day before the wedding, they get into a big fight, and the young couple decides to elope. This saves Phil from spending money he didn't really have on the reception.

Episode 8: Unaired   "The Ernie Williams Memorial Golf Course" (summary based on final draft script)

Director: Doug Rogers   Writer: Lan O'Kun

Phil has been invited to join the Neighborhood Business Association but needs $400 for an admission fee. He learns that a wealthy out-of-towner is coming to tour the neighborhood and has $5000 from his brother, Ernie Williams', estate to give to the community. He convinces the man that he could build a miniature golf course for $1000 with $400 upfront. The man gives Phil a check for $400. But Phil is unable to cash the check anywhere and learns that Ernie Williams was the head of the East Side mob. When Ernie's brother returns to see the golf course, Phil tries to get cash from him, but the brother is upset because all Phil did was turn the junkyard into the course. The Business Association shows up at the same time and advises Phil they are no longer allowing him to join the group because he is associating his business with a deceased gangster. Nat intervenes and tells the group that since the memorial golf course is really a junk yard, this shows how disgusted the Wheeler's are with what Ernie had done to the community. Embarrassed, the Association says it will waive all but $25 of the admission fee. Phil appreciates what Nat said but tells him that Ernie could not have been that bad since he left money to the community.

Farewell to *Arms*

The Sanford Arms was scheduled in the same time slot *Sanford and Son* had occupied and was opposite the *Donny and Marie Show* on ABC and *Wonder Woman* on CBS. The show, which ranked #100 for the 1977-78 TV season, was cancelled after only four episodes.

Secret Service Guy

Was to premiere in midseason 1996-97 on Fox

After inadvertently saving the President's life, a park tour guide becomes a secret service agent assigned to protect the President's daughter. Steve Kessler (Judge Reinhold) was the bumbling agent. Misty (Wendy Benson-Landes), the daughter; Frank McClellan (Michael McKean), Kessler's boss; George Vandenberg (David Burke), the President's chief of staff; Brett Michaels (Keith Diamond), a fellow secret service agent, and Weaver (Finn Carter), a female agent attracted to McClellan were other characters on this sitcom.

Background

David Silverman, Steven Pepoon, and Stephen Sustarsic created *Secret Service Guy* which was produced by Twentieth Century-Fox.

Episode Guide: 7 unaired episodes

Episode 1: "Pilot"

Director: Shelley Jensen   Writers: Steven Pepoon, David Silverman, and Stephen Sustarsic

Steve Kessler is a National Park Tour Guide at the Lincoln Memorial. When the President comes by for a visit to the Memorial, Kessler holds out a notebook to ask for his autograph and stops a bullet intended for the Commander in Chief. Kessler is rewarded by being made a secret service agent much to the chagrin of his new boss Frank McClellan. The President plans a trip to Egypt, and McClellan appoints Kessler to guard Misty, the President's daughter, to prevent Kessler from accompanying the President. However, Kessler encourages Misty to fly to Egypt with her dad so she can discuss some issues with him, and so he can also go. While in flight, Kessler accidentally spills hot coffee in the pilot's lap who then leaves Kessler in the cockpit with the plane on autopilot. McClellan gets Kessler out of the cockpit but locks the door behind him so that the pilot cannot get back in. Kessler ends up going into the passageway underneath the inside of the plane to open the cockpit door. He is assigned permanently to guard Misty.

Episode 2: "Mis-takeout"

Director: Shelley Jensen   Writer: George Beckerman

Kessler and Michaels are assigned to protect Misty while she is dating Victor Fresco, a radical environmentalist. At the restaurant where they go on their date, Misty skips out on the two secret service agents and is later found at the White House. When McClellan learns that they lost Misty, he assigns Kessler and Michaels to night stakeouts looking for counterfeiters. One of the counterfeiters, dressed as a pizza delivery guy, gets the drop on McClellan. Kessler sees the incident, and he and Michaels capture the counterfeiters and release McClellan.

Episode 3: "The Write Stuff"

Director: Jeff Meyer   Writer: Adam Lapidus

An anonymous author writes a tell-all book about the President's campaign. The President thinks that his running mate wrote the book and wants the Secret Service to investigate. Kessler reveals to the Vice President (Ed Begley, Jr.), who in the book is portrayed as a kleptomaniac, that he will be removed from the ticket. After the President asks for the VP's resignation, the Vice President takes the nuclear football for launching attacks. Kessler finds the VP hiding in a secret basement under his home along with all the things the he took from the White House. The Vice President threatens to launch a nuclear attack on Iraq. Even though it is revealed that Vandenburg, the Chief of Staff, wrote the tell-all book, Kessler suggests to the VP that he say he is "anonymous" to get back at the President and be a hero to people who don't like the Commander in Chief.

Episode 4: "Pup Fiction"

Director: John Fortenberry   Writer: Tim Schlattmann

When Weaver asks McClellan to watch her dog Stallone, he assigns the task to Kessler. Kessler takes the pooch to the White House with him for a summit with South American leaders. The dog snatches a brief case from a Chilean diplomat that turns out to be filled with cocaine. McClellan wants to take credit for the drug bust to impress his CIA buddies. However, Larson, his CIA friend, tells him that the drug bust ended a two-year undercover operation by the CIA to break up a drug cartel and that the cartel has put a hit out on McClellan. Kessler contacts the CIA who says there is no such undercover drug operation. Kessler, Michaels, Weaver, and McClellan find that Larson and other agents were laundering drug money from the cartel to purchase weapons for the Kurds in Iraq. Larson agrees to bust up the cartel if his scheme is not divulged to Congress.

Episode 5: "Jailhouse Hock" (summary from final draft script)

Director: John Fortenberry Writer: Rich Tabach

Kessler and Michaels are on the advance team for the President's trip to Singapore. McClellan joins them after he is advised that the psychological test he took as part of annual training showed he shouldn't be the head of Presidential security. While in Singapore, the trio are arrested and jailed for spitting out stinky fruit in public. Kessler finds a tunnel in their jail cell that leads to a caning room where they discover a political prisoner thought to have died. They get the keys from the prison guards and escape. McClellan is reinstated as head of security.

Episode 6: "Throw Kessler from the Train" (summary from final draft script)

Director: Terri McCoy Writer: Eric Shaw

The trial of the drifter accused of trying to kill the President is coming up, and Kessler will have to testify. Before the trial begins, the attorney for the accused says that Kessler was the mastermind behind the attempt and that he shoved the gun into the drifter's hand. Kessler finds that someone has video of the incident that will show he did not put the gun into the hand of the drifter, but the drifter's attorney gets the tape first. Kessler sees the lawyer on a train and heroically retrieves the video from him to prove his innocence.

Episode 7: "Where's Popov?" (summary from final draft script)

Director: Shelley Jensen Writers: Eva Almos and Ed Scharlach

President Popov of Uzbekistan has arrived in Washington to sign a nuclear disarmament treaty. McClellan reluctantly assigns Kessler to Popov's detail. When Kessler goes to Popov's hotel room with Michaels, an inebriated Popov, who is urinating out his hotel room window, accidentally falls and hits McClellan's parked car. The President doesn't want Popov's death known until the nuclear arsenal in Uzbekistan is dismantled. McClellan tries to hide the body but is arrested in Virginia for the supposed murder of Popov. Kessler and Michaels have to get McClellan out of jail and Popov's body out of the town morgue.

Kept Secret

Peter Roth replaced John Matoian as head of the Fox Entertainment Group and was not all that thrilled with his predecessor's shows. One of the series with which he was less than pleased was *Secret Service Guy*. Roth never let it debut. *Secret Service Guy* was Judge Reinhold's second sitcom (after *Raising Caines*) to be canceled before ever airing.

Teech

Premiered Wednesday, September 18, 1991, at 8:30 PM on CBS

Music teacher, Teech Gibson (Phil Lewis), who had been laid off from his teaching position at an inner-city Philadelphia school due to budget cuts, got a position as the only black teacher at all-white Winthrop Academy – an exclusive boys' school in suburban Philly. On his first day, he was mistaken by the headmaster's secretary for an electrician. Teech got assigned four troublemaking students being punished for pranks they pulled at the school. Athletic, not-so-bright George Dubcek, Jr. (Curnal Achillies Aulisio), the son of a former pro-football player; conniver Boyd Askew (Ken Lawrence Johnston), the spoiled son of a socially prominent family; Alby Nichols (Jason Kristofer, *Local Heroes*), an heir to a Philly cheese steak fortune, and the smart, handsome ringleader of the group, Kenny Freedman (Joshua Hoffman) were the troublemakers, dubbed "the gang of four." Somewhat of a "fish out of water," Teech found the students at Winthrop Academy needed his skills as a problem-solver as much as anybody. Also appearing on the series were Steven Gilborn as headmaster Alfred Litton, Maggie Han as Cassie Lee, the assistant headmistress who had hired Teech, and Jack Noseworthy as Adrian Peterman, a brown-nosing "perfect" student.

Background

David Frankel and Norman Steinberg created *Teech*, which was produced by Nikndaph Productions in association with Columbia Pictures. The theme song for the series was "Teach Me" performed by B.B. King.

Episode Guide: 4 aired; 9 unaired

Episode 1: September 18, 1991 "Pilot"

Director: Art Dielhenn   Writers: David Frankel and Norman Steinberg

Teech is offered the late Mr. Halworthy's position as the music teacher at Winthrop Academy conducting Introduction to Music classes. Dubcek, Alby, Freedman, and Askew had moved Mr. Halworthy's body, which was lying in state in the school's rotunda, to the headmaster's dining room, and, as punishment for this act, Headmaster Litton assigns them to Teech's music class. They are to learn the school song "The Halls of Winthrop" so they can sing it in front of Litton. Freedman refuses to participate because people make fun of him for singing in a high-pitched voice. Litton expels Freedman from school for his refusal, but Teech tells Freedman that, if he sings, he will get him back in school. In front of Litton, the four guys, including Freedman, sing the school song. Litton says he cannot hear Freedman, but Teech says that Freedman sings so high that only certain discerning people can hear him.

Kathy Kinney, best known as Mimi on *The Drew Carey Show*, played the headmaster's secretary on this episode.

Episode 2: September 25, 1991 "Stool Daze"

Director: James Widdoes   Writers: Norman Steinberg and David Frankel

Nichols has to wear the "stool of deprivation" since Litton thinks he brought a pizza into the dorm after curfew although it was really Teech who gave him the pizza. When Teech tells Nichols to take off the stool, Litton criticizes Teech's methods and threatens to terminate him. The guys move all of the furniture out of Teech's apartment because they think he has caved in to Litton. Teech goes to see his Uncle Isaac (B.B. King) for advice. Isaac advises him that change has to be gradual and to compromise with the school's administration. Teech then has his entire class wear stools of deprivation. Litton says that this form of punishment shouldn't be used on everyone and that Teech's students should remove the stools.

Episode 3: October 2, 1991   "Carnival Knowledge"

Director: Stan Lathan   Writer: Terri Minsky

Alby meets Suzanne, a girl from another school who had just turned down Freedman's advances. They begin dating, but Freedman subsequently phones her and asks her out. Not knowing that Suzanne is now also dating Freedman, Alby, Suzanne, and Freedman all go out together. When Freedman asks Suzanne to break off her relationship with Alby, she says she doesn't want to because she likes to teach him about life. Dubcek and Askew see Freedman kissing Suzanne and ask Teech for advice. When Teech makes Freedman feel guilty, he breaks off his relationship with Suzanne at the same time Alby stops seeing her because he felt like a student when with her.

Episode 4: October 9, 1991   "Teech vs. Dubcek"

Director: Art Dielhenn   Writer: Stacey Hur

Dubcek is playing football and doesn't have time to study for Teech's mid-term. Teech is being pressured to pass Dubcek anyway so he can play in the big game. Ms. Lee asks Teech to give Dubcek a retest, but Litton doesn't like the fact that it is an entirely new test. When Teech fails Dubcek again, Dubcek's father pressures Teech to pass his son. He says his son is "special," and so Teech has Dubcek dress in his football uniform and do workouts keeping him separate from the rest of the class. Dubcek realizes that his football helmet has turned into a dunce cap and asks Teech if he can retake the test.

Episode 5: Unaired   "Nervously Virgin on a Woman Breakdown"

Director: Art Dielhenn   Writers: Richard Christian Matheson and Thomas Szollosi

Returning from vacation, Alby tells the other guys that he had sex over the break, but it is obvious that he is still a virgin. Meanwhile, Litton asks Teech to help him write a song for a songwriting contest. When the guys find that both Alby and Ms. Lee were in Puerto Rico over the break, they conclude that Alby had sex with her. When Ms. Lee hears the rumor about her and Alby, she wants to confront him, but Teech says he has a better idea. She invites Alby to her apartment, tells him to call her Cassie, and says she wants to get married. Teech shows up, and they both explain to Alby that he has to confess to everyone that nothing happened between him and Ms. Lee. Alby informs the other students that he is still a virgin.

Episode 6: Unaired "Sink or Swim"

Director: Art Dielhenn   Writer: Susan Estelle Jansen

The father of one of the students at Winthrop wants to donate a state-of-the art aquatic center to the school, but all of the students and staff have to first pass a swim test to get the donation. Alby is afraid of the water and doesn't want to take the test. Teech advises him to face his fear. However, when Teech finds out he also needs to pass the test, he makes up a story about having a bad experience swimming to hide the fact that he doesn't know how to swim. Alby says he is not taking one of Teech's pop quizzes since he had a bad experience on a prior test. Teech confesses that he doesn't know how to swim, and Litton volunteers to train him. But someone filled the existing swimming pool with detergent so no one can swim. Litton promises the benefactor that everyone will take the swim test eventually. Alby passes the test, and Teech works on learning how to swim.

Episode 7: Unaired "Understudy"

Director: Art Dielhenn   Writer: Evan Katz

Litton wants Gibson to teach his niece, Annette, an actress, the cello for her next film role. When Annette appears to be interested in Teech, Litton gets Askew to find out what is really going on between the two. After Askew gets the help of the other guys in this endeavor, they decide to make Litton a little crazy by telling him that there really is something between Teech and Annette. Askew shows Litton some photos of Teech and Annette dancing and having breakfast together. When Litton goes to Teech's apartment to see if his niece is there, Teech says Litton is making wild accusations. Annette then appears from Teech's bathroom and says she is doing research for her character that falls in love with her cello teacher. After Litton leaves, Annette admits that she really wasn't doing research, but Teech wants her to go since she wasn't honest with him. The guys tell Teech they knew it wouldn't work out between Annette and him because he was shorter than her.

Episode 8: Unaired "Life's Little Lessons"

Director: Art Dielhenn   Writer: Lyla Oliver

The guys make up love letters to Adrian Peterman from a Deila Shaw, an attractive girl from another school. Straight A-student Peterman gets a B on a test and explains that it is because he is in love with Deila. He shows the letters to Teech. Teech finds out what the guys have been doing and instructs them to write a letter to Peterman breaking off the relationship with Deila. After Teech has the guys read their "Dear John" letter in front of Peterman and Deila, Deila asks Peterman out to lunch. Meanwhile, Litton invites Teech to dinner with his wife Cora. After the Litton's argue over whether he should play table tennis with Teech, Mrs. Litton tells her husband that he is not a good listener and kicks him out of the house. Teech eventually gets Litton to apologize to Cora.

Episode 9: Unaired "The Candidate"

Director: James Widdoes   Writer: Jonathan Feldman

Nichols is running against Peterman for junior class president. Askew also decides to get in the race to impress his dad who is coming to visit. Freedman is managing Nichols' campaign, but Askew gives Freedman money to manage his campaign. When Nichols says that he can't compete, Teech advises him to stay in the race and become a "man of the people." Teech shows Askew some old school newspaper articles about Askew's father that illustrate his dad was just like him. Askew, Peterman, and Nichols have a debate where both Askew and Nichols withdraw their candidacies. Teech lets Nichols know that he shouldn't have quit and that he and Askew should remain friends.

Episode 10: Unaired "Pizza My Heart"

Director: Stan Lathan   Writers: Thomas Szollosi and Richard Christian Matheson

When Freedman dates Rita, a waitress at Franco's Famous Pizza, Nichols, Askew, and Dubcek question him about why he is dating a "townie." Freedman initially invites Rita to the school's formal dance but then says that the dance is canceled after his friends point out that she doesn't have the same background as he does.

Instead, Freedman brings a girl from a prep school to the dance. Rita ends up delivering pizza to the dance and, when she sees Freedman, she throws a pizza on his tuxedo. Teech encourages Freedman to go into town to talk to Rita. However, when he does, she dumps another pizza on him. Teech advises the other guys that they shouldn't judge people who are not like them. Eventually Freedman successfully apologizes to Rita. They kiss and make up.

Episode 11: Unaired   "Loosiers"

Director: Paul Lazarus   Writers: Jonathan Feldman and Terri Minsky

The gang of four is in a losing competition with Litton's Lions in intramural basketball. Freedman is the best player on "Gibson's Gazelles" but is tired of not winning. Ms. Lee suggests that Teech add Peterman to his team, and Freedman then joins Litton's team. With Peterman, Gibson's Gazelles get into the playoffs with the Lions. However, Litton wants Freedman off his team because he is not a team player. When Freedman wants to rejoin the Gazelles, the other guys are opposed. Teech persuades the rest of his team to change their minds. In the playoff, although Gibson's team is defeated, the team remarks that they played a great game and Freedman became a team player. Teech says his team is the real winner since they learned about friendship.

Episode 12: Unaired   "In Charm's Way"

Director: Paul Lazarus   Writers: Richard Christian Matheson and Thomas Szollosi

Dubcek has lost his lucky penny that his father gave him and is worried about an upcoming wrestling match. The rest of the gang of four admits that they all have lucky charms, and, to help Dubcek, they give him theirs – socks, underwear, and a money clip. Teech tries to tell Dubcek that he will win regardless of whether or not he has his lucky penny. But, in the match, Dubcek loses and says he will never wrestle again. Litton wants Dubcek to resume wrestling and asks Teech to get him back. Gibson has the guys rig a poker game so that Dubcek wins and thinks his luck has returned, but Dubcek catches on to the scheme. Later, Teech has Dubcek's dad give him another lucky penny that the dad says is the real one. At the next match, Dubcek is pinned right away. He tells Teech that he knew the penny his dad gave him wasn't real because he finally found the original penny before the match. Dubcek comes to realize that luck doesn't matter and that the other guy was just a better wrestler than he was.

Episode 13: Unaired "Members Only"

Director: Thomas J. Thompson   Story: Rick Cunningham and Richard Marcus
Teleplay: Richard Marcus

The guys are being considered for membership in a secret Winthrop club called the "Quivers." After they all go through the initiation process, only one of the guys – Askew, is asked to join. The other guys don't think he should become a member without them, but he does anyway. When the Quivers want him to join them for lunch, he abandons the rest of the gang. Teech asks the guys to change Askew back to the way he was before he became a Quiver. But Askew doesn't change. He receives a letter telling him to have his roommate Dubcek move out so a Quiver member can become his roommate. After he makes Dubcek move, Teech informs him that he wrote the letter to see how far Askew would go in obeying the club's dictates. Askew tries to make amends to the other guys and has Dubcek return as his roommate. He tells the Quivers that he bought the trademark to their club's name and is forming his own Quivers club.

Phil Lewis (Teech) later played Mr. Moseby on *The Suite Life of Zack and Cody* and its spinoffs.

Early Dismissal

Lasting only four episodes, *Teech* was on opposite the more popular *The Wonder Years* on ABC and *Unsolved Mysteries* on NBC. The first episode of *Teech* ranked forty-fifth, but each episode after that scored lower ratings. The final episode ranked seventieth out of eighty-seven shows.

Waverly Wonders

Previewed on Thursday, September 7, 1978 before moving to Fridays at 8:00 PM on NBC

Former pro-football player Joe Namath starred on this series as unmarried, former pro-basketball player Joe Casey who was now teaching history and coaching at Waverly High School in Wisconsin. The basketball team, called the Waverly Wonders, had not won a game in three years.

Joe Casey reported to a female principal, Linda Harris (Gwynne Gilford) to whom he would make remarks like: "I only majored in history because they had the best-looking girls." Casey had played two years with the New York Knicks. Joe's high school basketball team consisted of John Tate (Charles Bloom), a shy player afraid to shoot the ball; Tony Faguzzi (Joshua Grenrock), the stereotypical Italian; William "Hasty" Parks (Tierre Turner), a teenage con artist, and Connie Rafkin (Kim Lankford), a young feminist who was the team's best player. Joe also had to deal with his belligerent predecessor, George Benton (Ben Piazza), the former coach, and was friends with fellow teacher Alan Kerner (James Staley). Many likened the *Waverly Wonders* to ABC's hit high school sitcom at the time, *Welcome Back, Kotter*. However, unlike *Kotter*, which dealt with a teacher returning to his old school to teach disadvantaged kids, the humor on the *Waverly Wonders* derived more from the team's ineptness and Joe's reputation as a ladies' man.

Background

William Bickley and Michael Warren wrote the pilot episode for this sitcom. They would go on to create more successful comedies like *Family Matters* (1989) and *Step by Step* (1991).

Reportedly, Larry Hagman was originally offered the lead role on this comedy but declined it in favor of a starring role on *Dallas*.[83] In the original script for the pilot, the main character's name was "Harry Casey." But then Namath was hired because of his name recognition. Casey's first name was changed from "Harry" to "Joe." Lorimar Productions produced the series.

Episode Guide: 4 aired; 5 unaired

Episode 1: September 7, 1978   "Pilot" (summary based on tape draft script)

Director: Bill Persky   Writers: William Bickley and Michael Warren

Former basketball star, Joe Casey, starts his first day as history teacher and basketball coach at Waverly High School. He gets off to a bad start when he mistakes the principal, Ms. Harris, for a secretary and calls her "Honey." After the first basketball team practice, Casey tells Ms. Harris that he wants to quit because he feels he has no hope with the students, but she makes him promise to stay at least until the end of the week. One of the basketball players hears that Casey is going to leave and calls him a quitter. After thinking more about his decision and after letting Connie Rafkin on the team, who turns out to be a really good player, Casey changes his mind about leaving.

Gwynne Gilford is the wife of actor Robert Pine (*CHiPs*) and the mother of actor Chris Pine (*Star Trek*).

Episode 2: September 22, 1978   "Tate vs. Tate" (summary based on final draft script)

Director: Dick Martin   Writers: Thad Mumford and Dan Wilcox

After losing another game, John Tate's dad lambasts his son in the locker room in front of his teammates. When his father leaves, John talks with Coach Casey about how he can no longer tolerate his dad yelling at him but that he is too scared to say anything to his father. Joe's fellow teacher Alan Kerner jokes that he had a friend who found it helpful to put a paper bag over his head when he got scared. That night, John goes to Joe's apartment saying he ran away from home and wants to stay at Joe's place. Joe makes John call his dad to let him know where he is. John hides in the bedroom when his father shows up and then comes out with a paper bag over his head yelling at his dad to stop embarrassing him in front of his friends. His father congratulates John for finally standing up to him and says that is what he had been waiting for.

Conrad Bain played the father in this episode and, after *Waverly Wonders* was canceled, Bain starred in its replacement, *Diff'rent Strokes*.

Episode 3: September 29, 1978   "Joe Checks Out the Librarian" (summary based on final draft script)

Director: Dick Martin   Writers: Larry Mintz and Alan Eisenstock

Joe asks the new librarian, Joyce Nesbitt, out on a date and the next day, the couple is the talk of the school. They go out three more nights, but Joe grows weary as Joyce becomes more attached to him and loves the attention she is receiving. She cancels all of her plans so they can go out every night. When he takes his class to the library to do research, Joyce mentions she is going to have him meet her parents. After Joe ends their relationship, Joyce gets really mad at him. In anger, she stamps Joe's arm multiple times with her date stamp in front of Alan Kerner who then proceeds to ask her for a date.

Dick Martin, who directed almost all of the episodes of *Waverly Wonders*, was better known as half of the comedy team of Rowan and Martin that hosted *Laugh-In*.

Episode 4: October 6, 1978   "Rafkin's Victory Dance" (summary based on final draft script)

Director: Dick Martin   Story: Sally Wade and Roger Garrett   Teleplay: Victoria Johns and Deborah Dawson

Connie mentions to Joe that she won't go to a school dance after the game because she doesn't have a date. All the guys think of her as one of them. Joe suggests she ask John Tate to the dance. Later, John tells Joe and Alan that he doesn't have a date for the dance, and they say he should invite Connie. When, during basketball practice, one of the cheerleaders makes fun of Connie for not having a date, Connie, in front of everyone, aggressively asks John to go to the dance. He says "no" because he is caught off guard, and Connie runs away mad. Joe advises Connie that if she wears a dress to school the next day, he is sure John will invite her to the dance. The next day, when everyone sees her in a dress, they make so much fun of her that, when Tate asks her to the dance, she screams "no" and runs away. After the game, Connie shows up late to the dance looking very pretty in a dress. All the guys are very nice to her since they felt guilty for making her feel bad, and Tate says that she looks sexy.

Sally Wade, who co-wrote the story for this episode, was married to the late comedian George Carlin.

Episode 5: Unaired   "Joe Goes to Press" (summary based on final draft script)

Director: Dick Martin   Writers: Deborah Dawson and Victoria Johns

After another loss by the Waverly Wonders, the local newspaper writes a scathing review of the team. Coach Casey decides he should write a letter to the editor in response. When fellow teacher Alan Kerner interrupts him and asks him to go to a happy hour, Connie volunteers to finish the letter. The next day the eloquent and thoughtful letter is published by the paper and boosts morale at the school. Joe takes full credit, and the paper asks if he could write an article for them on sports at the high school. Connie gets mad at Casey for not giving her any credit for the letter, but the coach says that the letter included his ideas anyway and that he should have no problem writing the news article. After Casey has writer's block and can't do the article, he apologizes to Connie and is honest with Ms. Harris about who wrote the letter to the editor. He comes up with the idea to have all his students write the article together as a team effort.

Episode 6: Unaired   "Pied Piper" (summary based on final draft script)

Director: Dick Martin   Writers: Thad Mumford and Dan Wilcox

Joe informs his history class that he will be giving a test on Friday. Hasty Parks asks Joe for some extra help since he is worried about not getting an A on the test. Joe tells Hasty to come to his apartment that night. However, Joe's friend and former teammate on his NBA team, Scooter, comes by and wants to party with him. Joe says "no" because he has to put together the test that night. Scooter goes to Joe's apartment anyway and brings two stewardesses with him. While the four are partying, Hasty comes to the door, realizes that Joe has forgotten their appointment, and leaves. The next day Joe misses class due to a bad hangover. Hasty and the rest of the class are mad at him for skipping the review he promised them before the test. When Scooter lets Joe know that he has another party planned for that evening, Joe refuses and says he has to focus on the kids. Scooter leaves, and Joe invites Hasty to come over that night so they can work together on the test.

Tierre Turner (Hasty) is now a stunt man as well as an actor.

Episode 7: Unaired   "The Revolution" (summary based on final draft script)

Director: Dick Martin   Writer: Jim Rogers

Ms. Harris leaves for a week-long seminar and former coach George Benton takes over as acting principal. He imposes a very strict set of rules on both the students and teachers. Casey is teaching his students about the Boston Tea Party, and he decides to rebel against one of Benton's new rules by not wearing a tie. His students start their own revolt called the "Casey Rebellion." Their first act is to violate the new rules about public displays of affection by having everyone kiss in the hallways. Tate and Rafkin get suspended after passionately kissing. The rest of the students revolt, and Benton suspends the entire school. Realizing he has gone too far, he pleads with Casey and the other teachers to help him get the kids back and win their respect. Casey plans an impromptu school assembly where Benton apologizes to the students.

Episode 8: Unaired   "The Kiss" (summary based on final draft script)

Director: Dick Martin   Story: Stephen Neigher   Teleplay: Thad Mumford, John Rappaport, Dennis Koenig, and Dan Wilcox

Joe receives a message from his old college that he didn't actually complete the exam in his last philosophy class and his degree is not valid. Ms. Harris advises Joe that he can take a state equivalency test in lieu of completing his degree in order to be qualified to teach. The test is offered only once a year, and it will be given next week. Joe begs Ms. Harris to help him prepare. Knowing Joe's reputation as a ladies' man which was reinforced by Alan who told her that Joe thought she is hot, when Ms. Harris gets to Joe's place, she thinks he's in the mood for something else even though all he wants to do is study. She kisses him, and, when he doesn't react right away, she gets mad and leaves. The next day she is embarrassed, apologizes, and promises to actually help him study. Later that day, Joe receives a phone call telling him that his college made a mistake, and he actually did graduate.

Writers Mumford, Rappaport, Koenig, and Wilcox all later wrote and produced episodes of *M*A*S*H*.

Episode 9: Unaired   "Mock Marriage" (summary based on final draft script)

Director: Dick Martin   Story: Bruce Kane   Teleplay: Thad Mumford, Dan Wilcox, Brook Smith

Fellow teacher Alan Kerner asks Joe to lend him $50,000 so that he can become a motel owner and get out of teaching. After Alan tells Joe he has lost the knack for teaching, Joe convinces him to change his teaching habits and teach more about life and not just stuff from textbooks. Alan sees an article in the paper about teen marriages ending in divorce and decides to have his students pair up and create mock marriages to teach them about human relationships. Among the students he pairs up are Rafkin and Faguzzi who hate each other. They complain to the principal which makes Kerner more depressed about teaching. When he talks with Casey about killing himself, Joe convinces him not to do this but to give Principal Harris at least two weeks' notice that he is leaving. The next day, Casey mentions to Rafkin and Faguzzi that Mr. Kerner has contracted a deadly disease and has only two weeks to live. To make Alan feel better, the two students ask if they can redo their marriage, and they begin acting as if they really like one another. When everyone wonders why the two are acting so nice to each other, Rafkin says it is because they love Kerner and think he is a great teacher. Alan is overwhelmed and agrees to reconsider leaving.

Wonders Cease

NBC had a special preview of *Waverly Wonders* on Thursday, September 7, 1978, before it settled into its regular time slot on Fridays where the premiere ranked fifty-ninth out of sixty-five shows. The sitcom lasted for four episodes.

Wednesday 9:30 (8:30 Central)

Premiered Wednesday, March 27, 2002, at 9:30 PM on ABC

This satire of the TV industry was scheduled by ABC at the same time as its title. David Weiss (Ivan Sergei), a young, idealistic theatrical producer, was hired by the owner of the fictional IBS network, Red Lansing (played by Monty Python's John Cleese), to be manager of current programming to improve the network's ratings. David tried to maintain his integrity while dealing with the indecisive network president Paul Weffler (Ed Begley, Jr.); the senior vice president of programming, Mike McClarren (James McCauley), who pretended to be gay when it was to his advantage; the neurotic head of comedy at the network, Lindsay Urich (Melinda McGraw), and Joanne Walker (Sherri Shepherd), the recently promoted vice president of programming.

Background

Wednesday 9:30 (8:30 Central) was created by Peter Tolan, who had also co-created the series *The Job* with Denis Leary, which *Wednesday 9:30 (8:30 Central)* had replaced. This sitcom, originally titled *The Web*, was produced by the Cloudland Company and Touchstone Television.

Episode Guide: 5 aired; 1 unaired

Episode 1: March 27, 2002   "Pilot"

Director: Ted Wass   Writer: Peter Tolan

David starts working at IBS and meets the network executives. He has been hired to give the network's shows a Midwestern perspective and thinks that sex on TV should be toned down. IBS' owner wants one of the network's comedies – *Just the Three of Us* – to see an immediate ratings improvement. David suggests that the female character played by Lori Loughlin be given more comedy to do. Lori asks David out to dinner, and they end up having sex. The next day David is critical of the new material given to Lori's character. She gets mad and says she was sexually harassed by network management. The story appears in *Variety* prompting the network president to fire David. However, the publicity over the lawsuit boosts the ratings for *Just the Three of Us*, and David is able to keep his job.

Episode 2: April 3, 2002   "The Art of Groveling"

Director: Ted Wass   Writer: David Baldy

Red orders David to do whatever it takes to get a demanding John Ritter for IBS. Ritter first asks David to take care of his "little brother," and then to fly to New York City to see if the person who lived in his apartment there left the iron on. Finally, he wants David to dispose of the body of a person he accidentally killed. The latter, however, was a gag John had perpetrated on David to see how far he would go in helping him. Meanwhile, Mike is competing with David to sign Ritter. After he tries to one-up David by contacting Ritter's doctor, Mike ends up having heart bypass surgery.

Episode 3: May 29, 2002   "Death Be Not Pre-empted"

Director: Robert Berlinger   Writer: Daphne Pollon

Red wants to air the execution of serial killer Ted Wayne Giblen (Ted McGinley) because he thinks the ratings will be tremendous. All of the staff meets with Giblen to convince him to sign with IBS, and Lindsay brings him some home-baked cookies. He says he will sign with the network if IBS's Lori Loughlin shares his last meal with him. Although David says he is against the broadcast, he chaperones the meal. It turns out that Ted really wanted to have dinner with David – not Lori, because he was into sexual experimentation during his final hours. David resists his advances. Ted eats one of Lindsay's cookies, has an allergic reaction to the peanut butter, and passes out. David thinks he is just pretending in order to get him to give Ted mouth-to-mouth resuscitation, but Ted ends up dying.

Melinda McGraw (Lindsay) later portrayed Kelsey Grammer's wife on the short-lived *Hank*.

Episode 4: June 5, 2002   "Chinese Baby"

Director: Peter Tolan   Writer: Jenji Kohan

David has to tell one of the stars of an IBS series that she needs to lose weight. The staff suggests that the actress check herself into rehab, be put to sleep for a week, and be given a 500 calorie drip. The network uses the cover story that the star is in rehab to kick a heroin addiction. The star agrees to this only if she gets the lead in the network's new miniseries. Meanwhile, on the advice of her therapist who says she has a lot of love to give, Lindsay adopts an infant daughter from China for $25,000 and five pairs of Levi's. She hires three nannies to take care of the baby. But since she is alone with the baby for ninety minutes each night when the nannies aren't around, she finds it difficult to put up with the baby's crying. Lindsay decides to give the baby to Samantha, the star of an IBS comedy which is filming its seventy-fifth episode. The star is due a gift from the network for every twenty-five episodes in which she appears, and she tells Paul she wants the baby as her gift.

This episode created some controversy. Parents of adopted children were upset over how the subject of adoption was addressed.[84] Lisa Rinna played Samantha on this episode.

Episode 5: June 12, 2002   "Fired"

Director: Ted Wass   Writer: Lesly Lieberman

When David comes to work one day, he finds David Hahn, the guy who used to hold his position, working in his office. Hahn is Paul's ex-wife's son who apparently was never told he had been fired. Subsequently, another guy, Jeffrey Jew, an Oriental hired by Red, claims David's job. Paul finally fires David Hahn and David Weiss and gives the job of manager of current programming to Jeffrey. Meanwhile, after Mike's name appears on a list of the 100 most powerful gay men in Hollywood, he invites David Weiss, as his date, to the gay power luncheon. Mike says he will try to get David's job back for him if he goes. But Mike becomes jealous when David, and not he, is invited to see Don, the gay godfather, and he informs David that he won't help him. David goes directly to Red to try to get his position back. Red is not sure he remembers David, but, after Don, the gay godfather, speaks to Red, David is rehired.

STARTING A BRAND NEW JOB

Episode 6: Unaired "Diversity" (summary provided by David Baldy)

Director: Unknown   Writers: Mike Martineau and David Baldy

IBS has finished last in the annual NAACP report on network diversity. They only had one person of color on any of their shows, and his character was killed off. Red approves an IBS diversity program, and Paul assigns David, Mike, and Joanne to head it. They start adding minorities to their existing series. For instance, on a show called *The O'Shannons*, set in an Irish bar, a black actor walks in declaring "I'm a former NBA player and I just bought the bar." As a result, the media accuses the network of pandering.

Name Change Didn't Help

Wednesday 9:30 (8:30 Central) was placed on hiatus after two low-rated episodes (the first episode ranked sixty-third; the second ranked seventy-second). Its title was changed to *My Adventures in Television*, and the comedy was brought back at the end of May 2002 for three more episodes after which the series was canceled for good.

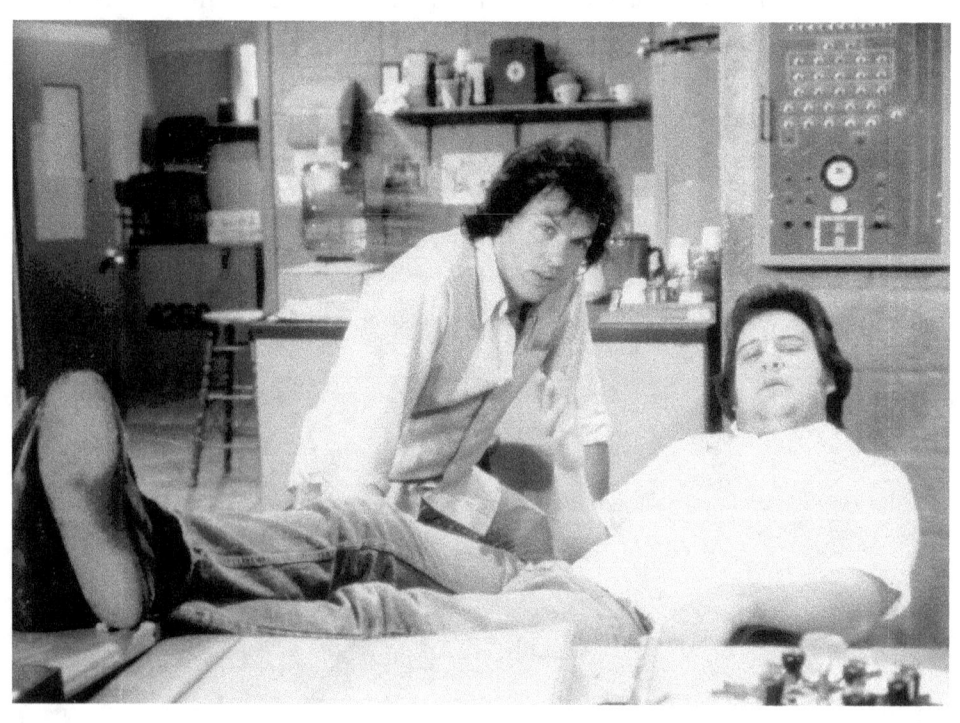

Working Stiffs with Michael Keaton and Jim Belushi

Chapter 11
Mostly Mismatched Workmates

Sitcoms centered on co-workers are a counterpoint to those focused on roommates. Workmate comedies usually have two or three people, often with opposite personalities or of different genders or of varying ages, who work together but do not necessarily live together. This concept has been used more successfully in TV police and detective shows (i.e., *Starsky & Hutch*, *Cagney and Lacey*, *Rizzoli and Isles*) than in workplace TV comedies. There have been a few moderately successful comedies built on this premise such as *Car 54, Where Are You?* The less-than-successful sitcoms involving co-workers are profiled in this chapter.

Ace Crawford, Private Eye

Premiered Tuesday, March 15, 1983, at 8:00 PM on CBS

Ace Crawford, Private Eye was another attempt by Tim Conway at sitcom stardom. In this series, Conway played a bumbling private detective with a part-time assistant but full-time accountant, Toomey (Joe Regalbuto), whose family issues often interrupted his work with Ace. Toomey idolized Ace and narrated each episode of the series. He was to Ace like Dr. Watson was to Sherlock Holmes. Ace hung out at The Shanty bar with Inch (Billy Barty), the bartender; Luana (Shera Danese), the singer at the bar, and Mello (Bill Henderson), Luana's blind piano accompanist. Lt. Fanning (Dick Christie) appeared at the end of each episode awed by Ace's skill in solving cases.

Background

Ron Clark, who had written several screenplays for Mel Brooks' features such as *Silent Movie* and *High Anxiety*, created *Ace Crawford* along with Tim Conway. This vehicle allowed Conway to do physical comedy and sometimes appear as characters he did on *The Carol Burnett Show*. For example, in the first episode of *Ace Crawford*, Conway disguised himself as the doddering old man he had portrayed in sketches on the Burnett series. Conway Enterprises Productions produced the sitcom.

Episode Guide: 5 aired episodes

Episode 1: March 15, 1983   "Murder at Restful Hills"

Director: Michael Preece   Writer: Ron Friedman

Ace investigates the claim of Luana's grandmother that the deaths at her nursing home are not the result of natural causes. Crawford goes undercover as Toomey's father and discovers that the nursing home's doctor is killing its residents to collect their life insurance by tying them to a fast-moving treadmill.

Shera Danese (Launa) was married to the late actor, Peter Falk.

Episode 2: March 22, 1983   "Bull Bates"

Director: Charles S. Dubin   Writers: Ron Clark and Tim Conway

Because she is tired of his murderous ways, Deedee, the girlfriend of gangster Bull Bates (Albert Salmi), wants to give Ace, Bates' book detailing everyone he has rubbed out. Ace asks Toomey to retrieve the book at Bates' warehouse, while he entertains Deedee. When Bates drops by Deedee's place unexpectedly, Ace eventually gets the drop on him.

Episode 3: March 29, 1983   "Inch in a Pinch"

Director: Michael Preece   Writer: Arnie Kogen

Inch is being shaken down by the bar's laundry service but refuses to give them more money. Ace gets involved in the case and wants to trap the head guy by having Toomey take a picture of Ace paying him off. Ace knocks out the guy, and Toomey gets the photo showing the payoff.

Episode 4: April 5, 1983   "The Microchip Caper"

Director: Michael Preece   Writer: Rudy DeLuca

Alexandra Rivers (Christine Belford), a representative of an insurance company, hires Ace to try to steal a valuable microchip to test a tech company's security system. Rivers along with her partner Klaus Goffman (John van Dreelen) plan to kill Ace after he gets the microchip so they can sell it on the black market for $1 million. Ace and Toomey break into the tech company and get the chip, but Rivers and Goffman take it from Ace. However, with Toomey's help, Ace gets the chip back, and the insurance company representatives are arrested.

Episode 5: April 12, 1983   "The Gentleman Bandit"

Director: Michael Preece   Writer: Mickey Rose

Maureen Duffy (Marian Mercer), owner and publisher of *Business Woman* magazine, hires Ace to investigate the robberies of several of her secretaries. Ace dresses in drag as the new girl in the typing pool to catch the robber. While Toomey, who is suffering from a cold, falls asleep in his car waiting for Ace to alert him to the presence of the thief, the bandit, who had worked for the company before being fired, tries to rob Ace. Ace tackles the thief, and the bandit is arrested.

Fifth Attempt

Ace Crawford, Private Eye was Tim Conway's fifth attempt at starring on a successful series. After *McHale's Navy* and before becoming a supporting player on *The Carol Burnett Show,* Tim had starred on two short-lived sitcoms – *Rango* and *The Tim Conway Show,* and one unsuccessful variety series, *The Tim Conway Hour.* Following the Burnett show, he tried another self-titled variety show in 1980 that ended after fifteen months. CBS did not renew *Ace Crawford* after the initial order of five episodes. The sitcom ranked seventy-fourth in the Nielsen ratings for the season. As a footnote to this comedy, in 1989, Forum Home Video released the first three episodes of *Ace Crawford* on VHS.

Buddies

Previewed Tuesday, March 5, 1996, at 9:30 PM before moving to Wednesdays at 9:30 PM on ABC

Dave Chappelle and Christopher Gartin starred on this series as Dave Carlisle and John Butler – friends since childhood who ran a small film and videotaping company in Chicago called Hi-Intensity. They both had apartments in the same building as their office. The building was owned by Dave's father, Henry (Richard Roundtree), who was a little like the character George Jefferson on *The Jeffersons*. Henry owned two apartment buildings and several gas stations and believed in "black-owned, black-operated." Dave had a permanent girlfriend, Phyllis (Tanya Wright), while John was married to Lorriane (Paula Cale) whose mother, Maureen (Judith Ivey) described herself as "the white-trash queen." In addition to exploring the relationship between the two friends and their significant others, the comedy also sought to deal with racial issues.

Background

Created and produced by Carmen Finestra, David McFadzean, and Matt Williams, the creators of *Home Improvement*, *Buddies* originally starred Dave Chappelle and Jim Breuer. Disney discovered Chappelle and Breuer at the Montreal Comedy Festival in 1994, and they were cast in an episode of *Home Improvement* in March 1995 that served as the introduction for their roles as two friends—one black, one white. In that episode, Tim Allen's character had an argument with his wife and ended up sharing the details with members of his *Tool Time* audience. He commiserated with two men –Dave and Jim – who were experiencing similar problems with their girlfriends. The women in the men's lives were upset with them for imparting this information on TV. According to Jim Breuer, originally he and Chappelle were to do three episodes of *Home Improvement* to introduce their characters, but this was reduced to one episode.[85] Apparently, Tim Allen was not too pleased with using an episode of his show as a spinoff for *Buddies*. When filming the *Home Improvement* episode, Allen would purposely call them by each other's names.[86]

Three episodes of *Buddies* with Chappelle and Breuer were filmed. The show was set in Detroit – not Chicago and Ari Meyers from *Kate & Allie* played Breuer's wife. *Buddies* was scheduled to debut in spring 1995 in the time period following *Home Improvement*, but at the last minute, ABC pulled the series.[87] Because the producers did not feel that Jim Breuer's acting style was quite right, he was dropped from the sitcom along with Ari Meyers as his spouse. Christopher Gartin was hired to replace him, and the actress Paula Cale (aka Paula Korologos) was cast as his wife. Episodes were reshot, and the comedy finally had a special preview on March 5, 1996, and then moved to its regular time slot on Wednesdays at 9:30 PM. The Wind Dancer Production Group produced *Buddies*.

Episode Guide: 4 aired; 8 unaired

Episode 1: March 5, 1996 "Lights, Camera, Yuck!"

Director: Paul Lazarus Writer: Peter Tolan

John has a client who wants the birth of his baby filmed, but Dave is somewhat disgusted by the idea. The client gives John and Dave a beeper so that they will know when the couple goes to the hospital. After the beeper goes off, the buddies head to the hospital where they find the dad has passed out at the sight of blood. John gets grossed out and leaves the delivery room. Dave is left with the mother and her doctor and sets up the camera to record the event. Meanwhile, Phyllis takes several outfits from the department store where she works to show Maureen who wants to attend a function at a country club. Maureen chooses an $800 outfit but comes back from the party with the outfit in tatters after having a fling with the club's gardener.

Episode 2: March 13, 1996   "A Room with a Pyew"

Director: John Pasquin   Writer: Trish Baker

A tenant dies in the apartment building where John, his wife, and Dave live. Dave's dad wants a black tenant to move in. However, Maureen likes the apartment and asks to rent it. Both John and Lorraine don't want Maureen as a tenant thinking that they will have no privacy. When John tells Maureen that he would prefer her not to rent the place, she feels like she isn't wanted. Finally, John relents and asks Dave to allow his mother-in-law to have the apartment, which he does. However, when Maureen moves in and Dave's dad stops by, she confuses him with a janitor. This irritates Henry, but John explains that he asked Dave to let her rent the apartment. Henry allows Maureen to stay but gives Dave all the responsibility for her as a tenant.

Episode 3: March 20, 1996   "Regarding Henry"

Director: Andrew Tsao Writer: Sharon D. Johnson

Henry is turning fifty, and Dave wants to buy him a gift. He and John go to a department store to purchase an expensive golf club for his dad. A race-conscious undercover security guard follows Dave around thinking he is a potential shoplifter. To prove a point, John shoplifts a few items, but the guard doesn't see him because he is too busy watching Dave. The store disapproves of John's "teaching" technique and has him escorted to the security office. Later, when Dave returns to the store to buy the golf club for his dad, he finds that the store only has a display model left which the clerk will sell for an outrageous price. Dave ends up giving his dad some gold toe socks that John and his wife had bought for Henry.

Episode 4: March 27, 1996   "Famous Last Words"

Director: John Pasquin Writer: Mark St. Germain

Henry wants the guys to tape Uncle Albert's will. During the taping, Uncle Albert says that Henry picks on Dave like Henry's dad picked on him and tells Henry to hug Dave. Meanwhile, Lorraine and John argue about how he organizes groceries in their kitchen. John videotapes Lorraine to show Dave how crazy she becomes over little things. She accidentally sees the tape and gets mad. Eventually John re-arranges the groceries and confesses to Lorraine that she is right about how to organize things and he was an idiot for taping their argument.

Episode 5: Unaired   "Marry Me…..Sort Of"

Director: Paul Lazarus   Writer: Daphne Pollon

The buddies have a video dating client, Janice (Vanessa Williams), who used to date Dave. Phyllis sees Dave flirting with Janice and becomes irritated. When Phyllis asks Dave if he wants to date others, he says "basically yes" and confesses that after Phyllis and he had broken up for a time he had dated Janice. Phyllis decides that Dave and she should not exclusively date each other. After John encourages Dave to win Phyllis back, Dave tells her she is the only girl for him. They kiss and make up.

Episode 6: Unaired   "Pet Peeves"

Director: John Pasquin   Writer: Robert Zappia

Dave gets a job filming a commercial for a pet store, Perry's Pet Palace, which involves spiders that John is afraid of. Also, John doesn't know that they will only get paid for the commercial if the client likes it. Much to John's dismay, the tarantula used in the commercial gets loose in their office. When John finds out that they may not get paid for their efforts, he argues with Dave and leaves Dave to film the commercial by himself. Finally Dave convinces John to help him with the spot. The pet store owner loves the commercial, and they get paid.

Episode 7: Unaired "The Content of their Character"

Director: John Pasquin   Writers: Daryl Rowland and Lisa DeBenedictis

Dave's dad gets him a possible job filming a promotional video for the Chicago Black Business Association and advises Dave that John should not be involved because he is white. Initially Dave agrees but then changes his mind and says both he and John need to go to the interview with the head of the association. Later, Henry informs Dave that they did not get the job. Dave goes to the association to see if the reason for the turn down was because John is white. The head of the Black Business Association informs Dave that the reason had nothing to do with John but was because they have not yet had enough experience in the business.

Episode 8: Unaired   "There Goes the Groom"

Director: John Pasquin   Writers: Todd Jones and Earl Richey Jones

The buddies are taping the wedding of Phyllis' younger sister. When they find that the groom is very nervous about the upcoming nuptials, as a joke, Dave and John tell him all the things that he will miss, like watching football, when he gets married. The groom decides to back out of the wedding. In the course of trying to get the groom to reconsider, Dave proposes to Phyllis, and Phyllis says "yes."

Episode 9: Unaired   "The PSA Story"

Director: John Pasquin   Writers: Bob Burris and Michael Ware

Dave and John are trying to come up with a slogan for a public service announcement on racism that they hope to film. However, they are turned down by the group financing the PSA because of their lack of experience. But, when Dave says that he can get Karem Abdul-Jabbar for the spot, the group agrees to give them the job. Phyllis had seen Karem in Chicago at the department store where she works, and Dave finds the hotel where Karem is staying. He and John go to the hotel's restaurant to talk with the basketball player, but are ushered out of the restaurant as Karem walks in. Trying for a second time to speak to Karem, Dave finally succeeds, and Karem agrees to do the PSA.

Episode 10: Unaired   "John, I've Been Thnking…."

Director: John Pasquin   Writer: Art Everett

John's wife, his mother-in-law, and Phyllis are all going to see a French film, while John and Dave play poker with some friends. Initially the poker game was to be in

Dave's apartment but, because his toilet isn't working, it is moved to John's place, which his wife said she didn't want. Because one of Dave's friends will soon go into the Army, the other friend ordered pizza delivered by two strippers. When the women return from the movie, neither John nor Dave tells them about the poker game or the strippers. Subsequently, John's wife finds a pair of red panties in his pants pocket and wonders why they are there even though they are hers. John confesses everything, they argue, and she leaves. After Dave talks to John's wife and says that he was the one who persuaded John to play poker, John and his wife patch things up.

Episode 11: Unaired "Engagement Hell"

Director: Andrew Tsao   Writer: Steve Gabriel

Phyllis is picking out wedding invitations, meeting with a minister, and picking a date for her wedding to Dave even though he has not committed to a specific date. Dave reads a magazine article about commitment phobia that he thinks applies to him and wants to postpone any wedding plans. Phyllis and Dave write down all of their concerns about marriage to try to cure his commitment issues. However, Phyllis thinks he is not taking her concerns seriously and calls off the wedding. When Dave says he loves her and that he wants to get married, Phyllis agrees, but they don't set a date.

Episode 12: Unaired "Whack & Blight"

Director: Andrew Tsao   Writer: Peter Tolan

The buddies get a job to do a music video for a rap artist whom Dave knew in school. Walter (Hill Harper), the rap artist, thinks white people are the oppressors and doesn't want John involved in the project. Dave won't take the job unless Walter hires them both and tells John about the problem with Walter. John invites Walter back to the office, but Dave ends up speaking with him to change his mind. Walter says that when he dated a white woman in school, he was beaten. Although Dave advises him not to give up on people, still Walter won't relent.

Never To Be Seen Again?

Buddies' debut episode ranked eighteenth but lost about 30 percent of the audience from its lead-in *Home Improvement*. When it moved to Wednesdays, the first episode in that timeslot ranked thirty-ninth. After four episodes, the series was canceled. With the success of *Chappelle's Show* on Comedy Central, Buena Vista Entertainment released ten episodes of *Buddies* on DVD in 2005 labeled as "the show Dave Chappelle doesn't want you to see."

Clerks

Premiered Wednesday, May 31, 2000 at 9:30 PM on ABC

This animated sitcom centered on the adventures of two clerks manning stores in a strip mall in Leonardo, New Jersey. Dante Hicks, voiced by Brian O'Halloran, was a clerk at the Quick Shop convenience store, while his friend Randal Graves, voiced by Jeff Anderson, worked at the RST Video store next door. Silent Bob Plutarski (Kevin Smith) and Jay (Jason Mewes) hung out with Dante and Randal.

Background

Clerks –The Animated Series was based on the independent black and white film of the same name made by Kevin Smith and was developed for television by Smith, David Mandel, and Scott Mosier. Touchstone Television, Miramax Television, View Askew Productions, and Woltz International Pictures produced the series.

Episode Guide: 2 aired; 4 unaired

Episode 1: May 31, 2000   "A Dissertation on the American Justice System by People Who Have Never Been Inside a Courtroom, Let Alone Know Anything about the Law, but Have Seen Way Too Many Legal Thrillers"

Director: Steve Loter   Story: Steve Lookner   Teleplay: Steve Lookner, David Mandel, and Kevin Smith

Jay falls on some spilled soda in the Quick Stop and threatens to sue. Randal berates a high-priced attorney to take Jay's case which he eventually does and sues Dante and the store for $10 million. Randal then defends Dante in court before Judge Reinhold and a jury of black basketball players. He calls several movie directors, like George Lucas and Steven Spielberg, to testify about their films which have nothing to do with the case. In the end, the jury finds Dante . . . The audience never knows the verdict because Korean animators had to finish the episode.

The premiere episode was actually the fourth episode produced.

Episode 2: June 7, 2000   "The Clipshow Wherein Dante and Randal Are Locked in the Freezer and Remember Some of the Great Moments of Their Lives"

Director: Nick Filippi   Story: Paul Dini, David Mandel, and Kevin Smith   Teleplay: David Mandel and Kevin Smith

After the Quick Stop is robbed, Dante gets new locks put on all the doors, and Randal and he accidentally get locked in the store's freezer. While in the freezer, they flashback to when they first met, when Dante lost his virginity, when Randal mistakenly ordered an Asian male bride, and other events in their lives. Jay and Silent Bob come into the freezer but lock the door behind them before Dante and Randal can say anything. Finally, Silent Bob produces a crowbar and pries the door open. However, Randal and Dante then lock themselves in the video store and flashback to their trips to London and India where they worked as convenience store clerks. The police finally let them out of the store.

Episode 3: Unaired   "Leonardo Leonardo Returns and Dante Has an Important Decision to Make"

Director: Chris Bailey   Writers: Kevin Smith and David Mandel

The son of the town's founder, Leonardo Leonardo, returns and unveils a big, new convenience store, Quicker Stop, which takes business away from Dante's Quick Stop. Dante discounts all the merchandise in the store to sell it. When Leonardo sees the money Dante is making on the sale, he offers Randal and Dante jobs as manager trainees, but Randal refuses the new positions. Randal and Dante gain evidence of Leonardo's plans for world domination and expose the plans at a town meeting, but no one listens. Finally, influenced by the UPN comedy *The Secret Diary of Desmond Pfeiffer*, Randal dresses in drag like Lincoln did in *Desmond Pfeiffer* and blows up the Quicker Stop.

This episode was actually the first one to be produced and scenes from it were included in the flashback episode number two.

Episode 4: Unaired   "Leonardo Is Caught in the Grip of an Outbreak of Randal's Imagination and Patrick Swayze Either Does or Doesn't Work in the New Pet Store"

Director: Chris Bailey   Writers: David Mandel and Kevin Smith

A new black character, Lando, is introduced in this episode which has Randal opening the Quick Stop and forgetting to bring a shipment of frozen burritos in from the curb. A pet store opens in the strip mall where Patrick Swayze is a clerk. Leonardo Leonardo returns for a photo spread in *Pet Store Weekly* and is bitten by a monkey at the store. He then eats one of the rancid burritos Randal left out in the sun. When he gets sick, Randal thinks it is because of the monkey bite, and the town is quarantined. Leonardo starts feeling better until he eats another burrito. Dante and Randal have to stop a bomber from destroying the town to prevent the supposed monkey virus from spreading. They talk to the pilot in the bomber who backs off after Dante says he is gay.

Episode 5: Unaired   "Dante and Randal and Jay and Silent Bob and a Bunch of New Characters and Lando Take Part in a Whole Bunch of Movie Parodies Including, but Not Exclusive to, *The Bad News Bears*, *The Last Starfighter*, *Indiana Jones and the Temple of Doom*, Plus a High School Reunion."

Director: Nick Filippi   Writer: Brian Kelley

Dante and Randal attend their tenth high school reunion, while Leonardo Leonardo attends his thirtieth. Randal meets several former girlfriends who are now all lesbians, but he is most enamored when he sees an old video game "Pharaohs" that he used to play. He tries to beat his old record on the game and, when he does, he is taken to a secret cult to help carry rocks to build pyramids. Meanwhile, at the reunion, Dante sees his old baseball team mates who don't remember him as their manager. Leonardo gives Dante the chance to coach his Little League team which becomes a winner when Jay joins the team. The team goes to the Little League World Championship where they find that a cult has kidnapped the competing team. Dante and his team go to the cult's lair where they find Randal and the kidnapped children. His team wins the championship against the malnourished, former child slaves.

Alec Baldwin was the voice of Leonardo Leonardo.

Episode 6: Unaired "The Last Episode Ever"

Director: Steve Loter   Writers: David Mandel and Kevin Smith

At a Fanta.Com. Convention, Randal and Dante are told by the attendees that the TV show should be more like the film *Clerks*. Back at the Quick Stop, Dante and Randal have to keep the store open longer because of a fair in town. Dante had a date with Caitlin Bree for the evening but now has to cancel it. Various bizarre customers come from the fair to keep Randal and Dante busy at the store including Jay and Silent Bob who constantly update them on events at the fair. Jay tells Dante that his date is at the fair with another guy. Gorillas get loose from the fair and rampage through the town; Leonardo drops by the store and asks the guys to play soccer against a Brazilian team, and Dante keeps getting phone calls from a guy who wants to tell him about *The Matrix*. After Randal makes a crank call to President Bill Clinton, the FBI comes to arrest him. However, the FBI has to graft the President's head to the body of a gorilla to save him from becoming a vampire. The President climbs up the Ferris wheel at the fair; it breaks loose and crushes an elephant. Dante's intended date starts making out with the Ferris wheel. In the end, the writers send Dante and Randal to Gilligan's island, and then they become contestants on the three-hour *Who Wants to be a Millionaire*.

Life after Cancelation

With advertiser defections over its content and with poor ratings, ABC canceled *Clerks* after two episodes. However, Miramax released *Clerks* on DVD in 2001, and the series was subsequently aired on Comedy Central in 2004 and on the Cartoon Network's Adult Swim between 2008 and 2010.

Cutters

Premiered Friday, June 11, 1993 at 8:30 PM on CBS

Billed as a "new comedy from the producers of *The Mary Tyler Moore Show* and *M*A*S*H*," *Cutters* was about a reluctant partnership between an old-fashioned barber shop and a more prosperous beauty salon. Joe Polachek (Robert Hays), a not-so-successful pro-golfer, moved from California to Buffalo, NY to take over the family barber shop when his widowed dad Harry (Dakin Matthews, *The Office*) decided to retire. Even though he was retired, Harry still came to work every day. Joe convinced his father to tear down the wall separating his shop from the beauty salon next door. "Adrienne of Buffalo" was run by Adrienne St. John (Margaret Whitton). The two businesses merged resulting in a clash of cultures between conservative Harry and the more progressive Adrienne. Other characters on *Cutters* included: Lynn Fletcher (Julia Campbell), Adrienne's partner in the beauty shop, who was infatuated with commitment-phobic Joe; Deborah Hart (Robin Tunney, *The Mentalist*), a manicurist; Troy King (Julius Carry, *Misery Loves Company*), a gay black stylist who had been an Olympic track star, and Chad Connors (Ray Buktenica), Joe's buddy.

Background

The summer tryout series was created by Allan Burns, who, with James L. Brooks, had created and produced Mary Tyler Moore's 1970s sitcom, and by Burt Metcalfe, who had produced *M*A*S*H*. The other creators were Lindsay Harrison and Howard M. Gould. According to Mr. Gould, the idea for *Cutters* came from Allan Burns.[88] Burns, Metcalfe, and Gould were in a writing- producing partnership at Grant/Tribune Productions and were interested in doing a battle of the sexes sitcom that included a generational strain between a father and a son. Lindsay Harrison was brought in to write the pilot with them. The pilot for the comedy was shot twice. The Harry Polachek character was originally played by Robert Prosky. But for some reason, the network did not like Prosky in the role. The producers then tested other actors, including George Kennedy and Peter Boyle, with Dakin Matthews finally chosen to portray the father on the series. Turnaround Productions and Grant/Tribune Productions in association with Disney produced *Cutters*.

Episode Guide: 5 aired episodes

Episode 1: June 11, 1993   Pilot

Director: Andy Cadiff   Story: Allan Burns, Burt Metcalfe, Howard M. Gould, and Lindsay Harrison   Teleplay: Lindsay Harrison

Joe persuades his dad to merge their barbershop with the beauty salon next door.

Burns, Metcalfe, and Gould first worked with Robert Hays on the NBC series *FM* which ran for thirteen episodes.

Episode 2: June 18, 1993   "Where's Harry?"

Director: Andy Cadiff   Writer: Unknown

Harry leaves the shop to study at a beauty college after one of his regular customers' defects to Adrienne's side of the business.

Episode 3: June 25, 1993   "Give 'Til It Hurts"

Director: Andy Cadiff   Writer: Howard M. Gould

To Joe's dismay, Chad dates Lynn and wins her over by giving her the impression he is a charitable person.

Episode 4: July 2, 1993   "Harry's Best Friend"

Director: Andy Cadiff   Writer: Lindsay Harrison

TJ, Harry's old buddy from school, visits. Harry wants to go with TJ to a Buffalo Bills football game, and a friend of Troy's offers the two of them seats in his company's sky box. At a bar after the game, TJ reveals he is gay which troubles Harry, but in the end, Harry decides to bid his friend good-bye when he flies back to Phoenix.

Episode 5: July 9, 1993   "Hi There, Sports Fans"

Director: Andy Cadiff   Writer: Unknown

A magazine's swimsuit edition makes waves at the shop leading to another quarrel between Joe and Lynn. The guys want to keep their *Playboy's* and sports magazines swimsuit issues, and the women want their *Cosmos*.

Cut

Cutters lost the ratings race to ABC's comedy *Step by Step* and was not renewed after its five episodes were broadcast.

Harry

Premiered Wednesday, March 4, 1987, at 8:30 PM on ABC

There have been sitcoms about police detectives, lawyers, doctors, but *Harry* has been the only sitcom to date centered on a hospital supply clerk. Alan Arkin, who had starred in movies like *Wait Until Dark* and *Freebie and the Bean* in the sixties and seventies, played Harry Porschak, a wheeler-dealer supply clerk in charge of the supply room at New York's Community General Hospital. His main nemeses were Nurse Duckett (Holland Taylor) and her toady Lawrence (Thom Bray), who was second in charge of the hospital's supply room. Harry had two assistants in the supply room—— Bobby Kratz (Matt Craven) and Richard Breskin (comedian Richard Lewis). Lewis' character on the series was a hypochondriac, similar to the persona he uses for his stand-up act and on *Curb Your Enthusiasm*. Wyatt Lockhart (Kurt Knudson) was the hospital administrator, and Barbara Dana, Arkin's spouse at the time, played Dr. Sandy Clifton, a psychiatrist.

Background

Harry was created by Susan Kramer and developed for television by Barry Levinson and Gary Jacobs specifically for Alan Arkin. Arkin was encouraged to do a television series by his agent who indicated that Arkin and his wife could work together, that the show would be produced in New York, near Arkin's upstate home, and that the line between TV and film was blurring.[89] In addition to being the star of the series, Arkin was also an executive producer. He stated that he had a five-year plan for developing his character, of learning who he is, where he comes from, and what he's about.[90] He needn't have bothered to develop such a plan. ABC originally ordered thirteen episodes of the comedy but then reduced the order to six episodes in addition to the pilot. Touchstone Television produced the sitcom.

Apparently there were conflicts between what ABC expected the series to be and what Arkin wanted. According to Thom Bray who played Lawrence on the series, "... ABC wanted Arkin to play 'a guy like Sergeant Bilko. He wanted a show with a lot of heart and didn't want the name-calling kind of comedy.'"[91] In order not to exceed the budget for the show, many of the cast took reduced salaries to work with Arkin and his concept of a gentle comedy laced with realism. Bray stated further that "... there were a lot of writing problems. It was a tribute to the production staff, the rest of the cast, director Bill Foster – and Alan's genius – that Alan was able to make something out of it."[92] Writers for the series agreed that Arkin and Holland Taylor gave stellar performances but disagreed about the quality of the writing. One writer pointed out that Arkin's wife's performance on the sitcom was not that great. Arkin also had his eighteen-year-old son Anthony act in a minor role. The network and studio told the writers to give them as little to do as possible, and that, in one episode, Tony Arkin was directed to read his one line with his head in a waste paper basket while his character was looking for something.[93]

Episode Guide: 4 aired; 3 unaired

Episode 1: March 4, 1987   "Meet Harry Porschak"

Director: Steve Robman   Story: Gary Jacobs and Ken Finkleman   Teleplay: Gary Jacobs

Harry is running a pool to bet on when a patient will pass a kidney stone. Lawrence informs Nurse Duckett that he can get her evidence of the pool. But, while in Harry's office to find the evidence, he discovers paperwork showing Harry has been selling hospital equipment and pocketing the money totaling $100,000. After the hospital administrator and Nurse Duckett confront Harry about the supplies he sold, he says he sold them to buy a much-needed new X-ray machine for the hospital and right then it is delivered for Nurse Duckett to see.

Episode 2: March 11, 1987   "How Do You Solve a Problem Like Nurse Duckett?"

Director: Bill Foster   Writer: Rich Orloff

Nurse Duckett discovers a shortage of surgical gowns which Harry has tie-dyed to sell to raise money to purchase a satellite dish. To satisfy Duckett, he needs to dye them back to green. Harry gives Nurse Duckett a ticket to a matinee of her favorite musical, *The Sound of Music*, and goes with her to keep her occupied while his staff dyes the gowns. When Nurse Duckett becomes infatuated with Harry, he goes over to her place to clear the air. Duckett thinks he wants to make love to her. However, Harry indicates he is not interested, and she has him leave. The next day, Harry is able to provide the green gowns to Nurse Duckett.

Holland Taylor, who played Nurse Duckett, became a regular on several series including *The Powers That Be* and *Baby Bob*, where she starred along with Adam Arkin, Alan Arkin's son. More recently she has been featured on the sitcom *Two and a Half Men*.

Episode 3: March 18, 1987   "This is the Army, Mr. Porschak"

Director: Steve Robman   Writer: Gary Jacobs

A military policeman visits Harry to tell him he has been AWOL for twenty-seven years. Apparently, Harry forged his own discharge papers from the Army. He now needs to complete the year of service out of which he cheated the military. Harry makes a deal with Lockhart that if he can stay out of trouble for one week, Lockhart will intervene with the military so Harry doesn't have to serve the additional time. However, Harry can't resist taking money from a doctor to give the doctor a better parking spot. Harry leaves for the military with Lawrence in charge of supplies. But Harry changed all the stock numbers before he left resulting in supplies not getting distributed. Lawrence ends up trying to call Harry to come back, but Harry has already returned having forged papers so the military will think he is serving his remaining time in Iceland.

Episode 4: March 25, 1987   "The Great Rat Race"

Director: Linda Day   Writer: Alan Mandel

Bobby makes friends with a rat that escaped from the hospital's laboratory. Harry proposes to Lockhart to have "rat races" to raise money for the hospital by selling bets and souvenirs on the races to hospital staff. Harry takes the money won from the first race and buys a video game for the supply room instead of giving the winnings to Lockhart. He hopes to make up the money on the next race, but Bobby's rat loses. Harry then convinces Lockhart to buy the video game for use by all the hospital staff.

Episode 5: Unaired   "Harry's Big Night"

Director: Unknown   Writer: H. Schireson

Sandy asks Harry to take her to the hospital fund-raiser dance. Initially he says "yes," but then has second thoughts and feels he might not fit in with the doctors and so backs out. Harry arranges for a doctor to take Sandy and later learns that Sandy turned the doctor down for him.

Episode 6: Unaired   "Mr. Imperfect"

Director: Unknown   Writer: David Tyron King

Lawrence quits after making a math error on an invoice. Harry is determined to get Lawrence's job back after learning that he will be replaced by a computer.

Episode 7: Unaired   "Rebel with Sort of a Cause"

Director: Unknown   Writer: Janet Leahy

Harry drops a box on his foot and ends up as a patient in the hospital being looked after by Nurse Duckett. He sees what conditions are really like for hospital patients and is determined to do something about them, but Nurse Duckett wears him down and he finally gives up.

Not So Wild about *Harry*

Harry debuted at thirtieth out of sixty-four shows, but its ratings decreased with each subsequent episode. After four episodes, the sitcom was history.

Following the demise of *Harry*, Alan Arkin starred on the dramatic series *100 Centre Street* and resumed his movie career, winning an Oscar for best supporting actor for *Little Miss Sunshine*.

In the Beginning

Premiered Wednesday, September 20, 1978, at 8:30 PM on CBS

"They've seen the light....but don't see eye to eye" was how CBS advertised *In the Beginning*. The comedy starred McLean Stevenson (formerly of *M*A*S*H*) as Father Daniel Cleary and Priscilla Lopez as Sister Agnes who worked together out of a storefront in a poor section of Philadelphia offering food and comfort to drunks, punks, street people, and ladies of the evening. Father Cleary, a fund-raising Catholic priest with good administrative skills who drove a Mercedes, found himself assigned to a ghetto parish with a streetwise nun who had once been a member of a gang, supported the idea of women as priests, and had also ridden on the Planned Parenthood float in the Thanksgiving Day parade. She called Father Cleary "Reverend Mean," and he called her "Attila the Nun." As a line from the series theme song said, "In the beginning, there was not one point of view we shared."

The cast also included Priscilla Morrill (*Dorothy, Baby Makes Five*) as Sister Lillian, Sister Agnes' superior, and Jack Dodson (previously on *The Andy Griffith Show*) as Monsignor Francis Barlow. Willie (Olivia Barash), a young teenage girl; Jerome Rockefeller (Bobby F. Ellerbee), a young black; Tony (Cosie Costa); Bad Lincoln (Michael Anthony), and Frank (Fred Lehne) were the kids that hung out at the mission. Mr. Brown (Will Hunt) was a homeless drunkard who was often at the mission.

Background

Gy Waldron created *In the Beginning*, which was developed by Norman Lear. Similar to other Lear sitcoms, the comedy involved a conservative character and a more liberal one. *In the Beginning* was originally called *Aggie*, and focused on a young nun battling the church bureaucracy.[94] But when McLean Stevenson was hired, the theme shifted from nun vs. bureaucracy to liberal nun vs. conservative priest. The comedy was then titled *Just the Beginning;* however that title was changed before the series aired. Initially CBS scheduled *In the Beginning* on Saturdays at 8:30 PM, but, before its premiere, the series was switched to Wednesdays at 8:30 PM. T.A.T. Communications Company produced *In the Beginning*.

Episode Guide: 5 aired; 4 unaired

Episode 1: September 20, 1978   "Mission Impossible"

Directors: Doug Rogers and Jack Shea   Writers: Jim Mulligan and Norm Steinberg

Stodgy, orthodox Father Cleary and feminist, street-smart Sister Agnes are assigned the task of opening a storefront mission to serve the poor and homeless. In the course of establishing the mission, they meet Willie, a young street-smart girl, and Jerome Rockefeller who is deaf but can read lips. Later Willie bursts into the mission pursued by two men. Sister Agnes wrestles one of the guys to the ground. He turns out to be a detective who wants to arrest Willie for delivering cocaine. The two detectives arrest Sister Agnes and Father Cleary along with Willie but then drop the charges against them and release Willie into their custody. Cleary wants to resign from the mission but says he would stay if Aggie quits. Sister Agnes leaves, but the people at the mission want her back. When she returns to get her things, she talks with Father Cleary, and he asks her to return.

Episode 2: September 27, 1978   "What's It All About?"

Director: Doug Rogers   Writers: Patti Shea and Harriett Weiss

Sister Agnes is amazed at the ignorance the teenage girls at the mission have about sex. She and Father Cleary realize the need for a sex education class. Cleary says that he taught such a class at his last parish. Aggie instructs the girls about birth control, while Father Cleary lectures the guys about sin. Since this is not what the guys want to know about, they leave Cleary's class and join Aggie's group. When Father Cleary hears the discussion in Aggie's class about birth control, he says that the only effective method is abstinence. He then talks about the gift of love coming before sex.

Episode 3: October 4, 1978   "Father Cleary's Crisis"

Director: Doug Rogers   Writer: Leonora Thuna

The mission is having a celebration for Father Cleary's forty-seventh birthday, and he thinks that on his birthday, the bishop will name him monsignor. Meanwhile, Cleary is trying to get Jerome a job as a mechanic at a car dealership. When Monsignor Barlow stops by to inform Cleary that the bishop decided to promote someone else as monsignor, Father Cleary does not take the news well. He becomes depressed thinking that he is over-the-hill. Sister Agnes says that he is just feeling sorry for himself. Jerome then announces that he did not go for his job interview since he thinks he is not good at anything because of his deafness. Father Cleary advises him that he is better than he thinks he is and that he should go to the interview. Aggie points out to Cleary the similarities between Jerome's attitude and his attitude about himself.

Episode 4: October 11, 1978   "The Good Thief"

Director: Will MacKenzie   Story: Liz Coe   Teleplay: Joe Bonaduce

Someone is stealing items from the mission, and Cleary assigns Sister Agnes and Sister Lillian the task of finding the thief. With Jerome, they stake out the mission at night. When Father Cleary comes to the storefront at night, Jerome mistakes him for the thief and chokes him. After the Sisters and Jerome take Cleary to the hospital, Willie breaks into the mission to steal the stereo. The next day, Father Cleary takes charge of the investigation and interrogates the guys from the neighborhood about the thefts. He threatens to call the police to report the crimes, but Willie confesses that she took the stuff to try to impress the older teens in the neighborhood who were treating her like a kid.

Episode 5: October 18, 1978   "Aggie's Love Story"

Director: Doug Rogers   Story: Gy Waldron
Teleplay: Patti Shea and Harriett Weiss

A musician, Beau Jennings (Rick Springfield), is mugged in an alley beside the mission and has his guitar stolen. After Father Cleary allows him to stay at the mission for a short while, Jerome finds Beau's guitar. Beau and Aggie sing a duet, and he kisses her. She says that she wanted to kiss him back. Aggie tells Father Cleary that she is not worthy to be a nun because she is physically attracted to Jennings. Cleary advises her that such feelings are normal and that's why there is a vow of celibacy. He suggests that she should not be so hard on herself.

Episode 6: Unaired   "The Poker Game"

Director: Randy Winburn   Writer: Ron Bloomberg

Aggie needs to rent three buses for a grade-schoolers' camping trip she has planned, but the mission doesn't have the funds. After Aggie, Lillian, and Father Cleary go to a testimonial dinner, a guy named Shark (Phil Leeds) stops by the mission and persuades Jerome to let him have a poker game there. When Lillian and Aggie come back unexpectedly and discover the game, Aggie wants to get in the game to win money for the bus trip. Father Cleary returns from the dinner, finds Sister Agnes and Sister Lillian playing poker, and stops the game. He agrees, however, to let them play one more hand, and Aggie wins $179 for the bus trip.

Episode 7: Unaired   "The Kook"

Director: Bob Lally   Writer: Michael Morris

A gentleman named Ron Burke (Jack Riley) comes to the mission asking for bus fare. Ron admits to just being released from a mental hospital for the criminally insane in Rockvale, Pennsylvania and says he is going back to the hospital since he isn't adjusting well to the real world. Father Cleary is worried that Ron might be violent. However, the Sisters learn that he caught his wife cheating, beat the other man, and his attorney pled him guilty by reason of insanity to lower the charge. Ron wants to return to the mental hospital because he feels that people don't trust him, but the Sisters encourage him to stay.

Episode 8: Unaired   "Well Healed"

Director: Marc Daniels   Writer: Stephen Miller

An elderly woman, Ms. Dumbroski, claims that Father Cleary performed a miracle when he shook her hand and cured her of diabetes. After the news media interview Cleary about the miraculous cure, Monsignor Barlow asks Father Cleary to maintain a low profile. Aggie and Lillian decide to investigate the woman's claim themselves. They find that Ms. Dumbroski has a twin and the twin pretended that she was the one with diabetes and had been cured. The twins thought that if the neighborhood gangs believed that Father Cleary was a miracle worker, they would listen to him and the twins would not be mugged anymore.

Episode 9: Unaired   "Wedding for Three"

Director: Doug Rogers   Story: Bill Larkin and Joe Calvelli   Teleplay: Chuck Stewart and Arthur Phillips

Peggy O'Neal, a young, unmarried, pregnant woman, shows up at the mission to see Father Cleary and requests that her baby be put up for adoption. She doesn't think that the father would be interested in knowing about the baby, but Sister Agnes wants to locate him before the mother gives birth. Father Cleary and Sister Lillian find the pizza shop where the father works and have him deliver pizzas to the mission. Father Cleary informs Tony, the delivery guy, that he is the father of Peggy's baby. Peggy tells Tony that she is going to place their child for adoption. Tony asks Cleary to marry them, but Peggy says she doesn't love him. In the end, Peggy finally agrees to marry Tony, and Father Cleary performs a quick ceremony as Peggy is rushed by ambulance to the hospital to give birth.

End of *the Beginning*

In the Beginning lasted for five episodes. The series followed *The Jeffersons*, and, in its first outing, ranked forty-fifth in the ratings. McLean Stevenson said that one reason for its cancelation was the restrictions that were imposed on the writers because the series did not want to offend the Catholic Church.[95] However, this reason seems to be contradicted by Sister Elizabeth Thoman, whose organization, The National Sisters Communication Service, served as consultants to *In the Beginning*. She indicated that the show's writers never grasped the profound effect on the Catholic Church of Vatican II and that they wrote out of presuppositions and traditional stereotypes about nuns and priests.[96] Ten days after *In the Beginning* was canceled, McLean Stevenson would begin filming the unremarkable *Hello, Larry*.

Nick & Hillary

Previewed Thursday, April 20, 1989, at 9:30 PM before moving to Wednesdays at 9:30 PM on NBC

Nick & Hillary was the resurrection of a comedy-drama *Tattingers* that premiered on October 26, 1988. *Tattingers* was axed in January 1989 because of dismal ratings.

Tattingers was a fancy New York City restaurant co-owned and managed by Nick Tattinger (Stephen Collins). Also starring on *Tattingers* was Blythe Danner as Nick's ex-wife, Hillary and Jerry Stiller as Sid Wilbur, their maitre d'. The premise for *Nick & Hillary* was that while Nick Tattinger was out of the country in Brazil searching for their accountant who had embezzled funds from the restaurant, Hillary took over the business and turned it into a hip nightclub. When Nick returned to the United States, he partnered with Hillary to try to keep the restaurant in business. Chris Elliott joined the cast as the new maitre d' of the nightclub, while Jerry Stiller's character became the full-time bartender and 10 percent owner. Nick and Hillary had two daughters – Nina (Patrice Colihan) and Winnifred (Jessica Prunell). Jessica Prunell replaced Chay Lentin who had played Winnifred Tattinger on the original series. The restaurant's chef was Sheila Bradey (Mary Beth Hurt), and the head waiter was Louis Chatham (Roderick Cook).

Background

Like *Tattingers*, *Nick & Hillary* was created by Tom Fontana, John Masius, and Blythe Danner's husband, the late Bruce Paltrow, and was developed by John Tinker, Robert DeLaurantis, and Channing Gibson. The comedy was produced by the Paltrow Group and MTM Productions. "Anybody's Guess" was the series theme song.

Episode Guide: 2 aired; 2 unaired

Episode 1: April 20, 1989   "Half a Loaf"

Director: Art Wolff   Writers: Tom Fontana, Channing Gibson, and John Tinker

After finding that the accountant who had embezzled funds has died in Brazil, Nick Tattinger comes back to the States to manage his restaurant and finds it changed into the "Nitery of the Nineties." Even though the new nightclub Hillary helped to create is making money, the business is spending money as fast as it earns it. Hillary wants to run the establishment with Nick, but Nick objects. However, when Nick sees Hillary stand up to threats from a mob-connected laundry service, Nick says he wants Hillary to stay to help manage the place.

Writer John Tinker is the son of Grant Tinker who, with his then-wife Mary Tyler Moore, had founded MTM Productions.

Episode 2:   April 26, 1989   "El Sid"

Director: Don Scardino   Story: John Tinker and Tom Fontana   Teleplay: Channing Gibson

The new maitre d', Spin (Chris Elliot) wants a raise for his non-talking assistant Marti. Nick says "no" to the raise, while Hillary says "yes." Hillary suggests that Sid settle the dispute. When Nick and Hillary find that Marti wants only $3 more a week, they give her the raise even though Sid finally decides not to grant the pay increase.

The producers apparently thought that baby boomers would like this reference to *The Adventures of Spin and Marty* on the old *Mickey Mouse Club*. David Letterman's band leader, Paul Shaffer had a cameo as a customer of the restaurant on this episode.

Episode 3: Unaired "Tour of Doody"

Director: John Whitesell   Story: Tom Fontana and Channing Gibson
Teleplay: John Tinker

Nick is playing chef while Sheila has the night off. She is in a booth at the restaurant fooling around with her boyfriend James. Nick and Sheila argue over whether James really loves her. Subsequently, when James breaks up with her, she blames Nick. Everyone at the restaurant wants Nick to apologize to her. Nick decides to fix Sheila up with a new busboy at the restaurant – Myron Treadwell (William B. Macy). Sheila finds that Myron and her both like skiing, and he offers to cook dinner for her. At dinner in his apartment, Sheila discovers that Myron also likes to dress up as Howdy Doody and wants her to be Clarabelle the Clown.

David Forsyth and Linda Dano, stars, at the time, of the soap *Another World*, made cameo appearances on this episode as patrons of the restaurant.

Episode 4: Unaired "Money Matters"

Director: Alan Metzger   Writer: Robert DeLaurentis

Hillary is buying a lot of new furnishings for the restaurant such as Tiffany salt and pepper shakers and hand towels from Paris which Nick says they cannot afford. Also, Nick and Hillary's daughter Nina has failed her Algebra mid-term and is upset because she has lost her confidence for math. When Hillary wants to hire a tutor for her which costs money, Nick suggests that Nina get a job at the restaurant. After Nina ends up working nights as a hostess in a skimpy outfit, Nick finally agrees to hire a tutor because Nina has decided to skip college and go into the restaurant business. Nick fires Nina as a hostess but has her work as the restaurant's accountant to improve her math skills.

Reboot Fails

The first episode of *Nick & Hillary* premiered on a Thursday right after *Cheers* and ranked eighteenth. However, when NBC moved the show to its regular timeslot on Wednesdays, the ratings sank. The second episode ranked fifty-fourth, and the two remaining episodes never aired.

Rewind

Was to premiere Thursday, September 11, 1997 at 8:00 PM on Fox

In this never-seen sitcom, Scott Baio and Mystro Clark played friends and co-workers whose thoughts about certain situations would flash back from the 1990s to the 1970s. Baio starred as Rob Di Paulo, a marketing executive at a beverage company, who sensed that many of the things he was experiencing, he had experienced when he was younger. Clark portrayed Harv, Rob's fast talking and rapidly rising buddy and co-worker in the company. When facing certain situations at work or in life, there would be flashbacks to parallel situations when Rob and Harv were teenagers. For example, to emphasize Harv's spendthrift ways, the audience would see a flashback to Harv buying expensive jeans and getting in trouble with his mother for not paying the dentist or, to highlight Rob's attraction to hot executive Dana who catches him staring at her chest, the scene would flashback to Harv and Rob as teens talking about breasts. Christine Taylor (*Party Girl*) was Dana Rogers, a smart executive in the company who was the girlfriend of Mike "the Hatchet" (Larry Poindexter)—a corporate downsizer. Playing the younger versions of the Baio and Clark characters were Milo Ventimiglia (*Gilmore Girls*, *Heroes*) and DeJuan Guy. Sherri Shepherd (*Wednesday 9:30*, *The View*) appeared as Janiece in the series – the guys' surly secretary.

Background

Rewind was created by Boyd Hale and Tom Burkhard, with Efrem and Susan Seeger as executive producers for Warner Bros. Television in association with Subway Productions. In the original pilot, Adam Zolotin was teenage Rob, and Chris Edwards played teenage Harv. They were replaced by Ventimiglia and Guy when the pilot was redone.

MOSTLY MISMATCHED WORKMATES

Episode Guide: 6 unaired

Episode 1: "The Jacuzzi and the Presentation" (summary based on final draft script)

Director: Shelley Jensen   Writers: Susan and Efrem Seeger

Rob, who has worked for the beverage company for about three weeks, has a big presentation about sparkling water coming up which he had forgotten about. Meanwhile, Harv has purchased a Jacuzzi to go with his nice apartment which he can't really afford. Later that day, Rob meets Dana, the company's international sales representative and briefly flirts with her at a bar. Harv tells Rob to cool it with Dana because she is dating Mike "the Hatchet" who is an executive that takes pleasure in firing people. Rob leaves the bar to go back to the office to work on his presentation. When Dana shows up drunk at Rob's office and passes out, he takes her to his apartment. The next day, Rob runs into "the Hatchet" in the men's room. Mike has heard about Rob and Dana and threatens to fire Rob after his presentation as well as terminate Harv who is also in the men's room. After Rob and Harv return to the office, they find that Harv's new Jacuzzi has been delivered right to the middle of the office. When the big boss walks in and sees the Jacuzzi, Rob spins it as part of his presentation on sparkling water – a bottle of sparkling water is like relaxing in a Jacuzzi in every bottle. The boss likes it, and the guys get out of trouble.

Episode 2: "My Place or Yours?" (summary based on final draft script)

Director: Rod Daniel   Writer: Tad Quill

A handyman is installing a fancy Jacuzzi-curtains-combo switch at Harv's apartment. Harv informs him that it will be a few days before he can pay for the work. In the meantime, Rob flirts with Dana at work who seems receptive to his charms, but Janiece tells him that Dana got a promotion and will be moving to London in a few days. Upset, Rob makes a move on Dana at happy hour. Harv gives Rob the keys to his apartment so Rob can impress Dana with his Jacuzzi (flashback to Harv telling Rob to lie to a girl by saying his dad is Peter Frampton – a seventies rock star). Harv meets a woman named Tanya at the bar and wants to go back to her place, but her ex-boyfriend is there. He has to go to his apartment to get the keys for Rob's apartment. At Harv's apartment, after Harv hides behind the sofa, Dana throws Rob's keys in the Jacuzzi as a sexy joke. The handyman knocks on the door to try to collect his money. Everyone ends up telling the truth. No one is upset, and the guys get their girls.

Episode 3: "The Box" (summary based on first draft script)

Director: Rod Daniel   Writers: Richard Levine and Lynnie Greene

When Rob cleans out his apartment, he and Harv find a box of old baseball cards that they think might be valuable. They take them to a sports collectibles store to try to sell them to pay for a summer beach vacation home. They learn that the cards are worthless, but as they leave the store, the woman who owns the shop sees the box the cards are in, and offers them $1500 for it. Rob says "no" because in a flashback it is revealed that the guys bought the box together in 1975, and Rob says it symbolizes their friendship. Harv later steals the box from Rob's apartment while Rob is in the shower and sells it for $3000. Even though Rob tries to act like he is not mad over Harv selling the box, Harv becomes irritated that Rob is not more upset over the matter. Although the guys end up not getting the beach house, Harv buys them season tickets to the Phillies to make up for it.

Episode 4: Unaired   "Ransom" (summary based on final draft script)

Director: Rod Daniel   Writer: Howard Meyers

While at a bar after work, Harv is talking about a promotion that he wants and what he would do with the money. Violet, an attractive young woman also in sales, introduces herself to Harv as his competition at the company. Also, at the bar, Rob sees an attractive blonde who mesmerizes him, but then she vanishes. At work the next day, Rob and Harv get Janiece to hack into the computer system to see who is doing better in sales – Harv or Violet. Harv shows everyone his lucky T-Bird Matchbox car that he thinks will win him the sales competition and says that Violet has a lucky purple dress that he needs to steal from her (flashback to Harv with the same lucky T-Bird model getting on the football team). Harv has a party at his apartment and spills a drink on Violet's lucky dress. However, instead of letting him take the dress to the cleaners, Violet asks Janiece to do it. Harv talks Rob into helping him get the dry cleaning ticket so he can pick up the dress. Harv gets the dress and, as he rips it, he gets a ransom note from Violet with one of the wheels from his T-Bird model. They arrange to meet to exchange items. The T-Bird model in the exchange is accidentally thrown in the street and run over by a car. Out of the car comes Rob's mystery blonde, a Victoria's Secret model, whom he takes home. Both Violet and Harv lose the sales competition to another sales associate.

Episode 5: Unaired   "The Car" (summary based on first draft script)

Director: Rod Daniel   Writers: Earl Richey Jones and Todd Jones

Rob is late for work because his old car broke down again, making him miss a meeting with the boss who has now left for a week-long conference. Rob had a big, time-sensitive sales pitch, and now he will have to go through Lawrence, the boss' right-hand man. Meanwhile, Harv convinces Rob that he needs to buy a fancy new car. Rob sees if he can purchase a car cheaper at an auto auction. At the auction, while Rob is off getting a drink, Harv bids on a Porsche with Rob's paddle (flashback to Harv destroying fine china in a science experiment when Rob stepped out of the room). Rob is furious at Harv and almost sells the Porsche until Lawrence compliments him about it and asks him out for drinks. At the restaurant, Rob and Harv try to impress Lawrence. They end up with a very expensive bill, and Rob still didn't have a chance to give his sales pitch. At work the next day, Harv is on the phone with a client who is complaining about a late delivery. He says he can't help because their delivery trucks don't have a homing device. Lawrence overhears Harv and says that is a great idea for the trucks. Harv calls Rob out of his office to have him tell Lawrence his own great pitch which Lawrence also likes. Thus, Harv makes up for Rob having to spend money on the Porsche and dinner.

Episode 6: Unaired   "Product Placement" (summary based on first draft script)

Director: Gerry Cohen   Writer: Leilani Downer

Rob and Harv complain at work about a party they went to the night before for Rob's cousin Vince who just became a big TV producer. After talking to Mike in the break room about the overzealous product placement in *The Lost World*, Harv decides that he will have Blackwell beverages placed on Vince's new TV show. Harv has a beer placed on the show, and almost gets in trouble for not asking for his boss' permission (flashback to Harv not asking permission to wear his older brother's jacket), but luckily Mr. Blackwell thinks it is a great idea. Harv and Rob see an early cut of the show where the beer bottle is used as a murder weapon. They freak out but are redeemed at the office viewing party where Mike tries to take credit for the product placement idea because he was the one that gave them the idea. Harv and Rob give him full credit just when the murder scene airs.

Unwound

Fox bumped *Rewind* from its fall schedule because, according to the network, ". . .'Rewind' is a series that's still evolving, and so rather than rush the creative process, we've chosen what we believe is the wiser course."[97] However, Fox never did air the sitcom.

Singer & Sons

Premiered Saturday, June 9, 1990, at 9:30 PM before moving to Wednesdays at 9:00 PM on NBC

Harold Gould starred on this comedy as Nathan Singer, an aging, widowed Jewish deli owner in New York City who had no children to take over his business. Esther Rolle (*Good Times*) played Sarah Patterson, Singer's housekeeper who convinced him to employ her sons – Mitchell (Bobby Hosea), her divorced younger son with a little daughter and a former executive, and her older son Reggie (Thomas Ford) who was more impetuous and had been a factory worker. The sons really did not get along together. Supporting characters on the sitcom were Claudia James (Arnetia Walker), a waitress at the deli, and Sheldon Singer (Fred Stoller), Nathan's timid nephew.

Background

NBC ordered four episodes of this comedy premiering the first episode after its hit *Golden Girls* before moving it to Wednesday nights. Bob Young and Michael Jacobs created *Singer & Sons*; Michael Jacobs Productions in association with Touchstone Television produced the series.

Episode Guide: 4 aired episodes

Episode 1: June 9, 1990   "Two Sons for Singer"

Director: Steve Zuckerman   Writers: Michael Jacobs and Bob Young

Tensions run high after Nathan hires Mitchell and Reggie to run the deli since the two brothers don't like each other.

Episode 2: June 13, 1990   "The Boxer Rebellion" (summary provided by Lisa Medway)

Director: Steve Zuckerman   Writer: Lisa Medway

Reggie is convinced that he was accidentally switched at birth and that he is really the son of famous boxer Floyd Patterson whose own son, Reggie thinks, was born in the same hospital and on the same day as he was. When he tracks down the Floyd Patterson in question, he turns out to be a white guy. Meanwhile, deli customers try to duplicate Nathan's late wife's blintzes.

Episode 3: June 20, 1990   "Once Bitten"

Director: Steve Zuckerman   Writer: Michael Jacobs and Bob Young

Nathan encourages his brother to reconcile with his ex-wife Felicity (Anne-Marie Johnson). However, Reggie remains skeptical thinking that Felicity is really a vampire.

Episode 4: June 27, 1990   "Our's Not to Reason Why Shmy"

Director: Steve Zuckerman   Writer: Neil Alan Levy

Someone is robbing all the shops in the neighborhood except Nathan's deli. When Reggie suddenly has money, Claudia thinks he is the robber, but he actually got the money from gambling.

Closed for Business

The ratings for the sitcom didn't merit NBC ordering more episodes. While the debut episode airing after *The Golden Girls* scored respectable ratings, subsequent episodes in the series regular Wednesday timeslot did not rate as well.

Work with Me

Premiered Wednesday, September 29, 1999, at 8:30 PM on CBS

Work with Me, a sitcom about married attorneys who worked together, starred Kevin Pollack as Jordan Better and Nancy Travis as his wife and co-worker, Julie. Jordan liked to plan everything; Julie, was more impulsive. Stacy (Emily Rutherford) and Sebastian (Ethan Embry) were Julie and Jordan's young assistants who were having a secret affair. A.J. (Bray Poor), a massage therapist, had an office next door to the Betters.

Background

Stephen Engel created and was the executive producer of *Work with Me*. Engel had been a lawyer before he got into show business. He saw the comedy as a way for the characters played by Pollack and Travis to interact with odd characters who sought their legal advice.[98] The show's leads often took different positions on issues and people. Stephen Engel Productions and Nat's Eye Productions in association with Universal and CBS produced the series.

Episode Guide: 4 aired; 5 unaired

Episode 1: September 29, 1999   "Pilot"

Director: Pamela Fryman   Writer: Stephen Engel

Jordan Better thinks he will make partner at the Wall Street firm where he has worked for ten years. What he doesn't know is that the head of the firm doesn't like him since he lost a golf game to Jordan. When Jordan is denied partner, he quits and goes to work with his wife Julie. He and Julie agree that they have to act like law partners and not spouses at work. However, Jordan is jealous of a handsome client (Ted McGinley) of Julie's whom he thinks is interested in her. Julie says the relationship with the client is platonic, but the client does flirt with her. After Julie tells Jordan about the flirtation, she insists that at the office, he still has to treat her as his partner – not his wife.

Episode 2: October 6, 1999   "The Best Policy?"

Director: Andrew D. Weyman   Writer: Sheila R. Lawrence

Jordan doesn't accept criticism well particularly from his wife. To create a more open relationship, Jordan and Julie decide to adopt an "honesty policy" and tell each other personal thoughts that they might otherwise have kept secret. After they exchange "constructive criticism" at the office, the honesty policy continues at home where they confess their sexual fantasies – she with the package delivery man, he with Wonder Woman. Lynda Carter (Wonder Woman) happens to be a client of Julie's, and, when she comes by the office and learns that she is Jordan's "fantasy girl," she decides to get another attorney. Julie and Jordan keep the honesty policy but don't apply it to their love-making.

Episode 3: October 13, 1999   "Time Apart"

Director: Andrew D. Weyman   Writer: Michael Curtis

Believing they are together too much, Jordan and Julie plan some time apart. Jordan goes to a bar with a reluctant Sebastian and A.J. where Sebastian tries to keep A.J. from asking Stacy out. Julie stays home and attempts to watch a tape of *The Mask of Zorro* but accidentally gets her hand stuck in the VCR.

Episode 4: October 20, 1999   "Crush"

Director: Andrew D. Weyman   Writer: Bill Kunstler

Sebastian's valentine to Stacy ends up with Julie who thinks she forgot the anniversary when Jordan proposed to her, and so she gets him a present to make up for it. However, when Jordan denies writing the valentine, and they find a copy of it on Sebastian's computer, Stacy says that Sebastian wrote it for Julie.

Episode 5: Unaired "'Til Death Do Us Partner"

Director: Andrew D. Weyman   Writer: Kari Lizer

Doctors Gail and Lewis Osborne, authors of a book called *'Til Death Do Us Partner*, monitor Julie and Jordan's work relationship. Julie and Jordan do exercises at home to build trust and intimacy even though Jordan is less than enthused about the exercises. The doctors keep making suggestions about their work habits which irritate Jordan. However, when Jordan shows the Osborne's his new billing system for the office, they are impressed which Julie doesn't like. Julie says that Jordan is trying to be the boss at work, and she goes off in front of the Osborne's. They tell Jordan and Julie that they had to dredge up all their fears and resentments for them to start "clean." Meanwhile, Stacy decides that she and Sebastian need rules for keeping their affair a secret at work.

Phil Lewis (*Teech*) portrayed Lewis Osborne on this episode.

Episode 6: Unaired "The Reception"

Director: Andrew D. Weyman   Writers: Cynthia Greenburg and Judy Toll

Jordan meets Eric, a colleague with a top law firm that has an opening for a litigation attorney. Jordan expresses interest in the position, but Eric offers the opening to Julie. Meanwhile, Julie throws a reception for Jordan to celebrate him joining her firm. However, she doesn't show up for the reception until very late having turned down the litigation position without knowing of her husband's interest in the opening. Jordan confesses that he tried to get the position and apologizes to Julie. In other storylines, Stacy wants Sebastian to give her a pet name, and A.J.'s latest "soul mate" is obsessed with suicide.

The comedienne Sarah Silverman appeared on this episode as A.J.'s soul mate.

MOSTLY MISMATCHED WORKMATES

Episode 7: Unaired "Better Legal Advice"

Director: Andrew D. Weyman   Writer: Gail Lerner

Julie becomes the host of a legal advice show on a public access TV channel with A.J. as her producer. On the first show, when no one calls in after an initial crank call, Jordan, disguising his voice, phones and begins asking questions. Julie thinks her debut was great but wants Jordan on her next show. Reluctantly, Jordan appears and becomes popular with the viewers by yelling at the callers. Julie says she hated what he did on the air, and so Jordan tells her she can be on her own for the next show. On the third show, the callers want to know why Jordan is not appearing. Jordan phones in and pretends to be a supportive caller, but Julie knows it is him. After three shows, she decides to give up the series.

Nancy Travis (Julie) subsequently became a regular of *Becker*, *The Bill Engvall Show*, and *Last Man Standing*.

Episode 8: Unaired "Thanksgiving"

Director: Andrew D. Weyman   Writers: Bryan Behar and Steve Baldikoski

Jordan wants Sebastian to date a potential client—a game show model who is suing her bosses for wrongful termination after she gained weight. Meanwhile, Julie's Thanksgiving dinner is not turkey with all the trimmings but instead is food from Turkey. At the dinner, Stacy is upset about the attention the model is giving Sebastian, and she confesses, when Julie and Jordan are out of the room, that she and Sebastian are dating. Eventually, Julie gets the model as a client by buying her a monkey.

Emily Rutherford (Stacy) later was the 'new Christine' Hunter on the comedy *The Adventures of Old Christine*.

Episode 9: Unaired "Daddy's Little Lawyer"

Director: Andrew D. Weyman   Writer: Sheila R. Lawrence

Julie's dad Leonard (Paul Sorvino) visits her in hopes of getting help with his will. Leonard informs Jordan that Julie's mother is his third wife and that he has to provide in his will for his second wife who left him for another woman. However, he doesn't want Julie to know about his prior wives. When Jordan finally confides these secrets to Julie, she confronts her dad. Leonard tells Julie that he was embarrassed to say anything to her about his second wife since she became a lesbian after their marriage.

Work Out

Work with Me premiered at fifty-seventh in the Nielsen ratings and subsequent episodes ranked even lower. The fourth and last episode ranked sixty-eighth.

Working Stiffs

Premiered Saturday, September 15, 1979, at 8:00 PM on CBS

Jim Belushi and Michael Keaton starred on this comedy as two brothers, Ernie and Mike O'Rourke, who shared the same apartment and sought success in the business world by beginning as janitors in their Uncle Harry's Chicago office building. The sitcom was somewhat like a male version of the hit *Laverne and Shirley*. The brothers had several bosses throughout the shows brief run. In the pilot episode their immediate boss was Charles Pressman played by Neil Thompson. Subsequent bosses were Falzone (Phil Rubenstein) and Al Steckler (Val Basoglio). Mike and Ernie lived in an apartment over Playland, a café, where they spent a lot of their off hours. Mitch Hannigan (Alan Arbus) owned Playland, and Nikki Evashervska (Lorna Patterson) was a waitress there. Paul Reubens (Pee Wee Herman) appeared on several episodes as Heimlich, a waiter at the cafe.

Background

Working Stiffs was on Saturdays against NBC's hit cop show, *CHiPs*. Bob Brunner, Art Silver, Marc Sotkin, and Harry Colomby created the series. Frog Productions and Huk Productions in association with Paramount Pictures Corporation produced *Working Stiffs*.

MOSTLY MISMATCHED WORKMATES

Episode Guide: 4 aired; 5 unaired

Episode 1: September 15, 1979   "The Preview Presentation"

Director: Penny Marshall   Writer: Marc Sotkin

The brothers go to their Uncle Harry (Michael Conrad) for a job and are hired as janitors. Their boss is super-efficient building manager Charles Pressman (Neil Thompson). Mike and Ernie mess up delivering a file cabinet to an office, and then have to install a light bulb on a large clock outside the top story of the O'Rourke Building which leads to a long scene of slapstick comedy.

Director Penny Marshall is better known as Laverne from the sitcom *Laverne and Shirley*.

Episode 2: September 22, 1979   "Looking for Mr. Goodwrench"

Director: Norman Abbott   Writer: E. Jack Kaplan

Val Basoglio as Al Steckler became the brothers' boss in this episode where Mike and Ernie master a new combo tool that gets their jobs done so quickly that they have a lot of free time. Steckler decides that he doesn't need to employ both brothers because of the new tool and lets it up to them to decide which one gets fired. Ernie elects to be the one terminated and tries to find another job. Meanwhile, nuns are coming to look at office space in the O'Rourke Building, and Steckler advises Mike to look his best. Mike begins to change his clothes but gets his hand stuck in the soda machine while he is in his underwear. Ernie comes by and is able to get his brother's hand unstuck, but Steckler will only give him his old job back if he pleads for it. When the nuns recognize Ernie and Mike as former pupils, they tell Steckler to make both Ernie and Mike's jobs permanent.

Director Norman Abbott is the nephew of the late Bud Abbott of Abbott of Costello fame.

Episode 3: September 29, 1979   "The Bank Robbery" (aka "Bomb Show")

Director: Norman Abbott   Writer: Al Aidekman

Michael witnesses a bank robbery and is stalked by the robber. When the robber comes to the O'Rourke Building and tries to kill Mike with an electric drill, Ernie isn't around and so doesn't believe him about the incident. After the robber plants a bomb in the elevator's phone box, the brothers get trapped inside the elevator. Steckler captures the robber, and the bomb squad arrives and instructs Mike and Ernie on how to defuse the bomb.

Episode 4: October 6, 1979   "My Boys are Having a Baby"

Director: Art Silver   Writer: Gail Honigberg

Nikki, the waitress at the boys' hangout, is having a baby, and her husband Ralph (Thomas Callaway), who has just returned from California, informs Ernie that he is leaving Nikki because he is too young to be a dad. Nikki overhears the conversation and demands that Ralph return to California. Ernie says that he will marry Nikki, but she doesn't want to get married again right away. Nikki goes into labor, and Mike and Ernie have to deliver what turn out to be twins.

Lorna Patterson (Nikki) later starred in the TV series *Private Benjamin* and is married to actor-director Michael Lembeck.

Episode 5: Unaired   "The Bosses"

Director: Greg Antonacci   Writer: David Duclon

In this episode, it is revealed that Charles Pressman from the pilot episode has been fired, and Mike and Ernie's uncle makes them the bosses of the maintenance staff on a trial basis. Office cubicles need to be installed for a major tenant in the building. The guys assign the project to Fred (Dick Balduzzi) who literally falls asleep on the job. Ernie fires Fred but then feels sorry for him since he has a family, and so rehires him with a raise. When Fred still doesn't complete the job, Mike and Ernie have to try to build the cubicles themselves and, of course, make a mess of things. Their uncle dismisses them as bosses and makes Falzone (Phil Rubinstein) their new boss.

Jim Belushi's youngest brother William had a cameo in this episode as a janitor.

Episode 6: Unaired   "Pal Joey"

Director: Dennis Steinmetz   Writer: E. Jack Kaplan

Mike meets an old friend, Joe (Ric Casorola) who is now a stockbroker with new offices in the building. Joe is having a party for his clients, and the guys volunteer to clean the office thinking that they are invited to the party. When Mike and Ernie show up at Joe's party with a six-pack, Joe is surprised to see them and asks them to leave. However, on their way out, Ernie discovers a fire in the hallway and goes to get the fire department since the phone hasn't been installed yet in the office. Mike tries to prevent panic among the party goers by having everyone evacuate through the air conditioning duct. Both Mike and Ernie are hailed as heroes.

Episode 7: Unaired   "The Old Man in the Building"

Director: Unknown   Writers: Alan Spencer and John Markus

Strange events in the office building prompt the guys' supervisor, Falzone to rent a guard dog.

Writer Alan Spencer went on to create the sitcoms *Sledge Hammer!* and *The Nutt House*.

Episode 8: Unaired   "Trading Up"

Director: Unknown   Writer: Susan Seeger

The brothers date women who are more interested in dessert than in them.

Episode 9: Unaired   "Sagebrush Estates" (summary based on shooting script)

Director: Unknown   Writer: Stephen Neigher

Ernie meets Valerie, a girl he knew from fifth grade, and asks her out to a baseball game. However, she gets a last minute invitation to a dance, and Ernie tells her it is all right to go to the dance instead of the game with him. Later, Mike sees an invitation in the trash of one of the executives in the building where they work. The invitation is for a free weekend to look at land, go square dancing, and have a barbecue at Sagebrush Estates. He suggests that Ernie invite Valerie to the event so she thinks he is a big land investor. Mike, Nikki, Ernie, and Val go, but the executive from the building also shows up, and they try, without luck, to avoid him. Ernie has to admit to the executive that he has no money to purchase land, and the four of them leave. Valerie wonders why Ernie portrayed himself as a big-land investor to impress her when all he had to do was to be himself. Valerie likes Ernie, and in the end, they kiss.

According to Paramount, eight episodes of *Working Stiffs* were produced. When contacted, writer Stephen Neigher could not recall if this episode was filmed or not.[99] It may be a script that was never produced.

Unemployed

Working Stiffs was originally scheduled by CBS to debut on Wednesdays at the beginning of the 1979-78 season, but the network flip-flopped the show with another new comedy, *Struck by Lightning*, which had initially been placed on the Saturday schedule. The change did nothing for either series. They both debuted near the bottom of the Nielsen ratings. The premiere of *Working Stiffs* ranked fifty-fifth out of fifty-seven series. By its third episode, it was the lowest rated show for the fall season and was canceled after the fourth episode. Six episodes of the series were subsequently released on VHS and Laserdisc by Paramount Home Video.

After the demise of *Working Stiffs*, both stars went on to more successful careers. Jim Belushi starred on the long-running sitcom *According to Jim*. Michael Keaton, after starring in one more short-lived sitcom, *Report to Murphy* in 1982, had a successful theatrical film career, starring in movies like *Mr. Mom*, *Batman*, *Batman Returns*, and *Beetlejuice*.

Zorro and Son

Premiered Wednesday, April 6, 1983, at 8:00 PM on CBS

Walt Disney Productions, which had produced the *Zorro* TV series in the late fifties, decided to resurrect the masked fighter against injustice in Spanish California as the focal point of a new comedy. The premise of *Zorro and Son* was that Don Diego (aka Zorro) was growing older and no longer fully capable of fighting against the excesses of the Spanish troops, and so his faithful manservant Bernardo (Bill Dana) sent to Spain for Don Diego's son, Don Carlos, to return from college to California and partner with his dad in the fight for justice. Portraying Don Diego was Henry Darrow; Paul Regina was featured as the son. Gregory Sierra (*Barney Miller, A.E.S. Hudson Street, Common Law*) played Commandante Paco Pico, Zorro's nemesis; Richard Beauchamp was his assistant Sgt. Sepulveda. Also on the series were John Moshitta (Corporal Cassette), who brought other characters up-to-date on the plot by rapidly repeating the storyline, and Barney Martin in a dual role as Brothers Napa and Sonoma.

Background

Eric Cohen developed *Zorro and Son*. The comedy was produced by Kevin Corcoran, who, as a child actor, had been featured in several Walt Disney Productions; he had played Moochie on *The New Adventures of Spin and Marty*. Guy Williams, who had been Zorro on the original series, was considered for the lead role in *Zorro and Son* but turned it down because he did not like the fact that the new series would be a comedy.[100] In a magazine interview, Williams said, "I found out that CBS was really in charge, not the Disney people. They decided to give *Zorro and Son* the 'cutes,' and then, in typical network fashion, they 'cuted' the 'cutes,' and it was an abortion. It happened because Walt wasn't there. I've seen Walt throw network people off the lot. If he had seen their script, he would have yelled bloody murder."[101]

Zorro and Son used the same theme song as the original *Zorro* TV show and the opening credits spliced black and white footage from the original series with color footage of the stars of *Zorro and Son*.

Episode Guide: 5 aired episodes

Episode 1: April 6, 1983   "Zorro and Son"

Director: Peter Baldwin   Writer: Eric Cohen

Bernando suggests to Don Diego that his son Don Carlos can help him fight for justice in Old California, and Don Diego reveals to Don Carlos that he is Zorro. He trains Don Carlos in the methods he uses, but Don Carlos prefers more scientific ways, like a concoction of onion gas he has made, to battle the Spanish troops. When Zorro Sr. tries to free Brother Napa, who is on trial for "selling wine before its time," from the Commandante, Zorro, Jr. arrives to help him.

Episode 2: April 13, 1983   "Beauty and the Mask"

Director: Gabrielle Beaumont   Writers: Eric Cohen and Nick Arnold

When Angelica, a flamenco dancer, seeks asylum from the Spanish troops, Don Carlos wants to help her. He takes her to the Vega hacienda but cannot reveal that he is Zorro Jr. The Commandante discovers that Angelica is helping the rebels and learns where she is hiding when Bernardo brings flamenco shoes to town for repairs. Paco tells her that if she gives up Zorro, he will not harm her mother who is living in Mexico City. After Zorro, Jr. rescues her from the Commandante, she confesses that she is being forced into spying for Paco. Zorro Sr. retrieves Angelica's mother from Mexico City, and Angelica joins the rebels.

Episode 3: April 20, 1983   "A Fistful of Pesos"

Director: Alan Myerson   Writers: Eric Cohen and Nick Arnold

The Commandante dressed as Zorro begins stealing from the poor giving Zorro a bad reputation. Bernardo tells Zorro Sr. that someone must be impersonating him. Initially, he thinks it is his son, but then they work to set a trap for the real imposter. Brother Sonoma brings a religious relic to their hacienda for the imposter to steal. Zorro Sr. subdues the imposter who is dressed like him. The soldiers think they are taking the real Zorro into custody, but it turns out to be the Commandante.

Episode 4: May 4, 1983   "Wash Day"

Director: Peter Baldwin   Writers: Eric Cohen and Nick Arnold

While Bernardo is laundering both the father and son's Zorro costumes, a strong wind blows them away and into the hands of Paco. Bernardo tries to retrieve the clothes, but the Commandante arrests and interrogates him hoping that he will reveal Don Diego as Zorro. Don Diego advises Bernardo to confess that he is Zorro. The Commandante doesn't believe him and plans to hang Bernardo in hopes that the real Zorro will show himself. While Don Diego is with Bernardo, Don Carlos finds the Zorro outfits in the mission, dresses as Zorro, Jr., and rescues Bernardo from the gallows.

Episode 5: June 1, 1983   "The Butcher of Barcelona"

Director: Gabrielle Beaumont   Writer: Nick Arnold

El Excellente (Dick Gautier), a life-long rival of Paco's, is coming to inspect the pueblo. El Excellente's bodyguard, Cpt. Jorge Mendez (H.B. Haggerty), known as the Butcher of Barcelona, is an old nemesis of Zorro's. Since Paco thinks that El Excellente wants to replace him with Mendez, he asks Don Diego to be his ally against El Excellente. Because of Zorro, El Excellente initially fires Paco but then says that if Paco can capture Zorro in twenty-four hours, he can get his old job back. Don Diego proposes that someone dress as Zorro so Paco can capture him. Diego thinks it is better to help Paco in order to prevent a greater evil. After Zorro Sr. wins a sword fight with Mendez, El Excellente decides to keep Paco in his position.

Maybe Guy Williams Was Right

CBS ordered five episodes of the comedy as a spring tryout. *Zorro and Son* attracted only about 13 percent of the viewing audience losing the ratings race to *Real People* on NBC and ABC's *The Fall Guy*. The network decided not to order additional episodes.

Do Not Disturb
Back Row: Jolene Purdy, Molly Stanton, Brando Eaton
Front Row: Jesse Tyler Ferguson, Niecy Nash, Jerry O'Connell

Chapter 12
Working as a Team

A group of people engaged in the same work activity is the theme of the situation comedies in this chapter. Long-running sitcoms such as *M*A*S*H*, *Barney Miller* and *WKRP in Cincinnati* have been built around this premise. The little-known shows here deal with sports teams, hotel staffs, police squads, military units, office workers, as well as TV production teams.

A.E.S. Hudson Street

Premiered Thursday, March 23, 1978, at 9:30 PM on ABC

Think *Barney Miller* in a hospital setting and that succinctly describes *A.E.S. Hudson Street*. The sitcom took place in an inner city hospital ward; "A.E.S." stood for "Adult Emergency Services." Gregory Sierra, familiar as Detective Chano on *Barney Miller*, was Dr. Antonio (Tony) Menzes, chief resident who had to deal with patients needing emergency care, a nutty hospital staff, and a bureaucratic hospital administrator. Other characters on the series included pregnant nurse Rosa Santiago (Rosanna DeSoto); nurse Rhonda Todd (Julienne Wells); ambulance driver Foshko (Susan Peretz) and her assistant Stanky (Ralph Manza); male nurse Newton (Ray Stewart); hospital administrator J. Powell Karbo (Stefan Gierasch); Dr. Jerry Meckler (Bill Cort); Dr. Glick, a psychiatrist (Allan Miller), Dr. Sorrentino (Jane Marla Robbins), and Dr. Paul Friedman (Bob Dishy).

Background

Danny Arnold, who had created *Barney Miller*, co-created *A.E.S. Hudson Street* along with Chris Hayward and Tony Sheehan. F. Murray Abraham, who would later win an Oscar for his role in the movie *Amadeus*, played Dr. Menzes in the original pilot but was replaced by Sierra when ABC ordered five episodes of the series as a spring tryout following *Barney Miller*. Also, Stefan Gierasch replaced Irwin C. Watson as the hospital administrator after the original pilot. The sitcom was produced by Triseme Corp.

Episode Guide: 5 aired

Episode 1: March 23, 1978 "Dr. No-No" (summary based on final draft script)

Director: Noam Pitlik   Writer: Roland Kibbee

A mental patient, Fenton Coody (Jack Dodson), dressed as a doctor, parades around the hospital and then leaves the building. Meanwhile, Karbo tries to get Tony to perform a secret vasectomy on one of the hospital's board members who keeps getting his mistresses pregnant, but Tony refuses based on moral principles. Stanky and Foshko bring in a man whose life was saved on the street by an anonymous doctor who performed an emergency tracheotomy on him. Karbo overhears this and asks the anonymous doctor to perform the vasectomy on the hospital board member. Tony discovers that the "doctor" is Fenton Coody, who had army medical experience but doesn't know how to perform a vasectomy. Tony has Coody explain what he did to the board member, and it turned out to be a harmless procedure.

Episode 2: March 30, 1978 "In the Black" (summary based on final draft script)

Director: Noam Pitlik   Writer: Roland Kibbee

A South African diplomat comes to the hospital feeling sick, and Dr. Banks, an African-American surgeon, tries to examine him but the diplomat asks for another doctor. Tony rebukes the diplomat because of his racism. Meanwhile, the hospital has a power failure while a pregnant woman and her husband are stuck in an elevator. Tony has to talk the couple through the delivery; the wife ends up having twins. Once the power comes back on, Dr. Banks informs Tony that the diplomat had to have surgery during which he needed a blood transfusion. Dr. Bank's blood was the only matching type in the hospital.

Episode 3: April 6, 1978 "Shutdown" (summary based on final draft script)

Director: Noam Pitlik   Writer: Bob Colleory

A black man is admitted to the hospital after being hit by a car. His six-year-old son James witnessed the accident and is in shock. Dr. Glick brings Tony a mental patient, Mrs. Hollis, who has been declared sane but doesn't want to leave the hospital because it feels like home to her. Glick suggests that Mrs. Hollis volunteer in the ER, and, it turns out, that she is the only one who can get James to talk. Meanwhile, Powell Karbo attends a meeting of the hospital's budget committee and announces to the staff that the hospital must close. Mrs. Hollis overhears Karbo's statement, becomes distraught, and goes up to the roof to jump. Dr. Glick and Tony try to talk her down. James, realizing that Mrs. Hollis is missing, makes his way to the roof and is able to convince her not to jump. Impressed with what the boy did, hospital bureaucrat Vernon Pratt promises to try to keep the hospital open for another few months.

Episode 4: April 13, 1978 "Diagnosis: Dead, Prognosis: Improving" (summary based on final draft script)

Director: Noam Pitlik   Writer: Tom Reeder

Dr. Menzes receives a job offer from Hawaii. But before he can reply to the offer, he has to deal with many emergencies. Mr. Toth, a construction worker, comes to the ER to get a physical for a life insurance policy. At first, Tony says that he will have to make an appointment with a regular doctor's office, but, after Toth explains how dangerous his job is and that he has a large family to care for, Tony gives him an examination. He finds that the patient needs immediate surgery for a heart problem, but Toth says it is against his religion. Tony demands that Toth bring in his religious mentor, Brother Wayne, to convince him otherwise. Tony explains to Brother Wayne that it was God's will to bring Mr. Toth to the hospital to be saved, and Wayne approves of the surgery. In the last scene, Tony calls the hospital in Hawaii to accept the position only to learn that they have found someone else.

Episode 5: April 20, 1978 "Dr. Freidman" (summary based on final draft script)

Director: Noam Pitlik Writers: Danny Arnold, Chris Hayward, and Tony Sheehan

Dr. Friedman has been through a few rough surgeries where his patients have died. His next patient attempted suicide via a gun shot, and the patient does not recover. After Friedman speaks with Dr. Glick about the hopelessness of being a doctor, Tony finds him in a room about to kill himself with a syringe full of potassium chloride. Tony and another doctor convince Dr. Friedman to get some rest in the psych ward. In the final scene, Friedman is recuperating and using his surgical skills to sew wallets.

From *Hudson Street* to *Stat*

A.E.S. Hudson Street failed to attract an audience and was not renewed after the initial order of five episodes. However, Danny Arnold updated the series in 1991. Titled *Stat*, the lead doctor was named Tony Menzes just like on *A.E.S. Hudson Street*. However, Dennis Boutsikaris took on the role. Arnold stated, "I didn't like the way *Hudson Street* was going. It was too much of a soap opera. But I thought that if I could update it and deal with current problems in medicine, I'd be interested."[102] *Stat* lasted for six episodes. Boutsikaris later starred on the short-lived *Misery Loves Company*.

Ball Four

Premiered Wednesday, September 22, 1976, at 8:30 PM on CBS

In advertisements, CBS said *Ball Four* was "all hits and no errors." On the series, Jim Bouton played Jim Barton, a pitcher for the fictional Washington Americans. Much to the chagrin of his teammates, in the first episode, they discover that he was writing a series of articles for *Sports Illustrated* on what really happens off the field in baseball. Other characters on *Ball Four* included:

- Raeford Plunkett (Marco St. John), a "good ole boy" relief pitcher;

- "Rhino" Rhinelander (ex-football player Ben Davidson), the not-so-bright catcher;

- C.B. "Cool Breeze" Travis (Sam Wright), the handsome, black outfielder;

- Orlando Lopez (Jamie Tirelli), a Panamanian utility man;

- Billy Westlake (David James Carroll), the naïve rookie pitcher;

- Lenny "Birdman" Seigel (Lenny Schultz), so named because he quacked like a duck and spent most of his time in the team's whirlpool;

- Pinky Pinckney (Bill McCutcheon), the team's coach, and

- "Cap" Capogrosso (Jack Somack), the manager of the team.

The comedy's theme song was "We're in Love with the Game" composed and performed by Harry Chapin.

Background

Jim Bouton, a former Major League Baseball player, authored a book, *Ball Four*, about his years with the New York Yankees, Seattle Pilots, and Houston Astros. Along with sportswriter Vic Ziegel and TV critic Marvin Kitman, Bouton used that book as the basis for a situation comedy on CBS.

Apparently the first episode was completed only a few days before the show's premiere because part of the original staff walked off the show, and more experienced personnel had to be brought in to save the episode. CBS Entertainment produced the sitcom.

Episode Guide: 5 aired; 2 unaired

Episode 1: September 22, 1976   "Work in Progress" (aka "Re-Sweetened Commissioner)

Director: Jay Sandrich   Story: Herbert Hartug
Teleplay: Jay Sommers, Jim Bouton, Greg Antonacci, and Dave Segall

From the newspaper, Barton's teammates find out that Jim is writing articles about baseball for *Sports Illustrated*. Thinking that the articles will be an unflattering portrait of them, his teammates give him the silent treatment so he won't have anything to write about. The team's PR office issues a memo saying that any articles have to receive prior approval from them, and Cappy and Jim are summoned to the commissioner's office. The commissioner, who has read Jim's first article and doesn't like it because it describes players' antics after the game, tells Barton to issue an apology which he refuses. The team owner wants to drop Barton, but Cappy says he wants to keep him.

Episode 2: September 29, 1976   "The Unpractical Joke"

Director: Unknown   Writer: Unknown

Barton and pitcher Plunkett (Marco St. John) perform practical jokes on each other.

Episode 3: October 13, 1976   "What's a Nice Watch Like You Doin' in a Place Like This?"

Director: Bob Lahendro   Writer: Greg Antonacci

Coach Pinckney tries to put his heirloom watch in the team's safe, but, since it is locked, he leaves the valuable watch on a stool outside his locker. After the game, the watch is missing. Barton comes under suspicion as the thief, but he concludes that Rhino took the watch to put it in a safe place. Rhino divulges that he indeed took the watch but forgot where he hid it. The watch is eventually found in Rhino's catcher's mitt.

Episode 4: October 20, 1976 "A Quiet Day at the Iroquois Hotel"

Director: Unknown   Writer: Unknown

Barton tries to rest before a rare nighttime starting pitching assignment in Cleveland, but his teammates use his hotel room for a hangout.

Episode 5: October 27, 1976 "The High-Flying Rookie"

Director: Unknown   Writer: Unknown

Jim helps a teammate who is hooked on uppers and downers.

Episode 6: Unaired "Rookie in Love"

Director: Stan Lathan   Writers: Tom Meehan and Tony Geiss

Billy Westlake, the rookie pitcher, receives a letter from his girlfriend saying they should start seeing other people. Barton hooks him up with a woman he knows, and, after three dates, Billy wants to propose to her.

David James Carroll (Billy Westlake) died of a pulmonary embolism in March 1992 at age forty-one. He had been suffering from AIDS.

Episode 7: Unaired "Closet Phobia"

Director: Bob Lahendro   Story: Janet Himmelstein
Teleplay: Marvin Kitman and Jim Bouton

On their way out of a hotel to get the team bus to their next game, Barton, Lopez, Westlake, Rhino, Plunkett, and Travis all get stuck in an elevator. When they ring the emergency alarm, the hotel manager thinks the players are just fooling around. The team finally boosts Plunkett up through the escape hatch to get help, but he ends up going off with two attractive ladies he sees in the lobby.

Strike Out

The September 29 episode of *Ball Four* ranked fiftieth out of sixty-six series with subsequent episodes rating even lower. The sitcom was canceled after five episodes even though the show had a good time slot between *Good Times* and *All in the Family*.

In subsequent editions of his book *Ball Four*, Bouton briefly discussed his experiences with this comedy saying that he, Kitman, and Ziegel submitted an eighty-page proposal to CBS for the TV version of his book. The network said that they would only purchase the series if the creators wrote the scripts, but then the network had the scripts rewritten anyway. Bouton said the main problem with the comedy (other than his wooden acting style) was the difficulty in conveying the reality of baseball. CBS wouldn't allow anyone on the series to spit, burp, swear, or chew tobacco.[103]

Battery Park

Premiered Thursday, March 23, 2000, at 9:30 PM on NBC

Following in the footsteps of *Barney Miller*, *Battery Park* was an ensemble workplace comedy set in New York City's Battery Park district starring Elizabeth Perkins as Capt. Madeleine Dunleavy, a tough sarcastic boss who wanted to become mayor and Louis Ferreira aka Justin Louis (*Local Heroes*, *Public Morals*) as Ben Harlin, a chief detective with a spotless record. Also in the cast were Jacqueline Obradors as Det. Elena Vera, an outspoken female detective; Robert Mailhouse as Det. Kevin Strain, a cop who owned Velvet Rope Security and moonlighted as a bodyguard for celebrities; Jay Paulson as Carl Zernial, the youngest member of the squad, and Frank Grillo and Bokeem Woodbine as detectives Stig Stigliano and Derek Finley, who found wacky fun in their jobs. Sam Lloyd played Ray Giddeon, a perpetual crime victim.

Background

Battery Park was co-created by Gary David Goldberg and Chris Henchy. Goldberg (*Family Ties*) had created a sitcom for ABC called *Sugar Hill* about a police captain and his squad starring Charlie Sheen. The cast of *Sugar Hill* included Duane Martin, Joe Pantoliano, and Teri Polo. ABC initially ordered ten episodes but then backed out of the deal. Goldberg and Henchy changed the title to *Battery Park,* made the police captain a female, and sold the comedy to NBC. DreamWorks produced the series.

Episode Guide: 5 aired; 2 unaired

Episode 1: March 23, 2000   "Pilot"

Director: Andy Cadiff   Writers: Gary David Goldberg and Chris Henchy

Ben and Elena investigate the shooting of Vincent DiCenzo, a member of the Gravante crime family. Madeleine has concerns that if DiCenzo dies, the precinct will not have the lowest homicide rate in the city which would interfere with her plans to be mayor some day. She likes the slogan: "Safest Precinct; Safest City." Meanwhile, John Taliando, a reputed drug runner is arriving at the airport from Columbia, and Derek and Stig want to arrest him. When Ben goes to the hospital to see DiCenzo, to stimulate him, he reads the newspaper comics. The precinct gets good publicity from Ben's treatment of DiCenzo leading it to be dubbed "The precinct that cares." Maria DiCenzo, Vincent's daughter visits the hospital, and asks Ben out for a beer because he was nice to her dad. In a subplot, Ray Giddeon, the precinct's perpetual victim, wants to file a complaint that women are having sex in his apartment, while he is not there.

Chris Henchy, who co-created *Battery Park* and co-wrote this episode, later helped to create the sitcom *I'm with Her* based on his marriage to Brooke Shields.

Episode 2: March 30, 2000   "Rabbit Punch"

Director: Arlene Sanford   Writer: Chuck Martin

Madeleine goes undercover to catch a suave con artist, Mike (Corbin Bernsen), who scams wealthy women out of their savings. When she begins to fall victim to his charms, it could endanger the police bust. Mike wants $50,000 from her. Madeleine gives him the check and says she won't arrest him, but Ben does. Meanwhile, Stig resents that Derek received a heroism commendation until he is overcome with remorse after accidentally grazing his partner with a gun shot during an arrest. Ray claims a giant Easter bunny (really a man dressed in a bunny suit) attacked him on the Staten Island ferry.

Episode 3: April 6, 2000   "How Do You Solve a Problem Like Maria?"

Director: Lee Shallat Chemel   Writer: Jane O'Brien

Maria DiCenzo stops by the police station to see Ben. He asks her to dinner, they kiss, and Internal Affairs snaps a photo. Both Madeleine and Internal Affairs question Ben about his relationship with Maria, and they keep the couple under surveillance. Ben announces to everyone that he and Maria will be dating and for everyone to back-off. Carl finds that his old English teacher has been arrested, along with her hookers, for working as a madam. Elena takes pity on Ray after his apartment burns down. He moves into his mother's place while she is in Italy, but someone breaks into his mother's apartment and steals everything while he is there.

Elizabeth Perkins (Madeleine) later starred on the Showtime series, *Weeds*. Writer Jane O'Brien is the younger sister of Conan O'Brien.

Episode 4: April 13, 2000   "You Give Law a Bad Name"

Director: Arlene Sanford   Writer: Mark Banker

The instructor for the precinct's sexual harassment seminar comes on to Ben. Madeleine doesn't believe the instructor is harassing Ben until she overhears her say she wants to have sex with him. Meanwhile, Madeleine wants to arrest Bon Jovi for trashing a hotel room twelve years ago. Elena and Kevin attend one of his concerts to make the arrest, but before they can, Madeleine phones Bon Jovi. He comes to her office, and she lets him off the hook. Stig and Derek arrest a man who thinks of himself as a crime fighting superhero known as The Hawk. When The Hawk says he knows about a robber holding up ATM machines, the detectives arrest the bandit with The Hawk's assistance.

Episode 5: June 17, 2000   "Walter's Rib"

Director: Arlene Sanford   Writer: Sheila R. Lawrence

Madeleine's ex-husband Walter (Henry Winkler) is prosecuting an important case in which she is supposed to testify, but she asks Ben to take her place. Walter, who is known for trying to settle all cases before they go to trial, wants to get back with Madeleine. Because Ben thinks that Madeleine should get involved so Walter takes this case to trial, Madeleine shows up at the trial. Walter calls her to the stand and asks her why she left him. She says he was wasting his potential. Meanwhile, Ray is mugged, and Stig and Derek think they can advance their careers by using Ray as bait to attract criminals. However, Ray eventually tires of being the bait.

Episode 6: Unaired   "Fast Times at Union High"

Director: Lee Shallat Chemel   Writer: Paul A. Kaplan and Mark Torgove

Carl poses as a high school student and Kevin as a substitute teacher trying to infiltrate a computer theft ring at a local high school. Carl gets carried away with the undercover assignment enjoying more popularity in school than he ever did as a real student, but he is disappointed when he doesn't make the wrestling team. Meanwhile, Ben has trouble committing to Maria and ends the relationship when she says her dad has retired and made her the head of the "family business." Stig and Derek lose a suspect in the building's heating ducts and crank up the furnace to get him out, and Madeleine thinks she has to give a speech before a Latino group which turns out to be a lesbian organization.

Episode 7: Unaired   "Black Monday"

Director: Arlene Sanford   Writer: Chris Henchy

Kevin is throwing an expensive birthday party for his model girlfriend on the day the stock market crashes. Because the crash affects his investments, he begins to disinvite people and ends up serving pizza. Ray feels that he is responsible for the crash because he gaveled the stock market opening and broke the gavel creating confusion. Two stockbrokers are on a ledge of a building threatening to jump, while Stig and Derek try to talk them off the ledge. Meanwhile, Madeleine wants to have a press conference to highlight how she is controlling the situation and asks Ray to be at the conference. However, as the market rallies, the media leave.

The actor who played Ray Giddeon (Sam Lloyd) is better known to audiences as the character Ted Buckland on *Scrubs*.

Dead *Battery*

Battery Park followed *Frasier* on Thursdays. It lasted for only four episodes, losing nearly thirty percent of the audience who watched *Frasier*, and was trounced in the ratings by ABC's *Who Wants to Be a Millionaire*.[104]

Do Not Disturb

Premiered Wednesday, September 10, 2008, at 9:30 PM on Fox

The setting for this ensemble comedy was a boutique hotel in New York City with a quirky staff. Niecy Nash was Rhonda, the human relations director at the inn; Jerry O'Connell played Neal, the hotel's manager. Nicole (Molly Stanton), the head clerk; Larry (Jesse Tyler Ferguson), the gay head of housekeeping; bellboy Gus (Dave Franco), and reservations clerk Molly (Jolene Purdy), who moonlighted as a plus-size model, made up the other characters on this sitcom.

Background

The comedy, originally called *The Inn*, was created by Abraham Higginbotham, who had previously produced *Will & Grace*. Brando Eaton was the original bellboy, but he was soon replaced by Dave Franco, James Franco's younger brother. Reveille Productions and Twentieth Century-Fox produced the series.

Episode Guide: 3 aired; 4 unaired

Episode 1: September 10, 2008   "Work Sex"

Director: Jason Bateman   Writer: Abraham Higginbotham

A local New York magazine called *Time Out* prints an article about the on-the-job sexual exploits of the staff of The Inn causing Rhonda to take action by having a sexual harassment seminar. She says that staff must have more self-control which causes Neal to try to be on his best behavior. But Rhonda can't resist the sexual advances of Bobby, the security guard. Neal catches Bobby and Rhonda in the basement and suspects they are having an affair. He pretends that he installed a security camera in the hotel's basement and wants Rhonda to watch some videos with him. She admits she is as bad as Neal. Meanwhile, Molly assists Nicole with her modeling career, and Gus helps Larry to be more sexual by having him flirt with a guy at a bar who happens to be a friend of Larry's lover Victor. In the end, it turns out that the magazine article was written about Molly by a male lover of hers.

Jesse Tyler Ferguson (Larry) later became a regular on the ABC sitcom *Modern Family*.

Episode 2: September 17, 2008   "The Birdcage"

Director: Gary Halvorson   Writer: John Quaintance

Rhonda doesn't approve of Neal's idea to place a life-size birdcage in the hotel's bar so he can put his best-looking female staff members on display. She tells staff that forms have to be completed before anyone can appear in the birdcage, but Neal goes ahead anyway and has skimpily-clad females in the cage. Nicole is not happy when she realizes that Neal has yet to ask her to work in the birdcage. She becomes depressed and fights with a girl in the cage so she can be on display. Meanwhile, Gus talks single female guests into giving him bigger tips by using insider information about them that Larry has provided and then splitting some of the tips with Larry. Molly catches on to the scheme and asks Gus to work with her. Rhonda finally puts a stop to it.

Episode 3: September 24, 2008   "Dosing"

Director: Gary Halvorson   Writer: Sally Bradford

When the staff finds out that it is time for them to be evaluated to see if they deserve bonuses, they are on their best behavior. Meanwhile, Rhonda is upset when Neal fires a bartender seemingly without cause. After Rhonda rehires the bartender, she and Neal argue over who has the authority to fire and hire staff. Their arguing delays the evaluations and causes staff to go to great lengths to resolve the conflict between

Rhonda and Neal. Meanwhile, the hotel's owner, RJ Novak (Jon Polito) and his wife stop by for a weekend visit. RJ wants Neal to keep his wife busy, while he goes out with his mistress. Neal comes on to RJ's wife at the bar because the bartender whom Neal had fired drugged his drink. While Rhonda fires the bartender, Neal ends up in a bubble bath in RJ's room. Rhonda intervenes before RJ's wife can get in the bathtub with Neal. She climbs in the tub with Neal to make it appear that the two are having an affair.

Episode 4: Unaired   "Pilot"

Director: Jason Bateman   Writer: Abraham Higginbotham

RJ, the owner of the hotel is arriving with a reporter from *The New York Times* who is doing an article about the Inn and the top ten places to stay in New York. Molly wants to get out of the reservations area and move to the front desk, but Neal won't let her because she is overweight. She wishes to work at the front desk since she is a singer and hopes to impress guests with her singing ability. Molly calls her dad who is a civil rights attorney, and he threatens to sue the hotel. RJ tells both Neal and Rhonda that they must resolve the problem with Molly. She agrees to drop her lawsuit if Neal lets her sing once a week in the hotel bar.

In the original pilot, the hotel's owner, RJ, was portrayed by Robert "RJ" Wagner.

Episode 5: Unaired   "Satisfaction"

Director: Jason Bateman   Writer: Abraham Higginbotham

The staff tries their best to put up with a high-maintenance guest. However, Nicole plots revenge on the guest. Meanwhile, Rhonda is tired of a friend who has been taking over her apartment. When Neal shows an interest in her friend, Rhonda attempts to help the relationship along so her friend will move out.

Although better known for his acting, Jason Bateman not only directed episodes of *Do Not Disturb* but also episodes of *Arrested Development* and *Valerie's Family* on which he starred.

Episode 6: Unaired   "Sorry, Charlie?"

Director: Bob Koherr   Writers: Sally Bradford and Kirk J. Rudell

Charlie Jenks, a writer, is staying at the hotel and always answers his door in the nude. When Rhonda goes to his room to tell him to stop answering the door naked, he says that part of his writing process is to be nude. However, while speaking to Rhonda, Charlie dies. His sudden death has an impact on the staff. Larry, who doesn't really want to marry his partner Victor, decides to make the most of his life before he dies and to propose to Victor. When Neal holds a press conference to inform reporters about the death of Jenks at the hotel in order to get publicity, the reporters tell Neal that he is exploiting the death. Rhonda advises Larry that he is not ready for marriage, and Victor is just thankful to him for thinking of proposing.

Episode 7: Unaired   "Break Room" (summary based on draft script)

Director: Rob Schiller   Writer: Kirk J. Rudell

Neal is having a hotel storage room turned into a break room which the staff thinks will be for their use, but Neal plans to make it an exclusive club for the public called the "Break Room." When the club opens, hotel staff is forbidden from going to the room. Despite this, Rhonda takes Larry, Gus, and Molly to the Break Room to celebrate Gus' birthday. Neal finally decides to shut the club down after one fabulous weekend to make it a legend. He turns the space into a real break room for the staff.

The Final Nail?

Do Not Disturb ran fourth in its time slot, averaged about four million viewers for its three episodes, and was savaged by critics. For example, "If there is one single person in America who can be found chuckling at any joke delivered on Fox's 'Do Not Disturb,' he or she should immediately be sent for a medical evaluation. This might be the worst, most offensive sitcom to make it on the air in quite some time." [105] In response to such critiques, the producers of the series sent a letter of apology to some writers stating: "We deserve all the criticism . . . and, yes, even the accusation that it very well could be the final nail in the multi-camera sitcom's coffin."[106]

A League of Their Own

Premiered Saturday, April 10, 1993, at 9:00 PM on CBS

Publicity for this comedy said that it was, "A bunch of rookies looking for a break. A washed up manager looking for a second chance. Together they're quite a team." Like the movie on which it was based, *A League of Their Own* was set during World War II when male baseball players were serving in the armed forces, and because of this, the women's professional baseball league was formed. The comedy focused on one team from that league—the Rockford Peaches. Reprising their roles from the movie were Tracy Reiner (Penny Marshall's daughter and Rob Reiner's adopted daughter) as Betty Horn, a pitcher whose husband had been killed in the war, and Megan Cavanaugh as Marla Hooch, a hitter. Other team members included Dorothy "Dottie" Hinson (Carey Lowell), the star catcher; Kit Keller (Christine Elise), Dottie's younger sister and one of the team's pitchers; Mae Mordabito (Wendy Makkena), the sexy outfielder; Doris Murphy (Katie Rich), the outspoken infielder, and Evelyn Gardner (Tracy Nelson). The team's manager, Jimmy Dugan (Tom Hanks in the film), was played by Sam McMurray. Pauline Brailsford was Miss Cutbert, the team's chaperone at their boarding house.

Background

Lowell Ganz and Babaloo Mandel, who had written the screenplay for the 1992 film, adapted it for television, and Penny Marshall (*Laverne and Shirley*), who had directed the movie, was one of the producers of the series and directed the first episode. The sitcom picked up where the movie ended. For example, in the film the character of Dottie Hinson left the team when her husband returned from the war. In the series, Dottie returns to the Peaches when her husband re-enlists. *A League of Their Own* was produced by Montrose Productions and Parkway Productions in association with TriStar.

Episode Guide: 5 aired; 1 unaired

Episode 1: April 10, 1993 "Dottie's Back"

WORKING AS A TEAM

Director: Penny Marshall   Writers: Lowell Ganz and Babaloo Mandel

Walter Harvey (Garry Marshall) threatens to disband the Peaches because they are not performing well. When the team says they need Dottie in order to be winners again, Harvey dispatches his assistant to Oregon to see her. Since her husband is back in the service, she returns to the delight of the team.

Jon Lovitz was Mr. Capadino, a role he played in the film *A League of Their Own*, in this episode of the series. However, now Capadino was Mr. Harvey's assistant and not a baseball scout as he was in the movie.

Episode 2: April 17, 1993   "The Fat Boys of Summer"

Director: Ted Bessell Writers: Lowell Ganz and Babaloo Mandel

Jimmy's old Major League teammates are in town for a reunion and challenge the Peaches to a ball game. Since his old teammates are overweight and hung over from the night before, they are losing to the Peaches six to nothing by the fourth inning. The women feel sorry for them and decide to play badly to let the guys catch up. Jimmy castigates the Peaches for not playing their best, and, by the ninth inning, the score is seven to five. The men's team has two on base and two outs. Mae robs Jimmy of a home run, and the Peaches win.

Director Ted Bessell played Marlo Thomas' boyfriend Donald on *That Girl*.

Episode 3: April 24, 1993   "The Monkey's Curse"

Director: Tom Hanks Writer: Doug McIntyre

Jimmy wins Benny the chimp in a card game and decides to make it the team mascot. The fans love Benny, and the Peaches win eight games in a row. However, when the chimp is injured by Dottie's line drive, the team starts losing games. Mr. Harvey wants Dottie to read a statement to the fans apologizing for hitting the monkey, which Dottie finds humiliating. After talking with Jimmy, Dottie decides to read the statement so she can play again. In the end, the monkey gets better, and someone purchases the animal from Jimmy.

Carey Lowell (Dottie) is married to actor Richard Gere.

Episode 4: August 13, 1993   "Marathon"

Director: Ted Bessell   Writers: Alan Eisenstock and Larry Mintz

Mr. Harvey enters the team in a dance marathon as a publicity stunt. The team encourages Betty to participate even though she feels guilty dancing with a man given the death of her husband. Betty challenges Mae for the dance marathon title and the $100 prize, while Doris meets an admirer played by Willie Garson (*Ask Harriet*, *White Collar*). Mae and her partner allow Betty and her partner to win the prize.

David Lander who played Squiggy on *Laverne & Shirley* with Penny Marshall and also appeared as a radio sportscaster in the film *A League of Their Own*, portrayed the dance marathon announcer on this episode.

Episode 5: August 13, 1993   "Drinking Problems"

Director: Harvey Miller   Writer: Barry Rubinowitz

After Jimmy's date walks out on him, he asks Dottie for advice about women. He wants Kit to go to the bar, the Suds Bucket, with him, but, when Dottie finds out, she goes to the bar to get her sister. Mae's boyfriend takes Kit home, and Jimmy and Dottie commiserate over drinks on what turns out to be her second wedding anniversary. When Miss Cutbert comes to the bar trying to find Mae and Dottie, Jimmy dances with Cutbert to distract her so Mae and Dottie can escape.

Episode 6: Unaired   "Shortstop" (summary based on shooting script)

Director: Unknown   Writers: Alan Eisenstock and Larry Mintz

The Peaches have won eight games in a row thanks to shortstop Ellen Sue. But she is marrying a rug salesman who doesn't want her to play baseball any longer. Jimmy conducts tryouts for a new shortstop. One of the candidates for the position is Madelyn "Bunny" Mintz—very attractive but not that good at shortstop. After Jimmy gets drunk and has sex with Bunny, the Peaches start losing games because of her at shortstop. Jimmy admits to Dottie that he made a mistake in putting Bunny on the team and has little choice but to fire her.

League Disbanded

Originally planned for six episodes, the series expired after three episodes were telecast. *A League of Their Own* performed poorly opposite the sitcom *Empty Nest* on NBC. The debut episode ranked fiftieth. CBS did burn off two other episodes of the series on August 13, 1993 where they ranked seventy-ninth out of eighty-eight shows.

No Soap, Radio

Premiered Thursday, April 15, 1982, at 8:00 PM on ABC

"Two elephants are sitting in a tub taking a bath. The first one says, 'Pass the soap.' The second elephant responds, 'No, soap radio.'" Not that this makes much sense, but then *No Soap, Radio* was not the typical TV sitcom. It did have a storyline about a rundown hotel in Atlantic City owned by Roger (Steve Guttenberg) who was assisted by Karen (Hillary Bailey). But each episode was punctuated by sight gags, blackouts, and comedy routines that more often than not had nothing to do with the plot. Routines included a news report that Mr. Potato was missing, a person with a terminal illness hearing on a television commercial that he was dying, a dummy with a basketball as its head coming to life, John Larroquette as a photographer whose model's head expanded, and Louis Nye as a monk at a Friar's Roast. In addition to the owner and his assistant, other characters on the series were Tuttle (Stuart Pankin, *Nearly Departed*), the house detective; Morris (Jerry Maren), the bellboy, and long-term residents, Mr. Plitzky (Bill Dana, *The Bill Dana Show, Zorro and Son*), and Mrs. Belmont (Fran Ryan).

Background

Les Alexander, Ron Richards, Michael Jacobs, and Richard Smith created the comedy which replaced *Mork & Mindy* on ABC's schedule for five weeks. Actress Brianne Leary appeared as Sharon in the pilot but was replaced by Hillary Bailey as Karen in the other episodes. The Alexander Smith Co. and Mort Lachman and Associates in conjunction with Alan Landsberg Productions produced the series.

Episode Guide: 5 aired episodes

Episode 1: April 15, 1982 "Pilot"

Director: John Robbins   Writers: Les Alexander and Dick Smith

Roger is receiving offers to sell the Pelican Hotel to the Tarantula brothers. He is not sure he wants to get rid of the place since it has been in his family for three generations. However, he is beginning to weaken before the persistence of the Tarantula brothers' attorney.

Episode 2: April 22, 1982   "Carmine the Squealer"

Director: Bill Hobin   Writers: Bill Richmond, Ron Richards, Fred Raker, Kevin Kelton, Tom Saunders, Robert Illes, and James Stein

The FBI has booked a room for Carmine "Meat Hook" Turner (Jerry Stiller), who is testifying against the mob. Turner is dressed as a woman, but Roger is still upset that he will be staying at his hotel. A hit man comes to the hotel to kill Turner, but Meat Hook is able to escape. After the attempt on his life, Turner has second thoughts about testifying, but Roger encourages him to go through with his testimony.

Episode 3: April 29, 1982   "Karen Fools Around"

Director: Bill Hobin   Writers: Bill Richmond, Ron Richards, Fred Raker, Kevin Kelton, Tom Saunders, Robert Illes, and James Stein

Roger wants Karen to take out an important client, Mr. Clavington, for dinner to drum up business for the hotel. When he sees that Clavington is very handsome, Roger become jealous over the time Karen is spending with him. Roger fires Karen when she calls him a hypocrite. However, he subsequently discovers that Clavington has a fiancé and that Karen got him to book a convention at the hotel, and so Roger apologizes and rehires Karen.

Episode 4: May 6, 1982 "Miss Pelican"

Director: Bill Hobin   Writers: Bill Richmond, Ron Richards, Fred Raker, Kevin Kelton, Tom Saunders, Robert Illes, and James Stein

Tuttle has arranged for the hotel to host a Miss Galaxy Beauty Contest, but Conroy, the promoter of the contest, doesn't show up. Karen finds out that Conroy is a con artist and will not be paying for the pageant. Since the contestants have no money to go home, Karen decides the hotel should put on its own "Miss Pelican" pageant. Tuttle sells his car to get the money to cover the hotel expenses.

Episode 5: May 13, 1982   "The Bum's Rush"

Director: Bill Hobin   Writers: Bill Richmond, Ron Richards, Fred Raker, Kevin Kelton, Tom Saunders, Robert Illes, and James Stein

The staff is expecting a hotel critic who often disguises himself as a bum. When a real bum comes into the lobby, Tuttle thinks he is the critic and invites him to spend the night.

No Soap, Cyberspace

After the initial five episodes were aired, ABC decided not to renew the series. However, many of the sketches from *No Soap, Radio*, such as a chair that eats people and a deer hunting a man, can be found on such websites as You Tube.

The Nutt House

Premiered Wednesday, September 20, 1989 at 9:00 PM before moving to 9:30 PM on NBC

A once fashionable New York hotel that had fallen on hard times was the setting for this situation comedy. The hotel was managed by Reginald J. Tarkington (Harvey Korman). Ms. Frick (Cloris Leachman), the oversexed head housekeeper always wanted to bed Tarkington. Freddy (Mark Blankfield), the nearly blind elevator operator; co-owner Charles Nutt III (Brian McNamara); Charles' secretary Sally Lonnaneck (Molly Hagan), and Dennis (Gregory Itzin), the hotel's desk clerk made up the rest of the hotel staff. The series had a lot of slapstick and sight gags such as the elevator operator having trouble getting the elevator level with the floor and a gate coming down in the hallway for a "tray crossing" when bellboys moved a train of serving carts.

Background

Mel Brooks and his protégé Alan Spencer created the sitcom. Spencer had previously created the ABC comedy *Sledge Hammer!* that in some respects was like *Get Smart*, a series Brooks developed with Buck Henry. *Nutt House* was produced by Touchstone Television which had produced the film *Big Business*. Brooks told Spencer that Disney (the owners of Touchstone) had a big, expensive set left after the completion of *Big Business* and suggested that the two partner on doing a TV sitcom using the set.[107] Spencer was basically in charge of the series with Brooks reviewing the scripts. Spencer hoped that the comedy would mark a return to physical and visual comedy on television. Leonard B. Stern, who produced *Get Smart*, was a creative consultant on *Nutt House*.

Episode Guide: 5 aired; 5 unaired

Episode 1: September 20, 1989   "Pilot" (special one-hour episode)

Director: Gary Nelson   Writers: Mel Brooks and Alan Spencer

When very old and almost bald Edwina Nutt (Cloris Leachman in a dual role) is in danger of losing her hotel to the owner of Texplex, a large hotel chain, she sends for her grandson, Charles Nutt III, a jet-setting playboy who has shown no interest in the family business. Mrs. Nutt makes her grandson co-owner of the place, and he attempts to manage the hotel in order to save it. A representative of Texplex arrives to purchase the place and offers cash to Charles. However, Charles refuses to sell, and the cash mysteriously disappears to cover the hotel's outstanding bills. When the Texplex representative says the hotel staff has falsified the books to make it look like the hotel has 600 guests, Charles gets 600 Swedish massage therapists to book rooms in the hotel, and Texplex abandons its takeover attempt.

Episode 2: September 28, 1989 "The Accidental Groom"

Director: Bill Bixby   Writer: Alan Spencer

An immigration official visits the hotel looking for illegal immigrants. When Ms. Frick cannot produce documentation showing she is legally in the United States, she needs to marry a U.S. citizen to stay in the country. Tarkington reluctantly agrees to marry her. However, at the wedding ceremony in the hotel lobby, Tarkington faints before he can say "I do." Charles finds that Ms. Frick is a citizen because her first husband was one, even though she married him in Europe.

Episode 3: October 11, 1989 "A Frick Called Wanda"

Director: Bruce Bilson   Writer: Jim Geoghan

Reginald is depressed, feeling that he has grown old and unattractive, until a pretty hotel guest starts spending more and more time with him. Meanwhile, a courier checks into the hotel with $200,000 in bearer bonds which Tarkington advises him to lock in a safe in his hotel room. The woman who is admiring Tarkington is conspiring with a thief to steal the bearer bonds. Tarkington doesn't believe Frick when she tells him that the two are in cahoots. When Tarkington is in the woman's room, the thief comes in with a gun and forces Tarkington to go to the courier's room to open the safe. Tarkington refuses, wrestles with the thief to get his gun, and the thief is arrested.

Episode 4: October 18, 1989 "21 Men and a Baby"

Director: Bruce Bilson   Writer: Alicia Marie Schudt

A professional basketball team, the Badgers, checks into the hotel before a playoff game and demands quiet. However, when a crying baby keeps them awake, Reginald orders the baby and mother evicted until Ms. Frick succeeds in quieting the infant. Tarkington demands that Frick look after the baby until the mother finds another place to stay. The mother abandons the child, and the basketball team loses their game with the team's manager blaming Tarkington for the loss. In the end, the mother has second thoughts about leaving her child and returns for the baby.

Episode 5: October 25, 1989   "Suites, Lies and Videotape"

Director: Roger Duchowny   Writer: Richard Day

The hotel has no guests, and its creditors have given Charles another deadline to pay the bills. He suggests that they get the President to stay at the hotel on an upcoming visit. As a way to promote the place to the President, the staff does a patriotic video with Tarkington as the star. The hotel receives a reply from the President that he will stay there, and the publicity results in increased reservations. When, at the last minute, the President cancels his visit, Tarkington decides to have Freddy impersonate the Commander in Chief for the news media. However, things change again, and the President actually shows up.

Episode 6: Unaired   "A Night at the Reunion"

Director: Bill Bixby   Writers: Mark Curtiss and Rod Ash

Charles books a big high school reunion at the hotel, but the fire inspector, who is trying to keep his job, won't let them have 300 people in the hotel's banquet room. Tarkington discovers that the school reunion is for his graduating class and decides to resign because he feels that he is not a success. Charles advises him to take a vacation instead of resigning, but the hotel staff persuades Tarkington to masquerade as a wealthy tycoon at the reunion. After the fire inspector reveals that Tarkington is really the hotel's manager, Tarkington apologizes to his former classmates but says that being a hotel manager is an honorable profession, and they forgive him.

Episode 7: Unaired   "To Tell the Truth"

Director: Art Wolff   Writers: Mark Curtiss and Rod Ash

Sally's mom requires surgery for which Sally needs $1170. Meanwhile, an escaped gorilla invades the hotel, tears up a room, and terrorizes Ms. Frick. Tarkington gives Sally $1170, but Charles thinks that Tarkington stole the money from the hotel's petty cash since that amount is missing. Tarkington says he got the money from gambling on the horses, and when that is proved to be correct, he investigates who really took the $1170 from the hotel. After he finds that a hotel guest stole the money, Ms. Frick wrestles with the guest who faints when she sees the gorilla. It turns out that Sally's mother needed the money for a nose job.

Episode 8: Unaired   "When Charles Met Sally"

Director: Roger Duchowny   Writer: Alicia Marie Schudt

The hotel hires Marla, a PR expert, to upgrade its image. She wants to make Charles the focus of the public relations campaign as the "sexiest hotel owner." Sally thinks that Marla and her are in competition, particularly for Charles' attention. Marla also decides to have a Valentine's Day party at the hotel three months before the holiday, and she steals an idea from Sally for a fashion show. When Sally finds that Marla's expenses are eating into the hotel's profits, Charles won't listen to her. Sally sabotages the fashion show Marla is putting on by using lingerie models which gets Marla fired.

Episode 9: Unaired   "My Man Tarkington"

Director: Tom Trbovich   Writer: Gerald Gardner

When the hotel cannot afford to give Tarkington his annual pay raise, he considers taking a position as a valet for a Japanese businessman. Charles encourages him to take the job and tears up his contract with the Nutt House. Charles hires a new manager, Jonathan Creel (Paxton Whitehead) from Britain, while Tarkington stays on during a transition period. The new manager fires Freddy and the hotel maids and brings in some staff from England. Tarkington changes his mind about leaving, but Creel refuses to quit since he has an iron-clad contract. After Charles gives all the staff iron-clad contracts, they conspire to force Creel to leave.

Episode 10: Unaired   "Nutt Cracker Suite"

Director: Bruce Bilson   Writer: Richard Day

When a Russian ballet troupe comes to the hotel, their lead male dancer is so enthralled by America that he wants to defect so he can party here all the time. Meanwhile, the KGB agent who is to monitor the activities of the troupe is attracted to Ms. Frick. The hotel staff tries to prevent the male dancer from defecting so as not to create difficulties for the establishment. The dancer eventually changes his mind and jumps on the roof of the troupe's bus as it is about ready to leave.

Episodes Never Produced

Three additional scripts were written for this series – "Phantom of the Nutt House," "Dennis and the Menace," and "I Can't Tark It Anymore."[108] However, the storylines of these scripts are not known.

House Closed

The *Nutt House* had a respectable premiere, ranking twenty-fifth. However, it lost audience share from its lead-in – *Night Court*. The second episode of the series ranked forty-third, and the third episode, fifty-eighth. The sitcom was canceled after five episodes. One reviewer foretold the fate of the series by saying "…it is just the kind of different, irreverent sitcom that usually gets canceled after about six weeks."[109]

The Office

Premiered Saturday, March 11, 1995, at 9:00 PM on CBS

Not to be confused with the NBC situation comedy that premiered in 2005, this workplace sitcom starred Valerie Harper, best known as Rhoda from *The Mary Tyler Moore Show* and its spinoff. Harper played Rita Stone, a secretary in the executive offices of Package Inc., a package design company. Rita, a divorcée who had been with the firm for nineteen years, was a highly competent secretary for her somewhat inept boss, Frank Gerard (Dakin Matthews, *Cutters*), a senior manager at the company. There were three other executives and three other secretaries in the office: Natalie Stanton (Lisa Darr), the company's only female executive and her secretary Beth Avery (Debra Jo Rupp, *If Not for You*), a working mother who was barely able to keep up with her family and job demands; Steve Gilman (Kevin Conroy), the company's top salesman and his secretary Deborah Beaumont (Kristin Dattilo-Hayward), who was working on her MBA, and Bobby Harold (Gary Dourdan),

WORKING AS A TEAM 449

the firm's temperamental graphic artist and his new, blonde secretary Mae D'arcy (Andrea Abbate).

Background

According to Susan Beavers, who co-created *The Office* with Barbara Corday, the comedy was based on her own experiences as a $75-a-week secretary.[110] CBS likened the show to the British series *Upstairs, Downstairs* with the company executives being the upstairs part and the secretaries being the hired help. Beavers, who had previously created another short-lived sitcom, *Dudley*, with Dudley Moore, would later help produce the hit sitcom *Two and a Half Men*. Her co-creator Barbara Corday is best known for creating the female detective characters Cagney and Lacey. Witt-Thomas Productions and A.M. Incorporated in association with Warner Bros. produced *The Office*.

Episode Guide: 5 aired; 1 unaired

Episode 1: March 11, 1995   "Pilot"

Director: Jay Sandrich   Story: Susan Beavers and Barbara Corday   Teleplay: Susan Beavers

Per a directive from headquarters, Frank informs all the secretaries that there will be no paid overtime anymore just when the executives need to come up with a new concept for a client and the secretaries will have to work past normal business hours. Bobby has a temporary secretary, Mae who criticizes Frank about the lack of paid overtime figuring she is a temp and has nothing to lose for speaking her mind. Under a perceived threat from the secretarial staff, Frank says he will find a way to move money around for overtime and will hire Mae full time.

Gary Dourdan would go on to co-star for several seasons on *CSI*.

Episode 2: March 18, 1995   "Laboring Pains"

Director: Jay Sandrich   Writer: Susan Beavers

Beth has to bring her sick son to work with her since the babysitter never showed up. Her son turns hyperactive in the office.

Debra Jo Rupp (Beth) is best known for her role as Kitty Forman on *That 70's Show*.

Episode 3: March 25, 1995   "Rita & Frank"

Director: Jay Sandrich   Writer: Ken Estin

After the other secretaries encourage Rita to date, Deborah suggests that Rita go out with her Uncle Kirby. When she does, she has a great time. Rita goes on another date with Kirby despite the fact that Frank wants her to work overtime. After Frank lets Rita know that he can no longer depend on her, the other secretaries say that Frank is just jealous that she is dating. Frank apologizes for over-reacting, and Rita replies that, to have her own personal life, she will not be able to give work as much time as she used to. Meanwhile, Beth and her husband are trying to resurrect romance in their lives, but the kids and work interfere. Finally Beth visits her husband at work during the lunch hour, and they make love.

Episode 4: April 8, 1995   "Power Playing"

Director: Jay Sandrich   Writer: Susan Beavers

The company is being sold, and Mae knows the prospective buyer intimately. After she dates the new buyer, the executives pump Mae for information. She begins to enjoy a position of power in the company and ignores her secretarial duties. The new buyer decides to go back to Boston and dumps Mae. Knowing that the executives are still relying on Mae for information about what the new owner's plans are for the current employees, Rita uses all her contacts to learn that the new buyer is just purchasing the stock in the company and will make no changes in personnel. Rita allows Mae to give this news to the executives herself.

Episode 5: April 15, 1995   "Judgment Day"

Director: Jay Sandrich   Writer: Susan Beavers

The new owner, Croft Industries, requires all employees to undergo an annual merit evaluation to see if they warrant a pay increase. None of the secretaries are pleased with this. Beth's evaluation shows she has others do her work for her. Mae tells Bobby he didn't spend enough time on her evaluation, and so he changes everything from "good" to "poor." Rita gets an excellent review from Frank, but she dislikes the process. Beth is really upset about having her evaluation done by Frank since her boss Steve is out of town. Meanwhile, the staff is dealing with a mistake made on the trial packages of Whitler's Oat Flakes. The "W" was left off the packages, and so they read "Hitler's Oat Flakes." Since Frank needs everyone to come together to handle this PR problem, he talks headquarters out of doing evaluations.

Episode 6: Unaired   "My Guy"

Director: Jay Sandrich   Writer: Ken Estin

Natalie and Deborah don't realize that they are both dating the same guy.

Axed

The Office received low ratings and failed to maintain the lead-in audience from *Dr. Quinn, Medicine Woman*. The show was axed after five of six episodes had aired.

On the Air

Premiered Saturday, June 20, 1992, at 9:30 PM on ABC

Filmmaker David Lynch, best known for directing movies like *The Elephant Man* and *Blue Velvet* and creating the TV series *Twin Peaks*, developed *On the Air* with his producing partner Mark Frost. *On the Air* was a parody of fifties television, and to fans of David Lynch, it is probably considered a cult classic.

The situation comedy, set in 1957, took place behind the scenes of *The Lester Guy Show*—a kind of variety show on the fictional Zoblotnick Broadcasting Corporation. Lester Guy (Ian Buchanan) was a fading actor who hoped for a comeback with his own TV series. Supposedly, Lester Guy had previously been cast in a B-movie in

England when virtually all other English actors were serving in World War II. While Lester couldn't act, sing, or dance, he was a trouper. With a wacky cast and incompetent crew, everything that could go wrong with the show did. Nevertheless, *The Lester Guy Show* became a hit for ZBC.

Betty Hudson (Marla Jeanette Rubinoff) played the dim-witted ingénue on the show. Other characters included Vladja Gocktch (David L. Lander, *Laverne & Shirley*), the show's director with a difficult-to-understand European accent; Dwight McGonigle (Marvin Kaplan), the incompetent producer; Bud Budwailer (Miguel Ferrer), the network boss; "Blinky" Watts (Tracey Walter), the sound engineer who had "Bozeman's simplex" and saw 25.62 percent more than anyone else, and the Hurry Up Twins (Raleigh and Raymond Friend) who often walked together across the soundstage saying "hurry up." The episodes were not shown in the sequence they were produced, but that didn't really matter, given the absurdity of the series.

Background

ABC committed to the comedy when *Twin Peaks* was initially a success. However, after *Twin Peaks* began to tank, the network became less eager to work with Lynch.[111] The network didn't broadcast *On the Air* until a full year had passed since the episodes were filmed. The sitcom was produced by Lynch/Frost Productions.

Episode Guide: 3 aired; 4 unaired

Episode 1: June 20, 1992   "*The Lester Guy Show*"

Director: David Lynch   Writers: David Lynch and Mark Frost

During the live premiere of *The Lester Guy Show*, props fail, there is no sound, Lester gets knocked unconscious, and the camera broadcasts scenes sideways. However, the trouper that she is—Betty Hudson carries on with the show. The audience loves it, and the show becomes a hit.

Marla Rubinoff (Betty), in addition to being an actress, became a licensed Marriage and Family Therapist.

Episode 2: June 27, 1992   "Weiner Takes All"

Director: Jack Fisk   Writer: Robert Engels

Lester plots to embarrass Betty since she is getting most of the fan mail. He has Professor Answer compete with Betty and her seventh grade teacher live on the air in a rigged quiz show. As luck would have it, Betty and her teacher win.

This episode was really the third one filmed.

Episode 3: July 4, 1992   "The Great Sylvia Hudson"

Director: Lesli Linka Glatter   Writer: Mark Frost

Betty's older sister, Sylvia (Anne Bloom), with whom she doesn't get along, is a special guest in addition to a puppet called Mr. Peanut. Sylvia does not want to do a skit with Mr. Peanut and makes him cry on live TV. But Betty and Lester buck him up, and Betty appeals to the audience to sing the Mr. Peanut song.

This was the fifth episode produced, and the final one to air.

Episode 4: Unaired   "My Dinner with Mr. Zoblotnick"

Director: Lesli Linka Glatter   Writer: Mark Frost

Betty gets a dinner invitation from Mr. Zoblotnick, the head of the network, and worries about what she will say to him. Lester does everything possible to sabotage the dinner including making Betty think that Mr. Zoblotnick is a wolf and planting a listening device in Zoblotnick's booth. However, Zoblotnick still enjoys his dinner with Betty.

Episode 5: Unaired   "An Almost Innocent Man"

Director: Jonathan Sanger   Writer: Scott Frost

A great English actor guest stars on *The Lester Guy Show* as Lester and the cast try to recreate the classic film, *An Almost Innocent Man,* wherein Lester plays a criminal about to be executed. However, as usual, things go wrong. Lester is knocked unconscious when a load of artificial ducks falls on him, and later, the electric chair in which Lester is sitting as the criminal about to meet his end launches Lester to the top of the TV studio.

Writer Scott Frost is the brother of *On the Air* co-creator Mark Frost.

Episode 6: Unaired   "The Gypsy Traveler"

Director: Betty Thomas   Writer: Robert Engels

The Great Presidio (I.M. Hobson), a Gypsy magician, is booked for the show, but he is not the performer he once was. Lester wants to learn magic so he can do tricks in place of the Great Presidio, but, of course, Lester's tricks go wrong. The Great Presidio gets his touch back and performs marvelously. Meanwhile, new plumbing creates havoc in the studio.

Episode 7: Unaired   "No Business Like Shoe Business"

Director: Jack Fisk   Writers: David Lynch and Robert Engels

Lester wants to book a Beatnik on the show – "the woman with no name"- who is a great boot maker. She ends up doing an avant-garde interpretative dance about shoes. Meanwhile, Betty tries to remember her mother's first name, and Lester's latest attempt to make Betty look bad involves him getting a recording of Betty's voice and modifying it so she sounds terrible. However, when Lester and Betty sing a duet on the show, instead of Betty's voice sounding bad, Lester's voice does.

Off the Air

On the Air was scheduled Saturdays during the low-viewing summer months. Its debut episode ranked eighty-eighth out of ninety-two shows, and succeeding episodes scored even lower ratings. After three of the seven episodes produced had been broadcast, *On the Air* was taken off the air.

As one newspaper critic put it: "…tonight's debut indicates "On the Air" will be without a doubt, the most gloriously, monumentally, yea, even spectacularly stupid

TV show in the history of the medium. But, then, that's exactly what Lynch was trying for."[112]

All seven episodes of the series were subsequently released on VHS by Worldvision.

On the Spot

Premiered Thursday, March 20, 2003, at 9:30 PM on the WB

Not quite just another comedy set at a hotel, *On the Spot* attempted to combine the traditional sitcom format with improvisational comedy. The series had the same cast of characters and a general storyline each week, but the plot was improvised in two ways – when a bell rang, the actor speaking the last line would have to change it in some way, and at various points during an episode, host Charles Esten would stop the action and ask the audience for suggestions on how the story should proceed. In addition to a host, this comedy also had a live stage band under the direction of Dweezil Zappa. Mr. Henderson (Tim Conway), the head of Global Properties, Inc. which owned a chain of hotels; Jeff Miller (Jeff B. Davis), the new manager of the Sun Spot Hotel in Malibu; Brenda (Erinn Carter Hayes), the ambitious assistant manager; Monty (Jordan Black), the hotel's bartender; Caramel (Arden Myrin), the hotel's maid, and Fifi (Mindy Sterling) and her partner The Professor (Michael Hitchcock), the lounge act comprised the cast of characters.

Background

Robert Cohen created *On the Spot* which was produced by Warner Bros.. In the original pilot, Omar Goodling was the series host but was replaced by Charles Esten. The WB ordered six episodes of the comedy.

Episode Guide: 5 aired; 1 unaired

Episode 1: March 20, 2003   "Pilot"

Director: Gerry Cohen   Writer: Robert Cohen

Mr. Henderson assigns Jeff from the mailroom to go to the Sun Spot hotel to see why it is not making money. Upon his arrival, Jeff meets Carl (Brian Doyle-Murray), the current manager and the other staff. Carl is subsequently found dead in his office, and Henderson makes Jeff the hotel's manager even though he knows little about running a hotel. When Jeff asks Fifi and the Professor to improve their act, they quit. He auditions new acts to take their place, but since he can't find any better entertainers, he rehires Fifi and the Professor.

Episode 2: March 27, 2003   "Little Brenda Dynamite"

Director: Michael Dimich   Writer: Dan Signer

The cast films a commercial for the hotel to drum up business. The commercial elicits an unexpected revelation about Brenda's past.

Episode 3: April 3, 2003   "Bachelorette Party"

Director: Gerry Cohen   Writers: Alec Holland and Melissa Samuels

Brenda throws a bridal shower at the hotel for a friend from college (Cheri Oteri), and things get rowdy when a male stripper arrives. Mr. Henderson tries to get a good night's sleep before an important meeting.

Episode 4: April 10, 2003   "Hooker Convention"

Director: Gerry Cohen   Writer: Michael Gordon

Brenda wagers Jeff that she can fill the hotel with guests in less than twenty-four hours, but what she doesn't tell him is that the guests are all prostitutes. To complicate matters, Mr. Henderson arrives at the hotel when his wife kicks him out of their house.

Episode 5: April 17, 2003   "One-Star Hotel"

Director: Michael Dimich   Writers: Ron Corcillo and A.J. Poulin

Andy Richter comes to the hotel to prepare for the role of a bellboy in a movie. An accidental bump on the head causes Richter to have amnesia and think that he is a real bellboy.

Episode 6: Unaired "Mr. Moneybags"

Director: Gerry Cohen   Writer: Michael Saltzman

A rival hotel-chain owner, J.P. Moneybags (Wayne Knight), interrupts a book-signing at the hotel and threatens to launch a hostile takeover.

Writer Michael Saltzman later co-created the unaired WB comedy *Misconceptions*.

Spot Off

The WB pulled the show after five episodes before May sweeps. As with several other series profiled in this book, *On the Spot* scored lower and lower ratings with each succeeding episode.

Park Place

Premiered Thursday, April 9, 1981, at 8:30 PM on CBS

Yet another *Barney Miller*-like sitcom but this one took place at a legal aid clinic. In charge of the Park Place Division of the New York City Legal Assistance Bureau was attorney David Ross (Harold Gould, *Singer & Sons*). His staff included Jeff O'Neill (David Clennon), the office jokester; Howie Beach (Don Calfa), who was seeking a case that would lead to a lucrative partnership; Jo Keene (Mary Elaine Monti), the only female lawyer; Mac MacRae (Lionel Smith), a wheelchair-bound black Vietnam veteran, and Brad Lincoln (James Widdoes), the newbie who had just graduated from Harvard. Frances Heine (Alice Drummond, *Frannie's Turn*), the administrative secretary for the group, often quoted Bible scripture, and Ernie Rice (Cal Gibson) was the office receptionist.

Background

Reinhold Weege, a former writer and producer for *Barney Miller*, created *Park Place* which had a four episode order from CBS after the pilot for the series was broadcast in April 1980. In the pilot written by Weege, the legal aid office filed an injunction against the owner of their building for not installing handicapped accessible facilities. But the owner finds that the Legal Assistance Bureau's lease has expired and wants to evict them. He finally relents on the eviction and promises to install the handicapped upgrades after seeing a wheelchair-bound person fall in the elevator and get back into his wheelchair without asking for help. Meanwhile, a man claiming to be 137-years old wants to apply for Social Security but lacks a birth certificate. The representative from the Social Security Administration won't accept the documents the man has as proof of age.

Starry Night Productions and Warner Bros. Television produced *Park Place*.

Episode Guide: 4 aired episodes

Episode 1: April 9, 1981   "Revenge"

Director: Peter Bonerz   Writer: Reinhold Weege

A Mrs. Rothman (Florence Stanley) comes to the Legal Assistance Bureau and announces that she has just murdered her husband. She realizes that the legal aid clinic is not a police station but explains that "I wasn't sure what was proper." It seems that she had an argument with her spouse over whether to have chicken or a roast for dinner. She shot him because he wanted the roast even though, as she reasonably argued, the chicken was already thawed.

Episode 2: April 16, 1981   "Benign Neglect"

Director: Jeffrey Melman   Writer: Tom Reeder

A young girl named Universe Kessler wants to be divorced from her permissive parents because they allow her to do anything she wants, like hitchhiking to California on her own. When the parents come to the office, they agree to permit her to remove herself from their custody. A hearing is held to determine if the parents should be charged with neglect. After the judge grants the neglect petition, David tells the parents they are abdicating their responsibility. In the end, the mother asks her daughter to go home with her and her dad.

Episode 3: April 23, 1981 "Marooned"

Director: Peter Bonerz   Writer: Reinhold Weege

A blizzard hits New York City, and the legal staff, together with a waiting room full of clients, is marooned in the building. Jo and Mac get stuck in the building's elevator, while Jeff's mother, who flew into see him, is stranded at the airport.

Episode 4: April 30, 1981 "Crazy Judge"

Director: Asaad Kelada   Writer: Reinhold Weege

Jeff, Howie, Jo, and Mac, each working on different cases, are all jailed for contempt of court by an overwrought judge (John Randolph). Brad is left in charge of the office. David, a friend of the judge, advises him that he needs psychological help which results in contempt charges against David. David is released from jail by the DA's office to try to help the judge. Everyone is released after David convinces the judge to take a leave of absence.

From *Park Place* to *Night Court*

Although CBS did not renew *Park Place*, NBC approached Weege about doing a comedy about a court. Based on his research with the New York legal aid society for *Park Place*, he came up with the idea of making the series *Night Court* about the real New York City arraignment court.

Public Morals

Premiered Wednesday, October 30, 1996, at 9:30 PM on CBS

Public Morals was a sitcom about a New York City vice squad unit that dealt with so-called victimless crimes like gambling and prostitution. Lt. Neil Fogarty (Peter

Gerity), forty-five-year-old veteran cop, well-meaning but a bit disillusioned with the world, headed the vice squad. Second in command was ambitious Sgt. Val Vandergoodt (Jana Marie Hupp). Other characters on the squad included Det. Ken Schuler (Donal Logue), thirty-three-years old, heavy-set, and obnoxious; Det. Corinne O'Boyle (Julianne Christie), a thirty-year-old voluptuous blonde; Det. Mickey Crawford (Louis Ferreira aka Justin Louis from *Local Heroes* and *Battery Park*), a recent edition to the squad who used to be Val's boyfriend; Officer Darnell "Shug" Ruggs (Joseph Latimore), twenty-eight, black and a cum laude graduate of Columbia University, and Det. Richie Biondi (Larry Romano), twenty-nine-years old, a handsome Italian who was the first member of his family to be on the side of the cell looking in. The series also had a gay administrative assistant, John Irvin (Bill Brochtrup), imported from *NYPD Blue*.

Background

Steven Bochco and Jay Tarses created *Public Morals*. Bochco is best known for developing dramas like *NYPD Blue*, although he did create the comedy *Doogie Howser, M.D.* Originally, Bochco tried to sell *Public Morals* to ABC, which turned down the series for a variety of reasons: they did not have a good time slot for an adult comedy, the humor was too risqué, and Bochco was not writing the show himself but letting Jay Tarses do the scriptwriting.[113] Tarses had created several critically successful but ratings-deprived comedies like *Buffalo Bill* and *The Slap Maxwell Story*. He had also created the unsuccessful *Black Tie Affair*. After ABC's rejection, Bochco took the series to CBS, which green-lighted it. The comedy was filmed in front of an audience using the conventional three-camera approach.

Bochco said that he took a "low-brow approach" with this comedy and described the show as "kind of raunchy"[114] *Public Morals* was produced by Bochco Productions and Twentieth Century-Fox.

Even before the show premiered, it created controversy. In the pilot episode, the vice squad was referred to as the "pussy posse" because of its sting operations against prostitution. At least one CBS affiliate said it would not air the show, and some advertisers threatened to withdraw their commercials. The line was cut from the pilot, but still CBS decided to air the second episode first. Bochco contended that the controversy stemmed from the fact that the sitcom was from his company and that CBS had historically been the most conservative TV network.

Episode Guide: 1 aired; 12 unaired

Episode 1: October 30, 1996   "The Blue Cover"

Director: Don Scardino   Writer: Jay Tarses

The detectives arrest some underage patrons at a bar who insult them by calling them "meter maids" and "pigs." John Irvin is added to the squad as the new administrative assistant. Meanwhile, Lt. Fogarty is feeling the stress of being acting commanding officer and is not sleeping well. The detectives return to the bar selling liquor to underage drinkers and shut it down.

Episode 2: Unaired   "The Yellow Cover"

Director: Don Scardino   Writer: Lisa Albert

Corinne's boyfriend is arrested for propositioning Val, but none of the detectives want to inform Corinne. When her boyfriend returns to their apartment, he accidentally tells her he propositioned a hooker, and Corinne breaks up with him. Corinne spends the night at the station where Mickey tries to hit on her. In the end, Mickey goes to Corinne's apartment and apologizes.

Episode 3: Unaired   "The Aqua Cover"

Director: Don Scardino   Writer: Matt Tarses

Ruggs comes to work without his pants saying that a nine-year-old boy mugged him with a gun. When the boy is arrested, Ruggs meets with him, and the boy steals Ruggs' wristwatch. Lt. Fogarty is on a cheese-only diet and becomes obsessed with a strange smell in his office until Ruggs realizes it is the lieutenant who smells. When Richie brings his dog to work because he feels it is lonely, he is persuaded by John to see if the dog likes his dog so the two dogs can have companionship. Schuler gets a date through the personal ads who then demands Schuler's shoes at gunpoint.

Episode 4: Unaired   "The Red Cover"

Director: Don Scardino   Writer: Beth Fieger Falkenstein

The squad accidentally raids the wrong room in a tenement building before breaking up an illegal gambling operation next door. One thousand dollars of the money confiscated subsequently goes missing. While Lt. Fogarty is acting strange from the flu, Richie goes to his priest to admit that a packet of money from the raid accidentally fell into his desk drawer and he didn't discover it until the next day. However, since he is from a family of cons, he is afraid no one will believe him. He is persuaded to tell the truth, but, when he returns to the squad room, he finds that everyone knows about the mistake and took care of the problem.

Episode 5: Unaired   "The White Cover"

Director: Andy Ackerman   Story: Steven Bochco and Jay Tarses
Teleplay: Jay Tarses

This is the pilot episode for the series that introduces the main characters. Lt. Fogarty is acting commanding officer for the squad while Captain Chung, the regular CO, is in the hospital. Corinne and Val go undercover as prostitutes arresting johns, and they plan a second operation – this time arresting prostitutes. In his office, Fogarty chastises Corinne for not arresting one of the johns on their initial undercover operation because he was a paraplegic. In the second sting operation, Fogarty, Biondi, and Schuler pose as insurance salesman and rent a hotel room to snare hookers, but Val, Corinne, and Shag prematurely burst into the room to arrest the women when one of the women inadvertently says a code word on which the detectives had previously agreed. The detectives had determined that the name "Mary Chapin Carpenter" would be their code word, and when one of the detectives asks a hooker what music she likes, she says "Mary Chapin Carpenter." In the second sting operation, the paraplegic comes to the hotel room looking for sex and is arrested this time. Also in this episode, there is a rumor that Val is a lesbian, and when a woman enters the squad room, Val kisses her. It turns out the woman is really Mickey Crawford in drag, and he is introduced as the newest member of the team.

In the original script for this episode, Fogarty calls Corinne into his office and says: "You know what we used to call ourselves in the old days when we'd round up prostitutes off the street?" Corinne responds: "The pussy posse." This was the line that caused the pilot not to be broadcast as the first show, and the line was cut from the episode. Also, in the original script for the pilot, the character of Val Vandergoodt did not appear. In her place was a female Puerto Rican detective named Maria Hidalgo.

Episode 6: Unaired   "The Green Cover"

Director: Don Scardino   Writer: Richard Dresser

Schuler and Corinne pose as a married couple looking for extra-marital sex at a brothel, which results in the arrest of the madam. The madam turns out to be the girl that Schuler worshipped from afar when in high school, and he thinks she will go out with him in return for preferential treatment. Meanwhile, Mickey feels he is not being treated as one of the team.

Donal Logue (Schuler) later starred on the sitcoms *Grounded for Life* and *The Knights of Prosperity*.

Episode 7: Unaired   "The Purple Cover"

Director: Don Scardino   Writer: Dan Greenberger

Crawford and Ruggs think they have spotted a porn peddler when the man offers them something strange and exotic, but it turns out to be a llama. John hosts a sensitivity seminar in the office. Richie prepares for his brother's bachelor party, and Schuler obtains some confiscated sex toys from the evidence room for the celebration. Fogarty has purchased a hat for his wife for their anniversary which is in the same type of box as the sex toys. John accidentally delivers the box with the sex toys to Fogarty's wife who seems to be very pleased with the gift. Richie has the bachelor party for his brother without much excitement except that he and Mickey fight over Corinne and Richie's cousin Sal brings a llama to the party.

Episode 8: Unaired "The Orange Cover"

Director: Don Scardino   Writers: Alan R. Cohen and Alan Freeland

Richie's brother Tony is arrested for gambling, and much to his mother's annoyance, he decides not to help Tony get out of jail before his sentencing. He wants his brother to learn a lesson. Fogarty doesn't know what to do when his second wife wants to have another child. He doesn't wish to have another kid, but Schuler gets him to reconsider.

Episode 9: Unaired "The Shrimp Cover"

Director: Don Scardino   Writer: Richard Dresser

The detectives accidentally expose another vice squad undercover operation at a bar. After Mickey overhears a phone conversation which says that someone is going to be "whacked" (i.e., fired) for the mishap, everyone is afraid for their jobs. When Schuler is called into Fogarty's office, everyone thinks he is the one getting fired, but Fogarty just wants to ask him about a hemorrhoid procedure he had since Fogarty is going to have the same procedure. When the detectives give Schuler a farewell gift, he says he is not getting fired. John then brings a fax to Fogarty which says that one of the other vice squad undercover cops was crooked and exposed the operation. As the detectives watch a TV report about the crooked cop's arrest, a cleaner arrives to say that someone called to have the squad room's floor "waxed."

Episode 10: Unaired   "The Cornflower Cover"

Director: John Ferraro   Writer: Lisa Albert

Val and Corinne go undercover at an upscale hotel where Val sees her favorite children's book author who propositions Corinne and is arrested. Val is upset by such an action from a childhood idol and can't stop crying. As part of "Bring Your Kids to Work" day, Rugg's daughter visits the squad room which is decorated for Christmas. Val feels even worse when the daughter overhears Val say that Santa Claus doesn't exist. Lt. Fogarty talks with Rugg's daughter and convinces her that there really is a Santa Claus. When Corinne asks Mickey to speak with Val about her crying episode, she says that the author ruined her childhood memories.

Episode 11: Unaired   "The Goldenrod Cover"

Director: John Ferraro   Writer: Matt Tarses

Fogarty finds that his office is too hot and asks Mickey to join him on the precinct's rooftop for a talk in the snow. Fogarty wonders if Mickey would like to go on a date with his daughter Maura from his first marriage. When Mickey sees that Corinne is attracted to Richie, he agrees to go on a blind date with Fogarty's daughter. They meet at the cops' hang-out where Schuler has also arranged for his ex-wife's new boyfriend to be questioned by Val to see if the man will flirt with her or remain faithful to Schuler's ex. The man shows no interest in Val, and Fogarty's daughter doesn't like Mickey. As Maura leaves the bar, she bumps into Schuler's ex-wife's new boyfriend. They are immediately attracted to one another and decide to go to another bar. Meanwhile, Val and Mickey console each other over coffee.

Episode 12: Unaired   "The Camel Cover"

Director: John Ferraro   Writers: Marc Flanagan and Lisa Albert

Fogarty arrests an older prostitute, Vivian La Rue, and asks her advice on his sexual problems with his younger wife who wants a baby. The pressures of acting as captain are making it difficult for him to satisfy her. A few days later, Fogarty informs the squad that Captain Chung has died, and he is now worried about giving the eulogy at Chung's funeral and the prospect of becoming captain. The detectives attend Chung's funeral where Fogarty initially refuses to give the eulogy, but, after talking to Corinne, goes ahead with a heartfelt speech. The lieutenant is promoted to captain and tells the prostitute that his wife is happy also.

Episode 13: Unaired   "The Tuna Cover"

Director: Jay Tarses   Writer: Richard Dresser

While John and Mickey are ordering sandwiches at Mario's Deli, an elderly man tries to rob the place. Mickey is too busy deciding what to drink to notice the situation, but John manages to get the gun away from the robber when he puts it down on the counter. Back in the squad room, despite Mickey's protestations that John was the hero, everyone believes that Mickey disarmed the robber. John later receives a special commendation from the mayor's office and becomes a local celebrity after the deli owner reports his brave act to the news media. The newfound celebrity goes to John's head, and he alienates the rest of the squad, particularly Mickey who feels his tough reputation has been undermined. Meanwhile, Fogarty wants his detectives to look better and persuades Schuler to see John's personal shopper to improve his slovenly appearance. Due to the mayor and assistant mayor being sick, John's commendation ceremony, which all of the detectives attend, is conducted by an intern who handles the ceremony very quickly with few words. However, Mickey congratulates John on his heroism in front of the other detectives, and John states that the publicity surrounding the incident did go to his head.

Once and Done

The comedy was pulled after only one episode along with two other shows that made up CBS' Wednesday night line-up from 9:00 to 11:00 PM. The other two shows were the sitcom *Almost Perfect* and the drama *EZ Streets*. Initially CBS said that all three series were going on hiatus, but the network cancelled the two sitcoms and only *EZ Streets* was later resurrected for another brief run. *Public Morals* was the second CBS sitcom to be axed after one airing—the first was *Co-Ed Fever*.

In an interview after the failure of *Public Morals*, all Bochco would say about it was "it was fun. It was different."[115]

The Rollergirls

Premiered Monday, April 24, 1978, at 8:00 PM on NBC

A girls' roller derby team from Pittsburgh was the focus of this short-run comedy. Terry Kizer starred as Don Mitchell, the somewhat shady owner-manager of the Pittsburgh Pitts made up of Mongo Sue Lampert (Rhonda Bates), known as the "Amazon from Arkansas;" J.B. Johnson (Carolyn Ann Brown), a black woman from Harlem; Selma "Books" Cassidy (Joanna Cassidy), a feminist intellectual who was proficient in four languages; Honey Bee Novak (Marcy Hanson), voted "Girl Most Likely To" by her Ohio high school class, attractive but not too bright, and Shana

"Pipeline" Akira (Marilyn Tokuda), an Eskimo-American. Howie Devine (James Murtaugh), the voice of the Pitts, had previously worked as an opera commentator on an FM radio station.

Background

NBC ordered four episodes of *The Rollergirls* as a spring tryout. Created and produced by James Komack (*Another Day, Chico and the Man, Mr. T and Tina, Snip, Welcome Back, Kotter*), the comedy was set in Pittsburgh because Komack though the "Pittsburgh Pitts" sounded good.

Episode Guide: 4 aired episodes

Episode 1: April 24, 1978   "Battle of the Sexes"

Director: Burt Brinckerhoff   Writers: Neil Rosen and George Tricker

The Pitts compete against an all-male team, the Atlanta Aces whose captain, Ralph (Jed Allan) once dated Cassidy.

Episode 2: May 1, 1978   "Come to Me, My Melancholy Mongo"

Director: Burt Brinckerhoff   Writer: Stan Cutler

When the girls decide that romance is the cure for a depressed Mongo, they secretly arrange a date for her with Don.

Episode 3: May 3, 1978   "Pilot"

Director: James Komack   Writers: George Tricker, Neil Rosen, Gary Belkin, and Stan Cutler

The team flashes back to how they came together. Mongo, Pipeline, J.B., and Books already knew one another although Mongo and Books disliked each other. The new addition was Honey Bee to whom Don is attracted. Don is always trying to keep the team afloat, but financial woes lead to the girls sleeping in the locker room instead of the apartment he had promised them. The players strike after their first paychecks fail to materialize.

Episode 4: May 10, 1978 "One of Our Players Is Missing"

Director: Burt Brinckerhoff Writer: Stan Cutler

Honey Bee is traded to the rival Rhode Island Hens, but she doesn't like her new team. She tells her former team that she won't skate hard against them. Don likes the fact that his team could actually win their game.

Just Quietly Rolled Away

The Rollergirls did well in the ratings when it was on Monday nights replacing *Little House of the Prairie* for its first two episodes. When it moved to Wednesdays for its final two episodes, it lost in the ratings to ABC's *Eight Is Enough* and CBS' *Spiderman* and was not renewed.

Shaping Up

Premiered Tuesday, March 20, 1984, at 9:30 PM on ABC

A work comedy set in a health club sums up the premise of *Shaping Up*. Buddy Fox (Leslie Nielsen), the owner of a Santa Monica health club, was in his sixties but physically fit. The manager of the club, young, athletic Ben Zachery (Michael Fontaine), was assisted by three attractive aerobics instructors – Shannon Winters (Jennifer Tilly), Melissa McDonald (Shawn Weatherly, Miss USA and Miss Universe, 1980), and Zoya Antonova (Cathie Shirriff). Jake Steinfeld of *Body by Jake* fame also appeared on the series.

Background

Sam Simon and Ken Estin, who produced *Cheers*, created *Shaping Up*. Estin and Simon had just joined health clubs and were impressed by the invigorating environment when they decided to develop the sitcom.[116] Originally they wanted Lloyd Bridges for the comedy, which was then titled *Welcome to the Club*. When Bridges said that he was too old for regular series work, they offered the role of the club owner to Leslie Nielsen. There was no pilot for *Shaping Up* because it was picked up as an on-the-air commitment. Initially Tim Robbins was cast as Ben, the club manager. But ABC and Paramount wanted a more handsome lead for this role, and so Michael Fontaine was cast. Estin-Simon Productions in association with Paramount produced the series.

Episode Guide: 5 aired episodes

Episode 1: March 20, 1984   "Baby Be Mine"

Director: Michael Lessac   Writers: Ken Estin and Sam Simon

After several failed marriages, Buddy Fox decides to adopt a child. He makes a deal with an unwed mother played by Alyce Beasley for her child.

Writer Sam Simon went on to help create and produce *The Simpsons*. He also married Jennifer Tilly (Shannon) in 1984. They divorced in 1991.

Episode 2: March 27, 1984   "Ex Pede Hercuelum"

Director: Michael Lessac   Writers: Ken Estin and Sam Simon

Ben suggests that Buddy perform a feat of strength to get publicity for the club. Buddy thinks this is a good idea until he tries the stunt – lifting the front of a VW.

This was the first episode shot and was to be the introduction to the series. However, ABC liked the "Baby Be Mine" episode better and so aired it first.

Episode 3: April 3, 1984   "Defusing the Muse"

Director: Michael Lessac   Writers: Ken Estin, Sam Simon, Merrill Markoe

Shannon has no time for Buddy's latest club recruit until she learns that he is an award-winning playwright.

Episode 4: April 10, 1984   "I Should Have Danced All Night" (aka "Tile Solution")

Director: Michael Lessac   Writers: Ken Estin and Sam Simon

Melissa goes to her first Hollywood party and has an all-night date, while Ben and Buddy have an all-night session on shower tile replacement.

Episode 5: April 17, 1984   "Mixed Nuts"

Director: Michael Lessac   Writers: Ken Estin and Sam Simon

The death of a friend has Buddy worrying about how his own funeral will be conducted. Meanwhile, Melissa loses Shannon's lucky earrings.

The Sitcom Is Dead?

Following *Three's Company* on the ABC schedule, *Shaping Up* performed well in the ratings. The last episode ranked fourth out of all shows for the week. However, ABC canceled *Shaping Up* in May 1984. The 1983-84 TV season was the end for a lot of comedies on ABC, such as *Happy Days* and *Three's Company*. According to Ken Estin, the network decided that the traditional form of TV comedy was dead.[117] ABC thought that the new form of comedy was the action comedy like CBS' *Scarecrow and Mrs. King*. They wanted to beat the other networks to the transition, and so they didn't renew a traditional sitcom like *Shaping Up* despite its good ratings.

The Six O'Clock Follies

Premiered Thursday, April 24, 1980, at 8:00 PM on NBC

"Meet those wild and wacky guys who brought you the news in Vietnam" was how NBC publicized this comedy-drama. Set in 1967, *The Six O'Clock Follies* was about the Vietnam War seen through the eyes of the staff who produced the Armed Forces Vietnam Network News and Sports, which aired every day at 6:00 PM in Saigon and was called *The Follies*. Major characters included:

- SP 4 Sam Page (A.C. Weary), a prize-winning, twenty-four-year-old TV newsman from Chicago before his ex-wife turned him in to the draft board who was now the co-anchor of AFVN-TV;

- Cpl. Don (Robby) Robinson (Laurence Fishburne), a twenty-three-year-old combat soldier who was a street reporter at the same TV station in Chicago as Page and was now Page's co-anchor;

- Col. Harvey Martin (Joby Baker), a career Air Force Colonel and the Officer in Charge of the AFVN-TV facility in Saigon;

- Lt. J.G. Vaughn Beuhler III (Randall Carver), a twenty-five-year-old ROTC graduate from the Deep South in charge of programming at AFVN-TV;

- Candace (Candi) DeRoy (Aarika Wells), a poor Southerner who came to Vietnam with the Bob Hope Christmas Tour and stayed to become the weather girl on AFVN-TV;

- Nick (Midas) Metkovich (Philip Charles MacKenzie), a twenty-two-year-old disciple of billionaire J. Paul Getty and talent coordinator of AFVN-TV whose real interest was in building a financial empire in Southeast Asia;

- Ho (George Kee Cheung), a nineteen-year-old Vietnamese janitor at AVFN-TV and Midas' financial liaison to the Vietnamese community who spoke perfect English, but only to Midas, and

- Lou Roskow (Howard Witt), a forty-five-year-old career journalist who was the Associated Press man in Saigon.

Impressionist Fred Travalena was the voice of President Lyndon B. Johnson on the series, and actors Phil Hartman and Bill Paxton also appeared in minor roles.

Background

Based on their experiences in opposing the Vietnam War, Marvin Kupfer and Norman Steinberg created *The Six O'Clock Follies*. The two lead characters, Sam and Robby, opposed the war, but obviously had limited opportunities to express this on their newscast. P.S. 235 Productions and Ella Productions in association with Warner Bros. produced the comedy-drama.

Episode Guide: 5 aired; 1 unaired

Episode 1: April 24, 1980   "Welcome, Robby" (summary based on pilot script)

Director: Bob Sweeney   Writers: Norman Steinberg and Marvin Kupfer

Sam helicopters out to a fire base at the front to pick up his former colleague, Robby Robinson, to co-anchor the news. When they get back to the TV station, Sam tells Robby that he hasn't told Col. Martin that Robby is black. At first, Martin is very hesitant about having Robby on the air, but Sam convinces him to give Robby a chance. The newscast goes off without a hitch, and Sam introduces Robby by saying he is the first anchorman who has actually been in combat. Later, Robby finds out that there has been a battle at his old base and wants to go back to be with his friends. After Sam tells him that that would be a bad move and that what they are doing on the air is really important, Robby broadcasts a message to his friends saying everyone's thoughts are with them and he will see them soon for some R & R.

Episode 2: April 24, 1980   "Goodbye, Candi" (summary based on revised draft script)

Director: Bob Sweeney   Writers: Norman Steinberg and Marvin Kupfer

Conservative Congressman Leon Bingham from Indiana is visiting Vietnam and sees Candi delivering the weather forecast in a mini-dress. He is livid and wants her fired. The troops protest her absence, and President Johnson intervenes to get Candi back on the air.

As an actor, director Bob Sweeney played Fibber McGee on the short-lived TV version of *Fibber McGee and Molly*.

Episode 3: April 26, 1980   "Rumors of Peace"

Director: Don Weis   Writer: John Steven Owen

WORKING AS A TEAM

The grapevine has it that something "really big" is about to happen in the war, causing many in Saigon to expect a cease fire. The news team goes all out to run down the truth.

Episode 4: August 2, 1980 "Ol' Yeller"

Director: Bob Sweeney   Writer: Norman Steinberg and Marvin Kupfer

The anchors rescue a German shepherd dog deemed a coward in action. They are rewarded when the dog detects a bomb that was planted at the Midas bar.

Episode 5: September 13, 1980 "The Surprise Party"

Director: Don Weis   Writer: Bob Baublitz

Robby's birthday celebration at the Midas bar is interrupted by a Viet Cong terrorist with an automatic rifle who holds the partygoers hostage.

Episode 6: Unaired "The Medal Winner" (summary provided by Marvin Kupfer)

Director: Bob Sweeney   Story: Norman Steinberg and Marvin Kupfer
Teleplay: John Boni

Robby and Sam want to do a story about a general (Richard Jaeckel) who is scheduled to receive the Medal of Honor. They find that the general did not participate in the battle for which the medal is being awarded but that he was actually in Cambodia rescuing prisoners of war at the time. Since the mission in Cambodia was a covert operation and the President thought he deserved a medal for that mission, the military came up with an alternative, fictitious justification for the honor.

Time's Up

Six O'Clock Follies never had an established time slot on NBC. Originally, it was announced that the series would have a six-episode spring tryout run. However, only a special one-hour episode and a regular half-hour episode aired in April 1980 with the one-hour episode ranking fifty-first. One more episode aired in August, one in September, which ranked fifty-ninth out of sixty series, and then it disappeared completely.

According to Marvin Kupfer, *Six O'Clock Follies* probably debuted at the wrong time in the country's history. On the night of its premiere, the producers held a party with the cast to view the one-hour special episode, which was interrupted by NBC news to report the failed mission to rescue the U.S. hostages being held by Iran. A number of soldiers were killed in the rescue attempt, and, after that, the viewing audience may not have been in the mood to watch a comedy-drama about the military.[118]

Chapter 13
Returning Home

Crumbs with Maggie Lawson, Fred Savage, Eddie McClintock, Jane Curtin, William Devane

"You can go home again" – at least that is the theme of the comedies in this chapter. Usually spurred by a personal or family life-changing event, the main characters in these sitcoms all return to their parental family and/or hometown.

The Building

Premiered Friday, August 20, 1993 at 9:30 PM on CBS

Bonnie Hunt not only starred on the series as Bonnie Kennedy but also created, wrote, and produced it. In *The Building*, Hunt played a struggling actress, who had appeared in local commercials as the "Randolph Carpet Girl," returning to her hometown of Chicago and moving into her old apartment in a building across from Wrigley Field. She was surrounded by a motley group— Holly (Holly Wortell), her loud best friend, Finley (Michael G. Hagerty), a fireman and part-time bartender, Big Tony (Richard Kuhlman), the building's super who was given to colorful language, Brad (Don Lake), an unemployed journalist, and Stan (Tom Virtue), a fellow actor to whom Bonnie seemed to be attracted. The gang often hung out at the Fire Escape Bar. Hunt and all the regulars were from Chicago's Second City improvisational comedy group.

Background

The show attempted to marry improvisational dialogue with the sitcom format. According to Hunt, at the time she was appearing on the sitcom *Davis Rules*, she had a good relationship with then CBS President Jeff Sagansky.[119] Hunt came up with the concept of the series in 1989, and, after *Davis Rules*, she presented the premise to CBS in the form of a play performed in an empty rehearsal hall. The network ordered six episodes. However, CBS wanted her to get a producing partner for the comedy since she had never produced a show before. Since she was friends with David Letterman, she asked him to help produce her sitcom. Letterman's Worldwide Pants Productions and Hunt's Bob & Alice Productions produced the series in association with CBS Entertainment Productions and Columbia Pictures Television. Although the network would have preferred *Oh Bonnie!* or *The Bonnie Hunt Show* for the title, she stuck with the title, *The Building*.

Episode Guide: 5 aired; 1 unaired

Episode 1: August 20, 1993   "Pilot"

Director: John Bowab   Writer: Bonnie Hunt

Bonnie moves into an apartment across from Wrigley Field in Chicago after her wedding is called off. Her former fiancé Jim calls from New York and says he is flying into Chicago for a day and wants to meet with her. Bonnie thinks that he is coming to apologize for calling off the nuptials. Jim sees Bonnie at the Fire Escape Bar and says that he is getting married to his new girlfriend who is now pregnant. However, he does tell Bonnie that he still wants to be friends with her.

George Clooney appeared in this episode as Bonnie's former fiancé Jim.

Episode 2: August 27, 1993   "Damned If You Do"

Director: John Bowab   Writer: Bonnie Hunt

Brad and Finley are planning a bachelor party for a friend, and Brad goes to the International House of Adult Films to get a movie for the party. Brad forgets his money and calls Bonnie to bring it to him. After she arrives, a robber in a ski mask shows up, and Bonnie and Brad become hostages as the incident is broadcast live on TV. The police finally come through the back door of the store and disarm the robber. Later Bonnie is at the Fire Escape Bar where the bachelor party is being held and hides in the big cake for the party. TV reporters come into the bar and take pictures of her as she is getting out of the cake.

David Letterman, in a ski mask, played the robber in this episode.

Episode 3: September 3, 1993   "The Waiting Game"

Director: Paul Kreppel   Writer: Elaine Arata

Bonnie gets a part-time job as a waitress at the Fire Escape Bar because she needs money that she lent Brad but doesn't want to ask him to pay back. While working at the bar, she refuses to take money from her friends for drinks, pays a cabbie to take a drunk home, and loans money to some others and so ends up owing more to the bar's petty cash account than she made in tips.

George Wendt from *Cheers* had a cameo as a bar patron who only wanted coffee in this episode, and Andy Dick appeared as a casting director – another bar patron.

Episode 4: September 10, 1993   "Father Knows Best"

Director: John Bowab   Writer: Bonnie Hunt

Bonnie auditions for a soap commercial with a very particular director, played by Richard Kind, and his assistant (Andy Dick). Her late dad used to sing the soap commercial's jingle to her, and Bonnie thinks he will be disappointed if she doesn't get the job. She finds that the final candidates have been narrowed to her and another woman, but in the end, she isn't selected.

Donald O'Connor appeared in a cameo as the ghost of Bonnie's father who says she was his favorite.

Episode 5: September 17, 1993   "Yakkity Yak Don't Talk"

Director: John Bowab   Writer: Bonnie Hunt

Bonnie is invited to appear on the *Billy Shoe Show* based on her portrayal as the Randolph Carpet Girl. She purchases a new dress for the show and thinks that staff at the TV station will do her make-up. But, when the make-up staff at the station leaves after making up Mr. Shoe, Bonnie asks Holly, who accompanied her to the station, to do her make-up. When she appears on the show, she has far too much make-up on. Bonnie takes a moment to say "hi" to her friends at the Fire Escape Bar, and Billy Shoe asks if she is a big drinker. She says she doesn't have a drinking problem, but then the price tag on her new dress pops out. She tears it off only to have the sleeve rip up the side, and Bonnie doesn't hear Billy's next question. During a commercial, Holly runs into the studio to wipe off some of Bonnie's excess make-up, and Billy wonders if they are lesbians. Bonnie's friends console her after the show.

Actress Ruta Lee appeared as one of the sales clerks in the dress store on this episode, and Jim Belushi played Billy Shoe.

Episode 6: Unaired "No Place Like Home"

Director: Unknown   Story: Elaine Arata   Teleplay: Bonnie Hunt

Bonnie and a former tenant share memories and lemonade on a hot day.

The Boys and *The Building*

The Building initially followed *The Boys* on Friday nights at 9:30 PM. But when it received slightly better ratings than *The Boys*, the time slots for the two shows were switched. This change did not really help either series, and they were both canceled after five of their six episodes had aired.

According to the *Washington Post*, *The Building* was not your standard sitcom. Characters would speak at the same time, and the dialogue of the foul-mouthed character would sometimes come out in bleeps. Even when not bleeped or overlapped, the dialogue was not "the standard set-up-punch line patter" of a sitcom.[120]

Built to Last

Premiered Wednesday September 24, 1997 at 8:30 PM on NBC

Royale Watkins put his career move to California on hold when his father, Russel (Paul Winfield), suffered a heart attack, and he took over management of his dad's business, Watkins Construction. Other characters on *Built to Last* were Royale's mother, Sylvia (Denise Dowse) and four siblings: eldest son, Robert (Geoffrey Owens), an architect; teenage Randal (Juan Lamont Pope); sister, Tammy (Natalie Desselle), and nine-year-old brother, Ryce (Jeremy Suarez). All of Royale's siblings lived at home except for Robert who had his own apartment. Royale lived in his parent's basement.

Background

Built to Last was another situation comedy centered on a comedian's stand-up act. Watkins was discovered by then-NBC entertainment President Warren Littlefield while doing his act at the L.A. Improv. Royale played himself on the series. In real-life, his dad was a general contractor with a wife and a very large family including thirteen siblings besides Royale: Ryce, Rome, Ramon, Romel, Rafe, Rase, Ramled, Lora, Ralph, Reginold, Tammy, Ronald, and Darryl. Greg Garcia, Warren Hutcherson, and Dave Duclon created the series. *Built to Last* was produced by Lightkeeper Productions and Warner Bros. Television. Garcia later created *Yes, Dear*, *My Name Is Earl*, and *Raising Hope*.

Episode Guide: 3 aired; 5 unaired

Episode 1: September 24, 1997   "Pilot"

Director: Michael Zinberg   Writers: Greg Garcia and Warren Hutcherson

While headed to California for a career as a computer-game designer, Royale learns that his dad has had a mild heart attack and can no longer work full time. He has a choice – either let the family construction business be sold to a competitor or take it over himself. He chooses the latter.

In the initial draft script for this episode, Royale was a sociology major at Princeton who worked for his dad while on breaks from college. He lived in his parents' guest house and was dating a girl named Linda. After his dad's heart attack, Royale decided to run the construction business while taking college classes at night.

Episode 2: October 8, 1997   "The Apple Doesn't Fall Too Far...." (summary based on revised table draft script)

Directors: Rod Daniel and Steve Zuckerman   Writers: Warren Hutcherson and Michael Ajakwe, Jr.

Royale's first day managing the company requires attitude changes from his siblings as well as from himself. Royale makes Randal carry a day planner that looks like a purse so that he can keep better track of his appointments. He has also added all of Tammy's files to a computer system that she doesn't know how to use. Both Tammy and Randal reject the changes and leave the office. The next day Royale gives Randal a cell phone instead of the planner and makes Tammy's computer files easier to use. They are happy with the changes and decide to stay.

Episode 3: October 15, 1997   "A Family Affair"

Director: Steve Zuckerman   Writer: Nancy Callaway

Royale is dating Olivia for whom his company is building a deck. The family loves Olivia, but Royale does not like her temper. After he tells Olivia that they don't connect, she still wants to pursue him, but he says "no." Olivia starts dating Robert because she likes being with the Watkins family so much. Royale advises Robert that Olivia is just using him to be part of the family. When she shows her temper in front of Robert, he breaks up with her. Meanwhile, Russel has bought a TV satellite dish and is spending all of his time watching TV.

Episode 4: Unaired   "Admitting Mistakes"

Director: Steve Zuckerman   Writer: Greg Garcia

Royale is dating Stephanie, but he says that he doesn't want to get serious with her and that they can date others. Royale and Randal take Robert bar hoping to meet some girls. When Royale sees Stephanie with another guy at the bar, he remarks that he is with his own date. He asks a girl at the bar to be his date. Because Stephanie is aware that the girl pretending to be Royale's date is a waitress at the bar, she knows he does not really have a date. Royale says he doesn't like it that Stephanie is dating someone else, and asks her to remove him from her list. Meanwhile, a friend of Ryce's tells him that he is an "oops" baby because he is the youngest in his family and wasn't planned. Ryce wants to run away, but his parents let him know that he was not a mistake but a surprise – a very good surprise.

Episode 5: Unaired   "Best Seats in the House"

Director: Rod Daniel   Writers: Dan Cross and David Hoge

Royale is dating Valerie, a girl he knows from college, who has passes to a skybox for a Redskins game. The whole family goes to the game to tailgate. Valerie has an extra ticket to the skybox, and so Royale invites his dad along with him and Valerie. Russel is loud and enthusiastic about the game, while everyone else in the skybox is rather sedate. When Valerie mentions to Russel that she thinks Royale is embarrassed by his behavior, Russel leaves. Meanwhile, Lynn Swan and Dick Enberg are invited to tailgate with the rest of the Watkins family. They give Tammy and Randal passes to the press box where Tammy brings some of her mother's BBQ ribs for Lynn and Dick to enjoy. When Royale leaves the skybox to find his dad, he sees Tammy and Randal in the press box. Royale and Randal have to fill in for Swan and Enberg on the air when the two announcers get too much of the hot sauce from the ribs. Royale then broadcasts that his dad can never embarrass him.

Episode 6: Unaired   "More Tricks Than Treats"

Director: Rod Daniel   Writers: Dave Duclon and Gary Menteer

On Halloween, Royale meets Mary, a young mother and her son who come to the Watkins house for treats. Royale walks them home, and then Bobby (Michael Clarke Duncan), her muscular and jealous ex-husband shows up. Mary asks Royale to hide in the closet. However, Royale reveals himself, and Bobby challenges him to a fight. It turns out that Russel was trying to scare Royale by getting Mary to pretend that she had a jealous ex-husband who would fight any guy who showed an interest in her. Meanwhile, Robert, Randal, and Tammy are at home watching horror movies. When they run out of candy for some teenage trick-or-treaters, the teenagers pummel the house with eggs. The siblings fight back with tomatoes and toilet paper.

Episode 7: Unaired   "The Car, the Loan and the Date"

Director: Rod Daniel   Writer: Michael Ajakew, Jr.

Randal is looking for another car; Royale wants him to buy a truck which is more practical and loans him $3000. But instead of buying a truck, Randal purchases a 1968 GTO for $1500 and uses the rest of the money for a new car stereo system. Late at night Royale removes the stereo system from the car and pretends thieves took it. When Randal admits he was stupid to buy the car, Royale says he will give him $1500 to fix up the car, sell it, and buy a truck. Royale thinks he will get the $1500 from selling the stereo system, but Randal finds it in the garage and wants to keep it for his new truck. Meanwhile, Tammy is dating Walter who feels intimidated by Russel. Tammy wants her dad to leave her dates alone which he reluctantly agrees to do.

Episode 8: Unaired "A Thanksgiving to Remember"

Director: Michael Zinberg Writers: Warren Hutcherson and Greg Garcia

Ryce has to do a family tree for school. Royale and his dad compete to see who can come up with the better family tree – Royale using the computer or Russel going through books and notes stored in the attic. Royale produces a long computer print out that shows the family has long-lost cousins in Cleveland – the Scott family, who happen to be visiting the DC area for Thanksgiving. Royale and Sylvia invite them to Thanksgiving dinner and, when they arrive, they find that the Scott's are white. After going through the boxes of notes in the attic, it turns out that the Scott's ancestors were slave owners. Although there is now some uneasiness between the families, they decide to be gracious and continue on with the day. Eventually, through finding similarities between the two families such as both Russell and Mr. Scott having been marines, they end up getting along and having a nice dinner.

Built to Last Didn't

Canceled after three episodes, the series ranked eighty-third out of 104 shows. After *Built to Last*, Royale Watkins went into scriptwriting himself, penning episodes of *All of Us*, *'Til Death*, and *Are We There Yet?*

Costello

Premiered Tuesday, September 15, 1998, at 8:30 PM on Fox

Costello starred comedienne Sue Costello as Sue Murphy, an outspoken barmaid at the Bull and Dog, a working-class bar in South Boston. Also working at the bar were Trish (Kerry O'Malley), Sue's best friend, and Lottie (Jenny O'Hara, *Highcliffe Manor*), her mother. Sue wanted to be more than just a barmaid and become better educated despite her family preferring that she get married and settle down. In addition to her mother, the Murphy family included Sue's dad, James (Dan Lauria, *The Wonder Years*), a carpenter, and her brother, Jimmy (Chuck Walczak), who had no regular job because he said he had back problems.

Background

Born in South Boston, the situation comedy was inspired by Sue Costello's real life. Costello co-created the series along with Cheryl Holliday. Matt Williams, Carmen Finestra, and David McFadzean were its producers. They were the team behind the hit series *Home Improvement*, and Williams had created *Roseanne*. Costello's character seemed like a young Roseanne. Fox originally ordered thirteen episodes of the series but reduced its order to eight. Touchstone Television and Wind Dancer Productions produced the series.

Episode Guide: 4 aired; 4 unaired

Episode 1: September 15, 1998   "Pilot"

Director: John Whitesell   Story: Cheryl Holliday and Sue Costello   Teleplay: Cheryl Holliday

Sue and her boyfriend, P.J. (Matthew Mahaney), break up because Sue wants to go to college instead of marrying him. She has to move back with her parents and brother since the lease on her and P.J.'s apartment is in his name. Sue also informs her family that she is in therapy to improve her self-esteem and realize her full potential. Her family doesn't understand why she left her boyfriend who had just gotten a promotion in Boston's transit authority or why she is in therapy. Later, when she finds out that P.J. was cheating on her with Mary McDonough (Josie DiVencenzo), her nemesis, she has a physical altercation with McDonough at the bar.

Episode 2: September 22, 1998   "Monkey Butt"

Director: Lee Shallat Chemel   Writers: Gabe Sachs and Jeff Judah

Sue receives an admissions application from the University of Massachusetts, but her family doesn't think she should waste time going to college. Her dad thinks she should become a welder. The application requires that Sue write a 500 word essay on a personal event that changed her world view. She decides to write about when her mother's dress was caught in her red panties at church exposing her butt to everyone since Sue says metaphorically that everyone's butt hangs out at some time. Mom is upset about the essay and accidentally spills coffee on the application and then tears it. The admissions office refuses to accept the form given its condition until Sue argues with them. She gets admitted to the university but is on the wait list.

Episode 3: October 6, 1998   "Sue Drives, Ya Suck Bag"

Director: Lee Shallat Chemel   Writer: Cheryl Holliday

Sue wants to learn to drive so she doesn't have to depend on others to get to her therapist's. First she asks Trish to teach her to drive, but Trish doesn't want to. Then she wants her brother Jimmy to teach her. When he takes her out for driving lessons, he drinks beer while Sue drives, and they are pulled over by the police. Jimmy runs and is arrested. Sue asks her mother for driving lessons, but her mother gets Sue involved in a road rage incident. Finally, Sue asks her dad to teach her. He does, but she doesn't listen to him about using the turn signal properly and ends up flunking her driver's test.

Kerry O'Malley (Trish) is the sister of actor Mike O'Malley.

Episode 4: October 13, 1998   "Sue Dates a Freakin' Dentist"

Director: Ted Wass   Writer: Lester Lewis

Unable to afford dental work when she breaks a tooth on some candy, Sue's mother suggests that she go to a dental school where they don't charge for tooth repair. Sue becomes infatuated with Brian, the Harvard-trained dental student she meets at the school. When she goes back to see him, they find they share a love of James Joyce short stories. He asks her out, and she suggests they meet at the bar where she works. When he comes to the bar, a drunk customer demands that Sue wait on him. Sue ends up hitting the customer, and Jimmy hits Brian because he thinks that Brian should have defended Sue. Sue goes to see Brian again to apologize, and, despite the problems he encountered at the bar, he still wants to date her. Meanwhile, Sue's mother doesn't want to attend the Carpenters Union dance with James who wants to win a dance contest. James goes alone but leaves before mom finally decides to attend the event. Mom and dad end up dancing together at home.

Episode 5: Unaired   "The Anniversary"

Director: Unknown   Writer: Alex Herschlag

Sue thinks that her parents should do something special to celebrate their thirtieth wedding anniversary. She takes her mother for a facial and a new hair style and has her dad make reservations at a fancy restaurant. But James decides to go to the place where he and his wife always dine, which serves an all-you-can-eat sausage buffet. Dad and mom argue over his choice of restaurant but make up, and Sue's dad gives his wife a pair of pearl earrings for their anniversary.

Episode 6: Unaired   "The Garage"

Director: Lee Shallat Chemel   Writer: Bob Daily

Sue needs to get the rest of her belongings out of her ex-boyfriend's apartment. While she is doing this, her ex, P.J. comes by, and they reconcile. When she decides to move back in with P.J., her family is thrilled. They invite P.J. to dinner where he says that he will "let" Sue take a college class and that Sue doesn't need to "think" anymore since she now has him. They fight again over how controlling he is. He breaks up with Sue this time, and she decides to live in her parent's garage.

Episode 7: Unaired   "Double Date"

Director: Unknown   Writer: Mary Fitzgerald

Sue and Trish go on a double date with Shawn, a guy from the bar, and his cousin Chappy. At the restaurant, while Trish and Chappy are away from the table, Shawn says he would like to hook up with Sue after the date with Trish. When Sue mentions to Trish that Shawn made a pass at her, Shawn tells Trish that it was really Sue that made a pass at him. None of Sue's friends will be truthful about Shawn.

Sue locks everyone in the bar and forces them to have shots until someone confesses the truth, which Shawn himself does eventually.

Episode 8: Unaired "Angie O'Plasty"

Director: Unknown Writer: Jane O'Brien

It's Halloween, and everyone in the Murphy family is trying to scare each other. Lottie has a pain in her left shoulder which won't go away, and Sue insists that she see a doctor. When she does, the doctor diagnosis acid reflux and sends her home. But at the bar, during their Halloween celebration, Sue's mom has a heart attack and ends up in the hospital. After Sue's dad leaves the hospital to go home to give out candy, Sue convinces him to go back to see his wife even if he is afraid of hospitals. In the end, the family and bar patrons give Lottie a surprise Halloween party after she gets out of the hospital since Halloween is her favorite holiday.

Near the Bottom

The comedy failed to find an audience; it lasted only four episodes. *Costello* ranked ninety-second out of 122 shows. Its main competition was *JAG* on CBS and *The Hughley*s on ABC.

Crumbs

Premiered Thursday, January 12, 2006, at 9:30 PM on ABC

Mitch Crumb (Fred Savage) was a screenwriter who returned home to Connecticut after he learned that his mother, Suzanne (Jane Curtin) was being released from Cedar Hill, a mental hospital. She had been committed when she tried to run over her husband, Billy (William Devane) with her car after finding out he was cheating on her.

Mitch, who was gay but had not divulged that fact to his family, had an older brother, Jody (Eddie McClintock), who resented Mitch because Mitch had written a movie about third brother Patrick's drowning death. Jody ran the family restaurant. The cast also included Maggie Lawson as Andrea Malone, Mitch's friend from high school who worked at the Crumb family restaurant – the Stone House Grill, and Reginald Ballard as Elvis, a black orderly at Cedar Hill. Each episode of the series began with a flashback to earlier times—many showing scenes when the family was together.

Background

A hybrid of the seventies sitcom *Soap* and the movie *Ordinary People* is how creator Marco Pennette described *Crumbs*, his comedy about a dysfunctional family.[121] While trying to adapt *The Parent Trap* into a sitcom for ABC, the network told him to create a comedy around some of the crazy stories he described in meetings about his own family.[122] While growing up, Pennette's mother tried to run over his dad with the family car after learning that the dad was having an affair. The mother was then admitted to a psychiatric hospital. Upon being released, she learned that her husband had fathered a child with his girlfriend and so sent the new mom a chicken dressed in a baby outfit. Pennette also lost a brother in a boating accident and witnessed his surviving brother deal with the guilt after the accident. Furthermore, Pennette himself struggled with revealing his homosexuality to his parents. All of these incidents were covered in the series' episodes.

Pennette indicated that writing the sitcom was cheaper than going through therapy. He hired his mother as casting director for the show, and the other members of the family seemed to be all right with the events described. Pennette said of his parents: "I bought them homes before doing this. It helps when you own the deed to their homes."[123] *Crumbs* was produced by Touchstone Television and Tollin/Robins Productions.

Episode Guide: 5 aired; 8 unaired

Episode 1: January 12, 2006   "Pilot"

Director: Ted Wass   Writer: Marco Pennette

After getting writer's block and ending his affair with his male therapist, Mitch Crumb returns home to deal with his mother about to be released from a psychiatric facility; his father who left his mother for Shelly, a restaurant reviewer, and his brother who feels that Mitch is there only to write about the family in order to make money. His father is now struggling to be a massage therapist, and has impregnated Shelly. When Mitch's mother learns of this, she threatens the father with a gun, which turns out to be a cigarette lighter.

Episode 2: January 19, 2006   'Whatever Happened to Baby Bodashka?"

Director: Ted Wass   Writer: David Walpert

Suzanne decides to adopt a baby from the Ukraine since her ex-husband and Shelly are having a baby. Suzanne's ex goes to Cedar Hill to complain that, when Suzanne was a patient there, she had an affair with Elvis, a hospital orderly. When his complaint inadvertently gets Elvis fired, Elvis gets a job at the Crumb family restaurant. Mitch, as restaurant manager, has to fire a waitress for stealing, which he has never done before. In the end, Suzanne decides that her sons still need her, and so she doesn't pursue the adoption.

Episode 3: January 26, 2006   "Friends in High Places"

Director: Ted Wass   Writer: Marco Pennette

Mitch is becoming a substitute for his dad with respect to Suzanne. At Mitch's urging, his mother joins a divorce support group but finds it boring, and so she joins a group of recovering drug addicts who end up seeing her as a role model. Meanwhile, Mitch's brother needs $2000 which Mitch gives him thinking it is for the restaurant but it is really for a car payment.

Episode 4: February 2, 2006   "Jody Crumb, Superstar"

Director: Ted Wass   Writer: Regina Stewart

Billy decides to run the restaurant after he loses his massage license when he said he would give an undercover cop a "happy ending" not knowing what that phrase meant. Mitch's dad and brother don't pay Mitch for his work at the restaurant thinking that he doesn't need the money, and he is too proud to tell them otherwise. Jody gets into an argument with his dad saying that Billy made him work in the restaurant and he had to give up a music career. Jody also believes that his dad blames him for Patrick's death. When Suzanne thinks that Mitch is moving out of her home to an apartment near Billy's place, she begins shoplifting. In the end, Mitch reconciles with his mom, and Jody reconciles with his dad.

Episode 5: February 7, 2006   "Six Feet Blunder"

Director: Ted Wass   Story: Marco Pennette   Teleplay: Hayes Jackson

Suzanne gets a job as a colonial re-enactor. Because Mitch wants to date a guy who is working with his mother, he tells the guy that his parents know that he is gay. When the guy finds out that Mitch was not honest with him about being out to his parents, he won't date Mitch. After another colonial re-enactor (Ben Franklin played by Martin Mull) hits on Suzanne, the sons and ex-husband speak to him about sexual harassment on the job. Meanwhile, Billy decides he would like to be buried in the family plot when he dies which Suzanne initially rejects but later accepts.

Episode 6: Unaired   "Tennis, Any Crumb?"

Director: Ted Wass   Writer: Heidi Perlman

Billy's pregnant mistress Shelly (Ilena Douglas) finally appears in this episode. Mitch's dad invites him to what he thinks is a baby shower for Shelly, but it turns out to be her nightclub singing debut. Apparently, Shelly likes to do something "scary" each day and today she is singing in a club. Mitch likes Shelly, and the two decide to see a museum exhibit together. When Jody finds out that Mitch and Shelly are going to a museum, he takes Suzanne to the same museum so she can bump into them. Suzanne becomes upset seeing the two together and dumps Mitch as her tennis partner in favor of Jody. Shelly encourages Mitch to attend the tennis tournament anyway to watch his mom and brother play. After Jody gets sick during the tournament, Mitch takes his place. At the end, to show how much he trusts his mother as a confidant, he tells her he is gay.

Writer Heidi Perlman is the younger sister of Rhea Perlman (*Cheers*) and the sister-in-law of Danny DeVito.

Episode 7: Unaired   "Maybe I'm Tony Randall"

Director: Ted Wass   Writer: Joel Stein

Suzanne wants to go to a gay bar with Mitch, while Billy tries to bond with Jody since Shelly told him that if he doesn't have a good relationship with his current children, he may not have one with his new daughter. After feeling uncomfortable at the bar, Mitch decides to date a girl from the video store who has shown interest in him. However, after a few dates, he goes back to the bar. Jody and his dad watch a fight on TV, but Jody thinks it is easier to give his dad some Photo Shopped pictures that show the two together as a way to prove to Shelly that the two bonded.

Eddie McClintock (Jody) went on to become a regular of the science fiction series *Warehouse 13*.

Episode 8: Unaired   "Sleeping with the Enemies"

Director: Ted Wass   Writer: Sung Suh

Billy hurts his back fixing his ex-wife's roof. Since Shelly is away, Suzanne takes him in and tries to win back his affection. When Billy wants to leave, Suzanne gives him pain killers to make him sleepy and keep him there. After Mitch finds that his dad is with Suzanne, he says that she can't pretend she still has the same relationship with his dad, and so Suzanne tells Billy to go home. Meanwhile, Mitch becomes jealous of an affair between Jody and his friend Andrea. However, from Andrea, Mitch learns that Jody may be more sensitive than he thought when she tells him that Jody visits Patrick's grave every Sunday.

Maggie Lawson (Andrea) later starred on *Psych*.

Episode 9: Unaired   "The Gift of the Magpie"

Director: Ted Wass   Writer: David Walpert

Suzanne decides to have Christmas four months late since she missed the holiday when she was in the psychiatric hospital. For her Christmas dinner, she invites Billy, Jody and Andrea, and Mitch and his ex-boyfriend, who happens to be in town.

Suzanne mistakes Billy's gift for Shelly as a gift for her, but, when she discovers it is engraved with Shelly's name on it, she tears down the Christmas tree. Billy tries to make things right by giving Suzanne a pair of gloves – a gift he gave her every Christmas during their thirty-three years of marriage.

Episode 10: Unaired   "Suzanne Gets Certified"

Director: Ted Wass   Writers: Les Firestein and Heidi Perlman

Suzanne has a date with Frank (Elliott Gould) a friend of Billy's and is so happy she signs the final divorce papers. When she finds out that Billy suggested that Frank date her, she has second thoughts about signing the papers and feigns mental illness to get her recommitted to Cedar Hill so that her signature becomes null and void. Frank visits Suzanne at the hospital and says that he really wanted to go out with her. After she is released, she gives Billy the final divorce papers. Meanwhile, Jody has been invited to join his former band in a gig but wants to back out at the last minute because of nerves. Mitch encourages him to play with the band.

Episode 11: Unaired   "A Loon Again, Naturally"

Director: Ted Wass   Writers: David Grubstick and Ray Brown

Suzanne likes the fact that people give her special treatment because they think she is still crazy. She doesn't want to be seen as normal because she believes she would lose her celebrity status. Suzanne becomes jealous when Camille (Rhea Perlman), who was a patient with her at Cedar Hill, gets publicity for the book she wrote about her nervous breakdown. Suzanne goes to Camille's book reading at a local bookstore and tells Camille her book is fiction and that she is more mentally ill than Camille. To prove this, she runs a forklift through the store. Meanwhile, Mitch is dismayed when his alumni book reports he is a restaurant manager and not a writer. When he finds that his dad provided this information, he argues with Billy and gets fired. Because Jody told Mitch that their dad always wanted to be a boxer, Mitch tries to get in his good graces by bringing back his dad's sparring partner and buying him a bathrobe that fighters use. Mitch finds that Jody was just making this up but tells his dad that he is not ashamed to work at the restaurant and that his writing career is over.

RETURNING HOME

Episode 12: Unaired   "He Ain't Hetero, He's My Brother"

Director: Ted Wass   Story: Regina Stewart   Teleplay: Les Firestein and Hayes Jackson

Shelly and Billy are finally getting married, and Suzanne decides to sell the family home. While Suzanne has an open house, Jody finds a gay magazine in Mitch's closet, and Mitch finally tells his brother he is gay. Suzanne wants to move in with Frank, but he isn't ready yet for such a commitment because he is still doing chores for his former wife. Suzanne decides to invite Frank's ex, Lorraine (Teri Garr), for lunch to discuss things. Lorriane shows up in a wheelchair because she has MS. Suzanne decides to get Lorraine a helper monkey so Frank can be free of her. However, Lorraine cannot let go of Frank, and he figures that both his ex-wife and Suzanne are manipulating him too much and leaves both of them. Meanwhile, Mitch throws a bachelor party for his dad which Shelly attends putting a damper on things. Shelly has concerns about becoming a suburban housewife when she marries Billy. The Buddhist Temple, at which the wedding ceremony is to take place, burns down and the wedding is postponed. Also, because Jody keeps threatening to tell Billy that Mitch is gay, Mitch sends his dad an email outing himself.

Episode 13: Unaired   "…And It All Came Crumbling Down"

Director: Ted Wass   Writers: David Walpert and Heidi Perlman

Suzanne leaves home and becomes a blackjack dealer at an Indian casino, and Billy, despite denying he read Mitch's email, changes his mind about Mitch being best man at his wedding. Mitch goes to see his mother and wants to stay with her, but she takes him back home and decides not to sell the house after all. Since Billy is getting married to Shelly, Suzanne decides to marry herself and face life on her own. When Mitch faces his dad about the email he sent him, Billy tells Mitch that he isn't normal and is throwing his life away. He also says not to come to the wedding. Shelly informs Billy that he cannot disown his son and calls off the wedding. Meanwhile, Elvis marries Suzanne to herself, and in the last scene, Billy returns to Suzanne.

Crumbling Down Indeed

ABC premiered *Crumbs* after the hit *Dancing with the Stars*. It failed to retain a majority of the viewers from *Dancing with the Stars*. Each successive episode of the series had fewer viewers going from an audience of nearly 12 million for its premiere episode to 9 million for its fourth episode. ABC scheduled a special Tuesday night installment of *Crumbs* on February 7, 2006, but it rated even lower with an audience of 7 million. After placing the comedy on hiatus in February, ABC officially canceled the series in May.

Chapter 14
Failing at Marriage

Snip with Lesley Ann Warren and David Brenner

Name a successful sitcom about divorce where the man and woman remain on friendly terms after separating. With the possible exception of *Happily Divorced*, it's difficult to think of one. The same cannot be said for little-known comedies on this subject. Here are three.

It's Not Easy

Premiered Thursday, September 29, 1983, at 9:30 PM on ABC

It's Not Easy centered on a couple who had divorced but still lived near each other so they could share custody of their children. After having two kids – a daughter Carol (Rachael Jacobs) and a son Johnny (Evan Cohen), Sharon Long (Carlene Watkins), a dental hygienist, divorced her husband, Jack Long (Ken Howard), who ran Long's Sporting Goods which he had inherited from his late father. She then married Neal Townsend (Bert Convy) who conducted consumer research and had a son of his own –Matthew (Billy Jayne aka Billy Jacoby). Sharon and Jack's kids stayed with their father who lived across the street from his ex-wife. Neal Townsend's former wife, Evelyn, the butt of many jokes on the series, was never seen. Ruth Long (Jayne Meadows), Jack's mother who lived with him, helped to take care of Carol and Johnny.

Background

Pat Nardo, who had written episodes of the *Mary Tyler Moore Show* and *Rhoda*, created *It's Not Easy* based on her own life. According to Nardo, her then-husband had an ex-wife and three children. She indicated that she was the only second wife in America who had a whole television series that she could use to dump on her husband's first wife.[124] Nardo wrote the pilot for *It's Not Easy*, titled "Stepping," in fall 1981 and initially cast Carlene Watkins and Gerald McRaney as the divorced couple and Larry Breeding as the wife's second husband.[125] However, when McRaney's detective series, *Simon & Simon*, got renewed, Ken Howard took the role as Jack. The actor Larry Breeding died in a car accident and was replaced by Bert Convy. Both incidents delayed the sitcom for a year. Patricia Nardo Productions in association with The Konigsberg Company and Twentieth Century-Fox produced *It's Not Easy.*

Episode Guide: 5 aired; 5 unaired

Episode 1: September 29, 1983   "Pilot"

Director: Robert Moore   Writer: Patricia Nardo

Jack's kids think that their dad is lonely until they meet Sherry Gabler (Christine Belford), the woman he has been dating. Sherry is a long-time neighbor whom Jack's ex-wife despises. However, Jack tells Sharon that she doesn't have to like Sherry since he is not married to her any longer.

Episode 2: October 6, 1983   "Did He or Didn't He?"

Director: John Tracy   Writers: Mitzi McCall and Anne Convy

Neal complains to Sharon about her amicable relationship with her ex-husband Jack. But Neal has a lot of explaining to do when his goodwill visit to his ex-wife results in an overnight stay; while Sharon attempts to hide her feelings about Neal's stay from Jack.

Bert Convy, who died of a brain tumor in 1991, was probably best known as the host of game shows like *Tattletales* and *Super Password*. Anne Convy, who co-wrote this episode, was Bert's wife when the series aired.

Episode 3: October 13, 1983   "Jack Kills Sharon's Grandmother"

Director: John Tracy   Writers: Prudence Fraser and Robert Sternin

Sharon's great-grandmother, Winnie, is coming for a visit, and her mother wants Sharon to pretend she is still married to Jack. Sharon's mother thinks that if Winnie finds out about the divorce, it will kill her. When she comes for dinner, Sharon, Jack, and their kids pretend they are still married. However, after one of the kids asks Winnie to stay longer and she says "yes," Jack decides to be honest with her about the divorce. Winnie dies, and Jack feels terribly guilty. It turns out that Johnny had told Winnie that his parents were divorced before Jack had told her, and so Jack no longer feels responsible for Winnie's death.

Episode 4: October 20, 1983   "Betrayal"

Director: John Tracy   Writer: Gary Kott

Jack confides to Sharon that he is bored with sex and suggests that he and Sharon make love as therapy for him. Sharon says "no" and informs Neal of what Jack proposed. When Neal gets upset, Sharon says that Jack has a problem with women. Jack learns of this and feels that Sharon betrayed his confidence. He gives Sharon the silent treatment. However, after Neal confides to Jack that he had the same lack of interest in women after he broke up with his ex-wife, Jack feels better and forgives Sharon.

Episode 5: October 27, 1983   "Teacher Pet"

Director: Tony Singletary   Writer: Michael Cassutt

Johnny's teacher wants to meet with Jack over his son's problem with authority. Sharon accompanies him to the meeting although she doesn't get along with the teacher. The teacher informs Jack that Johnny is pulling pranks in class with another student. Sharon then discovers that Jack is dating the teacher, and Johnny starts getting good behavior reports which Sharon thinks are due to Jack's relationship with the teacher.

Episode 6: Unaired   "My Dinner with Andrea"

Director: John Tracy   Writer: Carmen Finestra

When Jack sees Neal's co-worker Andrea (Mimi Kennedy), he decides that he wants to ask her out. They go together for three weeks, and Andrea asks Sharon and Neal to go to dinner with Jack and her. At dinner, she reveals that she had a fling with Neal before he married Sharon. This leads to awkward moments at the table with Sharon particularly upset that Neal never told her of the affair. Andrea announces that she doesn't want to get involved in the lives of Jack, Sharon, and Neal and leaves the restaurant.

Episode 7: Unaired   "Taking Sides"

Director: Tony Singletary   Writer: Robert Stevens

All of the adults are going out, and Matt is left to babysit Johnny and Carol. When Neal and Sharon return from the theatre, they discover that Matt had a party with some of his friends along with Carol and Johnny. Neal wants to punish all the kids, but Jack doesn't want Carol and Johnny to miss a football game for which he has tickets. Sharon initially declines to take sides between Neal and Jack over how her kids should be punished but finally says that Jack is right. She ends up going to the game with him and her kids. However, she leaves the game early and wants to make up with Neal. After Jack returns from the game, he tells Johnny and Carol that they have to obey Neal.

Episode 8: Unaired   "All Night Long"

Director: Charlotte Brown   Writer: Carmen Finestra

Neal and Andrea are working at his home on a report for work, while Matt and the other kids come down with the flu. Jack drops by the Townsend household, runs into Andrea, and they rekindle their relationship. However, Andrea is miffed when Jack has to take care of the kids, and she walks out on Jack again. She subsequently stops by Jack's house to say she is sorry, and the two eventually reconcile.

Episode 9: Unaired   "Neal Kills Johnny's Fish" (summary based on first draft script)

Director: Charlotte Brown   Writers: Anne Convy and Mitzi McCall

Neal and Sharon tell everyone they are going away for a weekend together but really plan to spend the weekend at home alone. Jack comes to Sharon and Neal's house thinking they are both out in order to get his daughter's allergy pills and finds Sharon and Neal together in the bathtub. Ruth comes into the bathroom looking for Jack, and Ruth's new boyfriend, who had spent the night with her, subsequently shows up. After Ruth and her boyfriend leave, Neal forbids Jack from ever setting foot in his house again. A few days later, Jack comes over to Sharon and Neal's house with Johnny who wants his dad to see his new fish. Since Jack is not permitted to come in, Johnny puts the fish in a coffee mug to show his dad.

After his dad leaves, Johnny temporarily places the mug on Neal's desk where Neal mistakes it for his own mug and swallows the fish. Johnny and Carol are not that upset over the demise of the fish, but they are concerned that Neal won't let their father in the house. Neal relents and invites Jack back.

Episode 10: Unaired "You Made Her Love You"
(summary based on shooting script)

Director: Charlotte Brown   Writer: Gary Kott

Neal's sister Ellen is visiting after breaking up with her boyfriend, and she is drowning her sorrows with food. Jack stops by after taking the kids to miniature golf and asks Ellen to the movies. Later, after Ellen returns to Neal and Sharon's place, she says that she and Jack had a romantic walk along the beach instead of going to the movies. Ellen says they are in love, but Jack says it was all innocent. The next day, Ellen, Jack, and the kids go to the zoo, and Ellen makes dinner for Neal, Sharon, and Jack. Sharon wants Jack to break things off with Ellen, and, when Jack tells Ellen it is all over between them, she confesses that she was just playing games with him and was not serious.

Viewers Tuned Out

Despite the delays in getting the comedy on the air, Nardo thought it would be a hit. ABC was committed for thirteen episodes. However, only ten were produced. The sitcom came in third in the ratings against its competition on Thursdays. Its debut ranked sixty-third and the October 13 episode ranked sixty-first out of sixty-six series. It was on opposite *Simon & Simon* on CBS and the Emmy-winning *Cheers* on NBC. The sitcom was canceled after five episodes. ABC felt that the viewing public just did not want to watch a show about divorce.

Snip

Was to premiere September 30, 1976 at 9:30 PM on NBC

Loosely based on the movie *Shampoo* that starred Warren Beatty, *Snip* was created by James Komack and developed by Stan Cutler. Komack's hit sitcoms *Chico and the Man* and *Welcome Back, Kotter* starred stand-up comedians Freddie Prinze and Gabe Kaplan respectively, and *Snip* starred another stand-up comic—David Brenner, making his debut as a womanizing hair stylist working with his ex-wife, Beverly, played by Lesley Ann Warren. Other characters on the series were Beverly's Aunt Cleo Fetcherly played by Hope Summers (*The Andy Griffith Show, Another Day*). A black manicurist, Daffney (Bebe Drake) and a gay hairdresser, Michael Robert St. James (Walter Wanderman) rounded out the cast of characters. The producers of the series actually hired a technical adviser for Wanderman to make sure his character didn't behave in ways that would offend gays. As portrayed on the sitcom, Wanderman's character was relatively subdued, at least compared to the more maniacal character played by Brenner. Wanderman looked like a very thin Gabe Kaplan with an Afro haircut and seventies-style moustache.

Background

The original concept of the series had Brenner playing a free-spirited hairdresser working in Cape Cod in a shop owned by Lesley Ann Warren. They lived together but were not married, and they also had a teenage daughter. The role of the teenage daughter was dropped, however, and the Brenner and Warren characters became a divorced couple.

The series' original producer and writers quit after the first five or six shows because they couldn't work with *Snip's* star, David Brenner and his ego. Five episodes of the sitcom were completed with two other episodes shot but needing editing when NBC pulled the plug on the comedy and never aired it. *Snip* was produced by James Komack Productions.

Episode Guide: 7 unaired

Episode 1: "David Makes His Move" (Pilot)

Director: James Komack   Writer: Stan Cutler

David and Beverly were co-owners of a Philadelphia beauty salon, had lived together for two years, got married, and then split up after six months because of David's womanizing. Beverly sells her share in the beauty salon and moves to Cape Cod where she sets up her own business called "Beverly's." David visits her in Cape Cod for the first time since the divorce. He confesses that he still loves her and wants to stay the night at her place, but she makes him sleep on the couch. After David tells Beverly that he no longer runs around with other women, a girlfriend calls him at Beverly's shop putting a lie to his claim. However, Beverly does let David stay on "temporarily" as a hair stylist in her salon.

Episode 2: "Out of the Closet" (aka: "Out of the Closet and Into the Fire")

Director: James Komack   Writers: Stan Cutler and Bob Shayne

When Michael's mother is coming to visit, he informs David that his mother doesn't know he is gay. David suggests that Michael pretend he has a girlfriend, and Michael asks Beverly to be his girlfriend while his mother is there. After dinner, Michael's mother decides to stay overnight on the couch where David sleeps, and she expects Beverly and Michael to share the same bedroom. Michael asks David to spend the night at his place with his three roommates, but David doesn't want to leave. The mother says that Michael used to be gay but then got married when he was twenty and subsequently got a divorce. David confronts Michael about this and demands that Michael tell his mother the truth about his sexuality which he does.

Episode 3: "Cat on a Hot Tin Plate"

Director: James Komack and Gary Shimokowa
Writers: Bob Shayne and Stan Cutler

David prepares a special tuna spread for the staff and patrons of the salon. Even though a cat comes in the kitchen window and eats some of the spread, David serves the rest of it anyway. He later finds the cat dead in the driveway. Believing his special tuna spread caused the cat's death, David calls a doctor who sends paramedics to pump everyone's stomachs. A customer subsequently stops back to tell everyone that she ran over the cat when she left the salon earlier.

Episode 4: "The Test"

Directors: James Komack and Gary Shimokawa   Writer: Stan Cutler

David receives a citation from an attractive lady inspector that he is not licensed as a hair stylist in Massachusetts. He has to take a test to get his license but hates tests. Bev, Daffney, and Michael all encourage him to take the exam with Bev helping him to study. David wants to go to a motel to study with Beverly similar to what the two had done when he took his first test for licensure in Philadelphia. When he and Bev go to the seedy motel room, David just jokes around because he thinks he can't pass the exam. Bev advises him to charm the lady inspector when she comes back the next day to give him the test. However, the next day, a male inspector arrives for David's test. David thinks he blew the test and begins packing to leave Cape Cod. It turns out that, when the male inspector saw what a good job David had done on styling the female inspector's hair the previous day, he passes David.

Episode 5: "Daffney Come Home"

Director: Jeff Bleckner   Writer: Peter Meyerson

Daffney has been doing a lot of work at the shop – her job as well as everyone else's. On top of that, David proclaims that hair is more important than nails. She is tired of being taken advantage of and quits. Beverly wants David to apologize to Daffney so she will come back to work. Daffney's boyfriend wants David to accompany him to a bar to say he is sorry to Daffney. Beverly goes with David to the bar frequented primarily by people of color. David makes a fool of himself by being very obvious that he is uncomfortable in an all-black bar. He tries to apologize to Daffney and eventually she returns to work because she doesn't like being unemployed.

In 1977, Bebe Drake (Daffney) became a regular on the short-lived comedy *The Sanford Arms*.

Episode 6: "Any Port in the Storm" (aka "Any Port in the Storm, but Champagne in a Hurricane")

Director: Dennis Steinmetz   Writer: Jack Kaplan

Beverly is nervous when a hurricane threatens Cape Cod. David tries to comfort her, while Daffney and Aunt Cleo go to volunteer at the emergency center. Michael wants to stay, but David asks him to leave so he can be alone with Beverly. Michael,

Daffney, and Aunt Cleo all return to the house because of the storm. The power goes out, and a tidal wave is threatening the coast. David ties everyone down in preparation for the tidal wave. He ties himself to Beverly. However, the tidal wave ends up striking further down the coast.

Episode 7: "The Jealousy Factor"

Director: Hy Averback Writer: Bob Shayne

When an attractive female named Bambi comes to the shop for a comb out, Michael suggests to David that he use Bambi to make Beverly jealous. David and Bambi flirt, and he asks her out to dinner. Beverly thinks it is a good idea that David is dating because she can then lead her own life. On his way to meet Bambi, David sees Glen, Beverly's date for the evening whom she invited for dinner. David decides to stay and have drinks with Glen and calls Bambi to tell her he will be late. When David starts serving Glen and Beverly dinner, Beverly asks him to leave. However, Glen decides that he is the one intruding and asks Beverly for a rain check on the evening. Beverly is upset with David who says he is sorry. Bambi then comes to the door, and the three of them have dinner.

Episodes Never Produced

At least two scripts were written for *Snip* but never filmed:

"They Kill Rabbits, Don't They?" (aka "The Only Good Rabbit is a Live Rabbit") (summary based on draft script)   Story: Jerry Cutler and Bucky Searles   Teleplay: Brad Buckner and Eugenie Ross-Leming

Mrs. Harris, one of the shop's customers, calls Daffney to cancel her appointment because the pet rabbit Beverly gave her daughter is sick. She calls back again and David takes the message that the rabbit has died. When David jumps to the conclusion that Beverly is pregnant and doesn't believe her when she says the message is about a pet rabbit, she tells him she is pregnant. David asks Beverly to remarry him, but she says that he is only proposing because he thinks she is pregnant. After Mrs. Harris' daughter stops by to show her new rabbit to everyone, David realizes that Beverly is not going to have a baby. However, he still asks her to marry him, but Beverly says "no"—that they need to take things one step at a time.

"David and the Potted Plant" (summary based on draft script)   Writers: Patricia Jones and Donald Reiker

David buys a lot of potted plants for the salon thinking that he can sell them to customers once he gets a license to sell plants. He unknowingly purchases marijuana plants with the regular house plants. A woman in her thirties comes into the salon for something "special," sees the marijuana plants, and wants to buy one. At first, David doesn't want to sell a plant to her since he doesn't have a license but changes his mind when she offers him $50. The woman turns out to be an undercover cop and arrests David, Beverly, Daffney, and Michael. The police drop the charges against everyone except David who makes bail. He decides he will defend himself in court. When the police woman comes by the shop to takes pictures of the crime scene, David secretly records a conversation with her in which he claims he was entrapped. He gets her to admit that maybe she did entrap him to get promoted. He shows her the tape recorder, and the policewoman agrees to have the charges against him dropped. Later David finds that he forgot to put a tape in the recorder.

Snipped

According to Bob Shayne, who was the story editor on *Snip*, NBC's original mandate was to "Go ahead, and do a sex comedy."[126] But then the executive management at the network changed, and the new leadership didn't want a sex comedy on the schedule.

NBC initially said they pulled the series off the schedule for "doctoring" and indicated the show would debut as a midseason replacement, which never happened. David Brenner believed that NBC got cold feet because the show had a gay character.[127] While that may have been true of NBC, *Snip* would not have been the first sitcom with a gay supporting character. Two sitcoms that predated *Snip* had such characters – *The Corner Bar* in 1972 and *Hot'L Baltimore* in 1975—both on ABC. Ironically, ABC premiered *The Nancy Walker Show* at the same time and date that *Snip* was to premiere, and, on that series, Nancy's male secretary was gay.

The Stones

Premiered Wednesday, March 17, 2004, at 9:30 PM on CBS

Robert Klein (from *Bob Patterson*) and Judith Light (from *Who's the Boss?*) starred on this comedy as Stan and Barbara Stone, who, on the eve of their twenty-fifth wedding anniversary, decided to get an amicable divorce – they were just tired of being a couple. However, their grown children didn't want their parents to split up. The son, Winston (Jay Baruchel), still living at home, was a workaholic geneticist who had a crush on Audra (Kimberly McCullough), a colleague at work. Winston's more free-spirited sister, Karly (Lindsay Sloane), a freelance photographer, decided to move back home after being evicted from her apartment. Together they tried to convince their parents to not get a divorce.

Background

Initially, *The Stones* was on CBS's fall schedule to air on Wednesday evenings but got bumped from the schedule when CBS decided to air additional episodes of *Becker* instead as a stronger lead-in to the new David L. Kelley drama, *The Brotherhood of Poland, NH*. CBS then reduced its order for *The Stones* from thirteen episodes to nine in addition to the pilot.

The creator of *The Stones* was Jenji Kohan, the sister of David Kohan who, along with Max Mutchnick, helped produce the series. David Kohan and Max Mutchnick are best known for creating *Will & Grace*. KoMut Entertainment and Warner Bros. Television produced *The Stones*.

Episode Guide: 3 aired; 7 unaired

Episode 1: March 17, 2004   "Pilot"

Director: James Burrows   Writer: Jenji Kohan

When the Stone family meets at a restaurant to celebrate the parents' anniversary, mom announces that she and her husband are getting a divorce. The dad, an orthopedist, moves out of the house and into an apartment above the garage.

Episode 2: March 24, 2004 "Seamus on You"

Director: James Burrows   Writer: Jenji Kohan

Seamus, Karly's friend from Ireland, arrives for a visit, but the parents won't let him stay in the daughter's bedroom. While mom and dad try to one up each other on giving "divorce" gifts, they forget their son's twenty-first birthday. However, Seamus reminds them of the event.

Episode 3: March 31, 2004 "The Lawyer Trap"

Director: Steve Zuckerman   Writer: Barry Wernick

Stan thinks that Barbara is on a spending spree using the family credit cards when it is really Winston who is purchasing a new wardrobe with Karly's help. Stan cancels all the credit cards which infuriates Barbara. She retaliates by hiring a lawyer and calling off the "friendly divorce." Stan hires a lawyer as well and moves back into the house. When Stan and Barbara see that their attorneys are making the atmosphere very hostile, they fire them.

Episode 4: Unaired "The Lonely Goatherd"

Director: Andrew Tsao   Writer: Linda Wallem

After Stan hurts his back, Winston stays home to take care of him, while Barbara and Karly attend a *Sound of Music* sing-a-long at the Hollywood Bowl dressed as characters from the movie. Although Stan wants to watch basketball, Winston has other ideas for his dad.

Episode 5: Unaired "Romancing the Stones"

Director: Micheline Lanctot   Writer: Elaine Aronson

Barbara and Stan start dating. When a pretty colleague flirts with Stan, he ends up asking her out. Barbara joins an internet dating service and arranges to meet one of her matches. As the two prepare to go out, Barbara attempts to undermine Stan's confidence while building up her own. Meanwhile, Karly interferes in Winston's dating life causing a mix-up that almost costs her a job she likes.

Episode 6: Unaired   "She Ain't Heavy, She's My Sister"

Director: Lee Shallat Chemel   Writer: Barry Langer

Barbara's previously overweight sister Gail (Wendy Malick) comes to visit and attempts to use her new looks to take advantage of a new opportunity. Initially Barbara is eager to help Gail in any way she can. But when Gail tries to pull one over on Barbara, she quickly learns that straight-laced Barbara isn't the pushover she thought she was.

Episode 7: Unaired   "The Perfect Episode"

Director: Unknown   Writer: Matthew Salsberg

Barbara's parents played by Orson Bean and Barbara Barrie come for a visit. Barbara tries to hide the fact that she and Stan are divorcing

Episode 8: Unaired   "Courting the Coopers"

Director: Unknown   Writer: Kristofor Brown

Stan and Barbara compete for the attention of some friends who just learned about the divorce. Karly discovers that her mom accidentally killed her cat two years ago, and Winston finds that Audra once dated his favorite professor.

Episode 9: Unaired   "Howard's End"

Director: Unknown   Writer: Katy Ballard

Karly asks Winston for advice after she falls for a science geek who works with Winston.

Episode 10: Unaired   "The Road Not Taken"

Director: Unknown   Writers: Jennifer Konner and Alexandra Rushfield

Barbara tries to sell homemade croutons, while Stan reconnects with a woman from his hippie past.

Dropped Like a Stone

When *The Stones* finally debuted in spring 2004, it came in fourth in its time slot, ranking sixty-second for the week. The network canceled the series after three episodes.

George Segal in *Take Five*

Chapter 15
Starting Over

Loss of fame, fortune, and/or position is the theme of the comedies in this section. The characters in these little-known sitcoms attempt, sometimes successfully, sometimes not, to regain their former status.

Ask Harriet

Previewed Sunday, January 4, 1998, at 8:30 PM before moving to Thursdays at 8:30 PM on Fox

Ask Harriet was a "drag" comedy about a divorced sports reporter, Jack Cody, who had been fired from his job at the fictional *New York Dispatch*. Without any other job prospects, he decided to take his best friend's suggestion and apply as a writer for the "Ask Harriet" advice column at his old paper. In order to fool his former boss, Melissa Peters (Lisa Waltz), Jack dressed in drag and assumed the name of

Sylvia Coco. He got the job and, as so often happens in such comedies, no one at the paper, except his best friend, Ron Rendell (Willie Garson), knew that Jack and Sylvia were the same person despite the height and facial similarities between them. Others characters on the series were Trey Anderson (Patrick Y. Malone), Jack's former assistant who took over his column, Old Man Russell (Ed Asner), the owner of the paper, Joplin Russell (Julie Benz), Russell's granddaughter whom he wanted to eventually become managing editor, and Marty (Damien Leake), a vagrant who solicited in front of the newspaper's building.

Portraying Jack/Sylvia on the sitcom was the actor Anthony Tyler Quinn (no relation to the late actor Anthony Quinn) who had previously starred on *Someone Like Me*. To make sure the viewing audience knew Jack was a 'real' man, the character had a young preteen daughter, Blair (Jamie Renee Smith) from an earlier marriage, smoked cigars, and tried to have sex with almost every woman he met.

Background

Ask Harriet was created by Billy Riback, a former standup comic and producer on *Home Improvement*, along with former teen idol, David Cassidy, and Jonathan Prince, best known for starring on the syndicated comedy *Throb*. The original concept for *Ask Harriet* was "Tootsie in the sports world." But instead of the sports world, Riback decided to set the series in a newspaper newsroom[128]. One problem that Riback had to overcome was not making Anthony Taylor Quinn as Sylvia Coco look too ravishing. Apparently Fox executives did not want male viewers thinking that Sylvia looked better than their wives. Quinn said he based the character of Sylvia Coco on two different women: the actor's Aunt Rosseila and Tina Louise's portrayal of Ginger Grant on *Gilligan's Island*.[129] *Ask Harriet* was produced by Montrose Productions.

Episode Guide: 5 aired; 8 unaired

Episode 1: January 4, 1998   "Pilot"

Director: Andrew D. Weyman   Story: Billy Riback, Jonathan Prince, David Cassidy
Teleplay: Billy Riback and Jonathan Prince

In his daily column for the *Dispatch*, Jack writes about a senator's wife fooling around with the entire offensive line of the Oakland Raiders leading to a $21 million libel suit against the paper and to Jack's dismissal. Melissa, the editor in chief of the *Dispatch* with whom Jack had had a brief fling, gives his column to Trey Anderson, Jack's former assistant. His firing from the *Dispatch* meant that Jack had been fired from every newspaper in New York City. He doesn't want to move to another city because his daughter Blair and ex-wife live in New York. The death of the *Dispatch*'s "Ask Harriet" advice columnist gives Jack a chance to stay in the city. He thinks he can write the advice column from home and fax it to the paper, and so submits samples to Melissa. She likes the samples but wants to meet the writer in person. Jack takes his best friend Ron's advice, puts on a dress and high heels, and gets the job as an advice columnist at his old newspaper.

Episode 2: January 8, 1998   "Hot Coco"

Director: Robert Berlinger   Writers: Billy Riback and Jonathan Prince

Ed Asner joins the series as Max Russell, the owner of the newspaper. Jack believes he can convince Russell to hire him back. When Russell makes his granddaughter Joplin, Melissa's assistant, Jack thinks he can date Joplin and persuade her to tell her granddad to rehire him. But, after Joplin says that her granddad gets mad if she dates employees, Jack decides to meet Russell as Sylvia to convince Russell to rehire him. Russell informs Sylvia that he will hire Jack again if Sylvia has sex with him. Joplin then comes to Jack's apartment when her granddad is there with Sylvia. Sylvia has to confess that she lives with Jack, and Russell finds out Jack was going to have sex with Joplin further cementing Jack's position as an ex-employee of the paper. In the end, Russell gives Sylvia a five-year contract with the paper.

Episode 3: January 15, 1998   "Help Me, Help Me, Rwanda"

Director: Robert Berlinger   Writers: Jimmy Aleck and Jim Keily

After Jack gets a job as a columnist for *National Sports* magazine, Sylvia says she will resign and go to Rwanda to work with the apes. Old Man Russell, not wanting her to leave, says he will rehire Jack if she stays. Sylvia agrees, and Jack is rehired. However, Sylvia sends a telegram to the *Dispatch* stating she went to Africa anyway.

Old Man Russell is upset, but since Jack signed an iron-clad contract, Russell can't fire him. Instead he gives Jack menial tasks to do and eventually makes Jack Trey's assistant. Jack finally quits, and Sylvia returns.

Episode 4: January 22, 1998   "Turn Your Head and Kafka"

Director: Robert Berlinger   Writer: Peter Murrieta

Jack has been Sylvia for a month but hasn't picked up any of her paychecks. He needs money to pay for his daughter's school tuition as well as for braces and so decides to get his pay. However, before he can, he has to have a medical exam dressed as Sylvia. At the gynecologist's office, after answering a series of questions about Sylvia's health, the doctor signs the necessary papers without performing a physical examination. When the doctor requires a urine sample to test for Sylvia's estrogen level, Jack switches samples with a woman who turns out to be pregnant.

Episode 5: January 29, 1998   "Lips That Pass in the Night"

Director: Ken Levine   Writer: Jim Keily and Jimmy Aleck

Old Man Russell's wife is having a charity auction where people bid on dates with celebrities. Russell wants Sylvia to be one of the celebrities. Sylvia tells Ron, who is also in the auction, to make sure he bids on her. However, when Ron gets distracted by an attractive woman during the auction, Trey wins the date with Sylvia. Melissa wins a date with Ron. Old Man Russell comes to the restaurant where Trey and Sylvia are on their date, and he and Trey compete to go home with Sylvia. Meanwhile, Ron and Melissa are having dinner at the office. Trey looses the competition to Old Man Russell, but then Sylvia defeats Russell in arm wrestling and leaves by herself. Sylvia goes to the office where she advises Ron and Melissa not to get involved in a co-worker romance.

Willie Garson (Ron) later was a regular on *Sex and the City* and *White Collar*.

Episode 6: Unaired   "Fat Ron"

Director: Robert Berlinger   Writer: Pamela Eells

Jack has invested in a new restaurant called "The Joint," and wants Ron, the paper's food critic, to give it a good review. For his reviews, Ron uses caricatures of himself such as "Fat Ron" meaning the food was great or "Wretching Ron" meaning it wasn't. When the Sunday magazine section of the paper wants to do a photo spread on Sylvia, Jack thinks Sylvia can give needed publicity to his restaurant. Jack suggests using Ron's mother's apartment for the photo shoot since it is more feminine than his. After the shoot, while Jack is still dressed as Sylvia, Ron's mother (Phyllis Newman) comes home unexpectedly and sees Sylvia's clothes. Initially she thinks her son is a transvestite, but he explains the clothes are his "girlfriend" Sylvia's. Ron's mother then wants to throw a family party to celebrate the fact that Ron finally has a girlfriend. Jack says he will attend the party as Sylvia provided Ron gives his new restaurant a great review. However, Ron gives it a "Wretching Ron" review since he had to have his stomach pumped after eating there. Jack doesn't want to go to the party as Sylvia because of the review, but he finally shows up dressed as her because of his friendship with Ron.

Episode 7: Unaired   "Surprise, Surprise"

Director: Robert Berlinger   Writers: Gabrielle Allan and Ria Pavia

The office staff wants to throw a surprise birthday party for Sylvia. Ron tries to tell Jack about the party, but Jack wants to be surprised. Meanwhile, Melissa sets Sylvia up on a blind date with her cousin Trevor who informs Sylvia that he is gay but for "some reason" is attracted to her. Jack later runs into Trevor who confides that Melissa is having a surprise party for Sylvia. Jack initially says to Ron that Sylvia won't attend the party but subsequently learns that the birthday present is golf clubs which he really wants. Sylvia goes to the party, is touched by the card Melissa gives her, and receives the golf clubs which turn out to be for ladies.

Episode 8: Unaired   "Good for the Goose, Good for the Gander"

Director: Robert Berlinger   Writer: Peter Murrieta

Jack burns all of Sylvia's clothes and wigs thinking he is getting a job with *Sports Week* magazine. At a Knicks game for which he is writing an article for his prospective job, Jack punches an abusive fan, is ejected from the game, and is banned from attending for a month. To still attend the games, Jack dresses as Sylvia in a blonde wig and runs into the abusive fan again. Sylvia punches him, and this time the fan is ejected. After Sylvia complains that she should be treated just like Jack was, she is also banned from the games for a month and thus unable to complete the assignment for the magazine.

Episode 9: Unaired   "Kiss Harass Good-Bye"

Director: Ken Levine   Writers: Eva Almos and Ed Scharlach

The newspaper is having a sexual harassment seminar which Sylvia attends. Sylvia says she was sexually harassed by Trey thinking that he will be fired and that she will receive compensation. However, she finds that she would have a better case if the harassment was done by a superior. Jack comes forth to say that he was sexually harassed by his former boss Melissa and that she fired him because she wanted him sexually. Old Man Russell suspends Melissa until Jack's complaint is resolved. Ron tells Jack of the suspension and that Melissa wants Sylvia to console her. Jack as Sylvia goes to see Melissa who says that she had hated to fire Jack. Jack feels guilty about filing the complaint against Melissa and informs Russell that he is withdrawing his lawsuit.

Episode 10: Unaired   "Exes and Ohs"

Director: Steve Zuckerman   Writers: Gabrielle Allan and Ria Pavia

Jack is attracted to Janet, an employee at the paper who has broken up with her boyfriend. While Jack is chaperoning a slumber party with his daughter and her friends, Ron calls to tell him that Janet is with Melissa and other females from the paper consoling her over the break up and that he thinks Sylvia should join them. Jack has Ron supervise Blair's slumber party, and he goes as Sylvia to see Janet and the other women. While there, Sylvia leaves the room and, as Jack, phones Janet to ask her out. Melissa answers the call and hangs up on Jack. When Sylvia returns to his/her apartment, Blair sees her and asks "Harriet" for advice on why her parents divorced. Sylvia explains to Blair that her parents weren't mature enough when they married.

Episodes 11 and 12: "Dis-guise in Love with You"

Director: Amanda Bearse   Writers: Perry Rein and Gigi McCreery

In this two-parter, Jack's ex-wife Valerie returns, and Jack tries to hide everything he bought with Sylvia's paycheck since, to his ex, he is still unemployed. The two start fighting but end up in bed together. The next day, Jack tries to resume their relationship in order to save alimony, but Valerie finds one of Sylvia's dresses and threatens to end the relationship. Jack then arranges for Valerie to meet Sylvia at the office. Unfortunately the fire alarm goes off at the office, preventing Jack from changing out of Sylvia's outfit. When he comes home as Sylvia, Valerie is waiting for him in a sexy negligee. Jack has to tell her the truth about Sylvia to save his relationship with Valerie.

Episode 13: "Pumps and Circumstances" (summary based on final draft script)

Director: Lillian McCarthy   Writer: Pamela Ellis

Sylvia is on the cover of *Total Woman* magazine, and, due to the publicity from the magazine article, she has been invited to be the commencement speaker at Darnell University – the school Sylvia said she attended in the article. Jack wants Sylvia to get an honorary degree from the university since he never attended college and his late father would be pleased. Old Man Russell is a trustee for the university, and Ron went to the school. Both attend the commencement along with Sylvia. At the reception before the commencement, Sylvia meets the professor whom she replaced as the commencement speaker. The professor subsequently finds out that Sylvia never attended the school and threatens to tell everyone until Old Man Russell says he will purchase one million copies of the professor's book, *The Erosion of Ethics*. Old Man Russell informs Sylvia that he and all the trustees knew she didn't attend the university, but they wanted the publicity to increase enrollment. During her speech, Sylvia confesses she never went to the school.

Ask Not

Fox previewed *Ask Harriet* on Sunday, January 4, 1998, before moving the show to its regular time period on Thursdays where it lost over 5 million viewers from its

Sunday premiere. The last episode of the comedy on Thursdays scored one of Fox's worst ever first-run ratings for its time slot.

The Brian Benben Show

Premiered Monday, September 21, 1998, at 9:30 PM on CBS

A divorced news co-anchor who had been replaced and demoted was the premise of *The Brian Benben Show*. Benben had been anchor of the news on a Los Angeles TV station, KYLA-TV, but was replaced, along with his co-anchor, by younger, more attractive news people—Chad Rockwell (Charles Esten) and Tabitha Berkeley (Lisa Thornhill). Brian became a human interest reporter on *LA Story* when the incumbent in that position was crushed to death by a lovelorn ape while doing a story at the local zoo. Station manager, Beverly Shippel (Susan Blommaert), Kevin La Rue (Wendell Pierce), the sports anchor, and Billy Hernandez (Luis Antonio Ramos), the gay weatherman comprised the other staff at the TV station. Brian's friend and next door neighbor was Julia Martin (Lisa Vidal).

Background

The comedy was originally called *Benben* and then *The Benben Show*, but tests showed that the public thought the series was a children's clown show and so the title was changed to *The Brian Benben Show*. Robert Borden, the creator of *The Brian Benben Show*, later wrote and produced episodes of *The Drew Carey Show* and *Outsourced*. Warner Bros. and CBS Productions produced the sitcom.

Episode Guide: 4 aired; 5 unaired

Episode 1: September 21, 1998   "Pilot"

Director: Andrew D. Weyman   Writer: Robert Borden

The manager at the TV station where Brian works as a news anchor decides to replace him and his co-anchor with a new, young duo – Chad and Tabitha. Brian is fired but is rehired when the station's human interest reporter Freddy Fontaine is killed at the zoo by an ape in heat. Brian tries to get his old anchor job back by sabotaging Chad's Teleprompter, but then Chad makes Brian go live on air with his human interest story before he is ready. His first feature is to interview a 102 year-old woman, the oldest living person in L.A. and a former vaudevillian, who made music by blowing on different size bottles.

Episode 2: September 28, 1998 "House of Blues"

Director: Andrew D. Weyman   Writers: Don Payne and John Frink

Brian's chances of getting his old job back are diminished when the new co-anchors' ratings are higher than his and his former partner. Since Brian took a big pay cut in his new job at the station, he has to rethink his finances. He holds a yard sale for some of his stuff and considers television endorsements for a portable toilet manufacturer. But he thinks the ads are degrading and so decides to sell his house. Chad offers to purchase the house from him in cash. However, Brian rejects Chad's offer when he learns he is only buying the house to rub it in Brian's face. Brian ends up doing the endorsements for the toilet manufacturer.

Episode 3: October 5, 1998 "Brian's Got Back" (Part 1)

Director: Andrew D. Weyman   Writer: Alex Reid

Beverly goes on vacation and leaves Chad in charge who uses the opportunity to continue to torment Brian. Brian asks Chad if he can do a story about a corrupt city councilman. Chad approves it but first wants Brian to do a human interest story on clowns. The clowns frustrate Brian who assaults them on the air. To prevent a lawsuit, his station manager offers to take him to anger management classes. Meanwhile, Chad is praised when he steals Brian's story about the councilman. Brian deals with his anger at Chad by eating chocolate every time he would like to smash Chad's face and ends up gaining a lot of weight.

Kathy Kinney from *The Drew Carey Show* played the anger management class facilitator in this episode.

Episode 4: October 12, 1998   "Brian's Got Back" (Part 2)

Director: Andrew D. Weyman   Writer: Betsy Borns

Brian decides to do something about his weight gain particularly when women stop succumbing to his advances. However, the additional weight seems to cause Tabitha to become attracted to him. When Brian sees pictures of Tabitha's old boyfriends at her apartment, he realizes that she likes very large men. He goes on a diet, and six months later is back to his old weight.

Episode 5: Unaired   "Of Mice and Benben"

Director: Andrew D. Weyman   Writers: Pang-Ni Landrum and Maggie Bandur

After Julie convinces Brian to pursue a love life, he dates a woman named Summer, a militant vegetarian and environmentalist. Brian pretends to share the same beliefs as her, and they both end up tied to a tree.

Episode 6: Unaired   "Chad Dates Julie"

Director: Andrew D. Weyman   Writer: Jace Richdale

Brian tries in every way to show Kevin and Billy the evil side of Chad but fails every time. He then places a small camera in Julie's earring when she starts dating Chad in order to capture his evil side.

Episode 7: Unaired   "Have One for the Show"

Director: Andrew D. Weyman   Writer: Gail Lerner

For a segment of the news broadcast, Chad and Brian have to demonstrate how drinking affects driving using a video game. Since a couple of drinks do not seem to affect them, Beverly gives them some additional alcohol, and they quickly get drunk. While drunk, Chad and Brian bond which makes Julie very happy since she is dating Chad and is friends with Brian. The friendship doesn't last, however, and Chad and Brian try to hide from Julie the fact that they still intensely dislike each other.

Episode 8: Unaired   "Billy Don't Be a Hero"

Director: Andrew D. Weyman   Writer: Bobby Bowman

The news broadcast is tested by a focus group. Brian turns out to be the most popular with the group, and Billy the least popular. After refusing to change his segment of the show, Billy quits and is replaced by Brian. Despite the fact that Brian wants to help Billy get back on the air, he accidentally does a great job making it even harder for Brian to persuade the station manager to rehire Billy. Brian ends up blackmailing the station manager over compromising photos. After Billy returns to the show, it turns out that the station manager read the focus group results incorrectly and that Billy's segment was highly popular.

Episode 9: Unaired   "Motivating Kevin"

Director: Andrew D. Weyman   Writer: Robert Borden

While Kevin is giving a motivational speech to kids in the studio, Brian is doing a live report from a new sports-memorabilia restaurant where the owner shows evidence of a really embarrassing moment in football history – Kevin's final fumble on the field which resulted in his early retirement from the sport. When Kevin becomes very depressed, Brian tries to raise his spirits by going to the opening night of the restaurant to steal Kevin's football but finds real athletes defending the "treasure."

Athletes Kurt Rambis, Florence Griffith Joyner, and Kareem Abdul-Jabbar appeared as themselves on this episode.

Bye Bye Benben

This comedy followed *Everybody Loves Raymond* at 9:30 PM Mondays. Failing to hold on to its lead-in's audience, *The Brian Benben Show* was canceled after four episodes. The situation comedy ranked sixty-eighth out of 122 shows. *Becker*, starring Ted Danson, replaced it.

The Dictator

Supposed to premiere Tuesday, March 15, 1988 at 8:30 PM on CBS

The Dictator, another situation comedy that was canceled before it premiered, starred Christopher Lloyd (*Taxi, Back to the Future*) as Joseph Paul Domino, a deposed dictator from the Bando Islands in the South Seas who was now living in Rego Park, Queens, New York with his family and running a coin-operated laundromat. Wife Isabel (Deborah Rush), son Andrew (J.D. Cullum), and daughter Reggie (Robyn Lively) made up Domino's family. General Vesuvio (Joe Grifasi), the dictator's loyal aid, had been banished with him and was now working at Macy's. Eddie (David Alan Grier) was the attendant at Domino's laundromat. While his family was adjusting to life in the United States, Domino, always dressed in military garb, was plotting a return to his island nation and spoke to his supporters back home almost every week by radio.

Background

The Dictator was created by Andrew Bergman and was produced by Bergman, Bob Fraser, and Rob Dames. Bergman had written the original screenplay for the Mel Brooks' film *Blazing Saddles* and would script other movies as well such as *In-Laws* and *Honeymoon in Vegas*. Andy Ackerman directed *The Dictator* which was shot in New York City. Supposedly the producers originally wanted Carol Kane from *Taxi* for the role of Christopher Lloyd's wife before Deborah Rush was chosen. Two episodes were finished before the 1988 writer's strike. According to Rob Dames, they were in the process of rewriting the third episode when the strike occurred.[130] CBS originally contracted for six episodes. Lobell and Bergman Productions and Touchstone Television produced the series.

Episode Guide: 2 unaired episodes

Episode 1: "Reading, Writing and Rebellion" (summary based on reading script)

Writer: Gary Jacobs

From his laundromat, the dictator is overseeing a coup attempt against the current regime of the Bando Islands. Isabel has second thoughts about the coup thinking that they should wait until their strategic position improves. The dictator goes to a travel agent to make plans to fly back to his island nation, but then he finds that the coup has failed – one of the two coup leaders could not get his car started. Domino becomes depressed. However, a Mr. Driscoll, representing a group of concerned Americans, tells the dictator that he can get him back in power with gunboats and mercenaries. But Domino's son Andrew is worried that people on the island will be hurt. The dictator agonizes over a new coup attempt and says he wants a bloodless coup or no coup at all. The planned coup is called off.

J.D. Cullum (Andrew) is the son of Broadway actor, John Cullum. Deborah Rush (Mrs. Domino) married the son of Walter Cronkite, Chip Cronkite in 1985. Joe Grifasi (General Vesuvio) went on to another short-lived sitcom, *Some of My Best Friends*, where he portrayed Joe Zito.

Episode 2: "The Infantiki's Birthday" (summary based on first draft script)

Writer: John Swartzwelder

Domino and his family are celebrating the anniversary of the Infantiki's birthday. The Infantiki had led the Bando Islands into its "Era of Great Happiness." The Infantiki was five-years old at the time, but as the dictator says, he had wisdom beyond his years. Compared to him, other five-year olds were like children. Unfortunately, the Infantiki died from the vapors three months after turning five. Andrew says he cannot participate in the celebration because he has an interview with the Social Studies Honor Society at his school. Domino decides to invite the two boys and one girl from the society to celebrate the Infantiki's birthday and also interview Andrew. The kids sit through most of the ceremonial celebration, but, as they leave, the head of the group tells Andrew that anybody who puts up with this kind of "crap" deserves to be a member of the honor society. Andrew doesn't like the comment and changes his mind about joining the club.

Writer John Swartzwelder has written more episodes of *The Simpsons* than anyone else.

Deposed by a Strike

This comedy was to premiere on Tuesday, March 15, 1988, as CBS attempted to establish a new comedy night on that day. However, after producing two episodes of *The Dictator*, production on the series was suspended due to the writer's strike. CBS decided to replace it with Pam Dawber's comedy, *My Sister Sam*. By the time the writers' strike ended, the cast of the series had already found other work and so production never resumed. According to the late Bob Fraser, the strike was a merciful end to what he termed a very "iffy" show.[131]

Hank

Premiered Wednesday, September 30, 2009 at 8:00 PM on ABC

Hank Pryor (Kelsey Grammer), who had been the CEO of a company that managed a chain of 170 sporting goods stores, had lost his job and moved his family from New York City to River Bend, a small town in Virginia where his wife had grown up. Hank had been married to Matilda ("Tilly") played by Melinda McGraw for nineteen years. They had two kids: eleven-year-old Henry (Nathan Gamble) and teenager Maddie (Jordan Hinson). Tilly's brother Grady Funk (David Koechner), a building contractor, picked out their new less-than-spacious house for them.

Background

The comedy, originally titled *Awesome Hank* and then *Pryors*, was created by Tucker Cawley. McMonkey Productions, Werner Entertainment, and Warner Bros. Television produced *Hank*.

Episode Guide: 5 aired; 5 unaired

Episode 1: September 30, 2009   "Pilot"

Director: Andrew D. Weyman   Writer: Tucker Cawley

Since he is no longer a CEO, Hank tries to get re-acquainted with his family. The first night in their new home, Henry can't sleep because of the strangeness of the new place; Hank comforts him by confessing that he is also afraid of starting over in a new place.

Episode 2: October 7, 2009   "Yard Sale"

Director: Kelsey Grammer   Writers: Bill Martin and Mike Schiff

Hank wants to get rid of stuff the family isn't using and so decides to have a yard sale. Grady thinks that the Pryor family is selling things because they need money, and he offers Hank a job as a bookkeeper. When Hank refuses the offer, Tilly decides to take the job for something to do. However, Hank thinks that Tilly wants the job because she doesn't believe he will ever be a success again. After Tilly gives Hank a pep talk, he goes back to work selling the rest of the stuff at the yard sale.

Episode 3: October 14, 2009   "Drag Your Daughter to Work Day"

Director: Andrew D. Weyman   Writer: Tucker Cawley

To earn money for her own computer, Maddie is hired at an ice cream stand in the mall which happens to have an opening for another server. Since he has emphasized the importance of work to Maddie, Hank reluctantly takes the other server job at Maddie's request. Hank makes so many recommendations for improvements in the job that the manager lets him go after he questions the manager's authority. Hank is upset but is proud of Maddie when she gets her first paycheck.

Episode 4: October 21, 2009   "Relax, Don't Do It"

Director: Andrew D. Weyman   Writers: Jackie and Jeff Filgo

Finding it difficult to do nothing while unemployed, Hank oversees various projects like having the stairs in the house enlarged. Tilly wants him to relax, and she has her brother take Hank hunting. Hank eventually relaxes, but when he returns home, Tilly tries to keep him from finding out that the carpenters removed the stairs and won't install the new ones for another week thinking the house had a staircase in the back. When Hank discovers the stairs are missing, he says that this is what happens when he relaxes.

Episode 5: November 4, 2009   "Hanksgiving"

Director: Andrew D. Weyman   Writers: Jackie and Jeff Filgo

When Hank's mother-in-law, Mrs. Funk (Swoosie Kurtz), comes to visit for the first annual suburban Pryor family "Hanksgiving," he wants Tilly to prepare the Thanksgiving dinner from scratch, but she needs help from Grady and his wife. When her mother compliments Tilly on the meal, Tilly says that Hank was responsible for the feast.

Episode 6: Unaired   "Got It"" (summary for this episode and the following ones provided by Mike Schiff)

Director: Kelsey Grammer   Writer: Ilana Wernick

Hank is annoyed with Tilly's habit of saying "got it, got it, got it" every time he speaks to her but is reluctant to tell her this. Since Tilly is working for her brother, Hank convinces Grady that he hates the phrase "got it" as much as Hank does and instructs him to tell her to cut it out.

Episode 7: Unaired   "Hank's Got a Friend"

Director: Andrew D. Weyman   Writer: DJ Nash

At a tire store, Hank meets a man who seems like a kindred spirit. The Pryors befriend the man and his wife a bit over-eagerly and blow off plans with Tilly's brother and his wife. However, Hank and Tilly end up scaring off their new friends.

Episode 8: Unaired   "The Pryor Name"

Director: Andrew D. Weyman   Writer: Steve Skrovan

Hank discovers that Maddie has been using a fake last name at school to avoid the stigma of the Pryor name since her dad has become somewhat infamous. Hank isn't pleased by this and encourages Maddie to be proud of his name.

Episode 9: Unaired   "Tree House"

Director: Andrew D. Weyman   Writers: Tucker Cawley and DJ Nash

Hank tries to build a tree house for Henry but with disastrous results. Meanwhile, Maddie skips her chores.

Episode 10: Unaired   "Dog"

Director: Gail Mancusco   Writers: Bill Martin and Mike Schiff

While Pryor Sporting Goods is re-opening as PSG, an extreme superstore, Hank lets the kids adopt a mangy mutt rather than the purebred he'd prefer. The kids quickly abandon the dog, but Hanks believes the dog is capable of greatness though the rest of the world can't see it. Soon, Hank is protecting the dog as if it were himself. Meanwhile, Hank visits PSG and is appalled by how they've removed anything he can recognize as his own from the place. The sales clerk doesn't even realize that the "P" stands for "Pryor." Feeling totally forgotten, Hank is depressed until the dog performs a trick Hank had been training him to do, proving that old dogs can learn new tricks. Hank announces that he has bought the abandoned storefront where his very first store had been. He doesn't know what he is going to do with it, but he sees a chance to begin anew.

This episode was an attempt to give the comedy a bit of a new direction, but by then it was too late.

Hank Yanked

Hank led off ABC's new Wednesday night of comedy for the 2009-10 TV season. The debut episode won its timeslot, but ratings for each subsequent episode declined. The second episode of the series ranked fifty-seventh out of ninety-three shows. *Hank* was canceled on November 11, 2009 with only five of ten episodes airing. For the 2009-10 season overall, this comedy ranked sixty-sixth out of 124 series.

Kitchen Confidential

Premiered Monday, September 19, 2005, at 8:30 PM on Fox

Chef Jack Bourdain (Bradley Cooper) was trying a comeback as a head chef at a top New York restaurant. Too much liquor, women, and drugs had cost him his previous job as a chef four years earlier. Pino Lugeria (Frank Langella) owned Nolita, the restaurant at which Jack was making his comeback. Jack's staff at the restaurant consisted of Steven Daedalus (Owain Yeoman), the sous chef as well as a thief; Seth Richman (Nicholas Brandon), the womanizing pastry chef; Teddy Wong (John Cho), the seafood chef; Jim (John Francis Daley, *Freaks and Geeks*, *Regular Joe*), the eager-to-please rookie; Tanya (Jaime King), the sexy hostess, and Ramon (Frank Alvarez), the dishwasher. Pino's daughter Mimi (Bonnie Somerville) also worked at Nolita.

Background

Kitchen Confidential was adapted from Chef Anthony Bourdain's autobiography, *Kitchen Confidential: Adventures in the Culinary Underbelly*. An attempt had been made to produce a movie called *Seared* starring Brad Pitt based on Bourdain's book, but, when that project failed, a sitcom was developed by David Hemingson starring Bradley Cooper. Monkey Proof Productions, Darren Star Productions, and New Line Productions in association with Twentieth Century-Fox Television produced the series.

Episode Guide: 4 aired; 9 unaired

Episode 1: September 19, 2005   "Exile on Main Street"

Director: Darren Star   Writer: David Hemingson

Thanks to Jack's current girlfriend sending out his resume to various restaurants, Pino Lugeria wants Jack Bourdain to take over as head chef at his restaurant and to assemble a crew in twenty-four hours. Jack goes back to his old friends offering them all a chance to work together again. While preparing food for opening night, Steven cuts the tip of his finger off, and it ends up on someone's plate of food.

Restaurant staff takes everyone's plates away looking for the finger tip. It ended up on a visiting food critic's plate, but she doesn't see it before her plate is taken. The critic likes what food she was able to eat. While she doesn't like the service, she does print in her newspaper that the food was excellent. However, Pino's daughter does not like her dad's decision and resents Jack taking over.

Director Darren Star created the series *Beverly Hills, 90210*, *Melrose Place*, and *Sex and the City*.

Episode 2: September 26, 2005 "Aftermath"

Director: Darren Star   Writer: David Hemingson

When Pino suspects Steven of stealing steaks, Jack wants to change Steven and himself from their old ways. It turns out that Steven was exchanging steaks for a certain type of mushrooms and then wanted to exchange the mushrooms for lobster. Tired of Jack's strict supervision of the staff, Seth and Steven take him to a bar to find a woman. At the bar, Jack runs into an ex-girlfriend whom he invites to the restaurant for dinner. When she comes to the restaurant, she and Jack make up, and she asks him to come back to her place. However, right before closing, a group of stockbrokers enter the restaurant, order $1000 bottles of wine, rack up an $18,000 bill, and then leave without paying it. Steven goes after them and gets them to pay. Jack finally leaves the restaurant to go to his ex-girlfriend's apartment but falls asleep before they can make love.

Owain Yeoman (Steven) later became a regular on the TV series *The Mentalist*.

Episode 3: October 3, 2005 "Dinner Date with Death"

Director: Michael Spiller   Writers: Joshua Sternin and Jeffrey Ventimilia

Jack's old mentor, Chef Gerard (John Laroquette) comes to the restaurant. He has been visiting all of the restaurants of his former students and eating rich food even though he has heart problems. He now wants to have his last meals at Nolita. Chef Gerard says he will dine at the restaurant every night until he dies. Meanwhile, a hot dog vendor sets up his cart outside Nolita to feed the overflow crowd much to the dismay of the restaurant staff. Jack prepares one last meal for Chef Gerard which he promises will kill him, but he cannot bring himself to serve it. Chef Gerard leaves the restaurant without eating, gets a hot dog from the vendor, keels over, and dies.

Episode 4: December 5, 2005   "French Fight"

Director: Henry Chan   Writer: Dan Sterling

A nearby French restaurant steals a lamb dish from Nolita's menu. Mimi goes to the restaurant to resolve the problem but ends up sleeping with Michel (Michael Vartan), the restaurant's owner. Nolita's kitchen staff declares war on the other restaurant, resulting in Nolita hiring the French restaurant's bread baker and then having their computer system crash in retaliation. Steven takes the compressor out of the refrigerators in the French restaurant spoiling their food with that restaurant fighting back by cutting off Nolita's electricity. Chef Jack has Jimmy deliver live rats to Michel's restaurant, but Jimmy ends up naked in ice with sardines. Finally, after Jack calls the Immigration Service about Michel, Michel faces deportation for tax fraud.

Episode 5: Unaired   "You Lose, I Win"

Director: Victoria Hochberg   Writer: Stacy Traub

Because Jack needs to spend more time with the restaurant's patrons in order for the business to succeed, he hires Becky (Erinn Hayes) to be the head chef which doesn't go over well with the rest of his staff. While the restaurant becomes successful, Jack becomes jealous of Becky. To make him feel needed again by the kitchen staff, he says that Becky's dish of short ribs is inedible despite the fact that all the diners love it. Meanwhile, Mimi's old loser friend, Jessica, shows up with a very handsome fiancé, causing Mimi to be jealous of her.

Episode 6: Unaired   "Rabbit Test"

Director: Dennie Gordon   Writers: Joshua Sternin and Jeffrey Ventimilia

Jimmy accidentally accepts a delivery of live rabbits for the restaurant, but no one has the heart to kill them. Julia, a woman who is a vegan, visits the restaurant, and Jack begins dating her. He gets her to eat pizza with sausage which she devours. She binges on meat and gets sick. Meanwhile, Jack institutes a no-dating policy among kitchen staff which prompts Becky and Steven to flirt with each other by taking pictures of themselves with few clothes on, and Becky teases Jimmy to the point where he has an erection every time he sees her. In the end, Becky and Jack have sex.

Episode 7: Unaired "Let's Do Brunch"

Director: Victor Nelli, Jr.   Writer: Richard Appel

Jack and Becky's secret affair continues, while Pino is opening another restaurant. Becky convinces Jack to start serving brunch despite the fact that the rest of the staff is against the idea. At Becky's suggestion, Jack puts her in charge of brunch. When Seth discovers that Jack and Becky are sleeping together, Jack swears him to secrecy. Seth is hit by a van and taken to the hospital where Teddy visits him and finds out about Jack and Becky. The kitchen staff becomes aware that they have to do brunch because Jack is sleeping with Becky. In the end, Nolita keeps brunch because it is very profitable, while Becky will be the head chef at Pino's new restaurant since her managing Nolita's brunch was so successful.

Episode 8: Unaired "Teddy Takes Off"

Director: Michael Spiller   Writer: Dan Sterling

Jack takes credit for a yellow fin tuna dish that Teddy prepared which is favorably reviewed in *Food and Wine* magazine. Teddy quits in anger, and Jack decides to hire Chet, another seafood chef, which doesn't set well with the kitchen staff. Teddy takes a job at Jazz Fish a restaurant where he is propositioned by two waitresses wanting a threesome. Meanwhile, after Jack's restaurant is flooded with requests for the yellow fin tuna dish reviewed in the magazine, Jack realizes he doesn't know how to prepare it properly. Also, the kitchen staff tries to break the new seafood chef with Steven finally drugging him. Jack fires Chet, kidnaps Teddy, and takes him back.

After *Kitchen Confidential*, John Cho (Teddy) starred on the unaired sitcom *The Singles Table*.

Episode 9: Unaired "The Robbery"

Director: Fred Savage Writer: Lesley Wake

Armed robbers target the restaurant and rob the diners and kitchen staff. The publicity causes the number of patrons to dwindle. Jack thinks he tempted fate by enjoying his success too much. He begins cold calling customers to come back but without positive results. When Jack invites a gossip columnist to dine at the restaurant to get some good publicity, a sewer line breaks near the establishment driving the few customers away. Steven throws a model party to try to revive business, but the staff realizes that the models eat the food only to purge it. Pino tells Jack that if a person has talent and works hard, customers will come back on their own which they do eventually.

Episode 10: Unaired "Praise be Praise"

Director: Peter Lauer Writer: Richard Appel

Jimmy tries to impress Jack with his initiative in the kitchen, but his good intentions turn against him leading Jack to give Jimmy the silent treatment. Jack institutes a "no send back" policy which annoys Mimi. He also hooks up with an attractive woman at a bar who rates chefs on their sexual prowess on her chef hunter website, and he does not rate all that well. Jack then finds that none of the women at the bar are interested in him. He goes back to the woman to ask for a second chance and ends up cooking for her. When he gets his second chance with her, she finds the experience so intimate that she doesn't want to write about it.

Episode 11: Unaired "An Affair to Remember"

Director: Lev L. Spiro Writer: Lesley Wake

Pino is having a party at Nolita for his wife, while Jack meets and beds the tenant who lives above the restaurant. The tenant turns out to be Pino's mistress and shows up at the party Pino is throwing for his wife. When she threatens to tell all, Pino asks Jack to entertain her. After she informs Pino that Jack is her new boyfriend, Jack advises Pino that that is just a cover story so Pino's wife doesn't find out about her. Pino gives the restaurant to Mimi because she is tired of covering up for her dad and his mistress, and he gives Jack the apartment above the restaurant since Pino is moving his mistress to Italy. Meanwhile, Steven, Teddy, and Seth plan to take Jimmy out to find him a girl, but instead they use the pitiful story they tell about him to pick up women themselves. However, Tanya, the restaurant's hostess, begins to show an interest in Jimmy.

Episode 12: Unaired   "Power Play"

Director: Matt Shakman   Writer: Stacy Traub

Mimi and Jack clash over control of the restaurant. Mimi takes over Jack's office and goes around him directly to the kitchen staff by having a contest for best appetizer to add to the menu and by buying the staff the equipment they want. A health inspector arrives for a surprise inspection while Mimi assigned Jimmy the task of cleaning the overhead duct work. When Jimmy falls on top of the inspector, Jack has to bribe the inspector so she will not cite the restaurant. Mimi and Jack then agree to cooperate in running the place.

Episode 13: Unaired   "And the Award Goes To…"

Director: Leo L. Spiro   Writer: Karine Rosenthal

The restaurant is nominated for an Epicure award. Becky drops by and sees that Nolita will prepare Portuguese eel for the contest judge. After Pino tells Mimi that his new restaurant is in competition with Nolita for the award, Jack gets mad that Becky hadn't told him this. However, he continues to have sex with her, and, when they have sex in the kitchen, she intentionally kicks a hole in the container holding the Portuguese eel causing them to drop to the floor and die. Meanwhile, Seth discovers that Jimmy is dating Tanya, and Ramon sees the Virgin Mary in a prize lobster. When the judge for the award arrives at Nolita, Jack wants to cook the prize lobster since he no longer has the Portuguese eel, but Becky brings Jack the eel she got to prepare at her restaurant for the judge.

The Kitchen Is Closed

Paired with *Arrested Development*, the two comedies failed to attract a large audience. After three episodes, *Kitchen Confidential* went on hiatus until the Major League

Baseball playoffs were over. It came back in December for one episode, which ranked fifth in its timeslot against the series on four other networks, and then the comedy was canceled. After *Kitchen Confidential*, Bradley Cooper became a star of feature films like *Yes Man*, *He's Just Not That Into You*, and *The Hangover*. In May 2007, Twentieth Century-Fox released all thirteen episodes of the series on DVD.

Take Five

Premiered Wednesday, April 1, 1987 at 8:30 PM on CBS

Take Five, which was paired with *Roxie* on Wednesdays, starred George Segal (*Just Shoot Me*, *Retired at 35*) as a newly divorced man who had also recently been fired from a public relations job by his ex-father-in-law. His character, Andy Kooper, played the banjo in a semi-professional Dixieland jazz quartet where one of the members of the quartet, Monty (Bruce Jarchow) was dating Andy's ex-wife. Other members of the Lenny Goodman Quartet were Lenny (Jim Haynie) and Al (Derek McGrath). Andy had two daughters – fourteen-year-old Katie and twenty-one-year-old Cynthia. Kooper had found a new position with a public relations firm where the recently retired boss, Max Davis (Eugene Roche) put his incompetent son, Kevin (Todd Field) in charge. Andy's job at the new firm was to clean up Kevin's messes without letting him know he was doing it. Laraine McDermott (Melanie Chartoff), the boss's secretary, disliked Andy because she had sought the position he got. Dr. Noah Wolf (Severn Darden) was Andy's psychiatrist.

Background

Ron Howard and Brian Grazer executive produced this series. The writing team of Lowell Ganz and Babaloo Mandel created *Take Five*. Previously they had adapted Ron Howard's movie *Gung Ho* into a short-lived series on ABC. Imagine Films and Empire City Productions, Inc. produced *Take Five*.

STARTING OVER

Episode Guide: 2 aired; 4 unaired

Episode 1: April 1, 1987   "Kooper with a K"

Director: Barnet Kellman   Writers: Lowell Ganz and Babaloo Mandel

Andy Kooper's wife leaves him after twenty-one years of marriage, and his father-in-law boss fires him. Andy takes his mid-life crisis to a shrink. He then discovers that Monty, one of the members of his jazz quartet, has been seeing his ex-wife, and Monty regales Andy with news of a tryst with Andy's former wife in a national park. Andy does find another job with Davis & Son, a PR firm where the retiring head of the firm wants him to run the company while retaining his bumbling son.

The title of this episode was the original title for the series.

Episode 2: April 8, 1987   "The Return of Monty"

Director: Barnett Kellman   Writer: David Misch

Monty shows up at practice for the Lenny Goodman Quartet to reconcile with Andy. Everything goes fine until Monty brags about the new drum set Andy's former spouse bought for him.

George Segal got the writers of the series to have his character play the banjo since Segal played the instrument in real life.

Episode 3: Unaired   "The Boss is Back"

Director: Michael Lessac   Writers: Bob Pekurny and Barry Rubinowitz

After returning from a training seminar, Andy's young boss, Kevin, finds that one of his employees has been undermining his authority behind his back. Kevin wants everyone to take a lie detector test to find the culprit. During the test, Andy denies that he has been defying Kevin's orders, but later he confesses that Kevin's dad hired him to manage the firm since the dad didn't think that Kevin could handle the business himself. Kevin thinks that Andy is just fantasizing and says he will forgive and forget.

Todd Field (Kevin) later became a writer/director of such feature films as *In the Bedroom* and *Little Children*.

Episode 4: Unaired   "George's Dream Girl"

Director: Michael Lessac   Writers: Andy Cowan and David S. Willinger

When Kevin wants Andy to go after an account for young urban professionals, Andy meets Maggie, a friend of his who works for a competing public relations firm. He asks her out but then says that he has a lot of conflicting emotions about dating again and asks for her patience. When Maggie doesn't return his phone calls, Andy's friends tell him that it is probably because he didn't have sex with her. Andy meets Maggie at the presentation for their prospective clients, and she lets him know that she can't deal with his hang ups. In the end, Andy has a dream that Maggie comes to him and values his beliefs, but it is only a daydream.

Episode 5: Unaired   "My Friend, Dad"

Director: Michael Lessac   Writer: Ron Zimmerman

Andy's oldest daughter Cynthia, who works for the *National Tattler*, writes an unflattering article about one of Andy's clients – a popular TV star. Andy wants his daughter to retract the story, but, when she won't, Andy gets the star to reveal his true self to the world.

Episode 6: Unaired   "Men Who Hate Men Who Hate Women"

Director: Michael Lessac   Writer: Marjorie Gross

Laraine suggests a guy named Gary as a replacement for an ailing Lenny in Andy's jazz quartet. Gary starts making advances to Andy's daughter Cynthia. Matters get complicated when Andy finds that Gary is Laraine's boyfriend. He feels obligated to discourage both Cynthia and Laraine from dating a womanizer.

Marjorie Gross who scripted this episode is best known for writing several episodes of *Seinfeld* such as "The Understudy" and "The Shower Head." She passed away in 1996 at age forty from ovarian cancer.

Take Over

Take Five premiered following *Roxie* and, like *Roxie*, was canceled after two episodes. The premiere of *Take Five* was ranked sixty-fourth out of seventy shows.

Jeffrey Kramer and Jack Elam in *Struck by Lightning*

Chapter 16
Surprising Arrivals and Unexpected Inheritances

T he premise of an unexpected visitor or long-lost relative showing up has been a sitcom staple for years, as has the idea of an individual or family coming into a sudden windfall. However, these ideas are usually themes of a single episode and not the underlying concept of an entire series. It is difficult to maintain the surprise element of such premises throughout a full series run – something with which the sitcoms described in this chapter did not really have to contend.

Beware of Dog

Previewed Tuesday, August 13, 2002, at 8:00 PM on Animal Planet

The cable network Animal Planet's first and only attempt at a situation comedy was about a stray, mix, bearded collie named Jack (after Jack Nicholson because of the dog's sexy charm) enticing a family to take care of him. Jack (Chip) feigned an injury in a grocery store parking lot to get the attention of the Poole family so they would take him home. Bill Poole (Richard Waugh) and his wife Mary (Carolyn Dunn) had two children – sixteen-year-old Jessica (Alex Appel) and twelve-year-old Matt (Gage Knox). What made *Beware of Dog* different from, say, the *Lassie* series, was that the dog provided voice-over narration to the viewing audience about the events in each episode. Jack was voiced by Canadian actor Park Bench.

Background

Rob Gilmer created *Beware of Dog*, which was produced by Nelvana Entertainment in association with Alexander/Enright and Associates. Only two episodes of the series were produced.

Episode Guide: 2 aired episodes

Episode 1: August 13, 2002   "Born to be Wild"

Director: Richard Martin   Writer: Rob Gilmer

While looking for a home, Jack stands behind the Poole family car as Jessica is backing out of a parking spot at the local grocery. He pretends to be injured in hopes of becoming part of the family. The Poole's intend to keep Jack just until he recovers, but he becomes a permanent member of the family after disrupting a family argument and saving Mark from a bully. Jack skateboards in this episode.

Episode 2: August 13, 2002   "Hit the Road Jack"

Director: Richard Martin   Writer: Rob Gilmer

Jack ruins Bill Poole's vacation plans and is kicked out of the house. However, the family begins to miss him, and, after Bill has a change of heart, the family starts to look for Jack.

Director Richard Martin is the son of the late comedian and director Dick Martin.

SURPRISING ARRIVALS AND UNEXPECTED INHERITANCES   541

Dog Gone

Beware of Dog was supposed to have been given a regular time slot on Animal Planet in 2003, but that never happened. According to Rob Gilmer, the comedy was an unsettling experiment for the cable network since it had never done half-hour sitcoms before.[132] The producers of the series lobbied Animal Planet to spend money on off-network ads to promote *Beware of Dog* to people who didn't usually watch the cable channel. They also wrote a series of TV spots and billboard copy for the comedy which were never used by Animal Planet.

Bram & Alice

Premiered Sunday, October 6, 2002, at 8:30 PM on CBS

Bram Sheppard (Alfred Molina), a novelist, and his estranged daughter who suddenly showed up in his life were the focus of this comedy. Bram, who had not published a new book in more than twenty years, was still living off the sales of his previous Pulitzer Prize–winning novel. Alice O'Connor (Traylor Howard) wanted to be a novelist and found that her real father was Bram Sheppard, with whom her mother once had a brief affair. Other characters on the comedy were Paul Newman (not the actor but Roger Bart), who was Bram's assistant; Katie Hoover (Katie Finneran), one of Bram's neighbors, and Michael (Michael Rispoli, *My Guys*), the bartender in the ground floor lounge of Bram's apartment building. Katie Hoover had an unseen Japanese boyfriend named Toshiro on the series.

Background

Two of the producers of the hit *Frasier*, Joe Keenan and Christopher Lloyd, created *Bram & Alice*. They had a deal with CBS to develop a situation comedy for the network and decided, after writing for a conscientious character like Frasier Crane for a number of years, to develop a comedy around a character who was incredibly shameless. Originally, *Bram and Alice* was scheduled to follow *60 Minutes* at 8:00 PM on Sundays. Ted Danson's comedy, *Becker*, was to follow *Bram & Alice*. However, CBS decided to flip-flop the two series before their fall premieres. Knotty

Entertainment and Picador Productions in association with Paramount produced the sitcom.

Episode Guide: 4 aired; 5 unaired

Episode 1: October 6, 2002   "Pilot"

Director: James Burrows   Writers: Joe Keenan and Christopher Lloyd

Six months earlier, Alice O'Conner had moved from Vermont to New York City to be a writer. Her mother comes to visit her and encourages her not to give up on her dream. The mother tells Alice that when prize-winning novelist Bram Shepherd was teaching at Vassar and she was a secretary there, she had a one-night stand with Bram and that he is Alice's dad. When Alice goes to see Bram at his apartment, he initially assumes that Alice is one of his former one-night stands that he could not remember, and so he flirts with her. Needless to say, Alice finds that Bram is not the man she had thought he was. Alice says that she is moving back to Vermont. However, when Bram shows her the guest room, and she volunteers to pay rent, Bram invites her to stay.

Episode 2: October 13, 2002   "Cat Burglar"

Director: Jerry Zaks   Writers: Joe Keenan and Christopher Lloyd

Alice moves in with Bram, and he meets Alice's boyfriend Billy, who is old enough to be her father. Bram jumps to the conclusion that Alice has a "daddy complex" and feels that he cannot be a good father. He takes out his frustrations by giving her cat to a neighbor who has a lot of cats. Alice breaks up with Billy and, on the same day, tells Bram that it is her birthday. Bram feels guilty for giving away her cat and sends Paul to get it back.

Episode 3: October 20, 2002   "Paul-Pot"

Director: Jerry Zaks Writer: Michael Davidoff

Because Bram hasn't been paying his bills, Alice tries to get his finances in order. To get some money, Bram plays poker with his downstairs neighbor Buddy who publishes a big and tall man's catalog. Things go wrong when he can't cover his bet, and he offers Paul's services as an assistant to the winner who turns out to be Buddy. When Paul refuses to work for Buddy, Bram promises Buddy that Alice will go to a jazz concert with him. He tricks Alice into going out with Buddy, but, when she finds out what he did before she leaves for the concert, she balks at going. In order to pay what he owes Buddy, Bram ends up as a model in Buddy's catalog.

Episode 4: October 27, 2002   "Goody Two Shoes"

Director: Jerry Zaks   Writer: Jennifer Crittenden

Alice is always doing good things for people like helping with a Girl Scout troop, while Bram is preoccupied with finding a woman whom he can escort to the big conservancy gala since he did not get an invitation himself. Alice invites a homeless man to the apartment to try on Bram's old suit. Meanwhile, Bram has bedded Patricia, a neighbor, whom he thinks will allow him to accompany her to the gala. Paul believes that Alice slept with the homeless man and informs Bram who makes fun of Alice's goody two shoes image in front of Patricia until Alice corrects him. Patricia then feels so ashamed about her one night stand with Bram that she doesn't go to the gala.

Episode 5: Unaired   "Required Reading"

Director: Jerry Zaks   Writers: Paul Corrigan and Brad Walsh

Bram holds a class for aspiring writers and hopes to have sex with one of his students, Kristen, who has written a novel she wants him to read. Bram, not wanting to spend time reading Kristen's book, asks Alice to read it leaving her under the impression that it is his new novel. Alice thinks that the book about a supermodel who becomes a marine biologist is really bad, but she doesn't want to hurt Bram's feelings. Alice does eventually tell Bram that she didn't like the book, and she also mentions the novel to one of her friends. The news of Bram's new book shows up in the newspaper, and, when Kristen stops by the apartment to find out what Bram thought of her work, Alice reveals to her that she – not Bram- read her book. Of course, this revelation ends the possibility of Bram having sex with Kristen.

Episode 6: Unaired   "Getting to Know You"

Director: Jerry Zaks   Writer: Adam Braff

Bram shows no interest in small talk with Alice. He's jealous that his rival Vernon Landry is getting a lot of publicity for his new book, while Bram hasn't published a new novel in many years. Paul tries to get Bram some publicity and finally lands an interview for him with *New York Magazine*. When the interviewer arrives at Bram's apartment, Alice is there because she has a very bad cold and can't go to her temp job. Because Bram doesn't want to reveal his relationship with Alice to reporters, he tries to keep Alice in the kitchen by giving her his special cold remedy. However, when coming into the living room where the reporter is, Alice is accidentally knocked unconscious by Bram. When the EMS techs arrive, Bram has to inform them that Alice is his daughter which the reporter overhears, but, when the EMS techs ask about Alice's medical history, Bram knows nothing which the reporter also hears. Anticipating that the magazine will not be kind to him with respect to his relationship with his daughter, Bram wants to learn more about Alice.

Episode 7: Unaired   "Book of the Dead"

Director: Jerry Zaks   Writers: Paul Corrigan and Brad Walsh

Bram is being pursued by two of his ex-wives for past due alimony payments and thinks that a writing assignment about the Orient Express will not only be adventurous but financially rewarding as well. However, he discovers the assignment is to review a chain of airport restaurants called the Orient Express and isn't about traveling across Europe in a train. When a neighbor in the apartment building dies, Bram remembers that he gave a first edition of his novel to the gentleman and that edition would now be valuable enough to cover his alimony payments. He decides to go to the memorial service being held in the old man's apartment to try to get the book. Alice discovers he is stealing the book and tells him to put it back. However, later he returns to the memorial service with his assistant and retrieves the book. In a subplot, Katie reunites with her ex-skating partner whom she still secretly loves but finds that she doesn't love him as much as she does Toshiro.

Katie Finneran (Katie) more recently starred on the Fox comedy *I Hate My Teenage Daughter*.

Episode 8: Unaired   "Scribbling Rivalry"

Director: Will MacKenzie   Writer: Jennifer Crittenden

Alice asks Bram to read a story she just finished and give her an honest opinion of it. She then meets Mark, one of Bram's students, and they agree to date. Bram tells Alice that her story was "solid," but, when Mark stops by to pick up Alice, Bram says that his story was "brilliant" and that he has a great future as a writer. Alice becomes jealous of Mark, and she subconsciously begins to harm him by, for example, accidentally hitting him. Bram gives Alice one of his early works to read, and she finds that he was not that great a writer at the beginning of his career. Bram explains that writers do get better as time goes on. Meanwhile, Katie asks Paul over to help her hang a picture. When Toshiro calls Katie and hears Paul in the background, he presumes that Katie is fooling around with Paul – a mistake that Katie exploits to make Toshiro jealous.

Episode 9: Unaired   "Alice Doesn't Live Here Anymore"

Director: Will MacKenzie   Writers: Ken Levine and David Isaacs

Alice tells Bram that he is not honest with her about things like picking up clothes from the dry cleaners. However, Alice doesn't mention to Bram that her mother Margaret (Harriet Samson Harris) is coming to visit and that she has yet to let her mother know that she is living in Bram's apartment. In front of Margaret, Bram has to pretend that he is meeting Alice for the first time. Alice says she didn't inform Bram about her mother coming to New York City because she thought that Margaret and Bram would try to rekindle their lust for each other. When Bram, in front of Margaret, offers Alice his guest room, Margaret thinks he is speaking to her and accepts. However, after she goes in the guest room and sees two pictures of her on the wall, she thinks that is creepy and decides not to stay. Bram then directly offers the guest room to Alice, and her mother thinks it is a great idea.

Traylor Howard (Alice) later became Monk's assistant on the series of the same name.

Poor Ratings, Poor Reviews

Citing the following dialogue from the first episode, *USA Today* said that it hoped that *Bram & Alice* would not become TV's first incest sitcom:[133]

> Dad: "I'm looking at your face to see if you might have my eyes or my nose."
>
> Daughter: "I nearly had your tongue an hour ago".

Other critics used the words "awful," "dreck," "dreadful," and "wretched" to describe this comedy. *Bram & Alice* lost viewers from its lead-in, *Becker*. The first episode ranked forty-second; the second episode rated fiftieth; the third, fifty-sixth, and the fourth and final one, seventy-third. *Bram & Alice* did later air on the Universal HD cable channel.

God, the Devil and Bob

Premiered Thursday, March 9, 2000, at 8:30 PM before moving to Tuesdays at 8:30 PM on NBC

Bob Alman (voiced by French Stewart) received a surprise visit from both God (James Garner) and the Devil (Alan Cumming) in this animated comedy. God was about to give up on the world but decided that if one soul can prove the world needs saving, he wouldn't destroy it. Having a sense of humor, God let the Devil choose the soul, and the Devil chose Bob Alman, a thirty-two year-old auto worker in Detroit. Bob was married to Donna (Laurie Metcalf), and the couple had two children – thirteen-year-old Megan (Nancy Cartwright) and six-year-old Andy (Kath Soucie). God appeared to Bob in human form with white hair and a beard wearing sunglasses and casual clothes. The Devil was attired in black and had a British accent and a faithful assistant named Smeck (Jeff Doucette). Besides Bob, his son Andy could also see God in human form.

SURPRISING ARRIVALS AND UNEXPECTED INHERITANCES

Background

The series was created by Matthew Carlson and produced by Vanity, Carsey-Werner Productions and NBC. Originally developed for the Fox network, NBC snapped up the comedy when Fox decided to pass on it because of the number of animated shows it already had. Robert Downey, Jr. was hired to voice the Devil, but Alan Cumming took on this role when Downey was forced to leave the project because of his addiction to drugs at the time.

Episode Guide: 4 aired; 9 unaired

Episode 1: March 9, 2000 "In the Beginning"

Director: Jeff DeGrandis   Writer: Matthew Carlson

God approaches Bob in a bar and opens up the earth to prove that He is real. The Devil wants to tempt and ultimately destroy Bob so the world is his. Bob feels he has no clue on how to save the world. From a wino, Bob gets the idea of helping the needy and then takes his daughter to the mall to cheer her up. She is depressed because she feels she is not like all her friends since she has yet to get her period. Bob tries to understand her problem. God says that helping Megan is a good start in saving the world.

Nancy Cartwright, who voiced Megan, is the voice of Bart Simpson.

Episode 2: March 14, 2000 "Andy Runs Away"

Director: Swinton O. Scott III   Writer: Matthew Carlson

When Andy's friends at school don't believe that his dad has been designated by God to save the world, Andy asks his dad to have God make an appearance. After God declines Bob's request, Bob pretends he is God. Andy's friends discover that his father is masquerading as God and make fun of Andy. Andy is upset and boards a train to Canada. Bob receives a call from a waitress in Canada about his son and goes to pick him up. Bob gets Andy and advises him that God summons him and not vice versa. Andy goes back to school, and, in the end, Bob and God show up at Andy's kickball game where Andy helps his team win.

Episode 3: March 21, 2000 "Date from Hell"

Director: Steve Ressel   Writer: Matthew Carlson

Because the Devil feels that Bob doesn't respect him, he disguises himself as Jordan, a teenager, on whom Megan develops a crush. Bob discovers that Jordan is really the Devil, but Donna and Megan don't believe him. When he asks God to stop the Devil from dating Megan, God advises him to have faith in her. Donna and Megan plot to let her see Jordan without Bob's knowledge. When he finds out that Megan is at the ice rink with Jordan, Bob rushes to get her back. At the rink, Jordan talks a lot about evil, while Megan goes on and on about her life and friends. Jordan is so bored with Megan that he dematerializes and goes back to Hell.

Episode 4: March 28, 2000 "The Devil's Birthday"

Director: Sherie Pollack   Writer: Matthew Carlson

After God forgets the Devil's birthday, the Devil thinks that God is taking him for granted. The Devil informs Bob that he is leaving the world and taking all the evil with him. Bob finds that his wife and daughter begin agreeing with everything he wants and that everyone at work is happy. God feels that the Devil leaving the world to concentrate on maintaining Hell has upset everything. He says, "Without evil in the world, 'good' is meaningless." God sends Bob to Hell to get the Devil back in the world. Bob invites the Devil and God to a barbecue at his place where he gets them to respect one another.

Episode 5: Unaired   "Neighbor's Keeper"

Director: Sherie Pollack   Writer: Matthew Carlson

God wants Bob to save his neighbors, Randy and Stacy's, marriage. Bob talks with Stacy about her adulterous ways. Donna is irritated that Bob keeps going over to Stacy's every night to help her from committing adultery. When he speaks with Randy, Bob says that Stacy feels that Randy doesn't listen to her and that if they both love one another, they should stay together. Bob then listens to Donna about her concerns over going back to college after fourteen years.

Episode 6: Unaired   "God's Favorite"

Director: Dan Fausett   Writer: Matthew Carlson

Bob thinks that God has made him indestructible after he survives a bad accident at work. Bob takes his wife and kids to a family fun center and is mugged outside the center when he uses an ATM. He stands up to the mugger who has a gun, and this incident further reinforces his idea that he is indestructible. Bob tries skydiving without a parachute. On the way down, God says that he is going to die and that it was just dumb luck that he survived the other events. Bob latches on to a skydiver with a parachute who saves his life.

Episode 7: Unaired   "Bob Gets Committed"

Director: Steve Ressel   Writer: Alex Reid

God wants Bob to put up a billboard with the word "smile" on it. After Bob paints over an existing billboard, a cop stops by, and the Devil makes Bob slap the police officer. Bob is arrested, and, when he says he is a messenger of God, he is committed to a mental hospital. The Devil disguises himself as Bob and goes to Bob's home where he pleads with Donna to have sex with him and then contracts the measles from Andy. Bob escapes from the mental hospital in a hot air balloon and, following the advice of another patient in the hospital, sings "Tie a Yellow Ribbon Around the Old Oak Tree" to send the Devil back to Hell.

Episode 8: Unaired   "Lonely at the Top"

Director: Dan Fausett   Writer: Alex Reid

God comes to Bob's workplace because He is lonely and wants to experience life as a human being. He visits with Bob at home to get better acquainted with Bob's family. The Devil would like God to go back to Heaven so things return to normal, but God wants to spend more time on earth. He wants to play on the company's baseball team that Bob manages although He is not a very good player. Bob's team loses when God strikes out, and He finally decides to return to Heaven.

Episode 9: Unaired   "Bob Gets Greedy"

Director: Swinton O. Scott III   Writers: Gary Murphy and Neil Thompson

God wants Bob to do volunteer work. When the Devil tries to talk Bob out of doing charitable tasks, he leaves his Palm Pilot behind which contains sports scores for games not yet played. Bob uses the information to bet on games and begins to win big. Donna finds out about his winnings and is thrilled. They go on a spending spree, but God reminds Bob that the Devil will be exacting something from Bob for using the Palm Pilot information. Bob decides to stop gambling. However, Donna places one more bet on the outcome of a Red Wings hockey game. Bob learns that if she wins, the Devil will take her soul. Bob gets the Red Wings to forfeit the game so she doesn't win, and he ends up in a dunking booth for charity.

Episode 10: Unaired   "There's Too Much Sex on TV"

Director: Sherie Pollack   Writer: Matthew Carlson

When Bob gets a new, big-screen TV, God says there is too much sex on television. He wants Bob to do something about it. Initially Bob writes a letter to network executives, but God says he needs to go to Hollywood to visit the studios. In Hollywood, Bob becomes frustrated when he can't get in to see studio executives and eventually leaves. Back in Detroit, when a local TV station advertises an upcoming feature about sex, Bob sneaks what he thinks is a family-friendly video onto the air. However, Bob had forgotten he taped over the family video to make an amateur sex tape with him and Donna. Viewers are turned off by the video and destroy their TV sets.

Episode 11: Unaired   "Bob's Father"

Director: Steve Ressel   Writer: Matthew Carlson

Bob's dad, to whom he hasn't spoken for a long time because he was abusive, is in the hospital in Phoenix. Bob flies to Phoenix to see him, but they argue and Bob tells him to go to Hell. When his father dies, Bob asks God to bring him back to life so he can say a proper good-bye, but God declines. Thinking his dad is in Hell, Bob finds the Devil and goes to Hell, but the Devil divulges that Bob's dad is not

SURPRISING ARRIVALS AND UNEXPECTED INHERITANCES

there. Upon learning that his father is in Heaven, Bob says he is done with morality. God explains to Bob that he didn't know what was in his dad's heart and that his dad was a better person than Bob's grandfather was. God brings Bob's dad back for a short time so that Bob and he can talk and Bob can say good-bye.

Episode 12: Unaired   "God's Girlfriend"

Director: Dan Fausett   Writers: Gary Murphy and Neil Thompson

Bob and his family are on vacation at a resort when God appears. The deity is trying to avoid Sarah, a woman that, according to God, He had a relationship with similar to the one He has with Bob. God has a dinner date with Sarah but decides not to go. While God is distracted by Sarah, the Devil goes to Heaven and says he wants to take some of Heaven's overflow. God reveals to Bob that his relationship with Sarah was something more than the relationship Bob and He have. God apologizes to Sarah for missing dinner; they reconnect but realize that, because of all of His commitments, their relationship is not going to work.

Elizabeth Taylor was the voice of Sarah in this episode.

Episode 13: Unaired   "Bob Gets Involved"

Director: Swinton O. Scott III   Writers: Gary Murphy and Neil Thompson

When someone writes the "F" word on Andy's lunchbox, Bob declares war on evil. The Devil gets a group of citizens to join Bob in his fight and gives the group $50,000 which they use to purchase surveillance equipment. The group decides to demonstrate against the play Donna is in – *Arsenic and Old Lace*. The play is canceled, but Donna vows to put it on elsewhere. The Devil helps Bob find where the play is being performed, and his group fights with the audience. Kevin Bacon appears and says to everyone they have to come together; everyone then begins dancing. Later God advises Bob that he needs to look inside himself first before declaring war on evil. Bob discovers that Andy wrote the "F" word on his Barney lunchbox since he doesn't like the Barney character.

God, the Devil, and the Affiliates

The show came in fourth in its timeslot. About twenty-two NBC affiliates, representing 5 percent of the country, refused to air the series based on pressure groups who thought it was blasphemous. After four episodes, NBC pulled the plug. Unaired episodes of *God, the Devil and Bob* did air on the Trio cable network in June 2003. The entire series also aired in certain countries like the United Kingdom and Brazil and on the Cartoon Network. A DVD of the comedy was released in 2005.

Highcliffe Manor

Premiered Thursday, April 12, 1979, at 8:30 PM on NBC

This parody of Gothic horror tales starred Shelly Fabares as Helen Straight Blacke, a widow who inherited a mansion that housed the Blacke Foundation after her husband, Berkeley Blacke, supposedly died in a laboratory explosion. The Blacke Foundation was a think tank where scientists and philosophers attempted to solve world problems. It was made up of an assortment of oddball characters including Frances Kiskadden (Eugenie Ross-Leming), a mad female scientist working to reconstruct a bionic man called Bram Shelley (Christian Marlowe) with whatever parts her assistant Cheng (Harold Sakata) could dig up; Dr. Felix Morger (Gerald Gordon), a former assistant to Helen's husband; Drs. Lester and Sanchez (David Byrd and Luis Avalos) who, among others, were trying to take over the foundation; Rebecca (Jenny O'Hara, *Costello*), a maid, and Wendy Sparkes (Audrey Landers), Helen's secretary. Also unexpectedly showing up at the Foundation were the Reverend Glenville (Stephen McHattie) and his man servant Smythe (Ernie Hudson), whom the reverend had met in a South African prison. Peter Lawford narrated the opening of each episode providing a recap of what had previously transpired.

Background

The writer Robert Blees created the series concept for T.A.T. Communications – Norman Lear's production company, and the comedy was developed by Eugenie

SURPRISING ARRIVALS AND UNEXPECTED INHERITANCES

Ross-Leming and Brad Buckner. Ross-Leming, who played Dr. Kiskadden on the comedy, and Buckner had previously written and produced the second season of *Mary Hartman, Mary Hartman*, as well as *Fernwood Forever*. Originally *Highcliffe Manor* was to be syndicated like *Mary Hartman* five times a week, but that idea was abandoned. Six episodes of the sitcom were produced for NBC as a spring tryout, hoping that this gothic answer to *Soap* with an ongoing storyline would be successful.

Episode Guide: 4 aired; 2 unaired

Episode 1: April 12, 1979   "The Blacke Death"

Director: Nick Havinga   Writers: Brad Buckner and Eugenie Ross-Leming

Helen goes to the part of the mansion she rarely visits where the Blacke Foundation is located, to attend her husband's funeral. The funeral happens to be on the same day as the Foundation's employee picnic. Because Doctors Lester and Sanchez want Helen to leave as soon as possible, they rush the funeral. They give Helen luggage and a one-way ticket to Brazil, but she stays at the mansion anyway interrupting the resident scientists' plans to clone the world's leaders. Berkeley's attorney arrives to read his will which states that he gives full control of the Foundation to Helen. The attorney is then murdered. The body of the Foundation's Dr. Larsen is also discovered, and the villagers put a curse on Helen. Meanwhile, Rev. Glenville and his man servant arrive on Highcliffe Island from South Africa after their canoe crashes in a storm. Glenville was trying to prove his theory that blacks are Native Americans who migrated to South Africa to avoid the cold winters of North America.

Episode 2: April 19, 1979   "Berkeley Cheats the Grave"

Director: Nick Havinga   Writers: Brad Buckner and Eugenie Ross-Leming

Bodies from the village cemetery are missing, and the villagers think that Helen is responsible. They steal Berkeley Blacke's coffin. With her husband's body missing, Helen stays on and tries to run her first board meeting. Reverend Glenville begins investigating the murders of Berkeley's attorney and Dr. Larsen from the Foundation.

Episode 3: April 26, 1979   "The Evil from Within" (summary based on shooting script)

Director: Nick Havinga   Writer: Earle Doud

Helen's "get-to-know-the-new-boss" party seethes with plots against her. Doctors Lester and Sanchez want to get rid of Glenville since he is protecting Helen, and they ask Felix Morger to help. Meanwhile, Bram kisses Frances, and she relates to Glenville and Morger that she thinks that zombies must be responsible for the missing bodies.

Episode 4: May 3, 1979   "Love Blooms" (summary based on final draft script)

Director: Nick Havinga   Story: Brad Buckner and Eugenie Ross-Leming   Teleplay: Rich Orloff

Glenville tries to hold an inquest on the murders and disappearances. Frances is attacked and taken away by the villagers. Rebecca tells Bram what happened to Frances which sends him into one of his spells where he reveals he is really Berkeley Blacke. Felix Morger tries to tell Helen he is in love with her but only convinces her that she loves Glenville. Sanchez and Lester hire George Langly, a professional murderer, to kill Glenville, and Helen and Glenville share their first kiss.

Christian Marlowe (Bram) is the son of the late actor Hugh Marlowe.

Episode 5: Unaired   "Sex and Violence" (summary based on second draft script)

Director: Nick Havinga   Writers: Brad Buckner and Eugenie Ross-Leming

Helen and Rev. Glenville try to make love, but he is intimidated by all of her husband's mementos in the bedroom. Rebecca asks Smythe to find Frances and confesses that her ancestors were criminals who went into hiding on Highcliffe Island. Helen's mother, Clarabelle Straight (Inga Swenson), visits, and the professional murderer tries to shoot Glenville. Depressed over the disappearance of Frances and the fact

SURPRISING ARRIVALS AND UNEXPECTED INHERITANCES

that he is not getting his new arms and legs, Bram tries to kill himself. However, Smythe finds Frances and brings her back to the Foundation. Wendy and Felix confront Helen over her liaison with Glenville. Lester and Sanchez overhear, and they all ask Helen to leave the Foundation.

Episode 6: Unaired "Stark Terror" (summary provided by Eugenie Ross-Leming)

Director: Nick Havinga Story: Brad Buckner and Eugenie Ross-Leming Teleplay: Carmen Finestra and John Surgal

The townsfolk are turning into zombies, while the Mr. Coffee machine at the Manor is doing the same thing to staff. Wendy confesses to Cheng and Ian that Helen is really her mother who gave her up at birth. Frances starts to perform surgery on Bram that he believes will restore him. He still doesn't remember that he is Helen's husband. A PR guy is spinning the Manor's existence so that the town will like Helen more and not blame her for the zombie-like trances. Felix demands that Helen give him one date, or he will no longer support her with the Board of Directors. Felix then goes into a zombie-like trance. Bram's heart stops during surgery, and George Langly holds a gun on Glenville and moves in with a lethal syringe.

Off the *Cliffe*

The producers hoped that viewers of *Mork & Mindy* on ABC would switch channels after that series and watch *Highcliffe Manor*. This never happened. *Highcliffe Manor* ranked sixty-sixth out of sixty-seven shows when it premiered. It was canceled after four of the six episodes had aired. Following *Highcliffe Manor*, Shelly Fabares appeared on sitcoms like *One Day at a Time* and *Coach*. She is married to Mike Farrell, who played B.J. Hunnicut on *M*A*S*H*.

Misconceptions

Supposed to premiere spring, 2006 on the WB

Amanda Watson (Jane Leeves, *Frasier*, *Hot in Cleveland*), a single mother and museum curator, had a thirteen-year-old daughter, Hopper (Taylor Momsen), conceived by artificial insemination. For her birthday, Hopper wanted to know who her father was. Amanda thought the sperm donor was an Olympic medalist and surgeon who had graduated from Yale University. She was very surprised when he turned out to be a loud-mouth Joe Sixpack by the name of Eddie Caprio (Adam Rothenberg) who unexpectedly decided to get to know his daughter. Eddie worked in a pool hall, and his buddies were Jimmy (David Anthony Higgins) and Trey (Eddie Shin who replaced Brian Klugman from the pilot). French Stewart (*3rd Rock from the Sun, God, the Devil and Bob*) was Horace, Amanda's co-worker.

Background

Twentieth Century-Fox, Imagine Television, and Scribbler's Pillory Productions produced the series, initially titled *Best Laid Plans*. Jeff Kleeman and Michael Saltzman created the comedy. Originally the WB ordered thirteen episodes but cut their order to six episodes in addition to the pilot.

Episode Guide: 7 unaired episodes

Episode 1: "Who's Your Daddy" (aka "Thirteen")

Director: Andy Cadiff   Writers: Jeff Kleeman and Michael Saltzman

To make Hopper happy for her thirteenth birthday, Amanda seeks out her daughter's father. She goes to the sperm donor's apartment looking for Dr. Caprio and finds Eddie Caprio, a slacker who thinks she is a prostitute. He reveals that he is the father of her daughter. Before leaving, Amanda tells him that she sought out the services of a sperm bank since her ex-boyfriend said he didn't want children. Eddie's friends say that he should try to see his daughter. He goes to Amanda's place; but, since Horace told Hopper that they just discovered her father had died, Eddie initially pretends he is her dad's brother. Amanda confesses the truth to Hopper, and Hopper invites Eddie to stay for her birthday. Eddie discovers that Hopper is a baseball fan just like him and asks her to go to a game.

Episode 2: "Got to Get You Out of My Life"

Director: Jerry Zaks   Writers: Jeff Kleeman and Michael Saltzman

Horace suggests that Amanda have Eddie get a DNA test to show he is really Hopper's dad. Eddie's friends also want him to get a DNA test to prove fatherhood. Amanda invites Eddie for lunch and stabs him with a corncob holder to obtain some blood, while Eddie sneaks into Hopper's room and takes a hair brush. When the results of the DNA test on the hair brush show that Eddie is not Hopper's father, he informs Amanda. However, the results of the test on Eddie's blood sample reveal that he is Hopper's dad. Eddie shows Amanda the hair brush he used for his test, and she tells him that it is a brush for Hopper's toy horse.

Episode 3: "Dial E for Eddie"

Director: Jerry Zaks   Writer: Eric Horsted

Eddie wants to see Hopper more than once every three weeks, but Amanda resists. Without Amanda knowing, Eddie gives Hopper a cell phone so they can talk whenever she wants. However, he finds that she likes to use the phone so much that it disrupts his work and love life. Eddie asks Amanda for advice without revealing he gave Hopper a phone. Amanda suggests that Eddie establish firm limits on its use. Because Hopper is talking on the phone so much, she is losing sleep, but Amanda thinks she may be on drugs. When Amanda follows Hopper to see whom she is meeting at a teen hangout, she discovers Hopper has a cell phone. She also runs into Eddie who came to the same hangout to see if Hopper needed help after she called him. In the end, Amanda says that she will think about allowing Eddie to visit Hopper more often.

Episode 4: "Family Outing"

Director: Mary Lou Belli   Writer: Heather Wordham

Amanda has devised a schedule for Eddie to see Hopper every second and fourth Tuesday of the month. However, when she realizes that the second Tuesday of the current month is the same day as open house at Hopper's school, Amanda informs Eddie to visit Hopper on Saturday to avoid him going with them to the open house. After Hopper calls Eddie and mentions the open house event on Tuesday, he decides to show up anyway. Amanda wants him to leave, but Hopper asks him to stay. He doesn't want Hopper to introduce him as her dad but instead as the family's insurance agent. When Hopper stands up in front of the other parents to thank Eddie for caring, Amanda reveals that Eddie is really Hopper's father.

Episode 5: "Bad Guy's Day Off" (summary based on second revised table draft)

Director: Mary Lou Belli   Writers: Bill Martin, Mike Schiff, and Michael Saltzman

Amanda says that Eddie spoils Hopper and doesn't make the tough decisions a parent has to make. Eddie wants to prove to her that he can be a real parent. Amanda takes a day off as the "bad guy" and lets Eddie escort Hopper to the mall to buy a battery for her PC. At the mall, Eddie has to stop Hopper from purchasing a lot of frivolous things like new clothes. When Hopper gets home, Eddie has to make sure she writes her school paper instead of wasting time surfing the web.

Episode 6: "Amanda Goes Wild"

Director: Joe Regalbuto   Writer: Bill Canterbury

Eddie takes Hopper to see his pool hall, and she meets Jimmy, Trey and Eddie's sister Angela (Krista Allen) who used to be a stripper. After the visit, Hopper puts on make-up and stripper shoes which upset Amanda. Amanda goes to the pool hall to tell Eddie that Hopper will never visit there again. Angela apologizes to Amanda and orders drinks for the both of them. The two women get drunk, and Amanda does a pole dance in a subway car. She has a hangover the next day and a tattoo on her back. She doesn't know how to explain the tattoo to her daughter. When Eddie comes over, he notices the tattoo as he helps Amanda zip up her dress. He thinks that Hopper should see it also so she knows her mother is not perfect, but, in the end, he keeps quiet.

Episode 7: "The Courtship of Eddie's Daughter" (summary based on first table draft)

Director: Joe Regalbuto   Writers: Jeff Kleeman and Michael Saltzman

After a boy asks Hopper to go on a date with him, she is afraid her mother won't permit it. Eddie mentions the date to Amanda, and she is fine with it. However, Eddie is not. When Travis, Hopper's date, arrives, Eddie has a talk with him to make sure he behaves. Still concerned that it is Hopper's first date, Eddie and Amanda follow them but find nothing out of the ordinary happens.

No *Misconceptions*

The 2005-06 TV season was the last one for the WB which merged with UPN to form the CW network for the 2006-07 TV season. As a result of the merger, the WB was never able to schedule *Misconceptions*.

Over the Top

Premiered Tuesday, October 21, 1997, at 8:30 PM on ABC

Hadley Martin (Annie Potts), a thrice-divorced mother of Gwen (Marla Sokoloff), her teenage daughter, and a seven-year-old son, Daniel (Luke Tarsitano), was the owner-manager of a small hotel in Manhattan. Her first husband, Simon Ferguson (Tim Curry), unexpectedly showed up for a visit. Simon, an actor who had left his last job on a soap opera after his character was killed, had been married to Hadley for a short time twenty years earlier. Simon was so charming that Hadley decided to let him stay at the hotel after finding that he was homeless. Also in the cast were Steve Carell (later the star of *The Office* and several films), who played the hotel's overemotional chef, Yorgo Galfanikos; John O'Hurley as Robert McSwain, an investor in the hotel, and Liz Torres as Rose, the hotel's head of housekeeping.

Background

Nat Bernstein and Michael Katlin, who had earlier developed the sitcom *Bringing Up Jack*, created *Over the Top*. The original pilot for the sitcom was filmed in May 1997 but never aired. In the pilot, Annie Potts' character's first name was Katie – not Hadley; Tim Curry's character on the soap opera was killed after his plane crashed and his body was torn apart by monkeys; the marriage between the two characters lasted for six months, not twelve days as indicated in the first episode broadcast; a different actress played the daughter Gwen, and the hotel that the Annie Potts' character owned, which she received in a divorce settlement from her second husband, was a very small one that looked like a Victorian mansion, and only one hotel staff appeared – Steve Carell as the hotel's chef. The storyline was similar to the series first episode with Tim Curry's character losing his job on the soap opera and coming to stay at Annie Potts' hotel. She lets Simon stay because he brings new customers to the hotel's bar and because the kids like him, but she puts him to work in the hotel. This comedy was produced by Columbia TriStar, Greengrass, Katlin-Bernstein Productions, and Panamort Television.

Episode Guide: 3 aired; 8 unaired

Episode 1: October 21, 1997   "I'm Bonnie, I'm Clyde"

Director: Michael Lembeck   Writers: Nat Bernstein and Mitchel Katlin

Free-spirited, actor Simon Ferguson, loses his role on the soap, *Days to Remember*, when his character is killed in a plane crash. He goes to the large Metropolitan Hotel in New York City that is managed (not owned as in the pilot) by his former wife, Hadley, to whom he was married for twelve days twenty years ago. Hadley has had three failed marriages and two children. Simon meets the kids and, on the first night, gets Hadley drunk in the hotel's bar where they reprise numbers from *Bonnie and Clyde, The Musical*, which they appeared in several years earlier. The next day, Hadley is not prepared to meet a major investor in the hotel, Robert McSwain, and so he leaves. Hadley wants Simon to leave the hotel as well, but when she finds he has lost his job and his money, she lets him stay. In the end, Simon persuades Robert McSwain to come back to the hotel and gets him drunk in the bar.

In December 2011, an actual musical based on the lives of Bonnie and Clyde premiered on Broadway, but closed by the end of the month.

Episode 2: October 28, 1997   "The Kernel"

Director: Michael Lembeck   Writer: Alex Reid

Simon receives a call to appear on his old soap opera, *Days to Remember*, as his dead character's evil twin. However, there are strings attached to his appearance relating to the network head's sister who has romantic designs on Simon. In order to keep his job on the soap, she makes him go to museums, concerts, and dog shows with her which he dislikes. However, when he has to sleep with the sister to perhaps get his own prime time series, he can't go through with it. In the end, the soap kills off the evil twin character.

Episode 3: November 4, 1997   "The Nemesis"

Director: Michael Lembeck   Writer: David Litt

Simon and Hadley's old friend Justin (John Ritter) arrives at the hotel with plans to steal a movie role from Simon. After Justin tells Simon that the part is beneath him, Simon initially backs out of the audition. However, when he learns that Justin wants the part, he talks himself back into auditioning. Justin persuades Hadley who convinces Simon that the audition requires actors to dress in drag which is not true. Not knowing this, Simon goes to the audition in Rose's dress and is immediately thrown out. Justin comes to the audition in a business suit and gets to read for the part, but Simon had put a note on his script that said the actor had to act like a four-year-old child. Neither actor gets the role.

Episode 4: Unaired   "Who's Afraid of Simon Ferguson?"

Director: Michael Lembeck   Writer: David Brownfield

Simon directs Daniel's school play, *Jack and the Beanstalk*, and stars as the giant when he thinks that the father of one of Daniel's classmates is a big-time TV producer. He makes the classmate the star of the play instead of Daniel. But the kid's dad is not a TV producer; he is a TV repairman. Meanwhile, Gwen takes romantic advice from Rose about dating a boy which doesn't work out, but Yorgo steps in to save the day.

Episode 5: Unaired   "Acting Out"

Director Michael Lembeck   Writer: David Litt

Gwen has gotten the acting bug and decides not to go to college but instead become an actress. Hadley blames Simon for this, but then Hadley decides to try to re-activate her career as an actress by attending an acting workshop. However, her job and family responsibilities cause her to leave the class. Meanwhile, Simon is re-evaluating his career as an actor by visiting his old acting teacher who tells him that he still has talent even if it is buried under layers of pretense. In a subplot, Yorgo tries to convince Simon and then Rose to murder his brother because the brother is marrying a woman promised to Yorgo. Simon phones Yorgo's brother long distance to have the two brothers make peace.

Writer David Litt subsequently created the long-running *The King of Queens* and the short-lived *Regular Joe*.

Episode 6: Unaired   "Fight Night at the Metropolitan"

Director: Michael Lembeck   Writers: Tom J. Astle and David Brownfield

Hadley introduces "Sports Sunday" at the hotel, and Simon fights with a bunch of bullies. Meanwhile, Rose gets upset when her ex-fiancé (Erik Estrada) stays in the honeymoon suite, and Gwen is tricked into a date with her nerdy Spanish partner.

Episode 7: Unaired   "The Review"

Director: Michael Lembeck   Writers: Josh Goldsmith and Cathy Yuspa

Martin Mull appears as a newspaper critic reviewing the hotel. He gets the best room in the place as well as a bouillabaisse prepared by Yorgo into which Simon accidentally dumps a spice rack. However, they serve it to the critic anyway; he loves it and gives the hotel a five-star rating. Upon leaving the hotel, Simon accidentally knocks the reviewer into unconsciousness with a baseball. He returns the next day suffering from short-term memory loss and doesn't remember reviewing the hotel. The staff has to do everything all over again, but they cannot recreate the bouillabaisse. The critic wants to give the hotel a negative review. But Robert McSwain happens to have been a college roommate of his, and, in the end, the critic decides to give the hotel a positive review.

Episode 8: Unaired   "Simon, We Hardly Knew Ye"

Director: Michael Lembeck   Writer: Lee Aronsohn

Hadley becomes Simon's publicist and books him appearances cutting the ribbon for a new washer at a laundromat, hosting a telethon, and judging a kids' kite flying contest. He is not pleased with these kinds of events and so fires her and decides to handle his own publicity. He reports his own death to the news media in the hopes of generating interest about himself. At his memorial service, Simon shows up in disguise and hears a producer say that he had a role Simon would have been perfect for if he were still alive. When he hears this, Simon reveals himself saying he wasn't really dead. However, the producer turns him down for the role because of the shameful publicity. Meanwhile, Robert wants to get closer to Hadley. Simon says that the way to do that is to become friends with Daniel by playing with him.

Episode 9: Unaired   "It's Gwen's Party and Hadley'll Cry If She Wants To"

Director: Michael Lembeck   Writer: Amy Sherman-Palladino

Robert asks Hadley out for dinner on the same night that Gwen wants to have a party at the hotel. Hadley reluctantly approves the party if Rose chaperones which she does with an iron fist, putting partygoers through metal detectors and taking photos of the attendees. Simon joins the party since Hadley is out and teaches the partygoers traditional dancing and romantic techniques. When he finds Gwen and her boyfriend alone in Gwen's bedroom looking at pictures, he makes them go back to the party. Meanwhile, at dinner, Robert bores Hadley with his conversation about corporate earnings and making decisions about what Hadley should order. Even though he seems like the "perfect" man, Hadley leaves him alone at dinner and ends up crying on Simon's shoulder about her choice in men.

Episode 10: Unaired   "The Bee Story"

Director: Mathew Diamond   Writer: Tom Astle

Daniel is in a fight with Oliver, a classmate, who called him "stupid" while rehearsing for a spelling bee. Hadley and Simon meet with Oliver's parents and the teacher at the school where Simon takes what he thinks is a copy of the list of words for the spelling bee. Daniel wins the contest, but Oliver says he cheated. Hadley and Simon along with Oliver's parents attend another meeting at the school with Daniel's classmates as the jury to resolve the dispute between the two classmates. Simon confesses that he gave the word list to Daniel to study, but the teacher says that the list Simon took was only a practice list – not the one used in the spelling bee. Therefore, Daniel won the contest fairly. Meanwhile, Yorgo tries to work up courage to ask Linda, the mail carrier out on a date.

Episode 11: Unaired   "The Southern Story"

Director: Michael Lembeck   Writers: Josh Goldsmith and Cathy Yespa

Hadley's mother has her come to Tennessee to pick up a prized armoire, but her real intent is to reveal to Hadley that she is getting married. Meanwhile, Rose and Yorgo quarrel when they are left in charge of Hadley's kids.

Not Quite the Top

Over the Top was up against *JAG* on CBS and *Newsradio* on NBC—both of which did a lot better in the ratings. The sitcom scored one of the lowest ratings ever for a first-run series on Tuesdays at 8:30 PM on ABC. It lasted only three episodes. The creators of *Over the Top* suggested that a reason the show was canceled was due to the end of a personal relationship between ABC network head Jamie Tarses (daughter of sitcom creator Jay Tarses) and Robert Morton, one of the show's producers.[134] Katlin said that *Over the Top* was getting better and better but that ABC failed to promote it.

Pauly (aka The Pauly Shore Show)

Premiered, Monday, March 3, 1997, at 9:30 PM on Fox

According to one critic, *Pauly*, starring comedian Pauly Shore, made *Married with Children* look like Moliere.[135] Pauly Sherman was the twenty-eight-year-old slacker son of Ed (David Dukes), a wealthy businessman. He lived in his dad's Brentwood mansion and sponged off his father's fortune. The father's sexy, younger fiancée, Dawn (Charlotte Ross), and her ten-year-old son, Zach (Theo Greenly) had just moved into the father's mansion with Pauly. Because Dawn wanted Pauly to move out, he tried to undermine his dad's relationship with her. Sumi (Amy Hill), the Sherman's housekeeper, and Pauly's best friend Burger (Kevin Weisman), a nerd who worked at a video rental store, rounded out the characters on the series.

SURPRISING ARRIVALS AND UNEXPECTED INHERITANCES

Background

Created by James Berg and Stan Zimmerman who had previously written and produced episodes of *Roseanne*, *Pauly* was a vehicle for the same type of character Shore had played in movies like *In the Army Now* and *Jury Duty*. The sitcom was produced by Twentieth Century-Fox Television.

Episode Guide: 5 aired; 2 unaired

Episode 1: March 3, 1997   "Pilot"

Director: Robert Berlinger   Writers: James Berg and Stan Zimmerman

Ed Sherman's new girlfriend Dawn, who has dollar signs in her eyes and is hostile to her future stepson, comes to live in the mansion. Pauly's dad met Dawn when she was teaching step aerobics at a San Diego resort. After Dawn arrives with her young son, she asks Sumi, the maid, to get her luggage. "Can you see to my chest?" she says. To which the maid responds: "Looks like a doctor beat me to it." Pauly tells his dad that he is trying to protect him from gold diggers, while Dawn announces that she thinks Pauly should be on his own. Pauly's buddy, Burger, hacks into Dawn's old computer and finds information on everyone Dawn's ever dated, and Pauly and Burger use it to come up with a guest list for an engagement party for Dawn. In the end, Ed tells both Pauly and Dawn to move out, but Dawn and Pauly agree to a truce for Ed's sake.

Episode 2: March 10, 1997   "Spies Like Us"

Director: Amanda Bearse   Writers: Dalina Soto-Loesser, Dan Berendsen, and Mark Amato

Ed and Dawn argue over the details of a prenuptial agreement. Meanwhile, Pauly and Burger think that Dawn is having an affair with an inept handyman she hired. When they discover a letter in the trash to "Potsticker" from "Love Stud Jake," they decide to use video surveillance to catch Dawn in the act, never thinking that "Potsticker" could be Sumi.

Amanda Bearse, who directed this episode, played next-door neighbor Marcy D'Arcy on *Married with Children*.

Episode 3: March 17, 1997   "Pauly Comes Home"

Director: Max Tash   Writer: Mark Amato

Feeling that Dawn is taking over, Pauly decides to run away from home. He ends up rooming with Burger. Initially, Ed doesn't realize that Pauly is gone since Dawn tore up his note and threw it in the trash, but Sumi puts the pieces together.

Episode 4: March 31, 1997   "Foreplay"

Director: Terri McCoy   Writers: Dan Berendsen and Dalina Soto-Loesser

Dawn tries to become friends with the neighborhood socialites who are more impressed by Pauly. Meanwhile, Pauly gets the family's help to attempt to change his image to win over a ruthless colleague of Ed's.

Episode 5: April 7, 1997   "Through the Ringers"

Director: Amanda Bearse   Writers: Mark Alton Brown and Dee LaDuke

Burger finds that Dawn made her acting debut in a movie called *Slammer Sluts*. Meanwhile, while Dawn searches for a celebrity to endorse her new charitable foundation, Pauly keeps driving off all of the potential celebrities. Dawn then hires her friend Mariah (Christina Applegate) to occupy Pauly's time, but, when Burger realizes that Mariah was Dawn's co-star in *Slammer Sluts*, Pauly tries to turn the tables on Dawn.

Celebrities who played themselves in this episode included Dionne Warwick and Erik Estrada.

Episode 6: Unaired   "The Babe Magnet"

Director: Matthew Diamond   Writer: Bernadette Luckett

After a girl locks Zach in his locker at school, Dawn is concerned that her son is not fitting in. Ed asks Pauly to teach Zach to be "cool." At the video store, Pauly finds that women are attracted to guys with kids, and so Pauly uses Zach to try to pick up women. Pauly meets an attractive woman at the mall who is a single mother, and they arrange a play date. Pauly thinks "play date" means fooling around with the woman, but he soon discovers its real meaning when the single mom brings her twins and older son to Pauly's home. The woman says that she also has a daughter at a friend's for a sleepover, and, when the daughter needs something from her mom, the mother leaves Pauly in charge of the twins.

Episode 7: Unaired   "Life's a Drag"

Director: Matthew Diamond   Writer: Dana Reston

Edward wants to judge a beauty contest, the Ms. Fabulous International Pageant, instead of going away with Dawn. But Pauly volunteers to judge the pageant unaware that the contestants are drag queens. To check up on Pauly, Edward and Dawn go to the hotel where the pageant is being held. Pauly can't keep his hands off one of the contestants – Ms. North Carolina who has a jealous boyfriend. When the boyfriend breaks into Pauly's room, Pauly escapes, goes to his dad's room, and puts on one of Dawn's dresses. He ends up on stage as one of the contestants.

Lyle Waggoner played the pageant's Master of Ceremonies, and Shirley Hemphill was one of the judges in this episode.

Poor *Pauly*

Fox originally scheduled *Pauly* for 9:00 PM on Mondays, but then decided to slot it after *Married with Children* at 9:30 PM. As might be expected, ratings for *Pauly* were poor, and the sitcom was canceled after five episodes.

Scorch

Premiered Friday, February 28, 1992, at 8:00 PM on CBS

Two years after the end of *ALF*, the sitcom about an alien puppet creature that became part of a family, CBS tried a similar theme in the series *Scorch*. Scorch was a 1300-year-old talking, fire-breathing, green dragon. Awakened from a long sleep, he flew around, was struck by lightning, and fell in front of the window of an apartment inhabited by a divorced dad and his daughter. The daughter, Jessica Stevens (Rhea Silver-Smith), liked the dragon, but her father, Brian (Jonathan Walker), an out-of-work actor, did not. Brian got a job as a weatherman at WWEN-TV in New Haven, Connecticut whose staff included the station manager, Jack Fletcher (Todd Sussman), and Howard Gurman (John O'Hurley) and Allison King (Brenda Strong), the news co-anchors. Rose Marie from *The Dick Van Dyke Show* played the Stevens' nosy landlady, Edna Bracken.

Background

Allan Katz (*Roxie*) created, wrote, and produced *Scorch*, which was developed by Zane Buzby, Bob Calderon, and Edgar Scherick. Ventriloquist Ronn Lucas created the puppet Scorch in 1983, and both had been featured on a British TV variety show for five seasons in the late 1980s. The soundstage on which *Scorch* was filmed was trenched with the live actors on platforms so that Lucas could work with his puppet standing up. Edgar J. Scherick Associates, Lorimar Productions, and Saban Entertainment produced *Scorch*.

Episode Guide: 3 aired, 3 unaired

Episode 1: February 28, 1992   "Pilot"

Director: Zane Buzby   Writer: Allan Katz

Scorch, the 1300-year-old dragon that has been asleep for 100 years, becomes part of the Stevens' family, and persuades Brian to take him in a large canvas bag to an audition for a weatherman at WWEN-TV. At the end of the interview, Brian bumps the bag against the doorway as he is leaving and Scorch says "ouch." Brian

SURPRISING ARRIVALS AND UNEXPECTED INHERITANCES

then pretends that he is a ventriloquist and Scorch is his dummy. The manager thinks they make a great team, and Brian is hired as weather announcer for the *New Haven at Noon* program.

Episode 2: March 6, 1982   "Dragon Flu"

Director: Zane Buzby   Writer: Allan Katz

Scorch comes down with the dragon flu which causes various symptoms like coughing, swearing, barking, memory loss, and unconsciousness. At the same time, the station's boss is to receive an award for "Man of the Year" from Gurman, but the boss asks Scorch to give him the award. Brian and Jessica try to cure Scorch before the award ceremony. The next day Scorch is still sick but goes on with the presentation on *New Haven at Noon*. While he gets over the flu during the presentation, he gives it to Brian who starts barking like a dog.

Episode 3: March 13, 1982   "You Gaslight Up My Life"

Director: John Squeglia   Writer: Bill Richmond

Scorch's picture appears on the cover of New Haven's Sunday TV magazine. Although Brian advises Scorch to keep a low profile about the publicity, of course, Scorch doesn't. Howard Gurman is envious of Scorch's publicity since he was never on the cover of the TV log. He complains to the station manager, but his complaints fall on deaf ears. Howard kidnaps Scorch and takes him home to keep him off the show. While he is sleeping, Scorch pretends he is the voice of a ghost and tells Howard to return Scorch or burn in hell. The next day, Howard returns Scorch claiming that he found him in a bag in the parking lot.

Episode 4: Unaired   "First Time"

Director: Zane Buzby   Writer: Lee Aronsohn

Jessica and Scorch want Brian to begin dating again. At the station, Brian bumps into Lisa, Jack's sister who is helping out, and Scorch asks her to dinner with Brian at his apartment. At dinner, Scorch is so foreword with Lisa that she leaves. The next day, Jack tells Brian that his sister was morally repulsed by what she thought

Brian was saying through Scorch. Brian apologizes to Lisa, and they both go for coffee.

Episode 5: Unaired   "Scorch Likes It Hot"

Director: Howard Storm   Writer: Joe Toplyn

Dr. Joyce Brothers guests on *New Haven at Noon* during which Howard and Scorch argue. Jack hires Dr. Brothers as a media consultant, and she advises that Allison should be the lead anchor and that Scorch should be replaced by a female puppet. Scorch becomes Scorchtina by putting on a dress. On the air, Scorchtina complains that her bra is too tight and begins arguing with Howard again. Dr. Brothers tells Jack that she screwed up in revamping the show.

Episode 6: Unaired   "Money, Money, Money"

Director: Jim Drake   Writer: Allan Katz

Scorch uses Brian's credit card to purchase $1160 in merchandise from a TV shopping channel. Since Brian can hardly afford the credit card payments, Scorch gets the idea of raising $1160 to pay the credit card bill by playing poker with the station staff. However, Scorch and Brian end up losing at poker.

Scorch Torched

Six episodes of *Scorch* were produced, but only half that number aired. The show was opposite the popular family comedy *Family Matters* on ABC, which spelled doom for the series. The premiere episode of *Scorch* ranked seventy-seventh out of ninety shows, and the ratings for the subsequent episodes were even lower.

Struck by Lightning

Premiered Wednesday, September 19, 1979, at 8:30 PM on CBS

Struck by Lightning dealt with an unexpected family inheritance that served as the basis for the retelling of the Frankenstein legend. Twenty-eight-year-old Ted Stein

SURPRISING ARRIVALS AND UNEXPECTED INHERITANCES

(apparently, along the way, the family name was shortened from "Frankenstein"), played by Jeffrey Kramer, was the great-great-grandson of the infamous doctor and a high school science teacher from Boston. Not only did he inherit a rural inn in Maine, but also one of his ancestor's creations, "Frank" (Jack Elam), who had mellowed over the past centuries. Frank, the inn's caretaker, was now a kinder and gentler creature. Also at the inn were Nora Furness (Millie Slavin), who had been managing the place for Ted's grandfather before his death; her ten-year-old-son Brian (Jeff Cotler); Glenn Diamond (Bill Erwin), long-time resident of the inn and a newspaper reporter, and Walt Calvin (Richard Stahl), a local realtor.

Background

This comedic take on the Frankenstein legend was created and produced by Michael Friedman along with Arthur Fellows and Terry Keegan. Fellows-Keegan produced the series in association with Paramount Television.

Episode Guide: 3 aired; 10 unaired

Episode 1: September 19, 1979   "Pilot" (summary based on revised second draft script)

Director: Joel Zwick   Writers: Fred Freeman and Lawrence J. Cohen

Young science teacher Ted Stein inherits the Bridgewater Inn, and tells Nora, the inn's manager, that he would like to sell the place because he could use the money. Ted meets the inn's handyman, Frank, who informs him that his great-great grandfather was the infamous Dr. Frankenstein and that Frank is the monster that the good doctor created. Frank shows Ted his great-great grandfather's secret laboratory and makes him aware that he needs a special serum to keep him alive. Ted changes his mind about selling the place right away after threats and pleas from Frank for Ted to rediscover the serum formula.

Jeffrey Kramer (Ted Stein) went on to produce series like *Ally McBeal* and *The Practice*.

Episode 2: September 26, 1979   "Toot Toot Tutor Goodbye" (summary based on final draft script)

Director: Joel Zwick   Writer: Joseph Bryan

Ted is offered a job as a tutor for a small child whose family travels the world. Frank is upset thinking Ted will move away before perfecting his life-giving serum. However, Ted promises Frank that he will continue to work on the formula even when he is gone. When Frank sees a small amount of green serum in the lab that Ted tested on a hamster, he drinks it. The next day Frank feels sick and fears he is dying. Also, the hamster is nowhere to be found. The following day Nora informs Frank that the hamster has been found and is healthy. Frank feels better, but continues to act deathly ill because he doesn't want Ted to take the new job. Ted is wise to what Frank is doing and pretends to call the family and tell them he can take the job right away because Frank is going to die any minute. After Frank confesses to Ted that he doesn't want him to leave, Ted says he already decided to stay since he would miss Frank too much if he left.

Episode 3: October 3, 1979   "The Movie"

Director: Joel Zwick   Writer: Michael Russnow

Ted is torn between fear and greed when he learns he can make $5000 from a movie company for letting them film a horror movie at the inn. The horror film features a typical Hollywood Frankenstein monster which Frank doesn't like at all.

Episode 4: Unaired   "Frank Meets the Press" (summary based on shooting script)

Director: Joel Zwick   Writer: George Zateslo

Connie Turner (Liz Georges), a pretty young reporter staying at the hotel, is there to write a story about old hotels but has found nothing interesting to write about. Ted introduces her to Glenn who tells Connie about Dr. Frankenstein. She asks Frank about the story, and he says that the only exciting thing that ever happened at the inn was an earthquake in 1882 that killed someone. Connie goes to the local library for research and finds a photo of Frank at the earthquake scene. After she calls her editor to come to the inn, Frank begins to make a getaway plan. But Ted convinces Frank not to leave. When the editor arrives, Ted informs him that he is indeed the great-great grandson of Dr. Frankenstein and that Frank is the monster.

SURPRISING ARRIVALS AND UNEXPECTED INHERITANCES

Frank, dressed like the monster, crashes through a door with his arms out. The editor believes that everything looks too perfect and calls Connie a novice. He fires her and goes back to New York City. Ted tries to console Connie by saying that he can get her a job at the town newspaper, and right after that Frank gets struck by lightning and walks away like Frankenstein's monster.

Episode 5: Unaired "Happy Birthday Frank" (summary based on final draft script)

Director: Joel Zwick   Writer: John Boni

Brian is having a birthday party, and Frank is upset that he has never had a birthday party in his over 200 years on earth. When Nora and Ted decide to celebrate his birthday, Frank makes a lot of demands like wanting to pin the tail on a live donkey. Frank decides to have a party just for himself, but Nora, Walt, and Glenn throw him a surprise party anyway.

Episode 6: Unaired "The Maine Event" (summary provided by Bruce Kalish)

Director: Joel Zwick   Writer: Bruce Kalish and Philip John Taylor

Ted has a gambling problem and loses $500 betting on a football game. Frank strongly disapproves of gambling, but reluctantly agrees to enter a local arm wrestling contest to help Ted pay off the debt. Frank wins, of course, and gets caught up in the crowd's adulation. He decides to go for the New England Arm Wrestling Championship. When Ted hears that Frank's true identity will be revealed, Frank ends up throwing the match.

When providing this episode description, Bruce Kalish said that what he remembered most about Jack Elam (Frank) was his sense of humor and playing Liar's Poker (poker with serial numbers of dollar bills) at lunchtime. Elam died of congestive heart failure at the age of eighty-two in 2003.

Episode 7: Unaired "Frank the Crank" (summary based on shooting script)

Director: Joel Zwick   Writer: John Boni

Frank is depressed because Ted still cannot find the right formula for his serum. To cheer him up, Ted suggests that Frank re-paint Glenn's room since he enjoys painting walls. Frank chooses to paint murals of dead animals all over the walls. Not wanting to upset him, Ted and Glenn compliment Frank on his work, and Glenn tells Frank he should attend classes at the art school in town. Frank takes a big piece of the wall mural to the director of the school who signs him up for classes at $50 a month for the next five years, and the director says he has already sold Frank's first painting. Frank continues to paint morbid scenes and sell the paintings. The director comes over to the inn to pick up more of Frank's paintings, but refuses to buy them when he sees they are not framed like the previous ones. Frank says he ran out of the antique frames that he was using. When the director informs Ted that he only wanted to buy Frank's paintings for the antique frames, Frank hits the school director over the head with one of his canvases. Nora and Ted are worried that Frank will become depressed again, but Nora hears Frank practicing the trombone horribly downstairs and figures Frank has moved on to a new hobby.

Episode 8: Unaired   "Rich Frank, Poor Frank" (summary based on shooting script)

Director: Joel Zwick   Writer: Bryan Joseph

Frank asks Ted for a raise. He wants money to buy luggage since it seems everyone has luggage except him. Ted says the inn is not doing well, and he can't give Frank a raise. Frank decides to quit working and use his forty-three years of accumulated vacation time. Walt says he can get Frank back to work and goes to his room where he finds that Frank is selling his possessions to raise money. Walt discovers that Frank has two dozen cases of vintage French wine that, after checking with an auctioneer, he says are worth $600 a bottle. He advances Frank $2000 pending the sale of the wine which Frank uses to purchase luggage. Walt invites some businessmen to the inn to discuss investments with Frank. They break open a bottle of the vintage wine and find that it tastes horrible – it has turned to vinegar. Frank ends up taking his old job back, but instead of making $2.50 an hour, he will earn $4.00 an hour.

SURPRISING ARRIVALS AND UNEXPECTED INHERITANCES

Episode 9: Unaired   "Looking Out for Number 2" (summary based on final draft script)

Director: Joel Zwick   Writer: George Zateslo

Frank is concerned when Ted comes home very late from a date and lets Ted know that he will only stop worrying when he can accompany Ted on his dates. When Ted gets a cold but still wants to go out on another date, Frank locks him in his room. Ted tries to leave through a secret passage but gets lost, and Frank directs him back to his bedroom. The next night, Ted attempts to escape through his bedroom window by tying sheets together as a rope, but Frank pulls him back in through the window. Finally Ted informs Frank that he wants him to stay out of his life. Frank leaves the inn and is gone for four days. Everyone misses Frank including Ted who finds him working as a bartender. Ted apologizes to Frank and asks him to come back to the inn as long as Frank doesn't treat him like a baby.

Episode 10: Unaired   "Frank the VIIIth" (summary based on revised final draft script)

Director: Joel Zwick   Writers: Bruce Kalish and Philip John Taylor

A rich older widow – Mrs. Fairchild (Dody Goodman) is the hotel's only guest and has made a large deposit to stay some length of time. Ted and Nora have begun to use her deposit to build a hot tub at the inn. Mrs. Fairchild appreciates Frank's morose sense of humor, but Frank initially doesn't like her. When Ted realizes that Mrs. Fairchild is only staying there because she likes Frank, he makes Frank take her for a walk. They end up having a fun time, and Frank begins to fall in love with her and thinks of proposing. He pops the question at a romantic dinner, and Mrs. Fairchild says "yes." However, when Frank learns that he will have to get a blood test and show his birth certificate, he realizes that he cannot marry a human. He tells her that they should wait on marriage. She agrees and says she had a good time with Frank anyway.

Episode 11: Unaired   "My Mystery Guest" (summary based on shooting script)

Director: Joel Zwick   Writer: John Boni

In the middle of a storm on the night before Halloween, two men come to the inn – one of whom is wrapped entirely in bandages. The man not wrapped in bandages checks the other guy into the hotel saying that his patient's brother will pick him up the next day. Upstairs the two men talk quietly about a surgery to make the one man unrecognizable in order to escape the Mafia that is after him. The next day, Frank and Ted find the man in bandages dead. Since they are afraid that if the police come, they will have to explain Ted's laboratory downstairs, they choose to act as if the man dubbed "Mr. Smith" is still alive. Frank hangs Mr. Smith on the coat rack to keep him upright. A large, brutish man comes to the inn asking for his brother. Frank points out the coat rack. The large man threatens Ted and Frank asking who put them up to rubbing out his Mr. Smith. The man tries to attack Frank with brass knuckles and then a shotgun, but Frank is strong enough to ward off the attacks. An agent from the FBI comes in to arrest the large man and take away the body of Mr. Smith. In the end, Brian is inspired to dress as a bandaged man for his Halloween costume.

Episode 12: Unaired   "Welcoming Matt" (summary based on shooting script)

Director: Joel Zwick   Writer: George Zateslo

Matt Stein, Ted's cousin, arrives at the inn. He is a research scientist who is on the run after accidentally blowing up the laboratory for the company for which he worked. Frank thinks Matt can perfect the serum formula he needs to sustain his life. Matt converts Ted's bedroom into a miniature laboratory trying to make imitation plastic. Matt subsequently discovers the secret lab at the inn in which Frank was created, and he wants to tell the world about it. To keep that from happening, Frank shackles him in the lab. Ted confesses to Matt that their great- great grandfather was Victor Frankenstein who created Frank, but Matt is not impressed. Ted has Matt look at the serum formula, and then Matt accidentally blows up the lab.

Episode 13: Unaired   "A Frank Sentence" (summary based on final draft script)

Director: Joel Zwick   Writer: Joseph Bryan

Ted is complaining that he will never come up with the right formula for Frank's serum because the chemicals he needs are too expensive. When Ted goes to bed, Frank says that he is going on a walk to the cemetery. The next day, Ted learns that there has been a robbery at the drugstore and finds Frank with a bag full of the chemicals he needs. Frank denies that he robbed the drugstore and says he found the chemicals in a pile at the cemetery. However, later that day, Frank is arrested because a witness spotted Frank behind the drugstore, and he is in possession of the chemicals. Frank really enjoys the bleak surroundings in jail which annoys his cellmates. When Frank goes to see the judge, he is found guilty after being questioned. As Frank is being brought back to his cell, his cellmate, who cannot stand to bunk with Frank any more, tells the judge that he is the one who robbed the drugstore and that he dumped the chemicals in the cemetery. The judge dismisses all the charges against Frank.

Struck Out

Struck by Lightning was originally scheduled at 8:30 PM on Saturdays, but, before it premiered, CBS switched the show to Wednesdays. The comedy lasted for only three episodes before being canceled. *Struck by Lightning* premiered at fifty-sixth in the ratings, and its second episode sank to sixty-third. Its main competition was the second half hour of *Eight Is Enough* on ABC.

That's Life

Premiered Tuesday, March 19, 1998, at 9:30 PM on ABC

Comedian Gerry Red Wilson and actress Kellie Overbey starred on *That's Life* as married couple Mike and Patty, who, like the Bunkers from *All in the Family*, lived in Queens, New York. Mike, who reminded some of a young Archie Bunker, got promoted to head of the meat department at the grocery store where he worked and hoped to use the pay increase to remodel his upstairs apartment into a man cave.

However, Patty's snobbish sister, Catherine (Nadia Dajani, *Emily's Reasons Why Not*), and her son, Kieren (Michael Charles Roman), left penniless and homeless when Catherine's husband abandoned them, needed a place to stay and so moved into the apartment. Mike got along with Catherine about as well as Archie Bunker got along with his son-in-law. Mike made fun of his nephew's non-macho tendencies, warning that he would grow up to be a figure skater. Also on the sitcom were Paula Perrette as Lisa, Patty's twenty-one year old sister, and Ron Livingston as Mitch, Mike's best friend.

Background

Eric Gilliland, who had written and produced episodes of *Roseanne*, created *That's Life* with Brian Burns. The show's working title was *These Are the Days*—reminiscent of the theme song of the classic *All in the Family*, "Those Were the Days." Eric Gilliland Productions in association with Twentieth Century-Fox Television produced the series.

Episode Guide: 5 aired; 1 unaired

Episode 1: March 10, 1998   "The First One"

Director: Michael Lembeck   Story: Eric Gilliland and Brian Burns
Teleplay: Eric Gilliland

After his tenants move out, Mike is ready to remodel the upstairs apartment into "Guy Town," but then his wife's older sister and her son arrive for a visit supposedly to help Patty pick out new curtains. Catherine confesses that she doesn't know where her husband Lawrence is and subsequently discovers that he lost all of their money in bad investments. Patty tells her that she can move into the upstairs apartment until she works things out. Also, Patty mentions to Catherine that she and Mike have been trying to conceive for a year, and Catherine thinks the problem may be with Mike. When Mike and Catherine argue about their respective lifestyles, she says he should see a doctor. Later Mike informs Patty that he will go to the doctor to determine if he is the reason she can't get pregnant.

Writer Brian Burns is the brother of actor/director Edward Burns.

SURPRISING ARRIVALS AND UNEXPECTED INHERITANCES

Episode 2: March 17, 1998   "The Second One, Believe It or Not"

Director: Gordon Hunt   Writers: Pat Bullard and Rich Kaplan

When Catherine goes to remove all of her belongings from her old apartment, she finds that her husband took everything. Because of this, Patty wants to help Catherine redecorate the upstairs apartment which irritates Mike who thinks Patty is spending too much time on the project. Meanwhile, Mike goes to a fertility doctor and finds that his sperm has low motility. He hesitates discussing the diagnosis with Patty but does eventually.

Episode 3: March 24, 1998   "Actually, The Third One"

Director: Steve Zuckerman   Writers: Norma Safford Vela and Lisa Albert

Much to Mike's dismay, Mitch and Patty's sister Lisa are dating one another. Mike tells Mitch to stop dating her. Lisa gets upset that Mitch wants to slow things down. Patty accuses Mike of breaking up Lisa and Mitch because Mike thought that he would lose Mitch as a friend. Mike explains to Mitch that he gave him bad advice, while Mitch confesses to him that he had to sleep with Lisa so she would not break off their relationship. Meanwhile, while Mike is babysitting Kieran, he encourages the boy to join Mitch and him in playing football, and Kieran breaks his arm. Kieran is sad when his mother forbids him from playing with Mike anymore, but she eventually relents and lets them get back together.

Paula Perrette (Lisa) would find greater fame as a regular on *NCIS*.

Episode 4: March 31, 1998   "94 to Syndication"

Director: Michael Lembeck   Writers: Rich Kaplan, Janet Leahy, Pat Bullard, and Lisa Albert

Mike complains that Catherine has become a financial burden and suggests that she get a job as hostess at a restaurant. Catherine says she is already lining up jobs as an interior decorator. Mike is having a party with his friends to watch a Mets game and invites Catherine to attend so his friends can see how snobbish she is. She decides to drop in, and, much to Mike's chagrin, she becomes the hit of the party.

After Catherine returns from a meeting with a potential client, she sees her son wearing a helmet with a nut dish on top, gets mad, and calls everyone at the party "glassy-eyed droolers" and "losers." Patty scolds Catherine for being such a snob. Catherine confesses that she didn't get the decorating job to which Patty responds that her sister needs to find a regular job because she and Mike need the money.

Episode 5: April 7, 1998   "The Easter Story"

Director: Michael Lembeck Writer: Eric Gilliland

When Kieren asks Mike to take him to church, his mother objects because she doesn't like the Catholic Church's position on birth control and homosexuality. After Mike, a lapsed Catholic who normally attends church only on Easter and Christmas, and Kieran attend a mass, the nephew says he liked going and wants to attend next week. When Catherine learns that her son's interest in the church focuses on the more bloody aspects of the crucifixion, she tells Mike to stop taking him——much to Mike's relief who prefers staying home on Sundays to watch football. However, Mike feels guilty about not attending church and talks with his nephew about other aspects of religion. Kieren asks him if Hitler could confess all of his sins, would he then go to heaven. Mike has no answer to the question but says he will still take Kieren to church.

The Catholic League of Religious and Civil Rights denounced this episode as "the most anti-Catholic television show ever."[136] ABC responded by stating that the show had already been canceled before "The Easter Story" episode was broadcast because of weak ratings.

Episode 6: Unaired   "The Sixth One to Air"

Director: Unknown   Writers: Stacie Lipp, Norma Safford Vela, Sid Youngers, and Mark McAdam

Mike sees his father in a different light after he finally beats him at hardball. Meanwhile, Lisa practices her flossing on Mitch.

That's It

That's Life was on Tuesdays between *Home Improvement* and *NYPD Blue*, but it failed to keep an audience. The series retained only 70 percent of the audience from its lead-in, well below the 80 percent retained by its timeslot predecessor *Grace Under Fire*. On a sad note, Gerry Red Wilson (Mike) died of undiagnosed meningitis about eight months after *That's Life* was canceled.

The Trouble with Larry

Premiered Wednesday, August 25, 1993, at 8:00 PM on CBS

In *The Trouble with Larry*, Bronson Pinchot played Larry Burton, who had been captured by rogue baboons while on his African honeymoon with his new wife Sally Easden Burton (Shanna Reed). He thought she was dead. She thought the same about him, and so she remarried. However, through a newspaper clipping, Larry found that his wife was still alive and returned to the States on a ship. Uninhibited Larry moved in with Sally, daughter Lindsay (Alex McKenna), and Sally's current, straight-laced husband Boyd Flatt (Perry King). Courteney Cox, who later became one of the stars of *Friends* and *Cougar Town*, played Sally's sister, Gabriella Easden. Also, featured on the sitcom was Marianne Muellerleile who played a different overweight character in each episode that Larry would insult ala Groucho Marx and Margaret Dumont.

Background

Andrew Nicholls and Darrell Vickers created and produced *The Trouble with Larry*. Originally titled *My First Husband*, Nicholls and Vickers had the idea of creating a sitcom about a deranged but charming guy who comes back into the life of the wife he last saw on their African honeymoon.[137] Before the series was cast, Nicholls and Vickers had drafted three scripts – the pilot, a script about Larry convincing Gabriella that he knew Robert Redford and they and the rest of the family venture to New York City to meet him, and a script where Larry thinks he has won a radio station contest for a house full of new furniture.[138] The latter two scripts were never used.

Bronson Pinchot had a development deal with CBS for a situation comedy and decided to make *The Trouble with Larry* his next project. The role of Boyd Flatt, Sally's second husband, was one of the last to be cast. Edward Herrmann and Peter McNichol turned down the role that was eventually offered to Perry King. Highest Common Denominator Productions and Melleager Productions in association with Warner Bros. produced the comedy.

Episode Guide: 3 aired; 4 unaired

Episode 1: August 25, 1993   "The Homecoming"

Director: Joel Zwick   Writers: Andrew Nicholls and Darrell Vickers

When Larry Burton returns after being presumed dead for ten years, he is surprised to learn that his wife remarried and is raising the daughter he fathered. He moves in with the family while supposedly writing his memoirs. Sally and Gabriella run an art gallery in Syracuse, NY that they may lose because a guy wants to rent their space for a video store. Sally's husband Boyd schedules a showdown with the new prospective tenant. Larry interrupts the meeting pretending to be a German deli owner next door to the art gallery. He talks the potential tenant into tearing up his lease for the space so the gallery is saved, and Larry gives credit for this action to Boyd.

Episode 2: September 1, 1993   "The Vigilantes"

Director: Robert Berlinger   Writer: Tom Finnigan

When his daughter's bike is stolen and his ex-wife's sister's apartment is broken into, Larry goes after the burglars. Larry and Gabriella check out the art gallery when someone reports a light on, and they are captured by the two thieves – a heavy-set woman and her short, older male accomplice. Larry and Gabriella are tied up, but Larry manages to get lose just as the burglars return. Larry says he wants to join their gang and tells the female burglar played by Marianne Muellerleile where she can make her last heist – at Boyd and Sally's house. Larry had hooked up the

SURPRISING ARRIVALS AND UNEXPECTED INHERITANCES

front door of the house to a Clapper and when the burglar claps her hands, she is knocked unconscious by the door.

Episode 3: September 8, 1993   "My Science Fair Lady"

Director: John Fortenberry   Writer: Lisa Rosenthal

Pretending to be a robot his daughter supposedly invented, Larry tries to help Lindsay with her science project. Although he doesn't get away with the fake robot idea, his knowledge of the jungle leads him to expose the science fair winner as another fake.

Episode 4: Unaired   "The Angel of Death and Taxes" (summary based on final draft script)

Director: Linda Day   Writer: Steve Billnitzer

Boyd is doing the family taxes trying to determine if they will have enough money to go on vacation to Florida. He finds that he will owe a few thousand dollars and won't be able to go to Florida. Larry offers to mail the tax forms, but before he sends them, he makes some changes resulting in the Flatt's getting a $40,000 refund. They go on vacation to Florida and purchase a lot of new things for the house. The family then gets a telegram from the IRS informing them of an audit. A repo man comes and takes everything they bought, and Boyd breaks down during the IRS audit. Larry and Gabriella dress up as Boyd and Sally to go the IRS to try to rectify the situation. When Larry turns up the heat in the room so that the auditor passes out, he makes the auditor think he is having a heart attack. Larry, pretending to be the voice of God, tells the auditor to let the Flatt's off the hook in order to save his life. The auditor agrees, and Larry turns down the heat.

Episode 5: Unaired   "Witless for the Prosecution" (summary based on final draft script)

Director: David Trainer   Writer: Art Everett

The Flatt's neighbor Carl is having a wall built to separate their properties. The construction workers are making a lot of noise and have blocked Boyd's car with a pile of dirt. Gabriella, Sally, and Lindsay go over to the neighbor's house to complain, but he is handsome and nice to them and offers to drive them to work and school. Larry and Boyd become jealous of Carl and decide to visit his place at night and let the air out of his tires. While doing this, Boyd gets stuck under Carl's vehicle where Carl finds him in the morning and decides to sue Boyd since he won't apologize. Larry defends Boyd in court, and Carl, since he is a lawyer, represents himself. He also knows the female judge (Marianne Muellerliele). Larry does a poor job defending Boyd until he pulls out a map of the properties that shows Carl has built the wall on the Flatt's land. The judge throws the case out, but Larry continues to insult the judge about her weight, and he and Boyd land in jail for the night.

Episode 6: Unaired   "Rhinestone Cowboyd"

Director: Mark Linn-Baker   Writer: Julie Thacker

When Sally gives Larry a kiss, he is sure that she is falling in love with him again and is afraid that she and Boyd will separate. Sally feels that Boyd is taking her for granted since, for their tenth anniversary, he wants to go to the same restaurant they always dine at for their anniversary. Larry has Boyd dress up in a fancy cowboy outfit, and they all go to a country and western bar. Larry dresses in disguise to pick a fight with Boyd so that Sally will think that her husband is a hero. In the end, Sally tells Boyd he made up for everything tonight.

Marianne Muellerleile played a waitress at the bar in this episode. Director Mark Linn-Baker co-starred with Bronson Pinchot on the ABC comedy *Perfect Strangers*.

Episode 7: Unaired   "Pinata Full of Bones" (summary based on table draft script)

Director: Robert Berlinger   Writer: Charlie Kaufman

On a trip to Egypt, Boyd discovers a lost tomb with a mummy and brings the mummy home with him. However, his homecoming is overshadowed by the family's focus on a news story about a circus chimp that fell and is in critical condition. Also, Lindsay is having a birthday party on Saturday, but Boyd receives a call from an Egyptologist who wants to see the mummy on Saturday. When Boyd moves Lindsay's party to Sunday, Larry decides to move it back to Saturday with

Gabriella's help. Larry finds the mummy, thinks it is a piñata, and paints it. It scares all the kids at the party when it is broken open. Sally comes home, sees the mess, and they all concoct a plan to steal the injured circus chimp covered in badges to take the mummy's place for Boyd's press conference with the Egyptologist. During the press conference, lightning strikes scaring the chimp who starts to move and frightens everyone.

Screenwriter Charlie Kaufman, who wrote this episode, was the executive story editor for *The Trouble with Larry*.

CBS Didn't Like *Trouble*

The Trouble with Larry was part of CBS's fall 1993 schedule and was given a special early start to the season. The first episode ranked sixty-third in the Nielsen ratings, and the comedy ended up being canceled before the fall season actually began. CBS apparently didn't like the direction of the sitcom. The network thought it too silly and wanted a series that was more heart-warming.[139]

Apple Pie with Jack Gilford, Rue McClanahan, Dabney Coleman

Chapter 17
Not Exactly the Family Next Door

While TV has sought to present comedies about stereotypical American families, it has also introduced viewers to many unusual families such as *The Addams Family*, the Bundys in *Married with Children*, and *The Simpsons*. Some not-so-typical families that didn't stay around for very long are described in this chapter.

Apple Pie

Premiered Saturday, September 23, 1978, at 8:30 PM on ABC

Set in 1930s Kansas City, Missouri, at the depths of the Great Depression, this comedy focused on a lonely, unmarried hairdresser and former tap dancer, Ginger-Nell Hollyhock (Rue McClanahan), who recruited a "family" by placing ads in the local newspapers. Ginger-Nell decided that she wanted a family who came together out of mutual affection for one another. Her ads were answered, and, after numerous interviews, she chose a son, daughter, grandfather, and husband. Among the family members were "Fast Eddie" Murtaugh (Dabney Coleman), her con-man "husband;" blind and cantankerous "Grandpa" (Jack Gilford); her "son" Junior Hollyhock (Derrel Maury) who wanted to fly like a bird and practiced radio sound effects, and "daughter" Anna Marie Hollyhock (Cattlin O'Heaney), a tap dancer whose ambition was to "tap dance for the Lord" in the Rev. Dudley Tuttle's Cavalcade for Christ Springtime Follies.

Background

Apple Pie, developed by Norman Lear, was based on the play *Nourish the Beast* by Steve Tesich. *Nourish the Beast* was first presented at The American Place Theatre in New York City on May 9, 1973 under the title of *Baba Goya*. Set in the 1970s, Goya would place ads in newspapers every time she lost a husband to death or divorce. Her current husband, Mario, thought he was dying, and so, this time, he placed an ad himself for a new husband for Goya. Both Goya and Mario had been orphans. Goya had a daughter, Sylvia, who was born out of wedlock, and a son Bruno, a police officer who Goya had adopted. Also in the household was a cranky old man who didn't like to be called Grandpa. He had responded to a previous ad Goya had placed for a husband but was too old for the "part." Goya offered him the "grandpa position." During the course of the play, Goya interviews a man who responded to Mario's ad. Since Mario really wasn't dying, and Goya didn't need a new husband right away, she gave the man a position has her distant cousin. He had originally wanted to be her brother, but Goya thought that when Mario did die, it would be better for her to promote a distant cousin to the position of her husband than a brother.

Lear took *Nourish the Beast* and made it less ethnic by changing the names of the characters, the time period, and setting to make it more middle American.

Originally, a one-hour pilot was shot and previewed for critics who were less than impressed. They didn't like the grandfather's slapstick blindness, who the family said could smell the comics when he had a newspaper in front of him. Also, in the pilot, there were two sons, one of whom walked around in chains and padlocks hoping to be a candidate for *Ripley's Believe It or Not*. The pilot was reduced to thirty minutes, the son-in-chains character, portrayed by Richard Libertini, was deleted, and the concept was changed to emphasize the relationship between Ginger-Nell and Fast Eddie.[140] T.A.T. Communications produced the series.

Episode Guide: 2 aired; 5 unaired

Episode 1: September 23, 1978 "Fast Eddie Slows Down"

Director: Peter Bonerz   Story: Richard Powell and Lawrence J. Cohen   Teleplay: Charlie Hauck

Ginger-Nell needs a father for her makeshift family, and the charming "Fast Eddie" responds to her newspaper ad. "Fast Eddie" may be the dangerous bank robber being sought by the police, but then the family does need money to make their mortgage payment of $43 by Friday or lose their home.

Rue McClanahan starred in *Apple Pie* right after she had co-starred in *Maude* with Bea Arthur. The two would later reunite in *The Golden Girls*.

Episode 2: September 30, 1978   "Ginger-Nell Goes Hollywood" (summaries for this episode and the following ones provided by Charlie Hauck)

Director: Peter Bonerz   Writer: Charlie Hauck

Eddie doesn't like to make long-term commitments, and so he won't commit to dancing the Peabody with Ginger-Nell five days away. Freddie Reardon (Ken Berry), an encyclopedia salesman, stops by and says he's a dancer on his way to Hollywood where he has been promised a part in a Busby Berkeley movie. However, he has to raise the money to get there. Ginger-Nell invites him to rehearse his dance routines with her. She also buys encyclopedias from him. Freddie asks Ginger-Nell to go to Hollywood with him to dance as partners in the movie. When Eddie becomes jealous, Ginger-Nell tells him that all he has to do is ask her to stay, and she will. But Eddie can't even make that commitment. He telegrams a friend in Hollywood to find out if Reardon is legit. When the day arrives for Ginger-Nell and Freddie to leave, Eddie finally brings himself to ask Ginger-Nell to stay. Freddie leaves, but Ginger-Nell stays. A telegram arrives from Eddie's friend stating the movie parts were for real. Eddie says he will go with Ginger-Nell to the Peabody dance contest.

Episode 3: Unaired   "Rich Man, Poor Girl"

Director: Peter Bonerz   Writer: Sy Rosen

Anna Marie is smitten by Tinkham Davenport, a young man from a very wealthy family. Ginger-Nell feels the young man will just take advantage of her daughter, but Eddie is in favor of the relationship. He feels that Anna Marie will have a chance to marry into a wealthy family. Anna Marie receives an engraved invitation to a formal ball at the Union Club. Tinkham is taking her. On the night of the ball, Tinkham and his mother and father stop by to meet the Hollyhocks. Ginger-Nell gets angry at the Davenport's snobbish attitude, and she wants to kick them out of the house. Eddie calms her down. But eventually the Davenport's go too far, and Eddie himself kicks them out. Anna Marie sees that Tinkham was worthless because he didn't stand up for her to his parents. But she is very sad to miss the ball. Grandpa finds his old tuxedo in a trunk, puts it on, and escorts Anna Marie to the dance.

Episode 4: Unaired   "The Tornado"

Director: Peter Bonerz   Writer: William Davenport

Ginger-Nell tells everyone to go down to the storm cellar when the family hears a tornado warning on the radio. Eddie and Grandpa have been working on a project down there and discourage the family from investigating. Eddie says the tornado will never get near them. Although Eddie and Grandpa claim they are making furniture polish, Ginger-Nell figures out that they're really making beer. News reports warn that the tornado is nearer. However, before they can get down to the storm cellar, there is an explosion. The beer vat has blown up, and the cellar is filled with beer. They kneel down to pray, hoping the storm won't hit the house. Eddie, a non-believer, does his best to talk to God to take responsibility for putting the family in danger, and the storm passes.

Episode 5: Unaired   "Ginger-Nell Loses Her Touch"

Director: Peter Bonerz   Writer: Arthur Julian

While Ginger-Nell is on an emergency errand, Grandpa convinces Fast Eddie, who had been an Army barber, to do an important lady's hair so Ginger-Nell won't lose her as a customer. The woman loves Eddie's work, and soon Ginger-Nell's other clients are asking for Eddie instead of her. When Anna Marie needs to have her hair styled so she can get an usherette job, Eddie folds under the pressure, and Ginger-Nell has to take over and saves the day. She and Eddie go back to their regular roles.

Episode 6: Unaired   "A Man from Ginger-Nell's Past"

Director: Peter Bonerz   Writer: Arthur Julian

When a small circus comes to town, Eddie is eager to set up his shell game on the midway. Earlier in her life, Ginger-Nell had traveled with the same circus and had had a fling with the owner, Congo Dwayne. Dwayne comes to visit Ginger-Nell, and she gets upset when he seems inappropriately interested in young Anna Marie. When he offers Junior a job of traveling with the circus and taking care of the elephant, Junior loves the idea. Ginger-Nell pleads with Eddie for help, and Eddie entices Dwayne into a shell game and wins his uniform, whip, and the elephant.

Episode 7: Unaired   "They Walk Among Us"

Director: Peter Bonerz   Writer: Sy Rosen

At Halloween, there are reports in the newspapers of a scientist claiming Martians have been assuming human form and living in towns in America. As the Hollyhocks get ready to go to a Halloween party at the Soldiers and Sailors Home, they realize that their radio keeps going on and off on its own. They conclude that one of them is a Martian. Clues point at Eddie since he's been very secretive about his valise which he has never unpacked since moving in. When the family forces him to open it, they find nothing but clothes. However, Junior sees something at the bottom of the valise that Eddie tries to hide. It turns out to be a photo of him as a boy with his beloved dog, and he had been ashamed of seeming sentimental. A visitor then comes by to report that all the radios in town have been going on and off on their own because of static electricity. The family goes to the party.

Only Two

Apple Pie was on Saturdays opposite *Good Times* on CBS, another Lear-produced show that was in its waning days, and *CHiPs* on NBC, one of the network's most popular shows at the time. Low ratings killed *Apple Pie* after only two episodes (its first episode ranked fifty-fourth and its last episode ranked last out of sixty-seven shows) —the quickest cancelation of a fall series up to that time.

Everything's Relative

Premiered Tuesday, April 6, 1999, at 9:30 PM on NBC

A sitcom about a dysfunctional family with the only seemingly well-adjusted member, Leo Gorelick (Kevin Rahm), being a mild-mannered comedy writer pretty much describes *Everything's Relative*. Leo's bossy father, Jake (Jeffrey Tambor, *Arrested Development, Twenty Good Years, Welcome to the Captain*), had divorced his mother, Mickey (Jill Clayburgh), a clinical therapist, about twenty years earlier. Leo also had a neurotic, self-centered brother, Marty (Eric Schaeffer), a surgeon. Trina (Maureen Cassidy) was Leo's writing partner for the *OFI Monday* TV show.

Background

If the premise of a sensible character surrounded by dysfunctional relatives sounds somewhat like *Arrested Development*, that is no coincidence since *Everything's Relative* was conceived by Mitchell Hurwitz who later created the Jason Bateman sitcom. Witt/Thomas Productions in association with Warner Bros. and NBC Studios produced the series.

Episode Guide: 4 aired episodes

Episode 1: April 6, 1999   "Where the Son Doesn't Shine"

Director: John Fortenberry   Writer: Mitchell Hurwitz (summary based on final draft script)

Leo has just broken up with his girlfriend, Christine, and Jake has fixed him up with a friend's daughter who likes Jake. Jake is also planning an engagement party for his son Marty who is getting married for the third time. Meanwhile, Mickey is thinking of selling the house she purchased with Jake many years ago and moving closer to Leo and to Jake. Leo announces to Marty that he would like to break up with his family since he feels they are too controlling. He is tired of doing everything for them with no time for himself. At the engagement party for Marty, Leo plans to explain to his mother and dad that he wants separation from them, but, before he can, Mickey tells him that he's always trying so hard to keep everyone together. Leo realizes that she may be right.

Kevin Rahm (Leo) subsequently starred on *Desperate Housewives* and *I Hate My Teenage Daughter*.

Episode 2: April 13, 1999 "Prisoner of Love"

Director: John Fortenberry   Writer: Mitchell Hurwitz

Leo's ex-girlfriend, Christine, calls, and Leo tries to pretend he is no longer as involved with his parents and brother as he was when they were dating. However, the pretense comes undone when they all get on the phone with him. Meanwhile, Mickey wants to throw another engagement party for Marty since Marty complained that he never got any of the cake at the first party. Leo and Marty reminisce about their childhoods with flashbacks showing them at Indian Camp where Marty says he didn't get to eat as much fish as the other kids. Leo decides to attend the second engagement party so Christine can see for herself that he can ignore his family. But on the way to the party with their dad, Leo and Marty argue, Jake throws away the car keys, and they are unable to make it to the engagement party.

Shia LeBeouf played the young Marty in the flashbacks on this episode.

Episode 3: April 20, 1999 "City of Flies"

Director: John Fortenberry   Writer: Mitchell Hurwitz   (summary based on final draft script)

Jake buys Leo an expensive Mexican basket which Leo is less than thrilled to receive but tries to act pleased. Later, when Mickey comes by looking for Marty, she sees the basket and jumps to the conclusion that collecting Mexican baskets is Leo's new hobby. To outdo the father's gift, Mickey purchases seventeen Mexican baskets at a garage sale and then goes to Mexico to purchase more. Leo tells her not to compete with his dad over buying these baskets, but nonetheless Mickey brings back more baskets from Mexico. She finds hiding in one a thirteen-year-old boy. She wants the boy to stay with her awhile as a substitute for her sons who, since growing up, seem to spend more time with their father than with her.

Episode 4: April 27, 1999 "Just My Luck"

Director: John Fortenberry   Writer: Mitchell Hurwitz

Mickey sends a video to Leo which shows her doing a stand-up comedy routine about the family. Mickey wants Leo to show the tape to his boss, which he won't. Jake gives Leo's boss the video, and he thinks the tape is funny and wants to put it on the show. At the last minute, Leo comes up with a comedy sketch with the catch phrase "Just My Luck" in place of his mother's video.

Relative No Longer

NBC ordered four episodes of *Everything's Relative* as a spring tryout series. Ratings declined with each successive episode, and the comedy was not renewed for the fall.

The Grubbs

Supposed to premiere Sunday, November 3, 2002 at 9:30 PM on Fox

The Grubbs, a family of self-satisfied underachievers, featured Mike Grubb (Randy Quaid), who fell off a forklift at work and milked a back injury for all it was worth in disability checks, enabled by his wife Sophie (Carol Kane). As Sophie said, Mike made more money with a bad back than he used to make with his whole body. Mike and Sophie had two sons: Jimmy (Brian Sites) who liked to blow up stuff and had been held back in school so that he was in the same class as his brother, Mitch

(Michael Cera, before he became a movie star) who was also an underachiever until his new English teacher, Ms. Heather Krenetsky (Lori Rom) inspired him to aim higher. Coach Garra (Ricardo Chavira) at Mitch's school was dating Ms. Krenetsky, and Mitch's classmate and next door neighbor, Cricket Widmer (Alexandra Krosney), was attracted to Mitch. The comedy was set in a depressed steel town called Hackville, and most episodes focused on Mitch and his attraction to Ms. Krenetsky.

Background

The Grubbs was based on the British series, *The Grimleys*, which focused on Gordon Grimley (the Mitch character in the American version) who was in love with his English teacher, Geraldine Titley. Gordon's nasty, impotent father, Baz, was a steelworker with a bad back who had been on strike so long that he turned into a couch potato leading his wife, Janet, to start looking at other men. The pilot for the British series revealed that Janet was having an affair with next-door neighbor Mr. Titley, who was Geraldine's dad and apparently also had fathered Gordon. In addition to his parents and brother, Darren, Gordon had a promiscuous sister Lisa with the nickname "Marge" because "she spread so easily."

Fox originally ordered thirteen episodes of *The Grubbs* but then reduced the order to eight. Jeffrey Ventimilia and Joshua Sternin were executive producers of the situation comedy, which was produced by Low Bar Productions in association with Granada, Universal, and Twentieth Century-Fox.

Episode Guide: 8 unaired

Episode 1: "Pilot"

Director: Andrew D. Weyman   Writers: Jeffrey Ventimilia and Joshua Sternin

Mitch has a crush on his new English teacher, Ms. Krenetsky, who turns out to be his next door neighbor, and he strives to do more than average work in school so he can have a better life than his dad. His father wants both Jimmy and Mitch to be steel workers like he and his father before him were. The new teacher wants the class to write an essay about their future. In order to impress the teacher, Mitch constructs a special shoebox diorama for English class which he carries with him at school, even taking it to gym class. Coach Garra places the shoebox in the middle of the track, and it gets destroyed. Mitch then writes an essay for English class on which he gets his first C+.

Episode 2: "Dancing Mitch"

Director: Andrew Tsao   Writer: Jeff Martin

Ms. Krenetsky is chaperoning the school dance but needs some parents to help her. To prevent the dance from being canceled, Mitch volunteers his parents. His father Mike teaches Mitch how to go with the music when dancing. Mitch wants to ask Ms. Krenetsky to dance but is afraid of rejection. When Coach Garra shows up at the event to dance with Ms. Krenetsky, Jimmy distracts him so Mitch can request her to dance. However, before he can, Cricket asks Mitch to dance. Finally, Mitch gets the chance to have the last dance with Ms. Krenetsky.

Episode 3: "Hoop Dreams"

Director: Andrew Tsao   Writers: Tyrone Finch and Tom Purcell

Coach wants Mitch to join the freshman basketball team to draw offensive fouls. Mitch joins because he thinks this will attract Ms. Krenetsky. Ms. Krenetsky wants Mitch to quit basketball before he's hurt, but he shows up at the last game and gets both teams disqualified for starting a fight with the opposing team. Meanwhile, his dad is upset thinking he will die because of his high cholesterol, and so he wants to leave a legacy by trying to break some Guinness record. In the end, Mitch's mother convinces his dad that Mitch can be his legacy.

Episode 4: "The First Time"

Director: Andrew Tsao   Writers: Joe Port and Joe Wiseman

Mitch is upset at the possibility of Ms. Krenetsky having sex with Coach Garra. His dad tells him that when a woman has sex with a man, she is ruined for all other men. Mitch vows not to let the Coach "ruin" Ms. Krenetsky. He interrupts their trysts by having the Coach's car towed, by inviting guys to a toga party at her house, and by visiting her to ask about his homework assignment. However, he cannot stop their assignation. Meanwhile, Sophie admits to Mike that she was not a virgin when they married. Mike seeks to find who Sophie slept with while in high school. He informs Sophie that, despite what she may have thought, he was a virgin when they married. Sophie confesses that she had sex with a boy in high school who is now the school's janitor. Mike goes to the school and wrestles the janitor to the ground.

Episode 5: "Drink Carrying Robot"

Director: Andrew Tsao   Writer: Jessica Kaminsky

Mike rips off the paper boy for scratch-off tickets in the newspapers. He wins and buys a drink-carrying robot with the money. Meanwhile, Sophie gets the book *Ordinary People* that Mitch had been assigned by Ms. Krenetsky banned from the school because she thinks it puts mothers in a bad light. This irritates Mitch who says that he doesn't need his mother anymore. Sophie then wants to have a baby so she can have someone to care for. Although Mike doesn't want another kid, Sophie gets him drunk, and they attempt to make love in the back of an old car parked in their backyard. In the course of the lovemaking, Mike hurts his back, and the drink-carrying robot, much like Lassie, goes to Mitch for help. Sophie comes to understand that Mitch is growing up but realizes that Mike will always need her.

Episode 6: "Bedlam"

Director: Andrew Tsao   Writers: Ron Corcillo and A.J. Poulin

Mike orders an adjustable bed in order to get a free TV. After Jimmy glues his classmates to their seats in Ms. Krenetsky's class, she wants to know what the Grubbs will do about his behavior. Sophie agrees to allow the teacher to spend time with Jimmy in the hopes of changing him. Mitch becomes envious of the attention Jimmy is getting from Ms. Krenetsky. He wants to become like Jimmy and so spray paints the school lockers. Since Ms. Krenetsky thinks Mitch should know better, she gives him a week of detention. After Mitch and Jimmy fight, Jimmy decides to go back to being bad, and Mitch is no longer jealous of him.

Episode 7: "Rock"

Director: Matthew Diamond   Writer: Tasha Goldstone

Mitch wants to play his guitar at the school's talent night. When he plays for his dad, Mike brings out his electric guitar to teach Mitch how to rock. Mitch suggests that they both play at the school's talent night, but his dad refuses because of stage fright. Mitch decides he will play alone and not be afraid. However, Mike finally joins him on stage, and they proceed to break up their instruments much to the delight of the crowd. Meanwhile, Jimmy is told that if he doesn't start doing his homework assignments, he will be held back again. Because he wants to continue to be in the same class as his brother, he decides to do his assignments. Sophie writes an essay about herself for Jimmy on which he gets a D. She is upset about the grade and divulges to Ms. Krenetsky that she wrote the essay. Krenetsky says that the essay received a D because she couldn't believe a woman could be so subservient. Upon learning that Sophie wrote the paper, the grade is changed to F. Jimmy has to write a new essay, and he writes about Mitch's performance at talent night.

Episode 8: "The Feud"

Director: Andrew D. Weyman   Writers: Jeffrey Ventimilia and Joshua Sternin

When Ms. Krenetsky invites Mitch and his parents to her housewarming party, he decides to get a housewarming gift for his teacher. He thinks he will get her a necklace, but ends up giving her a picture of himself which she displays in her living room. Meanwhile, Cricket's dad, Arthur, argues with Mike about leaving his garbage cans out in the street. When Arthur brings the Grubb's cans in off the street, Mike feels insulted, and they feud. Mitch is afraid his dad will ruin the housewarming party since Arthur will also be attending with his daughter. He tries to talk his dad out of doing anything against Arthur at the party. Mike apologizes to Arthur, but Arthur says his daughter Cricket is too good for Mitch. Mike then takes his clothes off to reveal he is wearing elephant underwear with the trunk sticking out in the front.

Dan Castellaneta, the voice of Homer Simpson, was Cricket's dad Arthur on this episode.

Exterminated

After reducing the episode order, Fox executives were still not thrilled with the sitcom after negative critical reaction at previews and so decided not to air it. The network scheduled *Andy Richter Controls the Universe* in its place.

In commenting on why *The Grubbs* was canceled by Fox, producer Joshua Sternin said, "We were not exactly critics' darlings, to say the least, and I can't imagine that didn't factor into their decision. But generally speaking, it's never a good idea to try too hard to fathom the logic of network programming. That way lies madness."[141]

Ivan the Terrible

Premiered Saturday, August 21, 1976 at 8:30 PM on CBS

This Cold War-era satire of Russian life in the 1970s set in Moscow revolved around the Petrovsky family and its patriarch Ivan Petrovsky (Lou Jacobi), the headwaiter in the main dining room of The Hotel Metropole in Moscow. In addition to Ivan, the family, who lived in a very tiny apartment, included:

- Olga (Maria Karnilova), Ivan's wife who worked on a construction crew;

- Vladimir (Phil Leeds), Olga's first husband to whom she had been married for six months twenty- three-years earlier and who played chess for a living;

- Tatiana (Despo Diamantidou), Ivan's mother-in-law who was a motor woman on the Moscow subway;

- Nikolai (Alan Cauldwell), Ivan's son, a cosmonaut trainee who tended to get nauseous two feet off the ground;

- Svetlana (Nana Tucker aka Nana Visitor), Nikolai's wife, a student ballerina with the State ballet;

- Sascha (Matthew Barry), Ivan's twelve-year-old son and the only family member who could control the heard-but-never-seen pet dog, Rasputin;

- Sonya (Caroline Kava), Ivan's daughter, a multi-lingual tourist guide, and

- Raoul (Manuel Martinez), a Cuban foreign exchange student enrolled in agricultural studies who could not speak Russian.

Christopher Hewitt (*Mr. Belvedere*) appeared in different roles but always as a Russian bureaucrat.

Background

Ivan the Terrible was developed by the late comedian Alan King, Rupert Hitzig, Peter Stone, and Herb Sargent from an idea by Harvey Stambler. CBS ordered five episodes of the series which was sandwiched between *The Jeffersons* and *The Mary Tyler Moore Show*. King-Hitzig Productions produced the series.

Episode Guide: 5 aired episodes

Episode 1: August 21, 1976   "Comrade Can You Spare a Ruble" (aka "Ivan's Out of Work") (summary based on production script)

Director: Peter H. Hunt   Writers: Mike Barrie and Jim Mulholland

The Petrovsky family's household expenses are increasing, and Ivan wants everyone to cut back. Vladimir persuades Ivan to ask for a pay raise from his boss, Mr. Yoshenko, and to inform his boss that another hotel wants to hire him as their headwaiter if the raise is not granted. When Ivan goes to his boss with the request, Yoshenko tells him to take the new job. Eventually, Yoshenko comes to the Petrovsky apartment to speak with Ivan. He says that the restaurant is in shambles since Ivan quit, and he wants him to return with a pay increase.

Episode 2: August 28, 1976   "I Am Not a Crook" (summary based on production script)

Director: Peter H. Hunt   Writers: David S. Meranze and Marc Alan Zagoren

Sasha brings home a letter from school stating that he has been suspended because he scored ninety-nine on a placement exam and the school officials think he must have cheated. When Ivan sees Sasha's teacher, the teacher says that no one has ever scored that high on the Trans Soviet National Student Vocational Placement and Annual Guidance General Information Examination which covers a wide array of subjects. Ivan requests a hearing on the matter. At the hearing, Sasha says he really did know the answers to all the questions based on what he learned at home from different members of the family. The hearing examiner quizzes Sasha on different subjects, and he responds with the correct answers.

Episode 3: September 4, 1976   "The Very Loud Family" (summary based on production script)

Director: Peter H. Hunt   Writer: Mike Barrie and Jim Mulholland

The Petrovsky's are chosen as the typical Russian family for an American TV interview show hosted by Tom Skyler. Bureaucrat Federov gives Ivan's apartment a complete makeover so Americans can see the high Russian standard of living. At the end of the interview, Ivan confesses that all of his family lives together in a small, crowded apartment. However, since Federov never got official approval from the Kremlin for the makeover, Ivan doesn't get in trouble for revealing the truth.

Episode 4: September 11, 1976   "The Great Red Hope" (summary based on production script)

Director: Peter H. Hunt   Story: Harve Brosten and Barry Harman   Teleplay: Tony Geiss and Tom Meehan

Ivan wants to find Vladimir a wife who has her own apartment. He met Masha Malakov (Shirley Stoler), an Olympian shot putter at the Metropole, and invites her to meet Vladimir. After two weeks, Masha and Vladimir decide to marry. However, Ivan finds that the apartment he thought Masha had is really only a room in the Palace of Sports – a women's dormitory in which no men are allowed. The couple decides to live with the Petrovsky's. Ivan advises Vladimir to get a divorce, but, in a shot put meet outside Russia, Masha wins a gold medal and decides to defect. She is later disqualified because she failed her chromosome test.

Episode 5: September 18, 1976   "Red Tape" (summary based on production script)

Director: Peter H. Hunt   Writers: Peter Stone and Herb Sargent

Svetlana announces that she and Nikki are going to have a baby. To get his daughter-in-law and her husband more space, Ivan goes to a Russian bureaucrat to ask for a one-room apartment. He gets the apartment but, since he didn't make it clear to the official that he wanted the new apartment in addition to the one he has, the family has to vacate their present abode. However, Ivan is able to talk the prospective tenants for his current apartment out of renting it.

This episode was actually the pilot for the series.

Episodes Not Produced

Contained in the Peter Stone Papers at the New York Public Library for the Performing Arts are several additional storylines for the series that were proposed. In fact, the network ordered eight more scripts for *Ivan the Terrible*, but, for reasons described below, they were never produced.[142] These storylines included:

"Guess Who's Coming to Dinner"   Writers: David Meranze and Marc Alan Zagoren

Sonya invites an African-American tourist from one of her tours to dinner, with the family thinking that this means marriage for Sonya.

"Raoul Is a Spy"   Writers: Nick Arnold and Diana Omkar Spencer

Ivan suspects that Raoul may be a spy. He discovers rolls of film Raoul hid under his overcoat, takes Raoul to the Minister of Internal Security, and finds the film is of Carmen Miranda dancing.

"Tomatoes"   Writers: Ethel and Mel Brez

A farmer in Kazakstan wins a chess championship and, out of gratitude to Vladimir, sends the Petrovsky's a lot of tomatoes. To can the tomatoes, Ivan has to get a permit from the government which first requires him to undergo a physical. The doctor thinks Ivan has a contagious disease because of the red splotches on his skin and tells Ivan to eat tomatoes. The doctor later calls Ivan to say he made a mistake in the diagnosis and that really Ivan is allergic to tomatoes.

"Divorce, Russian Style" Writers: Jim McDonald and Rob Gerlach

Olga receives a letter informing her that a computer check revealed that she failed to sign the divorce papers from Vladimir. She needs to signs the papers as quickly as possible. However, having tired of Ivan being inconsiderate toward her, Olga delays signing until Ivan also signs a document stating he will be kinder to everyone.

"Ivan's Rib" Writer: Marilyn Suzanne Miller

The women in the Petrovsky household are tired of working all day and still having to make dinner and do all the housework. The men want to prove to the women that it is possible to work and run a house. After they attempt to prepare a dinner, the women point out that they don't mind doing housework as long as they are not taken for granted and that household duties should be shared between the men and women.

"Bushinsky Boy"

The Petrovsky's share their kitchen with the family next door – the Bushinsky's. Sonya falls in love with their son.

"Used Car" Writers: Tony Geiss and Tom Meehan

The family can finally afford to buy a used car, but Vladimir, Raoul, and Ivan end up in the hospital after an automobile accident.

"Oldest Man in Russia" Writers: Mike Barrie and Jim Mulholland

Vladimir's 140-year-old uncle comes to visit.

"Red Shoes" Writers: David Meranze and Marc Alan Zagoren

Nikolai demands that Svetlana give up her ballet career.

"Svetlana's Parents"

Svetlana's parents come to visit from Leningrad.

"Lottery Winner"

Ivan wins the Russian version of the lottery, and after he spends almost all the money, he finds out that under Russian tax law, he owes 630,000 rubles.

"Game Show Contestant"

Ivan becomes a contestant on a Russian game show where the first prize is a private home. He has to become an expert in the Russian version of American history to win. His family and the Bushinsky's are his tutors.

International Complications

Ivan the Terrible got respectable ratings. However, CBS decided not to renew the comedy because of the risk of alienating the Soviet Union since the network was interested in obtaining the rights to broadcast the 1980 Olympics from Moscow. As it turned out, NBC got those rights, and the U.S. ended up boycotting the Olympics because of the Soviet Union invasion of Afghanistan. The producers tried to revive the series in first-run syndication, but their attempts were not successful.

The Kallikaks

Premiered Wednesday, August 3, 1977, at 9:30 PM on NBC

According to NBC publicity for this comedy, *The Kallikaks* were "loathsome, lying and lazy! And those are their good points!" The Kallikak family consisted of J.T. (David Huddleston), a former coal miner from West Virginia who moved his family to California when he inherited a gas station; Venus (Edie McClurg), his wife; Bobbi Lou (Buddy Ebsen's daughter Bonnie), their social-climbing daughter, and Junior (Pat Peterson), their mechanical genius son. Helping J.T. run the gas station was Oscar Heinz (Peter Palmer), a German who could barely speak English.

Background

NBC ordered five episodes of the sitcom, which was created by Roger Price and Stanley Ralph Ross. They apparently chose the name of the show from a book published in 1912 titled *The Kallikak Family: A Study in the Heredity of Feeble-Mindedness*. *The Kallikaks* was conceived as a countrified version of *All in the Family*. Originally, Kathleen Nolan who had played Kate on *The Real McCoys* was cast as the wife on the series and Damon Bradley Raskin had the role of the son, but they were replaced by Edie McClurg and Pat Peterson. The comedy's theme song, sung by Roy Clark, was "Beat the System"—which pretty much summed up J.T.'s approach to life. Neila Productions in association with NBC produced the comedy.

Episode Guide: 5 aired

Episode 1: August 3, 1977   "You Auto Buy Now"

Director: Dennis Steinmetz   Writers: Stanley Ralph Ross and Roger Price

J.T. gloats when he unloads an old car abandoned at the gas station on his daughter's new boyfriend for a large profit.

Episode 2: August 10, 1977   "The Bells Are Wronging"

Director: Unknown   Writer: George Yanok

J.T. complains about a $14 over-charge on his phone bill. The phone company's computer then makes a big error and sends him a $140,000 refund from which J.T. tries to profit.

Episode 3: August 17, 1977   "TV or Not TV"

Director: Unknown   Writers: George Yanok and Stanley Ralph Ross

A TV producer (Jack Carter) offers the Kallikaks $500 per month to watch his shows on a TV set they got from an audience rating service.

Episode 4: August 24, 1977   "I Coulda Been a Contender"

Director: Unknown   Writer: Stanley Ralph Ross

After seeing the movie *Rocky*, J.T. tries to turn Oscar into a prize-fighter and has to deal with two gangsters who want to manage Oscar's career.

Episode 5: August 31, 1977   "Swami, How I Love Ya"

Director: Unknown   Writer: Unknown

The Kallikaks hire a medium to find out if Venus' late brother left them an inheritance.

The Usual Reasons

Co-creator Roger Price had a falling out with Stanley Ralph Ross, and George Yanok was brought in to help produce and write the series. According to Yanok, Ross was a "set-up-and-joke" writer, and Yanok was not. That conflict, along with NBC programming executives not knowing what to do with the show, doomed it from the start. As Yanok indicated, "the network wasn't getting high enough ratings for a show they didn't particularly like in the first place."[143]

Mr. T and Tina

Premiered Saturday, September 25, 1976, at 8:30 PM on ABC

A widowed Japanese inventor, Mr. Takahashi (known as Mr. T), transferred by his company from Tokyo to Chicago, dealing with his free-spirited American housekeeper, Tina Kelly, summed up the premise of this situation comedy. Pat Morita, who had played Arnold on *Happy Days*, left that hit series to star as Mr. T; Susan Blanchard was Tina, the governess. In addition to Mr. T and Tina, the household included Sachi and Aki (June Angela and Eugene Profanato, sister and brother in real life), Mr. T's two small children; Matsu, his seventy-year-old uncle (Jerry Hatsuo Fujikawa), and Michi, his sister-in-law (Pat Suzuki). Also in the cast were Ted Lange as Harvard, the nosy apartment handyman, and Miss Llewelyn

(Miriam Byrd-Nethery) as the landlady. The song "Chicago," partially done in an Oriental style, was the theme for the comedy.

Background

According to Donald Reiker, who co-wrote one of the episodes of *Mr. T and Tina*, the original concept for this comedy involved a Japanese soldier, found on an island and relocated to Chicago, who didn't believe World War II was over.[144] Presumably this version of the series was not titled *Mr. T and Tina*. In any event, the situation comedy that premiered on ABC was created by James Komack who had developed other comedies profiled in this book, such as *Another Day*, *Snip*, and *The Rollergirls*.

Mr. T and Tina was related in different ways to Komack's more successful comedies. It reversed the ethnicities from *The Courtship of Eddie's Father*, on which he had been featured as an actor. In that series, a widowed American father and his son had a traditional Japanese housekeeper. *Mr. T and Tina* had the clash of cultures theme from *Chico and the Man*, except instead of the clash between Latino and Anglo cultures, *Mr. T and Tina* focused on the clash of traditional Japanese culture with less traditional American culture.

The pilot for *Mr. T and Tina*, which introduced the two main characters, was written by Stan Cutler and titled "The Ogallala Connection," identifying the town in Nebraska from where Tina came. The pilot was never broadcast.

Madelyn Davis and Bob Carroll, Jr., who had co-created the classic *I Love Lucy*, were brought in to help produce *Mr. T and Tina*. They scripted the premiere episode of the sitcom. To introduce the new comedy to viewers, Pat Morita played the Mr. T character on the second season premiere episode of *Welcome Back, Kotter*. In that episode, the high school where Mr. Kotter taught had a career day, and Mr. T came to show his inventions to the students. The second season premiere of *Kotter* occurred two days before the debut of *Mr. T and Tina*, and so presumably Mr. T's appearance on that show would help boost the audience for *Mr. T and Tina*.

Episode Guide: 5 aired; 3 unaired

Episode 1: September 25, 1976   "Tina Really Truly Gets Fired"

Director: James Sheldon   Writers: Madelyn Davis and Bob Carroll, Jr.

Tina loses a $200 kite in the winds of Chicago and, much to Mr. T's dismay, dresses his daughter in an outfit which shows her belly button. Mr. T is working on a new invention – a flight belt – which allows people to fly. Just like a scene from a Lucy show, Mr. T puts the belt on, flies around the apartment, and crashes to the floor when Tina pushes a button on the belt's remote control device. This is the last straw, and Mr. T fires Tina to the disappointment of the rest of his household. He then interviews new candidates for Tina's position. Tina in disguise applies for her old job back. Mr. T admits he is not perfect and rehires her.

The Sweathogs from *Welcome Back, Kotter* appear in the opening scene of this episode, wishing Mr. T well when he goes to Chicago.

Episode 2: October 2, 1976   "What Makes Sumo Run?"

Director: Unknown   Writers: Patricia Jones and Donald Reiker

Mr. T's cousin, a sumo wrestler from Japan, visits and is immediately attracted to Tina. Before Mr. T can tell him that Tina really doesn't love him, he challenges Mr. T to a wrestling match in the living room with Tina going to the winner.

When contacted about this episode, Donald Reiker, who wrote the episode with his wife Patricia, said he no longer has the script for "What Makes Sumo Run?," but if he did, he would burn it immediately – that was how bad it was.[145]

Episode 3: October 16, 1976   "Guess Who's Coming to Live"

Director: Unknown   Writer: Carl Kleinschmitt

In a flashback episode, Mr. T, newly arrived in Chicago, unwittingly hires a scatterbrained American girl as governess for his children and finds himself the unyielding object introduced to an invincible force.

Episode 4: October 23, 1976   "I'm O.K., You're All Bananas"

Director: James Komack and Gary Shimokawa   Writer: Jim Mulligan

Mr. T feels he gets no respect from his family since they came to America, and he blames Tina for this. He wants everyone to do things his way. Tina suggests they all have a sensitivity session so each can "walk a mile in the other person's shoes." Each family member acts like Mr. T, while Mr. T acts like each of them. Mr. T sees how he was too strict and says everyone can make their own decisions. However, Tina dislikes the new situation, and Mr. T says that he will go back to how he acted before and do away with democracy in his household.

Episode 5: October 30, 1976   "I Thought He'd Never Leave"

Director: Dennis Steinmetz   Writer: Morton Miller

An obnoxious houseguest arrives from Japan, and Mr. T's strict adherence to Japanese tradition requires him to put up with the guest because, when they were kids, Mr. T saved his life. Harvard and Mr. T devise a plan to get into an argument, have the house guest take sides, and then one of them would ask the house guest to leave. When this plan doesn't work, Harvard suggests that Mr. T pretend he is dying and have his last wish be for the house guest to go back to Japan. Finally, Mr. T confesses that he never really saved the man's life when they were kids and that he is no longer responsible for him. The house guest proclaims he is "free" and leaves.

Episode 6: Unaired   "Where is My Wandering Matsu Tonight?"

Director: Rick Edelstein   Writers: Madelyn Davis and Bob Carroll, Jr.

When Tina, the kids, and Uncle Matsu go to the university museum, Tina loses Matsu. She asks Harvard to find a cop to report the uncle missing. Eventually, Matsu phones Mr. T to inform him that he took the wrong train and went to Waukegan. Mr. T tells him to take the train back to Chicago, but Matsu phones again to say he ended up in Skokie. When he calls for the third time, Mr. T advises him to get a cab to bring him home. In the meantime, different police officers keep bringing elderly Japanese men to the apartment thinking they are Matsu. When the real Matsu finally arrives, Mr. T and Tina are asleep in the living room, and so Matsu goes upstairs to bed. He finally comes down from his bedroom to show everyone he has returned.

Episode 7: Unaired   "Reading, Writing and Rice"

Director: Rick Edelstein   Writer: Rowby Goren

Mr. T is afraid that his kids are losing their Japanese heritage. Tina suggests that she begin teaching the children Japanese culture, but, before he leaves for a business trip to New York City, Mr. T instructs her not to attempt this. She goes ahead anyway and involves not only Mr. T's kids but also other kids from the building who receive lessons in Kabuki theatre, origami, and Japanese folk dances from her, Harvard, and Michi. When Mr. T comes back early from the business trip, he discovers what she is doing, and Miss Llewelyn says that the school violates Mr. T's lease and that she will have to evict the family. However, after the kids show Mr. T that they got more out of the classes than he realized, he wants to continue the school. Mr. T entices Miss Llewelyn to act in a presentation of "Little Red-Riding Hood" that the class puts on, and Miss Llewelyn admits she was too rash in wanting the school closed.

The late Miriam Byrd-Nethery (Miss Llewelyn) was the wife of actor Clu Gulager.

Episode 8: Unaired   "The Americanization of Michi"

Director: Unknown   Writer: George Tibbles

When Mr. T's sister-in-law, Michi, decides to return to Japan because she feels she doesn't fit in with American culture, Tina's attempts to Americanize her throw the household into an uproar.

Sayonara, Mr. T

Almost from the start, *Mr. T and Tina* came under heavy criticism, not only from TV critics but also from the Japanese-American community for its stereotypical depiction of Asian-Americans. The Mr. T character had lines like: "You no nanny – you ninny" when speaking to Tina, and he called the landlady "Miss Rewerryn" instead of "Miss Llewellyn".[146]

The series' first episode ranked thirty-third out of sixty-three shows, but ratings declined after that with the October 2 episode ranking sixtieth out of sixty-six shows. After the fast cancelation of *Mr. T and Tina*, Pat Morita became a regular on the short-lived comedy, *Blansky's Beauties*, and then starred in the crime drama *O'Hara* and the sequel to *The Karate Kid* (Morita did the original *Karate Kid* before *Mr. T and Tina*). He passed away in 2005.

Nearly Departed

Premiered Monday, April 10, 1989, at 8:30 PM on NBC

"We're dead and we'll just have to live with that." This line from the debut episode of *Nearly Departed* basically sums up the concept. Like the 1950s sitcom *Topper*, *Nearly Departed* involved a married couple killed in an accident who came back to haunt their home. Unlike the TV show *Topper*, however, the couple in *Nearly Departed* died in an auto accident on a mountain road when rocks fell on their car, not a skiing accident involving an avalanche, and *Nearly Departed* lasted only four episodes, not two seasons as did *Topper*.

The stars of *Nearly Departed* were Eric Idle of *Monty Python* fame who played Grant Pritchard, a deceased English lecturer at the University of Chicago. Caroline McWilliams, who had been a regular on *Benson*, was his late wife, Claire. They haunted their former home while plumbing contractor, Mike Dooley (Stuart Pankin, *No Soap, Radio*); his wife, Liz (Wendy Schaal); their teenage son, Derek (Jay Lambert), and Wendy's father, Jack Garrett (Henderson Forsythe) moved in and redid the place. The only member of the family with whom the ghosts could communicate was the grandfather. NBC scheduled *Nearly Departed* after *ALF* on Mondays, apparently thinking that the fantasy elements of this sitcom would make it a good companion with the sci-fi comedy *ALF*.

Background

Created by Roger Shulman and John Baskin and initially called *Ghost Story*, *Nearly Departed* was produced by Baskin/Shulman Productions and by Lorimar. The comedy used no special effects as one might expect. Except for the grandfather, the rest of the cast simply ignored the presence of the characters Claire and Grant in each episode. Eric Idle sang the theme song, "Nearly Departed."

Episode Guide: 4 aired; 2 unaired

Episode 1: April 10, 1989   "Grant Meets Grandpa"

Director: John Rich   Writers: Roger Shulman and John Baskin

Claire and Grant come back as ghosts to haunt their old house now owned by Mike and Liz Dooley. Liz's father Jack is coming to dinner. He reveals that he has been evicted from his apartment which is being torn down and lost his job as a delivery van driver since his license expired. Liz says he can stay with them until he gets back on his feet. When Grant talks to the grandfather, the old guy can see and hear Claire and him. However, grandpa is afraid to say anything about this to Mike and Liz for fear they will think he is senile. The family tries to get the grandfather ready for his driver's test so he can renew his license. With help from Grant, he passes the test. However, he doesn't want his old job back. Since he wants to find a better job, he stays with Mike and Liz.

Episode 2: April 17, 1989   "Adventures in Babysitting"

Director: John Rich   Writers: Roger Shulman and John Baskin

Mike and Liz go to the symphony and leave grandpa in charge of fourteen-year-old Derek. When one of Jack's friends comes by to remind him that it is poker night, Derek insists he will be fine if grandpa leaves for an hour to play poker. Before he leaves, Jack asks Grant to babysit. After Derek invites a girl over, Grant keeps trying to interrupt them when they start kissing. Liz and Mike come home unexpectedly, and the girl leaves. When Jack comes home, Mike and Liz question why he didn't stay with Derek as promised. Later that night, Grant and Claire hear what they think are burglars in the house, but it turns out to be Jack packing to leave because he feels he let everyone down by playing poker. They go with him to the bus station where he plans to travel to Miami to be with his sister. At the bus station, a man tries to steal Jack's suitcase, but Grant scares the guy away. After grandpa returns to Mike and Liz's, Derek and Liz convince him to stay.

Wendy Schaal (Liz) is the daughter of actor Richard Schaal and the one-time stepdaughter of Valerie Harper.

Episode 3: April 24, 1989 "Altared States"

Director: John Rich   Writers: Sy Dukane and Denise Moss

The workmen building a home office for Mike find a box when they tear out an old closet. The box contains some of Grant's possessions including old love letters. In trying to get the box away from the Dooley's, Claire finds Grant's divorce papers from his first wife, Judith. Claire discovers that Grant was still married to Judith when Claire married him. When Liz reads aloud some of the love letters from the box, Claire overhears that one of the letters was to Judith. Claire feels that her marriage to Grant is a sham and informs him that she wants to get married again. Since they can't arrange a marriage ceremony themselves, they decide to attend another couple's ceremony. However, at the ceremony they choose, the groom gets cold feet and backs out of the marriage. Claire takes Grant back anyway since he at least made the effort to remarry her.

Episode 4: May 1, 1989 "TV or Not TV"

Director: John Rich   Writer: Neil Alan Levy

When Derek gets low grades at school, particularly in his science class, his mother thinks it is because he watches too much TV. His dad forbids him from watching any television until his science grade improves, and the set is moved to the basement meaning no one, including Grant, can view it. After Grant, Claire, and Jack all go to Derek's school, they discover that he is being bullied into doing another student's science homework. Since he doesn't like the bully leeching off him, Derek isn't doing the assignments that well. Jack says that he was bullied in school and that Derek should stand up to the bully. With Grant viewing the situation, Derek tells the bully that he isn't doing his homework anymore. Grant pulls the student's sweatshirt over his head and pulls his pants down, while Derek shoves him. The other boys that were being bullied turn on the student as well, and the bully leaves.

Episode 5: Unaired   "Grandpa's Date"

Director: John Rich   Writer: Daniel Palladino

Mike suggests that Jack start dating so he can get out of the house more. Mike knows a customer, Helen McCormick, whom he thinks Jack should ask out. Although hesitant initially, Jack finally asks Helen to a restaurant with Claire and Grant as chaperones. The couple eventually hits it off and begins dating on a regular basis. When Jack invites Helen for dinner at the house, Helen's ex-boyfriend shows up and wants Helen back. Jack then decides to break off his relationship with her.

Episode 6: Unaired   "Grant's Aunt"

Director: John Rich   Writer: Dale McRaven

When Grant's Aunt Millie (played by Eric Idle in drag) comes from England to surprise her nephew, the Dooley's have to inform her that Grant has died. Millie tells the Dooley's that she wants to have a séance to say her final good-bye to Grant. At the séance, Grant and Claire try to get the medium's attention but are not successful. Millie says she will come back with another medium if this medium is unable to communicate with Grant. Jack then says he hears something and tells Millie that Grant loves her and misses her. Millie is happy and is willing to leave with this final good-bye.

Caroline McWilliams (Claire) passed away in 2010 from complications of multiple myeloma.

Quickly Departed

Originally to air for six episodes, only four episodes of *Nearly Departed* were broadcast with each episode after the premiere having fewer viewers. The comedy ranked twenty-sixth out of seventy-four shows for its first episode; the second episode ranked thirtieth; the third, forty-second, and the fourth, forty-fifth. The full series was subsequently broadcast in England.

The Ortegas

Supposed to premiere Sundays at 8:30 PM during the 2003-04 TV season on Fox

A family with a TV studio in their backyard, *The Ortegas* was a part-scripted, part-improvisational comedy about a Mexican-American family that hosted a talk show with a live audience in Van Nuys, CA. The situation comedy starred Cheech Marin as Henry Ortega, a realtor, and Al Madrigal as his thirty-year-old son, Alejandro Oretga, who was the host of the talk show that welcomed real-life celebrities who had no knowledge of the script. Also in the cast were Terry Hoyos as Esmeralda Ortega, Al's mother, and Renee Victor as Henry's mother, Maria Ortega. Al's dad, mom, and grandmother joined him in interviewing each week's guests.

Background

Critics who viewed the first episode of *The Ortegas* thought it was very similar to a show on E! at the time called *The Michael Essany Show*. Essany had been doing a talk show on cable access since he was fourteen-years old, and by the time his show premiered on E!, Essany was a twenty-year-old college freshman in Indiana doing a talk show from his parents' home.

However, *The Ortegas* was really based on a British sitcom called *The Kumars at No. 42*, which premiered in November 2001. In that series, the Kumars were an Indian family who lived in Wembley with son Sanjeev fancying himself as a handsome, professional talk show host. The Kumars had bulldozed the garden in their backyard to build a TV studio for their son who would interview at least two celebrity guests during each show. Sanjeev's mother loved having guests around the house and always offered them food. Sushila was the grandmother who liked to ask celebrities naughty questions and flirted with handsome male guests. Sanjeev's dad, mother, and grandmother would all be in the studio and question the guests along with Sanjeev.

The American version of the show was the object of a bidding war between NBC and Fox with NBC producing a pilot that didn't make it into their fall lineup. The producers of the series then offered it to Fox which originally scheduled it between *The Simpsons* and *Malcolm in the Middle* on Sunday nights. The comedy was produced by Pariah Productions, Hat Trick, and Kumtegas, Inc.; executive producers were Wally Wolodarsky and Gavin Polone.

Episode Guide: 6 unaired

Episode 1: "The First Show"

Director: Linda Mendoza   Writer: Wally Wolodarsky

The guests on Al's show are Shannen Doherty and Tom Arnold. Al asks Shannen if she remembers him from the fan letters he wrote while she was on *Beverly Hills 90210,* and the family wants her to autograph DVD's of the film *Heathers* in which she appeared. Al asks Tom Arnold how he compares to other talk show hosts, and his dad does a Senor Wences impression. At the end of the show, mom gives the guests food to take home with them.

In a preview of the series shown to the press in July 2003, Denise Richards and Howie Mandel were the guests on the pilot. However, the episode described above was apparently the one intended for the first broadcast.

Episode 2: Unaired "Thanksgiving"

Director: Linda Mendoza   Writers: Julio Calderon and Roger Campo

To celebrate Thanksgiving, Al is dressed like a Pilgrim. Guest Tom Green French kisses Maria. Esmeralda complains on air that no one helps her in the kitchen and wants Henry to cook the Thanksgiving dinner. The second guest is Jamie Pressly who doesn't say much. After Henry starts a fire in the kitchen, he ends up apologizing to his wife for taking her for granted.

Episode 3: Unaired "The Fix Up"

Director: Linda Mendoza   Writer: Allison Adler

His parents want Al to date Chevy, the daughter of friends of theirs, who happens to be a dentist. Al meets the girl but comes on to her way too strong. Tommy Lee is Al's first guest, and he asks Tommy Lee about groupies. Chris Elliot is the second guest. At the end of the show, Al apologizes to Chevy, and she says he is cuter when he is himself. However, she leaves with Tommy Lee.

Episode 4: Unaired "Al and the Female Demographic"

Director: Liz Plonka Writer: Gigi New

According to Chet, a Fox executive who visits the Ortegas, women aged eighteen to thirty-five don't like Al, and Chet wants his parents to explain this to him. Rob Schneider, Al's first guest, does an Elvis impersonation and reveals that one of his first jobs was selling ladies shoes. The second guest, Alyssia Milano, brings a cactus plant as a gift. Esmeralda asks her what it is like to have a cookie named after her. In the time between the two guests, Esmeralda tells Al what the Fox executive said about his popularity with women which he does not take well.

Rob Schneider and Cheech Marin would later appear together on the short-lived CBS comedy *Rob*.

Episode 5: Unaired "The Fight"

Director: Liz Plonka Writers: Maya Forbes and Wally Wolodarsky

Jessica Simpson and Nick Lachey are Al's guests. Henry gets into a fight with Esmeralda because she said that Nick Lachey is cute. He ends up sleeping in the talk show studio. Al and Jessica get into a burping contest. Henry challenges Nick to a fight, but then Henry and Esmeralda reconcile.

Writer Maya Forbes is the wife of Wally Wolodarsky.

Episode 6: Unaired "The Funeral"

Director: Linda Mendoza Writer: Dino Stamatopolous

The Ortegas are hosting a funeral reception for a next-door neighbor who died. Al is afraid of death and doesn't want to express his sympathy to the neighbor's son who, like Al, lived with his mother. Shaquelle O'Neal is the first guest and gives Al the nickname of "Alamo." Tori Spelling, the second guest says a few words at the funeral where Shaq breaks down in tears. Shaq ends up helping to dust the top shelves in the Ortegas' kitchen.

Another Fox Last Minute Cancelation

Fox changed its fall 2002 schedule to move *The O.C.* from Thursdays up against *CSI* and *Will & Grace* to Wednesdays displacing *The Bernie Mac Show*, which moved into the time slot after *The Simpsons* where *The Ortegas* was supposed to premiere. Fox said that *The Ortegas* would premiere in the spring or summer of 2003, but that never happened.

The People Next Door

Premiered Monday, September 18, 1989, at 8:30 PM on CBS

The People Next Door was about a cartoonist, Walter Kellogg (Jeffrey Jones), with a vivid imagination—so vivid that things he imagined actually materialized in his presence like a mounted moose head that talked or entertainer Steve Allen playing the piano. Walter could not always control his imagination, especially when he was nervous. A widower, Walter fell in love with Abigail MacIntyre (Mary Gross), a psychologist from Ohio. In the first episode, Walter and his children, eleven-year-old Aurora (Jaclyn Bernstein aka Jaclyn Rose-Lester) and fourteen-year-old Matthew (Chance Quinn), move to Abigail's hometown in Covington, Ohio. As is often the case in fantasy sitcoms, when someone has special powers, they are kept a secret from others. In *The People Next Door*, Walter and his kids tried to keep his fantasies-come-to-life ability a secret, especially from Abigail's sister, Cissy (Christina Pickles), a beautician, and from Truman Fipps (Leslie Jordan) – the nosy postman who was infatuated with Cissy.

Background

The People Next Door was created by Wes Craven of *Nightmare on Elm Street* fame and by Bruce Wagner together with Madeline and Steven Sunshine. The title of the series came from the name of the comic strip drawn by the lead character.[147] Commenting on why one of his first ventures into television was a comedy and not a horror show, Craven indicated that he was typecast as only a horror director and always said that if he did TV it would be comedy.[148] According to Craven, comedy and horror were connected something like love-hate and were similar in the sense of working with the unexpected and the relieving of tension. The series was produced by The Sunshine Inc., Wes Craven Productions, and Lorimar.

Episode Guide: 5 aired; 5 unaired

Episode 1: September 18, 1989 "I Do, I Do or Married to a Mob"
(summary based on shooting script)

Director: J.D. LoBue   Writers: Wes Craven, Madeline and Steven Sunshine, Bud Wiggins

After a whirlwind courtship, Walter and his two kids move to Abigail's house in Covington, Ohio where they meet Abby's sister Cissy. While in Walter's new studio, Steve Allen appears singing and playing "Imagination Is Funny." Walter confesses to Abby that he can make things appear just by imagining them, but she doesn't believe him until right before the wedding ceremony, when she sees the mirror and a moose head speak to her. She says that she still loves him and will try to cope with his imagination coming to life.

Episode 2: September 25, 1989 "Town Without Pity"
(summary based on shooting script)

Director: J.D. LoBue   Writers: Madeline and Steven Sunshine

Walter is having difficulty coming up with a subject for his next cartoon. He is used to doing cartoons about city life but now that he has moved to Covington, he wants Abby to show him around so he can get inspired. Since she has patients waiting for her, he decides to accompany Truman Fipps on his postal rounds. When Walter returns from his day with Truman, he tells Abby that the town has a lot of juicy rumors floating around. The cartoon that he creates shows townsfolk with T-shirts dishing dirt into bowls. The T-shirts read: "Covintgton Dirt Dishing Derby Festival." When the town sees the cartoon, everyone is angry at Walter. The Chamber of Commerce wants an apology, but, when the head of the Chamber starts receiving orders for T-shirts, the Chamber realizes it can make some money from the publicity. At the end, Cissy confesses to Walter that she was the one calling the Chamber to order t-shirts.

The original *People's Court* judge, Judge Wapner, and comedian Henny Youngman had cameos in this episode.

Episode 3: October 2, 1989   "Dream Date" (summary based on shooting script)

Director: J.D. LoBue   Writer: Lee Aronsohn

Neal Farrell, an old friend of Walter's, sends him a letter. While reading the letter, Neal appears through Walter's imagination, and Cissy sees him. Walter has no choice but to introduce her to Neal. When Neal reappears later, Cissy asks him to dinner the following night. Before the dinner, Walter tries to contact the real Neal to visit him in Ohio. Neal is not available, but Walter leaves messages for him. For the dinner, Walter is not sure he can imagine Neal for the entire evening, but he doesn't want to disappoint Cissy. Eventually, the real Neal does show up wearing a different suit, looking a little older, and with his hair combed differently from what Walter imagined. Walter has to quickly modify Neal's outfit so Cissy isn't suspicious. In the end, Cissy drives Neal to the airport.

Dick Clark had a cameo in this episode.

Episode 4: October 9, 1989   "You Show Me Yours . . ." (summary based on shooting script)

Director: J.D. LoBue   Writer: Mark Masuoka

When Abby learns that Walter still has his apartment in New York City which he is subletting, she thinks this means that he is not committed to their marriage. Walter explains that he has kept the apartment because it is valuable real estate. Although she apologizes to Walter for overreacting, Abby believes that Walter is still in denial about the real reason he has the apartment. Walter admits to her that, when growing up, he never had a permanent home since his parents were in the theatre and traveled a lot. Walter then asks Abby to talk about her childhood. Abby admits that her dad, an egg farmer, one day got up and left his family and that she has abandonment issues.

Sigmund Freud and Dr. Joyce Brothers popped in and out of various scenes in this episode.

Episode 5: October 16, 1989 "Happy Birthday, Baby" (summary based on shooting script)

Director: J.D. LoBue   Writer: Bob Tischler

For Walter's fortieth birthday, Abby is planning a surprise party. When he looks in the mirror, Walter sees himself as a ninety-seven-year-old man. Because Abby realizes that he is upset about turning forty, she makes some changes to the guest list for the party. To prove that he is still young, Walter thinks that he and Abby should have a baby. During his discussion with Abby about this, he imagines himself pregnant. Abby and Walter go upstairs to further discuss the baby issue as the guests arrive for the party. When Abby leaves their bedroom, Walter runs after her and is surprised by whom Abby invited – all elderly people from a retirement home. They show Walter that he is not that old, and he says he no longer fears growing older.

Episode 6: Unaired   "Halloween" ("Night of the Living Walter") (summary based on shooting script)

Director: J.D. LoBue   Writer: Lee Aronsohn

At Halloween, Walter is imagining Halloween ghosts and goblins, like the Wolfman. Because he is having problems distinguishing real Halloweeners from the specters he conjures up, he doesn't want to attend Abby's Halloween Party. When he sees a man in a hockey mask with an axe enter the front door and go upstairs, he is not sure if the man is real or imagined. Walter encourages all the guests to leave Abby's party thinking the man with the axe is real. Abby tries to convince Walter that the guy is only a figment of his fears. Abby and Walter discover that the man in the hockey mask is really Walter or at least the part of Walter that he is afraid to look at. Walter confesses to Abby that he is fearful that his imagination will drive away the people he loves, and Abby tells him that she loves him with or without his imagination.

Episode 7: Unaired "Make Room for Abby" (summary based on shooting script)

Director: J.D. LoBue   Writer: Lauren Eve Anderson

Abby wants to play a larger role in raising Aurora and Matthew and thinks that Walter is shutting her out of parenting. Walter agrees to let Abby make breakfast for the kids, but he objects when she makes French toast which he thinks is too high in sugar and fat. Abby has Walter hold a family meeting to discuss how they all fit together as a family. He confesses that he doesn't know how to give up being both mother and father to the kids ever since their biological mother died. However, he finally tells the kids that things have changed and they now have Abby.

Ann B. Davis had a cameo in this episode as the maid from *The Brady Bunch*.

Episode 8: Unaired "A Jealousy Story"

Director: J.D. LoBue   Writer: Mark Masuoka

Lyle Vandenberg (Barry Van Dyke), a wealthy bachelor and Abby's former beau, is in town and wants Abby to become director of the clinic where she works and where he chairs the Board. Upon meeting Lyle, Walter become jealous and his imagination runs wild when Abby and Lyle work late at the clinic and go out for dinner together. Although Walter denies he is envious, Abby says he has nothing to worry about. When Lyle stops by to talk to Abby, Walter becomes a fly on the wall to eavesdrop on their conversation. Lyle explains that he is no longer in love with Abby and that he is getting married.

Episode 9: Unaired "House and Home"

Director: J.D. LoBue   Writer: Lauren Eve Anderson

When Walter and Abby want to remodel and go to the bank for a loan, they discover that Cissy had borrowed $75,000 against the house. Walter and Abby think that Cissy has a gambling problem and that is why she took out the mortgage. However, after Cissy reveals that the money was used to pay for Abby's college education, Walter agrees to take over the monthly mortgage payments.

Milton Berle had a cameo in this episode.

Episode 10: Unaired "No ZZZ's"

Director: J.D. LoBue   Writers: Dennis Danziger and Ellen Sandler

Walter is keeping everyone up at night with his incessant snoring. Abby wants him to see a doctor which he does reluctantly. The doctor diagnosis a deviated septum and recommends a simple operation. While Walter is afraid of surgery, he is finally convinced to have the operation which solves his snoring problem.

Bert Convy appeared as the host of *Win, Lose, or Snore* – a takeoff on a game show he hosted called *Win, Lose, or Draw*. Also, TV's *Ben Casey*, Vince Edwards, had a cameo on this episode saying that operations don't work.

Door Closed

The sitcom was canceled after five of the ten episodes produced had aired. The premiere episode beat *The Hogan Family* on NBC and ranked twenty-ninth for the week. However, after that, ratings dropped each week, and the series lost audience share sandwiched between *Major Dad* and *Murphy Brown*. The fifth episode ranked fifty-fifth.

The Pitts

Premiered Sunday, March 30, 2003, at 9:30 PM on Fox

The unluckiest family in the world—the Pitts—was made up of dad, Bob Pitt (Dylan Baker); mom, Liz Pitt (Kellie Waymire), and their two children, sixteen-year-old Faith (Lizzy Caplan) and twelve-year-old Petey (David Henrie). Bob and Liz ran a not very profitable "Mail Boxes & More" franchise store, which fit in with the main premise of the sitcom that unbelievably bad luck followed the family everywhere.

Background

The Pitts was created by two writers and producers from *The Simpsons*, Mike Scully and his spouse Julie Thacker-Scully. Taped in front of a live audience, the comedy was produced by Duh Productions in association with Twentieth Century-Fox.

Episode Guide: 5 aired; 2 unaired

Episode 1: March 30, 2003   "Pilot"

Director: Lee Shallat Chemel Writers: Mike Scully and Julie Thacker

The nanny Bob hires for his children was supposed to have been his prom date twenty-five years ago, but he never showed up. Now she wants revenge, but, for some reason, she is still intent on becoming Mrs. Pitt. Meanwhile, Faith doesn't have a date for her big homecoming dance.

Episode 2: April 6, 2003   "A Bug's Wife"

Director: Lee Shallat Chemel   Writer: Mike Scully and Julie Thacker

The parents buy Faith a haunted VW that falls in love with her, convinces her not to go to school, and takes her to Las Vegas to be married.

Episode 3: April 13, 2003   "Squarewolves"

Director: Katy Garretson Story: Julie Thacker-Scully   Teleplay: Alec Sulkin and Wellesley Wild

The family goes on a charity "Walk against Terrorism" and gets lost at night in the woods. Dad and mom are attacked by werewolves and turn into werewolves themselves when there is a full moon. The kids discover their parents are werewolves when they view a video the son made of their garbage cans with the parents rummaging through the cans looking for food. The next night of the full moon, after the parents are captured by animal control, the kids have to go to the animal shelter to free them.

Episode 4: April 20, 2003   "Dummy and Dummier"

Director: Tom Cherones   Story: Mike and Julie Thacker   Teleplay: Mike Scully

Petey's birthday party turns into a bust with lame games his dad devises like laser tag with flashlights until Bob gets his old ventriloquist dummy out of a suitcase in the basement. The magical dummy, Morty, has a grudge because Bob kept him in the suitcase for years, but he is a hit with the kids. The dummy wants to move in with the family. Unsuspecting Bob shows him the computer and gives him the password to the family's financial information. Morty gives the Pitts a gift certificate for spa treatments to get them out of the house, obtains all their financial information, and locks them out. Petey takes the family to a supposedly abandoned beaver dam to spend the night where they run into a live beaver. The next day, they take the beaver to their house and put him through the mail slot in the front door where he proceeds to gnaw Morty to death.

Episode 5: April 20, 2003   "Miss American Pipe"

Director: Matthew Diamond   Writers: Tom Gammill and Max Pross

Faith wants to participate in the filming of a rock video at her school. However, when dad blows up the hot water heater with a nail gun, Faith gets a water pipe stuck through her head which her doctor doesn't want to remove. Looking the way she does with a pipe sideways through her skull, she won't leave the house. Eventually, she goes to the video filming with hair wrapped around each end of the pipe, but the pipe causes feedback on the sound system. When the hair around the pipe comes off, Faith runs away. The family finds that she has joined Zeke's Freak Shows and tells her that they will also join the show if she doesn't quit. She leaves and goes back to filming the video. But a pipe breaks in the school, and ever-resourceful dad repairs the pipe with Faith who then becomes very popular. In the end, Faith's brother hits her with a door, and the pipe comes out.

Episode 6: Unaired   "Ticket to Riot"

Director: Lee Shallat Chemel   Writers: Mike Scully and Julie Thacker

After his car is ticketed and towed, Bob goes to court to fight the ticket and wins by default when no police officer shows up. However, he takes a bus home which turns out to be the bus to the prison. The family gets Bob out of prison, but, before they can leave, the prisoners riot and take the family hostage.

Episode 7: Unaired   "Bob's New Heart"

Director: Matthew Diamond   Writer: Brian Scully

The Pitts join a square-dancing club suggested to them by two customers at their store. The club turns out to be a cover for a satanic cult. After a dance, the Pitts become unconscious, and the devil's heart is transplanted into Bob. After committing evil deeds, Bob is asked by the cult to unlock the Doors of Hell, but his soul fights the force. The Pitts finally win back Bob's heart on eBay.

Kellie Waymire, who played Liz Pitt, unexpectedly passed away in November 2003 at age thirty-six from cardiac arrhythmia. Writer Brian Scully is the brother of series co-creator Mike Scully.

A Second Chance

The Pitts ran for five low-rated episodes on Fox following *Malcolm in the Middle*. Although it was canceled after five episodes, there was discussion about developing *The Pitts* as an animated cartoon series. A pilot was made for the animated version with Allison Janney voicing Liz Pitt, but Fox decided to pass on the revamped series.

The Secret Diary of Desmond Pfeiffer

Premiered Monday, October 5, 1998, at 9:00 PM on UPN

The first and, to date, only sitcom satirizing the Lincoln presidency, *The Secret Diary of Desmond Pfeiffer* starred Chi McBride as a butler to Abraham Lincoln (Dann

Florek) during the "fun" years of the American Civil War. Pfeiffer, a black, knighted English lord, had fled to the United States to avoid paying gambling debts and found work at the White House. He maintained a diary, which provided the storylines for the series. Christine Estabrook was Mary Todd Lincoln; Kelly Connell played Ulysses S. Grant, and Max Baker (*Talk to Me*) was Desmond's bumbling assistant, Nibblet.

Background

Mort Nathan and Barry Fanaro created *The Secret Diary of Desmond Pfeiffer* as a way, among other things, to poke fun at the Clinton presidency. Nathan and Fanaro deliberately picked Lincoln as their vehicle for satire, rather than a less revered president such as Grant because they felt, despite the fact that he was the first president to be assassinated and his spouse suffered from mental illness, that Lincoln was ripe for a satirical look.[149] According to director Matthew Diamond, UPN ordered a total of thirteen episodes of the series including the pilot, but only nine episodes were produced before the comedy was canceled.[150] Fanaro/Nathan Productions and Paramount Pictures Corporation produced the sitcom.

Episode Guide: 4 aired; 5 unaired

Episode 1: October 5, 1998 "A.O.L.: Abe On-Line"

Director: Matthew Diamond   Writer: Jim Gerkin

Desmond and Nibblet find a valuable ring inside a small box hidden in the White House kitchen that they think once belonged to Thomas Jefferson. But before Desmond can do anything with the ring, Mary Todd Lincoln takes it. Later, Desmond, listening through the door to the President's office, hears someone using the telegraph to send obscene messages. It turns out that Lincoln is doing this to try to spice up his sex life. Lincoln knocks over a kerosene lamp, burns his hands, and needs Desmond to continue to send telegrams. Meanwhile, in an effort to retrieve the ring, Nibblet, harnessed on a rope, is lowered into Mrs. Lincoln's bathroom while she is taking a bath, but he cannot get the ring since it is on her toe. Later, Nibblet gives Mrs. Lincoln a pedicure to attempt to recover the ring but is still unsuccessful. In the final scenes, the President and Desmond go to a bar to meet the woman who is corresponding through the telegraph with Lincoln. She turns out to be Mrs. Lincoln. The obscene telegrams inspire the Lincoln's to make passionate love, and the ring comes off Mrs. Lincoln's toe and falls through a crack in the floor. Over a hundred years later, Mrs. Clinton finds the ring and tells Bill Clinton that she knows how to pay for his legal bills.

Episode 2: October 12, 1998 "Up, Up and Away"

Director: Matthew Diamond   Writers: Marc Abrams and Michael Benson

Desmond, Nibblet, and the President go aloft in a hot air balloon when General Grant trips over the rope holding the balloon. They find themselves behind enemy lines after the balloon is shot down by Confederate troops. To avoid capture, Lincoln dresses in drag, and Desmond tells the rebels that they are on a secret mission to infiltrate the North. What the three are really seeking are secret rebel battle plans. They are taken to the home of a Confederate general where Lincoln has to fend off the general's advances. Nibblet eventually confesses that they are Northern spies, and the three are taken out to be shot. However, the Confederate soldier who is to shoot them is really a Northern spy and lets them go.

Sherman Hemsley (*The Jeffersons*) had a cameo in this episode as the Confederate soldier who, when he takes off his disguise, is a black Northern spy.

Episode 3: October 19, 1998 "Saving Mr. Lincoln"

Director: Matthew Diamond   Writers: Mert Rich and Brian Pollack

Desmond tangles with a member of the White House staff who is scheming to end his friendship with President Lincoln.

Episode 4: October 26, 1998 "Once Upon a Mistress"

Director: Matthew Diamond   Writer: Bill Boulware

When foreign dignitaries bring their mistresses to visit, President Lincoln finds temptation in the gift of a mistress from one of the dignitaries. However, Lincoln's mistress decides to give up her lifestyle and stay in America, and she persuades

NOT EXACTLY THE FAMILY NEXT DOOR

the other mistresses to do the same. Meanwhile, Nibblet creates a tonic for Mrs. Lincoln's headaches. They both drink the tonic which has some side effects. It cures headaches but makes Mrs. Lincoln's breasts larger and gives Nibblet bosoms. Being displeased with their mistresses leaving them, the foreign dignitaries challenge Lincoln to a duel. Pfeiffer suggests that they settle their differences over bowling. If Lincoln and his team win, Lincoln will receive money from them to continue the war. If the foreign dignitaries win, they get "to pass around Mrs. Lincoln" to whom they are attracted because of her ample bosoms. Thanks to General Grant, Lincoln's team wins.

Episode 5: Unaired   "Pilot" (summary based on writers' draft script)

Director: Matthew Diamond   Writers: Barry Fanaro and Mort Nathan

When Grant advises Lincoln to send Mary Todd away because the Civil War is not going well, Desmond thinks he will accompany her to England. Ever since the war began, Lincoln hasn't had sex with Mary Todd, and the only way she will ask her husband for Desmond to accompany her is if Desmond sleeps with her which he doesn't want to do. He talks Nibblet into posing as him to sleep with Mrs. Lincoln. Nibblet agrees to the plan and places an aphrodisiac in Mary Todd's brandy. However, the President's new, attractive secretary drinks the brandy, and Nibblet ends up having sex with her. Desmond decides to approach Lincoln directly about going to England with his wife. He serves the President brandy which brings out the President's latent homosexuality. The President talks about all the boys with "big biceps" and "washboard stomachs" going off to war and ends up hugging Desmond, stating, "It's not right for one man to own another—respect, care for, vacation together maybe." Lincoln decides to free the slaves and agrees Desmond can go to England. However, that night the President and Mrs. Lincoln finally have sex, and he calls off the trip because he needs his wife around to keep up his morale.

This pilot episode was never broadcast because of complaints from black activist organizations that the episode made jokes about slavery.

Episode 6: Unaired   "Pigeon English"

Director: Matthew Diamond   Writer: Unknown

When the President suffers an allergic reaction on the eve of Queen Victoria's visit, Mrs. Lincoln decides to hire a body double to impersonate her husband. The double doesn't realize that Mrs. Lincoln has another use in mind for him.

Episode 7: Unaired   "Kidnapped"

Director: Matthew Diamond   Writers: Mark Steen and Ron Nelson

When Confederate soldiers kidnap Mrs. Lincoln, Grant retaliates by kidnapping Robert E. Lee's wife.

Dann Florek, who played Lincoln on the series, became the captain on the long-running *Law & Order: Special Victims Unit.*

Episode 8: Unaired   "School Daze"

Director: Matthew Diamond   Writer: Unknown

Storyline unknown

Episode 9: Unaired   "Guess Who's Coming to Dinner"

Director: Matthew Diamond   Writer: Unknown

Storyline unknown

Desmond's Demise

Only four episodes of *The Secret Diary of Desmond Pfeiffer* aired on Mondays at 9:00 PM and then at 9:30 PM. The first episode ranked 116th out of 125 shows for the week. By the final episode, the comedy ranked 133rd out of 135 shows. The head of UPN said at the time that *Pfeiffer* was exactly the series the network wanted to put on the air to show that "we do cool TV too."[151] However, the sitcom not only had low ratings up against the comedies on CBS, *Monday Night Football* on ABC, and *Ally McBeal* on Fox, but it also was lambasted by critics. The *New York Times* called the series "jaw-droppingly witless."[152] *The San Francisco Chronicle* said, "Preposterously bad jokes pile on top of each other as this unimaginably bad premise manages to be even worse than expected."[153] Apparently, no one found humor in an inept, insensitive, sex-obsessed Abraham Lincoln.

Appendix
Series by Season and Network

1952-53

NBC – *Doc Corkle*

1966-67

ABC – *The Tammy Grimes Show*

1975-76

CBS – *Ivan the Terrible*

1976-77

ABC – *Mr. T and Tina*

CBS – *Ball Four, A Year at the Top*

NBC—*The Kallikaks, Snip*

1977-78

ABC – *A.E.S. Hudson Street, Free Country*

CBS – *Another Day*

NBC – *The Rollergirls, The Sanford Arms*

1978-79

ABC – *Apple Pie*

CBS – *Co-Ed Fever, Dorothy, Flatbush, Hanging In, In the Beginning, Mister Dugan*

NBC – *Highcliffe Manor, Waverly Wonders*

1979-80

ABC – *Semi-Tough*

CBS – *Struck by Lightning, Working Stiffs*

NBC – *The Six O'Clock Follies*

1980-81

CBS – *Checking In, Park Place*

1981-82

ABC – *No Soap, Radio*

CBS – *Herbie, The Love Bug*

1982-83

ABC – *Baby Makes Five*

CBS – *Ace Crawford, Private Eye, Zorro and Son*

1983-84

ABC – *It's Not Easy, Shaping Up*

1984-85

CBS – *Dreams*

1985-86

NBC – *Fathers and Sons*

1986-87

ABC – *Harry*

CBS – *Better Days, Roxie, Take Five*

1987-88

CBS – *The Dictator, First Impressions, Trial and Error*

1988-89

NBC – *Nearly Departed, Nick & Hillary*

1989-90

CBS – *The People Next Door*

Fox – *Molloy*

NBC – *The Nutt House, Singer & Sons*

1990-91

CBS – *You Take the Kids*

1991-92

ABC – *Arresting Behavior, Julie, On the Air*

CBS – *Princesses, Scorch, Teech*

1992-93

ABC – *Laurie Hill*

CBS – *The Boys, The Building, Cutters, Dudley, Frannie's Turn, A League of Their Own, Tall Hopes, The Trouble with Larry*

NBC – *Black Tie Affair*

1993-94

CBS – *It Had to Be You, 704 Hauser*

NBC – *Someone Like Me*

1994-95

ABC – *Bringing Up Jack*

CBS – *Daddy's Girls, The Office*

Fox – *My Wildest Dreams, Wild Oats*

NBC – *The Martin Short Show*

1995-96

ABC – *Buddies*

CBS – *If Not for You, My Guys*

Fox – *Local Heroes, Misery Loves Company*

NBC – *Raising Caines*

1996-97

ABC – *Common Law*

CBS – *Life... and Stuff, Public Morals*

Fox – *Love and Marriage, Lush Life, Party Girl, Pauly, Secret Service Guy*

1997-98

ABC – *Over the Top, That's Life*

Fox – *Ask Harriet, Rewind*

NBC – *Built to Last*

WB – *You're the One*

1998-99

CBS – *The Brian Benben Show*

Fox – *Costello*

NBC – *Everything's Relative*

UPN – *The Secret Diary of Desmond Pfeiffer*

WB – *Katie Joplin*

1999-00

ABC – *Clerks, Talk to Me*

CBS – *Grapevine, Love & Money, Work with Me*

NBC – *Battery Park, God, the Devil and Bob, M.Y.O.B*

WB – *Brutally Normal*

2000-01

ABC – *The Trouble with Normal*

CBS – *Some of My Best Friends*

NBC – *Go Fish*

2001-02

ABC – *Bob Patterson, Wednesday 9:30 (8:30 Central)*

Animal Planet – *Beware of Dog*

CBS – *Danny*

NBC – *Imagine That*

UPN – *As If, The Random Years*

WB – *My Guide to Becoming a Rock Star*

2002-03

ABC – *Lost at Home, Regular Joe*

CBS – *Bram & Alice, Charlie Lawrence*

Fox – *The Grubbs, The Pitts*

NBC – *The Jake Effect*

WB – *The O'Keefes, On the Spot*

2003-04

CBS – *The Stones*

Fox – *Luis, The Ortegas*

NBC – *Come to Papa, Coupling*

2004-05

Fox – *Life on a Stick*

2005-06

ABC – *Crumbs, Emily's Reasons Why Not*

Fox – *Kitchen Confidential*

WB—*Misconceptions*

2006-07

Fox – *Happy Hour*

NBC – *The Singles Table, Twenty Good Years*

2007-08

CBS – *Welcome to the Captain*

Fox – *The Return of Jezebel James*

2008-09

ABC – *In the Motherhood*

Fox – *Do Not Disturb*

2009-10

ABC – *Hank, Romantically Challenged*

2010-2011

NBC – *The Paul Reiser Show*

Endnotes

1 Brian Scully, Personal communication with author, February 2, 2012.

2 Lee Aronsohn, Personal communication with author, February 7, 2012.

3 Bill Carter, "The Media Business: Roseanne's Husband Playing Follow the Leader," *The New York Times*, November 20, 1992.

4 Rob Owen, "Brutally Normal' Is Just an Average Show," *The Post Gazette*, January 24, 2000.

5 "Brutally Talented Tangie Ambrose Comes to TV," *The Los Angeles Sentinel*, January 19, 2000.

6 Peter Bogdanovich, "NBC's Opposite of The Opposite of Sex?," *The New York Observer*, June 14, 1999.

7 Don Roos, Private communication with author, March 15, 2012.

8 Hal Boedeker, "'Someone Like Me' Not the Same Old 'Brady Bunch' Shtick," *The Chicago Tribune*, March 14, 1994.

9 Vance Muse, *We Bombed in Burbank: A Joyride to Prime Time*, (Reading, MA: Addison Wesley Publishing Company, 1994), 18.

10 "Church-Owned Stations Ban 'Coupling,'" *Studio Briefing–Film News*, September 22, 2003.

11 Alicia Kirk, Private communication with author, December 3, 2011.

12 Lisa de Moraes, "The TV Column: Steve's Reason Why Not," *The Washington Post*, January 22, 2006.

13 Kate O'Hare, "Fox Hopes 'Life on a Stick' Is as Funny as It Sounds," *The Vindicator*, March 19, 2005.

14 Paul Shaffer, *We'll Be Here for the Rest of Our Lives*, (New York: Flying Dolphin Press, 2009), 163.

15 Ibid., 144.

16 Bruce Fretts, "Hanging 'Tough,'" *Entertainment Weekly*, September 12, 2003.

17 Diane Werts, "Isn't It Romantic? Maybe, Maybe Not. 'If Not For You' Reflects the Quirky Vision of Creator Larry Levin," *Newsday*, September 17, 1995.

18 Lisa Schwarzbaum, "Enter Faye, Laughing," *Entertainment Weekly*, October 8, 1993.

19 Andrew Nicholls, *Valuable Lessons: How I Made (and Lost) Several Million Dollars Writing Over 100 Shows You Never Heard Of*, (Kindle Edition, 2010), 180.

20 From Tribune Wires, "'It Had to Be You' May Return to CBS-TV--But Without Faye Dunaway," *The Chicago Tribune*, December 4, 1993.

21 Andrew Nicholls, *Valuable Lessons*, 181.

22 Jay Bobbin, "Newlyweds Hope They're the Ones for Each Other in WB Comedy," *The Buffalo News*, April 19, 1998.

23 Harvey Laidman, Private communication with author, May 11, 2012.

24 George Yanok, Private communication with author, September 18, 2011.

25 Ibid.

26 Tim Brooks and Earle Marsh, *The Complete Directory to Prime Time Network and Cable TV Shows: 1946–Present*, 9th ed. (New York: Ballantine Books, 2007), 481.

27 Frank Mula, Private communication with author, February 13, 2012.

28 Ibid.

29 Larry Bonko, "From Lake Taylor High to 'Misery,'" *The Virginian Pilot*, September 30, 1995.

30 Tom Jicha, "Fine Times, Foul Shows 'Too Something' and 'Misery Loves Company': Too Much Sunday Misery," *The Sun Sentinel*, September 30, 1995.

31 John Crook, "Dysfunction is Not a Laughing Matter," *The Sunday Free Lance Star*, October 1, 2000.

32 Joe Saltzman, "After the Ax: Postmortem of a TV Series," *The Los Angeles Times*, August 20, 1978.

33 Liz Smith, "'Another Day' – Not Just Yet," *The Chicago Tribune*, January 8, 1978.

34 Elizabeth Forsythe Hailey, Private communication with author, August 10, 2011.

35 Susan King, "Laughing at Reality: ABC Breaks New Ground with this Fact-Based Comedy 'Arresting Bahvior,'" *The Los Angeles Times*, August 16, 1992.

36 Lon Grahake, "Sitcom Merry-Go-Round: ABC Shifts Midweek Shows," *The Chicago Sun-Times*, March 28, 1995.

37 Rob Reiner, Archive of American Television interview, November 29, 2004.

38 James Burrows, Archive of American Television interview, December 17, 2003.

39 Scott D. Pierce, "What's in a Name? 'Come Fly with Me' Is Transformed into 'Love and Marriage,'" *Deseret News*, August 1, 1996.

40 Rob Owen, "'O'Keefes' a Refreshing, Good-hearted Satire," *The Pittsburgh Post-Gazette*, May 21, 2003.

41 "HSLDA Reviews 'O'Keefes' Pilot," Home School Legal Defense Association website, May 2, 2003, retrieved August 2, 2011.

42 Shauna Snow, "Morning Report," *The Los Angeles Times*, May 8, 1996.

43 Michael Elias, Private Communication with author, April 28, 2011.

44 Ken Tucker, "You Take the Kids, TV Review," *Entertainment Weekly*, December 14, 1990.

45 Bob Nickman, Private communication with author, February 12, 2012.

46 David Bianculli, "Night of 100 Snores Too Typical of CBS," *The New York Daily News*, April 3, 1996.

47 Howard Rosenberg, "'My Guys' a Limo Ride of Cheesy, Uninspired Humor," *The LosAngeles Times*, April 3, 1996.

48 Mark Harris, "Decision Time for CBS," *Entertainment Weekly*, October 25, 1991.

49 Lee Goldberg, *Unsold Television Pilots Vol. 2: 1977-1989*, (Lincoln, NE: iUniverse.com, Inc., 2001), 450.

50 Bob Niedt, "Paul Rodriguez Tries Again with a New Latino Comedy," *The Chicago Sun-Times*, March 12, 1988.

51 Daniel Ruth, "Two Comedy Series Debut with Promise for Long Run," *The Chicago Sun-Times*, March 15, 1988.

52 Marsh McCall, "Twenty Good Years Live Blog," NBCUNI.com, October 11, 2006, retrieved May 7, 2012.

53 Fred Topel, "Twenty Good Years and Two Good Names," *CanMag*, October 11, 2006.

54 Marsh McCall, "Twenty Good Years," NBCUNI.com.

55 Eric Mink, "George vs. 'Frasier': 'Bob' to Duke It Out," *New York Daily News*, July 27, 2001.

56 Wesley Hyatt, *Short-Lived Television Series, 1948-1978: Thirty Years of More Than 1,000 Flops*, (Jefferson, North Carolina: McFarland & Company, Inc., 2003), 42.

57 Author Unknown, "Radio-TV News & Views," *The Chicago Tribune*, October 22, 1952.

58 Richard L. Bare, Private communication with the author, July 11, 2011.

59 Kate O'Hare, "Hank Azaria Uses His Imagination," *Osala Star-Banner*, January 8, 2002.

60 Lee Aronsohn, Private communication with author, February 7, 2012.

61 Scott Pierce, "'Life…and Stuff' Is Just Awful," *The Deseret News*, June 5, 1997.

62 Jeff Jarvis, "Life…and Stuff," *TV Guide*, June 21, 1997.

63 Suzanne C. Ryan, "New TV Shows Reflect Change in U.S. Values," *The Record*, May 25, 2002.

64 Andy Meisler, "At Lunch with: Martin Short, A Comic Chameleon at Play in Prime Time," *The New York Times*, September 28, 1994.

65 Michael Short, Private communication with author, December 27, 2011.

66 Laurie Parres, Private communication with author, November 29, 2011.

67 Alessandra Stanley, "An Idle Star with Time for Trouble," *The New York Times*, April 13, 2011.

68 Chris Willman, ""TV Reviews Julie Andrews Stars in Fish-Out-of-Water Comedy," *The Los Angeles Times*, May 30. 1992.

69 Tom Shales, "Laurie Hill Cut," *The Washington Post*, October 23, 1992.

70 Allan Katz, Private communication with author, January 1, 2012.

71 Alec Freeman, "Tammie [sic] Grimes Likes to Use the Telephone," *The Hartford Courant*, September 27, 1966.

72 Ron Green, "The Tammy Grimes Show," geocities.com/greenronny/g/Tammy, 2004, retrieved October 7, 2009.

73 Rick DuBrow, "Danny's Daughter Makes Successful TV Bid," *The Press-Courier*, September 9, 1966.

74 Vince Leonard, "Life's Rosier for Bill Dozier," *Pittsburgh Press*, January 11, 1967.

75 Michael Ausiello, "Nathan Lane Throws a Political Party," *TV Guide*, January 9, 2003.

76 Marla Gibbs, Archives of American Television interview, July 27, 2006.

77 Bob Carroll, Jr. and Madelyn Davis, Archives of American Television interview, November 24, 1997.

78 Keith Phipps, "Jason Bateman Interview," A.V. Club, March 24, 2004.

79 Les Brown, *Les Brown's Encyclopedia of Television*, 3rd ed. (Detroit, MI: Visible Ink Press, 1992), 358.

80 Charlie Hauck, Private communication with author, April 19, 2011.

81 Charlie Hauck, Private communication with author, August 31, 2011.

82 Wikipedia, "The Sanford Arms," retrieved November 12, 2009.

83 Internet Movie Database, "Waverly Wonders," retrieved September 4, 2009.

84 David Bauder, AP Television Writer, "Parents of Adopted Children Angry Over Network Comedy 'My Adventures in Television,'" June 18, 2002.

85 Jim Breuer, *I'm not High (But I've Got a Lot of Crazy Stories about Life as a Goat Boy, a Dad, and a Spiritual Warrior)*, (New York: Penguin Group, 2010), 135.

86 Ibid.

87 Brian Lowery, "ABC Pulls 'Buddies' Before Debut," *The Chicago Sun-Times*, April 13, 1995.

88 Howard M. Gould, Private communication with author, April 7, 2012.

89 Kathryn Baker, "Alan Arkin, Wife Dana Partnered in TV Series," *The Free-Lance Star*, April 4, 1987.

90 Ibid.

91 Marilyn Beck, "Outlook Not Good for Arkin's 'Harry' Series: Personalities," *St. Petersburg Times*, March 8, 1987.

92 Ibid.

93 Howard Kimmel, Private communication with author, June 18, 2011.

94 Sister Elizabeth Thoman, "Sad Saga of Sister Aggie," *Media & Values*, Fall, 1978.

95 Marilyn Beck, "Marilyn Beck's Hollywood: Stevenson Tries Again," *Bangor Daily News*, December 22, 1978.

96 Sister Elizabeth Thoman, "Sad Saga of Sister Aggie."

97 Daily News Wire Services, "News & Notes: 'Living Single' Gets FOX Spot Meant for Stalled Baio Vehicle," *Daily News* (Los Angeles, CA), August 29, 1997.

98 Rick Bentley, "Time to Judge: Actresses Rule the Courtroom in the New Lineup of TV Shows," *Fresno Bee*, October 24, 1999.

99 Stephen Neigher, Private communication with author, April 1, 2012.

100 Internet Movie Database, "Zorro and Son," retrieved September 7, 2009.

101 Mike Clark, "Guy Williams – Relaxed, Retired and 'Lost in Space,'" *Starlog Magazine*, January 1987.

102 Mark Harris, "Stat Man Danny Arnold," *Entertainment Weekly*, May 3, 1991.

103 Jim Bouton, *Ball Four Plus Ball Five*, (New York: Stein & Day Publishers, 1981), 421.

104 Brian Lowry, "'Battery' Not Included in NBC's Lineup," *Albany Times Union*, April 16, 2000.

105 Stuart Levine, MSNBC.com, Quoted in Brian Stelter, "Fox Cancels 'Do Not Disturb' After Producers Admit to Shaming Network," *The New York Times*, September 26, 2008.

106 Brian Stelter, "Fox Cancels 'Do Not Disturb'....".

107 Author Unknown, "Producer Enjoys Some Laughs as Brooks Creates Use for Set," *The Buffalo News*, July 27, 1989.

108 Bill Cotter, *The Wonderful World of Disney Television: A Complete History* (New York: Hyperion, 1997), 374.

109 Faye Zuckerman, "'Nutt House' Is Loony, and That's Good," *The Spokesman Review*, September 20, 1989.

110 Larry Bonko, "Just Another Show About 'The Office' with Valerie Harper," *The Virginian Pilot*, March 11, 1995.

111 "David Lynch – On the Air," lynchnet.com/ontheair/ retrieved August 26, 2009.

112 Scott Williams, "David Lynch's TV Revenge, *Reading Eagle*, June 20, 1992.

113 Nancy Hess, "Bochco Gets a Chance to Try a Laugh Track," *The New York Times*, July 14, 1996.

114 "Close Up: Public Morals," *TV Guide*, October 26, 1996, 192.

115 Steven Bochco, Archive of American Television interview, May 21, 2002.

116 Ken Estin, Private communication with author, January 15, 2012.

117 Ibid.

118 Marvin Kupfer, Private communication with author, February 12, 2012.

119 Susan King, "Bonnie Hunt: Building a Sitcom", *The Los Angeles Times*, August 15, 1993.

120 Michael E. Hill, "The Building: How Different Is Bonnie Hunt's Show? Let Us Count the Ways," *The Washington Post*, August 15, 1993.

121 William Keck, "It's a Gay, Gay World for Fred Savage," *USA Today*, January 25, 2006.

122 Richard Huff, "A Life of 'Crumbs': TV Series Came from Own Family," *New York Daily News*, January 15, 2006.

123 Ibid.

124 Howard Rosenberg, "'Easy' Didn't Get Chance To Do It," *The Los Angeles Times*, October 21, 1983.

125 Internet Movie Database, "It's Not Easy," retrieved November 16, 2009.

126 Bob Shayne, Private communication with author, March 5, 2011.

127 Wesley Hyatt, *Short-Lived Television Series 1948-1978*, 256.

128 Monica Collins, "'Ask' and Ye Shall Receive a Good Sitcom," *Boston Herald*, January 4, 1998.

129 Lon Grahnke, "Advice Is a Drag: Guy Poses as Female Columnist in 'Ask Harriet'," *The Chicago Sun-Times*, December 30, 1997.

130 Robert Dames, Personal communication with author, January 17, 2012.

131 Bob Fraser, Private communication with author, April 10, 2011.

132 Rob Gilmer, Private communication with author, August 30, 2011.

133 Robert Bianco, "'Bram & Alice': Get Me Rewrite," *USA Today*, October 30, 2002.

134 "Did Romance Break Up Undo TV Series," *Studio Briefing: Film News*, November 10, 1997.

135 Bruce Fretts, "The Perils of Pauly," *Entertainment Weekly*, March 1997.

136 Bill Carter, "Catholic Lay Group Accuses ABC of Biased Programming," *The New York Times*, April 17, 1998.

137 Andrew Nicholls, *Valuable Lessons*, 167.

138 Ibid, 167-68.

139 Ibid, 173.

140 Kay Gardella, "'Apple Pie' Sliced to Half Hour," *The News & Courier*, July 15, 1978.

141 Joshua Sternin, Private Communication with author, March 5, 2012.

142 Robin Adam Sloan, "Celebrity Corner," *Miami News*, March 19, 1977.

143 George Yanok, Private communication with author, February 27, 2012.

144 Donald Reiker, Private Communication with author, August 1, 2011.

145 Ibid.

146 Marilyn Beck, "ABC's 'Mr. T and Tina' Already Needs a Face-lift," *The Chicago Tribune*, October 5, 1976.

147 Vincent Terrace, *The Ultimate TV Trivia Book* (Winchester, MA: Faber and Faber, 1991), 169.

148 Tom Jicha, "Odd 'People' Risky Business", *Sun-Sentinel*, Sept. 18, 1989.

149 Terry Jackson, "UPN's New Secret Diary is Offensive Television," *Miami Herald*, July 29, 1998.

150 Matthew Diamond, Private communication with author, March 17, 2012.

151 "The Secret Diary of Desmond Pfeiffer," *Entertainment Weekly*, January 29, 2010, 41.

152 Caryn James, "Television Review, 'Daring Lincoln to Spin in his Grave,'" *The New York Times*, October 5, 1998.

153 Tim Goodman, "Running Out of Synonyms for 'Bad,' 'Pfeiffer' Comedy Could Cause an Epidemic of Unprintable Language," *The San Francisco Chronicle*, October 5, 1998.

Index

Ace Crawford, Private Eye – 377-80, 634
Ackerman, Andy – 65-66, 71, 73, 76, 156-160, 190, 269, 462, 522
A.E.S. Hudson Street – 423-26, 634
Aidekman, Al – 254-56, 415
Albert, Lisa – 461, 464, 579
Aleck, Jimmy – 15, 513-14
Alexander, Jason – 214, 263-64, 268
Almos, Eva – 358, 516
Amos, John – 196, 347
Andrews, Julie – xi, 307, 310
Aniston, Jennifer – xi, 18
Another Day – 163-71, 634
Antonacci, Greg – 211-15, 416, 428
Apple Pie – 587-92, 634
Arata, Elaine – 187-88, 477, 479
Archibald, Dottie – 19-20, 36
Arkin, Adam – 95, 394
Arnold, Nick – 180-182, 338, 420-21, 602
Aronsohn, Lee – xiii, 178, 283-85, 304, 562, 569, 620-21

Arresting Behavior – 171-73, 636
As If – 26-30, 638
Ask Harriet – 511-18, 637
Asner, Ed – 233, 512-13
Aspen, Jennifer – 264, 268
Azaria, Hank – 119, 122, 279

Baby Makes Five – 173-76, 634
Bailey, Hillary – 174, 441
Baker, Max – 319, 627
Baker, Phil – 112, 131-32
Baldikoski, Steve – 342, 413
Baldwin, Peter – 34, 182, 204, 419-20
Ball Four – 427-30, 633
Bandur, Maggie – 72, 75, 520
Baskin, John – 198, 611-12
Bateman, Jason – 248, 250, 339, 342, 434, 436, 592
Battery Park – 430-34, 637
Bearse, Amanda – 517, 565-66
Beavers, Susan – 220, 222, 449-50
Beckerman, George – 18, 356
Begel, Cindy – 296, 337
Begley Jr., Ed – 107, 357, 372
Behar, Bryan – 342, 413
Belushi, Jim – 414, 417-18, 479
Bendetson, Howard – 296, 336-37
Benson, Robby – 112, 176, 266
Berlinger, Robert – 120, 186, 201-02, 373, 513-15, 565, 582, 584
Bernstein, Nat – 176, 559-60
Better Days – 1-7, 635
Beware of Dog – 539-41, 638
Bicks, Jenny – 123, 125, 229
Bishop, Kelly – 105, 314
Bixby, Bill – 3-5, 50-54, 117-18, 445-46
Black Tie Affair – 30-37, 636

Bleckner, Jeff – 347-48, 503
Bob Patterson – 263-68, 638
Bonerz, Peter – 458-59, 589-91
Boni, John – 473, 573, 576
Boutsikaris, Dennis – 151, 426
Bowab, John – 318, 477-78
The Boys – 140-43, 636
Bradford, Sally – 67-68, 435, 437
Bram & Alice – 541-46, 638
Brewster, Paget – 128, 135, 156, 161
The Brian Benben Show – 518-21, 637
Bringing Up Jack – 176-79, 636
Brown, Mark Alton – 229, 566
Brutally Normal – 7-11, 638
Buckland, Marc – 8-9, 340-342
Buckman, Phil – 210, 214, 264
Buckner, Brad – 123-124, 504, 553-55
Buddies – 380-86, 636
The Building – 476-79, 636
Built to Last – 479-83, 637
Burmester, Leo – 135, 171, 173
Burris, Bob – 202, 398
Burrows, James – 91-93, 183-84, 506-07, 542
Buzby, Zane – 23, 568-69

Cadiff, Andy – 283-87, 391-92, 431, 556
Cahoon, Kell – 192, 228-29
Cale, Paula – 148, 150, 380-81
Canterbury, Bill – 137-38, 558
Carell, Steve – 268, 559-60
Carroll, Bob Jr. – 337-38, 607-09
Carry, Julius – 151-52, 390
Cassidy, Joanna – 220, 466
Cawley, Tucker – 100, 524-25, 527
Cendrowski, Mark – 65-67, 287

Chappelle, Dave – xiv, 380, 386
Charlie Lawrence – 332-35, 638
Checking In – 335-37, 634
Chemel, Lee Shallat – 74-75, 87, 157-59, 225-26, 240-43, 432-33, 484-86, 508, 624, 626
Cho, John – 94, 96, 528, 531
Clerks – 386-90, 637
Clohessy, Robert – 310, 314
Clooney, George – xi, 169, 477
Co-Ed Fever, 37-44, 634
Cohen, Gerry – 191-92, 407, 455-57
Cohen, Lawrence J. – 571, 589
Cohen, Robert – 21, 259, 445
Cohen, Ted – 92-93, 99
Come to Papa – 268-69, 639
Common Law – 111-15, 637
Conway, Tim – 377-80, 455
Cooper, Hal – 165, 183-84
Corcillo, Ron – 456, 597
Corrigan, Paul – 147, 149, 224, 543-44
Costello – 483-87, 637
Coupling – 44-49, 639
Cox, Nikki – 21, 340
Crumbs – 487-94, 639
Cunningham, Rick – 124, 365
Cutler, Stan – 467-68, 500-02, 607
Cutters – 390-92, 636

Daddy's Girls – 209-15, 636
Dajani, Nadia – 55, 578
Daley, John Francis – 230, 528
Damus, Mike – 7, 227-28
Dana, Bill – 419, 441
Daniel, Rod – 405-07, 480-82
Daniels, Mark – 40, 400

Danny – 216-19, 638
Danziger, Dennis – 278, 623
Dattilo-Hayward, Kristin – 148, 448
Davenport, Bill – 346-48, 350, 590
Davidoff, Michael – 291, 542
Davis, Madelyn – 337-38, 607-09
Dawber, Pam – 282, 285, 524
Day, Linda – 201, 203, 395, 583
DeBenedictis, Lisa – 177, 383
Diamond, Matthew – 87-89, 566-67, 598, 625-30
Dick, Andy – 11, 478
The Dictator – 522-24, 635
Doc Corkle – 270-75, 633
Dodson, Jack – 396, 424
Do Not Disturb – 434-37, 639
Dorothy – 337-39, 634
Doyle-Murray, Brian – 129-30, 149, 456
Drake, Bebe – 351, 501, 503
Drake, Jim – 41, 105-07, 174, 570
Dreams – 50-55, 635
Drescher, Fran – 239, 241, 243, 281
Dresser, Richard – 32-34, 36, 463-65
Drummond, Alice – 304, 457
Dubin, Charles – 116, 378
Duclon, Dave – 416, 480, 482
Dudley – 220-23, 636
Dunaway, Faye – xi, 122

Eells, Pamela – 241, 514
Eisenstock, Alan – 368, 440
Elias, Michael – 38, 40, 200
Emily's Reasons Why Not – 55-61, 639
Engelberg, Amy and Wendy – 17, 233, 344
Esten, Charles – 455, 518
Estin, Ken – 450-51, 468-70

Everett, Art – 125, 384, 583
Everything's Relative – 592-94, 637

Fabares, Shelly – 126, 552, 555
Faber, Steve – 159-60, 218
Falkenstein, Beth Fieger – 84-85, 462
Fathers and Sons – 180-82, 635
Ferber, Mel – 4, 327
Ferreira, Louis (aka Justin Louis) – 148, 430, 460
Filgo, Jeff and Jackie – 65-68, 525-26
Finestra, Carmen – 380, 484, 498-99, 555
First Impressions – 276-78, 635
Fisher, Bob – 159-60, 218
Fitzgerald, Mary – 96, 100, 486
Flanagan, Marc – 345, 465
Flatbush – 143-47, 634
Flender, Rodman – 78, 81, 195, 342
Fortenberry, John – 12, 357-58, 583, 592-94
Frankel, David – 62-63, 359-60
Frannie's Turn – 303-06, 636
Free Country – 182-85, 634
Freeman, Fred – 276-77, 571
Fresco, Victor – 70-72, 156-57
Friedle, Will – 11, 86-87
Fryman, Pamela – 129, 177-79, 410

Ganz, Lowell – 438-39, 534-35
Gardner, Gerald – 106, 447
Garrett, Roger – 113, 368
Garson, Willie – 440, 512, 514
Geiss, Tony – 429, 601, 603
Gewirtz, Howard – 42, 247
Glatter, Lesli Linka – 32, 453
Go Fish – 11-14, 638
God, the Devil and Bob – 546-52, 637

Gold, Brandy – 173, 175, 276-77
Gordon, Bryan – 15, 190, 300-01
Goren, Rowby – 106, 610
Gould, Harold – 408, 457
Gould, Howard M. – 213, 390-91
Gower, Andre – 173, 180
Grammer, Kelsey – 140, 319, 373, 524-26
Grapevine – 61-64, 637
Greene, Lyn – 237, 239, 406
Greenburg, Cynthia – 29, 58, 412
The Grubbs – 594-99, 638

Halvorson, Gary – 231, 333-34, 435
Hampton, James – 137-38, 345
Han, Maggie – 30, 36, 359
Hanging In – 350, 634
Hank – 524-27, 639
Happy Hour – 64-70, 639
Harrington, Jay – 44-46, 58
Harrison, Lindsay – 124, 390-91
Harry – 392-96, 635
Hart, Terry – 108-09, 146
Hauck, Charlie – 346-47, 350, 589
Havinga, Nick – 165, 553-55
Herbie, The Love Bug – 115-18, 634
Higginbotham, Abraham – 97, 434, 436
Highcliffe Manor – 552-55, 634
Hobson, I.M. – 18, 454
Hochberg, Victoria – 16, 530
Holland, Alec – 78, 80, 456
Hughes, Terry – 140-42, 257-60, 277
Hunt, Bonnie – 143, 476-79
Hunt, Gordon – 276, 579
Hupp, Jana Marie – 101, 104, 460

If Not for You – 119-22, 636
Imagine That – 279-81, 638
In the Beginning – 396-401, 634
In the Motherhood – 223-27, 639
It Had to Be You – 122-28, 636
It's Not Easy – 496-500, 635
Ivan the Terrible – 599-604, 633

Jackson, Hayes – 265, 267, 490, 493
Jacobs, Gary – 392-94, 522
Jacobs, Michael – 151-53, 286, 288, 408-09, 441
The Jake Effect – 339-42, 638
Jensen, Shelly – 66, 68-69, 84, 86, 356, 358, 405
Jones, Earl Richey – 384, 407
Jones, Patricia – 503, 608
Jones, Todd – 384, 407
Julian, Arthur – 346-48, 350, 590-91
Julie – 307-10, 636

The Kallikaks – 604-06, 633
Kaplan, Jack – 415, 417, 503
Katie Joplin – 343-46, 637
Katlin, Mitchel – 176-77, 559-60, 564
Katz, Allan – 317-18, 568-70
Kaufman, Charlie – 155, 584-85
Keily, Jim – 16, 513-514
Kelada, Asaad – 67-68, 305-06, 459
Kellman, Barnet – 119, 210, 264-67, 279-81, 535
Kirshner, Don – 26, 104-05, 109
Kitchen Confidential – 528-34, 639
Klein, Dennis – 120, 173
Klein, Robert – 264, 506
Kleinschmitt, Carl – 164, 608
Kling, Woody – 104, 352, 354
Kohan, Jenji – 373, 506-07

Komack, James – 164, 467, 500-02, 607, 609
Konner, Jennifer – 190, 223-24, 508
Kristofer, Jason – 148, 359
Kurtz, Swoosie – 82-83, 128, 132, 526

LaDuke, Dee – 229, 566
Lander, David L. – 440, 452
Lapiduss, Sally – 238, 241
Lathan, Stan – 3, 6, 102-03, 361, 363, 429
Lauer, Peter – 14, 81, 216-17, 532
Laurie Hill – 310-14, 636
Lawrence, Sheila R. - 411, 413, 432
Lawson, Twiggy – 122, 239, 243
Lazarus, Paul – 364, 381, 383
Leachman, Cloris – 132, 443-44
A League of Their Own – 438-41, 636
Leahy, Janet – 218, 395, 579
Lear, Norman – xiv, 26, 104, 107, 197, 346-47, 349, 351, 397, 552, 588
Leeds, Phil – 104-05, 155, 399, 599
Leeves, Jane – 258, 555
Lembeck, Michael – 83, 320, 416, 560-64, 578-80
Lerner, Gail – 136, 157, 160, 413, 520
Lessac, Michael – 129-34, 469-70, 535-36
Levin, Larry – 119, 121, 171-73
Levine, Ken – 514, 516, 545
Levine, Richard – 237, 239, 406
Levy, Neal Allan – 409, 613
Lewis, Phil – 359, 365, 412
Life . . . and Stuff – 282-85, 637
Life on a Stick – 70-76, 639
Light, Judith – 257, 506
Linville, Larry – 116, 335
Litt, David – 230-33, 561-62
Lloyd, Christopher (actor) – 248, 522
LoBue, J.D. – 205-06, 619-23

Local Heroes – 147-51, 636
Lookner, Steve – 281, 386
Lopez, Priscilla – 107, 396
Lorre, Chuck – xiv, 304, 306
Lost at Home – 285-89, 638
Love and Marriage – 185-89, 637
Love & Money – 128-35, 637
Luis – 289-93, 639
Lundy, Jessica – 140, 248
Lush Life – 235-39, 637

M.Y.O.B. – 14-17, 637
MacKenzie, Will – 54, 112-14
Macy, Bill – 20, 231, 349
Madrigal, Al – 98, 615
Mancuso, Gail – 68-69, 95, 187, 224, 244-45
Mandel, Babaloo – 438-39, 534-35
Manza, Ralph – 176, 424
Marcus, Richard – 278, 365
Margolin, Jody – 188, 246
Marrieta, Peter – 114, 514-15
Marshall, Penny – 415, 438-40
Martin, Andrea – 282, 294-95, 316-17
Martin, Bill – 94, 96, 525, 527, 558
Martin, Dick – 247-48, 367-71, 540
The Martin Short Show – 293-99, 636
Martineau, Mike – 186, 375
Matheson, Richard Christian – 166, 361, 363-64
Matthews, Dakin – 390-91, 448
McCarthy-Miller, Beth – 199, 224
McClanahan, Rue – 229, 587, 589
McCoy, Terri – 202, 358, 566
McFadzean, David – 380, 484
McGill, Bruce – 30, 246
McGinley, Ted – 332, 373, 411

McGraw, Melinda – 372-73, 524
McIntyre, Doug – 256, 439
Meehan, Tom – 429, 601, 603
Melman, Jeff – 290-91, 315, 458
Meloni, Christopher – 140-41, 151, 153
Mendoza, Linda – 226, 616-17
Metcalf, Laurie – 332, 546
Miner, Steve – 194-96, 310
Mintz, Larry – 368, 440
Misconceptions – 555-59, 639
Misery Loves Company – 151-55, 636
Mister Dugan – 346-49, 634
Mr. T and Tina – 606-11, 633
Molloy – 18-20, 635
Moore, Dudley – 209, 215, 220, 223, 449
Morgan, Harry – 132, 193
Morita, Pat – 155, 298, 606-07, 611
Morrill, Priscilla – 107, 173, 175, 338, 396
Mula, Frank – 148, 150, 296
Mulligan, Jim – 353, 397, 609
Myerson, Alan – 39, 105, 315, 420
My Guide to Becoming a Rock Star – 76-82, 638
My Guys – 227-30, 636
My Wildest Dreams – 314-16, 636

Nearly Departed – 611-14, 635
Neigher, Steven – 312, 370, 417-18
Nicholls, Andrew – 123, 581-82
Nick & Hillary – 401-04, 635
Nielsen, Leslie – 123, 468
No Soap, Radio – 441-43, 634
The Nutt House – 443-48, 635

O'Brien, Jane – 432, 487
The Office – 448-51, 636

O'Hara, Jenny – 484, 552
O'Hurley, John – 269, 559, 568
The O'Keefes – 189-93, 638
On the Air – 451-55, 636
On the Spot – 455-57, 638
Orloff, Rich – 394, 554
The Ortegas – 615-18, 639
Over the Top – 559-64, 637
Owen, John Steven – 122, 472

Palladino, Amy Sherman – 185-87, 244-45, 563
Palladino, Daniel – 245-46, 614
Pankin, Stuart – 441, 611
Pantoliano, Joe – 182, 431
Park Place – 457-59, 634
Parker, Rod – 346-47, 350
Parres, Laurie – 280, 298
Party Girl – 82-86, 637
The Paul Reiser Show – 299-301, 640
Pauly – 564-67, 637
Peaslee, John – 88, 250-51
Pennette, Marco – 233, 488-90
The People Next Door – 618-23, 635
Perkins, Elizabeth – 14, 430, 432
Petranto, Ross – 175, 352-53
Pilot, Judd – 88, 250-51
Pitt, Brad – xi, 254, 528
The Pitts – 623-26, 638
Pollon, Daphne – 129, 133, 373, 383
Port, Joe – 232, 596
Posey, Parker – 82, 243-44
Poulon, A.J. – 456, 597
Praiser, Ian – 42, 247
Princesses – 239-43, 636

Prosky, Robert – 216, 390
Public Morals – 459-66, 637

Quill, Ted – 280, 405
Quinn, Anthony Tyler – 21, 24, 304, 512

Rafkin, Alan – 108, 277, 350
Raising Caines – 193-96, 637
The Random Years – 86-90, 638
Reeder, Tom – 425, 458
Regalbuto, Joe – 346, 378, 558
Regular Joe – 230-33, 638
Reich, Andrew – 92-93, 99
Reid, Alex – 519, 549, 560
Reiker, Donald – 505, 607-08
Reinhold, Judge – 189, 192-93, 355, 359, 387
The Return of Jezebel James – 243-46, 639
Rewind – 404-08, 637
Rich, John – 120-21, 136, 338-39, 612-14
Richmond, Bill – 317, 442-43, 569
Riggi, John – 77-78, 81, 333, 335
Riley, Jack – 316-17, 399
Rispoli, Michael – 227, 229, 541
Riva, Diana-Maria – 112, 289
Robinson, Bumper - 18, 83
Roche, Eugene – 307, 534
Rogers, Doug – 354, 397-400
The Rollergirls – 466-68, 634
Romantically Challenged – 90-93, 639
Rosen, Sy – 174, 184, 350, 590-91
Rosenthal, Lisa – 86, 583
Ross, Michael A. – 71-72, 74, 158-59
Ross-Leming, Eugenie – 123-24, 504, 552-55
Rowland, Daryl – 177, 383
Roxie – 316-19, 635

Rubinowitz, Barry – 440, 535
Rudell, Kirk J. – 258, 260, 437
Rupp, Debra Jo – 119, 448, 450
Rushfield, Alexandria – 190, 223-24, 508
Rutherford, Emily – 45, 410, 413

Sacks, David – 178, 287
Salsberg, Matthew – 342, 508
Saltzman, Michael – 457, 556, 558
Samuels, Melissa – 78, 80, 456
Sandler, Ellen – 221, 278, 623
Sandrich, Jay – 333, 428, 449-51
Sanford, Arlene – 12, 431-33
The Sanford Arms – 351-55, 634
Saunders, Tom – 192, 228-29, 290, 293, 442-43
Savage, Fred – 300-01, 487, 532
Scardino, Don – 96, 104, 109, 402, 461-64
Scharlach, Ed – 358, 516
Schiff, Mike – 94, 96, 525-27, 558
Schiller, Rob – 23, 232-33, 437
Scorch – 568-70, 639
Scully, Brian – 127, 150, 266, 626
The Secret Diary of Desmond Pfeiffer – 626-31, 637
Secret Service Guy – 355-59, 637
Seeger, Efrem – 83, 404-05
Seeger, Susan – 84, 404, 417
Semi-Tough – 246-48, 634
704 Hauser – 196-99, 636
Shaffer, Paul – 104-05, 107, 109, 403
Shaping Up – 468-70, 635
Shea, Jack – 19-20, 198-99, 278, 336-37, 397
Shepherd, Sherri – 157, 372, 404
Shimokawa, Gary – 164, 502, 609
Shulman, Roger – 198, 611-12
Sierra, Gregory – 112, 419, 423

Silver, Art – 2, 12, 414, 416
Singer & Sons – 408-10, 635
The Singles Table – 94-97, 639
The Six O'Clock Follies – 470-74, 634
Snip – 500-05, 633
Solomon, Ed – 172-73, 280
Some of My Best Friends – 248-52, 638
Someone Like Me – 21-24, 636
Spencer, Alan – 417, 444-45
Spiro, Lev L. – 9, 80, 217, 532
Staley, Dan – 129, 142
Steckler, Doug – 296, 318
Steen, Nancy – 51-52, 334
Steinberg, Norm – 359-60, 397, 471-73
Steinmetz, Dennis – 417, 503, 605, 609
Stern, Daniel – 216, 230, 300
Sternin, Joshua – 529-30, 595, 598-99
Stewart, French   546, 556
Stewart, Regina – 113-14, 149, 489, 493
St. Germain, Mark – 277, 382
Stiers, David Ogden – 128, 132, 159
Stiller, Jerry – 317, 401, 442
The Stones – 506-09, 638
Storm, Howard – 3, 5, 277, 570
Struck by Lightning – 570-77, 634
Suh, Sung – 260, 491
Summers, Hope – 163-64, 501
Sunshine, Steven & Madeline – 307-08, 618-19
Szollosi, Thomas – 166, 361, 363-64

Take Five – 534-37, 635
Talk to Me – 319-22, 637
Tall Hopes – 200-03, 636
Tambor, Jeffrey – 98, 256-57, 592
The Tammy Grimes Show – 322-30, 633

Tarses, Jay – 30-33, 460-62, 465, 564
Tarses, Matt – 132, 461, 465
Tash, Max – 136-38, 186-87, 566
Taylor, Christine – 82, 84, 404
Teech – 359-65, 636
Teverbaugh, Mike – 73-74, 259, 315
Thacker, Julie – 584, 624-26
That's Life – 577-81, 637
Thomas, Betty – 172-73, 454
Thomas, Eddie Kaye – 7, 87
Thompson, Neil (writer) – 51-52, 550-51
Tolan, Peter – 372-73, 381, 385
Torres, Liz – 335, 559
Tracy, John – 152-55, 247, 315, 497-98
Trainer, David – 151, 153, 583
Trbovich, Tom – 51-54, 174, 447
Trial and Error – 252-56, 635
The Trouble with Larry – 581-85, 636
The Trouble with Normal – 156-61, 638
Tsao, Andrew – 290-92, 382, 385, 507, 596-97
Twenty Good Years – 256-61, 639

Vaupen, Drew – 112, 131-32
Ventimilia, Jeffrey – 529-30, 595, 598
Vickers, Darrell – 123, 581-82
Volz, Nedra – 107, 363
Von Scherler Mayer, Daisy – 59, 75, 82-83

Waldron, Gy – 105-06, 397, 399
Wallace, George – 197, 200
Walpert, David – 157, 159, 489, 491, 493
Walsh, Brad – 47, 49, 224, 543-44
Walter, Lisa Ann – 231, 314, 316
Ware, Michael – 202, 384
Wass, Ted – 85, 149-50, 228-30, 230, 232, 320-21, 372-74, 485, 488-93

Waverly Wonders – 366-71, 634
Wednesday 9:30 (8:30 Central) – 372-75, 638
Weege, Reinhold – 247, 458-59
Weisman, Sam – 200, 304
Weiss, Harriett – 174, 397, 399
Welcome to the Captain – 97-100, 639
Weyman, Andrew – 19-20, 45-49, 71-74, 253-56, 411-13, 512, 518-21, 524-27, 595, 598
Whitesell, John – 21-23, 295, 403, 484
Widdoes, James – 101-02, 249-52, 321, 360, 363, 457
Wild Oats – 100-04, 636
Williams, Matt – 380, 484
Williams, Michelle – xi, 193
Wiseman, Joe – 232, 596
Wolff, Art – 402, 446
Work with Me – 410-14, 637
Working Stiffs – 414-18, 634

Yanok, George – 144, 605-06
A Year at the Top – 104-09, 633
Young, Bob – 151, 153, 408-09
You're the One – 135-38, 637
You Take the Kids – 204-07, 635

Zaks, Jerry – 333, 542-44, 556-57
Zinberg, Michael – 180-81, 245, 480, 483
Zisk, Craig – 78-80
Zisk, Randall – 10, 181
Zolotin, Adam – 185, 404
Zorro and Son – 418-21, 634
Zuckerman, Steve – 84, 343-44, 409, 480-81, 507, 516, 579
Zwick, Joel – 2, 571-77, 592

www.ingramcontent.com/pod-product-compliance
Lightning Source LLC
Chambersburg PA
CBHW071710300426
44115CB00010B/1377